Social Security

Social
Security

ROBERT J. MYERS

Published for
McCahan Foundation
Bryn Mawr, Pennsylvania
by Richard D. Irwin, Inc., Homewood, Illinois

ISBN 0-256-01750-6
Library of Congress Catalog Card No. 74-29747
Printed in the United States of America

To my wife, Rudy

McCahan Foundation

The McCahan Foundation was created in 1955 by the American College of Life Underwriters of Bryn Mawr, Pennsylvania. It is named for Dr. David McCahan, fourth president of the American College, and world-renowned scholar in insurance and economic security.

It is the primary purpose of the Foundation to strengthen and encourage research on the nature, problems and issues pertaining to economic security mechanisms. Its activities include (1) the publication of monographs, papers, bibliographic studies and books that enhance understanding of the problems and issues regarding economic security programs; (2) the sponsorship of seminars, symposia and convocations in order to bring various points of view to bear on problems of economic security; (3) the improvement of communications among the academic, government and business communities on subjects related to economic security; and (4) the establishment of an information system embracing the literature of private and social insurance and related fields.

In Search
of Truth
About
Man's
Quest for
Security

Foreword

The social security system of the United States impacts in a direct or indirect manner on more than 200 million citizens. Some 79 million persons in the work force, and their employers, support the system through contributions (taxes). Some 31 million persons currently receive retirement, survivor, or disability benefit payments from the system. Almost all wives, husbands, widows, widowers, and children, whether paying taxes or not, are entitled to benefits based upon certain contingencies or eventualities.

In 1974, about $59 billion was paid into the system for old-age, survivors, and disability insurance by employed individuals, employing organizations, and the self-employed. An additional $13 billion was paid in for hospital and supplementary medical insurance under the Medicare program.

This volume is published 40 years after the social security system was established in the United States. In many respects the system is maturing, as would be suggested by its broad dimensions just described. In other ways, the system is changing, or is perceived to be changing, as demographic trends and economic problems impact upon it. It seems reasonable to conclude that more than ever in the past, there is broad public interest in how social security works and how well it will serve its present and future beneficiaries.

Robert J. Myers, currently Professor of Actuarial Science at Temple University, served as Chief Actuary of the Social Security Administration of the U.S. Department of Health, Education, and Welfare from 1947 to 1970. He is acknowledged as one of the world's foremost authorities on social insurance and has served as consultant to many nations. He is a past president of the American Academy of Actuaries and the Society of Actuaries, and is a distinguished Fellow of this latter body.

This volume is a major reorganization and revision of the author's *Social Insurance and Allied Government Programs* published in 1965 by Richard D. Irwin, Inc. The McCahan Foundation is privileged to make this publication available. In keeping with the Foundation's publication policy, it should be noted that the findings and conclusions in this volume are those of the author and should not be attributed to the McCahan Foundation.

DAVIS W. GREGG, Chairman
Governing Committee
McCahan Foundation

Preface

Since the dark days of the depression years of the 1930s, social security programs of many types have grown rapidly in the United States. Their effects have been very significant from social, economic, and political standpoints.

Before the 1930s, the only social insurance programs were the workmen's compensation laws, primarily state legislation. Allied with social insurance are the state-operated public assistance programs—both being a part of what is internationally known as "social security." In one form or another, many of the public assistance plans were operative before the 1930s, but with the advent of federal financial participation, these programs too have grown rapidly. In their effects, the social insurance programs and the public assistance programs are not generally independent of each other or competitive, but rather the latter should complement the former.

This book has been written for the purpose of giving a thorough factual description of the various social insurance and allied programs now operating in the United States. The emphasis is both on the general principles underlying the development of the systems and their present status, and on the general social and economic results developing from them. Necessarily, a certain amount of detail must be presented to indicate clearly the nature of the systems. The major emphasis is on the social insurance programs, rather than on public assistance. Furthermore, the greatest emphasis is on the largest program and the one which affects the most people—old-age, survivors, and disability insurance and Medicare, often referred to merely as "social security."

The closing chapter gives a brief summary of the general principles underlying a number of foreign social security programs, so that the reader may be aware of the diversity of methods used throughout the world in seeking to provide economic security. The book is intended to deal with both the factual aspects of the various social security programs and the underlying policy issues, and to make recommendations for program changes.

It is important to note that this book deals only with statutory programs. In many areas, such as retirement pensions, health care for the aged and the long-term disabled, and survivor benefits, significant protection supplementing that under statutory programs is provided through private-sector organizations (insurance companies, Blue Cross-Blue Shield plans, trusteed pension plans, and group practice prepayment plans). In other areas, such as temporary sickness cash benefits, workmen's compensation (work-connected injury or disease) benefits, and health care for the younger, working population, the protection is furnished predominantly by private-sector organizations (although workmen's compensation is a statutory program).

Not included within the types of protection dealt with in this book are such closely related programs as no-fault automobile insurance and state crime compensation programs. Although these possess some of the characteristics of social insurance or other types of social benefit programs, they do not seem to be comparable with the broad governmental programs dealt with here.

The author wishes to acknowledge the helpfulness of many friends and colleagues who reviewed and commented on one or more chapters of the final manuscript. These include Lawrence Alpern, ASA, MAAA, Daniel N. Price, Alfred M. Skolnik, and William M. Yoffee, Social Security Administration, Department of Health, Education, and Welfare; Charles E. Hawkins, Committee on Ways and Means, House of Representatives; James H. Manning, MAAA, and Margaret M. Dahm, Unemployment Insurance Service, Department of Labor; Abraham Benjamin, Railroad Retirement Board; Edwin C. Hustead, ASA, U.S. Civil Service Commission; Joseph B. Glenn, FSA, FCAS, Department of Defense; Nicholas J. Prendergast, ASA, Veterans Administration; Michael J. Romig, Chamber of Commerce of the United States; Abraham M. Niessen, ASA, MAAA; and Gordon R. Trapnell, FSA, MAAA.

A special word of appreciation is expressed to Dr. Charles E. Hughes, CLU, CPCU, Associate Professor of Insurance and Chairman of the American College's Department of Group and Social Insurance, for his wise counsel as to the structure of the book and his judicious review of the manuscript. Finally, thanks go to Helen L. Schmidt, CLU, of the McCahan Foundation, for her patient assistance in editing and preparing the manuscript. Of course, any factual errors or misstatements contained in this book are the sole responsibility of the author.

Washington, D.C.   ROBERT J. MYERS
May 1975

Contents

List of Tables

List of Abbreviations

AALL	American Association for Labor Legislation
AB	Aid to the Blind
ACE	Average current earnings (OASDI)
AFDC	Aid to Families with Dependent Children
AHA	American Hospital Association
AMA	American Medical Association
AMW	Average monthly wage (OASDI)
APTD	Aid to the Permanently and Totally Disabled
COES	Committee on Economic Security
CPI	Consumer Price Index
CRR	Commission on Railroad Retirement
CSR	Civil Service Retirement
DI	Disability Insurance
DIC	Dependents Indemnity Compensation (military benefits)
FAP	Family Assistance Plan
HEW	Health, Education, and Welfare (Department of)
HH	Home Health (services)
HI	Hospital Insurance (Medicare Part A)
HIAA	Health Insurance Association of America
HMO	Health Maintenance Organization
MA	Medical Assistance (Medicaid)
MAA	Medical Assistance for the Aged

MFB	Maximum Family Benefit (OASDI)
NHI	National Health Insurance
OAA	Old-Age Assistance
OASDHI	Old-Age, Survivors, Disability, and Health Insurance
OASDI	Old-Age, Survivors, and Disability Insurance
OASI	Old-Age and Survivors Insurance
PIA	Primary Insurance Amount (OASDI)
PSRO	Professional Standards Review Organization
RR	Railroad Retirement
RUI	Railroad Unemployment Insurance
SMI	Supplementary Medical Insurance (Medicare Part B)
SNF	Skilled Nursing Facility
SSA	Social Security Administration
SSI	Supplemental Security Income
TDI	Temporary Disability Insurance (cash sickness benefits)
UI	Unemployment Insurance
VA	Veterans Administration
WC	Workmen's Compensation or Workers' Compensation
ZPG	Zero Population Growth

PART I

Introduction

Economic security is one of the unfulfilled needs of man. Social security programs have been designed to aid man in his quest for economic security. Part I examines the underlying concepts of social security programs.

chapter 1

Social Security Concepts

In the past 40 years a vibrant new phrase has been introduced to the social and economic life of mankind—the magic words "social security." Although the types of programs generally described as social security had been in existence in some countries for many years, until 1935 their development was quite slow in the United States. In that year the Social Security Act was enacted, and this alliterative phrase came into being. Since then, many foreign countries, in developing new programs, or in modifying old ones, have used this phrase in place of those used previously (such as national insurance or social insurance).

QUEST FOR SECURITY

The very nature of man is to strive continually for material security of all types for himself, his family, his community, and his nation. But by his very human nature, man is destined to have, at best, incomplete success in this quest.

From the first dawning of history, man faced serious physical dangers—from wild animals, from the cold, from famine and drought, and from his fellow man. Over the many centuries, the frequency and severity of these threats to physical security have been lessened, and in some instances virtually eliminated, as man has developed mentally and spiritually. Despite this, even today, in many countries of the world, most of the people have very little real security as to basic human needs for food, shelter, and medical care. In the economically more developed countries, material conditions are at a quite favorable level, so that most of the population, especially those in families containing workers, are reasonably well off, at least as long as the worker is employed.

This great improvement in the material well-being of the population in economically well-developed countries has, without exception, been the result of rapid industrialization and a changeover from a rural economy to a highly urbanized one. Formerly, families produced or bartered for most of their needs and had only small supplementary cash income. Under the monetary economy resulting from industrialization, with its accompanying increasingly high standard of living, few people own any means of production, and many do not even own their own homes. Thus the loss of earning power to a family in an industrialized economy poses a problem completely in contrast with the situation in an agrarian economy. Although the industrial age has greatly aided man in his eternal quest for security by eliminating or diminishing many problems that have confronted him for centuries, certain new problems have arisen.

METHODS OF ATTAINING SECURITY

In the earliest days of civilization, man attempted to achieve security completely by his own efforts. Soon, families banded together for both productive and protective efforts. This growth continued until there were villages, towns, cities, provinces, and nations.

In our industrial economy the first method of attaining security of all kinds naturally devolves on the individual concerned. But this is only the beginning. Group action of all types is necessary. For physical security, we have the police forces, the military forces, the courts, and international agencies.

With reasonable assurance of physical security, there is still the problem of security against various risks of stoppage of earnings. Again, the primary responsibility rests with the individual, but our modern society and forms of government have prescribed certain responsibilities in this direction on the part of the employer and the government.

The individual's responsibility for providing his economic security may be termed as "private individual provisions." Cooperative arrangements involving both the individual and his employer (or, under certain circumstances, groups of individuals) may be termed "group provisions." The combination of private individual provisions and group provisions may be termed "private-sector provisions." Finally, programs established by governments may be termed "social security."

CONCEPT OF SOCIAL SECURITY

The phrase "social security," when considered as to its basic composition, is so broad as to be virtually meaningless. The "security of the whole society" would encompass all activities of mankind—not only physical and mental, but even spiritual. As "social security" is commonly used, however, it connotes measures for economic security under governmental auspices.

Some individuals hold a very broad concept of social security, considering it to include such diverse programs as public education, vacations with pay, community organization and planning, counseling services, school lunch programs, research in health problems, and so forth. Generally, however, social security is defined as including only a more restricted scope of programs, namely, (1) those providing cash payments to persons and families whose income from earnings has ceased or diminished, either temporarily or permanently; (2) those furnishing medical care to persons and families receiving benefits under item 1 or, under certain circumstances, to all persons of a given category; and (3) those providing cash payments in respect to all children of a given category, regardless of the presence or absence of parents who could support such children, and regardless of whether such support is being given or in what quantity.

In this country, the term "social security" is widely, though incorrectly, used to refer to the combination of the cash benefits provided by the old-age, survivors, and disability insurance system (often called OASDI for short) and the health benefits provided by the Medicare system, both established by the Social Security Act.

Types of Social Security Programs

Many different types of programs can fall within this latter, more restrictive, definition of social security. It may be said, however, that there are really only nine distinct branches or types of programs—as set forth in the International Labor Organization's Convention No. 102, "Minimum Standards of Social Security."[1] These may be classified as either short-term or long-term risks, depending upon the length of payment for individual cases.

Three branches involve entirely long-term risks, namely, old-age benefits, survivor benefits, and disability benefits. Old-age benefits are payable for life after attainment of a certain age, often with certain requirements as to retirement. Survivor benefits are payable after the death of the breadwinner, either for life or for a period of years. Disability benefits, sometimes known as invalidity benefits, are payable generally during the continuance of permanent and total disablement. In the subsequent chapters, these three branches will be treated simultaneously, since social security systems for one of these branches usually include one or both of the other two. A fourth branch, family allowances, is to some extent a long-term risk, since payments are made during the years when there are young children.

The branches covering primarily short-term risks are unemployment benefits, sickness benefits, medical care, and maternity benefits. The first two may, but usually do not, provide for payments over an extended period. Unemployment benefits are usually paid after a short waiting period and for a limited number of weeks in the event of the wage earner being out of work. Medical (or health) care benefits are either cash reimbursement or services granted in varying degrees and for varying periods to the individual, and sometimes to his family, in the event of illness. Sickness benefits, sometimes referred to as temporary disability benefits, are payable after a short waiting period for a limited period of time, with benefits under the disability branch entering in when the disablement becomes permanent in nature. Maternity benefits consist of both medical care and periodic cash payments; in reality this branch is a combination of the two branches, sickness benefits and medical care, for the special risk of maternity.

The ninth branch, industrial injury benefits, is a combination of short-term and long-term risks, since it includes sickness benefits, disability benefits, and medical care for the individual who is injured at work and survivor benefits for his dependents if his death results from such injuries.

---

[1] For details on this convention, see Robert J. Myers, "New International Convention on Social Security," *Social Security Bulletin,* October 1951.

Besides these nine branches, there can be broad general income-supplementation programs applicable to the entire population, generally on the basis of a means test. Such programs include guaranteed annual income plans, negative income tax plans, and food stamp plans.

Social security programs can be subdivided according to their general nature, as well as according to the particular risk with which they deal. Perhaps, five broad categories may be distinguished—social insurance systems, social assistance systems, universal benefit (or demogrant) systems, mandatory employer plans, and subsidized voluntary insurance. In some instances, the classification is not clear-cut.

Generally speaking, social insurance systems involve definite benefit amounts and qualification conditions prescribed by law, with the cost being met by contributions from the covered individual and/or his employer and, sometimes, in part from general government funds. Administration of social insurance programs is always done by governmental organizations (on this point, however, note the subsequent discussion). Coverage of such programs is compulsory, with certain minor exceptions, and applies to workers of a considerable number of employers. Appendix A gives a definition of social insurance, as developed by the Commission on Insurance Terminology. The OASDI system and the hospital insurance portion of Medicare are examples of a social insurance program, as are also the wage-related pension systems of Canada and many Latin American and European countries, and the unemployment insurance systems of Canada and the United States.

Social assistance systems have considerably more discretionary features than social insurance systems, with the amounts of the payments being based on individually determined need and being financed from general governmental funds. Just as in the case of social insurance programs, social assistance programs are always administered by governmental organizations. The several federal-state public assistance programs in the United States are examples of social assistance systems, as are also the similar programs in Canada and the national assistance program in Great Britain.

Universal benefit systems generally cover the entire population of a country, rather than merely the employed population, and condition the payments on demographic elements (for this reason, such programs have sometimes been termed "demogrant" systems) such as age, residence, family status, and so forth. At times, the benefits provided by such systems involve an income and/or assets test that is mathematically administered and so is not a needs test on an individual basis (and, accordingly, the system may then properly be classified as different from a social assistance program). In certain instances, these programs may be partially financed by direct earmarked contributions, such as a percentage of each resident's gross or net taxable income, but they are distinguished from social insurance systems because there is no relationship between benefit receipt and contribution payment. Universal benefit systems are always administered by governmental organizations. The Canadian old-age security program (flat benefits to persons aged 65 and over) is an example of a universal benefit system, as are also the similar programs of Australia, New Zealand, and the Scandinavian countries. The supplemental security income program for the aged, the blind, and the disabled inaugurated in the United States in 1974 is also an example of a demogrant system.

The mandatory employer plans are those under which employers are required by law to establish certain types of benefits for their employees. These plans either are administered by the employer or are contracted-out with a private insuring organization—at times with the alternative possibility of using a competing governmental organization. In many respects, these plans are similar to social insurance systems—especially if the exact form and amounts of the benefits are prescribed by law—but the distinguishing characteristic of social insurance systems is the mandatory governmental administration. The original version of the Ontario Pension Benefits Act, which would have required certain employers to establish pension plans with certain benefit standards, was an example of a mandatory employer plan, but this provision was not contained in the final legislation. So also are the state workmen's compensation systems in the United States (other than those that require the employers to purchase protection *only* from the "monopolistic" or "exclusive" state fund). Some authorities, however, would classify workmen's compensation as social insurance, since the benefits are prescribed by law and the administration either is performed by a government agency or is under the close supervision of such an agency. The proposal of the Nixon administration in the area of national health insurance, as made in 1972–74, is also of the mandatory employer approach.

Subsidized voluntary insurance plans are those under which the government encourages individuals to protect themselves against certain risks by subsidizing part of the cost for those who opt for coverage. Such programs can be administered by the government or by private organizations. The supplementary medical insurance portion of Medicare is an example of a program of this type, as are also the medical care programs in some European countries that are operated through mutual benefit societies.

Individual Equity and Social Adequacy

Whenever a social security system involves contributions from the potential beneficiaries, the question of individual equity versus social adequacy arises. Individual equity means that the contributor receives benefit protection directly related to the amount of his contributions —or, in other words, actuarially equivalent thereto. Social adequacy means that the benefits paid will provide for all contributors a certain standard of living. The two concepts are thus generally in direct conflict, and social security systems usually have a benefit basis falling somewhere between complete individual equity and complete social adequacy. Usually, the tendency is more toward social adequacy than individual equity. A classic and monumental discussion of this subject was presented by Reinhard A. Hohaus in 1938 and still remains valid (see Appendix B).

Individual private insurance policies are, of course, necessarily based on the individual equity concept. This does not mean that each individual will necessarily always get exactly his money back plus interest, as in the case of a savings bank account or some government bonds. Rather, insurance company contracts have premium rates actuarially determined for the benefits provided, so that policyowners in the same risk class pay the same premium amount for the same benefit. Due to random chance, the relationship between premiums paid and benefits received under a private insurance company contract will vary considerably for a given selected group of presumably identical risks. But in advance, no one can foretell which of the group will die early and thus receive benefits far in excess of premiums, and which will die after many years of premium participation and thus receive benefits well below their premiums accumulated at interest.

The concept of social adequacy must, of necessity, play a large part in group plans and in social security systems. If too much individual equity were to prevail when a system was started, the benefits paid would be relatively small. Thus, many years would elapse before the system would begin to meet the purposes for which it was established. Nonetheless, it is quite common to maintain a certain degree of individual equity in group plans and social security systems, although more stress is placed on social adequacy.

Somewhat related to the elements of individual equity and social adequacy is the matter of what might be termed group equity. From the standpoint of fair and equitable treatment, it seems highly desirable that in any social insurance or other social benefit program, persons with virtually identical circumstances should, as much as is feasible, receive the same benefits. In other words, there should be as few sharp borders as possible. For example, the benefit amount should not differ greatly for persons with identical earnings records who reach the normal retirement date on December 31 of a particular year as compared with those who do so on the next day. However, sharp borders cannot always be avoided, as, for example, in the case of persons who just miss acquiring the necessary coverage eligibility requirements.

Relative Cost of Social Security versus Private Insurance

Sometimes statements are made that social security programs are much less expensive than private insurance. At times, when considering the experience in the early years of operation of a long-term benefit program, this seems to be strikingly so. The explanation, however, is largely that for those initially granted benefits, the social adequacy concept applies so much more importantly than the individual equity concept.

One argument of those who state, or imply, that social security systems can do the job so cheaply is the application of the so-called "magic of averages." Under this theory, presumably because social security systems are so large as to number of persons covered and amount of contributions collected, relatively low benefit costs are inevitably expected to result. This belief is, of course, fallacious. It seems to be a direct parallel to the classic economic fable of the storekeeper who pays 50 cents a dozen for eggs and sells them for 4 cents apiece, but claims that he can nevertheless make a profit if he sells enough.

Actually, a social security system is not a magical machine. A contribution or tax of $1 put into one end cannot result continuously in $10 of benefits at the other end. It is basic logic that the cost of a system is determined solely by the benefits and the administrative expenses paid. Accordingly, if in the aggregate the relative benefit cost of a social security system is the same as that of a private individual plan or a group insurance program, the only difference in total cost arises from any differences in administrative expenses. Generally, however, administrative expenses represent only a small fraction of benefit costs, so that any cost advantage that a social security system possesses because of its size arises primarily on this account. Large systems have one other advantage over smaller ones. Since fewer sizable accidental and random fluctuations of experience are likely to occur in a large-coverage program, less need exists for providing margins for contingency reserves.

The real reason for having a social security system, in addition to private insurance coverage, is not primarily from a cost standpoint, but rather that social benefits on a social adequacy basis can only in this way be provided to a large sector of the population.

Social Insurance as "Insurance"

At times, the issue has been raised as to whether it is really proper to use the word "insurance" in connection with social security or social insurance. It would seem that this is justified because of the broad pooling mechanism utilized in social security systems, even though, from a strictly legalistic standpoint, proper usage of this word might also require that there be present a lawful and binding contract. The OASDI-Medicare system does not involve any contractual arrangements, although the covered individual does have statutory rights to benefits that are legally enforceable. Specifically, *Webster's Seventh New Collegiate Dictionary* (Springfield, Mass.: G. & C. Merriam Co., 1972), gives the following as the definition of "insurance": "1 a: the action or process of insuring: the state of being b: means of insuring 2 a: the business of insuring persons or property b: coverage by contract whereby one party undertakes to indemnify or guarantee another against loss by a specified contingency or peril c: the sum for which something is insured."

Social insurance seems to qualify under item 2b of this definition, since indemnification against loss by a specified contingency is certainly what is being done under such programs. For example, the "indemnification" is the benefits payable, the "loss" is the presumptive loss due to not being able to work, and the "contingency" is such things as old age or disability retirement. The fact that this protection must be furnished under a contract according to the definition does not preclude social insurance from being termed "insurance" on the grounds that it is not a "contract" enforceable by law. In fact, social insurance benefits are statutory rights, enforceable by law, and the term "contract" is actually defined broadly in the dictionary as being an agreement between parties to do something.

It is recognized that the use of the term "social insurance" may result in some misunderstanding of the basic nature of a social security program by the general public, who will tend to think of it in terms of their acquaintance and knowledge of private insurance, or even government insurance involving a contractual relationship (such as the National Service Life Insurance program for those in, or formerly in, military service; crop insurance; and parcel post insurance). Nonetheless, the term "social insurance" is a very popular one both here and abroad, and by usage and dictionary meaning seems proper.

There has been considerable public discussion to the effect that the Supreme Court has declared that the OASDI system is not "insurance." Such statements are based on the decision in the Nestor case (*Fleming v. Nestor*, 363 U.S. 603, 1960), which dealt with the constitutionality of a provision prohibiting payment of OASDI benefits to persons who had been deported for subversive activities. Actually, the decision stated that "the Social Security system may be accurately described as a form of social insurance, enacted pursuant to Congress' power to spend money in aid of the general welfare." At the same time, the Supreme Court recognized that a covered employee has a noncontractual interest that "cannot be soundly analogized to that of the holder of an annuity, whose right to benefits are bottomed on his contractual premium payments." In this respect, it is true that the government brief made a statement that has frequently been incorrectly understood, namely, that "the OASI program is in no sense a federally-administered 'insurance program' under which each worker pays 'premiums' over the years and acquires at retirement an indefeasible right." The foregoing statement must be viewed as a whole; because of the absence of a comma after "program," it does not state that OASI is not an insurance program of some other type than that described.

Furthermore, it should be noted that Congress has referred to OASDI benefits as "insurance benefits" and has designated the part of the Internal Revenue Code that levies the employer and employee taxes to support the OASDI system as the "Federal Insurance Contributions Act."

Regardless of the conflict over the applicability of the term "insurance" to social insurance programs, it is clear that social insurance and private insurance (including governmental insurance plans on a contractual basis) have certain elements in common and certain elements that are distinctly different. This is not to say that because of any such differences, one form is good and the other form is bad. Rather, both forms have important—and complementary—roles to play in economic and social life.

Among the areas in which social insurance and private insurance are similar are the following: a widespread pooling of the risks against which protection is provided; specific, and generally complete, descriptions of all conditions pertaining to coverage, benefits, and financing; precise mathematical calculations of benefit eligibility and amounts; and specific tax or contribution (or premium) rates that are computed to meet the estimated costs of the system. On the other hand, the areas in which social insurance and private insurance are, to some extent or other, dissimilar are the following:

1. Private insurance must be based on individual equity. Social insurance, although possibly having certain individual equity features, must generally contain a considerable degree of emphasis on social adequacy principles.
2. Private insurance is on a voluntary basis as to participation (under some employee benefit plans, the employee must paticipate, but the employer's action in establishing the plan is voluntary—even under collective bargaining). Social insurance almost invariably is based on compulsory participation.
3. Private insurance involves complete contractual rights between the two parties (the insurer always has the right to terminate the contract on nonpayment of premiums; but usually, it must continue the contract in force for the period specified—but note the cancelable type of health insurance and the variable rate provisions in some noncancelable health insurance). Social insurance does not involve a strictly contractual relationship, although the benefits involve a statutory right (but the statutory provisions can be changed from time to time by the legislature).
4. Private individual insurance must be fully funded so that the rights of the insureds are protected, and this is a desired goal of private pension plans (but note that under the latter, full funding is often not present, especially with regard to prior-service benefits). Social

insurance, because of its compulsory and statutory nature, need not be fully funded—in fact, it is generally thought that from an economic standpoint, full funding is undesirable.

Originally, the criticism of the use of "insurance" came from persons associated with the private insurance business. Admittedly, the Social Security Board (now, the Social Security Administration) very definitely overstressed the insurance concept in the early days of the program. This was done primarily to build up and maintain public support for the social security program—by drawing upon the good name and reputation of private insurance.

More recently, some economists have attempted to discredit the insurance principle under OASDI.[2] Such individuals seem to consider insurance as involving only individual policies, which, by their very nature, must be founded on individual equity. They fail to consider the various group insurances, which have many of the same characteristics as social insurance. Under the group insurances, quite properly, employees do not usually share equally (or proportionately with salary) in the employer's contributions.

Social security is not completely analagous to private insurance, although certain characteristics are common. Despite what such economists assert, the cost of the OASDI program can be actuarially evaluated in a reasonably reliable manner, just as much as can group plans of a private nature, which are just as subject to future change. Again, benefits under OASDI are equally on a predetermined basis with those under private plans. The fact that OASDI is compulsory has no connection with whether or not it is insurance. The basic essence of insurance is broad pooling of the risks involved, and OASDI does this as a social insurance program.

Necessity for Compulsory Coverage under Social Insurance Programs

As indicated in the definition of social insurance in Appendix A, one basic distinguishing principle and feature thereof is compulsory coverage, with only minor exceptions, of all categories of persons subject thereto.

The question is raised as to why people should not be allowed individually to decide whether they wish to participate in the social

---

[2] For example, see John A. Brittain, *The Payroll Tax for Social Security* (Washington, D.C.: The Brookings Institution, 1972).

insurance program, especially those who are financially well off and who can (or believe they can) take care of themselves. Sometimes, those who express this view add the requirement, for such opting-out of social insurance coverage, that the individual must provide private-sector benefit coverage which is at least equal to that under the social insurance program.

Quite obviously, such an approach of voluntary coverage has great "political" appeal. Those who wish to be covered will be, and those who do not want coverage will have what they want, too.

The only difficulty—and one which in fact is controlling—is that with such voluntary coverage being operative, there would be significant adverse antiselection against the program. The low-cost risks (young persons, high-salaried persons, nonmarried persons, and women who expect to receive benefits from their husband's earnings record) would tend to opt-out, and those with high costs would tend to remain in. This, in turn, would completely disrupt the financing of the program and would necessitate higher tax rates or some other source of funds, which might cause still more persons to opt-out.

Another disadvantage of permitting general voluntary coverage is that some low-income persons for whom coverage might be financially advantageous would, nonetheless, opt-out "because they need the money now." In the long run, such persons would probably be destitute when old age, disability, or death strikes; and so governmental relief or assistance would be required. It seems preferable to take care of such cases by the social insurance approach as much as is possible.

If there is the requirement of having at least equivalent protection in order to opt-out, certain of the antiselection will be avoided (as will, too, the problem of those low-income persons imprudently opting-out). But yet there will remain so much antiselection in balance that the financing difficulties will be great.

In summary, then, although permitting general voluntary coverage might seem attractive at first glance, it is not at all feasible to do so from the standpoints of the program being adequately and reasonably financed and of it doing the protection job for which it is intended.

CONCEPT OF POVERTY

Historically, the concept of poverty was not developed as a result of a scientific determination, such as has been done in evaluating the speed of light or the distance to the moon. Instead, it was developed as a political stratagem for the reelection campaign of President Kennedy in 1964. After his assassination, this theme was taken over by President Johnson for his campaign.

Initially, a figure of $3,000 per year was arbitrarily taken as representing the poverty threshold, without specifying size of the family or its location. Subsequent refinements sharpened the concept so that this figure applied to a nonfarm family consisting of a married couple with two children. Then an entire framework of poverty levels was developed and was projected into the future on the basis of changes in the cost of living. No surveys were made at all as to what this initial "magic" $3,000 figure really meant in terms of living standards. Nor, in measuring poverty, is account taken of whether the family had assets such as home ownership or support from relatives.

As an example of a rather common situation where the individual is classified as being in poverty, but by any reasonable standard really is not, consider an aged widow. Assume that she has annual income of $1,600 (mostly from OASDI) and lives in her mortgage-free home worth $25,000. Suppose further that she has a small garden, or that her children help her out frequently by gifts in cash or in kind, or even that her married son and his family live with her and pay a substantial part of the operating expenses of the house. Certainly, she is making out reasonably well and is not really in "poverty"—and she, no doubt, is proud of being able to take care of herself from a financial standpoint.

Before this mechanistic definition of poverty was invented, the term "poverty" had more generally been used for the grinding type of depressed living and starvation that is so widely prevalent in many overpopulated, economically undeveloped countries. Little of this is actually present in the United States, although its different usage of this term has no doubt been quite enthusiastically accepted for propaganda purposes by some of its political opponents who can claim that, based on their definitions, their countries have no poverty, while this country admits to having a significant amount thereof.

SOCIAL SECURITY IN THE UNITED STATES

A system of "social security" programs has been adopted in this country. The purpose of this book is to examine the nature of these programs and to illustrate their significance as they act to assist in man's search for economic security.

The primary "social security" program in the United States is, of course, the old-age, survivors, and disability insurance system and the health benefits provided by Medicare. The magnitude and importance of this program is such that its description occupies the major portion of the book. Parts II and III are devoted exclusively to OASDI and Medicare. Part IV describes various related programs, including public assistance, unemployment insurance, workmen's compensation, the various cash sickness programs, the railroad retirement system, and other special programs. Finally, Part V provides a comparative survey of programs in foreign countries.

PART II

Old-Age, Survivors, Disability Insurance

The Social Security Act of 1935 initiated a program designed to alleviate the economic security problems faced by individuals entering the retirement years of their lives. In the years that followed, this program was broadened or expanded to include survivorship benefits, disability benefits, and health care benefits. This social security program is examined in detail in Parts II and III.

Part II will describe old-age, survivors, and disability insurance (OASDI). This Part begins with a detailed examination and description of the basic principles and present provisions of the OASDI system. This is followed by an historical review tracing the development of the OASDI program. Then, the important financing basis of the program is discussed. Part II concludes with a discussion of some issues involved in OASDI and a survey of some possible directions of future developments of the system.

chapter 2

Basic Principles and Present
Provisions of OASDI System

The old-age, survivors, and disability insurance system (OASDI) can best be understood by considering the basic principles underlying it before giving a description of its provisions. The latter can be considered under several broad headings: coverage, benefit provisions, and financing. Each of these is taken up in turn, including explanations of why the provisions were adopted. Appendix C includes a summary of the current provisions of OASDI as of the beginning of 1975, including the increases in benefits which will occur for June 1975, as a result of the automatic-adjustment provisions.

Before proceeding, it would be well to define several terms. By "workers" is meant both wage and salaried employees and self-employed individuals. By "wages" is meant both the wages of non-salaried employees and the salaries of salaried employees. By "earnings" is meant both wages and self-employment income. The terms "contributions" and "taxes" are here used interchangeably, since both are so used in the Social Security Act.

BASIC PRINCIPLES OF OASDI SYSTEM

There are a number of what might be termed "basic principles" of the OASDI program. These were the basic principles initially, and they have not been changed greatly in more than 35 years of operation. Among these are the following: (1) the benefits are based on presumptive need, (2) the benefits should provide a floor of protection, (3) there should be a balance between social adequacy and individual equity, (4) the benefits should be related to earnings, and (5) financing should be on a self-supporting contributory basis. It should be mentioned, however, that there is not universal agreement on all these principles by students of social security, as will be mentioned in the following discussion.

Benefits Based on Presumptive Need

Certain categories of social risk are established by the law, and benefits are, in general, paid when these eventuate. Thus, for example, old-age benefits are not payable automatically upon attainment of a stated minimum retirement age, such as 62, but rather only upon retirement. Likewise, benefits for eligible surviving widows are generally payable for their full lifetime, subject to their not being substantially gainfully employed, or to their meeting certain remarriage limitations.

The retirement condition for receipt of benefits is frequently misunderstood as being a means test or needs test. When considered in that light, some critics believe that the retirement, or earnings, test is unfair because only earned income is used as a criterion for paying benefits, while investment income is disregarded. This procedure, however, is essential if there is to be a system paying retirement benefits and not a charity or welfare program based on individual needs as determined by social workers. The latter would be an inimical basis insofar as the nation is concerned, because individual and group thrift would then be discouraged.

It is sometimes said that social security benefits are intended to be a replacement of earnings when certain risks take place, but this is not entirely correct. In many instances, retirement benefits are paid, and quite properly so, even though the individual had not been substantially gainfully employed for some years before the minimum retirement age. Under such circumstances, it can be argued that the benefits are logically payable because the individual, by working in his younger years, was accumulating certain deferred retirement benefits.

"Floor-of-Protection" Concept

It is generally agreed that social security benefits should provide only a minimum floor of protection against the various risks. There is, however, a great diversity of opinion as to how far apart the floor and the ceiling should be. At one extreme are those who believe that the floor should be so low as to be virtually nonexistent. At the other extreme, some believe that the floor should be high enough to provide a comfortable standard of living, completely disregarding any economic security that private or group methods might provide. This viewpoint implies that a floor-of-protection concept is not really valid. The middle viewpoint is that the benefits under a social insurance system should, along with other income and assets, be sufficient to yield a reasonably satisfactory minimum standard of living for the great majority of individuals. Then, any individuals still in need should be taken care of by a supplementary social assistance program.

In considering the level of OASDI benefits, it should be kept in mind that they are not subject to personal income tax, whereas pre-retirement earnings are subject to such taxes (and others too). However, this exemption from income tax is a valuable feature only for persons with high OASDI benefits and for persons with other income. Those with small or moderate OASDI benefits only would not have to pay income tax even if such benefits were taxable, because of the double personal exemption for those aged 65 or over and the standard deduction for low-income persons.

Relationship between Individual Equity and Social Adequacy

The OASDI system emphasizes social adequacy in the benefit structure more than individual equity, although some elements of the latter are present. In general, the higher the average wage the covered individual has, the larger will be his benefits. Also, the longer he is actually in covered employment in proportion to the period in which he could potentially be covered, the larger will be his benefits. The increase in benefits for higher amounts of earnings or for higher proportions of covered participation are by no means proportionate, but they are present. The social adequacy basis is also evident through the provision of relatively high minimum benefits and through the imposition of maximum benefit provisions.

Over the years, the OASDI benefit structure has shown a trend away from individual equity principles and toward more social adequacy. The provisions of the original act also placed emphasis on social adequacy, although it did have considerable emphasis on individual equity through the provision "guaranteeing" that total benefits payable with respect to a covered worker would always at least equal the employee taxes paid plus an allowance for interest. This guarantee was in an amount of $3\frac{1}{2}$ percent of total lifetime covered wages, as against the maximum ultimate tax rate being 3 percent, although starting off at 1 percent. The 1939 amendments eliminated this provision and instead substituted monthly survivor benefits, payable only in those cases where eligible dependents are left.

Even today, many people incorrectly believe that complete individual equity prevails under OASDI and that their taxes are accumulating at interest in the headquarters of the Social Security Administration in Baltimore. To some extent, this view is encouraged by the many references of the SSA to people's social security accounts that it maintains. Actually, these accounts record only the creditable earnings of each covered worker, and not the taxes paid or interest thereon.

This misconception prevails in some high places too. For example, Senator Barry Goldwater in an article in *The Reader's Digest* for August 1974 stated that OASDI benefits "are a repayment of our own earnings, which we have deposited in trust as a regular contribution deducted from our salaries and from our employers on our behalf." This statement was made to support the view that OASDI benefits should be paid at age 65 regardless of retirement from substantial employment.

Earnings-Related Benefits

Because of social adequacy and the floor-of-protection concept, it seems desirable that benefits should be relatively larger for those with low earnings than for those with high earnings. Accordingly, the benefit formula under the OASDI system has always been heavily "weighted," so that a higher benefit rate applied to the lower portion of average earnings than to the higher portion. However, since contributions are related to earnings up to the maximum earnings base, there is some appeal to the public in the fact that the higher an individual's earnings, the higher his benefits will be.

Because of a conflict between the two principles, social adequacy and earnings-related benefits, an anomaly (some would say gross inequity or injustice) arises under OASDI in the first few decades of operation.[1]

---

[1] For a more complete and critical discussion of this matter as it applies to both the Canadian social insurance system and OASDI, see James L. Clare, "Financing Social Security," *Proceedings*, 60th Annual Conference, National Tax Association, Tax Institute of America, 1973.

If benefits are to be earnings related, and if reasonably sizable benefits are to be paid in the early years of operation, the *absolute* actuarial bargain under individual-equity considerations will go to the highest paid persons, even with a heavily weighted benefit formula being applicable. Under such circumstances, the *relative* actuarial bargain will be larger for the low-paid persons in the short run; over the long run, the low-paid persons will make out much better than the high-paid persons when the value of benefits and taxes is compared, both relatively and absolutely.

As an illustration of this, consider the situation for individuals retiring at age 65 in January 1940. The monthly benefit for a nonmarried individual with maximum creditable earnings was $41.20, and this had an actuarial present value then of about $4,940. The corresponding benefit for earnings of $1,200 per year (approximately the average earnings of a full-time worker then) was $25.75, with a present value of about $3,190. The total employee taxes paid were $90 for the maximum case and $36 for the average case. Thus, the average individual had a benefit value that was 89 times the taxes he paid, as against a ratio of 55 times for the maximum case. But the absolute actuarial bargain was $4,850 for the maximum case versus only $3,154 for the average case. More computations along these lines are presented in the appendix to Chapter 5.

Some would term this situation as "upside-down welfare" and therefore as being indefensible. But it should be noted that the only way to avoid this situation if there is to be a social insurance plan is to have flat benefits—or to have only a public assistance plan. Those who believe in the desirability or necessity of an earnings-related social insurance system argue that the long-range advantages thereof offset the short-term anomaly discussed above.

Self-Supporting Contributory Basis

In brief, the principle of self-support means that no general revenue appropriations or subsidies will, over the long run, be needed to finance the benefit payments and the administrative expenses. The contributions (taxes) from workers and employers will be available for such purposes, as will be the interest earned on the trust funds that result from the excess of income over outgo of the system, which is, by law, invested only in United States government securities (or in securities guaranteed by the government). Such interest does not represent "contributions" or "financial support" from either the General Treasury or the general taxpayer, since the interest on these investments would have to be paid, regardless of whether the securities were held by the trust fund or by private investors.

The basic financing principle adopted by Congress in 1950, and since maintained for OASDI, is that the program should be completely self-supporting from taxes of workers and employers. Self-support can be achieved by any number of different tax schedules—ranging, at one extreme, from a schedule higher in the early years than in the later, thus tending to produce a "fully funded reserve," to the other extreme, a schedule so slowly graded up that "pay-as-you-go" or current-cost financing would, in effect, result. The actual basis adopted initially for OASDI was between "pay-as-you-go" and "fully funded"—probably nearer the former.

It should, however, be noted that this long-standing—some would say time-proven—principle of complete self-support from contributions of workers and employers is under attack. Some groups believe that a government subsidy (or more euphemistically, government contribution) is desirable because the heavy, and readily apparent, burden of payroll taxes is a strong deterrent to the benefit liberalizations which they espouse. This subject is discussed in more detail later, especially in Chapter 5.

Efforts to destroy the self-supporting principle of financing OASDI have been given impetus by the change in the railroad retirement system in October 1974, whereby a significant amount of its financing will come from the General Fund of the Treasury. This is discussed in detail in Chapter 12. It could be argued that such action is not really a precedent for the OASDI system, because there is a significant difference between a small group being subsidized by the whole nation and the entire citizenry being subsidized by itself.

Over the years, the various amendments have moved closer toward current-cost financing, especially insofar as the next few years after the legislative change would be concerned, but still showing considerable buildup of the trust fund balance in the long range. As a result, the actual experience showed close to current-cost financing, with the trust fund balance in recent years being about one year's outgo in size.

The amendments in 1972 recognized this principle of current-cost financing for the OASDI system by establishing a tax schedule that would accomplish this general result for all future periods. The principle is not stated explicitly in the law, although it is brought out clearly in the House and Senate committee reports, which have considerable influence in expressing congressional intent.

In carrying out this principle of self-support, the basis has been adopted that the employer and employee should share the cost equally, each paying a percentage tax rate on earnings up to a certain specified maximum amount. This equal-sharing basis was adopted on purely arbitrary grounds, and not for actuarial reasons. From a logical standpoint, it seemed a reasonable approach, since both parties have an interest in the matter, the employee because of his self-concern and the employer because of replacing in a humanitarian way his superannuated staff.

When self-employed individuals were first covered by the system, their tax rate was set at 75 percent of the combined employer-employee rate. This was a "political" and "practical" compromise between the position of paying only the employee rate and that of paying the combined employer-employee rate. This 75 percent basis was also "supported" by several other arguments. One was that self-employed persons report income which is partly the result of presumed interest earnings on the invested assets in the business, and this might perhaps average 25 percent of their total income. Therefore, they should not pay tax on this amount. The fallacy here, however, is that this 25 percent should not be included as a benefit credit, but it is being included.

Another argument for the 75 percent basis for the self-employed was that this category has a lower cost than does the category of employees, largely because they are apt to defer retirement longer. This may be true, but again the argument can be of doubtful relevance, because experience rating does not, and should not, play a role in OASDI as between other low-cost or high-cost categories. For a long-range risk like OASDI, it would be virtually an impossible task to develop any reasonably valid experience rating system.

Actually, from the standpoint of logic, and considering the financing of the system, the self-employed should pay the same rate as the employer and employee combined. The trust funds should receive the same amount of taxes for a particular amount of earnings credits no matter who earns them.

The 75 percent basis seemed politically necessary because the tax burden on the self-employed would otherwise seem too high, and many in this category are considered to be politically potent. Moreover, initially the self-employed paid the tax in one lump sum each year, when they filed their income tax, so that the tax amount was very apparent, as compared with employees who pay by the less painful way of periodic payroll deduction. Currently, the self-employed pay the social security tax along with the quarterly estimated income tax.

Even the 75 percent basis for the self-employed seemed onerous to them, and so a 7 percent ceiling on the OASDI rate was inaugurated for the self-employed in the 1965 amendments, with the ceiling first becoming effective in 1973. Likewise, to satisfy the complaints of the self-employed, when the hospital insurance (HI) portion of Medicare was established in 1965, it was decided that the self-employed should pay only the employee tax rate (i.e., 50 percent of the combined employer-employee rate).

When the system receives lesser amounts from the self-employed than from other covered categories, someone must make up the difference. Therefore, it can be said that all the tax concessions made to self-employed persons under OASDI and HI mean that the employers and employees must pay somewhat more than they otherwise would. Specifically, if the self-employed paid the full employer-employee rate, the 11.7 percent rate applicable for 1974 for OASDI and HI combined could have been reduced to 11.4 percent, a not insignificant decrease!

COVERAGE PROVISIONS OF OASDI SYSTEM

Virtually all gainfully employed persons are covered under the program or could be covered by election. The major exceptions are policemen with their own retirement systems in a majority of states, federal government employees under the civil service retirement system, low-income self-employed persons, and farm and domestic workers with irregular employment. Railroad workers are, in essence, covered under the OASDI program as a result of the provision for transfer of the wage credits of employees with less than 10 years of service and as a result of the financial interchange provisions applicable to all railroad employees (see Chapter 12). The numbers of covered workers and noncovered workers, by category, for June 1974, are shown in Table 2.1.

It is significant to note that in recent years the wages and salaries of persons covered by OASDI has represented 89 percent of all wages and salaries in the country. Further, the wages and salaries of persons

TABLE 2.1

Estimated OASDI Coverage in Effect among Persons
in Paid Employment, June 1974
(in millions)

		Noncovered Persons	
Employment Category	*Covered Persons*	*Coverage Not Elected*	*Excluded from Coverage*
Nonfarm self-employed..................	4.87	0.15	0.79
Farm operators........................	1.47	0.31	0.05
Ministers.............................	0.20	0.02	—
Employees in industry and commerce.....	56.83	—	0.35*
Employees of nonprofit organizations.....	3.13	0.22	0.16
Employees of state and local governments.........................	7.87	3.38	0.32
Employees of federal government, civilian.............................	0.29	—	2.46
Employees of federal government, military.............................	2.17	—	—
Farm employees........................	1.02	—	0.32
Domestic employees....................	0.91	—	0.39
Railroad employees.....................	0.60	—	—
Total employed persons.............	79.36	4.08	4.84

* Consists of newsboys under age 18.
Source: Social Security Administration.

covered under other governmental retirement systems (railroad retirement, civil service retirement, and state and local government retirement systems) but not under OASDI represented another 8½ percent. Thus, the wages and salaries of persons with governmental retirement plan protection were as much as 97½ percent of all wages and salaries in the country.

Nonfarm Self-Employed

All nonfarm self-employed persons are covered—both nonprofessional (such as store owners) and professional (such as lawyers and physicians). They report their net earnings annually on the income tax return, with no coverage when such earnings are less than $400. This provision was introduced for administrative reasons, since coverage enforcement would be extremely difficult for cases of very low earnings. It should be noted, however, that many persons are required to file income tax returns for social security purposes even though they have no income tax to pay (because the personal exemptions are in excess of their net income, despite the latter being $400 or more). Undoubtedly, much such required coverage is not actually effectuated.

It may be noted, however, that there has been a gradual "hidden" extension of coverage over the years in this area of employment because the $400 limit on earnings is now *relatively* much lower than when it was adopted initially for 1951, due to the significant increase in the general earnings level since then.

A special limited simplified reporting procedure applies to the nonfarm self-employed when they have low net earnings as compared with gross earnings. This is similar to the general provisions applicable to self-employed farmers, although much more restricted, and will be described in detail in the following section.

About 16 percent of the nonfarm self-employed persons who worked in June 1974 were not covered in such employment because of the minimum earnings requirement for coverage. Another 3 percent could have elected coverage under the simplified reporting procedure. Most of these low-income individuals were not dependent on such employment for their livelihood.

Farm Operators

Farmers are covered on the same general basis as other self-employed persons, except for a broader special simplified reporting option for those with low incomes. This option is available for low-income farmers because they frequently do not maintain good financial records, and do not need to do so for income-tax purposes, because no such tax liability exists. Coverage for farmers includes landlords who participate materially in farming operations.

Under the simplified reporting basis, applicable for all years, a farmer with gross income of not more than $2,400 a year may, instead of itemizing income and expense, use two thirds of his gross income as earnings for OASDI purposes. Consistent with this, a farmer with gross income of over $2,400, but net income of less than $1,600, may report earnings of $1,600, instead of actual net income. The procedure for the simplified reporting method for other self-employed persons is similar except that it can be used only in five reporting years, and then only in years when net earnings were less than both $1,600 and two thirds of gross income, and also only if net earnings were at least $400 in two of the preceding three years.

About 24 percent of the farmers who worked in June 1974 were not compulsorily covered in such employment even though they might have had gross earnings of at least $600; they could then have "elected out" by using the net-earnings alternative if these were less than $400. Some 85 percent of this category could have elected coverage under the simplified reporting option based on gross income.

Ministers

Ministers, unlike other occupational groups, may opt-out of coverage on the grounds of being opposed to public insurance of the OASDI type on account of conscience or religious principles. No specific proof of such grounds is necessary. The statement of the minister that such is the case is sufficient. Their earnings are considered as self-employment income even if their compensation is in the form of regular salary. Members of religious orders who have taken a vow of poverty (although, in a sense, not in paid employment) are eligible for coverage if their order agrees irrevocably to cover them, on the employer-employee basis, with their "earnings" to be based on the subsistence provided them, with a minimum not less than $100 per month. The election to opt-out of coverage by ministers must, in general, be made within two years after coverage is first available to the individual as a result of his having at least $400 of ministerial income. Ministers serving abroad who are United States citizens are covered in the same manner as in the United States, regardless of their employer and regardless of whether they have maintained a United States residence—for example, a United States citizen who has served a Canadian congregation for many years.

This special coverage basis for ministers resulted from the strong feeling of some denominations that ministers are not employees and from some ministers believing that participation in a governmental insurance program would violate the principle of separation of church and state. On the other hand, some denominations are quite willing to have their ministers covered on a compulsory basis. The present basis prevails because of the "least common denominator" element.

In passing, it is interesting to note a special exemption for members of certain religious faiths, which applies primarily to certain Amish groups. Exemption from coverage as a self-employed person may be granted to any individual who is a member of a sect which is conscientiously opposed to public or private insurance of the form of OASDI benefits.

About 90 percent of the ministers who are eligible for coverage are actually covered, with a higher proportion being among those at the older ages than at the younger ages.

Employees of Nonfarm Private Employers

All employees in private industry and commerce, including mining, transportation other than railroads, service industries, and so forth, are compulsorily covered, with no minimum restrictions as to amount of earnings or length of employment, except that newsboys under age 18 are excluded. Full-time life insurance agents and certain other types of salesmen are defined by the law to be "employees," regardless of their common-law status.

Employees of Nonprofit Organizations

Coverage for almost all employees of nonprofit organizations of an educational, religious, or scientific nature such as churches, private hospitals, and private schools and colleges, is at the option of each employing unit. Certain categories, such as students employed by their colleges, student nurses, and persons paid less than $50 in a calendar quarter, are not eligible to be covered. The employees in service at the time of election of coverage have an individual election whether or not to be covered. Once coverage is established however, it is compulsory for new employees.

This voluntary coverage basis was adopted because of the traditional tax exempt status of this type of organization. The requirement for compulsory coverage of new entrants and the stringent limitations on canceling the agreements serve to prevent antiselection against the program. In June 1974, about 93 percent of those eligible for coverage by election were actually covered.

Employees of State and Local Governments

Employees of state and local governments can be covered at the option of the state and of the employing unit. In addition, where there is an existing retirement system, a majority of the employees therein must vote in favor of coverage. However, policemen under an existing retirement system cannot be covered under any circumstances, except in specified states. In addition, there are a number of special provisions for designated states that facilitate coverage extension to employees under existing retirement systems by making subdivisions thereof, with each part being separately considered for coverage.

This voluntary coverage basis was adopted because of constitutional necessity—the federal government is not allowed to tax state governments, although it could tax the employees—see the later discussion as to how employees of international organizations and foreign governments are covered. The many complex provisions and alternatives for this coverage result from congressional courtesy. If one state wishes special treatment not disadvantageous to other states, it is readily granted. The requirement for compulsory coverage of new entrants and the stringent limitations on canceling the agreements serve to prevent antiselection against the program.

In June 1974, about 70 percent of all employees who were eligible for such elective coverage were actually covered, and of this group actually covered, about 70 percent also had coverage under a state or local retirement system.

Employees of Federal Government

Virtually all federal civilian employees not under the civil service retirement system or some other retirement system and all members of the uniformed services are covered on a regular contributory basis.[2] The military are covered in this manner only on their cash base pay. Also, OASDI coverage on a coordinated basis is provided for two small existing retirement systems, namely the Tennessee Valley Authority and the Board of Governors of the Federal Reserve Board.

This significant exclusion of most government employees from coverage results from the pressure of government-employee unions. The unions apparently prefer to have a separate, noncoordinated pension plan. This gives the unions more influence over the nature and development of their pension plan. It also permits the develop-

---

[2] The minor exceptions to coverage include such small categories as the President, the Vice President, members of Congress, congressional employees, and temporary employees hired on an emergency basis because of a natural disaster such as a flood.

ment of dual benefit protection by concurrent or subsequent social security employment, which may be very advantageous to the individuals involved, since they will receive relatively high social security benefits in relation to the taxes which they pay. By the same token, this antiselection is costly to the social security system.

On the other hand, short-service federal employees may be at a disadvantage by not receiving any benefits under civil service retirement and having a blank period in their social security. The unions, who oppose coordination of the two programs, appear not to be as much concerned with this category as with career workers. It is noteworthy that the government requires private employers with pension plans to coordinate them with social security (rather than permit contracting-out or exemption for those with suitable plans), but does not do so itself! The separate retirement programs for employees of the federal government and employees of state and local governments are described in Chapter 16.

Employees of Foreign Governments and International Organizations

United States citizens employed in the United States by foreign governments and international organizations are compulsorily covered. Their earnings are considered self-employment income, despite the fact that they are really salaried employees. This was done because of the diplomatic immunity from taxes for the employers involved.

Farmworkers

Farm employment is covered if cash wages in a year from a particular employer amount to at least $150. As an alternative, coverage is applicable if there are 20 or more days of employment remunerated on a time basis (rather than a piece-rate basis). Currently, this alternative is not of much applicability, because wage rates are such that the general provision will apply. Foreign farmworkers admitted on a temporary basis are not covered. In June 1974, 24 percent of the farmworkers who were then employed were not covered because of these earnings and other rules.

Domestic Workers

Domestic servants are covered in their employment for a particular employer if cash wages are $50 or more in a quarter from that employer. When this limit was established in the 1950 act, it represented about 10 days of employment by a day worker, but currently it is only about three or four days. About 30 percent of those who were employed in this type of work in June 1974 were not covered because of this earnings rule.

The dollar limits on coverage for both agricultural and domestic workers have been left unchanged for over two decades, despite the significant increases in general earnings levels. As a result, a gradual "hidden" extension of coverage has occurred over the years for these employment categories.

Tips

Tips to employees by the patrons of the employer are covered if they amount to at least $20 in a month. Under such circumstances, the employee must report the tips to the employer, and the latter must then include them in the social security tax returns as employee earnings in his employment, but only the employee tax is paid thereon. This unusual approach was taken because of the opposition of the employers involved, who protested that they had no control over the remuneration received as tips and therefore should not be taxed thereon.

Employment Abroad

The preceding discussion of coverage conditions relates to employment in the United States (including American Samoa, Guam, Puerto Rico, and the Virgin Islands) and on American vessels and airplanes. In addition, United States citizens working for American employers abroad are covered. Also, United States citizens working for foreign subsidiaries of American companies can be covered if the American employer so elects and guarantees payment of the taxes. A self-employed person working abroad is covered if he maintains a residence in the United States.

Military Service Wage Credits

"Gratuitous" wage credits of $160 a month were provided for military service after September 15, 1940. These terminated at the end of 1956, and regular contributory coverage began. Similar wage credits, at the rate of $300 for each calendar quarter in which the individual has military service, are given for service after 1956 as an allowance for remuneration furnished in kind. The OASDI system and the hospital insurance program are reimbursed by the General Fund of the Treasury for the cost of the additional benefits paid as a result of these wage credits.

Somewhat similar gratuitous wage credits are given to United States citizens of Japanese ancestry who were interned during World War II. The amount of such wage credits is based on the minimum wage then applicable under general law or, if higher, on the actual past wage of the individual. The cost of the additional benefits arising from these wage credits is reimbursed to the trust funds by the General Fund of the Treasury.

It is important to note that the gratuitous wage credits granted for service before 1951 have relatively little cost effect, since the vast majority of benefit computations are based on earnings after 1950.

BENEFIT PROVISIONS OF OASDI SYSTEM

The term "benefit provisions" includes such elements as (1) eligibility conditions that determine the extent of coverage required for benefits or "insured status," (2) beneficiary categories that identify the types of persons to whom payments are made, (3) benefit amounts including how payments are calculated, (4) an earnings test to establish the level of earnings permitted for benefit payments to be made, and (5) payment of benefits abroad. Whenever the general benefit level is considered, it is important to keep in mind the fact that OASDI benefits are not subject to federal or state income taxes.

Insured Status Conditions

There are three kinds of insured status: "fully," "currently," and "disability." The first yields eligibility for all types of old-age and survivor benefits; the second gives eligibility for certain survivor benefits; and the third is part of the requirement for the "disability freeze" and for disability monthly benefits, except in the special case of blind persons.

Insured status is defined in terms of quarters of coverage, either $50 of wages paid in a calendar quarter or $100 of self-employment income credited to that quarter, except as noted hereafter. With certain minor exceptions, such as death in the particular year, covered self-employed individuals are always credited with 4 quarters of coverage each year, since they are not covered unless they have $400 of earnings in the year. This is also the case for persons with the maximum amount of taxable wages in a year. Special rules similar to those for self-employed individuals apply to farmworkers, whose coverage depends on an annual rather than a quarterly earnings amount. Specifically, they receive credit for 1 quarter of coverage for each full $100 of farm wages earned in a year up to a maximum of 4 quarters of coverage for a calendar year. Naturally, persons with several types of employment can receive credit for no more than 4 quarters of coverage in a particular year. As was the case in connection with the coverage conditions based on dollar amounts, there has been a gradual "hidden" liberalization of the requirements for quarters of coverage, since under current earnings conditions it is much easier to earn $50 a quarter than it was when this limit was set in the 1939 Act.

The annual basis for allocating quarters of coverage for the self-employed and for farm workers was necessary because the coverage provisions for these categories are on an annual reporting requirement.

Fully insured status is achieved if the individual's quarters of coverage equal at least the number of years elapsing after 1950 or year of attainment of age 21, if later, and before the year of attainment of age 62. Somewhat stricter conditions apply, however, for men attaining age 62 before 1975. This will be discussed later. A person attaining age 65 in 1980, for example, must have at least 26 quarters of coverage to qualify for old-age benefits, even if he claims them at age 62. In death and disability cases, the measuring period ends with the year before the year of death or disability. The law provides for a maximum of 40 quarters of coverage being required for fully insured status, but this provision is now redundant since such a result actually occurs under the regular definition for the "maximum case" of those attaining age 21 after 1950. It was previously applicable when the closing computation point was age 65. It should be noted that the required quarters of coverage do not necessarily have to be obtained in the measuring period, but rather can also be obtained before 1951, before age 21, or in or after the year of attaining age 62. In any event, there is a minimum requirement regardless of the foregoing rule, namely, 6 quarters of coverage.

Men attaining age 62 before 1975, or age 65 before 1978, have somewhat less liberal conditions for obtaining fully insured status.

Before the 1972 amendments, an age-65 computation point was applicable to men but not to women. Thus, men attaining age 62 in 1972 had to have 24 quarters of coverage to be fully insured rather than the 21 quarters which would be required under the new computation method. This 24-quarters requirement was made applicable for men attaining age 62 in 1973–75. As a result, for attainments of age 62 in 1975, the requirement is the same for both sexes, and remains so thereafter as it increases 1 quarter for each elapsing year, to the maximum of 40 quarters for those attaining age 62 in 1991 and thereafter.

This discrimination against men attaining age 62 before 1975 is not very serious since most persons have far more quarters of coverage than needed to obtain fully insured status. The parallel discrimination with regard to computation of benefit amounts, discussed later, is much more significant.

Currently insured status is achieved by having 6 quarters of coverage in the 13-quarter period ending with the quarter of death, disability, or attainment of age 62 (or actual retirement, if later).

Disability insured status is achieved by having 20 quarters of coverage in the 40-quarter period ending with the quarter of disablement. Persons under age 31, who may not have had much opportunity for coverage, have alternative special, more liberal, rules— namely, (1) for those aged 24–31, quarters of coverage in at least half of the quarters after age 21, and (2) for those under age 24, 6 quarters of coverage in the last 12 quarters. Note that these two rules for persons under age 31 have a smooth junction at age 24 and that anybody satisfying them will also satisfy the requirements for fully insured status. In a relatively few cases, a young disabled worker can meet the regular "20 out of 40" requirement, and thus qualify—even though he cannot meet the special requirement.

Years containing a qualifying period of disability for individuals who have both fully insured status and disability insured status do not "count against" the individual in measuring the elapsed period for any of the insured status categories. This is the "disability freeze" provision to be described later.

Beneficiary Categories

Individuals are eligible for a monthly old-age insurance benefit at ages 62 or later if fully insured. The amount of this benefit is 100 percent of the primary insurance amount, PIA (defined later), except in the case of a worker first claiming the benefit before age 65. In the latter case, there is a reduction in the benefit of 5/9ths percent for each month below age 65 at time of retirement. Thus, a person retiring at exact age 62 receives a 20 percent lifetime reduction, which closely approximates an "actuarial equivalent" basis, so that no additional cost to the system arises on account of early retirements.

If an individual retires before age 65 but does not remain retired and instead returns to substantial employment, thereby losing some benefits under the earnings test to be described later, he receives an upward adjustment in his benefit when he attains age 65. Specifically, the reduction factor of 5/9ths percent is then applied only to the number of months before age 65 in which he had received the full benefit, without reduction under the earnings test. Thus, a person first claiming benefits at age 62, but who returns to substantial employment for 1½ years between ages 62 and 65 would have a 10 percent lifetime reduction after age 65.

When a general benefit increase is legislated or occurs under the automatic adjustment provisions (described subsequently), the amount of the increase is reduced on the basis of the then attained age with respect to those retiring before age 65. This is, of course, the actuarially equitable approach, even though somewhat burdensome from an administrative standpoint. As an example, consider an individual with a primary insurance amount of $200 per month who retired at age 62 and thus received a benefit of $160. If 1½ years later a 5 percent benefit increase becomes effective, his PIA is increased by $10, and his actual benefit is then raised by $9 (i.e., a 10 percent reduction factor is applied). Then, if three or more years later a 10 percent benefit increase occurs, his actual benefit rises by $21 (i.e., 10 percent of the sum of $200 and $10).

Payments are made only after an individual files a claim and is, in effect, substantially retired (retirement test provisions are described hereafter). Retroactive payments for as much as 12 months before filing of the claim may be made with respect to all monthly benefits.

An individual is eligible for monthly disability insurance benefits, in the amount of the PIA, if (1) he is totally disabled so that he cannot engage in any substantial gainful activity, has been so disabled for at least five months, and can be expected to continue to be so disabled for at least 12 months in total, or until prior death; and (2) he has both fully and disability insured status. Persons who are blind need to satisfy only the fully insured status requirement. If the individual was disabled as a result of a work-connected accident or disease and is receiving workmen's compensation benefits, the OASDI benefit may be reduced, as will be discussed later in connection with benefit amounts.

Total disability is defined as the "inability to engage in any substantial gainful activity by reason of any medically determinable physical or mental impairment." Blindness, statutorily defined as "central visual acuity of 20/200 or less in the better eye with the use of correcting lens" or limitation of vision such that "the widest diameter of the visual field subtends an angle no greater than 20 degrees," qualifies as a permanent disability.

It should be noted that the waiting period of five consecutive months of disability is not a presumptive period which, if satisfied, would "prove" the existence of a qualifying permanent disability. The effective waiting period between date of disablement and date of first benefit payment is 6½ months on the average, since the first payment is made at the end of the calendar month following five full months of disability, and then only if the individual is alive and disabled. In the case of an individual who recovers from his disability and within five years becomes disabled a second time, this waiting period need not be satisfied again.

The determinations of disability are made by state agencies, generally the vocational rehabilitation unit. The Social Security Administration reviews these determinations and may reverse the finding of disability, but may not reverse a denial of the existence of disability, except on a direct appeal of the claimant.

The determination of continuance of disability is made by the state agencies. Individuals must, in general, undertake vocational rehabilitation training. During the first nine months thereof, benefits will be paid regardless of earnings. The costs of the rehabilitation services for disabled workers and other disabled beneficiaries are paid from the trust funds which pay the cash benefits; that is, the DI Trust Fund pays the cost of this service for disabled workers and disabled children of such beneficiaries, and the OASI Trust Fund pays for other disabled children and for disabled widows and widowers.

There are two limitations on payments for rehabilitation. First, this benefit is available only if there is a good likelihood that the result will be rehabilitation of the maximum number of such beneficiaries into productive activity. Second, no more can be paid out in this manner in any fiscal year than 1½ percent of the benefit payments to disabled beneficiaries in the preceding year.

Benefits are paid during the first nine months of any other trial work period of a disability beneficiary who has not medically recovered from his disability. With this exception, there is no permitted amount of earnings, as there is for retired workers and for dependent and survivor beneficiaries under the earnings test. Rather, a disability beneficiary might have small earnings and still continue to receive benefits so long as he is considered not able to engage in any substantial gainful activity.

The disability benefits terminate at age 65, and the beneficiary then goes on the old-age benefit roll. If the medical condition of a disability beneficiary improves to the extent that he is no longer disabled within the meaning of the law, benefits are nonetheless continued for three months. Thus, for those having a trial work period, 12 months of benefits are payable after such period begins.

If the retired or disabled individual has a wife aged 65 or over (or, regardless of her age, if she has a child under age 18 in her care, or a child of any age who has been disabled since before age 22, using the same definition that is applicable for insured workers), an additional benefit of 50 percent of the worker's PIA is payable, with a similar addition for each eligible child. A child aged 18–21 who is in full-time school attendance is also eligible for child's benefits. Benefit eligibility continues until the end of the semester or quarter during which the student attains age 22 if he has not completed the requirements for a bachelor's degree, or if the school is on a "course" basis rather than by semester or quarter, until the end of the course, although for not more than two months. Such a child does not make the mother eligible for wife's benefits. Under such circumstances, the theory is that she is capable of employment, just as in the case when she is under age 62 and with no eligible child under age 18 or disabled. The term "child" includes not only natural children but also stepchildren and adopted children, although with certain restrictions to prevent abuse.

In certain instances, child's benefits are payable on the earnings record of a grandparent. Such child's parents must be dead or disabled, and the grandchild must have been living with and have been supported by the grandparent for at least a year. Considering these stringent conditions and the great likelihood that the child would receive benefits from one of his parents, relatively few of these grandchild's benefits will be payable.

A wife between age 62 and age 65 without an eligible child can elect to receive reduced benefits. These are based on the 50 percent benefit, but with a reduction factor of 25/36ths percent for each month under age 65 at time of claiming benefit being applied. This reduction continues during the joint lifetime of the couple. Thus, a wife claiming benefit at exact age 62 has a 25 percent reduction. This is somewhat less than the approximately 30 percent needed on an "actuarial equivalent" basis (a larger reduction than for women workers claiming benefits before age 65 being required because it applies during the shorter joint lifetime with the spouse, as compared with the single lifetime of the woman worker). The 25 percent basis was adopted, despite involving some added cost to the program, because the 30 percent reduction actuarially called for "seemed too large" from a political viewpoint insofar as the sponsors of the change were concerned.

A former wife who was divorced after at least 20 years of marriage is also eligible for a wife's benefit at age 62 or over, with such benefit being on a reduced basis if first claimed before age 65. Thus, more than one wife's benefit can be paid on a particular earnings record.

Husband's benefits, computed in a similar manner to wife's benefits for a wife without an eligible child present, are payable in respect to a retired or disabled female worker if the husband is aged 62 or over and has been chiefly dependent on her. The law, as it stood in early 1975, contained this dependency requirement. It also did not provide for father's benefits comparable with the mother's benefits for widows with young children or husband's benefits for retired or disabled female workers when the husband was under age 62. A unanimous Supreme Court decision in March, 1975, declared that the failure to pay such father's benefits was unconstitutional and that such must be done. It seems certain that, either by change in the law or by further court decisions, the dependency requirement and other differences in treatment by sex will be done away with, including those for widowers (as described next).

Widow's benefits are payable at age 60, or at age 50 if disabled, if the deceased husband was fully insured (including death after retirement). Parallel benefits are also payable with respect to dependent widowers. A divorced former wife can qualify for widow's benefits. The definition of disability for widows and dependent widowers is stricter than that applicable to disability benefits for insured workers. It requires the disability to be so severe as to prevent the individual from engaging in *any* gainful activity, not merely "any substantial gainful activity," which term is broadened by the law to take into account his age, education, and work experience. Moreover, the disability must occur no later than seven years after the death of the insured worker or, in the case of a widow with eligible children, no later than seven years after she ceases receiving mother's benefits. The reason for this seven-year "grace period" is that by the end of that time the widow or widower should, if not disabled before then, be able to have worked and acquired disability insured status on his own earnings record.

The widow's (or widower's) benefit, except as noted hereafter, is 100 percent of the PIA if the initial claim is made at ages 65 or over, 71½ percent at age 60, and 50 percent at age 50, with proportionate amounts at intermediate ages at time of award. These results are achieved by using a factor of 19/40ths percent for each month below 65 down to age 60 (which is somewhat smaller than the factor used for benefits for retired workers at ages 62–64 and is thus not quite on an approximate actuarial basis, so that some added cost to the program is involved) and a factor of 43/240ths percent for each month below age 60 down to age 50. The latter factor is purely arbitrary, developed to produce the 50 percent benefit rate established for age 50.

If the deceased insured worker had claimed a reduced old-age benefit before death, the widow (or widower) may receive a benefit which is less than the amount derived from these factors. Under such circumstances, the survivor benefit cannot exceed the larger of (1) the reduced old-age benefit or (2) 82½ percent of the PIA. This complex provision resulted from the change in the 1972 amendments providing for a 100 percent widow's benefit for widowhood at or after age 65, on the grounds that a single survivor needed as much to live on as a single worker. Following this argument to its logical conclusion, then, a widow should not receive *more* than the retired worker on whose earnings the survivor pension is based. The 82½ percent provision reflects the fact that this was the benefit rate previously for widows aged 62 and over.

The foregoing provision can result in considerable inequities and can make for difficult choices for persons who file claims for benefits. For example, consider a worker aged 62 with a wife aged 65. If he files a claim and becomes entitled to old-age benefits, his widow's benefit rate when he dies will be 82½ percent. But if he does not file, her rate will be 100 percent. It can make a tremendous financial difference if he files for early benefit and then dies within a few months after age 62.

When a fully insured worker dies, parent's benefits are payable at age 62 to parents who have been dependent upon such individual. The benefit is 82½ percent of the PIA if one parent receives benefits, and 75 percent each if two parents receive benefits. This is done in order that two parents will not receive more than a retired worker and spouse.

When a fully or currently insured individual dies leaving a child under age 18 (regardless of age if permanently and totally disabled since before age 22), or aged 18–21 and in school (and slightly beyond age 21 as in the case of a child of a retired or disabled worker), benefits are payable to such child and to the widowed mother having care of a child under 18 or disabled. A divorced former wife, as described previously, except that she does not have to meet the requirement of 20 years of marriage, is also eligible for mother's benefits. Just as in the case of retired and disabled workers, a child aged 18–21 who is in full-time school attendance does not make the widowed mother eligible for mother's benefits. These child survivor benefits are equally applicable with respect to the death of an insured female worker, except that no father's benefits are available. Valuable permanent survivor protection is thus available for women who leave the labor market to take up the job of raising a family if they have worked in covered employment long enough to be fully insured at time of potential death (40 quarters of coverage will always be sufficient)—see later example. The benefits are 75 percent of the PIA, both for the widowed mother and for each child. If the widowed mother can receive a larger amount as a widow's benefit (generally if she is age 61 or over), such payment is made, rather than a mother's benefit.

Special benefits payable at age 72 or after are available for two categories of persons who are not fully insured. Transitional-insured benefits can be qualified for under the same circumstances as old-age benefits (and wife's and widow's benefits can also then arise) for individuals who would meet the fully insured conditions except that they do not have the 6 quarters of coverage required, although they must have 3 to 5 such quarters. This provision applies only to men who attained age 72 before 1964 and to women who attained age 72 before 1967. Wife's benefits (but not husband's benefits) of 50 percent of the primary benefit are payable for wives who attained age 72 before 1969. Widow's benefits (but not widower's benefits) of the full primary benefit are payable for widows who attained age 72 before 1969 and whose deceased husbands similarly failed to meet the requirements of fully insured status, but had 3 to 5 quarters of coverage.

Transitional-noninsured benefits are available on only an individual basis for persons who either attained age 72 before 1968 or attained age 72 later and had 3 quarters of coverage for each year after 1967. This provision does not apply for men who attained age 72 after 1971 and for women who attained age 72 after 1969, since for these cases, fully insured status was as easy to meet. Persons, to be eligible for these benefits, must be residents of the United States (defined here so as to exclude American Samoa, Guam, Puerto Rico, and the Virgin Islands—on the grounds that federal income tax is not payable there) and must also be citizens or lawfully admitted resident aliens with at least five years of continuous residence. These benefits are not payable if the individual is receiving public assistance (including the supplemental security income program, as described in Chapter 11), and they are reduced on a dollar-for-dollar basis for any other governmental pension received (such as a state teacher retirement pension). If both husband and wife are eligible for these benefits, the wife's benefit is reduced by 50 percent.

The primary benefit amount is a flat figure for both types of special age-72 benefits. Such amount initially (1965 for transitional-insured benefits and 1966 for transitional-noninsured benefits) was $35 per month. Subsequently, this amount has been increased at the same time that general across-the-board increases were made in the regular benefits, and beginning June 1975 it is $69.60. The transitional-insured benefits are financed completely from the OASI Trust Fund (i.e., from the payroll taxes), whereas practically all the transitional-noninsured benefits, although paid through this trust fund, are financed out of general revenues; the only exception is for transitional-noninsured benefits for persons with at least 3 quarters of coverage, whose benefits are financed from the OASI Trust Fund.

In all cases of death of a fully or currently insured individual, a lump-sum death payment of 3 times the PIA is payable. This payment, however, may not exceed $255, which was the maximum amount available under the 1952 Act. It is important to note that this has not been increased by the subsequent amendments. Following the amendments in 1972, the minimum amount was $253.50, so that virtually no range in the amount of the lump sum was present. As a result of the amendments in 1973, for deaths after February 1974 the lump sum is $255 in all cases. The lump sum is payable in full to a surviving spouse, but in other cases it may not exceed the actual burial costs. This benefit must be claimed, in general, within two years of death, although later filing is permitted on a showing of good cause.

In order to be eligible for wife's benefits, the wife must have been married to the primary beneficiary for at least a year, or else be the mother of his child or have been eligible for widow's, parent's or disabled-child benefits on another earnings record (such eligibility can be of a deferred nature—that is, benefits would later have been available, upon attainment of age 62). Similarly, to be eligible for widow's benefits, the surviving wife must meet any one of the foregoing requirements (only nine months of marriage required, instead of one year, or no duration required if death was due to accidental causes or while in the uniformed services or if the couple had previously been married for at least nine months), or an alternative one, legally adopting a child while they were married. Corresponding requirements apply for husbands and widowers, in addition to the dependency requirement. Eligibility for parent's benefits extends not only to natural parents but also to stepparents and adopting parents when such status was achieved before the worker involved attained age 16. To be eligible for child's benefits, a child must be a natural or legally adopted child, or a stepchild who had such status for at least a year.

In those instances where dependency must be proved (parent's benefits and formerly—it would appear as a result of a Supreme Court decision in March 1975, which outlawed unequal treatment by sex in OASDI—husband's and widower's benefits), the proof thereof must be filed within two years of the worker's retirement, disability, or death, as the case may be.

Benefits are paid in full for the initial month of entitlement even though the beneficiary is not eligible for the entire month (e.g., as to retired workers, for the month of attainment of age 62; as to survivors, for the month of death of the worker). Conversely, benefits are not paid for the month of termination. In other words, whether or not benefits are paid for a month depends on the person's status at the end of the month. In essence, the nonpayment of pro rata benefits is balanced out by the payment of a full benefit for the initial month and no benefit for the final month.

Benefits terminate not only for death, recovery from disability, and attainment of age 18 for a nondisabled child beneficiary who is not attending school or attainment of age 22 for a nondisabled child beneficiary who is attending school, but also for other reasons for some of the beneficiary categories. Remarriage is, in general, a terminating cause for widows and widowers, while a marriage after the worker's death is generally such a cause for parent's benefits. Similarly, marriage usually terminates child's benefits. Marriage does not, however, terminate a survivor benefit when the person married is also receiving a survivor benefit or a disabled-child benefit, nor does it terminate a disabled-child benefit when the person married is a beneficiary of any type. Also, remarriage after age 60 for a widow or dependent widower to another person than described in the previous sentence does not terminate the benefit, although this does reduce the benefit amount to 50 percent of the PIA. This peculiar provision was adopted, as a compromise, to handle the problem of an aged widow "living in sin" with an aged man who was not an OASDI beneficiary (as reportedly occurred with some frequency in localities which were havens for the aged!).

School-attendance benefits for a child terminate if he ceases full-time attendance (after age 18 and before age 22) and is not disabled. Benefits are paid for months during summer vacation if full-time school attendance precedes and follows such months. Adoption of a child beneficiary is not a terminating event (although before the 1972 legislation it had been except when adoption was by a close relative).

Certain limitations apply to the benefit amounts described previously. No individual can receive, for any month, the full amount of more than one type of monthly benefit. For instance, if a woman has an old-age benefit in her own right and a wife's or widow's benefit from her husband's earnings, then, in effect, only the larger of the two benefits may be received, although in actual practice the old-age benefit is always payable, plus any excess of the secondary benefit.[3] Also, an eligible remarried widow (who remarried after age 60) can receive only the larger of her widow's benefit and the wife's benefit from her new husband. In addition, there are certain minimum and maximum benefit provisions (described subsequently). Also, certain restrictions on payment of benefits may apply in the case of persons convicted of crimes affecting the security of the nation.

---

[3] If benefits are claimed before age 65 and are thus on a reduced basis, when the secondary benefit which would be payable at age 65 is larger than the old-age benefit on the woman's earnings record which would be payable at age 65, then the procedure is to compute separately the reduced old-age benefit and a reduced residual secondary benefit based on the difference between the two full benefits. For example, assume that a woman has a primary benefit based on her own earnings of $100 and that her husband's primary benefit is $300. Then, if she claims benefits at age 62, her reduced primary benefit is $80 (80 percent of $100), and her reduced wife's benefit is $37.50 (75 percent of the residual unreduced wife's benefit of $50—50 percent of $300 minus $100), making a total benefit of $117.50. Note that this procedure is not the same as computing only the reduced full wife's benefit, which would be $112.50 (75 percent of 50 percent of $300).

If an individual who is receiving reduced benefits because of early retirement (at ages 62 to 64 for workers, wives, and husbands, and at ages 50 to 64 for widows and widowers) has them withheld for one or more months before reaching age 65—for example, as a result of the earnings test—an automatic benefit recomputation is made at that age. The benefit is recalculated by eliminating those months from the reduction period. For example, suppose a man claims his old-age benefit at his 62d birthday, but during the next three years he returns to work to such an extent that some or all of his benefit is withheld for nine different months in that period. Then, after age 65, his benefit will no longer be reduced by 20 percent but rather by 15 percent (the 27 months for which full benefits were paid times the 5/9ths percent factor).

TABLE 2.2

Summary of Eligibility Requirements and Benefit Rates for OASDI Benefits

		Requirement as to—	
		Insured Status	Benefit
Type of Benefit	Age	of Worker	Rate*
For Insured Worker			
Old age..........................	62 or over	Fully	100%†
Disability......................	None	Fully and disability	100
For Dependents of Retirement or Disability Beneficiary			
Wife, no child present............	62 or over	Fully	50%†
Wife, eligible child present‡.......	None	Fully	50
Child of worker..................	Under 18§	Fully	50
Husband........................	62 or over	Fully	50†
For Survivors of Insured Worker			
Widow...........................	60 or over‖	Fully	100%†
Widow, eligible child present‡.....	None	Fully or currently	75
Child of worker..................	Under 18§	Fully or currently	75
Widower........................	60 or over‖	Fully	100†
Dependent parent...............	62 or over	Fully	82½#
Lump sum......................	None	Fully or currently	300**

* Expressed as percentage of primary insurance amount, before effect of maximum benefit provisions. Monthly amounts in all cases, except for lump-sum death payment.
† A reduction applies if benefit is claimed before age 65.
‡ A child is not considered "eligible" for the purpose of this benefit if receiving benefits only because of school attendance. As the result of a Supreme Court decision in March 1975, also applicable to widowers (and likely also to husbands).
§ Regardless of age if disabled since age 18, or if attending school at ages 18–21.
‖ Or as low as age 50 if disabled.
If two parents, 75 percent each.
** Limited to $255.

A summary of the foregoing eligibility conditions and benefit rates is shown in Table 2.2.

Benefit Amounts

The benefit amounts are computed by first determining the primary insurance amount (PIA) of the insured worker and then applying to it the appropriate beneficiary percentages and any applicable reductions for "early retirement" (as shown in Table 2.2). Finally, the resulting benefits are subject to overall minimum and maximum family benefit provisions. Actually, the PIA is calculated in two steps. First, the average monthly wage (AMW) is computed. Second, the PIA is determined from the benefit table in the law by entering it with the resulting AMW. Furthermore, the benefit table will be automatically adjusted in the future (beginning in 1975) if the cost of living rises.

Determination of AMW.   The concept of average monthly wage used in OASDI is, in essence, an average computed over the entire potential period of coverage, but with certain periods of low earnings being disregarded. In general, years before 1951 (or age 22, if later) are disregarded. Depending upon the individual's years of attainment of age 62, or year of death or disability, if earlier, a number of years to be used in computing the AMW is determined.

In brief, except for men attaining age 62 before 1975, this measuring period is the number of years which have elapsed after 1955 (or, if later, the year of attainment of age 26) and before the year in which the worker attains age 62 (or dies or becomes disabled, if earlier). The years after 1950 with the highest earnings are used in the computation. The minimum period is two years, applicable in cases of death and in rare cases for age retirement preceded by a long period of disability. For age retirements and recomputations after 1960, the minimum period has generally been five years, although for men attaining age 65 in 1975, it was 19 years (but only 16 years for women under similar circumstances—the reason for the difference will be discussed later). The measuring period will increase gradually to an ultimate value of 35 years—that is, from the calendar year of attainment of age 27 through the year of attainment of age 61.

The use of 1956 as the starting point for determining the period over which the AMW is to be computed, even though earnings back through 1951 can be used in the computation, allows for a five-year dropout of years with low earnings. For example, an individual attaining age 62 in 1975 has his average wage computed over his highest 19 years after 1950, including, if advantageous, the year of attainment of age 62 and any later years. In other words, years of high earnings at and after 62 (possibly as a result of the maximum earnings base being increased over the years) can be substituted for earlier years of lower earnings.

Furthermore, in computing the AMW, the "disability freeze" can be utilized. Years that include qualifying periods of disability are eliminated from the measuring period. To qualify, the disability must be of at least five months' duration, and the individual must have both fully insured status and disability insured status at the time of disablement.

Men attaining age 62 before 1975 (i.e., age 65 before 1978) have less liberal condition for computing the AMW because prior to the 1972 amendments, an age-65 computation point was applicable to men (but not to women). Thus, men attaining age 62 in 1972 had to use 19 years for the measuring period (as against 16 years for women). This 19-year period was made applicable for men attaining age 62 in 1973–75, instead of increasing by one year each year. As a result, for attainments of age 62 in 1975, the requirement is the same for both sexes (and remains so thereafter as it increases one year for each elapsed year, to the maximum of 35 years for those attaining age 62 in 1991 and thereafter). Looking at the situation from the viewpoint of year of attainment of age 65, the periods for computing the AMW are as follows for attainments in 1971–79:

Year of Attainment	Number of Years in Computation of AMW	
	Men	Women
1971..................	15	12
1972..................	16	13
1973..................	17	14
1974..................	18	15
1975..................	19	16
1976..................	19	17
1977..................	19	18
1978..................	19	19
1979..................	20	20

Then, having determined the number of years in the measuring period, that number of years (not necessarily consecutive), with the highest earnings (excluding years before 1951) is used to compute the AMW, regardless of whether these years occurred before age 21 or after age 62. If there are not sufficient years with earnings, then zeros must be used to "fill out" the measuring period. Earnings in the year of retirement (whether for age or disability) are not used in the computation of benefits for that year, but they are used for subsequent years. On the other hand, earnings in the year of death are applicable immediately for survivor benefits. Similarly, earnings in a year after the year of retirement are used for recomputation of the benefit for the following year. The resulting average, if not an even integral dollar, is rounded down to the next lower dollar (i.e., the cents are dropped).

The earnings used in computing the AMW cannot, for a particular year, exceed the maximum taxable earnings base (sometimes referred to as the contribution and benefit base). This base is $3,000 for 1937–50, $3,600 for 1951–54, $4,200 for 1955–58, $4,800 for 1959–65, $6,600 for 1966–67, $7,800 for 1968–71, $9,000 for 1972, $10,800 for 1973, $13,200 for 1974, and $14,100 for 1975. After 1975, it will be automatically adjusted for changes in the level of earnings in covered employment (as will be discussed later).

As an illustration of how the AMW is computed, consider a man who attains age 62 in 1975 and who had qualified for a disability freeze for 1955 and 1956 (having then recovered). His AMW must be computed over a period of 17 years (1974, minus 1950, minus five years' dropout, minus two years' disability freeze). If his covered earnings were $2,400 per year in 1951–54, $3,000 in 1957–59, $3,600 in 1960–65, and $5,000 in 1966–74, then his best 17 years would be 9 years at $5,000, 6 years at $3,600, and 2 years at $3,000. His AMW would be $355 (total earnings of $72,600, divided by 204 months and rounded to the next lower dollar). If he worked in and after the year he attained age 62, his AMW might be increased. For example, if his covered earnings were $3,300 in 1975, $2,800 in 1976, and $3,700 in 1977, his earnings in 1975 and 1977 could be substituted for the lower earnings of $3,000 per year for two years, and his AMW would be $360 ($73,600 of total earnings divided by 204 months).

As another example, consider the case of persons who have always had maximum covered earnings, and examine the effect on them of the increases in the earnings base that have been made in the past—assuming no further increases over the $14,100 base in 1975. An individual who has no covered earnings in the years after attaining age 62 cannot have the maximum AMW of $1,175 that is possible under the law as it stood in 1975 unless he is age 27 or under in 1975, because he will have to count some years before 1975, during which years the earnings base was less than $14,100. For example, such an individual attaining age 62 early in 1976 would have an AMW of $573, based on 20 years (1 year at $14,100, 1 year at $13,200, 1 year at $10,800, 1 year at $9,000, 4 years at $7,800, 2 years at $6,600, seven years at $4,800, and three years at $4,200). This man could achieve the maximum AMW of $1,175, and thus the maximum old-age benefit of $522.80, only by working for 19 years beyond age 62 (although, of course, it is quite likely that in the meantime the maximum earnings base, as well as the maximum benefit amount, would have been increased beyond the present levels).

Another example of interest is in connection with women workers who spend much of their potential working lifetimes in the home raising a family. Consider a young woman who attained age 21 in 1958 and who worked in covered employment for the following 10 years at $400 per month (so that she acquired the necessary 40 quarters of coverage to obtain fully insured status regardless of subsequent employment) and then performed no more such work. At age 62, her AMW would be $114 ($48,000 of wages divided by 420 months), so so that she would, in effect, be considered as a low-wage person. If she died at age 42, her AMW for purposes of computing survivor benefits would be $266 ($48,000 divided by the 180 months after the year of attainment of age 26 and before the year of attainment of age 42).

A peculiar, and perhaps illogical, situation occurs for young workers in computing the AMW for purposes of disability and survivor benefits. Consider workers who are aged 28 or under in 1976 and who have the maximum covered earnings of $14,100 per year in 1975 and 1976 (neglecting the higher base possible in the latter year due to the automatic-adjustment provisions, described later). The AMW for such individuals who die or become disabled early in 1977 is based on only the two highest years and is thus $1,175, the maximum possible under the law as it stood in January 1975. This is well above the AMW of $595 for a person attaining age 62 at the beginning of 1977 (or for a person dying then who was at least age 26 in 1950) who has had maximum covered earnings ever since the program began in 1937.

Certainly, it does not appear equitable to treat the short-term new entrant so much more favorably than one who has contributed for many years at the maximum tax amount! Several possible solutions to this anomaly are discussed in Chapter 5.

As the final example, consider the computation of the AMW for persons who work well beyond age 62. As a result of substituting high years at this age and above for lower years before then, they can achieve high AMWs (and even the maximum possible one in the benefit table if the earnings base remains unchanged in the future after 1975). For example, the then maximum AMW of $1,175 could be obtained by 1980 by persons who attained age 65 in 1961 or before (and who are thus aged 83 or older in 1979) if they have the then maximum creditable earnings of $14,100 per year in 1975–79.

The AMW may also be computed back to the beginning of 1937 on the same basis as described previously, if this will produce a larger benefit. However, only rarely will such a result be obtained. This is because earnings in that period were much lower than subsequently. This method, for example, would be used for a person who worked in covered employment only (or principally) during World War II.

The AMW as so described is essentially on a career-average basis. In times of rising earnings, such as the United States has had for many years (especially since 1940), questions may be raised as to the use of a career-average wage, as contrasted with a final-average wage computed only over the most recent years preceding when the risk of retirement, disability, or death occurs. Under these circumstances, it may be argued, the career-average basis will produce unrealistic results because of utilizing the low wages of long-distant past years.

As a practical matter, however, the manner in which OASDI benefits have been adjusted in the past to reflect increases in the cost of living, and the manner in which they will be adjusted automatically for changes in the cost of living in the future, has been such as to produce about the same results as if a final-average basis had been used for determining the AMW. The reason for this is that each time that benefits have been increased in the past, the benefit percentage factors also have been correspondingly increased for those who will be beneficiaries in the future. This same approach has been written into the law by the 1972 amendments as being the procedure for the automatic adjustment of benefits relative to changes in the cost of living. In other words, the use of a career-average wage and dynamic benefit factors can produce about the same result as using a final-average wage and static benefit factors.[4]

The Benefit Formula. In all previous laws before the 1958 amendments, there was a definite benefit formula prescribed. For example, the 1954 Act benefit formula applicable to earnings after 1950 was 55

---

[4] For more details, see Robert J. Myers, "New Insight As to the True Basis of Social Security Benefits," *Pension & Welfare News,* August 1971.

percent of the first $110 of AMW, plus 20 percent of the next $240 of such wage (reflecting the $4,200 earnings base then in effect).

Under the 1958 amendments, an apparently considerably different procedure was used. They contained a benefit table giving the PIA for various ranges of AMW (e.g., where the AMW was $114–$118, the PIA was $66). The benefit table also provided for conversion of benefits for those on the roll before January 1959, so as to result in an increase of about 7 percent in the PIA (or $3, if larger). The benefit table also showed the maximum family benefit applicable for each PIA (e.g., $99 where the AMW was $114–$118). A similar procedure has been followed in subsequent legislation. The 1972 amendments not only contained a benefit table but also provided complete instructions as to how to derive the new benefit table when benefits are automatically adjusted for changes in the cost of living.

Actually, the benefit table in the law is based on a definite formula and on definite minimum and maximum benefit provisions, which are built into the table, and there is really no change in the basic principle that had prevailed in the past. Obviously, certain approximations have been made because of the grouping involved in rounding the benefits to the nearest dollar.

The approximate benefit formula underlying the benefit table for months beginning June 1975 is 129.48 percent of the first $110 of AMW, plus 47.10 percent of the next $290 of such wage, plus 44.01 percent of the next $150, plus 51.73 percent of the next $100, plus 28.77 percent of the next $100, plus 23.98 percent of the next $250, plus 21.60 percent of the next $175 (except that, in some cases, for average wages under $94, a slightly higher amount is payable, so as to fit in with the minimum benefit). The maximum PIA is $522.80, based on an AMW of $1,175 (which, as indicated previously, cannot be obtained for many years, except for workers dying or becoming disabled at a young age or for workers at the very oldest ages). The minimum PIA in the benefit table is $101.40 a month, applicable to AMWs of $76 or less.

A close approximation in a simplified form to this complicated seven-factor formula for the PIA is 46½ percent of AMW, plus $92. This duplicates the PIA in the benefit table within about $2 for AMWs between $110 and $675.

One might well ask how such a complicated benefit formula developed and what is its underlying basis. As mentioned previously, whenever the benefit level has been increased following 1954, this was accomplished by an across-the-board uniform percentage rise. This increase was applied not only to benefits in force at the time but also, for consistency, to the benefit factors in the formula, so that future beneficiaries would have the same treatment. As stated before, this has the effect of offsetting the career-average basis for the AMW, and thus producing about the same effect as would a final-average basis.

Specifically, the 55 percent factor applicable to the first $110 of AMW under the 1954 Act formula was increased successively by 7 percent (1958 Act), 7 percent (1965 Act), 13 percent (1967 Act), 15 percent (1969 Act), 10 percent (Act of March 1971), 20 percent (Act of July 1972), 11 percent (Act of December 1973), and 8.0 percent under the automatic adjustment applicable for June 1975 to yield the 129.48 percent factor in the present formula. In the same way, the 20 percent factor applicable to the next $240 of AMW under the 1954 Act formula was increased to the present 47.10 percent, and this factor was made applicable to the next $290 of AMW (in excess of the first $110) when the maximum creditable AMW was increased to $400 in the 1958 Act. Actually, this was not the most appropriate procedure, as will be indicated later.

Then, in the 1965 Act, when the maximum AMW was increased by $150 (to $550), the benefit factor applicable to the new band of AMWs at the top of the range was taken at the same percentage (21.4 percent) as had been applicable to AMWs between $110 and $400 in the 1958 Act. This was a more appropriate procedure, but perhaps not the best one. This factor was then increased successively by the percentage benefit increases of subsequent legislation, yielding the 44.01 percent factor in the current formula.

Next, in the 1967 Act, when the maximum AMW was increased by $100 (to $650), the benefit factor applicable to the new band of AMWs was taken at a percentage such that the maximum PIA would be the same as if the benefit factor applicable to the second band of AMWs (i.e., $110–$400) had applied to all of the AMW in excess of $110. Specifically, the formula then was 71.16 percent of the first $100 of AMW, plus 25.88 percent of the next $290, plus 24.18 percent of the next $150, plus 28.43 percent of the next $100. This use of a relatively high benefit factor on the new band of AMWs produced the desired result of the maximum PIA of $218 being the same as would have been derived from the "simple formula," 71.16 percent of the first $110 of AMW, plus 25.88 percent of the next $540. In other words, the factor applicable to the newly added band of creditable AMW had to be higher than the preceding one in order to average out at the higher level of the second preceding one. Unfortunately, this was a most inappropriate procedure.

The 1969 Act did not increase the maximum AMW, and so all benefit factors previously applicable were merely increased by 15 percent.

The legislation of March 1971 increased the maximum AMW by $100 and followed the appropriate procedure of applying a 20 percent factor (the same as in the second step of the 1954 Act formula) to such increase. At the same time, the benefit factors previously applicable were, quite properly, increased by 10 percent.

Similarly, the legislation of July 1972 increased the AMW by $250 (reflecting the $12,000 maximum taxable earnings base to be effective in 1974) and applied the 20 percent benefit factor thereto. The benefit factors applicable to the part of the AMW below $750 were increased by 20 percent (which was the general benefit increase then legislated).

Then, the legislation of December 1973 increased the AMW by $100 over that of the 1972 legislation (reflecting the change in the earnings base for 1974 to $13,200), and the 20 percent factor was applied thereto. The benefit factors applicable to the part of the AMW below $1,000 were increased by 11 percent, the general benefit increase then enacted, effective June 1974 (a 7 percent increase being effective for March–May 1974).[5] When the earnings base was increased to $14,100 for 1975, as a result of the automatic-adjustment provisions, the 20 percent factor was also applied to the additional $75 of AMW resulting therefrom.

In the automatic adjustment of benefits for June 1975, all benefit factors were increased by 8.0 percent. In this connection, it is interesting to note that President Ford, for purposes of governmental economy, proposed that this increase should be limited to 5 percent. However, he received virtually no support in Congress for the necessary legislative change to do this.

A minimum PIA (in terms of dollars) has always been provided. Originally, this was done for facility-of-payment reasons (so as not to

---

[5] The two-step approach was adopted because, in the short time available between enactment of the legislation and March 1974, it was not possible to make "exact" increases for all beneficiary categories (notably those involving more than one type of benefit). Accordingly, the "rough" 7 percent increase effective for March 1974 was to be completely overridden by the 11 percent increase effective for June 1974.

pay nominal, small amounts). Later, the minimum was increased disproportionately on the grounds that low-income workers needed some sort of reasonable amount on which to live. Still later, and currently, it has been realized that the minimum often goes to workers with spasmodic work histories (e.g., federal employees who have a second job) and not only to regularly employed low-earnings workers, and so it has been increased only in line with the general benefit level.

In summary, the most appropriate way to modify the benefit formula underlying the benefit table in the law whenever benefits are increased by a uniform percentage across the board and the maximum AMW is also raised, is to apply the percentage benefit increase (or perhaps some other percentage increase, such as half of the percentage increase in the wage level, if lower—for reasons that will be discussed later) to the previously applicable benefit factors, and to apply a 20 percent factor to the new band of AMWs at the end of the table. The fact that this results in a lengthy, apparently complicated, benefit formula is not important, because only the derived benefit table actually appears in the law. This procedure of using the same percentage increase for both those on the roll and the benefit formula was adopted in the automatic-adjustment provisions that were incorporated in the law in 1972.

It is interesting to note that if this procedure had been followed in the past, from the starting point of the 1954 Act formula, the current benefit formula would have been 129.48 percent of the first $110 of AMW, 47.10 percent of the next $240 of AMW, plus 44.01 percent of the next $50 of AMW, plus 41.13 percent of the next $150 of AMW, plus 36.40 percent of the next $100 of AMW, plus 28.77 percent of the next $100 of AMW, plus 23.98 percent of the next $250 of AMW, plus 21.60 percent of the next $175 of AMW. This would have yielded a maximum PIA of $502.10, or 3 percent lower than the actual figure of $522.80 in the current law.

Table 2.3 gives several fragments of the current benefit table as it relates to the cases where the AMW is computed for periods beginning with 1951.

The benefit table also provides for the determination of the PIA when it is more advantageous for the beneficiary to compute the AMW back to 1937 and to use the benefit computation method of the 1939 Act. Illustrative results under these circumstances are shown in Table 2.4.

Some may question that the benefit factor applicable to the first

TABLE 2.3

**OASDI Benefit Table Applicable
when Average Monthly Wage
Is Computed for Periods Beginning with 1951,
Effective June 1975**

Average Monthly Wage	Primary Insurance Amount	Maximum Family Benefit
$ 76 or under...............	$101.40	$152.10
77–78.....................	103.00	154.50
79–80.....................	105.30	158.00
81........................	107.30	161.00
.	.	.
.	.	.
.	.	.
107.......................	139.10	208.70
108–109...................	141.40	212.20
110–113...................	143.60	215.40
114–118...................	145.60	218.40
.	.	.
.	.	.
306–309...................	235.80	391.40
310–314...................	238.20	397.70
315–319...................	240.20	404.10
320–323...................	242.30	409.20
.	.	.
.	.	.
.	.	.
986–990...................	482.60	844.50
991–995...................	483.80	846.70
996–1,000.................	485.00	848.70
.	.	.
.	.	.
.	.	.
1,161–1,165...............	520.60	911.00
1,166–1,170...............	521.70	913.00
1,171–1,175...............	522.80	914.80

$110 of AMW exceeds 100 percent (which occurred for the first time in the 1972 amendments). Is it appropriate for benefits to exceed previous earnings? The explanation rests in the fact that the AMW is on a career-average basis and almost always will not be indicative of recent earnings prior to retirement, but will be significantly lower. Therefore, if the resulting benefits are measured against such recent earnings, the ratio will be much lower (and well below 100 percent for almost all categories of workers).

Special-Minimum Benefits. The PIA can alternatively be computed under a special-minimum formula based solely on years of coverage, and thus is not at all earnings related, as is also the case for the "regular" minimum in the benefit table.

A year of coverage is defined as a year in which covered earnings totaled at least 25 percent of the maximum taxable earnings amount. A special rule applies for years before 1951, because of the manner in which the earnings records are maintained, since that period is not

TABLE 2.4

OASDI Benefit Table Applicable when Average Wage Is Computed for Periods Beginning with 1937, Effective June 1975

Benefit Computed Under Method of 1939 Act	Primary Insurance Amount
$10	$101.40
15	101.40
20	111.50
25	134.50
30	156.50
35	174.10
40	191.60
45*	209.70

* Maximum possible is $45.60 (which produces same primary insurance amount as $45).

often used for the benefit amounts actually payable. The total earnings in 1937–50 are divided by $900, and the number of full units of $900 (although, of course, no more than 14 such units) are considered to be the years of coverage in that period. The $900 unit is used, instead of the $750 resulting from taking 25 percent of the $3,000 earnings base in 1937–50, as a partial offset to considering total earnings in the 14-year period rather than a year-by-year analysis.

The special-minimum formula for the PIA is $9 times the years of coverage in excess of 10, but not in excess of 30. The maximum such special-minimum benefit is thus $180 per month. If the years of coverage are 21 or less, the formula produces less than the "regular" minimum of $101.40, with 21 years yielding $99. In practice, however, the special-minimum formula is not possibly applicable for those with 22 to 24 years of coverage, because even with minimum qualifying earnings for such lengths of coverage, the benefit table produces larger amounts.

Minimum and Maximum Family Benefits. The minimum family benefit for survivors (applicable only when there is one such survivor, since in other cases the family benefit will always be larger than the prescribed minimum) is $101.40 a month, prior to any reduction for a widow or widower claiming benefits before age 65. The general principle is that the minimum family benefit is the same as the minimum PIA. It may be noted that this creates an anomaly as between widow's benefits and parent's benefits when claimed at age 62. As indicated later, in Table 2 of Appendix C, the widow's benefit is generally slightly higher, because it is at a rate of 82.9 percent of the PIA, versus 82.5 percent, but for low AMWs it is significantly smaller because of the manner in which this minimum operates.

The maximum family benefit (MFB) is shown in the benefit table for each range of AMWs, or, in other words, for each PIA.

Before the legislation in 1971, the MFB was, in general, a percentage of the AMW. Specifically, the MFB in the 1969 Act was determined approximately from the following formula: 80 percent of the first $436 of AMW, plus 40 percent of the next $214, except that it could not be less than 1½ times the PIA (which exception applied for AMWs of $239 or less). This procedure produced anomalies when all benefits were increased by a uniform percentage across the board and, in the case of benefits for a family, were permitted to rise above the stated MFB (for purposes of ease of public understanding, such that it could be stated that all beneficiaries received an "x" percent increase). As a result, persons coming on the roll shortly afterward who were affected by the MFB could have lower benefits than if they had come on the roll just before the effective date.

For the foregoing reason and, perhaps more importantly, because of the recognition of the need for dynamic benefit factors to offset the career-average wage basis, the 1971 legislation changed the procedure for determining MFBs. The resulting method is to increase the MFBs in the previous benefit table by the same percentage as the PIAs are increased and to make the MFBs for the new band of AMWs which is added at the upper end of the table be 175 percent of the applicable PIAs, which was about the same ratio as the maximum MFB held to the maximum PIA in the 1969 Act table. This procedure was adopted in the automatic-adjustment provisions that were incorporated in the law in 1972.

Table 2.5 shows the formula relationship of the MFBs to the AMWs and the PIAs. One might well question that for AMWs of $436 and less, the MFB is higher than the AMW. Should benefits paid exceed previous income? The answer to this apparent overliberality is the same as mentioned before in connection with the PIA—the use of a career-average wage for determining the MFB—so that benefits payable are not likely to be high relative to final earnings.

It will be noted that contrary to the general principles of social insurance, the MFB is relatively lower for the smaller AMWs than for the middle and higher ones. Specifically, for AMWs of $239 or less,

TABLE 2.5

Approximate Formula for Maximum Family Benefits, Effective June 1975

Average Monthly Wage	Primary Insurance Amount	Maximum Family Benefit*
$ 76– 239........	$101.40–203.20	1½ times PIA
240– 436........	205.10–294.20	126.6% of AMW
437– 627........	296.70–384.20	$276 plus 63.3% of AMW
628–1,175........	386.00–522.80	1¾ times PIA

* Percentages are applicable to upper end of AMW band for each PIA in benefit table.

the MFB is 150 percent of the PIA. This ratio then rises gradually until it reaches 187.8 percent for an AMW of $432 to $436 and thereafter declines, to 175 percent for AMWs of $628 and above. It would logically seem that at the lower end of the AMW range, the MFB should be 175 percent of the PIA (and this would then apply to AMWs up through $356). It could even be argued that the MFB should logically be a uniform percentage of the PIA throughout the entire range, such as the 187.8 percent present maximum value or a rounded 190 percent (or even 200 percent). This, however, raises both cost considerations and the desirability of even higher family benefits for the highest AMWs, where the level already seems excessive (especially for young workers).

The maximum family benefit provision applies to the total of the benefits payable before account is taken of reductions due to early retirement (before 65 for workers, wives, and widows and widowers) and of the increase in the primary benefit due to the delayed-retirement increment (discussed in the second following subsection) but after account is taken of nonpayment of benefits to one or more beneficiaries in the family group as a result of the earnings test. The benefit payable to a divorced wife (either as a wife's benefit or as a widow's benefit) is not subject to the maximum family benefit provisions.

The maximum family benefit has a special exception when child survivors are eligible on more than one earnings record, most commonly when both the mother and father die. Under these circumstances of full orphans, the children do not merely draw benefits on the earnings record of the parent who had the highest PIA and be limited by the corresponding MFB. Rather, the maximum is the sum of the two MFBs, but not in excess of the highest MFB in the benefit table. In other cases where not all children involved are eligible on all earnings records—as, for example, in the case of a couple having children of their own and the husband also having stepchildren by a former marriage—there are complicated rules which attempt to give the various children the highest benefits possible.

Illustrative Benefits.   Table 2.6 shows illustrative monthly benefits for various beneficiary categories, giving consideration to the applicable benefit proportions, the minimum and maximum benefit provisions, and the applicable reductions for persons claiming benefits before age 65. The figures in this table do not make any allowance for the effect of the delayed-retirement increment (discussed in the next subsection).

Examination of this table might lead one to wonder about the apparently high level of the benefit payments and what effect this will have on the role of the private sector in providing economic security. Thus, for example, the maximum primary benefit of $522.80, or the maximum benefit for a married couple of $718.90 or the maximum family benefit of $914.80 would seem to leave little room for supplementation for those with moderate earnings levels.

But once again, it must be remembered that the AMW is computed on the career-average basis. The maximum primary benefit for men attaining age 65 at the beginning of 1973 (and retiring then) was $266.10 under the table in effect then, with a maximum family benefit of $490.10—or 35 percent and 65 percent, respectively, of the maximum creditable earnings in 1972. Such figures for men attaining age 65 in January 1975 based on the table in effect then were $316.30 and $573.90, respectively—or 29 percent and 52 percent, respectively, of the maximum creditable earnings (at a rate of $13,200 per year)

2. Principles and Present Provisions of OASDI System 63

ABLE 2.6

llustrative Monthly Benefits under OASDI System for Various Family Categories, Based on Earnings after 1950, Effective June 1975

all figures rounded to the nearest dollar)

Average Monthly Wage*	Worker Alone	With Wife or Husband Who Claims Benefit at—		Worker, Wife and 1 Child†
		Age 62	Age 65	
Disabled Worker or Retired Worker Aged 65 at Time of Retirement:				
$76 or less	$101	$140	$152	$152
100	131	180	196	196
200	185	255	278	278
300	232	319	347	380
400	280	385	420	511
600	372	511	557	657
800	437	601	656	765
1,175	523	719	784	915
Retired Worker Aged 62 at Time of Retirement:				
$76 or less	81	119	132	132
100	104	153	170	170
200	148	218	241	241
300	185	272	301	334
400	224	329	364	455
600	297	437	483	583
800	350	514	568	678
1,175	418	614	680	810

Survivor Benefits

Average Monthly Wage*	Dependent Parent Aged 62	Disabled Widow Aged 50‡	Widow Aged 60‡	Widow Aged 65‡	One Child	One Child and Mother§	Maximum Family Benefit‖
$76 or less	$101	$ 57	$ 75	$101	$101	$152	$152
100	108	65	93	131	101	196	196
200	153	93	133	185	139	278 ‖	278
300	191	116	166	232	174	347	380
400	231	140	200	280	210	420	511
600	307	186	266	372	279	557	657
800	361	219	313	437	328	656	765
1,175	431	261	374	523	392	784	915

* When the average wage is based in part on earnings before 1976, it is affected by the lower earnings bases then in effect. Thus, an average wage of $1,175 will be difficult to obtain for many years (except for young survivor and disability cases).

† Also applies to worker, husband aged 65, and one child.

‡ Also applies to widower.

§ Also applies to two children, to two parents, and to father and one child.

‖ Payable to two or more children and mother or father, to three or more children, to disabled or retired worker, spouse, and one or more children, and to disabled or retired worker with two or more children.

Note: The above figures for retired workers do not include the effect of the delayed-retirement increment for those who work beyond age 65.

in 1974. Thus, there still seems to be ample room for private supplementation, and this will continue to be so in the future, if the benefit formula is not expanded beyond what the automatic-adjustment provisions will produce, and if the automatics operate properly (as will be discussed later).

Table 2.7 presents further data on the maximum primary benefits

TABLE 2.7

**Illustrative Monthly Benefits for Men Retiring at Age 65
or at Age 72 with Maximum Creditable Earnings
in All Previous Years, Based on Table in Effect
for June 1975**

Year of Attainment of Age	Man Retiring at Age 65		Man Retiring at Age 72	
	Nonmarried	Married	Nonmarried	Married
1972	$311.10	$466.70	$347.40	$519.40
1973	319.10	478.70	360.40	537.10
1974	329.30	494.00	379.00	563.00
1975	341.70	512.60	405.30	600.20
1976	364.00	546.00	425.20	627.70
1977	386.00	579.00	429.30	636.80
1978	403.50	605.30	453.30	665.10
1979	410.70	616.10	461.30	676.90
1980	416.50	624.80	466.40	684.30
1990	453.90	680.90	511.30	750.20
2000	492.50	738.80	533.70	812.40
2009 and after	522.80	784.20	559.40	820.80

Assumptions:
 1. Man attains age at beginning of year.
 2. Wife is same age as worker.
 3. No change in benefit table due to increases in cost of living or in taxable earnings base after 1975.
Note: Figures for attainments of age 65 in 1978 and after (or of age 72 in 1985 and after) are also applicable to women workers. For earlier years, figures for women workers are somewhat higher.

possible. It shows how the effect of the higher earnings bases which have gone into effect over the years and the age-62 computation point for men will gradually raise the level of the primary benefit. This is, of course, exclusive of the effect of the automatic-adjustment provisions for benefit amounts and the earnings base, which will be operative in the future if the CPI and earnings levels rise.

The lump-sum death payment for deaths after February 1974 shows no variation by AMW level, because it carries a $255 maximum, which is less than three times the minimum primary benefit. This maximum, first established in 1954, was enacted in order to limit the amounts payable to undertakers so as to discourage elaborate funerals and has not been changed since, despite large increases in the general benefit level. Under the 1972 legislation, the minimum lump-sum death benefit was $253.50, and the maximum of $255 was paid for all AMWs of $77 or over.

Delayed-Retirement Increment. The primary benefit (for the retired worker) is increased by 1 percent for each year (actually, by $\frac{1}{12}$ percent for each month) that the worker does not receive benefits because of the earnings test (described in the next section) in the period beginning with the month of attainment of age 65 (or January 1971, if later) and ending with the month before attainment of age 72, when benefits are payable regardless of the amount of earnings. Thus, the maximum increase for this factor is 7 percent of the PIA. This increase applies only to the primary benefit based on the benefit table and not to the special-minimum benefit based on years of coverage, and it is not passed on to benefits for dependents or survivors.[6] No credit is given for benefits withheld before 1971, because of the administrative difficulties that would have been involved, since the legislation adding this feature was enacted in 1972.

The delayed-retirement increment is applicable only to workers who have not received reduced benefits for retirement before age 65. This can result in some serious anomalies. For instance, consider a person who retires at age 62, draws actuarially reduced benefits for one month, and then returns to work because retirement was so unsatisfactory. He will not receive the significant increase of the delayed-retirement increment if he goes on working until age 72, although all but one month's actuarial reduction in his benefit will be restored. This is quite a penalty for one month's work at age 62!

Table 2.7 also presents illustrations of persons who have always had maximum covered earnings and who retire at age 72, or first claim benefits then. This shows the effect of both the delayed-retirement increment and the substitution of years of high earnings after age 62

---

[6] The best-of-all-worlds' treatment is given in those cases of beneficiaries with dependents where the special minimum produces a higher PIA, but such PIA is lower than the PIA under the regular formula increased by the delayed-retirement increment. For example, consider a man retiring at age 70 with 30 years of coverage and with a wife age 65. If his PIA by the regular formula is $178, so that with the increment his benefit becomes $186.90, he receives this amount instead of the $180 under the special minimum, while his wife receives 50 percent of the special minimum, or $90, instead of 50 percent of $178.

in computing the AMW, and also the higher age used as the computation point for men attaining age 62 before 1975.

Automatic Adjustment of Benefit Table. Beginning in 1975, the benefit table will be automatically adjusted, according to changes in the cost of living, as measured by the Consumer Price Index, developed by the U.S. Department of Labor. If the CPI for a particular base quarter rises by at least 3 percent from what it was in the last previous base quarter, the benefits in payment and the benefit factors in the benefit formula are increased by the percentage rise (rounded to the nearest 0.1 percent), effective for the next following June.[7] This is accomplished through action of the Secretary of Health, Education, and Welfare, which must be announced within 30 days after the end of the base quarter.

The base quarter is initially the second quarter of 1974 (since the 11 percent benefit increase legislated in December 1973 was effective for June 1974). Subsequent base quarters for the automatic operation of this provision are the first quarter of each year (beginning with 1975) if the 3 percent increase occurs. The special-minimum benefit based on years of coverage is not affected by this automatic adjustment, but it does apply to the flat-rate benefits for transitional-insured and transitional-noninsured beneficiaries.

For example, if the CPI had risen by only 2.8 percent from the second quarter of 1974 to the first quarter of 1975, the latter would not be a base quarter. If the rise measured from the second quarter of 1974 to the first quarter of 1976 were 3.4 percent, the latter would be the new base quarter, and benefits would be increased by this amount, beginning with June 1976.

As will be discussed later, when benefits are increased as a result of the automatic-adjustment provision, the earnings base that determines the maximum amount of earnings creditable for benefit purposes (and also taxable) may also be increased, as are also the annual

---

[7] The automatic-adjustment provisions as originally enacted in the July 1972 legislation provided for benefit increases being effective for Januarys, beginning with 1975, and based on base quarters of the second quarter of each year. The December 1973 legislation modified this approach, as stated here. In hindsight, one might ask why did not the automatic-adjustment provisions as to benefit levels become effective for January 1974, instead of a year later. Technically, this would have been quite feasible. Probably, it was thought that the nine-month measuring period then resulting would not have been long enough to affect the 3 percent trigger (although, in fact, it would have). Had this been done, there probably would not have been the two quickie legislations of 1973.

and monthly exempt amounts in the earnings test. When this is done, the benefit table is extended to the new band of earnings added, and a benefit factor of 20.00 percent is made applicable thereto.

The automatic-adjustment provision is made temporarily inoperative, however, when Congress enacts an across-the-board benefit increase.[8] For example, if such a law is enacted in 1975 and is first effective for benefits payable in a month of that year, the provision would not apply for 1976, and the new base period would be the quarter in which the legislated benefit increase is effective. Furthermore, if the benefit increase is effective for a month in the year after the legislation is enacted, the provision is inapplicable for two years. For example, if the legislation increasing benefits is enacted in October 1975, to be effective for benefits for January 1976, the provision cannot be operative until 1977, and the new base period will be the first quarter of 1976 (which would be compared with the first quarter of 1977).

The law also provides that Congress should be notified by the Department of Health, Education, and Welfare whenever it seems likely that the automatic-adjustment provision will become operative for benefits for the following June.[9] In any event, Congress is to be notified by April 30, when the CPI data for the preceding quarter are available, if an increase is certain. It does not seem at all unlikely that under such circumstances and based upon past performances, Congress will then legislate an increase and thus make the automatic provision inoperative. In this manner, some might say, members of Congress would get the credit for the benefit increase, rather than some actuary or statistician in the Executive Branch.

The CPI for the first quarter of 1975 increased 8.0 percent over that for the second quarter of 1974. Therefore, beginning with the benefits payable for June 1975, there was this increase in all monthly benefits.

---

[8] The legislation enacted in July 1973 that provided a 5.9 percent benefit increase for June–December 1974 (which was subsequently negated and superceded by the increases provided by the December 1973 legislation) specifically stated that this action would not be considered as affecting these provisions for suspending the automatic adjustment of benefits. In other words, the automatic provisions would have become operative for January 1975, with the 1972 benefit formula being increased on the basis of the rise in the CPI from the third quarter of 1972 to the second quarter of 1974. At the same time, the benefit increase provided by the 1974 legislation would have lapsed, or thus have been overridden.

[9] This notification is to be given as soon as the CPI published for any month has risen by at least 2½ percent over that for the last previous base quarter.

It will be observed that benefits are not decreased if the CPI were to decrease by 3 percent or more. Although logically this should be done, political considerations seemed to dictate otherwise. In any event, however, historically the CPI has rarely decreased this much and even then soon increased again.

Certain figures have been developed to show what will arise under the automatic-adjustment provision (whose pros and cons will be discussed in the next chapter, along with the reasons why it was adopted). For example, assume that each year after 1974, wages increase by 5 percent and that the CPI rises at an annual rate of 3 percent (which are the long-range assumptions currently used in the 1974 official actuarial cost estimates for the program). Under these circumstances, based on the December 1973 amendments, the primary benefit payable to a person retiring at age 65 in the year 2000 with maximum creditable earnings in all previous years (back to his youth) would be $1,257 per month, and the taxable earnings base for the previous year would be $44,700, yielding an annual employee tax of $2,883 at the 6.45 percent rate then called for according to present law.[10]

The foregoing figures are, at first glance, truly alarming, but they must be considered in relative terms rather than absolute ones. After all, the assumed wage level will be about 3.4 times higher than now. The maximum primary benefit payable will then represent only 33.7 percent of the maximum taxable earnings in the previous year, a ratio that does not seem excessively high in light of the ratio currently prevailing (as discussed in the previous subsection). Furthermore, the price level resulting from these assumptions will also be significantly higher—about twice as high.

Even more startling figures result when these projections are carried out to the year 2050. The maximum primary benefit in such case would be $16,220 per month, and the taxable earnings base for the previous year would be $514,200. The ratio of the benefit to the earnings base would then have risen to 37.9 percent, which indicates a significant rise in the relative benefit level. In other words, under these economic assumptions, the benefit structure gets somewhat "out of control," and correspondingly the cost of the program rises, and higher tax rates are required, especially in the long run, than currently

---

[10] It seems likely, as will be discussed later, that this rate is too low to finance adequately the present benefit structure.

scheduled. The official actuarial cost estimates made in 1974 showed such a result.

It is important to note that stability of the ratio of the primary benefit to the earnings in the year prior to retirement at age 65 (sometimes referred to as the "replacement ratio") prevails only when the assumed increase in the CPI is about half as large as that in wages. Such a condition did prevail in the two decades before the mid-1960s, when the technical work in developing the automatic-adjustment provision was done. But in recent years the CPI has been increasing almost as rapidly as wages (and in some years more).

If the CPI increases just half as fast as wages, the ratio of the primary benefit for the maximum-earnings case to the earnings base in the year before retirement at age 65 is very close to 32 percent in all future years for the assumed wage increase being 4 percent per year. This prevailed in the past, as shown in Table 2.8. The ratio has generally been between 30 and 32 percent, except for unusual years when the earnings base increased sharply (such as 1967–69 and 1975) or when the benefit level rose considerably (such as 1959, 1965, and especially 1973). Under the economic assumptions made in the computations for the next few years, the ratio rises significantly in 1977–78; this is a clear indication of the inherent instability of the existing automatic-adjustment provisions under likely future economic conditions.

If the wage increase rate is more than 4 percent, stability will occur but at a lower level, and vice versa. For example, for a wage increase of 6 percent per year and a corresponding CPI increase of 3 percent, the ratio levels off at about 28½ percent.

If the CPI does increase more rapidly than only half the increase in wages, the benefits will become an increasingly higher proportion of final wage. For example, for the maximum-earnings case, the ratio of the primary benefit in the year of retirement to the wage in the preceding year under the assumption of the CPI rising 4 percent per year and wages rising 5 percent per year is 42.9 percent for the retirant in 2000 and 62.7 percent for the retirant in 2050.[11] Such a developing trend would have serious effects on the financing of the system or, to look at the other side of the coin, on the reasonableness

---

[11] See Albert Rettig and Orlo R. Nichols, "Some Aspects of the Dynamic Projection of Benefits under the 1973 Social Security Amendments (P.L. 93–233)," *Actuarial Note No. 87*, Social Security Administration, April 1974.

TABLE 2.8

Ratios of Primary Benefit for Man Retiring at Age 65 at Beginning of Year with Maximum Covered Earnings in All Previous Years to His Earnings in Year before Retirement, 1953–78

Year	Primary Benefit (on annual basis)	Earnings Base in Previous Year	Ratio
1953*	$1,020.00	$ 3,600	28.3%
1954	1,020.00	3,600	28.3
1955	1,182.00	3,600	32.8
1956	1,242.00	4,200	29.6
1957	1,302.00	4,200	31.0
1958	1,302.00	4,200	31.0
1959	1,392.00	4,200	33.1
1960	1,428.00	4,800	29.8
1961	1,440.00	4,800	30.0
1962	1,452.00	4,800	30.2
1963	1,464.00	4,800	30.5
1964	1,476.00	4,800	30.8
1965	1,580.40	4,800	32.9
1966	1,592.40	4,800	33.2
1967	1,843.20	6,600	27.9
1968	1,872.00	6,600	28.4
1969	1,926.00	7,800	24.7
1970	2,277.60	7,800	29.2
1971	2,557.20	7,800	32.8
1972	2,593.20	7,800	33.2
1973	3,193.20	9,000	35.5
1974	3,295.20	10,800	30.5
1975	3,795.60	13,200	28.8
1976	4,368.00	14,100	31.0
Illustrative Projection for 1977–78†			
1977	4,980.00	15,300	32.5
1978	5,500.80	16,500	33.3

* First year for which "new-start" average monthly wage method was fully available.

† Based on 7 percent increase in benefits for June 1976 and 5 percent increase in benefits for June 1977 and on 8 percent increases in the earnings base for both 1976 and 1977.

of the OASDI benefit structure and its effect on the private-sector role in the economic security field.[12]

Conversely, if the CPI does increase less rapidly than half the

---

[12] For a challenging and incisive demonstration and discussion of this aspect, see Geoffrey N. Calvert, *New Realistic Projections of Social Security Benefits and Taxes* (New York: Alexander and Alexander, Inc., 1973).

increase in wages, the benefits will become a lower proportion of final wage. In what seems currently the unlikely event that the CPI will increase only 2 percent per year, as against 5 percent for wages, the ratios for 2000 and 2050 would be 26.5 and 23.7 percent, respectively.

Workmen's Compensation Offset. When a disabled worker is entitled to workmen's compensation monthly benefits (WC) as well as to OASDI benefits, an offset may be made against the latter so that total benefit income will not be so large as to discourage rehabilitation and return to work. This offset does not apply to the disabled worker after he attains age 62, nor does it apply to survivor benefits. Further, the offset is not applicable when the WC program provides for an offset or reduction when OASDI disability benefits are payable. This provision is applicable only to workers becoming disabled after June 1, 1965.

In determining the amount of the offset (if any), a new concept is involved—average current earnings (ACE). This term is defined as the largest of (1) the AMW, (2) monthly average of *total* earnings in covered employment in the highest five consecutive years since 1950, or (3) one twelfth of the highest annual *total* earnings in covered employment in the period consisting of the year of disablement and the preceding five years. It will be noted that the second and third methods consider earnings without regard to the maximum earnings base. In the vast majority of the cases, the third method will produce the most favorable result and will be used.

The offset applies only if the total of the WC benefit and the OASDI benefit (including dependents' benefits) exceeds 80 percent of ACE. No increases in the OASDI benefit due to legislation or the general automatic-adjustment provisions are considered for purposes of the offset provision. If such 80 percent of ACE is exceeded, then the OASDI benefit is reduced by such excess, but never to the extent that the total of the WC and OASDI benefits is smaller than the OASDI benefit alone.

As an example, assume that a disabled worker has an OASDI disability benefit of $260 before offset (including dependents' benefits), a WC benefit of $100, and an ACE of $400. Then, his OASDI benefit would be reduced to $220 (80 percent of $400, minus $100). If the ACE were $450 or more, no offset would be applicable. Or if the ACE were $300, the OASDI benefit would be reduced to $160, so that the total of WC and OASDI would at least equal the original OASDI amount of $260; the application of the general offset method would have yielded an OASDI benefit after offset of $140 (80 percent of $300, minus $100), or total benefits of only $240.

Every three years, effective for the third January after the year of the first benefit receipt and every third January thereafter, the ACE is adjusted to reflect any increases in the general earnings level. Thus, the limit for the offset based on 80 percent of ACE will increase if earnings rise, and the amount of the offset will be reduced, or even eliminated. The adjustment is made in exactly the same manner as is done under the automatic-adjustment provisions for the maximum taxable earnings base. In fact, this procedure as used for the WC offset was the model for such automatic-adjustment provisions enacted in 1972) since it was initiated in the 1965 amendments. Table 3.6 in the next chapter presents actual operating data that are used to determine the percentage increases which have been made in these offset cases.

As an example of how the automatic adjustment of ACE operates, consider a worker first entitled to disability benefits in 1975, with an OASDI benefit of $260 before offset (including dependents' benefits), a WC benefit of $100, and an ACE of $400. For 1975–77, his OASDI benefit would be reduced to $220 (plus any automatic benefit increases on his OASDI benefit of $260 based on rises in the CPI). Suppose that average first-quarter wages reported under OASDI increase 10 percent from 1975 to 1977. Then, his ACE for benefit purposes for 1978–80 will be $440, and his corresponding OASDI benefit after offset will be $252 (i.e., an $8 offset). It is likely that the general earnings level would rise sufficiently from 1977 to 1980 so that, after 1980, no offset would be applicable. Of course, if at any time the OASDI benefit were reduced because one or more dependents were no longer eligible, the offset would be recomputed (and probably eliminated). Furthermore, if the beneficiary reached age 62 or died during 1975–80, the offset would automatically terminate.

Earnings Test

Benefits for retired workers and their dependents and for survivors are, in general, not paid when the beneficiary is engaged in substantial employment, nor are benefits paid to dependents of a retired worker when he is engaged in such employment. This provision is sometimes termed the "retirement test"—to some extent a misnomer in regard to young beneficiaries. It might better be termed the "earnings test."

For 1975, benefits are payable for all months if the annual earnings from all types of employment, whether or not covered by the program, are $2,520 or less. This figure was determined from the $2,400 applicable in 1974 adjusted by the automatic provisions—the 5.94 percent increase in average wages in covered employment between the first quarter of 1973 and the first quarter of 1974 (see Table 3.6) was applied to $2,400, and the result of $2,543 was rounded to the nearest even multiple of $120.

If earnings exceed $2,520, then $1 of benefits is withheld for each $2 of earnings. As a result, a beneficiary who earns more than $2,520 in a year will always have more total income than if he held his earnings to exactly $2,520. In no event are benefits withheld for a month in which the individual has wages of $210 or less and does not render substantial self-employment services.[13] Moreover, the test is not applicable at all after the individual reaches age 72, and his earnings in and after the month of attaining age 72 are not considered in applying the test. For self-employed persons, the reported annual earnings are prorated by months in the year of attainment of age 72.

Some explanation as to the reasons for the complexities in the earnings test is in order. On the whole, they are needed to produce reasonable transition from full employment to full retirement, so as to lessen disincentives for the aged to work. This is the reason for the annual exempt amount and the reduction of benefits for earnings above this by only $1 for each $2 of such earnings.

The monthly portion of the earnings test is intended to take care of situations where the individual has very substantial earnings in some months, but not in others. A prime example of this is when the person retires in midyear after having high wages and then is completely retired during the remainder of the year.

The age-72 provision in the earnings test is really an anomaly. It changes the basis from retirement benefits to strictly annuity benefits, which is not the underlying philosophy of the program. This provision, as will be discussed later, came about as a result of political compromise when groups were covered who claimed that their members rarely retired and thus would never draw benefits if the "retirement" basis applied without limit as to age.

---

[13] The term "substantial self-employment services" is not defined in the law but rather by regulations, which are based partly on congressional intent as expressed in committee reports. More than 45 hours of work per month are generally considered substantial, but as few as 20 hours (or even less) can be so considered if they involve management of a large business or are in a very highly skilled occupation.

A special test applies to beneficiaries under age 72 outside the country who work in other than covered employment. Under these circumstances, no benefits are paid if the beneficiary works on any part of seven or more days in a month. This procedure, based on days of employment rather than on earnings, is necessary because of the widely differing earnings rates as between nations.

As an example of how the test operates, consider a retired worker under age 72 with an entitled wife, whose family benefit is $220 per month. If he is employed at $500 per month during March through September 1974, he will without question receive benetfis for the other five months. His benefits of $1,540 for March to September will be reduced by $550, since the excess of his earnings over $2,400 is $1,100, and there is a reduction of $550 therefor. In the actual administration, he might receive his benefits not only for January, February, and October–December, but also for March–June, and then have them suspended for July–September, with a final accounting and adjustment after the end of the year. Any earnings that the wife may have can affect only that portion of the family benefit which is the wife's benefit.

In the case of survivor families and disability-beneficiary families, the earnings of any beneficiary can affect only his own benefit. The earnings test does not apply to the disabled-worker, disabled-child, or disabled-widow beneficiary, since presumably he cannot engage in substantial gainful work except when he is in a trial work period while being rehabilitated.[14] For example, if the widowed mother beneficiary has substantial wages, this will have no effect on the benefits payable to the children (and, in fact, may not even decrease the total payable

---

[14] Although the law does not prescribe any dollar amounts to test whether the disabled beneficiary has demonstrated the ability to engage in substantial gainful activity (and thus no longer be considered disabled), regulations have been established doing this. In early 1974, these regulations provided that when, over a period of time, the person has earnings as an employee averaging over $140 a month, this will ordinarily prove that he is not disabled for benefit purposes. Similarly, if such wages are less than $90, this will not bar him from benefits, while for wages between $90 and $140, individual consideration of the circumstances will be made. Interestingly, and somewhat anomalously, the $140 amount was established when this was the monthly exempt amount in the earnings test (in 1968–71), but it was not changed subsequently when the latter was increased. In September 1974 the regulations were changed so as to bring them in conformity with earnings test; the $140 figure was increased to $200, and the $90 figure was increased to $130. If the individual is working in a sheltered workshop and has earnings averaging $200 or less per month, he will ordinarily not be considered as having established his ability to engage in substantial gainful activity.

to the family if the maximum family benefit available can be paid on the basis of the children's benefits alone).

Persons retiring during the year must count their earnings before retirement in applying the annual test, but nonetheless the monthly test will assure them of benefit payments for all months subsequent to a complete retirement. For example, a married individual without eligible children fully retiring on June 30, 1974, after having earned $15,000 would receive benefits for the last six months of the year, but would not receive any benefits for the first six months because the applicable reduction ($6,300) would be larger than the six months of benefits. However, if he retired only partially and earned somewhat over $200 each month, it is likely that he would not receive any benefits at all for the year. On the other hand, if his earnings in the first six months of the year were $2,400 or less, and he did not work thereafter, he would get benefits for the entire 12 months (if he had reached the minimum retirement age at the beginning of the year).[15]

In the year of death, the annual exempt amount is the monthly exempt amount times the number of months elapsed, including the month of death, with the $1-for-$2 reduction band then being applicable.

Automatic-adjustment provisions apply to the annual and monthly exempt amounts of earnings for 1975 and after. The adjustment is made in exactly the same manner as for the maximum taxable earnings base, as will be discussed later—that is, based on changes in average earnings in covered employment and done only for a calendar year when there has been an automatic adjustment of the benefit level in the previous year. Any such increases in the annual and monthly exempt amounts are rounded to the nearest $120 and $10, respectively. When such an increase is to occur for a calendar year, the Secretary of Health, Education, and Welfare must announce it on or before the previous November 1.

Payment of Benefits Abroad

Benefits are not payable in the case of deported persons, whose rights are terminated until they are subsequently lawfully admitted, and in the case of persons residing in certain countries where there is no reasonable assurance that checks can be delivered or cashed at full

---

[15] A beneficiary aged 62–64 could opt not to take benefits for such first six months, so as to have a smaller actuarial reduction for early retirement.

value. In the latter instance, the benefits are withheld but are credited to the individual and can subsequently be claimed if conditions change, but with only 12 months' payments for those who are not United States citizens. Otherwise, United States citizens (and also aliens who were on the roll in 1956) can readily receive benefits while abroad.

For aliens residing outside the United States coming on the roll after 1956, benefits are payable beyond six months only if the insured worker had 40 or more quarters of coverage or resided in the United States for 10 or more years, or if the country of which he is a citizen has a reciprocity treaty with the United States. There is a further restriction on the payment of benefits of those aliens who meet the 40-quarters or 10-years-of-residence requirements. If their country has a social insurance system of general application, it must pay full benefits to United States citizens while they are outside that country, or else OASDI benefits will not be payable to such aliens.

As a practical matter, the various restrictions are so lenient and so easy to meet that relatively few beneficiaries residing abroad do not receive benefits for which they have met the age and insured status requirements. The principal applicable restrictions relate to those living in some of the communist nations, such as mainland China and Cuba (but not the Soviet Union).

Actually, a number of countries have changed the provisions of their systems so that their citizens could meet the OASDI requirements, and thus reciprocity resulted for United States citizens. On the whole, far more aliens were benefited thereby than were United States citizens.

OASDI FINANCING PROVISIONS

The OASDI benefits and the accompanying administrative expenses are paid out of two separate trust funds. The old-age and survivor benefits come from the Old-Age and Survivors Insurance Trust Fund, while the monthly benefits for disabled workers and their dependents come from the Disability Insurance Trust Fund.

The income to these trust funds is derived from contributions (taxes) from covered workers and employers (see Table 2.9) and from interest earnings on investments. The total tax income is subdivided so that for 1974–77, an amount based on a combined employer-employee rate of 1.15 percent (.815 percent for the self-employed) is allocated to the DI Trust Fund, and the remainder goes to the OASI

Trust Fund. For 1978–1980 the allocation is 1.2 percent for the combined employer-employee rate (0.85 percent for the self-employed), while it is 1.3 percent (and 0.92 percent) for 1981–85, 1.4 percent (and 0.99 percent) for 1986–2010, and 1.7 percent (and 1 percent) after 2010. The allocation for the DI Trust Fund with respect to the self-employed is derived from the allocation for the employer-employee rate multiplied by the ratio of the self-employed total tax rate to the employer-employee total tax rate.

As indicated previously, the tax schedule in the law is intended to provide sufficient income to finance the program adequately over a long-range period, 75 years. However, as will be discussed in more detail in the appendix to Chapter 4 and in Chapter 10, the official actuarial cost estimates made in 1974 indicated a significant actuarial deficit, which will necessitate higher tax rates than those now scheduled in the law. Such higher tax rates will primarily be needed several decades from now rather than in the immediate future.

The indicated deficit, on a long-range basis, was 2.98 percent of taxable payroll, which means that for OASDI to be financed adequately over the next 75 years with the present benefit provisions, the combined employer-employee tax rate would have to *average* almost 3 percent higher than the presently scheduled rates.

However, this does not mean that the tax rates must be boosted so much in the near future. Rather, under the current-cost financing principle that is now followed, smaller increases in the near future will suffice, but this, of course, means larger ones later. Based on those official estimates, the combined employer-employee OASDI tax rate will probably have to be somewhat as follows if the present benefit provisions remain unchanged:

Period	*Present Law*	*Probably Necessary*	*Increase*
1975–1987	9.9%	10.5%	0.6%
1988–2003	9.9	11.3	1.4
2004–2007	9.9	11.7	1.8
2008–2010	9.9	12.7	2.8
2011–2015	11.9	14.0	2.1
2016–2020	11.9	15.5	3.6
2021–2025	11.9	16.3	4.4
2026 and after	11.9	17.6	5.7

But it should be noted, as has been discussed earlier, that the present benefit structure is somewhat "out of control." If this were remedied, the tax rates would not have to increase as much as shown, but some rise would still be needed.

The foregoing increased tax rates would have to be even higher if the economic assumptions used in the official actuarial cost estimates made in 1974 are too optimistic (as the author believes). But then the benefit structure would be even more "out of control," and remedying this situation would avoid such further increased tax schedule being necessary.

Two expert groups of actuaries and economists were established in 1974 to analyze the actuarial status of the OASDI system as it was shown to be according to the 1974 official actuarial cost estimates. The consultants to the Advisory Council on Social Security, which is a statutory body appointed by the Secretary of Health, Education, and Welfare concluded, although not unanimously, that these estimates gave a reasonable picture of the actuarial status of OASDI, but the deficit was more likely to be higher than lower.

The panel appointed by the Senate Finance Committee, however, concluded that the deficit was about 6 percent of taxable payroll, rather than 3 percent. On a year-by-year basis, most of the increase in the estimated deficit was after the year 2000. Thus, the deficiency in the combined employer-employee tax rate for the year 2050 was estimated by the panel to be 12.0 percent, as compared with 5.3 percent according to the official estimate. The increase in the estimated deficiency over that in the official cost estimate was primarily due to assuming lower mortality rates, lower fertility rates in the short range, and less favorable economic elements.

Both of these expert groups pointed out that a significant part of the deficit was due to the manner in which the automatic-adjustment provisions operated under the economic conditions which seem likely to occur. Each group proposed a solution to this portion of the problem, as will be described in Chapter 3.

The 1975 official actuarial cost estimates, presented in the 1975 Trustees Report, showed a considerably increased deficit, namely 5.32 percent of taxable payroll. This was caused by two factors, (1) the effect of the automatic adjustment of benefits for June 1975, which was 8.0 percent instead of the 4.4 percent estimated in the previous report, and (2) the use of higher assumptions as to wage and price increases (namely, as to the ultimate annual increase rates, 6 and 4 percent, respectively). Thus, the financing situation was shown to be even more critical.

The tax rates are applied to the earned income of the covered workers, up to a maximum annual amount, which is termed the earnings base (sometimes referred to as the contribution and benefit base). This base was $9,000 in 1972, $10,800 in 1973, $13,200 in 1974, and is $14,100 in 1975.

If a worker is employed by more than one employer (either concurrently or consecutively), the maximum taxable earnings base applies to each one separately. Under these circumstances, the employee receives a refund, on his income tax return, of the taxes which he has paid in excess of those on the earnings base. No such refund is payable to the employers under such conditions, in part because of the administrative problems so involved and in part because then the personal liberties of the employee would be violated (since each employer would then know that his employee was working elsewhere and, to some extent, what his other earnings were).

If a worker is both an employee and self-employed, his taxable self-employment income cannot be larger than the excess, if any, of the earnings base over his taxable wages.

After 1974 the base is to be adjusted automatically whenever benefits were similarly adjusted in the previous year (the benefit increase in 1974 under the December 1973 amendments being considered as an automatic adjustment for this purpose). The adjustment for a particular year, however, is based on changes in covered wages in the first quarter of the calendar year, rather than on changes in the CPI (as for benefits). Specifically, for a particular year, the base is that for the previous year multiplied by the increase in the average covered wage per person with wage credits as between the second preceding year and the preceding year, with the result being rounded to the nearest $300. The first quarter is used since then the effect of the earnings base is negligible, because few persons reach this maximum before the end of the quarter, so that in reality total wages in covered employment are being considered. When such an increase is to occur for a calendar year, the Secretary of Health, Education, and Welfare must announce it on or before November 1 of the previous calendar year.

Specifically, for 1975, since benefits are considered to have been automatically increased for June 1974, the average taxable wages of all employees for the first quarter of 1974 was compared with the similar figure for 1973. (Note that earnings of the self-employed and agricultural workers are not considered, because they are reported on an annual basis.) The actual increase of 5.94 percent was applied to the

$13,200 base effective in 1974, and the result of $13,984 was rounded to the nearest $300 to yield the $14,100 base applicable for 1975. If no such increase had occurred, the figure for the first quarter of 1973 would have continued to have served as the base point for subsequent determinations of the earnings base. The actual past experience with regard to such increases in first-quarter wages is shown in Table 3.6.

The total tax rates for the OASDI system are shown in Table 2.9, as well as those for this program and the hospital insurance (HI) portion of Medicare combined. The basis for determination of the self-employed rate for OASDI is three fourths of the combined employer-

TABLE 2.9

OASDI Contribution Rates

	OASDI		OASDI and HI	
Calendar Year	Combined Employer-Employee Rate	Self-Employed Rate	Employer-Employee Rate	Self-Employed Rate
1974–77	9.9%	7.0%	11.7%	7.90%
1978–80	9.9	7.0	12.1	8.10
1981–85	9.9	7.0	12.6	8.35
1986–2010	9.9	7.0	12.9	8.50
2011 and after	11.9	7.0	14.9	8.50

employee rate (rounded to the nearest $\frac{1}{10}$th percent), but not to exceed a rate of 7 percent. The 7 percent limit was established so that the tax burden on the self-employed would not be "excessive" and thus be complained about by this category. Beginning in 1973, this limit has been reached. The basis for determination of the self-employed rate for HI is merely the employee rate (established by the 1965 legislation initiating that program—again, the relatively low basis for the reason indicated before).

It may be observed that the total employer-employee cost of OASDI and HI combined, which is now 11.7 percent, first exceeded 10 percent of covered payroll in 1971 and is scheduled to increase over the years to 14.9 percent eventually.[16] There is real question as to how high

---

[16] As has been discussed previously, the tax rates set forth in present law are too low according to the official actuarial cost estimates made in 1974. Further, the author believes that the actuarial assumptions underlying these actuarial cost estimates are, in certain respects, too optimistic.

this tax burden can rise without either a taxpayer revolt or a serious, destructive effect on the provision of economic security through the private sector. In the early 1960s, both political conservatives and political liberals were asserting that a social security tax rate of 10 percent for the employer and employee combined was the absolute maximum!

The assets of the trust funds are invested by the Secretary of the Treasury solely in United States government obligations, other than for a relatively small cash working balance. The securities can be any of three types—obligations bought on the open market, obligations bought at issue (as part of a new issue offered to the public), and special issues. In the actual operations in the past, most of the investments have been in special issues. The law provides that the special issues shall bear an interest rate equal to the average market yield rate on all United States government obligations with at least four years to go until earliest maturity (as of the issuance date of the special issue), rounded to the nearest ⅛th percent. There is no specific provision as to the period until maturity for the special issues, but in practice, in the past there was an attempt to have them in a maturity schedule spread equally over a period of 15 years. However, because of a statutory limit of 4¼ percent on the interest rate of most bonds (which have durations of at least seven years), when interest rates rose so greatly after the mid-1960s, the policy was changed to one of purchasing the longest duration of notes (seven years). This statutory limit was removed in mid-1974 insofar as trust fund investments were concerned. Investment is also permitted in debt obligations that are guaranteed as to both principal and interest by the United States government.

ADMINISTRATION OF OASDI

The OASDI system is administered by the Social Security Administration in the Department of Health, Education, and Welfare. Thus, with one minor exception, it is a completely federally administered program. The earnings records are maintained in a central office in Baltimore, Maryland. SSA staff in about 1,250 district and branch offices make personal contacts with covered workers and their employers, and perform other functions such as assigning account numbers, receiving and adjudicating claims applications, and giving out information. Benefit claims are reviewed and authorized in six program centers located in various parts of the country. The continuing certification of monthly benefits is also handled by these centers.

The Treasury Department collects the taxes, prepares the benefit checks according to the certifications of the Social Security Administration, and maintains the OASI and DI Trust Funds. The Social Security Administration has the responsibility for preparing the actuarial cost estimates that serve to monitor the long-term financial soundness of the system and to provide the basis for the tax schedule in the existing law and as may be needed for proposed changes in the program.

The trust funds are the general responsibility of the board of trustees which is composed of the Secretary of the Treasury, the Secretary of Labor, and the Secretary of Health, Education, and Welfare. The Secretary of the Treasury serves as managing trustee and has the responsibility for the operation of the trust funds (including making the investments, holding the investments, and accounting for the financial operations). The trustees make an annual report, required to be submitted by April 1 (although in recent years this requirement has not been complied with), which contains both an analysis of the long-range actuarial status of the system and estimates of its operation during the next five fiscal years. The board also is authorized to recommend changes in the program, especially as to financing matters. Further, the board is to report immediately to Congress whenever it believes the size of either trust fund is too low (such a report has never been made).

Determinations of disability are, according to the law, made by state agencies (usually the vocational rehabilitation agency) under agreements with the Secretary of HEW, and on a reimbursable basis. The determinations of the state agencies are reviewed by the Social Security Administration to assure consistency and conformity with national policies. This review, however, may not reverse a state finding that no disability exists, although such reversal is possible in a formally appealed case.

chapter 3

Development of OASDI System

The preceding chapter described the old-age, survivors, and disability insurance system (OASDI) as it stands after the amendments of 1973. This chapter will describe how the program took its present form through sometimes gradual, sometimes rapid, evolution over the almost four decades it has been in existence. The presentation will be in the form of tracing through the legislative changes within each of the broad categories of coverage, benefits, and financing, but will not consider in any detail the changes and developments in connection with the financing basis, which will be discussed in the next chapter. One section will describe legislation passed by both the House and the Senate in 1973 but not finally enacted, since this is a good indication of possible future changes. Another section will present the recommendations of the 1974 Advisory Council on Social Security. The procedures by which changes have been made will also be brought out.

COVERAGE

The 1935 Act covered essentially all employees under age 65 in industry and commerce other than railroad workers. The 1939 Act extended coverage only by eliminating the age-65 restriction.

The 1950 Act brought coverage to virtually all employees of private and public employers, including regularly employed farm and domestic workers, except those already under some type of governmental retirement system. Coverage for all employees then brought in was not automatically provided, since for certain categories such as employees of nonprofit organizations and of state and local governments, it was available on a group elective basis. Coverage was extended beyond employees to include most nonfarm self-employed persons other than those in certain professions. The geographical limits of coverage were extended beyond the original bounds of the continental United States, Alaska, and Hawaii (plus certain maritime employees) to include Puerto Rico and the Virgin Islands, and also Americans working abroad for American employers.

The 1954 Act extended coverage even further by bringing in self-employed farmers and, on an elective basis, most state and local government employees under existing retirement systems. As a result, relatively few substantially gainfully employed persons were not covered, or could not be covered by an election. The most important groups still excluded were federal employees (including the military) under an existing retirement system, self-employed persons in the fields of medicine and law, and policemen and firemen under existing retirement systems. In addition, railroad workers were not directly covered, although as a result of amendments to the Railroad Retirement Act in 1951, those who obtain less than 10 years of railroad service were covered under OASDI. In effect, even those with 10 or more years of service were covered from a financial standpoint as a result of the financial interchange provision.

The 1956 Act brought in the remainder of the professional self-employed persons, except for physicians, and gave more opportunities for coverage for state and local government employees under existing retirement systems. Also, ministers were covered (on the self-employment basis, even though they might be employees) on an individual voluntary election basis, with strict rules to minimize antiselection. Other legislation enacted in this year changed the temporary gratuitous coverage of members of the armed forces to regular contributory coverage.

The original planners of the Social Security Act in 1935 had viewed coverage of all types of employment as the desirable goal for the system, after administrative and constitutional problems could be solved. In subsequent years, all studies of the program had reaffirmed this principle. Furthermore, all supporters of the program, regardless of their views as to the broadness of the scope of the benefit protection, believe in this principle. The 1954 legislation meant the almost complete realization of this aim. The 1956 legislation moved even further in this direction.

The 1958 and later amendments added only slightly to the coverage of the program by bringing in a small number of individuals in certain categories, principally in state and local government employment. The 1960 amendments added a small amount of coverage by adding certain rather interesting categories, such as employment in American Samoa and Guam and employment of American citizens employed by foreign governments and international organizations in the United States. The 1960 legislation also eliminated the requirement of two-thirds participation by existing employees of nonprofit institutions for elective coverage by such an organization to become effective.

The 1965 amendments covered self-employed physicians (and interns in hospitals as well, in order to maintain consistency). This was done at the same time that Medicare was legislated, both over the strong opposition of organized medicine.

The 1965 Act also covered tips paid to employees, which had been a particularly vexsome problem over the years. The employee is required to report them to the employer, but only the employee contribution is payable. From an actuarial standpoint, the system suffered no loss because the wage credits arising from tips were in addition to the normal wages paid by the employer and so produced additional benefits in the upper, less heavily weighted, portion of the benefit formula.

The 1967 amendments changed the coverage basis for ministers so as to be on a compulsory basis, but with opting-out permitted on grounds of conscience or religious principles. This change was made because many ministers, particularly younger ones, were not electing coverage because of economic or political reasons; and it had not been the intent of the original basis so to do. The opting-out is based solely on the word of the minister that he has the grounds for so doing.

The 1972 amendments provided for coverage of members of religious orders under a vow of poverty, on the employer-employee basis, if the order so elects, and for coverage of ministers who are United States citizens who are employed outside the country regardless for whom they work. Also, the optional simplified reporting procedure previously applicable to farmers was extended on a limited basis to other self-employed persons. Further, noncontributory gratuitous wage credits, somewhat similar to those applicable to members of the armed forces, were granted to persons of Japanese ancestry who were interned during World War II.

BENEFICIARY CATEGORIES

The 1935 Act provided monthly benefits only for retired workers aged 65 or over. The 1939 Act changed drastically the character of the system by adding benefits for dependents and survivors, including the wife aged 65 or over and the child under age 18 of the retired worker, and the surviving widow aged 65 or over, the surviving dependent parent aged 65 or over, the orphaned child under age 18, and the mother of such child. Subsequent legislation broadened and extended these dependent and survivor beneficiary categories, often in minor respects, as particular "deserving" and "noncontroversial" cases were called to the attention of members of Congress.

The 1950 Act added a few relatively minor beneficiary categories, including dependent husbands and widowers aged 65 or over, and wives of retired workers regardless of the wife's age if a child under 18 was present. The addition of husband's and widower's benefits was the first of a series of changes of relatively little effect, and thus low cost, that make for greater equality of treatment of male and female workers and of male and female beneficiaries. This change had relatively little effect because relatively few men are financially dependent upon their wives, and even then the man may have previously earned a benefit from his own employment that would be offset against the benefit coming from his wife's earnings.

The 1952 Act included a provision for a disability freeze, which protects the disabled worker's insured status and his average monthly wage for benefit computation purposes against the diminishing or destructive effect which would otherwise occur because of having no creditable earnings after becoming disabled. This is similar to the disability waiver-of-premium clause in life insurance policies. Because of an unusual legislative maneuver, since the House of Representatives and the Senate could not agree on this provision, it was not actually operative. However, the 1954 Act included such a provision on a fully effective basis.

The 1956 Act reduced the eligibility age for benefits payable to women from 65 to 62, except that for women workers and wives retiring before age 65, benefits are reduced for such early retirement.

This change was made because of the pressure to provide wife's benefits for men retiring at or just after age 65 where the wife was a few years younger. In turn, this required reducing the minimum age for widow's benefits, although there was considerable sympathy for making this change on its own merits, so that no "dry spell" would occur for a wife, coming on the roll at or just after the minimum age, who became widowed before age 65. And then, in the interest of equity to working women, the minimum retirement age had to be reduced to the same age 62. The reductions for claiming benefits before age 65 were introduced for female-worker and wife's benefits in order to hold down costs. No reductions, however, were made applicable to widow's benefits because of the general sympathy for widows.

In addition, the 1956 legislation added two major beneficiary categories, permanently and totally disabled workers aged 50 to 64 (but with no benefits for dependents), and children aged 18 and over who are eligible as dependents or survivors if they were permanently and totally disabled before age 18. These age limitations on the availability of disability benefits were introduced not only because of cost considerations but also because of the uncertainty as to how well the program could be administered and whether malingering would occur. The latter was thought to be more likely if the benefit level were high (as it would be if dependents' benefits were available) and also more likely for younger beneficiaries with long potential periods of benefit receipt. The disability benefits for disabled workers were subject to reduction by the amount of any other federal disability benefit (such as a veterans' benefit) or any workmen's compensation benefit. This offset provision was eliminated in 1958.

The 1958 Act made dependents of disabled worker beneficiaries eligible for benefits on the same basis as dependents of retired workers. The 1960 Act made the very significant change of eliminating the age-50 requirement for monthly disability benefits. Both of these changes seemed feasible because the cost experience of the program seemed favorable (although, as it turned out later, it was not so much as it seemed to be).

The 1961 Act reduced the eligibility age for men to 62, similar to what the 1956 Act had done for women except that the computation point for both insured status and benefit amounts was left at age 65, although it had previously been reduced to age 62 for women. The introduction of this anomaly of discrimination against men resulted for cost reasons and was not remedied until the 1972 legislation (and then only prospectively, being completely equal treatment by sex for purposes of insured status and benefit computation only for those attaining age 62 after 1974).

The 1965 amendments added two new beneficiary categories: child school-attendance benefits (payable at ages 18–21) and wife's and widow's benefits with respect to divorced wives when the marriage had lasted for at least 20 years. Also, the minimum age for widow's benefits was reduced from 62 to 60, but an actuarial reduction factor, at the same rate per month of early retirement as for retired workers, is applied to the basic benefit rate (then 82½ percent of the PIA). Further, a workmen's compensation offset provision against the amount of the disability benefits was introduced (or, rather, reintroduced, since a somewhat similar provision was in the 1956 amendments, but repealed in 1958). This was necessary so as to prevent payment of total benefits that would be excessively high, and thus likely to discourage rehabilitation and a return to work.

The 1965 legislation also liberalized the definition of disability by changing it from a "permanent and total" definition to the basis of total disability which is expected to last at least 12 months or to result in prior death. The principle of the disability preventing engagement in substantial gainful employment was continued. The 1967 amendments clarified and extended this basis by specifying that such inability to engage in employment referred to work which exists in the national economy, and not merely in the locality where the disabled person lives. The change to the 12-month basis was not as great as might seem to be the case, because previously the "permanent" definition was generally considered as really meaning for a period of about 18 months.

The 1965 amendments provided benefits at a flat rate that was lower than the regular minimum to the few persons aged 72 or over who had at least 3 quarters of coverage and who would have been fully insured except for the 6-quarter minimum requirement. This affected only workers who attained age 72 before 1964 in the case of males, and before 1967 in the case of females. An amendment in 1966 extended this benefit to all persons who attained age 72 before 1968, even though they did not have any quarters of coverage (and to the small number of persons who attained age 72 in the next few years—in any event before 1971—who had a few quarters of coverage but not sufficient to be fully insured).

The flat benefit rate has been increased over the years by the same percentages as the regular benefits, except in 1967, when the increase was 14.3 percent instead of 13 percent, and in 1971, when it was 5 percent instead of 10 percent. For the future, the automatic-adjustment provisions apply to this benefit in the same manner as to the regular benefits.

These changes of a blanketing-in nature were made to satisfy those who pointed out the great "actuarial bargains" received by those who were fully insured on the basis of a few quarters of coverage (at least 6) as against those affected by these two amendments who had previously not been eligible for any benefit. The provisions, however, were carefully drawn up so as to apply to only a closed group so that they would phase out and not be of a permanent nature that could tempt some persons to avoid, or else not seek, OASDI coverage because they could get these benefits anyhow. These benefits, except for persons with at least 3 quarters of coverage, are financed from the General Fund of the Treasury; the reason for this is to "maintain the contributory principle of OASDI."

Further, the 1965 amendments liberalized the definition of disability by requiring that it be expected to last for only 12 months (or result in prior death), instead of the previous basis of being of a long-continued and indefinite duration. This might appear to be a very significant change, but in fact the previous definition had been interpreted on an approximately 18-month basis, because physicians felt that this was the best that they could do. The definition was further liberalized for blind persons, so that at ages 55–64, it was inability to engage in the usual occupation; this could be a precedent for a similar change for all types of disability.

The 1965 amendments also provided for the payment of the costs of rehabilitation services out of the trust funds for cases where this would be "profitable" to OASDI by removing persons from the benefit rolls when they recover and can return to productive activity. Originally, there was a limit for such payments for a fiscal year of 1 percent of the benefit payments to disabled beneficiaries in the preceding fiscal year, but in the 1972 amendments this was increased to 1½ percent for fiscal year 1973 and 2 percent thereafter.

The 1967 amendments provided widow's and dependent widower's benefits beginning at age 50 if the beneficiary is disabled, but with very large early retirement reduction factors being applicable, depending upon the number of months below age 62 when first claiming benefits, and with a more stringent definition of disability than for disabled workers and disabled children, namely by requiring inability to engage in *any* gainful activity, rather than in *any substantial* gainful activity. This restrictive basis was adopted, because of the possibility of adverse experience with a category of persons who have generally not been in the labor market and whose ability to perform gainful work thus is difficult to test.

The 1967 amendments also made two important changes in insured status requirements. First, these requirements as they applied to women workers for child-survivor benefits were made less stringent by eliminating the requirement of currently insured status for married women generally, so that there would be complete equality between the sexes in this respect. Second, an alternative, more liberal, disability insured status provision was instituted for young workers, in recognition of the fact that they might become disabled shortly after entering the labor market.

Several changes in beneficiary categories of a lesser nature were made by the 1972 legislation. Divorced wives no longer need show any support requirement with respect to the insured worker. Child's school-attendance benefits are payable until the end of the semester or quarter in which age 22 is attained instead of ending before the month of attainment. Children disabled before age 22 (previously, before age 18) are eligible for lifetime benefits as survivors or as dependents of retired or disabled workers. Dependent widowers who are not disabled are given equal treatment with widows by having the minimum eligibility at age 60 (instead of 62).

For the first time, grandchildren can be eligible for benefits on the earnings record of an insured worker, as a result of the 1972 amendments. But this will occur only in the very rare case when the parents are dead or disabled and the child was living with and being supported by the grandparent. Generally, under such circumstances, benefits will be payable to the child on the earnings record of the parent; and these will be offset against the benefit coming from the grandparent, perhaps to the extent that nothing will be payable on the record of the grandparent.

The 1972 legislation significantly increased widow's and dependent widower's benefits by making the basic benefit rate 100 percent of the PIA when benefits are first claimed at age 65 or after, but with smaller benefit rates for earlier ages at claim and with a possible further reduction if the deceased spouse had received actuarially reduced early-retirement benefits. This change was made under the "logic" that the widow needs the same size benefit as the single (or widowed) retired worker. In many plans in the United States and abroad, the widow's benefit rate is lower than that for the retired worker on the grounds that the latter "made contributions toward his benefit."

For widows claiming benefits between ages 60 and 65, a reduction factor applies to grade in on a linear basis between the 100 percent factor at age 65 and the 71½ percent factor at age 60 that applied under previous law. This results in a factor of 82.9 percent at age 62, as against the previous one of 82.5 percent and was done so as to have the factors move smoothly by age at claim, rather than to have a linear basis between ages 60 and 62 (as before) and a different linear basis between ages 62 and 65.

As an exception to the foregoing basis for determining widow's benefits, the amount payable cannot exceed the reduced old-age benefit of the retired worker (if he had received one) or, if larger, 82½ percent of the PIA. The reason for this exception was to be consistent with the previously mentioned theory that the widow's benefit should be equal to the worker's benefit, but overriding this, it should not be reduced below 82½ percent of the PIA (otherwise, it might have reduced it to as little as 80 percent of the PIA), since this was the benefit rate previously applicable for widowhood at age 62 or over. This is a vivid example of how permanent complexities can be introduced into the program to preserve vested rights and prevent deliberalizations!

A Supreme Court decision in March 1975 ruled that father's benefits for a widower with young children must be paid on the same terms as mother's benefits for a widow with young children. This was done even though the law contained no such benefit provision, even with a test of dependency, as for aged husbands and widowers. It seems only a matter of time before a change in the law or a court decision will strike out the dependency requirement for such benefits and produce completely equal treatment by sex.

BENEFIT FORMULA

Fifteen different formulas for the determination of the primary insurance amount (PIA), which is used in determining all benefit amounts, have been in existence. Here, "benefit formula" will be construed broadly to include not only the formula itself but also the applicable minimum and maximum provisions. An important feature in benefit determination is the average monthly wage to which the formula is applied. Table 3.1 sets forth these formulas, along with a general description of the basis of computing the average monthly wage in connection with each one.

The benefit formula contained in the 1935 Act never became operative; before monthly benefits became payable, it was superseded by the formula in the 1939 Act. The formula established by the 1950 amendments went into effect in April 1952; but after five months of operation, it was replaced by that in the 1952 Act. That formula, in turn, was virtually superseded by the new one in the 1954 amendments. The 1952 formula continued to be used, as a minimum guarantee, until the 1958 amendments.

The 1972 amendments introduced two new (and complicating) features into the computation of primary benefits. Curiously, both of these moved in the direction of more individual equity and away from social adequacy.

The first was a delayed-retirement increment of $\frac{1}{12}$th percent increase in the PIA (but not for purposes of dependent or survivor benefits) for each month that an insured worker delays filing for benefits after age 65 (and before age 72) because he continues to work. This increase would not be applicable, of course, to those who claimed benefits before age 65. This change was made to recognize the sizable public complaint about the apparent inequity of the earnings test in taking away benefits which, some people believe, had been "bought and paid for at age 65," without any concomitant increase when retirement later occurred.

The second new feature in the computation of the PIA was the provision of a special minimum based on $8.50 per year of coverage, defined as years in which covered earnings were at least 25 percent as large as the maximum amount possible, for years in excess of 10, but not in excess of 30. In practice, this can apply only for those with at least 23 years of coverage, and it will actually apply to relatively few individuals (initially, only 150,000, or about ½ percent of the total beneficiaries).

The intent of this special minimum was to counter demands to have a much higher "regular" minimum than $84.50, which it was argued should be $150–200, so that "it would be above the poverty level, and people could live on it." This argument did not recognize the fact that many, if not most, persons getting the regular minimum do so because they are only intermittently in covered employment and often have

TABLE 3.1 OASDI Benefit Formulas under the Social Security Act and Its Amendments

Formula Enacted in—	Primary Insurance Amount	
	Basis	Percentages Applied
1935.........	Cumulative wage credits	$\frac{1}{2}\%$ of first \$3,000 plus $\frac{1}{12}\%$ of next \$42,000 plus $\frac{1}{24}\%$ of next \$84,000
1939.........	Average monthly wage* after 1936	40% of first \$50 plus 10% of next \$200, all increased by 1% for each year of coverage
1950.........	Average monthly wage* after 1950	50% of first \$100 plus 15% of next \$200
1952.........	" " "	55% of first \$100 plus 15% of next \$200
1954.........	Average monthly wage* after 1950, excluding four or five years of lowest earnings	55% of first \$110 plus 20% of next \$240
1958.........	Average monthly wage† after 1950, excluding five years of lowest earnings	58.85% of first \$110 plus 21.40% of next \$290
1965.........	" " "	62.97% of first \$110 plus 22.90% of next \$290 plus 21.4% of next \$150
1967.........	" " "	71.16% of first \$110 plus 25.88% of next \$290 plus 24.18% of next \$150 plus 28.43% of next \$100
1969.........	" " "	81.83% of first \$110 plus 29.76% of next \$290 plus 27.81% of next \$150 plus 32.69% of next \$100
1971.........	" " "	90.01% of first \$110 plus 32.74% of next \$290 plus 30.59% of next \$150 plus 35.96% of next \$100 plus 20.00% of next \$100
1972.........	" " "	108.01% of first \$110 plus 39.29% of next \$290 plus 36.71% of next \$150 plus 43.15% of next \$100 plus 24.00% of next \$100 plus 20.00% of next \$250
1973‡.........	" " "	119.89% of first \$110 plus 43.61% of next \$290 plus 40.75% of next \$150 plus 47.90% of next \$100 plus 26.64% of next \$100 plus 22.20% of next \$250 plus 20.00% of next \$100
1975§.........	" " "	129.48% of first \$110 plus 47.10% of next \$290 plus 44.01% of next \$150 plus 51.73% of next \$100 plus 28.77% of next \$100 plus 23.98% of next \$250 plus 21.60% of next \$175.

* Total credited earnings divided by months elapsed after year of attainment of age 21 or after "starting year" shown, whichever is more favorable.

† Total credited earnings divided by elapsed months for a number of years equal to number in the measuring period.

‡ Formula in December 1973 amendments effective for June 1974 (which overrides formula in July 1973 amendments—never effective—and formula under December 1973 amendments effective only for March–May 1974). For January–May, 1975, there is the same formula except that the 20.00 percent factor applies to the next \$175 instead of the next \$100, as a result of the earnings base rising to \$14,100.

§ Formula effective for June 1975, as a result of the automatic-adjustment provisions.

other pension income from noncovered employment (e.g., under the federal civil service retirement program).

It is also significant to note that the special minimum is not subject to the automatic-adjustment provisions added by the 1972 amendments, as are all other monthly benefit amounts. The December 1973 amendments, however, did increase the amount from $8.50 to $9 per year of coverage in excess of 10 years but not in excess of 30 years, an increase of 5.9 percent, or well below the general 11 percent increase legislated then. If no changes are made in the amount of the special minimum by legislative action in the future, it could gradually "wither away" as other benefit amounts are increased when the cost of living rises.

Supplementary information about each of these formulas is given in Table 3.2, which shows the minimum and maximum PIAs, the mini-

TABLE 3.2

Minimum and Maximum Benefit Provisions under OASDI
(monthly amounts, except for lump-sum death payments)

Year of Legislation	Primary Insurance Amount		Family Benefit		Lump-Sum Death Payment	
	Minimum	*Maximum*	*Minimum**	*Maximum†*	*Minimum*	*Maximum*
1935.........	$ 10.00	$ 85.00	‡	‡	§	§
1939.........	10.00	60.00‖	$ 10.00	$ 85.00	$ 60.00	$360‖
1950.........	20.00	80.00	15.00	150.00	60.00	240
1952.........	25.00	85.00	18.80	168.75	75.00	255
1954.........	30.00	108.50	30.00	200.00	90.00	255
1958.........	33.00	127.00	33.00	254.00	99.00	255
1961.........	40.00	127.00	40.00	254.00	120.00	255
1965.........	44.00	168.00	44.00	368.00	132.00	255
1967.........	55.00	218.00	55.00	434.40	165.00	255
1969.........	64.00	250.70	64.00	434.40	192.00	255
1971.........	70.40	295.40	70.40	517.00	211.20	255
1972#.......	84.50	404.50	84.50	707.90	253.50	255
1973#.......	93.80	469.00**	93.80	820.80**	255.00	255
1975#.......	101.40	522.80	152.10	914.80	255.00	255

* Applicable only to case of one survivor beneficiary (prior to any reduction for early retirement).

† In some cases, slightly larger amounts can be paid as the result of the provision for rounding benefit amounts (t next higher 10 cents for each beneficiary).

‡ No benefits provided for dependents of survivors.

§ No minimum or maximum provided (potential maximum was about $5,000).

Not including the effect of the delayed-retirement increment (which can increase the PIA by a maximum of 7 per cent) or the special minimum benefit based on years of coverage. Figures for 1975 are based on the automatic adjustmer made for June 1975.

‖ Assumes that 50 years of coverage is the maximum possible.

** These are the figures contained in the law, effective for June 1974, when it was enacted. The increase in th maximum taxable earnings base in 1975, as a result of the automatic-adjustment provisions, resulted in the benefi table being extended. As a result, as of January 1975, the maximum PIA in the table is $484, and the maximum fam ily benefit is $847.

mum and maximum family benefits, and the minimum and maximum lump-sum death payments. In considering this table, the major distinction between the benefit provisions in the 1935 law and those in subsequent legislation should be kept in mind. The original Act provided only retirement benefits for the insured worker, while the subsequent amendments have, in addition, provided supplementary benefits for the dependents of retired workers and for survivors of deceased workers—a move toward social adequacy and away from individual equity. The 1939 legislation adjusted the benefit amounts so that retired workers without dependents would receive, in the long run, less than they would have been paid under the original law and so that retired workers with dependents receive more.

At the same time, the 1939 legislation eliminated the money-back guarantee of the 1935 Act, which provided that every worker would get back somewhat more than the employee taxes he had paid. This was one of the few instances when the program has been deliberalized and was, of course, a distinct move away from individual equity and toward social adequacy. The savings from eliminating this refund benefit were, in effect, used to meet part of the cost for the survivor monthly benefits which were then added.

It should also be borne in mind that the 1950 legislation gave increasing recognition to presumptive family needs when it raised current benefit levels and at the same time eliminated the increment provision (1 percent increase for each year of coverage). An increment results in the payment of larger benefits in the later years of the program than in the early ones and also larger survivor benefits with respect to workers who die at the older ages than those who die at the younger ages. This change reflected the increasing emphasis on social adequacy, as against individual equity. But note the partial reversal of this change in the 1972 amendments when an increment was reintroduced for delayed retirement beyond age 65.

In the years since the original law was enacted, the minimum old-age benefit has increased so that in mid-1975 it is about 10 times the original level, while the maximum old-age benefit has gone up to only about 6 times its original level. In fact, the formulas in each of the first three major amendments resulted in a maximum old-age benefit equal to or less than the original amount. As indicated previously, however, consideration of the adequacy of the benefits cannot be viewed solely in terms of the changes in the old-age benefits. The introduction in the 1939 Act of family benefits for dependents and survivors resulted in a better distribution of social protection at roughly the same aggregate cost.

The trend in the minimum old-age benefit has resulted from two different philosophies as to its purpose. Originally, it was instituted for administrative reasons—as a facility-of-payment provision. Later, it was viewed as a payment applicable to low-income workers and hence, according to social insurance principles, should be raised proportionately more than other benefit amounts.

In more recent years, it was realized that a large proportion of those receiving the minimum benefit are not necessarily low-income workers living at poverty levels, but rather are recipients of other pensions (such as federal civil service retirement, state or local government retirement systems not coordinating with OASDI, or railroad retirement) or are only intermittent workers (such as many wives, whose husbands are eligible for sizable benefits). Thus, in the 1969 amendments the minimum was increased by the same 15 percent that applied to all benefits (but the result was rounded to the next higher dollar). In the amendments of March 1971 and later, the same procedure was followed (with no such rounding). This is in contrast with the action taken in the 1967 amendments, when the general benefit level was raised 13 percent, but the minimum went up 25 percent.

A married man has the protection, both before and after retirement, not only of monthly benefits for his survivors but also of supplementary benefits for eligible dependents that are available at his retirement. Specifically, for a retired worker whose wife is eligible and is not entitled to a benefit based on her own earnings, the maximum benefit was raised 125 percent by the 1958 Act from the amount payable under the 1935 Act. The increase at that time for a worker without an eligible wife was only 50 percent.

The minimum family benefit has likewise increased by 10 times since 1940, when these benefits were first paid, while the maximum family benefit is about 11 times what it was originally. The reduction in the maximum old-age benefit from $85 in the 1935 Act to $60 (in effect) in the 1939 Act is less significant than it might at first appear, because at the same time a maximum of $85 was made possible for a worker with an eligible wife.

The minimum lump-sum death payment is now four times the minimum specified in 1939; the maximum is about 30 percent lower than the potential maximum under the 1939 law, and is about 7 percent less than the highest amount actually paid under that law ($273.60).

It is noteworthy that the maximum lump-sum death payment has been held fixed at $255 ever since 1952, as a result of the 1954 amendments placing this overriding maximum on the normal amount of three times the PIA, and such limitation never having been changed. In fact, before the 1973 legislation there was virtually no spread in the size of this lump sum—only from $253.50 to $255—and now there is none at all, since $255 is available in all cases. The reason that this benefit has been frozen, despite the substantial increases in the overall benefit level, is that even those who wish to expand the scope of the OASDI program greatly have no desire to make more money available for funerals, which they believe will be wasted, and, instead, would rather spend what funds are available for other benefit purposes.

The first change in the benefit formula, made in 1939, reflected a change in philosophy. Benefits payable in the early years of the program's operation were made relatively larger, and presumptive family needs were recognized by provision of supplementary benefits for dependents. Offsetting these two changes, benefits for long-term contributors and for those without dependents were reduced. The second change in the benefit formula (in 1950) carried further the philosophy underlying the payment of larger benefits currently, by making no distinction in benefit amount based on years of coverage (for those continuously in covered employment). The change consisted primarily of adjustment to changes in the cost of living, with the average increase for those on the roll being about 77 percent. The third change (in 1952) was also primarily a result of wage-level and cost-of-living changes as a result of the Korean War, with the increase averaging about 15 percent. The fourth change (in 1954) reflected both an adjustment for higher wage levels and an increase of about 10 percent in the relative adequacy of the benefits, with the average benefit increasing about 13 percent. The fifth change (1958) again paralleled the increase in the cost of living since the previous change, and averaged about 7½ percent.

The sixth change in the benefit formula (in 1965) also paralleled the increase in the cost of living since the previous change, and averaged about 7 percent. The next three changes (13 percent in 1967, 15 percent in 1969, and 10 percent in 1971), however, were all somewhat more than the cost-of-living rises—by about 5 percentage points in each case—so that there was a significant "real" expansion in the benefit level of the program in 1967–71, as there also was in 1972.

The next change in the benefit formula, resulting from the 1972 legislation, was 20 percent. This was well above the 5.9 percent increase in the cost of living that occurred between the effective date of the previous increase (January 1971) and that of this increase (September 1972).

During the first Nixon administration (1969–72), the three benefit increases amounted to 51.8 percent on a cumulative basis. This compares with a cost-of-living rise of only 23.4 percent between the effective date of the 1967 benefit increase and September 1972, so that there was a real increase in benefit levels of 23 percent (151.8 ÷ 123.4 − 100). The Nixon administration urged increases only equal to the rise in the cost of living each three times that the legislation was being considered, but the actions of Congress produced the significant expansion of the benefit level which occurred.

The last four changes in the benefit formula resulted from the two 1973 amendments. The effect of the July 1973 amendments was an increase of 5.9 percent, based on the change in the CPI from June 1972 to 1973, whose amount was not known when the legislation was enacted. That benefit increase would have applied only for June–December 1974, and then would be overridden by the automatic-adjustment provisions, which were scheduled to go into operation first in January 1975.

The benefit formula under the July 1973 amendments never became operative because it was overridden by the two formulas of the December 1973 amendments. The first such formula, applicable only for March–May 1974, was an increase of 7 percent over the formula of the 1972 amendments, while the second one was an increase of 11 percent over the 1972 formula.[1] The 11 percent increase was justified on the grounds that this would approximate the CPI rise from September 1972 (the date of the last previous benefit increase) to June 1974; the actual rise was somewhat more than this, 16.4 percent. At the same time, the automatic-adjustment provisions for the benefit formula were changed to be effective for Junes (instead of Januarys), to be based on CPI changes between the first quarters of various years (second quarter as to 1974), instead of second quarters. As a result of

[1] The two-step approach was taken for administrative reasons. A completely precise procedure for adjusting benefits in payment could not be accomplished in the time available before the first effective month (March 1974), so an approximate basis (precise, in most cases) was prescribed for the benefits for the first three months.

this provision, the benefit formula applicable for June 1975 was derived by increasing all benefit factors by 8.0 percent.

It was interesting and significant to note that the increase in the CPI from September 1972 to the *first* quarter of 1974 was 12.0 percent, or virtually the same as the 11 percent benefit increase effective for June 1974. On this basis, equity to the beneficiaries with regard to the automatic adjustments could have been achieved by basing the adjustment for June 1975 on the change in the CPI from the *first* (instead of the *second*) quarter of 1974 to the first quarter of 1975.

One might ask whether the 1973 legislation was yet another expansion of the social security program and thus a further step away from having the private sector bear significant responsibility in the economic security field. Actually, the 11 percent benefit increase was reasonable, although it might have been accomplished in a somewhat better manner technically. When the 20 percent benefit increase was enacted in 1972, effective for September, inflation seemed to be diminishing, so that another benefit increase would not be needed in the next two years to maintain the purchasing power of the benefits.

Also, one might well ask why the original version of the automatic-adjustment provisions did not provide for them to go into effect in January 1974.[2] If this had been done, the benefit increase would have been based on the change in the Consumer Price Index from the third quarter of 1972 to the second quarter of 1973. The result, as the actual experience has turned out, would have been an increase of 4.5 percent beginning for January 1974, with another increase of 7.1 percent be-

---

[2] Interestingly, the Senate version of the July 1973 legislation did provide for the effective month to be January 1974 (but not using the logical method for determining the period for the increase in the CPI—i.e., the basis provided for all future years in the 1972 legislation). The sponsor of moving up the first date for the automatic adjustment of benefits, Senator Ribicoff, had initially proposed this simple, and correct, procedure of merely changing such date to January 1974 and not changing the measurement basis.

The first effective month was changed from January to June at the insistence of the Nixon administration, which was concerned about the incidence of the increased outgo on economic conditions and the budget (rather than about social insurance principles and social considerations). As to the latter, making the increase effective for June 1974 (with the first increased check going out at the beginning of July) would produce no effect on the budget for the fiscal year ended June 30, 1974.

In September 1973, the Senate voted to advance the first payment date for the 5.9 percent increase from June 1974 to whatever would be the month of enactment of the legislation, but the House did not concur.

ginning for January 1975. In hindsight certainly, the automatic-adjustment provisions should logically have been first operative for January 1974, and then the 1973 legislation would not have been necessary.

One encouraging aspect of the 1973 legislation occurred from the standpoint of those who believe that the automatic-adjustment provisions might take arguments about the magnitude of benefit changes out of politics. The change made was based solely on a change in the CPI. There was no "competitive bidding" between those who wanted much larger increases than the CPI indicated, as there had been when benefit increases were enacted in 1969, 1971, and 1972. Likewise, the automatic increase effective for June 1975 was made without any attempt in Congress to increase its amount, although an unsuccessful effort was made to have it be retroactive to January, with the added benefit cost to be met from general revenues.

Every change in the benefit formula since 1954 has been based on the formula in the 1954 law. The procedure has been merely to increase the various percentage benefit factors in the formula by the uniform percentage increase in the general benefit level of beneficiaries then on the roll (as described in the previous chapter). This same procedure is prescribed under the automatic-adjustment procedure enacted in the 1972 legislation.

Considering the fact that the four across-the-board benefit increases in the 1967, 1969, 1971, and 1972 amendments represented a rise of 29 percent in real terms, after deflating by the change in the cost of living, one can well ask whether the floor-of-protection concept has been abandoned in favor of having social security be a virtually complete national retirement system. Further in this direction there should also be considered the fact that other OASDI changes made in the 1972 legislation (principally, increased widow's benefits) represented, in effect, an additional increase of about 8 percent.

One particular situation occurs where OASDI has been expanded to the point that it fills the entire economic security needs. If a young worker aged 29 or under dies at the end of 1975 after having had the $13,200 maximum creditable annual earnings in 1974 and $14,100 in 1975 and leaves a widow and two children, the family benefit will be $901.60 per month. As against this, his net take-home pay (after considering federal and state income taxes and social security taxes) was about $950 per month. Thus, the survivor benefit is 95 percent of take-home pay, and the family income needs are less because of no work expenses and one less person.

The foregoing situation arises because of a technical defect in the benefit provisions, as discussed in the previous chapter. For a similar family, except that the worker is aged 41 or over in 1975 (and has had maximum covered earnings in all years from 1951 on), the corresponding survivor benefit is $648.40 per month, or only 68 percent of final take-home pay. This anomaly should be remedied—several ways in which this can be done are discussed in chapter 5.

The special benefits payable to persons aged 72 or over, as legislated in 1965 and 1966, were initially at a flat amount basically of $35 per month, intentionally somewhat below the minimum PIA of $44 then in effect. This special benefit rate of $35 was increased to $40 in the 1967 amendments (i.e., by about the same 13 percent as the general benefit level, but not nearly as much as the 25 percent increase in the minimum PIA). In the 1969 amendments, the rate for these special benefits was increased to $46, or by the same 15 percent rate as applicable to all other benefits.

The amendments in March 1971 provided only a 5 percent increase for these special benefits—to a rate of $48.30—as against the 10 percent increase in all other benefits. Evidently, the Congress did not view these special benefits, which are based on little or no covered employment, as being very needy of being liberalized beyond any changes necessary to keep up with rises in the cost of living. This approach was not followed in the 1972 and 1973 legislation, which applied the same 20 and 11 percent increases to these benefits as to all others and produced benefit rates of $58 and $64.40, respectively. The automatic-adjustment provisions continue this practice of the special benefits being increased at the same rate as the regular ones.

For workers retiring currently, the benefits paid are larger than the original program would have provided, both in terms of dollars and also in relation to wage at time of retirement. The relative size of the benefits was increased significantly by the 1954 amendments (and was maintained by the 1958 and 1965 amendments) and by the 1967, 1969, 1971, and 1972 amendments, a fact that is, of course, reflected by the increased financial support of the program provided by the higher ultimate tax rates scheduled in the law.

In considering the benefit formulas, it is necessary to recognize that in the 1939 and later acts the benefits are based on the career-average wage insofar as the "ultimate" condition is concerned (when persons would have the possibility of a full lifetime under the system). Certain modifications in this general principle have, however, been introduced over the years so that, in fact, up to now the average wage has been based on the earnings of a much shorter period. On the whole, this was done so as not to disadvantage newly covered groups, while at the same time giving the same advantages to those workers previously covered.

Thus, in the 1950 Act, the important change was made that the relatively low earnings before 1951 (in many cases of newly covered persons, no earnings at all) could be omitted. Likewise, as a result of the 1954 and 1956 Acts, the five lowest years of earnings are dropped out (in part, to be beneficial to groups newly covered in 1955, such as farmers), and this is also done for years in which the individual was permanently and totally disabled. The 1960 Act made a significant change by permitting years of high earnings after attainment of minimum retirement age to be substituted for prior years with low earnings instead of, as previously, having an alternative of computing the average wage up to the actual time of retirement rather than merely to the minimum eligibility age.

When the minimum retirement age for women was reduced from 65 to 62 in the 1956 amendments, the computation point for retirement benefits for them was also moved down to age 62. This resulted in a woman working until age 65 having three less computation years than a similar man—or, conversely she could substitute years of high earnings at ages 62–64 for years of low earnings before then, whereas a man could not.

When the minimum retirement age for men was similarly reduced by the 1961 amendments, no change was made in the computation point for men (because of cost considerations). Such a change, resulting in equal treatment of men and women, was made in the 1972 legislation, but only being applicable for men attaining age 62 after 1974.

Although the average monthly wage is computed on a career-average basis, the interacting effect of using dynamically adjusted benefit factors (as has been described previously) is to produce about the same results for benefits as if a final-average wage had been used in conjunction with static benefit factors. In other words, the basis for computation of benefits which has been followed in the past two decades adequately offsets the apparent illogical approach of having a career-average wage being applied in a period of significantly rising earnings.

Thus, a change to a final-average wage basis, such as the high five years, while at the same time retaining the procedure of dynamically adjusting the benefit factors through the automatic-adjustment provisions as the cost of living rises, would represent an unnecessary change, unless the intent were to expand the benefit level by any means possible.

AUTOMATIC-ADJUSTMENT PROVISIONS

For some years, proposals had been made to adjust automatically both benefit levels and the maximum taxable earnings base (the former by the Consumer Price Index and the latter by changes in the level of wages in covered employment). As precedents, this was done in several foreign social insurance systems and also, as to benefits, in the retirement plans for federal civilian employees and for the uniformed services. Also, the 1965 Act contained a provision involving automatic adjustment of the the maximum on combined social security disability benefits and workmen's compensation benefits. The procedure was exactly the same as was later adopted in the 1972 legislation with respect to the earnings base. It is also very significant to note that the manner in which the automatic-adjustment provisions for benefits operate is exactly the same as Congress has done in making all the ad hoc increases after 1954.

Although there was great popular pressure for such automatic-adjustment provisions, most organized groups opposed them. Politicians frequently were not in favor because then "the actuarial and statistical bureaucrats would get credit for benefit increases, rather than us." Most business groups opposed automatic adjustment because they feared that overliberalization would result, since politics would produce legislated increases on top of the automatic ones. These groups also opposed the automatics on the grounds that benefit increases resulting therefrom might come at the wrong time in the economic cycle and thus add to the fires of inflation.

On the other hand, most labor organizations were in opposition because they were afraid that the benefit level would be straight-jacketed at its then relative height, and they believed the automatics were desirable only after the benefit level had been substantially boosted. Quite obviously, the business and labor views were based on diametrically opposing logic, and if one were right, the other would be wrong!

Those who favored the automatic-adjustment provisions argued that the ad hoc procedures of the past had increased benefits about as much as would have the automatics, although in some instances with significant lag (as during 1958–64, when no increases were legislated, despite some rise in the cost of living), which seemed unfair to the beneficiaries. In certain other instances, the benefit increases exceeded what would be called for by changes in the cost of living (as during the first Nixon administration, 1969–72). It was the hope of those favoring the automatics that they would better control such political bidding up of the benefit level and thus take the program to some extent out of politics.

Shortly after President Nixon took office, he recommended a small number of obviously needed benefit changes. These included a 10 percent benefit increase (to make up for the rise in the cost of living that had occurred since the last previous benefit increase) and automatic-adjustment provisions. The benefit increase was enacted rapidly —at a bargained-up 15 percent.

The automatics were opposed by Chairman Wilbur D. Mills of the House Ways and Means Committee, an extremely powerful and well-informed person, but were supported strongly by Congressman John W. Byrnes, the ranking Republican member of that committee, who had favored this idea for some years. In early 1970, the bill containing the President's recommendation was changed by the Ways and Means Committee to exclude the automatics, but on the floor of the House, in an unusual and almost unprecedented manner, Chairman Mills was reversed, and the automatics were included. The Senate, too, approved these provisions, but because of long delays for other reasons (principally, the fight over the public assistance provisions, see Chapter 11), the bill was not enacted by the time Congress adjourned.

Provisions for automatic adjustments were included, without any serious controversy, in the legislation enacted in 1972, and are applicable to all types of monthly benefits, except those payable under the special-minimum provision (based solely on years of coverage). One significant change in the provisions was made as compared with the original recommendations. The Congress is to be informed, at least by August 15 (by April 1, as a result of the changes made by the December 1973 amendments), if the automatic-adjustment provisions would become effective in the next few months. Also, Congress is to be informed whenever the CPI has increased by 2½ percent since the last base quarter.

Under such circumstances, Congress could enact new benefit levels so as to get the political credit for the benefit increases. In fact, it is not inconceivable that the automatics may actually never go into effect, but rather will serve merely as warning signals of the need for congressional action! Accordingly, political competition can continue to be present, as it has in recent years. Nonetheless, it would seem that the presence of the automatics gives some hope, though no guarantee, of control over unwarranted expansion of the benefit level.

TABLE 3.3

Derivation of OASDI Benefit Increases Which Would Have Resulted If Automatic Adjustment Provisions Had Been Enacted in 1965, Effective for 1967

Year	CPI for Second Quarter of Previous Year*	Increase in CPI		Actual Benefit Increase Legislated†	
		From Previous One	Cumulative	In Year	Cumulative
1966.........	94.3	n.a.	n.a.	—	—
1967.........	96.9	2.8%	2.8%	—	—
1968.........	99.4	2.6	5.5	13.0%	13.0%
1969.........	103.5	4.1	9.8	—	13.0
1970.........	109.1	5.4	15.7	15.0	30.0
1971.........	115.7	6.0	22.6	10.0	43.0
1972.........	120.8	4.4	28.0	20.0	71.6
1973.........	124.7	3.2	32.1	—	71.6
1974.........	131.5	5.5	39.4	8.2‡	85.7

* On base of 1967 = 100.
† Shown in year when first effective.
‡ Reduced from the actual 7 and 11 percents legislated to allow for their being effective for only 10 months of the year.
n.a. = not applicable.

It is interesting to compute what would have been the effect if the automatic-adjustment provisions for benefits had been enacted in 1965, when the first automatic-adjustment provisions were incorporated into the program (for the workmen's compensation offset with respect to disability benefits). The results of a similar exercise are presented later with regard to the maximum taxable earnings base.

Table 3.3 shows the annual increases in the OASDI benefit level that would have occurred since 1965 if the automatic-adjustment provisions for benefits had been enacted then, instead of in 1972. It is assumed that the provisions would have been first effective for January 1967 (since the 1965 amendments increased the benefit level effective for January 1966) and that no ad hoc benefit increases were made. The result would have been benefit increases in January of each year except for 1967, when the 3 percent trigger point would not have been reached. The total cumulative increase in benefits up through 1974 would have been 39.4 percent under the automatic-adjustment method, or only about half of the actual increase of 85.7 percent. To put it another way, there was a real increase in the benefit level over what was called for by adjustment for changes in the cost of living of about 33 percent from 1966 to 1974.

As indicated previously, the automatic-adjustment provisions applicable to the benefit amounts did go into effective operation for June 1975. In the early part of 1975, President Ford proposed, for federal budgetary reasons, that the increase thereunder should be limited to 5 percent, just as he also recommended for the automatic adjustments under the Supplemental Security Income, the Civil Service Retirement, and the military pension programs. This proposal was greeted with a great lack of enthusiasm by Congress. It may, however, have had an effect on preventing action for a larger increase.

In fact, it was proposed in the Senate, when the tax reduction bill was being considered, that the increase should be paid retroactively back to January. This proposal carried the curious logic that the cost of the retroactive benefits should be met from general revenues. This would seem to imply that the regular increase resulting from the automatics was a "fully-financed insured payment," while the retroactive payment was welfare or public assistance.

The Senate did not adopt this proposal, but instead it provided in the bill for a uniform lump-sum payment of $100, financed from general revenues, for all beneficiaries under OASDI, railroad retirement, and the supplemental security income plan. This provision, however, was reduced to $50 in the joint conference on the legislation between the House of Representatives and the Senate.

MINIMUM RETIREMENT AGES

The original selection of age 65 as the minimum retirement age for insured workers was, to a considerable extent, arbitrary and empirical. Age 70 seemed too far advanced and unlikely of achievement, although many private pension plans, particularly those in the railroad industry, had such a minimum age in the mid-1930s. On the other hand, age 60 was too low an age, both in view of general employment practices and costs. Accordingly, the compromise "even quinquennial" age of 65 was selected.

The minimum eligibility age for wives, widows, and female dependent parents was reduced to 62 in the 1956 Act. This action was taken because wives are generally somewhat younger than their husbands, and so it was desired to have wives qualify at the same time as the worker retired. However, note that this reasoning was based on averages, and many wives are more than the *average* three-year differential between age of husband and age of wife prevailing at the older ages. Then, by the "domino theory," the minimum age for widows had to be reduced, because it would seem illogical to pay benefits to a woman as a wife and then to cut them off at the husband's death because she was still under age 65. The wife's benefits were reduced when claimed between ages 62 and 65 (on close to an actuarial basis, but not quite as much—because such a large reduction would have resulted), but no reduction was made for widows or parents—because of the general sympathy for these categories.

At the same time, it seemed necessary also to lower the minimum retirement age for women workers. This was done on the grounds that they had made direct contributions, whereas dependents of insured workers had not, and that, therefore, they should be treated as liberally. The early-retirement provision, however, provided for reduced benefits with the reduction factors being on an approximate actuarial basis, so that no "bargain" was involved for the beneficiaries, and likewise no additional cost occurred for the program. Actually, the only added cost involved was the small one arising from reducing the computation point for insured status and average monthly wage for women from age 65 to 62, thus requiring slightly less quarters of coverage and a somewhat shorter period for calculating the average wage.

The 1961 Act lowered the minimum retirement age for men to 62 for insured workers and dependent husbands, widowers, and male parents, with the reduction procedure for early retirement being the same as for women. No change was made in the year of attainment of age 65 as being the terminal point for computation of insured status and the average monthly wage. Such terminal point was not lowered for men because of cost considerations, even though this produced illogical results (such as different PIAs developing for males and females with identical dates of birth and employment histories). As mentioned previously, the 1972 legislation corrected this anomaly and lowered the terminal point for men to age 62 (but only for those attaining this age after 1974).

The 1965 amendments lowered the minimum eligibility age for widows from 62 to 60, but with actuarially reduced benefits. Parallel treatment for dependent widowers was not given until the 1972 legislation.

The 1967 amendments reduced the minimum eligibility age for both widows and dependent widowers to 50 if total and presumably permanent disability was present. The benefit rate, however, was sharply reduced from the 82½ percent rate payable at age 62 at first claim.

BENEFIT PROPORTIONS FOR DEPENDENTS AND SURVIVORS

When benefits for dependents and survivors were first introduced by the 1939 Act, the benefit proportion for all categories was 50 percent of the primary benefit payable to the worker (for deaths before retirement, the benefit that would have been payable if the individual had been eligible to retire), except for widows, for whom the proportion was 75 percent. The 1950 Act changed these proportions by increasing that for parents from 50 percent to 75 percent and by, in effect, giving the first survivor child beneficiary also 75 percent (but retaining 50 percent for all other child beneficiaries).

The 1960 Act increased the benefit proportion for all child survivor beneficiaries to 75 percent, thus establishing the uniform principle that all survivor beneficiaries receive 75 percent of the primary benefit and all dependents of retired or disability beneficiaries receive 50 percent (subject in all cases to the maximum family benefit). This principle was changed by the 1961 Act, under which widows, widowers, and dependent parents aged 62 and over at first claim had the proportion increased by 10 percent relatively, to 82½ percent (except that 75 percent was retained for parents in two-parent cases, so as to produce the same 150 percent family benefit as payable for a retired worker and spouse).

Over the years, many people had advocated that widows should receive the full PIA, and the change from 75 to 82½ percent of the PIA in the 1961 Act was a step toward this goal. The argument in favor of this was that when a married couple both over age 65 at claim were living, the benefit rate was 150 percent of the PIA, and when the wife died first the rate was reduced to 100 percent, so why should the rate for the widow be less than 100 percent if the husband died first? In answer to this argument, it was pointed out that this would result in unfair treatment to women workers, who received only a 100 percent benefit even though they had paid contributions toward it (and, in many cases, their PIA would be low because of their lower wages than married men).

President Nixon included a provision for 100 percent widow's (and dependent widower's) benefits when first claimed at age 65 or over, with graded-down amounts before then, in his proposals in 1969. These were eventually included in the 1972 legislation, although with an additional proviso that the amount payable could not exceed the benefit previously payable with respect to the deceased worker (applicable in cases of early retirement). Thus, the uniform principle was now, once again, present for all benefits for insured workers and their living or surviving spouses (but not for dependent parents) that full-rate benefits are payable only if claimed at or after age 65, with reduced benefits for earlier claim.

INSURED STATUS

The 1935 Act required aggregate covered wages of $2,000 and covered employment in any part of five different years in order to be eligible for monthly old-age benefits. The 1939 Act changed this basis completely so as, in a sense, to require coverage equal to half of the potential period (after 1936 or age 21, if later, up to attainment of the minimum retirement age or death, if earlier) in order to produce "fully insured" status so as to be eligible for old-age or survivor benefits. The 1950 Act liberalized this requirement—in large part, for the benefit of newly covered groups—by changing the measuring period so as to begin in 1951, but allowing coverage before then to count to meet the "one out of two" requirement, as does also coverage before age 22 or after attainment of retirement age.

The 1954 and 1956 legislation, which brought more groups into coverage, contained special alternative provisions that would yield fully insured status if there was continuous coverage, but with such provisions "washing out" in a few years. The 1960 Act considerably liberalized the fully insured-status provision by requiring coverage equal to only one third of the years after 1950 or age 21, if later, while the 1961 Act reduced this proportion to one fourth. These changes had a largely temporary effect, since the maximum coverage requirement for old-age benefits remained at 40 quarters of coverage (although only for persons attaining age 62 in 1991 will this "permanent" provision first apply).

Although the 1961 Act lowered the minimum retirement age (as to receipt of benefits) for men from 65 to 62, the measuring point for fully insured status for men was left at age 65, unlike the case for women, where it has been age 62 since the 1956 Act. Just as in the case of computation of the average monthly wage, cost considerations required that no change be made. The 1972 legislation moved the measuring point for men down to age 62 (but only for those attaining this age after 1974), so that eventual equality of treatment has been achieved.

At all times since the 1939 Act, the minimum requirement for fully insured status has been 6 quarters of coverage. The 1965 amendments provided special flat-rate benefits (at a basic rate of $35 per month) for persons aged 72 or over who would have met the requirement for fully insured status if the minimum provision had been 3 quarters of coverage instead of 6—the so-called transitional-insured benefits. Amendments in 1966 provided for similar benefits for persons aged 72 or over with no coverage (or, in some cases, with a few quarters of coverage being needed although less than would be needed for fully insured status), but with certain restrictions on the receipt of other governmental benefits—the so-called transitional-noninsured benefits.

Throughout the entire period following the 1939 Act, an alternative requirement, currently insured status, was permitted for young-survivor benefits. This, in a sense, requires coverage for half of the quarters in the last three years. That provision has remained essentially unchanged throughout the entire period. Initially, this was one of the requirements for the "disability freeze" (enacted in 1954) and for monthly disability benefits (enacted in 1956). In the 1958 Act, however, the requirement of currently insured status for both such benefits was eliminated, because in certain cases of gradually progressive disability, it proved to be a difficult requirement to meet.

Also, currently insured status was initially required for eligibility for certain benefits arising from the earnings record of a working woman (child's, husband's, and widower's benefits). However, in the 1967 Act, this special additional requirement was eliminated, which was a significant move in the direction of equal treatment of men and women.

The requirement for disability insured status remained unchanged since it was established in the 1954 Act (20 quarters of coverage out of the last 40 quarters) until the 1967 amendments. Then, special lower requirements were introduced for workers under age 31, since they might not as readily have the opportunity to acquire the 20 quarters of coverage needed. A similar provision had been included in 1965 for the blind, which thus pointed the way for this provision.

EARNINGS TEST

A test of retirement was implicit in the original act. For any month in which the individual received covered wages from "regular employment," monthly old-age benefits would not be paid. Regular employment was not specifically defined, however.

The 1939 amendments permitted payment of benefits if the beneficiary had earnings in covered employment of no more than $14.99 a month. The test was on an "all or none" basis. Earnings of $14.99 or less did not affect payment of the full benefit, but earnings of even slightly more than this amount meant that the entire benefit for the month was lost.

The earnings test was still $14.99 a month when the 1947 Senate Advisory Council on Social Security was formed. Because of changes since 1939 in the wage level and other factors, it was generally agreed that this amount was too low. Furthermore, there was the important question of working out a basis for the test which would be more equitable than the "all or none" basis and which would also be reasonably simple to administer. The advisory council stated that modification was necessary so that beneficiaries should not have their total income from benefits and employment reduced because of working.

One possibility considered was the general principle of a "one for one" reduction. Full benefits would be paid if monthly earnings were $35 or less, while if earnings were larger, the benefits would be reduced by the amount of the difference. Operation on this principle would permit a smooth transition from full-time employment to part-time employment and then to full-time retirement. Individuals earning more than the amount permitted for payment of full benefits would thus, within a certain range, maintain their total income from benefits and earnings combined, instead of having a reduction in total income, as under the "all or none" retirement test. Of course, this approach would not offer any incentive to work beyond the $35 limit, but it was a vast improvement over the "all or none" basis. The council recognized, also, that minor modifications would be necessary to facilitate administration to some extent, since month-by-month adjustments and calculations would be costly to make. Accordingly, it recommended quarterly adjustments.

The advisory council recognized that some modifications would have to be made for the self-employed, since their earnings would be reported annually. No specific proposals, however, were presented for this group.

Another recommendation made by the advisory council was that the earnings test should not apply to beneficiaries aged 70 and over. It was recognized that this proposal would involve some significant increase in cost, but not nearly as much, of course, as if the test were completely eliminated. In essence, then, the proposal was a compromise with those persons who held that the test was a restriction on their activity and who considered the benefits as something that they had paid for and that therefore should be payable automatically as an annuity at age 65. Furthermore, the elimination of the test for persons aged 70 or over would be attractive particularly to farmers and other self-employed persons (for whom the advisory council recommended coverage), since it had been argued that these groups generally "never retire."

The 1950 amendments raised from $14.99 to $50 a month the amount of wages permitted under the earnings test, but continued it on an "all or none" monthly basis for wage earners. A "unit reduction" procedure was adopted for the self-employed, who were brought into coverage and who report their earnings annually. Benefits were not withheld if the covered self-employment earnings reported for the year were $600 or less, but one month's benefit was withheld for each $50 (or remaining fraction thereof) of the amount of such earnings in excess of $600. The test was made inapplicable at age 75 and over (in order to make the program more attractive to the newly covered self-employed); this change, however, represented a breach in the underlying philosophy of the program to provide *retirement* benefits by having them be on an *annuity* basis at age 75.

The 1952 Act merely raised the exempt amount for wages to $75 a month. Correspondingly, the exemption for self-employment income was increased to $900 a year, with $75 units for subsequent withholding of monthly benefits. Under the 1952 Act, a number of situations occurred that aroused considerable criticism, particularly with respect to wage earners. A retired person who had wages of more than $75 a month, but not as much as $75 plus his benefit amount, had a particular problem. If, for example, a man's primary insurance amount was $60 and he had a wife aged 65 or over, the benefit for the couple was $90. In the month that this beneficiary had wages of $75, he would have available a total income of $165. If he earned $80, he lost his own benefit and his wife's benefit, and had only the $80 from his work, or a loss of $85 because of earning $5 more. The problem became less acute for him, of course, as his wages approached the amount of his benefits plus $75. In actuality, most beneficiaries who worked and were affected by the earnings test earned substantially more wages than their withheld benefits plus the $75 exempt amount.

There was also a problem for the beneficiary who worked only occasional months at wages that, while moderate, were more than $75 and who thus lost benefits for such months. He was, in fact, substantially retired, certainly to the same extent as a $75-a-month, 12-month worker, who perhaps had been able to adjust his wages downward so that he could receive benefits in all months.

Self-employed beneficiaries did not have the same problem because the earnings test operated differently for them. They had an undue advantage, moreover, when they had wages as well as self-employment income, since then a "double exemption" feature applied.

Another inequity existed because the earnings test applied only to covered employment. Thus, individuals who engaged full time in noncovered employment and were by no means retired could at the same time receive full benefits. Noncovered employment, for which earnings reports are not available through the collection of payroll taxes, was not counted in the operation of the earnings test principally because of the administrative problems involved under the limited coverage of the system. With the virtually universal coverage achieved by the 1954 amendments, such problems would be much smaller.

Accordingly, the 1954 amendments drastically revised the earnings test. Wages, as well as self-employment income, were considered on an annual basis. Noncovered earnings were taken into account along with covered earnings. Also, the test was, for the first time, made applicable to noncovered earnings of beneficiaries living abroad. The annual exempt amount was increased to $1,200, and $80 units of earnings thereafter were provided for the withholding of units of monthly benefits. Furthermore, under the monthly test, benefits were paid in any event if the beneficiary both had wages of $80 or less (changed to $100 or less by the 1958 amendments, and in every instance thereafter maintained at $\frac{1}{12}$th the annual exempt amount) and also did not engage in substantial self-employment. The age at which the test does not apply was reduced from 75 to 72, so that the program would have more appeal for self-employed farmers, who were first covered by this legislation.

The 1960 Act made a very significant change in the earnings test, and in fact, considerably changed its general philosophy. The $100 monthly test and the $1,200 annual exempt amount were continued, but under the annual test, the first $300 of earnings in excess of $1,200 resulted in a benefit loss of $1 for each $2 of such earnings, while for earnings in excess of $1,500 in the year, $1 of benefits was withheld for each $1 of such earnings. There was thus established the logical and equitable basic principle that earnings in excess of the annual exempt amount will always result in more total income (from benefits and earnings combined) than if earnings were held down to $1,200, which was not always the case under the previous basis of the earnings test. Nonetheless, there still remained the disincentive (because of the $1-for-$1 reduction band) for work producing earnings beyond the $1-for-$2 band, until total earnings were sufficiently high so as to offset the loss of all benefits.

The 1961 Act increased the $1-for-$2 reduction band from $300 to $500. The 1965 amendments, while increasing the annual exempt amount from $1,200 to $1,500, increased the band to $1,200. The 1967 amendments raised the annual exempt amount to $1,680 (and the monthly test to $140), but did not change the $1,200 band.

The 1972 legislation increased the annual exempt amount to $2,100 and eliminated the $1-for-$1 reduction band (or, in other words, extended the $1-for-$2 band indefinitely). This was another important change in philosophy; persons did not merely have no reduction in income from benefits and earnings when they worked, but, rather, higher earnings always mean higher total income. Moreover, under the former basis, when individuals were in the $1-for-$1 band, an additional dollar of earnings actually produced less *net* income than the dollar of benefits lost, because the earnings were subject to income tax and social security tax, whereas the benefits were tax exempt. The

1973 legislation simply increased the annual exempt amount from $2,100 to $2,400.

Another significant change brought about by the 1972 amendments provided that the annual and monthly exempt amounts would be adjusted automatically upward (no earlier than 1975). This will only be done when the automatic-adjustment provisions are effective for the benefit level. The adjustment for the exempt amounts will be made in the same manner as for the maximum taxable earnings base— from the change in average wages in covered employment—which seems reasonable, since both such elements are related to earnings levels (whereas benefit adjustments are related to cost-of-living changes).

The increases in the annual exempt amount that have been made from time to time since 1954 have been due to pressure from the general public. Many people erroneously see the earnings test as preventing them from working. Such is really not the case, however, because if employment conditions are really attractive, the wages involved will usually far more than offset the benefits lost. There is need, though, for the earnings test to be on a flexible, equitable basis, with as little disincentive for work as possible, and it would seem that this has now been accomplished by the action taken in the 1972 legislation.

One might wonder whether real increases have been made in the annual exempt amount over the years since such basis was first adopted to be effective in 1955, at $1,200 then, versus $2,400 in 1974. The increase in the 19-year period was 100 percent, but during the same time, average earnings in covered employment rose by about 115 percent. Thus, the annual exempt amount has not been overexpanded in recent years, despite the large dollar increases therein.

Although, in many ways, the earnings test has been liberalized from time to time, it furnishes one of the few examples where deliberalizations in the OASDI program have been made. In essence, the earnings test was deliberalized in 1950, when it was made applicable to new types of covered employment, and again in 1954, when it was made applicable to all types of covered employment, and again in 1954, when it was made applicable to all types of employment, whether covered or not. Some persons who were receiving benefits in 1950, despite being self-employed, were cut off the roll in 1951, when such employment was first covered. They felt that they had been maltreated because the terms of their "contract" had been altered, to their disadvantage, unilaterally without their consent. The same thing occurred in 1955, when the test was made applicable to all employment (e.g., in the case of a beneficiary then working for the federal government).

TAX RATES

The 1935 Act provided a long-range tax schedule, with the combined employer-employee rate rising by three-year steps of 1 percent each from 2 percent in 1937–39 to an ultimate rate of 6 percent in 1949 and thereafter. The 2 percent rate, however, was "frozen" by various legislative actions during the 1940s, although it did rise to 3 percent in 1950.

This action to hold down the tax rates in the 1940s was taken because the fund was growing rapidly. This resulted from the naturally low disbursements in the early years while the beneficiary roll was building up and as a result of the economic conditions arising from World War II (higher tax receipts due to increased wage levels and lower benefit outgo due to deferred retirements). Many people, especially in Congress, believed that a large fund was not desirable, or at least was not necessary, and that there should be reductions in the tax rates for this "separate and independent" social insurance system to offset partially the high general tax rates necessary to finance the war. This theory of separateness is in sharp conflict with the current economic and budgetary viewpoint as to the close interrelationship of the financing of OASDI and the national economy, which will be discussed in detail in a subsequent chapter.

The 1950 Act set up a new long-range tax schedule, rising from a combined employer-employee rate of 3 percent to an ultimate rate of 6½ percent in 1970 and thereafter (see Table 3.4). This change, as well as all subsequent ones, had the purpose of establishing a tax schedule with gradually increasing rates that would, according to the best actuarial cost estimates available, fully finance the program over the long-range future on a completely self-supporting basis (i.e., with no government subsidy).

The 1954 Act further changed this schedule by increasing such ultimate rate to 8 percent, effective in 1975. The 1956 Act added a flat ½ percent to the schedule, so as to finance the monthly disability benefits then added. The 1958 Act added a further flat ½ percent to

TABLE 3.4

Ultimate Tax Rates for OASDI and HI Systems

Year of Legislation	Year When Ultimate Rate Would Be Effective for Employer-Employee Rate†	Ultimate Tax Rate	
		Employer-Employee	Self-Employed
	Old-Age, Survivors, and Disability Insurance		
1935	1949	6.0%	*
1950	1970	6.5	4.875%
1954	1975	8.0	6.0
1956	1975	8.5	6.375
1958	1969	9.0	6.75
1961	1968	9.25	6.9
1965	1973	9.7	7.0
1967	1973	10.0	7.0
1971	1976	10.3	7.0
1972	2011 (1973)	11.7	7.0
1973	2011 (1973)	11.9	7.0
	Hospital Insurance		
1965	1987	1.6	0.8
1967	1987	1.8	0.9
1972	1986	2.9	1.45
1973	1986	3.0	1.5
	Both Programs		
1965	1987	11.3	7.8
1967	1987	11.8	7.9
1971	1987	12.1	7.9
1972	2011 (1986)	14.6	8.45
1973	2011 (1986)	14.9	8.5

* Not applicable.
† For OASDI, ultimate self-employed rate was effective in same year as combined employer-employee rate until 1972 legislation; figure in parentheses is year of ultimate rate for the self-employed.

the schedule and advanced future increases, so that they would be at three-year intervals beginning with 1960 (rather than five-year intervals), such increases being necessary in part because of the unexpected higher benefit costs arising from the coverage of farmers. The 1961 Act added yet a further flat ¼ percent to the schedule and advanced by one year the date when the ultimate rate would be effective (from 1969 to 1968). This action was taken in order to finance the cost of the benefit liberalizations then enacted.

The 1965 amendments reduced the combined employer-employee tax rate scheduled for the next few years by about ½ percent, but raised the ultimate rate (whose initial year was postponed from 1968 to 1973) by about ½ percent. At the same time, and somewhat more than offsetting, a new payroll tax was introduced, for the hospital insurance (HI) portion of the Medicare program enacted then.

The reduction in the OASDI rate in the 1965 legislation was made for economic reasons, since it was believed (quite erroneously) by the economic planners that the problem was deflation, and so it was desirable to reduce the so-called fiscal drag of the social security taxes. Actually, the problem was just the reverse—the coming inflation as the Viet Nam War activity increased! This was the beginning of the use of the OASDI and HI programs, as to their tax income, for overall national fiscal purposes (to be discussed in more detail later).

In the 1967 Act, the OASDI tax rates for the first few years were reduced slightly, to offset the increase in the HI rates needed to finance the higher costs for that program than had been originally estimated. On the other hand, the ultimate rate was increased by 0.3 percent (to 10.0 percent) in order to make up for the decreased rates in the early years and to help to finance the benefit liberalizations made in that legislation.

No change was made in the tax rates in 1969, since the benefit increases enacted then could be financed from the actuarial surplus present, which resulted from the increase in covered earnings since the previous actuarial valuation. The 1971 benefit increases, however, required additional financing; and part of this was derived from increasing the ultimate rate to 10.3 percent, thus for the first time breaking what some people thought was the absolute maximum tax rate desirable for OASDI of 10 percent.

The legislation enacted on July 1, 1972 (providing a 20 percent benefit increase) significantly changed the financing basis—by moving to a current-cost approach—and also changed the actuarial methodology (as will be discussed later). As a result, the OASDI combined employer-employee tax rates were decreased for the next four decades (until 2011)—by about 1 percent—but were increased by 0.4 percent (to 10.7 percent) in the ultimate years. At the same time, the corresponding HI tax rates were increased (to finance the long-range, and even short-range, deficiency in the financing of this program) by 0.4–0.6 percent in all future years, with the ultimate rate (for 1993 and after) being 2.4 percent. Thus, under this legislation, the ultimate rate for OASDI and HI (reached in 2011) was 13.1 percent, as compared with 12.1 percent under the previous law.

The foregoing tax schedules never went into effect because they were changed by the legislation enacted on October 30, 1972. As compared with the rates in effect in the law before 1972, the new combined employer-employee rates for OASDI were lower by about 0.7 percent until 2011 (but only by 0.3 percent for 1973–75), but were increased by 1.4 percent (to 11.7 percent) in the ultimate years. At the same time, the corresponding HI tax rates were increased by about .7 percent for the first five years and about 1.1 percent thereafter over the rate schedule in effect before 1972 (to finance both the previously existing deficiency and the cost of extending benefit protection to certain disabled beneficiaries). Thus, under this legislation, the ultimate rate for OASDI and HI was 14.6 percent, as compared with 12.1 percent under the law in effect before 1972.

The December 1973 legislation further increased the ultimate combined employer-employee tax rates for both OASDI and HI—from 11.7 percent to 11.9 percent and from 2.9 percent to 3.0 percent, respectively. At the same time, the near-future rates were maintained at the same level as to the total program, but were increased slightly for OASDI and correspondingly lowered for HI.

This general result for the OASDI program occurred because of the higher cost resulting from the relatively large increases in the CPI as compared both with increases in the general earnings level and with what had been assumed for the future, and because of the higher cost experience of the DI portion of the program. The tax schedule for the HI program could be reduced in the early years because of the sizable increase in the taxable earnings base (which resulted in more tax income, but no additional benefit outgo). A slight increase in the ultimate rate was needed, however, to maintain long-range actuarial balance.

Table 3.4 shows a very clear trend as to the size of the ultimate tax rate—ever upward. In part, this has been due to a change in the funding philosophy away from the accumulation of large reserves and toward current-cost financing. It has also been due to the expansion of the program, both an increase in the relative benefit level and the addition of new types of benefits.

As to the first year for which the ultimate rate is to be effective, the tendency has been to keep pushing this off further in the future, although this has not always been done. If current-cost financing is to be followed (as most experts in the field believe desirable and as has been done in connection with the financing of the 1972 legislation and subsequently), the tax schedule must be spread out further. To do so, however, results in the required ultimate rate being larger, since to have lower rates in the early years necessitates higher ones later. The enactment of such higher rates poses political problems, since considerable public attention is paid to them (and quite properly so).

The self-employed, with their initial coverage in 1951, were required to pay three fourths of the combined employer-employee rate. Beginning in 1962, this was an approximation, since the resulting rates were rounded to the nearest $\frac{1}{10}$th percent. In the 1965 amendments, the decision was made to provide a 7 percent ceiling for the self-employed OASDI tax rate, regardless of the "three-fourths" rule. In 1973, as a result of the 1972 amendments, this point has been reached, so that for all future years this rate will be frozen at 7 percent.

This lower tax rate basis for the self-employed was adopted for political reasons, to placate this group when it was initially covered. From the standpoint of the overall financing of the system, the proper

TABLE 3.5

Past and Future Contribution Rates and Earnings Bases for OASDI System

Calendar Years	Earnings Base*	Combined Employer-Employee Rate	Self-Employed Rate
1937–49	$ 3,000 (92.0%)	2.0%	†
1950	3,000	3.0	†
1951–53	3,600 (81.1%)	3.0	2.25%
1954	3,600	4.0	3.0
1955–56	4,200 (80.3%)	4.0	3.0
1957–58	4,200	4.5	3.375
1959	4,800 (79.3%)	5.0	3.75
1960–61	4,800	6.0	4.5
1962	4,800	6.25	4.7
1963–65	4,800	7.25	5.4
1966	6,600 (80.0%)	7.7	5.8
1967	6,600	7.8	5.9
1968	7,800 (81.7%)	7.6	5.8
1969–70	7,800	8.4	6.3
1971	7,800	9.2	6.9
1972	9,000 (78.4%)	9.2	7.0
1973	10,800 (81.8%)	9.7	7.0
1974	13,200 (85.8%)	9.9	7.0
1975–2010	‡	9.9	7.0
2011 and after	‡	11.9	7.0

* Figure in parentheses is percentage of total earnings in covered employment which is taxable in first year that base became effective.
† Not applicable.
‡ Base is subject to automatic adjustment after 1974 and is $14,100 for 1975.

basis would be to have the self-employed pay the full employer-employee rate. The fact that less than this is payable merely means that the employer-employee group is paying a higher tax rate for OASDI (by about 0.3 percent of taxable payroll) than they otherwise would if the self-employed paid the full employer-employee rate.

Table 3.5 shows the tax rates for the OASDI system, separately as to the combined employer-employee rate and the self-employed rate, for various past years and as scheduled for the future.

ALLOCATION TO DI TRUST FUND

The original allocation (in the 1956 Act) of the combined employer-employee tax rate to the Disability Insurance Trust Fund was 0.5 percent of payroll for all future years. The early experience seemed to indicate that this financing was not only adequate for the provisions originally enacted but also sufficient to meet the cost of extending the benefits to disabled workers below age 50 and to dependents (which was done). However, in the early 1960s, it was found that the experience had turned adverse, and thus more financing was needed.

Accordingly, the employer-employee allocation was increased to 0.7 percent of payroll by the 1965 Act and then to 0.95 percent by the 1967 Act. A further increase to 1.1 percent was made in the 1969 amendments, largely as a result of the substantial increase in the overall benefit level then. The allocation did not need to be changed when benefits were increased in the 1971 legislation, so that the entire increased financing from the higher ultimate tax rates then provided went to the OASI portion of the system.

The legislation enacted in July 1972 changed the DI allocation basis from a level, uniform one to a graded one that more closely paralleled the future trend of the cost of this portion of the program. Thus, the allocation was changed from 1.1 percent of payroll in all future years to 1.0 percent in 1973–77, 1.1 percent in 1978–2010 and 1.4 percent after 2010, which schedule was roughly equivalent to the level 1.1 percent rate. The legislation enacted in October 1972 liberalized the DI program in several ways, so that the foregoing allocation schedule had to be superceded before becoming effective by a new schedule of 1.1 percent for 1973–77, 1.15 percent for 1978–2010, and 1.5 percent thereafter. The December 1973 amendments further changed this schedule by recognizing the higher current disability experience—1.15 percent in 1974–77, 1.2 percent in 1978–80,

1.3 percent in 1981–85, 1.4 percent in 1986–2010, and 1.7 percent thereafter.

The allocation of the self-employment taxes to the DI Trust Fund was at a rate equal to three fourths of the allocation rate for employer and employee combined until the 1972 legislation. This applied in all future years, despite the 7 percent ceiling on the self-employment OASDI tax rate.

Under the 1972 legislation, the DI allocation basis for the self-employment tax was changed for years when the self-employment OASDI tax had reached the 7 percent ceiling. In such years, the self-employment DI allocation rate is the employer-employee DI allocation rate times the ratio of the self-employment OASDI tax rate (i.e., 7 percent) to the combined employer-employee tax rate (with rounding of the resulting allocation rate to the nearest 0.005 percent). As a result, the DI allocation for the self-employment OASDI tax rate under the 1972 amendments was 0.795 percent for 1973–77, 0.840 percent for 1978–2010, and 0.895 percent after 2010. The last figure, for example, is derived by multiplying 1.5 percent by the ratio of 7 percent to 11.7 percent, yielding 0.8974 percent, which is rounded to 0.895 percent. The corresponding schedule under the 1973 amendments is 0.815 percent for 1974–77, 0.85 percent for 1978–80, 0.92 percent for 1981–85, 0.99 percent for 1986–2010, and 1.00 percent thereafter.

TAXABLE EARNINGS BASE

The maximum earnings from a particular employer subject to tax was $3,000 a year from 1937 through 1950. The 1950 Act increased this amount to $3,600, effective in 1951. This 20 percent increase was far less than the rise in the general earnings level from the mid-1930s to 1951. That is indicated by the fact that the $3,000 base covered 92 percent of all earnings in covered employment when it was first effective, whereas the corresponding figure for the $3,600 base was 81 percent. This is one of the few instances where the program has not been kept up to date with changes in economic conditions and seems to be indication that Congress believed that the original base had been too high relatively.

As Table 3.5 indicates, the base was increased a number of times after 1950. In each instance until the 1972 amendments, the increases closely approximated the rises in the general earnings level and thus could not be said to represent a real expansion of the program, although the absolute amounts of the increases might make it seem so. This is shown by the fact that the ratio of taxable earnings to total earnings in covered employment in the first effective year for a new base remained at about the 80–81 percent level up through the 1971 amendments (which raised the base to $9,000 for 1972).

The 1972 amendments violated this precedent of more than two decades by making real increases in the earnings base. Thus, the $12,000 base which it scheduled for 1974 would likely have covered about 82½ percent of all earnings in covered employment, or significantly above the previous level of about 80–81 percent, but well below the 92 percent of the 1935 Act.

The 1973 amendments increased the scheduled base for 1974 from $12,000 to $13,200, which covered about 85 percent of all earnings in covered employment in 1974. This change was made in order to finance the liberalization made then in the earnings test. It would seem that liberalizations such as this should properly be financed by increases in tax rates, rather than through the indirect method of raising the earnings base.

An extremely important change affecting the earnings base was made by the 1972 amendments—namely, providing for automatic adjustment of the base (not earlier than 1975). This would be done only when the benefit level is also automatically adjusted. The adjustment, which can only be upward, is based on the change in wages in covered employment and is exactly the same procedure as was adopted in 1965 for automatically adjusting the "80 percent of wage" maximum applicable to combined disability benefits and workmen's compensation benefits.

An interesting demonstration can be performed with regard to the level of the earnings base in recent years and the effect that automatic-adjustment provisions might have had as compared with the ad hoc legislative changes actually made. It may be assumed that the procedure was adopted in 1965, when the precedent procedure for the workmen's compensation offset against disability benefits was enacted (effective for 1966 and after). Let it be assumed that the procedure was based on the $6,600 earnings base that was then enacted for 1966 and was thus first effective for 1967. The requirement that the earnings base cannot be changed unless an increase in the cash-benefits level is made will be ignored.

Table 3.6 shows the underlying data of the average taxable wage per

TABLE 3.6

Derivation of Maximum Taxable Earnings Bases
Which Would Have Resulted If Automatic-Adjustment Provisions
Had Been Enacted in 1965, Effective for 1967

| Year | Average Wage in First Quarter* | | Base Resulting from Automatic Adjustment | Actual Base |
	Amount	Increase from Previous Year		
1965	$1,026	—	—	—
1966	1,071	4.39%	$ 6,600	$ 6,600
1967	1,139	6.35	6,900	6,600
1968	1,219	7.02	7,200	7,800
1969	1,282	5.17	7,800	7,800
1970	1,348	5.15	8,100	7,800
1971	1,430	6.08	8,400	7,800
1972	1,555	8.74	9,000	9,000
1973	1,635	5.14	9,900	10,800
1974	2,007.69	5.94†	10,500	13,200
1975	n.a.	n.a.	11,100	14,100

* These data are used in the automatic-adjustment provisions for the offset of workmen's compensation benefits against disability benefits. For 1965–73, these data represent the average wage per wage item, which is the quarterly report that each employer makes for each employee, so that some employees have more than one wage item in a quarter. For 1973 and after, a more refined method has been used, and the data are the average wage per person with covered wages in the quarter.

† Based on a figure of $1,895.04 for 1973 on the modified method that was adopted for 1974 and after (see preceding footnote).

n.a. = not available.

wage item reported by employers (which is indicative of the average wage in covered employment) in the first quarter of each year during 1965–74 and the percentage increase from one year to the next. Also shown are the resulting earnings bases which would have resulted from the application of the automatic-adjustment provisions, as contrasted with the actual bases that were in effect. The bases resulting from the automatic-adjustment provisions closely parallel the actual ones for 1967–72 (except for 1971), but are significantly lower for 1972–74. In fact, the $13,200 base actually in effect for 1974 would have been only $10,500 if the automatic-adjustment provisions had been applicable since 1966, or about the same level as the actual base was for 1973.

COMBINED OASDI AND HI TAXES

Table 3.5 summarized the actual combined employer-employee tax rates and the maximum taxable earnings base in effect in the past and as scheduled in the future for the OASDI system. Table 3.7 gives similar data for the tax rates for the HI system and for OASDI and HI combined (the same earnings base prevails for both programs).

The total OASDI and HI taxes paid by an employee with maximum creditable earnings each year from 1937 on amounted to $6,043.20 at the end of 1974 (without allowance for interest), with the employer having paid the same amount. The corresponding figure for a self-employed person covered since this was first possible in 1951 was

TABLE 3.7

Past and Future Contribution Rates for OASDI and HI Systems Combined

Calendar Year	HI System Only		Combined OASDI-HI Systems	
	Combined Employer-Employee	Self-Employed	Combined Employer-Employee	Self-Employed
1966......................	0.7%	0.35%	8.4%	6.15%
1967......................	1.0	0.5	8.8	6.4
1968......................	1.2	0.6	8.8	6.4
1969–70..................	1.2	0.6	9.6	6.9
1971–72..................	1.2	0.6	10.4	7.5
1973......................	2.0	1.0	11.7	8.0
1974–77..................	1.8	0.9	11.7	7.9
1978–80..................	2.2	1.1	12.1	8.1
1981–85..................	2.7	1.35	12.6	8.35
1986–2010................	3.0	1.5	12.9	8.5
2011 and after............	3.0	1.5	14.9	8.5

$8,063.40. Although these amounts seem quite sizable, they do not look so large when compared with the annual benefit of $3,795.60 that would be payable to such a male individual who became age 65 at the beginning of 1975 and retired then ($5,693.40 for man and wife both aged 65). In other words, such a male employee receives in benefits in 1.59 years what he paid in taxes over a 38-year period (or in 1.06 years if married). The extent of the relative "actuarial bargain," which would be present to a somewhat lesser extent if interest were taken into account, is greater for persons with lower earnings levels and persons who retired in previous years.

Likewise, the total OASDI-HI taxes paid will be much larger for future entrants than for workers who came in the system at the beginning. For example, an employee entering covered employment at the beginning of 1975 at age 21 and working at maximum creditable wages until age 65 will pay total taxes of $37,638 according to the schedule in the present law, without taking into account any increase in the earnings base after 1975 as a result of the automatic-adjustment provisions.

Table 3.8 shows the maximum annual taxes paid by employees and

TABLE 3.8

Maximum Annual Taxes Payable under OASDI and HI Combined in Various Past Years

Years	Maximum for Employees*	Maximum for Self-Employed
1937–49	$ 30.00	†
1950	45.00	†
1951–53	54.00	$ 81.00
1954	72.00	108.00
1955–56	84.00	126.00
1957–58	94.50	141.75
1959	120.00	180.00
1960–61	144.00	216.00
1962	150.00	225.60
1963–65	174.00	259.20
1966	277.20	405.90
1967	290.40	422.40
1968	343.20	499.20
1969–70	374.40	538.20
1971	405.60	585.00
1972	468.00	675.00
1973	631.80	864.00
1974	772.20	1,042.80
1975	824.85	1,113.90

* Equal amount for employer tax.
† Not then covered by program.

by self-employed persons in various past years and at present for OASDI and HI combined. Such amount for employees increased from $30 at the start of the program in 1937 to $825 for 1975, while for self-employed persons the rise was from $81 in 1951 (the first year that they were covered) to $1,114 in 1975. Although part of these large increases were due to the inflationary conditions prevailing and to the method of financing (i.e., on a current-cost basis, under a situation of rising year-by-year costs), a significant portion was due to the expansion of the benefits provided.

The very considerable amounts of social security taxes presently paid by persons with maximum taxable earnings can cause considerable dissatisfaction and complaints. The 22 percent increase from 1973 to 1974, which may be considered a rise in the price of social insurance protection, is far more than the increase in prices generally—about which the general public is much concerned.

LEGISLATION PASSED IN 1973 BUT NOT ENACTED

In the latter part of 1973, it appeared to the Congress that the 5.9 percent benefit increase contained in the amendments enacted on July 9, 1973, to be effective for June 1974 would not be sufficient to reflect recent changes in the cost of living. Accordingly, action was begun to provide larger increases, and this resulted in the 7/11 percent increase described previously.

The House passed a simple bill in November merely providing for such increase, a modification in the automatic-adjustment procedures, and in the financing of the program (and also raising the payments under the supplemental security income program—see Chapter 11). About the same time the Senate passed a very extensive bill doing the same as the House, plus many other changes in both OASDI and Medicare. The final legislation closely paralleled the House bill, and the various Senate amendments, by a complex legislative procedure, were still held pending in conference. However, no conference agreement was reached on them in 1974, and so they died with the end of the 93rd Congress.

An account of these amendments is of value as an indication of possible future congressional action, at least insofar as the Senate is concerned. The most important such OASDI provisions adopted by the Senate Finance Committee were as follows:[3]

1. Automatic-adjustment provisions would apply to the special minimum based on years of coverage.
2. Agreements with other countries could be made to provide limited coordination between the United States social security program and that of the other country.[4] Totalization provisions would

---

[3] See Chapter 7 for the Medicare provisions.

[4] Such an agreement has already been negotiated with Italy, but has not yet become effective since it must be authorized by legislation of each country.

apply so that beneficiaries would not have impaired or reduced benefit rights when work had been performed under the systems of the two countries. Also, each country would not cover citizens of the other country when they work in its territory if they are covered under the system of the other country. Both business and labor organizations favored this change, so that it is likely to be adopted in the near future.

Then, on the Senate floor, the following major OASDI provisions were added:

1. Widow's benefits would be available at ages 55–59, with the same reductions as are applicable for disabled widows and widowers first claiming benefits at those ages.
2. The annual exempt amount in the earnings test would be increased to $3,000 (and the monthly test would be raised to $250) and the age at which the test would not apply would be reduced from 72 to 70.
3. Blind persons would be insured for disability benefits if they had 6 quarters of coverage at any time (instead of needing fully insured status), and then benefits would be paid without regard to earnings, ability to work, or refusal of vocational rehabilitation services.
4. Significantly, no additional financing was proposed to meet the additional costs involved in items 2 and 3.

1974 ADVISORY COUNCIL ON SOCIAL SECURITY

The Social Security Act provides that an Advisory Council on Social Security is to be appointed every fourth year, namely in each year following a presidential election. The council is to consist of 13 members, appointed by the Secretary of Health, Education, and Welfare, representing organizations of employers and employees in equal numbers and representing self-employed persons and the public. The council is to report not later than the January 1 of the second year following the year in which it is supposed to be appointed.

The council is charged with the responsibility of reviewing the financial status of the OASI and DI Trust Funds and of the two Medicare trust funds and of reviewing the scope of coverage, the adequacy of benefits, and all other aspects of these programs.

The 1973–74 council was not appointed until April 1974, more than a year after it could have first been named and well after the deadline of December 31, 1973, specified in the law. As a result, the council had an unusually short time to perform its work and, in fact, did not release its report until March 1975, or more than two months beyond its legal deadline.

The council reaffirmed that OASDI should remain the primary means of providing economic security in the event of retirement, disability, or death and should continue in its same general nature as a floor of protection.

The main concern of the council was about the financial status of OASDI, which has been discussed in Chapter 2, and will be discussed in more detail in Chapters 4 and 10. The recommended solution to this problem was first to correct the flaw in the automatic-adjustment provisions which are applicable to the benefit amounts of those newly coming on the rolls. This would be done by the decoupling procedure described in Chapter 5. Under that procedure, past earnings would be adjusted according to a wage index, and a revised benefit formula would then be utilized. Benefits for those on the roll would be adjusted from time to time according to changes in the CPI, just as under present law.

The second step in solving the financial problems of OASDI that was recommended by the council was to gradually reallocate the Hospital Insurance tax rate to the OASDI system as additional financing for the latter is needed. Then, the lost income to the HI system would be replaced by a government subsidy, so that eventually it would be completely financed in this manner, instead of by payroll taxes. The rationale behind this recommendation was that the hospital benefits are not earnings-related. At the same time, the council recommended that the OASDI employer and employee tax rates scheduled in present law should not be increased.

A minority of the council opposed this approach and instead believed that the financing problems of OASDI should be solved by direct increases in payroll tax rates. President Ford, in an unprecedented action, issued a statement immediately after the council made its report public, stating his support of the council's endorsement of the basic principles of the OASDI system and its recommendation for stabilization of the benefit structure, but his strong opposition to the financing of the HI program out of general revenues. Such opposition was based on his belief in the "earned rights" principle that has always been a basic feature of the program.

At one point in its deliberations, the council had favorably considered obtaining some additional financing for OASDI by increasing the earnings base to $24,000. However, after considering that this action would materially reduce the scope for providing economic security through private-sector means, the council rejected this approach.

The council also saw another possible method of alleviating the financing problems of OASDI, namely by increasing the minimum retirement age. However, it believed that such action would not be necessary or even advisable until about 35 years from now, when the demographic picture will be quite changed. At that time, the ratio of persons aged 65 and over to the working population will rise significantly, as a result of the cohorts of the post-World War II baby boom then reaching retirement age. Accordingly, the council recommended that Congress should consider such a change at some later time. Of course, somewhat the same cost effect could be obtained under the present retirement age conditions if persons worked longer than they now do, and if employers imposed less strict compulsory-retirement rules.

The Council also made a number of other recommendations for changes in the OASDI program, as follows:

1. The earnings test should be revised so that the reduction in benefits for earnings in excess of the annual exempt amount should be only $1 for every $3 of the excess earnings up to an additional amount equal to the annual exempt amount, and then $1 for $2 for additional earnings. On the other hand, the test should be deliberalized by eliminating the monthly portion for years after the initial year of entitlement.

2. Equal treatment should be provided for men and women, so that benefits would be payable to aged husbands and widowers without the present test of dependency and also to young widowers with children. At the same time, supplementary and survivor benefits (for both men and women) would be reduced, under the antiduplication provision, by the amount of any governmental pension based on the employment of such beneficiary, rather than only by the amount of any primary OASDI benefit as at present. The latter change would partially, or perhaps completely, offset the added cost for benefits to male dependents being payable in more cases. Such added cost, however, would not be large because of the earnings test and the antiduplication provision. It should be observed that the first part of this recommenda-

tion has, in effect, been carried out by the Supreme Court decision in March 1975, referred to previously.

3. The general minimum benefit, for persons with very low AMWs, should be eliminated over a period of time. It would be phased out by being frozen at its present dollar figure, instead of being increased by the automatic-adjustment provisions. The proposed restructured benefit formula, as described in general form in Chapter 5, would ultimately provide a PIA equal to 100 percent of the average monthly indexed earnings for those with low earnings, and not be subject to any dollar minimum. This would provide more logical treatment with regard to persons with minimal coverage at earnings just sufficient to acquire eligibility, who are in noncovered employment most of their working career and seek to obtain a windfall from OASDI (as they can now).

4. The definition of disability should be liberalized, so that, at ages 55–61, it would apply to inability to perform work for which the person has had considerable regular experience, rather than to perform any substantially gainful activity. The benefit rate for such lesser degree of disability would be 80 percent of the PIA, the same as for early-retirement at age 62. This change was recommended on the basis of easing administrative determination problems. However, it would seem that moving the definitional boundary would only create new boundary problems. Also, there would be problems in administering two definitions of disability, with different resulting benefit amounts, at ages 55–61.

5. The basis for the tax rate for the self-employed should be changed back to the original procedure of 75 percent of the combined employer-employee rate. This would be done by eliminating the 7-percent maximum on the rate, which was first effective in 1973.

The net effect of the foregoing recommendations is an estimated increase in the long-range average-cost of only 0.13 percent of taxable payroll. The largest increase, also 0.13 percent, is for the change in the definition of disability, with the other changes having relatively small costs, or savings, which counterbalance each other.

The Council also made a number of recommendations and suggestions not involving legislative changes in the OASDI system. These included the following points:

1. Coverage should be universally applicable to all types of employment. In particular, ways should be found to extend coverage to all

public employment (federal, state, and local), with appropriate co-ordination with the staff retirement systems for such workers.

2. Study should be made as to whether the automatic adjustment of benefits for changes in the cost of living should be done more frequently than annually.

3. A general study of the program should be made by a full-time nongovernmental body. This should cover such matters as funding versus pay-as-you-go financing, effects of the system on productivity, proper size of the trust funds, and the incidence of payroll taxes.

LEGISLATIVE PROCEDURES

When the OASDI system was initially developed in 1935, and also in all subsequent amendatory action, no single person or group was ever solely responsible for the action taken. The original act resulted from studies made by the Committee on Economic Security, which was headed by four Cabinet members and the Federal Emergency Relief Administrator. The committee had a small technical staff that made the basic studies on which recommendations could be based. In addition, its conclusions were determined from recommendations made by an advisory council representing labor, industry, and the general public. In the legislative process, the proposals of the committee were significantly modified both by the executive branch and by Congress before the final legislation resulted.

This same pattern of the influence of many groups and agencies in the legislative process has continued over the years. The procedure of obtaining the views of an advisory council has been followed in a number of instances. In 1937, an advisory council was appointed jointly by a subcommittee of the Senate Committee on Finance and the Social Security Board. In 1947 the Senate Committee on Finance appointed another advisory council. In 1953 an advisory group was convened by the Department of Health, Education, and Welfare.

The 1956 amendments provided for periodic advisory councils to review the status of the OASDI system, with particular emphasis on its financing. The first such council was appointed by the Secretary of Health, Education, and Welfare in 1957, and the second was appointed in 1963 (with it specifically having been assigned the broader responsibility of comprehensively reviewing the entire program). The law was changed in 1965, so that advisory councils were to be appointed in or after February 1969 (and every fourth year thereafter) to study the financing, the scope of coverage, and the adequacy of the benefits, both for the OASDI system and the Medicare program. This cycle was established so that the council would be named at the start of each presidential administration and could never be a "lame duck" one. It was also provided that the 13 members of the council should be selected so as to represent organizations of employers and employees (in equal numbers) and also to represent self-employed persons and the public.

Generally, the legislative procedure involved in any amendments that have been enacted has started with study and recommendations made by the Social Security Administration (at times, following the recommendations of an advisory council). The Secretary of Health, Education, and Welfare and the Executive Office of the President then approve these recommendations (possibly with some modifications), and a bill embodying them is introduced in the House of Representatives and sometimes also in the Senate. Under the Constitution, the House must initiate legislation in the field of taxation—and thus, too, in regard to OASDI and Medicare matters.

The Committee on Ways and Means of the House of Representatives is assigned the responsibility for social security legislation and usually holds public hearings on any administration proposals. At times, the Ways and Means Committee itself has initiated legislation without prior administration recommendation. In any event, this committee goes over the pending legislation very thoroughly in its executive sessions, and there has never yet been an instance where it did not make a number of significant changes in legislation proposed to it.

For many years, the executive sessions were closed to the press and the public. Now, however, all such sessions are open to all. In some ways, this may appear to be a desirable change, from the standpoint of doing away with so-called deals in smoke-filled rooms. In practice, though, events that transpired in the executive sessions were not kept very secret and frequently were leaked to the interested public. One problem with open sessions is that committee members may feel hesitant to expound their preliminary and tentative views for fear of being made to look ridiculous in case, on further deliberation, they take another stance. Also, the press might report the initial position, but not the final one, or the public might see only the former.

The bill embodying the results of the deliberations of the House Ways and Means Committee is almost invariably considered by the House of Representatives under a "closed rule" that does not permit amendments other than those desired by the committee. This procedure has been followed because of the complexity of the legislation and the procedural and technical difficulties that might arise if a large number of members of the House wish to amend different portions of the bill under consideration. (Recent action of the Democratic Caucus of the House of Representatives may result in a change in this closed-rule procedure.)

After the legislation is passed by the House of Representatives, it goes to the Senate and is referred to the Committee on Finance. This committee, too, holds public hearings and extensive executive sessions before reporting a bill to the Senate floor. This bill may be (and usually is) significantly modified as compared with the House version. Amendments can be freely made during the debate in the Senate, unlike what has been the situation in the House in the past.

The version of the bill enacted by the Senate then goes to a conference committee, which has the responsibility of reconciling the differences between it and the House version. This committee consists of the top-ranking members of both parties from the House Ways and Means Committee and the Senate Finance Committee. The version of the bill that is agreed to by the conference committee is then referred back to both the House and the Senate for approval, which almost invariably will automatically be given, and then it goes to the President for his approval.

chapter 4

Financing Basis of
OASDI System

As has been indicated previously, the OASDI system derives its primary source of financing from a specific contribution (or tax) schedule contained in the law. What might be called secondary financing comes from interest earnings on the accumulated funds. The Congress has frequently expressed its intent that the system should be self-supporting—insofar as the best available actuarial cost estimates indicate—from these sources, without any contributions or subsidies from the General Treasury. In this respect, it should be noted that interest earnings of the trust funds are not subsidies (as is sometimes incorrectly stated by some critics of the program, as will be discussed later). Likewise, this is also the case for the contributions payable in respect to the wages paid by the federal government to its covered employees (such as temporary workers and the military forces), since these are really "employer" contributions.

A potential threat to the long-established principle of the OASDI program being financed on a self-supporting basis may develop from amendments to the Railroad Retirement Act enacted in October 1974 (discussed in more detail in Chapter 12). These provide for a government subsidy to the railroad retirement program payable from general revenues, so as to remedy its serious financial problem. This action might be considered a precedent for similar action in connection with OASDI.

A question may be raised whether this is really a valid precedent. There is certainly a significant difference between a subsidy paid for by the entire body of taxpayers to a small group and such a subsidy paid by the entire group of taxpayers to essentially itself. After all, the incidence of taxation as between payroll taxes and general revenues is not so vastly different, especially after tax impacts are absorbed and redistributed among groups. And certainly almost all the same persons are involved in the payment of payroll taxes as in the payment of the taxes which produce the general revenues.

The possibility of a government subsidy to OASDI has also considerably increased with its growing financial problems. In fact, efforts were made by the Senate in March 1975 in connection with proposals to pay temporary increases in benefits to OASDI beneficiaries as part of legislation to lower income taxes and to finance the cost of such increases from general revenues. Such action, however, was not taken by Congress.

In order to understand more fully the financing basis of the OASDI system, examination must be made first of such broader points as why a fund develops, and the concept of actuarial soundness as it applies to social insurance. Then, the specifics of the actuarial basis of the system as it has developed over the years and as it is now may be considered. As related matters, consideration can be given to the relationship of the funds and the general budget, and to investment procedures, including the interest basis of the investments and possible alternative approaches. Finally, there will be considered the relationship of the OASDI and railroad retirement systems in regard to the financial interchange provisions, which integrate the financing of the two programs.

WHY A FUND DEVELOPS

Under almost any pension system, the cost of the benefits will rise for many years after the program is inaugurated. There are many factors that produce this result, but not all the factors are present in every instance. Among such factors are (1) the increasing proportion of the aged in the population (almost entirely as a result of the maturing population and the continual improvement in mortality at all ages in the past); (2) the greater proportion of younger persons than of older persons covered when the system is established (partly because of the omission of all or some of the current aged who are already retired); and (3) the basing of benefits to a greater or lesser degree on the length of time contributions are made (so that benefits in the early years of operation are smaller than those that will be paid ultimately).

If the rising benefit cost is to be met by a level contribution rate, contribution receipts in the early years of operation will exceed benefit disbursements, and thus a fund will be built up. After the early years (or perhaps decades) of operation, the reverse situation will occur. If the system is in "actuarial balance," with the level contribution rate properly and precisely determined, interest on the fund that is developed in the early years will meet the excess of benefit disbursements over contribution income in the later years.

As an alternative to financing a pension plan with a level contribution rate, a schedule providing for a lower rate in the early years and a series of increases thereafter can be used. The ultimate rate under such a schedule will, of course, have to be higher than the level rate mentioned previously. The size of the fund that develops will depend on the gradation of the contribution schedule. If there were very little gradation (that is, if the initial rates were only slightly below the level rate, and the ultimate rate was attained in a short period and was accordingly very little above the level rate), then the developing fund would be almost as large as under the level-rate basis.

At the other extreme, if the contribution schedule starts out very low and rises very slowly, but ultimately to a fairly high level, virtually no fund might be developed, and yet the system would be in actuarial balance. In fact, this situation—in which the contributions are determined, to all intents and purposes, so that they equal the estimated benefit payments in each future year—is one form of "pay-as-you-go" financing. The term also applies to a situation that involves no definite benefit commitments but instead the paying of whatever benefits would be possible with the prescribed contribution income or, conversely, raising whatever money would be necessary to meet benefit obligations determined in advance.

There are, of course, an infinite number of variations possible in the contribution schedule that, under the assumptions made, would result in a self-supporting system. As still another alternative, plans can be financed by having higher contribution rates in the early years and lower ones thereafter. This procedure, naturally, produces a larger fund than financing through the use of a level rate and is fairly common in financing private pension plans. The accrued liability for service performed before the inception of the plan and the additional cost arising from the fact that the initial group has a higher average age than future new entrants can both be financed by amortization over a period of years.[1] After this time, the contribution rate would be relatively low— at the level necessary for new entrants coming in at the younger ages. Furthermore, at such time the system would be fully funded and meet the most rigid definition of actuarial soundness (to be discussed in some detail later). Thus, the assets on hand would be sufficient to meet all the benefit obligations that have accrued. If the system were to be terminated, both as to collection of contributions in the future and crediting of future service, the accrued benefit obligations could be met only if the computations had assumed no discounting for gains from future withdrawals or for deferred retirements and, of course, if all other actuarial assumptions were realized.

It may be noted further that if by reason of the provisions of the plan, the cost of the benefits does not rise sharply in the future, the resulting fund, even with a level contribution rate, will be much smaller than under a plan that has a sharply rising benefit cost. In fact, if a plan is developed in which the benefit cost (related to payroll) would be the same for every future year, then obviously the corresponding level contribution rate would just meet the benefit disbursements each year, and no fund would develop.

One disadvantage of having an increasing contribution rate is that those who retire in the early years of operation do not pay as high a rate for the benefits they receive as do those who retire in subsequent years. Even with a level contribution rate, those who retire in the early years usually receive far more in benefits than their contributions would have purchased on an actuarial basis. Through one method or another, they receive credit for service performed before the inception of the plan and, accordingly, only a small portion of their benefit is "purchased" by their contributions. This procedure is customary under both private pension plans and social insurance. Otherwise, if benefits are related to contributions made or to length of service after the plan began, inadequate pensions would be provided for the first few decades of operation of the system. Accordingly, the program would not really be serving the purpose for which it was established.

Another problem arising with increasing contribution rates is that

---

[1] In theory, these liabilities could be paid off in one initial lump sum, but in practice this procedure is not followed, if for no other reason than tax considerations.

ultimately the employee rate (particularly if the employer and employee rates are equal) may be higher than individual equity would suggest—that is, the young entrant would be able to purchase more protection with his own contributions from an insurance company than is furnished under the social insurance system. If this situation were to arise, one possible solution would be to lower the ultimate contribution rates and make up the difference by a government subsidy to the system in the later years of operation. On this basis, there could be graded contribution rates starting at a low level, with the employee rates not rising beyond the "individual equity" level. At the same time, a relatively small fund would be built up. This solution would involve the concept of an ultimate government contribution or subsidy.

Alternatively, if the employer contribution rate were significantly higher than the employee rate, it is likely that the latter would never rise beyond the individual equity level. Of course, if there is also a government contribution to the system (especially if it is at least equal to half of the combined employer-employee rate, as is frequently the case in many systems), then it is even more unlikely that the ultimate employee contribution rate under a graded schedule would ever exceed the individual equity level.

CONCEPT OF ACTUARIAL SOUNDNESS

In discussions of any type of long-range benefit program, the phrases "actuarial soundness" or "actuarially sound" occur from time to time. Essentially, these terms relate to the ability of the given plan to provide the benefits established. Many different definitions may be given in the absence of any strict legal requirements applicable (as, for instance, is the case with reserve requirements for life insurance and annuity reserves of insurance companies). For noninsured pension plans, there tends to be a somewhat broader range of definition. For social insurance plans, the range is even broader.

At perhaps one extreme for private pension plans might be the definition that a plan is actuarially sound if the fund on hand is large enough to pay all future benefits for those currently on the roll. In other words, no allowance is made for the accrued benefit rights of those not yet retired. At the other extreme is a plan under which the existing fund is sufficient to pay for all benefit rights accrued to date. This basis would be somewhat difficult to attain for a newly organized plan which assumed considerable liabilities on account of past service. Accordingly, some actuaries define an actuarially sound plan as one:

> . . . where the employer is well informed as to the future cost potential and arranges for meeting those costs through a trust or insured fund on a scientific, orderly program of funding under which, should the plan terminate at any time, the then pensioners would be secure in their pensions and the then active employees would find an equity in the fund assets reasonably commensurate with their accrued pensions for service from the plan's inception up to the date of termination of plan.[2]

This definition permits a long period before all the past-service credits are fully funded.

Other actuaries have a somewhat less stringent definition of an actuarially sound system:

> One which sets forth a plan of benefits and the contributions to provide these benefits, so related that the amount of the present and contingent liabilities of the plan as actuarially computed as of any date will at least be balanced by the amount of the present and contingent assets of the plan actuarially computed as of the same date.[3]

How do these concepts of actuarial soundness apply to the OASDI system? According to the first definition, this program is not actuarially sound; according to the second definition, it is. Acceptance of the basis of the first definition, however, does not mean that the converse is true—that the system is actuarially unsound and therefore, by implication, is bankrupt and should be liquidated. Rather, the author of the first definition stated in the same paper that he did not "see any point in rigorously applying actuarial reserve techniques to a broad national system. Such a system transcends 'actuarial soundness' criteria of the usual kind. What purpose would be served if reserve assets in the actuarial amount of $150 billion were now on hand? They would not be used; the system is not going to terminate, calling on a liquidation of the reserve for benefits."

Even though it is generally agreed by actuaries that the first and

[2] Dorrance C. Bronson, "Pension Plans—The Concept of Actuarial Soundness," *Proceedings of Panel Meeting: "What Is Actuarial Soundness in a Pension Plan?"*, sponsored jointly by the American Statistical Association, the American Economic Association, the American Association of University Teachers of Insurance, and the Industrial Relations Research Association, Chicago, December 29, 1952.

[3] George B. Buck, "Actuarial Soundness in Trusteed and Governmental Retirement Plans," ibid.

more restrictive definition of actuarial soundness does not apply to OASDI, it may be of interest to present certain quantities pertinent to it.

Such calculations can readily be made, and this has been done by the Social Security Administration on an appropriate basis, even though it is recognized by its actuaries that the resulting figures can be misunderstood and misused—and, in fact, have no real significance for a social insurance system. One concept of measuring the actuarial condition of a pension plan is to develop the "deficit for present members." This merely means the amount required at the present time that, together with the existing fund and the present value of future contributions from present members will support future benefits for those on the roll, for present active members and their survivors, and for survivors of previously deceased members who have not reached the minimum eligibility age for survivor benefits. In other words, this is a "closed-group" concept, under which the system would be continued for present members but would have no new entrants and no employer contribution income in respect to new entrants.

The situation for the OASDI program under this concept is shown in Table 4.1 as of the middle of 1971, 1972, 1973, and 1974 (the 1972 and 1973 figures include the effect of the 20 percent benefit increase and the automatic-adjustment provisions enacted into law on July 1, 1972, while the 1974 figure also includes the effect of the 11 percent benefit increase under the 1973 amendments). This concept, it should be realized, is only of theoretical interest and is not of true significance under a long-range social insurance program. However, it has been required by law since 1967 (Sec. 402, P.L. 89–809) that such figures should be computed annually in accordance with legislation requiring the Treasury Department to report to Congress all unfunded accrued

TABLE 4.1

Actuarial Status of OASDI, 1971–74 (on "closed-group" basis)

		Amount (billions)		
Item	1971	1972	1973	1974
1. Present value of future benefits and expenses	$1,044	$2,859	$3,231	$4,025
2. Present value of future taxes	570	950	1,068	1,519
3. Existing trust fund	41	44	44	46
4. Net deficit, (1) − (2) − (3)	433	1,865	2,118	2,460

Note: These valuations have been carried out at an interest rate of 6% for 1972–74, and 5¼% for 1971.

liabilities of the United States government. Corresponding data on an "open-group" basis for a 75-year future period are also prepared. These are presented subsequently in Table 4.3. No such "closed-group" data are prepared for the HI system.

Under this closed-group concept, there was an actuarial deficit of $433 billion in mid-1971, or about 11 times the amount of the then existing trust fund. The actuarial deficit one year later was much larger—$1,855 billion (i.e., almost $2 trillion), or 42 times the amount of the then existing trust fund. This astounding figure resulted largely from changing the cost-estimating method, by using dynamic economic assumptions as to earnings levels and price levels (which, in turn, affect benefit levels). The actuarial deficit in mid-1973 rose by 14 percent— as a result of the further liberalizations included in the October 1972 amendments—to $2,118 billion, or 48 times the amount of the then existing trust fund. The actuarial deficit as of mid-1974 rose by 16 percent—largely as a result of the 11 percent benefit increase—to $2,460 billion, or 53 times the amount of the then existing trust fund.

Still another concept of actuarial soundness applicable to private pension plans may be considered in respect to the OASDI system, namely, the present value of all benefits in current payment status. In a sense, this corresponds to the terminal-funding concept of private pension plans. At the beginning of 1973, benefits in current payment status were being paid at a rate of about $3,885 million a month. These had a present value at 5 percent interest of about $360 billion, about 8½ times the then existing trust fund. But it should be kept in mind that this relationship has no direct bearing on the actuarial soundness of the program, although it is an interesting summary measure of the obligations incurred and facilitates comparisons with other systems.

Paul A. Samuelson, an economist from Massachusetts Institute of Technology, expressed some rather unique and startling views on the concept of actuarial soundness as it applies to OASDI and on the financing of OASDI in his column in *Newsweek* for February 13, 1967, where he stated in regard to that program:

> The beauty about social insurance is that it is *actuarially* unsound. Everyone who reaches retirement age is given benefit privileges that far exceed anything he has paid in. And exceed his payments by more than ten times as much (or five times, counting in employer payments).
>
> How is this possible? It stems from the fact that the national product is growing at compound interest and can be expected to do

so for as far ahead as the eye can see. Always there are more youths than old folks in a growing population. More important, with real incomes growing at some 3 percent per year, the taxable base upon which benefits rest in any period are much greater than the taxes paid historically by the generation now retired.

Dr. Samuelson was in error in his understanding of the concept of actuarial soundness as it applies to OASDI, since he seemed to believe that this term was equivalent to full-reserve financing. But even more, he erred in believing that OASDI possessed a magic, Ponzi-type machine involving economic perpetual motion. Less than a decade has passed, and now we have conditions such that both continuous population growth and economic expansion due to increasing productivity no longer seem likely.

Finally, the question may be raised as to whether a long-range social insurance system with "pay-as-you-go" financing (defined to mean that annual receipts and annual disbursements are approximately in balance) could ever be considered actuarially sound. It could not, of course, under the first definition of actuarial soundness. Under the second definition, however, it would be possible that such a program could be actuarially sound if a gradually rising contribution schedule were determined so as to approximate closely the estimated future disbursements year by year.

Regardless of whether the concept of actuarial soundness in its usual meaning can be applied to the OASDI system, there must be thorough actuarial analysis and cost estimates for the program—essential factors in considering and determining the long-range benefit structure of the program.

ACTUARIAL BASIS OF OASDI

The original 1935 legislation did not provide for any government contribution or subsidy to the system, even though this had been the recommendation of the presidential committee that studied the matter. The cost estimates indicated that the system would be self-supporting from the contributions of employers and employees. There was—and still is—considerable misunderstanding of the financing basis, since many people believed that a full actuarial reserve system was being developed, especially since the estimated ultimate fund of $47 billion in 1980 seemed so large, slightly greater than the national debt in 1935. Such was not the case, however, because the cost estimates showed the system to be self-supporting only when it was considered as operating into perpetuity. At any particular date, the fund available would by no means be sufficient to meet the accrued liabilities without the help of the scheduled future contributions.

Other evidence that the original act was not on a so-called full-reserve, actuarial basis can be found from the benefit structure. A worker retiring at age 65 at the beginning of 1942 (the earliest possible date) with typical earnings of $1,000 per year would have contributed $60 (with his employer paying the same amount), and he would have received a monthly benefit of $16.67. Thus, in four months, he would have received more in benefits than he had paid in taxes—hardly an actuarial, individual-equity plan!

The 1939 amendments changed the financing basis to what was generally believed to be a "pay-as-you-go" basis or, more properly, a contingency fund basis. The Social Security Advisory Council of 1937–38 recommended the development of a relatively small contingency fund, with government contributions eventually. However, the law did not specifically adopt this recommendation, and the program has not developed in this pattern. The 1939 amendments "froze" the tax rate for the three years 1940–42 at the initial level (2 percent for employer and employee combined), and subsequent congressional action continued this freeze throughout the 1940s. This action further strengthened the belief of many persons that the system was being financed—or would be financed—on a "pay-as-you-go" basis, despite the fact that because of the economic situation due to the war, income was very considerably in excess of outgo and a sizable fund had accumulated.

No specific provision was made in the 1939 act for any government subsidy, despite the fact that, according to some individuals, a contingency-reserve financing approach had been adopted. However, the 1943 legislation that continued the 2 percent employer-employee tax rate incorporated a provision authorizing appropriations to the trust fund from general revenue if needed to finance the program. No appropriations were made under this provision, since the trust fund grew rapidly, and none seemed to be required.

The Social Security Advisory Council of 1947–48, somewhat paralleling the action of the previous advisory council, recommended a financing basis under which a relatively small contingency fund would develop, with eventual federal contributions (or subsidies) equal to half the combined employer-employee taxes. This advisory council also recommended an immediate increase in the contribution rate, despite the fairly sizable fund that was continuing to develop. This action was based, in large part, on "psychological" grounds rather than actuarial ones, in order that the general public would realize that the considerably liberalized benefits recommended meant additional costs and consequently higher contribution rates.

Congress, in enacting the 1950 amendments, did not concur in the financing recommendations made by the advisory council, but instead quite clearly and strongly expressed the intent that the system be completely self-supporting from the tax income provided. This basis has subsequently been maintained. The tax schedule has been revised from time to time as additional benefits have been provided and in accordance with needs indicated by revised actuarial cost estimates.

Until the 1972 amendments, the self-supporting principle was implemented by having an upward-graded tax schedule that reached its ultimate level in a few years. Frequently, the scheduled increases were not put fully into effect when the time for them came, but rather they (and subsequent scheduled increases as well) were postponed at least in part, for a few years.

One reason that the approach of grading up the tax schedule rapidly, with the ultimate rate coming within a few years, was that then such ultimate rate would not have to be as high (and thus not disturb the public as much) as if it were long deferred. For example, consider a simplified example of taxable payrolls being constant in all future years and with a trust fund interest rate of 5 percent. Suppose that a tax schedule of 6 percent rising to 10 percent in three-year steps of 2 percent each were desired to be stretched out to have the ultimate rate occur 30 years hence (instead of six years) with equal steps every decade. Then, such steps would have to be 2.63 percent each, and the ultimate rate would be 13.89 percent.

An illustration of how this basis worked out can be found by considering the situation as it was at the time of enactment of the 1971 amendments. The OASDI tax schedule would reach its ultimate level in a few years (1976), while benefit disbursements would rise for a number of decades. In accordance with the self-supporting financing basis of OASDI, this means that a sizable fund would develop. In fact, in the intermediate-cost estimate made then, the ultimate size of the trust fund was well in excess of $250 billion (it was about $40 billion at the end of 1971).

The 1972 amendments did not change the self-supporting principle, but moved the financing basis for the future to current-cost or pay-as-you-go from the previous modified-reserve procedure. It is important to note that in the past decade, the actual experience had been close to current-cost financing, due to the freezing of the tax rates or the postponement in part of scheduled increases. This is indicated by comparing the fund on hand with the outgo (for benefits, administrative expenses, and financial interchange with the railroad retirement system) for the next year.

Such ratio was about 17 in 1940, when payment of monthly benefits first began. It then rose to about 20 in 1943–44, but thereafter it declined to about 14 in 1949 and then dropped sharply to about 8 in 1950, after the benefit level was raised significantly to recognize the increase in the cost of living in the World War II period. After 1950, the ratio continued to decrease and by the beginning of 1964 it was only 1.1. In all years from 1965 through 1971, the ratio was close to 1.0.

The 1971 Advisory Council on Social Security recommended that the program be financed on a current-cost basis, with the trust funds maintained at a level approximately equal to one year's expenditures. The council recognized that this had been the case in the recent past, that this recommendation was "nothing new," and that many persons had "recognized that the funds should be held to such a contingency function." The council further recommended that the ratio of the fund to the next year's outgo should not fall below 75 percent or rise above 125 percent (under either of which circumstances the board of trustees should immediately report to Congress whenever it perceives that this will be the case for the next year).

The future tax schedule for OASDI for the 1972 amendments was developed by Congress along the lines recommended by the advisory council, although the reporting requirement for when the ratio of fund to annual outgo falls outside the 75–125 percent range was not written into law. As a result of the large benefit increases in the 1972 amendments, the test ratio for OASDI fell to 80 percent when computed at the beginning of 1973. Under the tax schedule adopted, it will not rise to 100 percent until about 1990. It would appear that the legislation was framed so as to hold down near-future tax rates by "riding at the bottom of the range" of the ratio and thus financing benefit liberalizations by depleting the fund relatively.

The December 1973 amendments continued the same financing approach as the 1972 amendments. However, because of anticipated relatively large short-range increases in benefits due to changes in the

CPI, the test ratio for OASDI of funds on hand at the beginning of the year to expenditures in the year was then estimated to decrease over the next few years from 72 percent for 1974 to 62 percent for 1978.[4] There is some indication that Congress established the "tradition" of a test ratio of 75 percent (i.e., riding the lower end of the range) when it enacted the July 1973 amendments (which, to a large extent, were overridden by the December 1973 amendments), since then the Senate Finance Committee stated that this ratio was "considered by the Congress last year as an acceptable level of contingent funds on hand."[5] As will be noted, however, this tradition was soon broken (or at least badly fractured) by the December 1973 amendments.

Moreover, estimates made in 1974 showed an even more significant deterioration of this test ratio for OASDI. The ratio of assets on hand at the beginning of a calendar year as a percentage of the expenditures in the year, as shown in the 1974 Trustees Report, is estimated to decrease from 74 percent for 1974 to 48–51 percent for 1978.

The automatic-adjustment provisions introduced by the 1972 amendments did not directly affect the financing basis of OASDI. As mentioned in Chapter 3 and as will be brought out in more detail in the appendix to this chapter and in Chapter 10 when the actuarial cost estimates are discussed, the effect of the necessary economic assumptions as to wage and price trends can be very significant and serious as to the financing of the system.[6]

As part of these automatic-adjustment provisions, it is provided that when they produce a benefit increase, the Secretary of Health, Education, and Welfare is to report also to Congress as to the extent that the increased cost of the benefits is met by the increase in the taxable earnings base triggered thereby.

Up to the present point, reference has been made to "trust fund" in discussing the OASDI program. Actually, following the 1956 amendments, there are two separate trust funds—one for the old-age and survivors insurance benefits and the other for the disability insurance benefits. This subdivision has no real significance in regard to

---

[4] Computed from data on page 14, "Report of the Committee on Ways and Means, United States House of Representatives, to Accompany H.R. 11333," House Report No. 93–627, November 9, 1973.

[5] See page 19, "Report of the Committee on Finance, United States Senate, to Accompany H. R. 8410," Senate Report No. 93–249, June 25, 1973.

[6] For a challenging and incisive demonstration and discussion of this aspect, see Geoffrey N. Calvert, *New Realistic Projections of Social Security Benefits and Taxes* (New York: Alexander and Alexander, Inc., 1973).

the financing of the program. It was adopted as a "guarantee and assurance" that the newly provided disability benefits would not bankrupt the trust fund (if all benefits were to be paid from a single fund) in the event that the disability experience proved much less favorable than estimated.

Over the years, the actuarial cost estimates prepared in the Social Security Administration have been used by Congress as the basis for its consideration of changes in the OASDI program. Particularly since the positive recognition and adoption of the self-supporting principle in 1950, the cost estimates have tended to play a very important role in its legislative development.

Before any legislative action, Congress studies carefully the cost of proposed benefit liberalizations in the light of the financial situation of the existing system—that is, whether any additional financing is necessary, or conversely, whether an actuarial surplus is present that can be used to liberalize benefits without additional financing being needed. At times, Congress has determined that liberalizations were too costly, and they have been trimmed down or eliminated. For example, in 1956, the House voted to pay full benefits at age 62 (instead of at age 65) to all categories of female beneficiaries and to provide monthly disability benefits beginning at age 50. This was to be financed by a 1 percent increase in the combined employer-employee tax rate in all future years. The controlling reason for restricting disability benefits to those aged 50 and over was the cost aspect. The Senate, however, was not in favor of an increase in the contribution schedule as large as 1 percent and so provided actuarially reduced, rather than full, benefits for women workers and wives (but full benefits for widows) claiming them before age 65. This action, permitting the increase in the combined employer-employee tax rate to be held to ½ percent, was agreed to by the House and was enacted.

Before the 1972 amendments, the OASDI system was financed neither on a full-reserve basis nor on a pay-as-you-go current-cost basis. Rather, it may be said to have been on a partial-reserve financing basis. The trust funds then were expected to serve two roles—to provide interest earnings so that ultimate tax rates can be somewhat lower than if there were no accumulated fund, and to be used as contingency funds to meet any excess of outgo over income in years when this would result from poor economic conditions or from the operation of the graded tax schedule. Under the law prior to the 1972 amendments, the OASI Trust Fund was estimated to grow rapidly in the future, as a result of the scheduled increases in the tax rates in 1973 and 1976. Over the long run, it was estimated that under the financing basis of that law, interest receipts would meet about 10 to 15 percent of the benefit costs.

The question had been raised in some circles of economic thought as to whether such large funds (with resulting interest income) should be allowed to develop—because of the possible deflationary effect on the economy. For example, in connection with the legislation considered in 1964, Secretary of Health, Education, and Welfare Anthony J. Celebrezze testified before the Senate Finance Committee as follows: "Under this schedule the contribution rates would increase more slowly and gradually than under present law, so that excessive accumulations of funds in the next several years, with possible depressing effects on the economy, would be avoided."

The change in the 1972 amendments to a current-cost basis was intended, among other things, to make the effect of the OASDI system on the overall economy relatively neutral. The trust funds will continue to play the two roles that they have in the past, although to a much lesser extent with regard to providing some of the financing for the system through the interest earnings. Nonetheless, such earnings will meet 5–6 percent of the cost each year (if the trust fund balance is about one year's outgo and if the interest rate is about this level), or about three times as much as needed to pay for the costs of administration, which represent only about 1½ to 2 percent of total outgo. Or it might be viewed that the interest is used first to increase the size of the trust fund so that it maintains its same relative level as compared with outgo, in which case it is largely used up to do so.

Although, in some quarters, there has been considerable criticism of the fact that since 1950 legislative action has liberalized the OASDI system about every two years, there is one important point that should be kept in mind. Each time there has been legislative activity, the Congress—particularly the important, controlling legislative committees concerned—has very carefully considered the cost aspects of all proposed liberalizations. Any changes made have been reasonably fully financed according to the best actuarial cost estimates available. Thus, Congress has attempted to keep the system on a self-supporting basis by keeping benefit costs very closely in balance with tax income. The committees have always been anxious to be able to say that the program is "actuarially sound." Certainly, the program can be said to have staunch financial safeguards as long as Congress continues to be cost conscious, as it has been in the past, and to finance benefit liberalizations adequately.

SOCIAL SECURITY AND THE UNIFIED BUDGET

Until the late 1960s, the operations of the social security trust funds were not reflected in the general budget of the United States government. In other words, the trust fund operations were considered to be completely separate from other governmental operations and did not affect the budget balance (or imbalance). Beginning with the budget for fiscal year 1969 (July 1968 through June 1969), such trust fund operations—as well as those of other trust funds administered by the federal government—were reflected in a unified budget. This was done because economic planners asserted that they were interested in all financial activities and operations of the federal government, and therefore this basis should be used for the budget.

Some confusion and public misunderstanding has occurred as a result of the unified budget. There are those who believe that the social security taxes are merely placed in the General Fund of the Treasury, and then are unaccounted for and are used for other purposes. This is not so, since there is strict accounting, and all monies in excess of what is needed for current expenditures are invested in interest-bearing issues.

Others are puzzled that it can happen—and it did in fiscal year 1969—that the budget can show a surplus and yet the national debt has increased. The reason for this is that OASDI had a sizable excess of income over outgo (which was used to purchase government obligations and thus was reflected in the national debt) that was large enough to more than offset the lack of balance in the "regular" budget.

It seems essential that the operations of the social security trust funds should be relatively neutral insofar as the economy is concerned. Likewise, the operations of the trust funds should not be manipulated, as some economic planners would like to do, so as to stimulate or slow down the economy (as the economic planners thought best) or so as to affect the balance situation of the budget. The 1971 Advisory Council on Social Security expressed its views on this subject as follows: "Even though the operations of the social security trust funds and other Federal trust funds programs are combined with the general operations of the Federal Government in the unified Federal budget, policy decisions affecting the social security program should be based on the objectives of the program rather than on any effect that such decisions might have on the Federal budget."

In March 1974, Chairman Wilbur D. Mills of the House Ways and Means Committee introduced a bill (H.R. 13411) that contained a section providing for removal of social security trust fund operations from the budget presentations. Although action was not taken on this matter during 1974, considerable significance can be attached to these views of this knowledgeable member of Congress, who at that time wielded great power.[7]

INVESTMENT PROCEDURES

Throughout the entire period of operation of the OASDI program, the method of investing the assets of the trust funds has changed relatively little. In general, it may be said that the trust funds, which are under the direction of the Secretary of the Treasury, receive the tax income and pay the benefits and administrative expenses. The excess of the income over the outgo is invested in obligations of the federal government, and the interest therefrom augments the income of the system.

Since the middle of 1940, the tax collections have been automatically appropriated to the trust funds as they are received by the Treasury Department (initially, this is done on an estimated basis, but with retroactive adjustments based on actual posted reported earnings). From 1937 through the middle of 1940, a somewhat different procedure was followed. The authorized appropriations to the Old-Age Reserve Account (as it was called then) were not specifically to be measured by the taxes collected, but rather were to be "an amount to be determined on a reserve basis in accordance with accepted actuarial principles." Underlying legal and constitutional aspects made a distinct division between the taxes collected and the benefits paid seem desirable. In actual practice, however, this language was interpreted to mean that the appropriations should be the estimated net proceeds of the taxes, after deduction of the estimated administrative expenses (which procedurally were paid out of the General Treasury but, of course, in practice came from the gross tax receipts).

After the program was declared to be clearly constitutional in 1937, this indirect procedure was no longer necessary. As a result, the 1939

---

[7] See page E1521, *Congressional Record*, March 18, 1974, for Mr. Mills' supporting statement for this proposal.

amendments provided for the current automatic-appropriation basis. At the same time, "insurance" terminology was introduced in referring to the program, both in the law and in public explanations presented by the Social Security Administration. In part, this was proper, since OASDI is social insurance, but this approach was somewhat overdone, so as to draw on the good name of private insurance to build up confidence in and support for OASDI.

Because the original method of appropriation was on an estimated "net" basis, there was not an exact balance between net income (after deducting actual administrative expenses) and appropriations made. In the 3½-year period, the total excess of tax collections over appropriations was $141 million. Offsets against this are administrative expenses during the same period of $76 million and tax refunds paid by the General Treasury and not reimbursed by the trust funds, for the period through June 1952 (after which refunds were chargeable to the trust funds), amounting to $38 million. As a result, a sufficiently close balance had, in essence, been achieved for the period of the first 3½ years of operation, when there was not completely precise accounting of tax income.

The investments of the trust funds can be either in special issues or in any other securities of the federal government, bought either on the open market or at issue. Some regular issues have been bought, both on the open market and when they were offered to the general public. Special legislation has provided that certain semigovernmental issues—such as those of the Federal National Mortgage Association (so-called Fannie May)—can be purchased by the trust funds, even though they are not guaranteed as to both principal and interest by the government.

Most of the investments, however, have been in special issues. Before 1940, it was provided that these special issues should bear an interest rate of 3 percent. From then until the 1956 amendments, they carried an interest rate slightly below the average coupon rate on all interest-bearing obligations of the United States outstanding at the time of issue of the special issues.

The 1956 Act changed the interest basis for special issues so that it was determined from the average coupon rate on all *long-term* government obligations (issued initially for five or more years), rounded to the nearest ⅛th percent. The 1960 Act revised this interest basis, so that the interest rate is now determined from the average *market yield* rate on government obligations that are not due or callable for at least four years from the date of determination.

In 1940–43, the new special issues were for durations of four or five years. Beginning in 1944, some new special issues were for durations of one year (or less); and beginning in 1945, all new special issues were of this duration. Accordingly, beginning in 1947, the entire investment portfolio was reinvested each year (on June 30). This procedure was followed until 1957, when a transition was begun—toward spreading the investment portfolio of each of the trust funds over the following 10 years. Investments during a fiscal year are made in certificates which mature on the following June 30. At that time, the funds from the maturities are reinvested in long-term notes (up to 7 years until maturity) or bonds (of 7 years or more).

Then, in 1959 the permanent portfolio of special issues was spread more or less equally over the next 15 years, and this principle was followed until the late 1960s. In order to be equitable to the trust funds as interest rates rose above 4¼ percent then, this principle was suspended, and new special issues were given a maturity of seven years, since other provisions of law prohibited a higher rate than 4¼ percent for longer term securities. Such prohibition was removed in mid-1974, and then blocks of special issues at an interest rate of 7⅝ percent were purchased with the funds then available for investment, in equal amounts maturing in each year of 1981–89.

This special-issue interest rate was initially 2½ percent (in 1940), but as large volumes of long-term government bonds were floated to finance the war effort, the rate gradually decreased and reached a low of 1⅞ percent in the period from May 1943 to July 1946. Thereafter, there was a gradual rise to 2⅝ percent for the period from July 1958 to September 1960, which was the last month before the new basis provided by the 1960 amendments went into effect.

When the interest basis was changed by the 1956 amendments (effective for October 1956), there was no change in the rate actually made available to the trust funds. As it happened, under the conditions prevailing at that time, the new method of basing the rate on long-term obligations (rather than on all obligations) produced a slightly lower unrounded rate, but the change in the rounding procedure produced a final result that was exactly the same as the previous basis.

The new basis under the 1960 Act produced a sharp increase in the special-issue interest rate, yielding rates of 3⅝ to 4 percent for issues purchased in the last three months of 1960, or appreciably in excess of the 2¾ percent rate that would have been in effect then under the old basis. During 1961–65, this interest rate was generally between 3¾ and 4¼ percent, but thereafter it rose significantly, reaching a high of 7⅞ percent in February 1970. Since then, the rate fell somewhat and was at a level of about 6 percent during 1971–72, but rose to about 6¾ percent during 1973, and then it increased in 1974, reaching a peak of 8⅛ percent in September, but fell off to 7⅜ percent by the end of the year.

Although there has been considerable opposition to investing the excess income of the system in government bonds, no positive support has been offered for any other form of investment. All other possibilities have seemed to be objectionable in the United States for overwhelming reasons.

One possible investment practice would be to purchase securities of private concerns, either bonds or stocks. There are several objections to this approach. First, with the large amount of money available, the government would control a considerable portion of the private industrial economy, which would, in effect, result in "socialism by the backdoor method." Another practical disadvantage would be the need for a far-reaching and deep-searching investment policy that would permit the trust funds to obtain an adequate rate of interest with reasonable security. Under such a policy the government would, in effect, be setting itself up as a rating organization, since the investment procedures would naturally have to be open to full public view. If no preference were shown for different types of securities, but rather investments were made widely and indiscriminately, there would be a serious danger of loss of capital and diminution of investment income.

Another possible procedure would be to invest the funds in social and economic activities such as the construction of housing, dams, hospitals, and the like. This method would be open to some objection on the grounds mentioned previously—government entry into private fields of activity. Even more serious is the argument that any use of public funds for such purposes should be under the control of the elected representatives of the people (Congress) rather than the indirect and less visible approach of having a social insurance organization making decisions as to what is best for the country.

RELATIONSHIP WITH RAILROAD RETIREMENT SYSTEM

The railroad retirement system (described in detail in Chapter 12) provides benefits similar to those under OASDI for workers in the railroad industry. In virtually all ways, these benefits are more liberal than under OASDI, and the Railroad Retirement Act provides that the benefit amounts will be at least 10 percent larger than the same wage record would have produced under OASDI. The law provides for a coordination of railroad compensation and covered earnings under OASDI in determining not only survivor benefits in all cases but also retirement benefits for persons with less than 10 years of railroad service. All survivor and retirement benefits involving less than 10 years of railroad service are to be paid by the OASDI system.

An important element affecting the financing of the OASDI system arose through amendments made to the Railroad Retirement Act in 1951. The financial interchange provisions are designed to place the OASI and DI Trust Funds in the same financial position they would have held if there never had been a separate railroad retirement program. Each year, computations are made on the basis of a small sample of railroad beneficiaries, completely investigated as to how much the OASDI benefit and administrative expense outgo would have been increased if railroad earnings had been covered under OASDI. This takes into account any OASDI benefit rights obtained by other employment. The additional tax income if railroad employment had been under OASDI is estimated from aggregate railroad retirement coverage data. The calculation of the transfers necessary is readily made from these data.

It is estimated by the Social Security Administration that the net effect of these financial interchange provisions will be a relatively small net loss to the OASDI system. The estimated reimbursements from the railroad retirement system will, over the long run, be somewhat smaller than the net additional benefits paid on the basis of railroad earnings.

It was determined that the "initial amount" due the OASI Trust Fund from the Railroad Retirement Account as of the middle of 1952 was $488 million.[8] The law provided that interest, and no principal, would be transferred to OASI as long as any part of this initial amount due remained and that when the initial amount had been completely eliminated by the annual excesses of additional outgo over additional income under OASDI if railroad employment had been covered thereby, transfers of such excess amounts would occur. Accordingly,

---

[8] Such "initial amount" was also determined for previous years. It increased from zero at the beginning of 1937 to $513 million at the end of 1950 and then decreased to the $488 million figure.

each year the interest on the net amount due was transferred from the Railroad Retirement Account to the OASI Trust Fund, and the principal was steadily reduced by the aforementioned excess of additional outgo over additional income that was determined under the actual developing experience.

By 1957—because of the relatively older age of railroad workers as compared with the covered population under OASDI—the entire initial amount had been liquidated; and beginning in 1958, payments have been made each year from the OASI Trust Fund to the Railroad Retirement Account, amounting to some $300 to $400 million per year in the early 1960s, $500 to $700 million annually through 1972, but $783 million in 1973 and $909 million in 1974. In regard to the DI Trust Fund, there was no "initial amount" but rather immediate transfer beginning in 1958. For the first two years, relatively small amounts were paid from the Railroad Retirement Account to the DI Trust Fund. Thereafter the flow has been in the other direction (at about $15 to $30 million per year).

In the near future the OASI Trust Fund will continue to make substantial payments to the Railroad Retirement Account; but after a decade or so, these will become smaller and, in fact, quite likely after some years the flow of payments will be reversed. This trend will result from several factors—the age distribution of the OASDI coverage will become older, and the effect of duplicating and overlapping benefits will be more significant (i.e., a greater proportion of railroad beneficiaries will also have OASDI benefits in their own right, and the financial interchange results in the railroad retirement system getting credit only for the *additional* benefits that would be payable if railroad employment were under OASDI).

APPENDIX

Methodology for Actuarial Cost Estimates
for Social Security Programs

Quite naturally, in programs as broad and diversified as are social security programs generally, there are no neat mathematical formulas for cost estimates and valuations—just as is the case in connection with the complex pension and employee benefit plans that have developed over the years—as against the relative simplicity of the actuarial valuation formulas used for individual life insurance and annuity policies. This appendix will deal with cost-estimating procedures for all types of social security programs, but the main emphasis will be devoted to the cost estimates for the OASDI system. Similar discussion for the Medicare program is presented in the appendix to Chapter 8.

COST ESTIMATES FOR LONG-RANGE
SOCIAL INSURANCE PROGRAMS

Making actuarial cost estimates for long-range social insurance programs of a pension nature involves a number of problems similar to those encountered in making such estimates and valuations for private pension plans. Conversely, there are many problems peculiar to each. A precise dividing line cannot be drawn, partly because a system may contain certain benefit features characteristic of each.

The OASDI system is clearly social insurance, since it is a national program covering virtually the entire working population, and no direct relationship exists between contributions paid and benefits received. To put it another way, OASDI emphasizes social adequacy at the expense of individual equity.

Another of our national programs, the railroad retirement system, adheres in large measure to the principle of individual equity and thus includes features often found in private pension plans. For instance, retirement and disability benefits are directly proportional to length of covered service (although there are certain minimum benefit provisions, and although benefits are heavily weighted for low-paid workers), and for many years, although no longer, total benefits paid were guaranteed at least to equal employee contributions. However, the survivor benefits are similar to those of OASDI.

The civil service retirement system (and to a certain extent, many similar plans for state and local government employees) tends to be much closer to a private pension plan than to social insurance. Nevertheless, certain elements of social insurance have been introduced into CSR, possibly because of a fear among certain groups of "encroachment" by OASDI. In many cases, CSR disability and survivor benefits bear little relationship to length of service, but rather are based on social adequacy principles.

This appendix, in discussing the general methodology of preparing and presenting long-range actuarial cost estimates, draws largely upon the procedures under OASDI, but other systems are also considered. In order to lay a foundation for the discussion, there are first considered (1) valuation methods used, (2) variability of cost estimates, and (3) the concept of open-end groups as against closed groups.

Valuation Methods

Two methods of presenting actuarial valuations are commonly used. Historically, the most common is the familiar "balance sheet" method, which to a certain extent follows the format, although not the substance, of standard accounting procedures. The assets and liabilities, both actual and potential, are determined on a given date. Such determination for social insurance systems is usually made not only for present covered workers but also including all future new entrants as well. On the other hand, for private pension plans the concept is generally on the basis of presently covered workers only. Under one approach, future assets are valued on the basis of actual scheduled contribution rates, and the resulting deficit or surplus (in monetary units or as related to payroll) is derived. Under another approach, assets and liabilities are "balanced" by determining the contribution rate needed to achieve this result. Even though the actuarial valuation does not show an actual balance sheet but rather the resulting annual costs in dollars and in percentage of payroll, one made by this procedure may still be said to be of the balance sheet type.

The other procedure, the "projection" method, involves a presentation of year-by-year figures in the future for many years (perhaps at quinquennial or decennial intervals) for such elements as covered workers, beneficiaries, covered payroll, contribution or tax income, interest income, benefit disbursements, administrative expenses, and balance in the fund.

The balance sheet method has the advantage of ease of preparation, since in most cases well-established actuarial techniques permitting the use of existing tables and computational shortcuts may be followed when "static" assumptions for the various cost factors are made. This is particularly important when dealing with small systems, for which extensive work is usually not warranted. On the other hand, when "dynamic" assumptions, such as continuously improving mortality, are used, the projection method may prove less difficult.

Another advantage sometimes claimed for utilizing the balance sheet method is that it is not necessary to make assumptions for experience extending many years into the future. This is not the case under either method when, as is customary in connection with social insurance plans, the costs are figured for many years, even sometimes into perpetuity, because of the assumption of continuing groups of new entrants. Under these circumstances, the balance sheet method may be less realistic because static future conditions as to new entrants, mortality rates, retirement rates, and the like, are usually assumed.

Most laymen look upon valuations of the balance sheet type with complete mystification, sometimes even with skepticism. Comments are often made that the figures from such valuations are "only actuarial costs and not indicative of real costs." This probably occurs because the present values of all future benefit disbursements, the only ones shown, are so much higher than current costs. If the projection method is used, such criticism is greatly lessened. The immediate and near-future situation is clearly recognized and portrayed. This, in turn, lends credibility to the graphic picture presented for the more distant future.

One argument often made in favor of the balance sheet method as against the projection method is that the former must be used when there is limited experience under the system. Under such circumstances, the actuary must use actuarial data from the experience of other systems, sometimes even those of other countries. This argument is not valid. An ingenious actuary can use the projection method under almost any circumstances.

In conjunction with cost estimates developed on the projection basis, it is possible to derive "level premium" or "level cost" figures, both for benefit and administrative costs and for tax income. The "level cost" is the percentage of covered payroll that if charged from the present into the future over the entire period considered in the valuation, would produce sufficient tax and interest income to the fund to meet the cost of the benefit payments and administrative expenses. The "level cost equivalent of the tax rates" is the percent of covered payroll that if charged from the present over the period considered in the valuation, would produce the same amount of income to the fund, taking into account interest, as would be produced by a graded schedule of tax rates. The use of these two figures, after taking into account the in-

TABLE 4.2

Comparison of Effect in Valuations of OASDI System of Using Level Costs as Compared with Average Costs (all figures are in percentages of taxable payroll)

Item	Level Cost	Average Cost
Valuation for Amendments in Mid-1972		
Benefits*.............................	9.79%	9.77%
Taxes.................................	9.87	9.84
Net actuarial balance....................	+0.08%	+0.07%
Valuation in 1974 Trustees Report		
Benefits*.............................	13.70%	13.89%
Taxes.................................	10.82	10.91
Net actuarial balance....................	2.88	2.98

* Including also the effects of the administrative expenses, the railroad retirement financial interchange, and the existing trust fund balances at the valuation date.

terest on the existing fund at the time of the valuation and the development of a future fund balance such that it, at the end of the valuation period, has a size equal to one year's outgo, gives an indication of the long-range actuarial balance of the system.

In 1972 the procedure of using the level cost concept was changed to one of "average cost." The latter is merely the simple arithmetic averaging of the annual costs over all the years in the valuation period expressed as percentages of taxable payroll. The failure to consider interest for payments made at different time periods is largely counterbalanced by the nonrecognition of the larger dollar costs over the years as the system matures. The net difference between the two concepts is relatively small, as shown in Table 4.2.

Actuarial valuations of private pension plans, both in this country and abroad, have almost always been done by the balance sheet method.

On the other hand, the cost estimates for the OASDI system have always been prepared by the projection method. The balance sheet method has generally been used for both the RR and the CSR systems, although at times, projection estimates have been made for these programs. Cost estimates for foreign social insurance programs have usually been made by the balance sheet method, although in recent years there seems to be some trend toward the projection method. Countries that have adopted this latter course of action include Great Britain, Israel, and Sweden.

Variability of Estimates

Long-range actuarial cost estimates and valuations, regardless of type, cannot be precise, no matter how accurately and meticulously prepared. Considerable differences will inevitably arise between actual experience over the long-range future and the estimates. Although it cannot be expected that the figures will be precise, such estimates must be made to indicate future cost trends. One difficulty in making comparisons of actual experience with previous assumptions is that the underlying program frequently changes as a result of legislative action.

Because of the variations that will almost certainly occur between the actual experience and the actuarial assumptions, it can be argued that cost estimates or valuations serve their purpose best if they are on a "range" basis. This procedure has very definite value, although it involves considerable extra work. Even when the range procedure is followed, a single intermediate estimate is frequently required. This will not necessarily be any more accurate or "probable" than either of the range estimates. Such a single estimate may, however, be needed for establishing long-range schedules of tax rates.

The actuarial cost estimates for the OASDI system that were developed during 1937–70 were of the range type. The original estimates for the 1935 act were on the single estimate basis. The 1971 Advisory Council on Social Security recommended that "contribution rates should be based on a single, best estimate derived from a single set of assumptions that reflect likely future trends . . . , rather than on an average of a low-cost and a high-cost estimate." The council also recommended that other estimates should be made on the basis of variations in the major cost factors. The author does not agree with this procedure, even though in practice it produces about the same result, because one is fooling oneself if it is believed that a "best" estimate is precisely possible. The current OASDI estimates are on the basis recommended by the council.

Open-End Groups versus Closed Groups

Valuation of the actuarial liabilities of an insurance company is done completely on the "closed-group" basis. In other words, it is assumed that there will be no new entrants in the future, so that the existing group of policyholders must "stand on their own feet" financially. This is the method required by law and is the only reasonable and proper basis—as has been evidenced by the past financial failures of assessment and similar organizations that completely depended for their solvency on new entrants.

Private pension plans operate under many different financing methods, almost all of which are on the "closed-group" basis insofar as the financing is considered from a percentage-of-payroll cost basis, or when a full balance sheet is presented. It is, of course, true that many such plans are not completely funded at the present time, although definite plans are generally in effect for this to be accomplished at a specific future date. In any event, the vast majority of plans do not anticipate a continual flow of new entrants and an indefinite continuation of the plan to assure financial solvency.

The financing basis of the CSR system differs somewhat from that of most private pension plans in that an "open-end group" technique is followed. The payroll is assumed to remain level in all future years at the current figure, and interest on the unfunded accrued liability, which in essence is permitted to increase slightly until the early 1980s and then is "frozen," is measured against this payroll. This cost is thus spread over perpetuity and is added to the new-entrant, or normal, cost to yield the level premium cost of the program. For example, in the valuation as of June 30, 1970, the normal or new-entrant cost was estimated at 12.95 percent of payroll, and the total level cost at 25.65 percent, of which the employees contribute 7 percent.[9]

Most actuarially guided state and local government employee retirement systems are financed on a "closed-group" basis, since the un-

---

[9] The total level cost was derived by the author from data on the total annual contributions required from the government on the basis of paying in the next year only 10 percent of the interest accruing on the unfunded liability (see "Fiftieth Annual Report of the Board of Actuaries of the Civil Service Retirement System," House Doc. No. 93–37, January 3, 1973).

funded accrued liabilities are intended to be amortized over a definite future period. In many cases, however, the period is so long that there is relatively little difference between this approach and the "open-end-group" basis, under which a continuous flow of new entrants is assumed and interest is paid into perpetuity on the "frozen" unfunded accrued liability.

The valuations of the RR system and of OASDI and HI are of a truly "open-end-group" nature—even though the former basically uses the balance sheet method and the latter uses the projection method. For the RR system a projection of annual taxable payrolls is made for the next several decades, with a leveling off assumption thereafter, and this series is equated to an equivalent level annual payroll that is then used as the basis for the balance sheet method computations. The estimates of future railroad payrolls are based on population projections and estimates of future railroad traffic. On the other hand, for OASDI and HI, the coverage of the system and the resulting payrolls are determined from population projections running for almost a century into the future, with relative stability and maturity assumed thereafter, and on estimated trends in the labor force participation rates by age and sex. The RR valuations are made on a perpetuity basis, while the OASDI ones cover a 75-year period, and the HI ones cover a 25-year period. The shorter period for HI reflects the much greater difficulty involved in projecting its assumptions (i.e., for health care unit costs and utilization). Under neither system is there any attempt to "freeze" the unfunded accrued liability, as in the CSR system.

The actuarial status of the OASDI system is usually expressed as a percentage of taxable payroll. The same procedure is followed for the HI system. Specifically, the 1974 trustees reports showed the OASDI system to have an actuarial deficit on a long-range basis of 2.98 percent of taxable payroll. The corresponding figure for HI was the relatively negligible actuarial surplus of 0.02 percent. However, it is also possible to express the actuarial status on a balance-sheet basis.

Table 4.3 gives data on the deficits of the OASDI and HI systems in terms of dollars as of certain recent dates on the open-group basis. Such deficit on a valuation date is (1) the present value of future benefit payments and administrative expenses, both for current beneficiaries and workers and for future entrants, minus (2) the present value of future taxes for present workers and new entrants, minus (3) the existing trust fund.

Under this open-group, limited-period concept, there was a small

TABLE 4.3

Actuarial Status of OASDI and HI on Open-Group, Limited-Period Basis as of June 30, 1971–74

		Amount (billions)			
Item		*1971*	*1972*	*1973*	*1974*
OASDI System					
1. Present value of future benefits and administrative expenses............		$1,185	$4,717	$5,526	$6,532
2. Present value of future taxes...........		1,132	4,813	5,306	5,174
3. Existing trust fund...................		41	44	44	46
4. Net surplus or deficit, (1) − (2) − (3)..		+12	+140	−176	−1,312
HI System					
1. Present value of future benefits and administrative expenses............		$ 276	$ 272	$ 414	$ 465
2. Present value of future taxes...........		140	282	428	465
3. Existing trust fund...................		3	3	4	8
4. Net surplus or deficit, (1) − (2) − (3)..		−133	+13	+18	+8

Note: These valuations have been carried out at an interest rate of 6 percent for 1972–74 and 5¼ percent for 1971.

actuarial surplus for OASDI as of mid-1971 and mid-1972, because the system was then estimated to be in close actuarial balance. A deficit of $176 billion occurred as of mid-1973, when there was a small estimated lack of actuarial balance, but this soared to $1.3 trillion in mid-1974, when the actuarial lack of balance was almost 3 percent of taxable payroll.

The actuarial deficit for OASDI under the open-group basis tends to be much more volatile than under the closed-group basis discussed previously, for which figures were presented in Table 4.1. This is because the situation under the open-group basis depends to a considerable extent on the amount of taxes that will be paid by new entrants in long-distant future years, when the tax rate is much higher and when the assumed level of taxable earnings under the dynamic economic assumptions is so much higher. In contrast, under the closed-group basis, the taxes considered are almost entirely those to be paid in the next 45 years, so that little effect is present for the higher ultimate tax rate scheduled after 2010.

This can be illustrated by considering the actuarial deficits for mid-1974 under the two concepts. The closed-group concept shows a deficit of $2,460 billion, as against only $1,312 billion, or 53 percent as much, for the open-group concept. However, the situation is quite different when the several components are considered. In moving from the closed-group concept to the open-group one, the present value of the future taxes is 3.4 times as large, whereas the present value of the future benefits is only 62 percent higher.

Under the closed-group, limited-period concept, the HI system has shown relatively small actuarial surpluses in all years in 1972–74, amounting to roughly $10–20 billion on this present-value basis. This situation occurred because the program was estimated in close actuarial balance under the tax schedules and earnings bases in effect at the time of the valuations, as discussed in Chapters 8 and 10 (see especially Table 10.10). The large deficit shown for mid-1972 was because this determination was made before the HI tax schedule was increased significantly by the July 1972 amendments, so as to remedy the previously-existing long-range financing problem of this program.

LONG-RANGE OASDI COST ESTIMATES

Principal Elements and Factors

The following principal quantities are estimated for various future years and are used in deriving the cost estimates for OASDI:

1. Total population in all geographic areas covered by OASDI, by age groups and sex, for five-year time intervals.
2. OASDI-covered workers as percentages of total population by age-sex groups.
3. Number of covered workers, derived from items 1 and 2.
4. Proportions of covered workers with 4 quarters of coverage in a year.
5. Average annual creditable earnings of covered workers, by coverage classification and by sex.
6. Total annual creditable earnings of covered workers, derived from items 3, 4, and 5.
7. Effective annual taxable payrolls, from item 6 after adjustment for tax lags, for employer tax on amounts in excess of individual wage maximum, and self-employment tax rate differential as compared with combined employer-employee rate.
8. Annual tax receipts, from combined employer-employee tax rates applied to item 7.

9. OASDI-insured population (potentially eligible for retirement, disability, or survivor benefits) as proportions of total population.

10. Insured population, derived from items 1 and 9. Female insured population subclassified as "steady" or "nonsteady" workers.

11. Number of old-age beneficiaries in current payment status, from insured population over retirement age (item 10), reduced to allow for effect of earnings test (and also for persons claiming the actuarially reduced benefits available before age 65).

12. Gross number of wife beneficiaries aged 62 and over, derived from male old-age beneficiaries (item 11) multiplied by proportions married. This is reduced for wives already included in item 11, and then is increased for wives receiving residual wife's benefit in addition to old-age benefit.

13. Deaths of insured male workers, derived from mortality rates applied to item 10.

14. Gross number of widows aged 60 and over, derived from item 13 by applying proportions of deceased insured male workers leaving widows, and using rates of termination due to mortality and re-marriage. This is adjusted in the same manner as item 12 to take into account widows entitled to old-age benefits.

15. Number of children of old-age beneficiaries, derived from number of old-age beneficiaries (item 11) by applying factors based on past experience.

16. Number of survivor children of insured workers, derived from total child population (item 1) by applying factors representing number of orphans of insured workers as proportion of total child population.

17. Number of mothers of child-survivor beneficiaries, derived from number of survivor children (item 16) by applying factors based on past experience; similarly, number of wife beneficiaries under age 62 of old-age beneficiaries, derived from number of children of old-age beneficiaries (item 15) by applying experience factors.

18. Number of survivor parents, based on factors representing number of eligible parents as proportion of total aged ineligible population.

19. Number of lump-sum death payments, derived from mortality factors being applied to insured population (item 10).

20. Disability incidence rates.

21. Number of disability beneficiaries, developed from incidence rates (item 20) applied to insured population (item 10), after adjust-

ment for the more restrictive "disability insured status" requirements, using assumed rates of termination due to death, recovery,
and attainment of age 65.

22. Number of dependents of disability beneficiaries, developed from
projections similar to those listed for dependents of old-age beneficiaries (items 12, 15, and 17).

23. Average primary insurance amounts for beneficiaries in current
payment status, projected from current averages to ultimate
averages, based on items 4 and 5.

24. Annual amounts of benefits, from appropriate proportions of
average primary insurance amounts (item 23) applied to numbers
of beneficiaries (items 11, 12, 14, 15, 16, 17, 18, 19, 21, and 22).
Proportions based on applicable fraction of primary insurance
amount, with adjustments for effects of family maximum provisions, actuarial reductions in benefits for "early" claims, increases in benefits for delayed retirement, and residual benefit payments.

Earnings Assumptions

The long-range OASDI cost estimates were based on level earnings
assumptions until 1971. This, however, did not mean that covered payrolls were assumed to be the same each year; rather, they rose steadily
as the population at the working ages was estimated to increase. If in
the future the earnings level should be considerably above that which
prevailed at the time of the estimate, and if the benefits for those on
the roll were at some time adjusted upward so that the annual costs
relative to taxable payroll remained the same as estimated for the
present system, then the increased dollar outgo resulting would offset
the increased dollar income. This is an important reason for considering
costs relative to taxable payroll rather than in dollars.

If the general level of earnings rises in future experience above that
assumed in the cost estimates based on level-earnings assumptions, and
if all other experience factors closely conform with the assumptions
made, then the cost of the program relative to taxable payroll would be
lowered. In other words, a saving would be generated that could be
utilized to liberalize the benefit provisions—or, perhaps more accurately stated, to keep them up to date. The reasons this occurs are
because of the method of computing the average wage for benefit
purposes over the potential covered lifetime (rather than, say, on the

final wage) and because of the weighted nature of the benefit formula.

In regard to the latter, as earnings increase (up to the maximum taxable and creditable amount), the tax payable rises proportionately, but the benefits being derived increase less than proportionately. For example, under the 1973 law, if a $300-a-month worker suddenly becomes a $400-a-month worker, his taxes rise by 33 percent; yet the benefit rate for an average monthly wage of $400 is only 21 percent higher than for a $300 wage; moreover, there is the further dampening factor that under these circumstances the benefit eventually payable would be based on less than a $400 wage in many instances, because some of the period of the $300 wages would be used in the calculations.

The same result of a reduction in the cost of the system—or a saving —arises in somewhat similar fashion when the maximum earnings base is raised, and the only benefit provision change is to extend the benefit table to the additional covered earnings merely by applying the lower factor at the upper end of the formula (20.0 percent) thereto.

It should be kept in mind that in the absence of automatic-adjustment provisions, although the element of the likelihood of rising earnings in the future represents a significant safety factor insofar as the OASDI cash benefits are concerned *if level earnings assumptions are used*, the reverse is the case as to any benefits in kind, such as medical care.

The cost estimates made before 1971 did not take into account the possibility of a rise in earnings levels, although such a rise has characterized the past history of this country. If such an assumption had been used in the cost estimates—along with the unlikely assumption that the benefit structure would not be changed—the cost relative to taxable payroll would, of course, have been lower. If benefits were adjusted to keep up to date with the cost of living and to reflect rising earnings trends, the year-by-year costs as a percentage of taxable payroll would be unaffected. In such case, however, the level cost would be higher, since under such circumstances the relative importance of the interest receipts of the trust funds would gradually diminish with the passage of time. If earnings consistently rise, thorough consideration would need to be given to the financing basis of the system because the interest receipts of the trust funds would not meet so large a proportion of the benefit costs as anticipated.

In a very real sense then, the use of a level earnings assumption was a safety factor in the cost estimates that would and could (and did) arise to offset any adverse experience of other actuarial factors (although its primary purpose, as indicated previously, was to keep the benefits up to date in the event of rising earnings levels).

The 1971 Advisory Council on Social Security recommended that the level-earnings assumption should be discarded in favor of using assumed increasing earnings. This was done on the grounds that it is more realistic and that it prevents the overstatement of the role of interest earnings of the trust funds. The author does not agree with these arguments against the use of level earnings if such practice is clearly understood (as has been described previously).

The use of rising-earnings assumptions in connection with a program which has static benefit provisions is incorrect, and deceptive of the true costs. It is inconsistent and unrealistic to use dynamic economic assumptions along with static benefit provisions. Nor is it reasonable, or proper, for the actuary to make assumptions that the benefit provisions will be dynamic and how they will change.

Nevertheless, a good argument can be made for using rising-earnings assumptions when the system is automatically adjusted, as to benefit levels and the maximum taxable earnings base, for changes in economic conditions. The advisory council supported such automatic adjustment, as had been recommended by President Nixon in 1969.

The problem with using rising-earnings assumptions over a long period of years is the sensitivity involved in the relationship between the assumed rate of increase in the earnings level and that in the Consumer Price Index, which affects the benefit level. When the basis was changed in late 1971, the assumptions made resulted in a large "actuarial surplus," and this was utilized to provide most of the financing for the 20 percent benefit increase legislated in 1972. More discussion of this matter is given in Chapter 10.

In deciding upon appropriate assumptions over the long range as to the rates of increase of earnings and the CPI, examination of the past data should be made. Of course, projection for the future from such data should not be made in a purely mechanistic manner but, rather, any changed elements or trends of significance should be taken into account. This does not mean that undue importance should necessarily be attached to any current situation. However, when the current experience differs significantly from the long-range assumptions decided upon, grading in the assumptions over a short period of years is logical.

Table 4.4 presents data on the rates of increase of total wages in covered employment (i.e., disregarding the effect of the maximum taxable wage base) and of the CPI since 1940. It should be noted that

TABLE 4.4

Comparison of Annual Rates of Increase of
Consumer Price Index and Wages in Covered Employment*
(measured from previous year to year shown)

Year	(1) CPI	(2) Wages	(3) Column (2) Minus Column (1)	(4) Ratio of Column (2) to Column (1)
1940.............	0.82%	5.55%	4.73%	6.8
1941.............	5.12	10.12	5.00	2.0
1942.............	10.72	13.15	2.43	1.2
1943.............	6.16	16.40	10.24	2.7
1944.............	1.66	8.34	6.68	4.0
1945.............	2.28	−2.59	−4.87	†
1946.............	8.45	5.18	−3.27	0.6
1947.............	14.41	16.45	2.04	1.1
1948.............	7.71	10.37	2.66	1.3
1949.............	−0.95	2.44	3.39	†
1950.............	0.96	6.41	5.45	6.7
1951.............	7.98	6.64	−1.34	0.8
1952.............	2.25	5.57	3.32	2.4
1953.............	0.79	6.48	5.69	8.2
1954.............	0.35	1.72	1.37	4.9
1955.............	−0.26	3.89	4.15	†
1956.............	1.45	6.28	4.83	4.3
1957.............	3.48	3.69	0.21	1.1
1958.............	2.77	2.30	−0.47	0.8
1959.............	0.79	4.99	4.20	6.3
1960.............	1.58	3.31	1.73	2.1
1961.............	1.07	1.42	0.35	1.3
1962.............	1.15	4.70	3.55	4.1
1963.............	1.24	2.86	1.62	2.3
1964.............	1.31	4.65	3.34	3.5
1965.............	1.67	2.51	0.84	1.5
1966.............	2.91	5.52	2.61	1.9
1967.............	2.83	5.67	2.84	2.0
1968.............	4.20	6.37	2.17	1.5
1969.............	5.37	6.56	1.19	1.2
1970.............	5.92	5.37	−0.55	0.9
1971.............	4.30	5.09	0.79	1.2
1972.............	3.30	6.60	3.30	2.0
1973.............	6.23	6.80	0.57	1.1
1974.............	10.97	6.49	−4.48	0.6

* Based on estimated *total* wages in covered employment (i.e., without regard to the effect of the taxable earnings base); excludes self-employment earnings.
† Not meaningful.
Source: Social Security Administration.

many factors affect the trend of such wages besides the general economic ones and the war conditions. For example, the composition of the coverage of OASDI has changed considerably over the years (but note that the diverse effect of covering the self-employed beginning in 1951 is eliminated by considering only wages). Also, it should be observed that a general economic law is that the differences between increases in wage remuneration (cash wages plus fringe benefits) over increases in the price level are an indication of increases in productivity.

Both the absolute and relative differences between the annual rates of increase of wages and the CPI have fluctuated widely over the years. This occurred often for obvious reasons, such as the effect of wars and their cessation, business depressions and booms, and imposed wage and price controls and the aftermath when removed.

The official actuarial cost estimates made in 1972–73 assumed that earnings would increase at an annual rate of 5 percent in all future years (after a short grading-in period) and that the CPI would increase at an annual rate of $2\frac{3}{4}$ percent. In addition, these estimates included a safety margin of $\frac{3}{8}$ percent per year applicable on a compound basis to the benefit outgo for all years until 2010. This safety margin was intended to be applicable for all the various elements considered in the actuarial cost estimates. If it is assumed to apply only to the CPI element, then it could be stated that the CPI was assumed to increase at an annual rate of $3\frac{1}{8}$ percent until 2010 and $2\frac{3}{4}$ percent thereafter.

Such estimates made in 1974 included no safety margin and used the same assumption as to earnings, but a level 3 percent assumption as to the CPI, which by and large averaged about the same as the previous one if the entire safety margin is assumed to be applicable to the CPI element. These assumptions, which involve about a 2 percent difference in the two rates and a ratio of such rates of 1.67 to 1, seem reasonable *if the experience of the last three decades is projected to continue in the future, although with some slight closing of the spread between them.*

The two expert groups of actuaries and economists, appointed in 1974 by the Advisory Council on Social Security and the Senate Finance Committee, respectively, particularly examined the assumptions as to future changes in prices and wages. The Advisory Council group concurred, although not unanimously, in the 5-percent and 3-percent set of assumptions as to wage and price increases in the long run, although expressing the thoughts that the 2 percent differential might be somewhat too large and that the level of both the wage and price increases might be somewhat too low. The Senate Finance panel used a 6-percent and 4-percent set of long-range assumptions, although it believed that a differential of 1¾ percent would have been as equally reasonable as the 2 percent one used.

The official cost estimates contained in the 1975 Trustees Report shifted from the 5-percent and 3-percent assumptions to 6-percent and 4-percent ones for the long-range, but had higher, grading-in assumptions in the first few years.

But is it reasonable and desirable to make such a direct projection of the past? The author believes that such spread will be diminished over the long-range future, not primarily because of the experience in the 1970s when, on the whole, the two rates increased in about the same manner, but, rather, due to other factors that seem to be of a permanent nature and represent real changes from the past. These include the following factors that will tend to bring the trends of the two rates closer together:

1. The growing scarcity of raw materials and the higher prices relatively that will have to be paid to the developing countries which supply them.
2. The costs to promote ecology, since cleaner air, water, and general environment requires more expense to produce a given item.
3. Changes in life styles and attitudes, so that workers are more concerned with leisure and pleasant working conditions than productivity and income (i.e., the lessening importance attached to the work ethic).
4. The increasing proportion of service industries, for which productivity increases are more difficult to achieve.
5. The decreasing proportion of the remuneration of employees that is paid as cash wages, with more as fringe benefits, so that the difference between increases in cash wages and increases in the CPI will be lower than such increases between total remuneration and the CPI (i.e., productivity increases).
6. The decreasing average workweek, which results in less rapidly increasing *annual* wages, on which benefits are based.

As a result, the author believes that the spread between annual increases in earnings and in the CPI over the long-range future will not be as large as is currently assumed in the official actuarial cost estimates. Such assumed differential should, the author believes, be somewhere between 1 and 1½ percent. If this were to be done, the result would be higher costs than shown in the official estimates—and likewise a benefit structure which would go out of control over the long range by providing benefits much higher relative to final wage than is the case currently or in the near future.[10]

Rather than assuming that earnings increase continuously forever—and thus reach astronomical levels in terms of dollars—it would seem more prudent to project earnings for only a decade or so (for which reasonable predictions can be made), and then to assume level earnings. Or else it should be assumed that, after a few years, earnings and the CPI rise at the same rate.

General Methodology for OASDI Cost Estimates

The long-range actuarial estimates for OASDI involve, as a first step, projections of the total population of the United States, including not only the 50 states and the District of Columbia but also Puerto Rico, the Virgin Islands, Guam, American Samoa, and armed forces and civilians temporarily outside the United States, since all these categories are affected by the provisions of the system. The basic population projections, subdivided by age groups and sex, are prepared for five-year time intervals.

Certain subpopulation groups are obtained from the basic population projections by applying projected percentage factors obtained from consideration of past data and trends. Among the more important subpopulations derived are the "covered population" (persons having any OASDI-covered employment during the particular year), the "insured population" (persons fully or currently insured, or both, in the middle of the particular year), the married male population aged 62 and over, and the female population aged 60 and over, subdivided according to marital status.

The basic cost quantities—taxable payrolls, tax receipts, and benefit expenditures—are projected from these subpopulations and from average earnings and benefit patterns. As a final step, the projected trust fund balances are obtained, using the given tax rates and the hypothesized interest rates. Similarly, "level costs" or "average costs" can be obtained to give a summarized view of the actuarial status of the system.

The procedure may be considered in slightly more detail. First, in

---

[10] Calvert, *New Realistic Projections.*

respect to computation of taxable payroll, the earnings assumptions when applied to the covered population produce the "credited payroll," covered annual earnings not in excess of the earnings base prescribed by law. The credited payroll is then adjusted to reflect (1) the lags in actual payment of taxes from the time the earnings were received and (2) the employer taxes on individual wages in excess of the earnings base for persons working for more than one employer during the year. Such earnings are not creditable for benefits, and the employee taxes on them are refundable (through being claimed on the income tax return); the employer taxes on such earnings are not refundable.

The numbers of old-age or primary beneficiaries (retired workers) in current payment status come from the total insured populations over the minimum retirement age, after reduction for individuals who are earning more than the earnings test permits. Average "primary insurance amount" patterns computed with reference to the patterns of average earnings, when applied to this group, give total old-age benefit disbursements. Special treatment, however, is necessary to recognize the actuarial reductions in benefits applicable for those claiming benefits at ages 62 to 64.

Application of the proportion of the males married to the number of male old-age beneficiaries in current status gives the gross number of wife beneficiaries in respect to retired workers. This gross number, however, must be adjusted for wives who have already been included as old-age beneficiaries on the basis of their own earnings. For the latter group, allowance is made for those cases where the wife's full benefit exceeds her primary benefit, so that the difference is payable as a partial wife's benefit. The total disbursements for wife's benefits are obtained by multiplying the numbers of such beneficiaries by the average benefits. The full amount, when payable, is 50 percent of the primary insurance amount. A lower average is, of course, used for wives who receive only a partial wife's benefit because of having a primary benefit based on their own earnings. Further, reductions in the wife's average benefit are made to allow for women who are under age 65 when their husbands retire. This group is assumed to apply for the actuarially reduced wife's benefit payable at ages 62 to 64 at their earliest point of eligibility.

The widow's benefit is the primary insurance amount of the deceased worker and is payable upon attainment of age 65 if the widow has not remarried, or at a reduced rate if first claimed at ages 60–64.

The number of widow beneficiaries is obtained by computing the number of widows created annually from deaths among the male insured workers. These widows are then projected by mortality and remarriage rates. Comparison of the overall results with the appropriate subpopulations is made so as to assure consistency. Just as in the case of wife's benefits, an adjustment is necessary to allow for widows who have acquired primary benefits on the basis of their own work history. Adjustment is necessary for those claiming benefits at ages 60 to 64, since "actuarial reduction" is applicable to widow's benefits (and also for disabled widows at ages 50–59).

The number of child beneficiaries of old-age beneficiaries is obtained by multiplying the number of old-age beneficiaries by appropriate ratios from the actual experience, subdivided by age groups. The number of child survivor beneficiaries is estimated from the total child population by projecting the proportions of such children who are orphans of insured workers. These proportions are obtained through intermediate steps involving the use of life-table techniques to estimate the total orphan population in the country in various future years, with further adjustment to develop the proportions having insured parents. Allowance has been made in these factors for the lower mortality both of married males as compared with total males and of insured workers as compared with other persons. The disbursements for child's benefits are obtained by multiplying the numbers of such beneficiaries by the average benefits, which are computed by taking into account the trends in the primary insurance amounts and the proportion of the primary insurance amount received, depending upon the number of children in the family.

The mother of a child receiving child's benefits is eligible for so-called mother's benefits. The number of such beneficiaries is obtained by multiplying the number of child beneficiaries arising from male insured workers by a factor derived from actual experience. This factor reflects the important fact that many of these mothers engage in substantial employment and so forego their benefits because of the earnings test. The average mother's benefit is determined from the appropriate average primary insurance amount and the proportion that the mother's benefit represents of the primary insurance amount, after allowance for the effect of the family maximum provision on the combined child's and mother's benefits for a particular family.

Lump-sum death payments are obtained by computing the numbers of deaths among the insured population in a particular year and multiplying them by the average payments, which are derived from the average primary insurance amounts, taking into account the effect of the maximum provision for lump-sum death payments.

Monthly disability benefits are payable to persons having the required insured status. Supplementary dependents' benefits are also available for spouses and children, under the same circumstances as for old-age beneficiaries. Disability incidence rates, by age and sex, are applied to the estimated insured populations to obtain the new cases. These are then projected by termination rates (for death, recovery, and attainment of age 65) to yield the disability beneficiary roll.

The disbursements for disability benefits are obtained by applying average primary insurance amounts to the derived numbers of beneficiaries. The number of wife and child beneficiaries in respect to disability beneficiaries, and the total amount of their benefit payments, are derived in a manner paralleling that used in respect to old-age beneficiaries.

It is much more difficult to select reasonable assumptions for disability cost estimates for a new program than to make assumptions for programs providing only retirement and survivor benefits. The latter are influenced by such factors as mortality and retirement rates that can be accurately estimated within a relatively narrow range of variation. On the other hand, rates of becoming disabled and rates of mortality and recovery for disabled persons are subject to wide fluctuations, being affected by such elements as interpretation of the definition of disability, economic conditions, public awareness of the benefits available, and psychological outlook of the covered persons. In fact, it has been stated, quite properly, that the potential disability costs can be determined only by instituting the plan and then studying its experience. But this must be qualified to the extent that the early experience is not necessarily sufficient to give a complete, accurate picture—as many past disability experiences have evidenced. Even after a number of years of operation, the experience of a disability benefits plan can change drastically, due to economic conditions or other factors, as has been so in the case of the DI program since 1970 (as will be discussed in more detail in Chapter 10).

Determination of OASDI Tax Schedule

The OASDI tax schedule is reviewed from time to time to determine whether it should be revised because of the actual experience or because of any modifications deemed appropriate in the assumptions used in forecasting experience. A similar review is also undertaken when major amendments in the benefit or other provisions are under consideration.

The first step for reviewing the schedule of tax rates is to estimate the disbursements for benefit payments and administrative expenses for many decades in the future. The next step is to convert these figures into percentages of taxable payrolls for the various years to determine what the yearly rates would be if the financing were solely on a "pay-as-you-go" basis.

The third step is to compute the average cost of the benefits and administrative expenses, expressed as a percentage of taxable payroll over the valuation period. From this, there is deducted the estimated average equivalent of the interest earnings on the amount in the trust fund as of the date of calculation, expressed as a percentage of taxable payroll. Then there is added the corresponding figure representing the expenditures necessary over the years to build up the trust fund balance so that its size at the end of the valuation period is equal to one year's outgo.

Finally, there is computed the estimated average equivalent of the tax rates, which is the percentage of covered payroll that is equal to the arithmetic average of the tax rates for all years in the valuation period. If this estimated level equivalent of the tax rates differs considerably (more than any empirically decided-upon margin of allowable deficit or surplus, as the case may be) from the estimated net level cost of the disbursements, then adherence to the present financing basis for OASDI requires a compensating change in the tax schedule. This same procedure is applied not only when the existing system is being reviewed but also when a "package" of proposed changes is being examined.

Table 10.8 and 10.9 present data on such valuations for OASDI in previous years, while Table 4.3 has shown these results for certain recent years in terms of dollars on the present-value basis.

chapter 5

Directions and Issues in OASDI

In considering possible future developments of the OASDI system, it may be stated broadly that there are three philosophies of what role a social security program should play in a nation's economic and social life. At one extreme are those who may be termed to be of the laissez-faire philosophy. They, in essence, believe that there should be no social security program—and certainly not on a social insurance basis. Instead, they believe that people should be completely self-reliant and take care of themselves (or have their family do so) when some economic risk befalls them. Under our Judeo-Christian culture, this philosophy is extended so as to have any unmet needs taken care of by private charity or, failing that, by governmental relief or public assistance programs, possibly involving considerable stigma on the recipients.

The laissez-faire philosophy is held by relatively few persons or, at least, it is not widely asserted publicly these days. Besides the moral and ethical questions of stigmatizing large numbers of persons who, for one reason or another, have not been able to provide adequately for themselves, there is the criticism against this approach that it can often produce the opposite effect from what its advocates really desire.

If there would be an extensive and fairly liberal public assistance program—which is what would likely occur in our highly industrialized, urbanized, politically active society in the absence of a social insurance program—many people would not bother to save through the private sector. To do so would not be productive, because any private pension or other income from savings would, in many cases, only be deducted from the assistance payment otherwise available, and total income would not be affected. Thus, the incentive to take care of one's self would be destroyed or greatly diminished for many.

At the other extreme are the expansionists, who sincerely believe that full economic security for those who can no longer obtain their financial support from current earnings should, for the vast majority of such persons, be provided by governmental programs. This result would, according to this philosophy, largely be accomplished through a greatly expanded social insurance program.

At the extreme, under this philosophy, the OASDI system would be extended to the point where virtually all economic needs for those affected by any long-term social risks would be provided. The benefit level would be raised such that, for the vast majority of beneficiaries, the benefit would approximate the most recent take-home pay. The expansionist philosophy of social security, if followed, could lead to the virtual elimination of private-sector activities in the economic security field.

The third philosophy may be called the moderate one. Moderates believe in the complementary roles of social insurance and the private insurance system, and believe that a governmentally imposed fully expanded social security system would produce undesirable results. They believe that full economic security provided in this manner would be bad for the character and moral fiber of the nation. This moderate philosophy holds the view that the level of benefits and the scope of protection should remain about the same *relatively* as at present. This would mean that benefits should be adjusted upward from time to time to reflect rises in prices and that the taxable earnings base should be similarly adjusted to reflect rises in wages.

The moderates also point out a serious related problem if the expanionist goal of providing virtually all economic security through the governmental sector is achieved. Such procedure would result in a significant decrease in capital formation through the private sector, since there would no longer be large pools of investments through private pension plans and life insurance companies. In turn, this would place more and more reliance on the government to fill these capital needs and thus inevitably more governmental control of business and industry.

These philosophies are by no means equal in their number of adherents or in their importance, nor, except between the two extreme philosophies, is it always possible to determine exact boundaries separating them. Nevertheless, the future development of the OASDI system will be influenced by the relative acceptance of these philosophies.

SPECIFIC DIRECTIONS FOR DEVELOPMENT

Future changes in the OASDI program will probably take various directions. New developments may occur in benefits, the maximum taxable and creditable earnings base, the earnings test, retirement age, coverage, definition of disability, earnings of married women, equal treatment of men and women, tax rates, and in many other areas.

Benefits

Probably the most important element from the standpoint of cost and economic effect in the OASDI program is the general benefit level. For present retirants at age 65 or over, the benefits now average about 31 percent of recent gross earnings for those with earnings at about the maximum creditable amount; such married retirants with wives at least age 65 get benefits of about 47 percent of pay. Based on the automatic-adjustment provisions in the law, if prices and wages rise in the future as may be expected, the general benefit level, as well as the taxable and creditable earnings, will move upward as a result of periodic adjustments.

Under these circumstances, the aforementioned ratio will soon rise significantly, reaching 40 percent for nonmarried persons and 60 percent for married couples. This increase will be the result of the faulty operation of the automatic-adjustment provisions, unless this is corrected.

In addition to the changes in benefit level to keep up to date with prices, there may be proposals for drastically raising the benefit level, possibly by as much as 50 percent, probably in gradual steps. This could be accomplished by increasing the factors in the benefit formula and by changing the method of calculating the average wage so that it is on a "final earnings" basis. This can be accomplished by granting more dropout years, or similarly using the average wage in the last or highest five years, rather than a lifetime average. This would mean that within the range of earnings covered by OASDI, single workers would get benefits of about 60 percent of final pay, and married workers about 90 percent of final pay, which would be very close to their former take-home pay. If this procedure were followed, it could, of course, largely eliminate the function of private pension plans and individual savings for old age.

Still other proposals have been made with regard to changing the automatic-adjustment procedure for benefit amounts. As was indicated in the appendix to Chapter 4, the present method possesses the potential danger of running out of control and producing inordinately high benefit amounts in relation to prior earnings. Beneficiaries on the roll would continue to have their benefits adjusted by changes in the CPI, just as at present, under all the proposals to be described hereafter.

One proposal to remedy this situation is to limit the adjustment of the factors in the benefit formula to the *smaller* of the increase in the CPI, or 50 percent of the increase in the earnings level, instead of merely being based on the increase in the CPI as would be done for beneficiaries on the roll.

Another solution to this problem would also be along these same lines of "decoupling." Under this approach, beneficiaries on the roll would continue to have their benefits adjusted according to changes in the CPI, but the benefit formula would be changed in a different manner. In particular, it would be expressed as a dollar amount plus a percentage of average monthly wage (AMW), such as $95 plus 43 percent of AMW. This formula would rather closely approximate the amounts currently derived from the present benefit formula. The adjustment of the benefit formula under this approach would be made merely by increasing the dollar amount annually according to changes in the general wage level, as is done under the current automatic-adjustment provisions with regard to the taxable earnings base.

Still another solution to the difficulties arising under the present automatic-adjustment procedure would be to index all past earnings credits so that they would be expressed as a proportion of the maximum taxable earnings base in the particular year. Then, the AMW would be computed on a relative basis, such as for a particular individual being 78 percent of the maximum, and this figure would be applied to the current earnings base. Then each year in the future, if wages increased and the maximum taxable earnings base was adjusted upward in the same manner as at present, all the benefit amounts would correspondingly rise as, for example, the AMW used in the benefit formula always being 78 percent of whatever the base became. Naturally, under this procedure, the benefit formula would be a percentage of the indexed AMW plus a uniform dollar amount, which would be dynamically adjusted in future years for changes in the earnings level. Such a benefit formula would initially be something like $92 plus 29 percent of AMW if it is desired to maintain about the same relative benefit level as is presently being paid.

Yet another approach in using the indexing procedure would be to index the earnings recorded for each past year according to either the *estimated* average earnings of all persons in covered employment in that year or the *actual* average covered wages in the first quarter of that year expressed on an annual basis. The latter basis is that used in the automatic-adjustment procedure applicable to the maximum taxable earnings base (for example, see Table 3.6 for the actual past data for such average wage).

As an illustration, suppose that the earnings record of a particular individual is to be indexed up to 1980 and that the average covered wage in the first quarter of 1980 is at the rate of $9,600 per year. Then, if the actual credited earnings in 1972, for example, were $8,000, this would be indexed up to $12,347—$8,000 times the ratio of $9,600 to $6,220 (derived from 4 times the quarterly figure shown in Table 3.6). The indexed earnings for all the various past years would be obtained in similar manner and would then be used to compute an AMW just as under present procedures. The benefit formula would be revised along the lines indicated previously and, for 1976, might be $95, plus 29 percent of the first $900 of average indexed monthly wages, plus 20 percent of the remainder of such average wage.

The 1974 Advisory Council on Social Security recommended this approach in a slightly modified form, so as to phase-out the minimum-benefit provision, by proposing a benefit formula of the following type: 100 percent of the first $134 of average indexed monthly wage, plus 29 percent of the next $766 of such average wage, plus 20 percent of such average wage in excess of $900. This formula gives the same results as the previously-mentioned one for average wages of $134 or more.

If any of these decoupling procedures involving indexing is adopted, it would probably be necessary to continue the present method of computing benefits as an alternative, so that nobody is penalized by the changeover. The present method would be gradually phased out if the benefit formula as applicable to future retirants and other claimants were frozen in its present form—that is, with the benefit factors not being increased for changes in the CPI.

An important side effect of any of these decoupling proposals is that the anomaly that younger workers have unduly high benefit protection as compared with that for similar older workers would be corrected. Such correction could be accomplished in other ways if decoupling is not done—for example, by a provision preventing younger workers from having a higher PIA than can be obtained by long-service workers covered since 1956 (or before).

Taxable Earnings Base

Closely related to the question of the benefit level is the maximum earnings base subject to taxes and creditable for benefits. This is an area of great controversy. One school of thought would argue for maintenance of this maximum base at the same relative level as it is under present law for 1975 ($14,100), and as it will be automatically adjusted thereafter in accordance with changes in the general wage level. Others might argue that the base should be decreased somewhat, or not be allowed to increase for a few years, so that it would maintain the same position as had been held when the base was changed to $3,600 in 1951, $4,200 in 1955, $4,800 in 1958, $6,600 in 1966, $7,800 in 1968, and $9,000 in 1972. Those bases covered the full earnings of about half the regularly employed male workers—or, viewing it from another aspect, about 80 percent of the total payroll. As earnings rise in the future, according to this theory, the maximum base would be advanced from time to time in a proportionate manner, as has been done since 1951, when the base was set at $3,600.

The remaining school of thought would increase the earnings base to a level such that virtually all except the very highest paid workers would have all their earnings covered, as was the case with the original $3,000 base in the late 1930s. The required base would, in 1975, have had to be about $20,700, which relative level the proponents would recommend reaching gradually over the next few years, and which, by 1977, would have to be about $24,900. Such a proposal, when interrelated with that for a sizable increase in the benefit level, would mean that virtually all workers could derive sufficient economic support from the OASDI system so that little supplementary savings for old age, either on a group or on an individual basis, would be necessary—other than perhaps home ownership.

At one point in its deliberations, the 1974 Advisory Council recommended increasing the earnings base to $24,000. This action was taken merely to provide additional financing to bolster up the deficiency situation of OASDI. Later, this proposal was rejected, when it was realized that the level of the earnings base plays such an important role in the extent to which the private sector can provide part of the economic security for the people of the nation.

Interestingly, the labor movement opposed such a sharp increase in the earnings base. Bert Seidman, the social insurance expert of the AFL-CIO, has said that such a move is not justified "now or even a long time in the future," although stating that there may be a need for a gradual rise (AFL-CIO, Labor News Conference, January 15, 1975). He went on to propose a government subsidy to solve the financial problems of OASDI.

Retirement Test

Another important area where changes may occur in the OASDI system is in regard to the earnings or retirement test. If public opinion on desired changes were measured by the number of bills introduced in Congress, the popularity leader by an overwhelming margin would be the repeal or liberalization of this test. In the past the congressional committees responsible for OASDI legislation have recommended only moderate changes in this provision (largely, to keep the dollar figures in it up to date with changing earnings levels—as the automatic-adjustment provisions will do in the future), apparently recognizing that most of the public criticism has been due to misunderstanding. Furthermore, most interested national groups, such as labor organizations and business associations, have always strongly favored such a test.

The major reason for the earnings test is that the OASDI program is designed to provide benefit protection against presumed loss of earnings arising from the risks covered by the program. This basis, insofar as retirement benefits are concerned, naturally differs from private insurance, which necessarily provides annuities at a prescribed fixed age. The test is a condition of eligibility for benefits and is not a prohibition of benefit payment (or, for that matter, a prohibition against working).

Cost considerations are also important in connection with the earnings test. The increased cost of eliminating it is substantial, being about 0.4 percent of taxable payroll on a long-range basis, while the increase in the rate of current outgo would be about $4 billion a year.

Paying benefits to fully employed persons is not considered socially necessary. On the other hand, to pay partial benefits or even full benefits to those in part-time or low-paid employment is desirable. The improved earnings test provided by the 1972 amendments goes a long way toward eliminating inequities and anomalies. It provides some incentive for aged persons to engage in partial employment and to "taper off" as they become older.

Those who argue for the elimination of the earnings test do so on several grounds.[1] First, they assert that the taxes plus accumulated interest belong to each person individually and purchase his own benefits, so that he should get them at age 65, and the system should not "profit" by his continuing to work and not get benefits. This point is countered by the fact that the taxes are not accumulated on an individual-equity basis and that the risk insured against and for which the financing under the tax schedule in the law is developed is the risk of retirement after age 65. Admittedly, the underlying philosophy on which this argument is based is violated to some extent by the test not applying at and after age 72, which was the result of political compromises.

Second, the argument to eliminate the earnings test is made on the grounds that people would be encouraged to work thereby and that they need the additional money in order to have enough to live on. Countering this is the fact that only about 10 percent of those over age 65 have any significant earnings at all, and many of these earn far less than the maximum possible for full receipt of benefits. It would seem that many aged persons who cannot be gainfully employed use the earnings test as perhaps an unnecessary alibi to explain their not working. Moreover, if some people need substantial earnings to supplement their OASDI benefits to live on, then it would seem that the entire benefit level is too low for the vast majority of the aged who cannot work.

Third, it is argued that the earnings test is unfair because it does not take into account unearned income, such as private pensions and investment income. To do so would change the nature of the OASDI

---

[1] For a vigorous exposition of this viewpoint, see Senator Barry Goldwater's article, "This Law Robs Our Senior Citizens!" in *The Reader's Digest,* August 1974, which was discussed in Chapter 2 as to the underlying nature of the OASDI taxes and the resulting individual equity-social adequacy aspects thereof.

program from social insurance to public assistance. Moreover, such a change would probably have the opposite effect of what advocates for elimination would want since the result would be far less private savings. Unless one could amass a very large income from private savings or private pension plans, why would one want any private-sector income since it would only result in a reduction in the OASDI benefit payable?

Fourth, the advocates of eliminating the earnings test deny that such action would have the high cost stated. They assert that after elimination, many people would work far more and would pay more OASDI taxes and more income taxes, too. In the author's view, this effect would be relatively small and really of no relative significance. As indicated previously, relatively few persons over age 65 not now working seem to have the possibility of doing so under any circumstances. Even for those few now working, not many seem to restrict their earnings so as to fall just below the maximum allowable for full benefit receipt.

There are still other ways that have been proposed to solve or lessen the "problems" associated with the earnings test. The 1 percent delayed-retirement increment inaugurated in the 1972 amendments was enacted for this purpose. Some persons advocate increasing the rate of the increment from such a "niggardly low" level to a higher rate. If such rate were to become as large as 10 percent, it would have the same cost effect as if the earnings test were eliminated. In other words, the increment would then be at the actuarial-equivalent level.

Still another proposal along these lines to soften the "inequity" of the earnings test is to eliminate the employee tax after age 65. The "logic" of this is that the persons affected should not be penalized twice, by paying taxes and by not receiving benefits. This approach ignores the fact that the taxes paid "purchase" larger eventual benefits through the 1 percent increment and generally through a higher average monthly wage for benefit purposes resulting. The cost of this proposal is about equivalent to the cost of increasing the delayed-retirement increment from 1 percent to $2\frac{1}{2}$ percent.

Another possible liberalization of the earnings test would be to reduce the present proportion of benefits withheld for earnings in excess of the annual exempt amount. Such reduction could, for example, be only $1 of benefits for every $3 of excess earnings, or even $1 for every $4. This could be done for all such excess earnings or for only a band thereof. Some people view this proportion as a "tax" on such excess earnings and assert that the present basis is like a 50 percent tax rate, which is unduly high.

The problem with this change is that it results in paying partial benefits to persons with high earnings who have by no means retired. For example, consider a husband and wife both over age 65 with a family benefit of $500 per month. If the annual exempt amount is $2,520, and the proportion is $1 for $3, then some benefits would be payable as long as annual earnings are less than $20,520. This situation would seem peculiar and illogical to some people.

Retirement Age

The minimum retirement age, too, is a matter of considerable significance. Just as in the case of the earnings test, there is strong popular pressure for lowering this age. From a logical standpoint, considering the improvements in health conditions and mortality of aged persons that have occurred in the past and that are likely to occur in the future, it could well be argued that the retirement age should be gradually increased in the future. This has been done in a few countries, even though it is politically difficult. It is not impossible that such action might occur at some future date in this country, especially if great breakthroughs occur in the field of medical care for the aged. Such a change could greatly lessen the financial problems facing OASDI at the close of 1974, part of which arose from the projected future demographic trend of lower fertility.

Nonetheless, at the present time the trend seems to be in the opposite direction. The miniumum retirement age for men was reduced to 62 by the 1961 act, but with actuarially reduced benefits. The strength of this movement to lower the minimum retirement age arose from the fact that in certain areas of the country, there were relatively high levels of long-term unemployment among workers just below age 65, in large part because of automation, and these were not covered by the unemployment insurance program. Further, as the argument goes, making this change will have no cost effect on the program. Underlying this argument is the thought that making available reduced retirement benefits at an earlier age will not generally result in voluntary early retirement or in changed employer retirement policies. If such is not the case, however, there could be very significant effects on our national economy through loss of production by having a reduced labor force, so that the absence of cost considerations may not be the controlling factor.

In the event of high levels of unemployment at the older ages or of employers compulsorily retiring workers at ages below 65, there may be pressures to lower further the minimum retirement age and, at the same time, to reduce or even eliminate the actuarial reduction factors. This may be necessary so that benefit adequacy will not be too greatly decreased. The higher cost of the system would, of course, have to be met from the national product in the form of larger taxes from covered workers and employers. It can be argued that this is feasible, as well as equitable, since increased productivity can absorb this cost and should be used first for this purpose.

There may also be developments in the direction of lowering the minimum eligibility age for widows who do not have eligible children in their care below the present age-60 limit. The problem is particularly serious for those widowed at the older ages or those whose last child ceases to be eligible when they are not quite old enough to qualify for widow's benefits. Proposals have been made from time to time to lower the minimum eligibility age or to provide for a continuation of mother's benefits after the last eligible child has reached age 18. These proposals, however, involve both significant cost considerations and matters of equity and consistency in comparison with the situation for women workers, who must wait until age 62 to be eligible for benefits.

Coverage

Probably all students of social security, whether they be of the moderate or expansionist philosophy, believe that all gainful workers should be covered under OASDI if at all administratively feasible. Over the years since the system began operations in 1937, through one means or another, this goal has now been virtually achieved.

At present, the only significant categories not covered are civilian employees of the federal government under a retirement system of their own, some state and local government employees, low-paid or very irregularly employed farm and domestic workers, low-earning self-employed workers, and unpaid family workers. From one viewpoint, railroad workers are not covered under OASDI, but in fact from a financing standpoint and to a considerable extent from a benefit standpoint, they really are covered by virtue of the RR system.

The low-income groups of farm and domestic workers and self-employed persons who are not covered are relatively small. Administrative difficulties would seem to preclude any attempt to extend coverage further to these categories. In actual practice, even present coverage compliance and enforcement is not nearly complete, and the federal government is not doing all that it really should to obtain the complete coverage under present law.

Also, it may be noted that in a real sense, coverage of these groups will automatically be extended in the future as general wages rise. The fixed-dollar requirements for coverage mean that a growing proportion, asymptotically approaching 100 percent, will be covered over the years. For example, in the domestic-worker area, coverage depends upon having at least $50 of wages from the particular employer in a quarter. In the mid-1950s, this generally represented about ten days of work, while now it is about three days, and some decades from now it may be only one day, so that even the most casual workers will be covered.

The case for OASDI coverage of federal civilian employees under a retirement system is the clearest of all. There are no constitutional or administrative problems whatsoever. The need for such action is obvious—some federal employees have gaps in their OASDI coverage and thus reduced OASDI benefits, with no corresponding benefits from a government retirement system, if they have short, intermittent federal service, while others receive overly large dual benefits.

Clearly, the logic for such coverage of government employees under OASDI is great; if the government requires private employers to be under OASDI even though they have an adequate pension plan of their own, why should not the government do the same thing with respect to its own employees? But the practical political facts of life are that such coverage cannot be achieved. The unions and other organizations of federal workers are strongly opposed to such coverage, largely because of the dual-benefits "bonanza" that is taken advantage of by many long-service workers and because such organizations would have less influence in the fringe-benefits area if part of the protection were transferred to OASDI.

About one third of all employees of state and local governments are not covered under OASDI, because their employing units have not elected to be covered or because the employees themselves do not want to be covered (for the same reasons as are applicable to federal employees). Most, but by no means all, such noncovered employees have coverage under a retirement system of their governmental unit. Constitutional reasons prevent the federal government from compelling these governments to be covered under OASDI.

A practical way to extend coverage completely to state and local government employees does, however, exist. It would be perfectly legal and constitutional to cover (and tax) compulsorily all such employees directly (as is done for personal income tax). The tax rate could either be at the self-employed rate or at the combined employer-employee rate. There are precedents for both the self-employed rate (namely, ministers and American-citizen employees of international agencies and foreign governments) and the combined employer-employee route (namely, tips unreported to the employer).

Persons engaged in unpaid family work (defined as employment in other than maintaining and operating the home, usually work on small farms) number relatively few. There seems no great problem here, especially since many so involved are children who have no need for current coverage and will, in any event, very likely be covered in other employment when they become older, or wives who will have benefit protection through their husband's earnings record.

With the growing impact of the women's liberation movement, a new approach in the area of OASDI coverage has been suggested. Earnings credits (on which OASDI taxes would be paid) would be made available to all homemakers. This could involve either voluntary individual coverage election (which would have problems of antiselection) or compulsory coverage (which would entail significant administrative problems of compliance enforcement). The amount of the presumptive earnings to be credited and taxed could either be uniform for all (which would lead to problems as to the proper level at which it would be set) or optional, depending upon individual choice (which would have problems of antiselection).

Another type of change that has been talked about for many years has been the so-called "blanketing-in" of persons aged 65 or over (or, alternatively, aged 72 or over) for the minimum OASDI benefit. This is argued for on the grounds that this group has been treated unfairly in contrast to the many beneficiaries who have received benefits based on covered earnings but, from an actuarial standpoint, have "purchased" only a small proportion of their benefits. On the other hand, the proposal is opposed on the basis that it would destroy the incentive to extend and maintain contributory coverage, since some groups (such as farm and domestic workers) might prefer not to contribute and yet receive the minimum benefit.

The financing of the blanketing-in proposals would be accomplished by several alternative procedures—completely from the funds of the OASDI system; completely from the General Treasury; or partially from each of these sources. One such dual financing basis would have the General Treasury make a lump-sum payment with respect to each blanketed-in person that would equal the maximum cumulative combined employer-employee contributions that would have been paid with respect to a person receiving the minimum benefit, plus compound interest. Some persons strongly oppose any such financing that relies in whole or in part on payment by funds of the OASDI system, on the grounds that this would be a "raid" on the trust fund and that it would destroy the basic contributory principle.

The arguments in favor of a permanent blanketing-in of the uninsured age become less strong as time goes by, since the group involved decreases steadily in numbers. The blanketing-in of persons who became age 72 before 1968 for a lower-than-minimum benefit was a step in this direction, but it seems most unlikely that this will be extended to other than the closed group involved.

Definition of Disability

Another type of change is in connection with the definition of disability, which now is on a relatively strict basis and involves a waiting period that is, in practice, six months. Proposals have been made that the definition should be changed from a "permanent and total" basis to an "occupational" basis—at least for those at the older ages (50 or 55 and over). The occupational basis would be either with regard to the last regular occupation or, more strictly, for inability to engage in substantial gainful activity requiring skills or abilities comparable to those required in a past activity in which the person had engaged with some regularity over a substantial period.

Also, proposals have been made to shorten the waiting period— say, to three months (or less). If the waiting period were to be reduced to only one week, the program would be broadened so as to include temporary disability benefits on a nationwide basis (thus replacing the few state programs in this area—see Chapter 15).

Other changes that have been proposed with regard to disability benefits are the elimination of the recency-of-employment requirement (20 quarters of coverage out of the last 40 quarters) and paying full-rate benefits to disabled wives (and husbands) and widows (and widowers), regardless of age—rather than significantly reduced benefits for disabled widows (and widowers) aged 50 or over.

Earnings of Married Women

Still another change that has been actively proposed—and, in fact, was in the House version of the 1972 legislation, but was dropped in conference—is to give more recognition to the earnings of married women in computing benefits. One way of doing this (as was contained in the House bill) is to combine the earnings record of the husband and wife and pay a benefit of 150 percent of the resulting primary benefit if this produces a larger amount than the sum of the two separate primary benefits. Another approach is to pay the woman worker the larger of the benefit based on her husband's earnings record and the benefit based on her own record plus a fraction (say, one fourth or one half) of the smaller of the two such benefits, instead of the present basis of paying only the larger of the two benefits.

Another proposal is to pool the earnings of the married couple each year, even though only one might have earnings, and to divide them equally between the husband and wife. In the event of death of one spouse, the other would inherit the entire earnings record. Dependents and survivors benefits for aged spouses and widows would be eliminated.

Equal Treatment of Men and Women

It would be possible, with relatively little additional cost, to have completely equal treatment of men and women under OASDI. All references to sex would be eliminated. Husbands and widowers would not be required to be dependent on their wives. Young widowers with children would be eligible for father's benefits. The additional cost would be nominal because of the earnings test (almost all young widowed fathers will be in substantial employment) and the antiduplication provision (almost all men will have a larger benefit on their own earnings record than that arising from their wife's record).[2] Apparently, this change will be completely achieved, either by future legislation or court decisions, as a result of the Supreme Court decision in March 1975.

---

[2] Provisions would be needed to take care of the situation where the man is under another governmental plan, such as CSR, but not under OASDI.

Other Changes

In any program as complex as OASDI, there are a great many relatively minor areas where extensions of protection may be urged. Among these are such matters as providing benefits for such other dependents as brothers and sisters, disabled dependents (such as wives and widows) regardless of age, and so forth. Space, however, does not permit considering in detail each of these changes. No doubt some of them will be adopted in the future. However, from a cost standpoint, and in overall economic significance, they are not so important as the items previously discussed.

The possible developments in the benefit protection afforded by the OASDI system have been discussed without mention of the necessary financing. Each time legislative activity has occurred in the past, Congress—particularly the controlling committees concerned—has carefully considered the cost aspects of the proposed changes. The enacted provisions have been financed fully, according to the best actuarial cost estimates available. Thus, Congress has attempted to maintain the system on a self-supporting basis by keeping benefit costs very closely in balance, over the long range, with tax income.

TAX RATES

In recent years there has been much public discussion as to how high the OASDI tax rates should ultimately go. Secretary of Health, Education, and Welfare (now, Senator) Abraham A. Ribicoff stated before the Senate Committee on Finance in 1961 that the ultimate rate should never exceed 10 percent for the employer and employee combined, and the late Senator Harry F. Byrd heartily agreed with him. Since then, many other persons have supported this view. It may be noted, however, that in the Senate debate on the 1964 amendments, Mr. Ribicoff (as a Senator) voted for a hospital-benefits proposal that, combined with OASDI, had an ultimate rate of 10.4 percent and has subsequently never referred to this 10 percent limit.

The scheduled ultimate OASDI rate (i.e., exclusive of the HI rate) for the employer and employee combined did not exceed 10 percent until the 1971 amendments were enacted, when a rate of 10.3 percent was called for in 1976 and after, as compared with the previous 10.0 percent. Interestingly, scarcely any mention was made at that time about the first breach of the 10 percent limit. As the result of the 1973 amendments, the combined employer-employee OASDI rate is scheduled to be slightly under 10 percent (9.9 percent actually) for the next 35 years, but the ultimate rate of 11.9 percent in 2011 and after will far exceed this "limit," and the 1974 official actuarial cost estimates indicate that a much higher rate will be necessary.

On the other hand, the counterargument has been made that there is no "magic" about this arbitrarily selected 10 percent figure and that a higher rate would not be deleterious to the national economy. In this connection it may be noted that the contribution rates for social security programs in many foreign countries (including such "free enterprise" ones as West Germany) are well over 20 percent.

One change that will most certainly be necessary in the OASDI program in the next few years is a strengthening of its financing, especially as to the tax rates for the long-range future. As has been indicated in Chapter 2, the 1974 official actuarial cost estimates indicated a significant actuarial deficiency. In part this occurred because of changes in the demographic assumptions, and in part because of the economic assumptions and the manner in which they affect the automatic-adjustment provisions as they apply to benefit increases. An even larger deficit would be shown if less optimistic economic assumptions were used, as was done in the 1975 official actuarial cost estimates.

If the automatics are changed to a basis that will result in stability, in one of the ways discussed previously in this chapter, increases in the tax schedule will still be necessary. However, they will not be nearly as large as if present law as to the automatics were left unchanged.

In considering the sizable increase in OASDI costs, and thus tax rates, from about 2010 on, there should be kept in mind that an at least partially counterbalancing factor is present. Demographic trends, especially if zero population growth tendencies prevail, indicate a much higher proportion of aged in the population then, and this is the basic reason for higher OASDI costs. However, offsetting this is the fact that the proportion of children will be correspondingly lower. It may be said in broad terms that the higher cost of providing for the nonproductive aged will tend to be counterbalanced by the lower cost for supporting dependent children.

Closely related to the matter of the maximum desirable tax rate for the OASDI system is the size of the maximum earnings base. For example, based on 1974 earnings levels, a tax rate of 10 percent combined with an earnings base of $23,700 has about the same aggregate tax impact (i.e., brings in the same amount of income) as a rate of 11 percent on a $13,200 earnings base—although, of course, with different impacts on low-earnings and high-earnings persons.

Or, to consider the situation from another viewpoint, compare the relative OASDI tax cost to employers in 1974 as it actually was with what it would then have been expected to be when looking ahead from the time the original law was enacted in 1935. The actual rate for 1974 was 4.95 percent—65 percent higher than the rate of 3 percent prescribed by the 1935 act for 1949 and after. However, the $3,000 earnings base in the 1935 act covered 92.0 percent of the total payroll at that time, while the $13,200 base covered only 85.8 percent of the actual 1974 payroll. Accordingly, the employer in 1935 looked forward to an ultimate tax cost of 2.76 percent when measured against total payroll (3 times 0.920), whereas the actual tax cost was 4.25 percent (4.95 times .858), or 54 percent higher.

A proposal has been made to increase the maximum taxable earnings base only as it is applicable to the employer tax. This would, of course, have considerable impact in providing additional financing, since there would be no additional benefit liabilities created, as is the case when the base is raised for the worker taxes. The effect of such a change for the employer tax is to provide additional financing of about 6.6 percent relatively—e.g., it could finance an across-the-board benefit increase of this amount.

Interestingly, the net long-range financial gain to the OASDI system of increasing the earnings base for *both* workers and employers is about the same as if this is done only for employers. In other words, the long-range cost of the additional benefits resulting is about the same as the long-range value of the worker taxes. This again indicates that increasing the base is as much of a benefit-level policy matter as it is a financing matter. Of course, for the HI system with its uniform benefits, raising the taxable earnings base, whether for employers only or for both employers and workers, results in a full gain from a financing standpoint.

It seems probable that the careful cost consideration by Congress will continue in the future. Accordingly, the most significant development likely in connection with the financing is whether the program should remain self-supporting from solely the taxes of workers and employers, or whether, as is common in some countries, and as some persons urge here, a specific government subsidy should be introduced.

Such a government subsidy has been argued for on the basis of a more equitable distribution of the cost of the program among the taxpayers. It is stated that the present OASDI taxes are in certain respects regressive, in that they are a uniform percentage on the first $14,100 (in 1975) of earnings. In rebuttal, however, it can be pointed out that the taxes are not regressive when they are considered in combination with the benefits, which are heavily weighted for persons with the lowest earnings.

As a practical political matter, it could be argued that a general government contribution might become necessary if the tax rate rises to a relatively high ultimate figure, made necessary by liberalizations in the general benefit level. Such liberalizations, combined with extension of the program into other areas, could readily result in an overall ultimate cost of 20 to 30 percent of payroll. Although such cost seems high in contrast with that for the present program, advocates of such an expansion can point to the fact that costs of this magnitude are involved in the more liberal private pension plans now in existence in this country and in many foreign social insurance systems. Diverting part of the cost of the OASDI system to a government subsidy from general revenues would tend to obscure its cost implications, although in most instances the covered individuals would still be paying the tax indirectly in large part.

A government subsidy for OASDI is advocated on several other grounds. First, it is pointed out that many other countries have this source of financing in their social security programs. Second, it is argued that the existence of a contributory national pension system results in a substantial reduction in public assistance costs, and accordingly, the government should share some of these savings with the social insurance program.

Third, the argument is advanced that, just as the employer generally does in private pension plans, the government should pay the cost of the unfunded initial accrued liability for past service credits applicable when the system began. This, over the long range, would result in the government subsidy meeting about one-third of the total cost.

A fourth argument for a government subsidy is that the "welfare" element, the portion of benefits not actuarially-purchased by the employer-employee taxes, should be financed by general revenues. This principle, as well as the preceding one, is much easier to state than to apply in practice.

Still another argument that has been advanced in favor of a government subsidy is that this is now present in the payments that meet the costs of the gratuitous military service wage credits, the special age-72 benefits, the HI benefits for the initial uninsured group, and the matching payments for the SMI enrollee premiums. However, in rebuttal, it should be pointed out that the first item is really being paid as an employer cost, the next two items are for limited closed groups, and the last item is for a program not involving payroll taxes, a subsidized voluntary insurance plan.

The Committee on Economic Security, which made the studies underlying the initial Social Security Act, recommended a government subsidy for its proposed contributory old-age benefits plan. Such subsidy would not have been initiated until 1965, about three decades after the inception of the program, but would eventually have met about one-third of the annual outgo. President Roosevelt, however, rejected this approach in favor of the self-supporting basis, and Congress concurred. He did this perhaps in view of the public criticisms of his unbalanced budgets (not very large in the light of the current situation!) and his desire not to be criticized for proposing legislation with built-in large federal subsidies for long-distant future years.

In the author's view, the foregoing arguments for a government subsidy for OASDI, or in fact any payroll-tax-supported social insurance program, are either not valid or not convincing. The self-supporting principle, whereby the system is completely financed by visible payroll tax rates, seems much more desirable since it clearly shows to the citizenry the real costs of the program. It should never be forgotten that taxes used to obtain general revenues to provide the government subsidy are paid by people in the long run. Although there may be some difference in the incidences of taxation for various taxes, these tend to gravitate in the same direction over the long run.

Supporters of government subsidies to social insurance programs often forget or disregard this fact that the government is not an independent, self-sufficient entity. For example, in a minority statement in the report of the 1974 Advisory Council on Social Security, a member associated with the National Council of Senior Citizens, argued in favor of a government subsidy to the Social Security system in the following manner: "Thus, in the long run, I see a social security system covering both cash benefits and health insurance financed partly by employer contributions, partly by employee contributions, and partly by contributions from the government in recognition of society's stake in a well-functioning social insurance program."

In reading that statement, one would think that "the government" or "society" was something completely separate, with its own financial resources, from the employers and workers, who constitute almost the entirety of the nation's population.

Advocates of a government subsidy to the OASDI system have had their position somewhat strengthened by the change in the railroad retirement system in October 1974 that provides a significant amount of its financing through monies from the General Fund of the Treasury (see Chapter 12). Others would argue that this is not necessarily a precedent, because the subsidy of a small group by the whole body of taxpayers is different than the latter attempting to subsidize themselves.

Because of the argument of some economists that the employer payroll tax for OASDI is directly passed on to employees in the form of lower wages than would otherwise have been paid, some persons have suggested that it should be eliminated. Instead, the corporation income tax would be used to help finance OASDI. Quite obviously, other taxes would then have to be increased to fill in the gap in general revenues thereby created. This proposal seems just another strategy to make less obvious to the general public what the true cost impact of the OASDI program really is.

The matter of the tax rate for self-employed persons relative to that for employees has been considered from time to time—especially as both the rate and the earnings base have risen. The tax burden on the self-employed is particularly evident since their tax is customarily paid in a lump sum quarterly, when income tax payments are made—rather than by the "painless" method of withholding from pay, as is done for employees. Although the self-employed OASDI rate is scheduled to be "frozen" at its present level so that it will more closely approximate the employee rate (as the latter rises according to the schedule in the law), there may be a question as to whether this is really equitable. Conversely, there may be moves to lower the self-employed rate to the employee rate, as has been the case under the hospital insurance program since its inception in 1966.

Martin Feldstein, professor of economics at Harvard University, has advocated a position as to OASDI financing in his paper "The Optimal Financing of Social Security," published in the Harvard Research Reports series, that goes to an opposite position from current-cost financing. In fact, what he advocates goes far beyond full-reserve financing.

Feldstein proposes that an extremely large fund should be built up within a decade, by more than doubling the OASDI payroll tax rates. Then, this fund would be of sufficient size so that no payroll taxes would be necessary in the future, since the interest income will then be sufficient to meet the outgo of the system. Such a result would be accomplished by having the fund's investments earn the "social rate of return," which would be about 13 percent, representing the actual average rate of investment earnings of business corporations *before* income tax. Quite obviously, the excess of such rate over what the government normally pays on its debt obligations would be a hidden subsidy to the system.

The author believes that the Feldstein proposal, which certainly can be classified as unique and innovative, is completely impractical and undesirable, as well as having no popular appeal to the people of the country. It would seem impossible to convince the current workers to pay such high tax rates so that future generations of workers would have none to pay. Also, there is serious question as to whether the prescribed size of the fund (a mere $600 billion) would be sufficient as an interest-earning endowment fund to finance the program over the long range, even at the artificially high interest rate of 13 percent. Significantly higher tax rates than double the present ones, if they are to be levied for, at most, a decade, would probably be necessary to build up such an endowment fund.

The basic idea behind the Feldstein proposal seems to be to strengthen the capital structure of the nation. If this is to be done, it would seem far better to do so outside the OASDI system, which should have as neutral an effect on the economy as possible, and should not be used as a general economic tool.

All in all, students of social security can expect to have some interesting years ahead—not only in analyzing the developments as they occur but also in predicting what will come next.

ISSUES

Social insurance is a subject that has never suffered from a lack of debatable issues, especially when individuals embracing different philosophies come together. Four issues are included here as being representative of current debate. These include the question of who pays the tax, whether or not the tax is regressive, whether OASDI should be partially financed from general revenues, and whether or not OASDI is a good buy for a young person.

Who Pays the Social Insurance Taxes?

Over the years, economists have considered the very interesting topic of who really pays social insurance taxes. To the man on the street, and even to members of Congress, this matter seems quite simple—the law clearly states that the employee pays a certain social security tax and that the employer matches it, while the self-employed pay a rate somewhat more than that of the employee.

But to economists, life is not that simple. Great intellectual exercise can be obtained from speculating on the real incidence of the social security taxes. All sorts of answers can be derived in theory. Moreover, the use of statistics (possibly also with elegant simulation exercises on electronic data processing machines) can make the matter even more challenging and add the appearance of scientific precision.

Is the employer tax passed along to the consumer in the form of higher prices? Or is it really paid by the employees through lower wages than otherwise? Or does it result in lower profits? Or is it paid partially by the federal government (and thus by the general taxpayer who is largely in the employee category), because employer social security taxes are counted as a business expense and thus result in lower employer income taxes?

Then, as to the employee tax, does the worker really pay it himself? Or does the employer pay it as a result of wage demands being higher on account of such tax deductions? After all, many employees are consciously or unconsciously economics-minded. What they really consider is not their gross pay, but rather their take-home pay.

Many economists currently are of the view that the employee taxes are really part of the total compensation of employees. Therefore, they conclude that the employer social security taxes are paid by the employees. There is question, on grounds of general reasoning, whether this can actually be proven. In the field of mathematics, it is not possible to accomplish a solution for every problem posed. In fact, it can be shown in some cases that solutions are impossible—for example, squaring the circle. The same situation also prevails in the field of economics.

The incidence of taxation—although a fascinating subject and problem—is not, in this real world, susceptible to precise solution, because the initiation of a tax will often, if not generally, change the situation completely. For example, with the high personal income tax rates that we now have on upper incomes, salary increases for executives are made relatively large, so as to produce a given net result after taxes. Similarly, when self-employed professional people establish their fees, they consider not the gross amount to be asked but rather the net result desired.

For the moment, accept the conclusion of many economists that social security taxes are, in the long run, borne by employees in the aggregate. However, then, one cannot logically or reasonably jump from that conclusion to the conclusion that each employee is himself really paying the employer tax levied on his earnings. Some economists take that jump in the dark, because they do not give adequate consideration to the mechanics of fringe benefits generally—both social-insurance and private-sector benefits.

In private employee benefit plans, the employer cost is usually expressed as an average percentage of payroll, but this does not by any means indicate that the employer is paying the same relative amount for each employee. In actual practice, it is usually the case that much more proportionately is paid by the employer for older employees, especially under pension plans and group life insurance plans, although the reverse can occasionally be the case (e.g., maternity benefits). Similarly, the employer cost, although stated as an average for all his employees, may differ widely as between various departments or branches of his business. Yet, it is not customary to allocate such fringe-benefit costs on an experience basis between the segments of the firm.

In the same way, under the social security program, assume that in the aggregate for the country as a whole, the employer taxes are really part of the remuneration of the employees and are therefore borne by them. Then, no reason exists to assert that the employer tax is allocated to each employee directly and individually. Instead, it seems more reasonable and logical to consider that the high-cost employee (the older one, or the low-paid one, or the one with dependents) receives a much higher amount from the employer tax than the amount of his own tax. Since the system is a nationwide one with universal pooling, such allocation can occur beyond the walls of the particular employer.

Thus, his employees might really be said to have allocable employer contributions from other firms. Or, conversely, the employees of a particular employer might, on this risk-allocation basis, have less assigned to them in the aggregate than the amount of taxes paid by their employer.

A vivid example of the difficulty in determining who is really paying the social insurance taxes is in connection with the railroad retirement system (which is dealt with in detail in Chapter 12). From its inception in 1937, the payroll tax was shared equally by the employer and employee. In 1973, the scheduled total rate (including the tax rate for the hospital insurance portion of Medicare) was 21.2 percent, or 10.6 percent for each party. Beginning in October 1973, as a result of collective bargaining between management and labor, the employee rate was reduced to the same amount as under the social security system (5.85 percent) and the employer rate was correspondingly increased (to 15.35 percent).

At first glance, this would seem to indicate that some of the employee cost of railroad retirement (namely, 4.75 percent of payroll) was shifted to the employer. But really it was not, because at the same time the railroad labor unions agreed to take only a 4 percent wage increase for an 18-month period, whereas most wage increases then being given averaged about 9 percent for such a period (i.e., at an annual rate of 6 percent). Thus, the employer cost for wages and RR tax was about the same as if the RR tax basis had remained essentially unchanged, and a 9 percent wage increase had been given. At the same time, the employee net take-home pay (gross minus RR tax) also was about the same, although he did obtain a financial advantage insofar as income tax is concerned.

The foregoing discussion has referred only to the incidence of the employer tax and how it should logically be allocated to employees on a risk basis, rather than directly and individually proportionately. It may be reasonable to assume that the employee tax is paid entirely by each employee individually, although even this assumption is not necessarily and absolutely so. In fact, legally it has no foundation; the tax is a liability of the employer who is permitted to deduct it from the employee's wages.

Similarly, the self-employed can logically be considered to be a combination of worker and employer. Any excess that they pay over what the employee tax would have been on their earnings can be presumed to be employer taxes, which are pooled for the benefit of the system as a whole.

Regressivity of Social Insurance Taxes

Critics of the payroll taxes that are used to finance social insurance programs are quick to point out that they are regressive (and therefore presumably undesirable, so that this financing basis should be changed).[3] Their argument points out, correctly, that the tax rate is a constant percentage up to the maximum taxable earnings base. Thus, the same tax rate is paid by all persons earning under the base, whereas those earning above it pay an *average* rate that is lower. For example, the average tax rate for a person earning five times the maximum base is only one fifth that of a person earning the base amount or less. Obviously, say the critics, this is an extreme, deplorable situation of regressive taxes.

But when both sides of the coin are considered—both benefits and taxes—OASDI is definitely *not* regressive. Looking merely at the tax side is playing ostrich. The benefits are heavily weighted in favor of the low-paid workers, as is discussed in Chapter 2 (and, as far as HI is concerned, the benefits are uniform, regardless of earnings level). Moreover, no significance can be attached to the fact that the average tax rate for those earning above the base is lower than for those at or below it, because no benefits rights are created on earnings above the base.

The critics of the payroll tax also make the argument that for many people the social security taxes are larger than the personal income tax. This seems to be an irrelevant point because they are not really comparable. The same statement could be made, especially for low-income persons who pay little or no income tax, if the illogical comparison of automobile expense and income tax were made. The whole intent of the progressive income tax is to have the low-income group pay little or no income tax.

OASDI and HI benefits can properly be considered as just another type of service and commodity that individuals are purchasing. The fact that the law compels them to make this purchase seems no more important than that they are compelled by a law of nature to consume

---

[3] See John A. Brittain, *The Payroll Tax for Social Security* (Washington, D.C.: The Brookings Institution, 1972).

food (which they must purchase). It seems democratic that the prices of goods and services should be the same for everybody, so that people are not subject to the stigma of being second-class citizens to whom government-required lower prices are applicable.

Those who argue that the social security payroll taxes are regressive have several solutions to offer. One is to increase the maximum taxable earnings base to a much higher level. In this way, the alleged regressivity would be reduced, although not eliminated. Such an approach seems undesirable, because it would unnecessarily expand the scope of social security benefits for the highest paid and thus diminish private-sector activities in the economic security field.

Another approach that is suggested by the critics of the payroll tax is to give special exemptions to lower income workers so that all or part of the payroll taxes that they paid will subsequently be refunded to them through the income tax return. For example, the taxes on the first $600 might be refunded for everybody, so that the *average* net tax rate paid would have a decreasing trend as wages increase. Or a basis can be developed so that the reduction applies only for the lowest income group and then gradually phases out as earnings increase.

But looking at the situation from the standpoint that social security is a type of financial service that individuals purchase, why should low-wage persons not maintain their dignity and feeling of personal pride and self-reliance by paying the same for it (as a percentage of their income) as does the next person?

The crux of the problem seems to be that those who favor so-called tax relief from the payroll tax for the poor do not recognize that the problem is on the income side and an attempt should be made to solve it directly and forthrightly—not merely by considering and acting upon only one of the expenditure items.

In early 1975, when efforts were made to combat the decline in the economy by providing massive tax reductions, one proposal was to include a social security tax reduction for low-income workers. The more general form of treatment suggested in the previous paragraph was, however, followed in the bill which passed the House. Specifically, for 1975 only, there would be a tax refund of 5 percent of the excess of (1) earned income up to $4,000 over (2) twice the excess of the individual's adjusted gross income (or, if larger, the earned income) over $4,000. The effect of this is to phase out the refund for earned income of $6,000 or over.

The House committee report was quite clear on the purpose of this proposal and its relation to the social security program. It stated that:

> It is appropriate to use the income tax system to offset the impact of the social security taxes on low-income persons in 1975 by adopting for this one year only a refundable income tax credit against earned income. Although the earned income credit may be viewed as a method to help compensate wage earners of low income families for much of the social security taxes they pay, your committee wishes to have it clearly understood that this provision of the bill is not intended to provide a way of reducing social security taxes paid by low income wage earners. (House Report No. 94-19, February 25, 1975)

The final legislation related only to families with children, but the tax refund rate was 10 percent, phased out at incomes of $8,000. As with many other "temporary" measures in the social welfare area, this provision may well be made permanent, rather than only for one year.

Should OASDI Be Partially Financed from General Revenues?

Some persons claim that the social security payroll tax is regressive, considering only the employee tax, and that therefore relief should be provided by having partial financing from general revenues, or what is euphemistically referred to as a "government contribution," but might better be termed a "government subsidy." Others go further and believe that the situation is doubly bad because the employee, in reality, pays the employer tax. The latter group suggest eliminating the payroll tax and substituting general revenue financing, preferably obtained by raising income tax rates. They assert that what they consider to be the myth of the "insurance" concept in the OASDI program is what is really thwarting their efforts and that if they can only destroy it, all will be well. Actually, as discussed in Chapter 1, the insurance concept is not a myth and is, in fact, one of the underlying strengths of the program. To destroy this concept would very likely result in the destruction of OASDI and change over to a public assistance program, with all the inherent weaknesses of such an approach.

Some persons who favor significant expansion of OASDI so as to have much higher benefit levels strongly oppose the views of those who question its insurance principle and seek to weaken greatly the payroll-tax financing basis. Nonetheless, such expansionists favor the infusion of some government subsidy into the program, hoping that a little such subsidy (proportionately) will not weaken the insurance principle. Their reason for such a compromise suggestion is that the general level of the payroll tax is now so high that covered workers are complaining about this. Thus, any further benefit increases beyond those necessary to keep the benefits up to date with the cost of living will be difficult to accomplish if there is solely payroll-tax financing.

This is the reason why no government subsidy should be introduced into OASDI on a permanent ongoing basis. If the system is financed on a completely self-supporting basis in the future, as in the past, the covered workers and their employers will be fully cognizant of the costs involved, as a result of the observable direct impact of the payroll taxes. They can then decide, on an informed basis, just how much further expansion of the governmental program they desire. Thus, full financing through the payroll tax makes the cost of OASDI readily apparent and therefore serves as a highly desirable cost control.

Those who advocate a government subsidy for OASDI propose several different ways of doing so and also different rationales. One approach, which is based on aesthetic logic and also the practice of some foreign systems, is equal tripartite financing—that is, the government subsidy would be equal to 50 percent of the combined taxes from workers and employers.

Another approach rests its case on the "accrued liability for the initial group of covered workers" concept. According to this, the government should meet the higher cost involved for those who entered the system at the start at an older age as compared with the cost for young new entrants in the future. A parallel is sought to be drawn by those who advocate this approach with the situation under contributory private pension plans, under which almost always the employer meets the costs for the initial unfunded accrued liability. On the whole, this procedure would involve about the same amount of general revenues cost as the tripartite one.

A third approach is to attempt to separate the "welfare" elements from the "true insurance" ones, such as by assuming that the heavily weighted portion of the benefit formula is "welfare" and that the remainder is "insurance" that is actuarially purchased by the worker and employer taxes.[4] The latter is not so; the determination of what is

---

[4] The benefit formula for the primary insurance amount which is first applicable for June 1975 has, in essence, a flat amount of about $235 per month for insured persons with an average monthly wage of at least $650, plus about 25 percent of such average wage (both below and above $650). Or this can be

purchasable, considering different ages and family structures, is just not a precisely determinable matter. Again, this procedure would involve about the same amount of general revenues cost as the tripartite one.

Any of these proposals for a government subsidy would require large expenditures from the General Fund of the Treasury immediately —somewhere in the neighborhood of $25 billion per year initially and increasing steadily thereafter. Obviously, this would be quite a strain and jolt to the federal budget. So, the advocates of this approach often suggest a gradual phasing in to make their proposal more palatable politically and fiscally. For example, under the equal tripartite approach, the government subsidy might be 5 percent of the combined worker and employer taxes in the first year, 10 percent in the second year, and so forth, until reaching the desired goal of 50 percent in the 10th year.

Some advocates of a government subsidy assert this is nothing new and that it was recommended in 1934 by the President's Committee on Economic Security, to be first payable in 1965; President Franklin D. Roosevelt, however, overrode this recommendation before submitting the proposal to Congress. Such advocates also assert that, in fact, a government subsidy is already in effect. They point out that payments from general revenues are currently being made with respect to the cost of (1) gratuitous wage credits for certain military service, (2) hospital benefits under Medicare for certain uninsured aged persons initially blanketed-in, (3) uniform cash benefits for certain persons aged 72 and over who attained such age before 1972, and (4) the matching amounts with respect to the premiums paid for persons covered by supplementary medical insurance.

None of these instances is really a precedent for a government subsidy on a permanent, ongoing basis to the portions of the social security program that are supported by payroll taxes. The military service wage credits merely involve the government as the employer. The two blanketing-in benefit provisions for benefits for persons already aged when the new protection was added relate to special transitional groups that will be phased out over a period of years. Finally, the matching of the SMI enrollee premium is essential in order to have a *voluntary* insurance program with uniform rates that is a good buy for all persons eligible.

---

expressed for average monthly wages under $650 as follows: $92 plus 46½ percent of such average wage.

In summary, it seems to the author that it is very undesirable to inject general revenues into the financing of OASDI (or the hospital insurance program either) as a permanent matter. To do so confuses the economic picture as to what the program really costs and who is paying for it. It is pure deception if workers—and employers, too—are convinced by the expansionists that a government subsidy will come out of somebody else's pocket, and not their own, in the long run.

Does the Young Person Get His Money's Worth?

From time to time, individuals pose the question of whether OASDI benefits are a good buy for an individual as compared with what he could obtain by investing the OASDI taxes in a private insurance program. Invariably, because of the nature of OASDI, the individual who is at middle age or older when he first entered the program will receive far more therefrom than he could obtain under a private insurance program with premiums equal to the OASDI taxes.

When the young new entrant is considered, different analysts obtain quite different results. Some find that the young new entrant receives very poor treatment under OASDI, whereas others conclude that he is being fairly treated (even though he is not receiving the actuarial windfalls which the older persons receive). The reason for this wide divergency of findings generally rests entirely on the assumptions made. Some specific computations of this type are presented in the appendix to this chapter.

Probably the most important assumption is whether the analysis should be made only on the basis of the employee tax or whether the employer tax should be included as well. Quite obviously, under the latter approach, the purchasable benefits from the private source will be significantly larger, and the comparison with OASDI will be much more favorable for the private approach.

Many economists assert that the employer tax is really paid by the employee and should be so assigned. However, it seems more logical that any such comparison should be confined only to the employee tax. Even though the employer taxes might, in the aggregate, be considered as part of the remuneration of employees and thus fully assignable to them, it does not follow that the assignment should be on an individual-by-individual basis according to wages. Rather, it would be reasonable (as is done in private pension plans) to make such assignment of the employer tax on a risk basis (i.e., much more proportionately for older and high-cost workers than for younger and low-cost workers).

Other assumptions for such analyses are also important. For example, there might be considered only single workers who retire (if they survive) at a relatively advanced age. Under such circumstances, the purchasable annuity under private insurance would compare very favorably with the OASDI benefit. But this does not seem a fair approach, because there should be considered a broad spread of individuals with all types of family composition and all ranges of retirement ages. Similarly, comparisons should not be restricted solely to high-paid individuals.

Still another important assumption concerns what will be the future course of the benefit level. This is especially significant now that automatic-adjustment provisions have been incorporated in OASDI, so that an assumption needs to be made about the future trend of the cost of living (which controls the future benefit adjustments).

Another assumption—and one which is closely related to the previous one as to the future course of the benefit level—is the rate of interest to be used in making the calculations about what private insurance benefit protection can be obtained. Frequently, these comparisons are made on the basis of what private insurance could theoretically be obtained, rather than for actual policies, since the latter seldom (if ever) can duplicate exactly the OASDI benefit protection to be compared. If a low interest rate is used in the calculations, this will make the OASDI benefit protection appear much more favorable—and vice versa.

Moreover, there is an important relationship between the two foregoing assumptions—future level of OASDI benefits and interest rate. Some expansionists argue that the program is always a good buy for the younger worker, even if the combined employer-employee tax rates are considered, because there will be significant increases in the benefit level over future years as the automatic-adjustment provisions apply.

The error in their analysis usually lies in the fact that they select a relatively low interest rate, such as 4 or 5 percent, for their calculations. In all logic, however, they should use an interest rate of 8 or 9 percent to conform with the dynamic economic assumptions which they make in regard to increases in the benefit level. If this were done, then OASDI would be shown to be a poor bargain for young new entrants when the combined employer-employee tax is considered, but a reasonably good buy when only the employee tax rate is considered. After all, as long as OASDI is financed entirely by payroll taxes, it possesses no "magic machine" so that it can produce benefits that are an actuarial bargain for everybody when the entire tax rate is considered individually allocable to each employee.

On the other hand, some critics of the OASDI program develop assumptions under which the taxes will purchase much larger benefit protection under private insurance than is actually obtained under OASDI. Frequently, these comparisons use the combined employer-employee tax rate, which does not seem a valid approach.

Sometimes such a result—although of a much lesser degree of superiority of the privately based benefit over OASDI—can be shown when only the employee tax rate is considered. However, such comparisons are usually invalid because they are incomplete on account of ignoring certain factors such as the availability of dependents and survivors benefits, or by using an excessively high interest rate, or by making some other assumption that is not a reasonable one.

In summary, then, it is literally impossible to make a precise comparison of the value of OASDI benefit protection as against what could be obtained under private insurance by using the OASDI taxes as premiums. The general statement can be made, however, that the average young new entrant receives somewhat more than his money's worth under OASDI if one considers only the employee taxes which he pays. On the other hand, if one considers the combined employer-employee taxes (which is not really a valid approach), the reverse will be true.

As to self-employed persons, who pay somewhat more than the employee tax rate, OASDI is not a bargain for the young person who expects to be in the self-employment category during his entire working lifetime. But, in this case, the result can be rationalized by asserting that part of what he pays is really an employer tax, pooled for the benefit of all workers under OASDI (just as is the case with respect to employees).

The recent change in the *prospective* financing basis of OASDI to a current-cost approach (which, by and large, had been followed in the past) is relevant in the discussion of this topic. For about the next 35 years (until 2011), the tax rate will be 17 percent lower than the ultimate rate. Thus, new entrants during this period will fare somewhat better than those coming in later. Nonetheless, the conclusions drawn above are still valid for near-future new entrants, both when considering only the employee tax and when considering the combined employer-employee tax. Roughly speaking, a young new entrant at the present time on the average "pays" with the employee tax for about 70–75 percent of his benefit protection, while for the ultimate new entrant, this proportion will be about 90–95 percent.

APPENDIX

Comparison of Actuarially Purchasable Benefits with Actual Ones

Frequently, interest is expressed in the question of the relationship of the size of OASDI retirement benefits which could be actuarially purchased with the taxes to the actual amounts payable. Often, this is directed to the matter of whether the young worker gets his money's worth from the taxes that he pays.

This is an apparently simple question. But it is one which is very difficult to answer—perhaps even impossible to respond to in an accurate manner. For one thing, as discussed in this chapter, there is the important question as to whether, for an individual, employer taxes paid on his wages "belong" to him or whether only the employee taxes should be considered in the analysis. Then, too, the comprehensive and complex benefit structure of OASDI (with its heavy reliance on dependents' benefits, earnings test, and provisions preventing duplicate benefits) is difficult to analyze or match private insurance coverage against.

It is almost obvious that persons retiring in the early years of operation of the OASDI system received tremendous actuarial "windfalls" because of the necessary social-adequacy nature of the program. But consider now the extent thereof.

Under the original 1935 law, a person retiring at age 65 at the earliest possible date (January 1942) would have received a monthly benefit of $25 if he had maximum covered wages ($3,000 per year), and the employee taxes paid would have been $180 ($30 per year during 1937–39 and $45 per year during 1940–41). Based on the U.S. Total Males Life Table for 1949–51 at 3 percent interest (a reasonable rate then), the present value of the benefits as of January 1942 was $3,009 for this case. The accumulation of the employee taxes to January 1942 at 3 percent interest was $193. Thus, the employee taxes "purchased" only 6.4 percent of the benefits, and the individual received a "windfall" of $2,816.

Next, consider the case of a similar individual under the 1935 provisions, except that he had the minimum wages needed to qualify for benefits ($1 of wages in both 1941 and 1942, at a tax rate of 1½ percent, and a total of $1,998 of wages during 1937–39, at a tax rate of 1 percent). His benefit would have been $10 a month, and its present value was $1,204. Thus, the taxes accumulated at interest, amounting to $23, "purchased" only 1.9 percent of the benefits. The "windfall" for this low-earnings individual was $1,181, or only 42 percent of that for the maximum-earnings person.

The 1935 provisions never went into effect; and, instead, those of the "more socially adequate" 1939 legislation became operative for retirements after 1939. Consider the case of a man retiring at age 65 in January 1940, with a wife the same age. For the person with maximum covered wages, the monthly benefit was $41.20 for the worker and $20.60 for the wife ($30.90 if she became a widow). These benefits had a present value of $8,264 as of January 1940 (on the same basis as used in the previous example). At the same time, the accumulated employee taxes ($90 in total) amounted to $94, so that they "purchased" only 1.1 percent of the benefits, and he had a "windfall benefit" of $8,170.

For such an individual with the minimum amount of wages to qualify for benefits (with 6 quarters at $50 each), the monthly benefit was $10 for the worker and $5 for the wife ($10 if she became a widow). These benefits had a present value of $2,119 as of January 1940. The accumulated employee taxes ($3 in total) amounted to $3.15, so that they "purchased" only 0.15 percent of the benefits, and the "windfall benefit" was $2,116, or only 26 percent of that for the maximum-earnings case.

In actuality, beginning in 1950, the benefits were increased for the 1940 retirant and his wife (and now amount to $209.70 for the worker if he is still alive and to $104.90 for the wife or $209.70 for the widow). If the increases that actually have taken place were taken into account in the foregoing computations, the "purchased" ratio would, of course, have been even smaller (although not very much so because the same benefit rates were maintained for the first decade and because of the discounting effects of mortality and interest).

Some of the approximately 32,000 persons who were paid benefits for January 1940 as retired workers aged 65 or over are still receiving benefits. At the beginning of 1970, this group had dwindled to 373.[5] But, by an unusual circumstance, the beneficiary designated as being the first person to receive a social security check, since it bore the number 1, Ida Fuller of Brattleboro, Vermont, was still alive in September 1974, when she had her 100th birthday.[6] Her initial monthly benefit, for January 1940, was $22.54, which was close to the average benefit then awarded, and the one for August 1974 was $109.20. The total benefits which she had been paid through August 1974 amounted to $20,447.52, as compared with the total employee taxes she had paid of only about $22. Miss Fuller died in January 1975.

Next, consider the situation for a man with maximum covered wages in every year since 1937 reaching age 65 at the beginning of 1975 and retiring then. Only the OASI employee taxes will be considered since it might be said that the DI taxes "bought" the disability benefits protection which he had had, and the HI taxes would "buy" the HI benefits protection he will have in the future. This procedure ignores both the survivor-benefits protection that he may have had in the past and the considerable "forfeiture" that he would have had in the past if he had died without leaving dependents who would have received benefits on his wage record, which elements are at least partially counterbalancing.

The OASI taxes for this case have been accumulated at an assumed interest rate of 3 percent for 1937–49, 4 percent for 1950–59, 5 percent for 1960–64, and 8 percent for 1965–74 (which are rates reasonably approximating those generally available in these periods). The total accumulation as of January 1, 1975, amounts to $10,532.

---

[5] See Francisco Bayo and Margaret A. Lannen, "Mortality of Charter Beneficiaries," *Actuarial Note No. 78*, Social Security Administration, August 1972. The author estimates that only about 50 of this group were living in January 1975.

[6] Based on information from an Associated Press dispatch of September 7, 1974, and from the Social Security Administration.

The monthly benefit payable is $316.30 if the man does not have an eligible wife. Assume that the CPI will increase at an average of 4 percent per year over his future lifetime. The present value of his monthly benefits, including the effect of the automatic-adjustment provisions, using the U.S. Total Males Life Table for 1959–61 (the latest available complete official table) at 8 percent interest (a reasonable rate under present circumstances), is $35,908. Thus, his OASI taxes "bought" only 29 percent of his benefits, and his "windfall benefit" was $25,376.

If the man in the foregoing example had been married to a woman of the same age (with no benefit based on her own earnings), the present value of the benefits would be $63,569. Accordingly, only 17 percent of the benefits would have been "bought" by the employee taxes, and his "windfall benefit" was $53,037.

Individuals currently retiring with wage histories less than the maximum level in all past years back to 1937, of course, have lower "bought" ratios than those derived above. Even if the employer tax were counted as well (which does not seem proper analytical procedure), the current retirants will not have "bought" their benefits—or even close thereto. For example, if the man who does not have an eligible wife in the foregoing example had wages each year in the past of only half the maximum, his monthly benefit would have been $202.10 per month (i.e., 64 percent of the $316.30 for the maximum-earnings case). The accumulated value of his taxes would have been $5,266, and the present value of his benefits would have been $22,943. Thus, he would have "bought" only 23 percent of his benefits and would have had a "windfall benefit" of $17,677.

It will be noted that although the "bought" ratio is lower for the low-paid man than for the maximum-earnings case, the latter *still* has a larger "windfall benefit" in terms of dollars ($25,376 versus $17,677, so that the latter is 70 percent of the former). As was indicated in the discussion in Chapter 1, this situation can, from some aspects, be subject to severe criticism. If the windfall were computed on the basis of the combined employer-employee tax, the situation would be somewhat different—a windfall of $14,844 for the maximum-earnings case versus one of $12,411 for the low-paid one, or 84 percent as much.

Finally, consider the situation for young new entrants currently—namely, a male who is covered from age 21 in 1976 until age 65, with maximum earnings in all years. It is assumed that the interest rate is 6 percent, that wages rise at 5 percent per year, and that the CPI increases 3 percent annually. These economic assumptions are reasonably consistent with each other; the wage and CPI assumptions are those used over the long range in the official actuarial cost estimates made in 1974, while historically the interest rate has generally been about 3 percent higher than the rate of CPI increases. As to mortality assumptions, the U.S. Total Population Life Tables for 1959–61 rated down two years (to allow for mortality improvement in the future) are used.

It is most important to note that the assumption is made that the tax rates presently scheduled will be applicable. As discussed previously, the latest official actuarial cost estimates indicate that higher tax rates will be needed, especially in the long run. As a consequence, the resulting ratios of the value of taxes to the value of benefits are likely understated. This element is not of great importance for the current new entrant, because the increases in the tax rates that will apparently be required will be relatively small for a number of years and will be sizable only after about three decades.

The monthly benefit payable to this new entrant at the time he retires in 2020 will be $3,576 per month; his earnings in the year before retirement would be $119,100, yielding the reasonable benefit ratio of 36.0 percent. The accumulation of the employee OASI taxes to age 65 would be $293,130, while the present value of the benefits then if he does not have an eligible wife would be $466,878. Thus, he has "bought" 63 percent of his benefit, so that he would have had a "windfall" of $173,748. On the other hand, if he has an eligible wife of the same age, the present value of the benefits would be $841,524, so that he would "buy" 35 percent of his benefits and have a "windfall benefit" of $548,394.

It will, of course, be noted that if the employer taxes were included as well as the employee taxes, his "bought" benefit would have been considerably more than the actual one if he has no eligible wife, which will generally be the case in the long range, because most women will then have benefits based on their own earnings credits which are larger than the wife's benefit coming from their husband's earnings record. But it does not seem proper to so assign the employer taxes.

The foregoing analysis is, of course, an oversimplified one. Varying a number of factors would change the results significantly. For example, a later age of retirement than 65 would considerably reduce the "bought" ratios, but a lower age would have little effect, because of the actuarial reduction factors then applicable. Still another important factor is the interest rate.

Some people, in attempting to portray the OASDI program as a bargain for all persons, including new entrants, point out the presence of the automatic-adjustment provisions as providing a virtually unmatchable advantage. They inconsistently (and erroneously) use dynamic assumptions for wages and the CPI, but a low interest rate. If, in the foregoing case of a man without an eligible wife, an interest rate of only 4 percent had been used, the situation would be drastically changed. The accumulated OASI employee taxes would be $195,184, and the present value of the benefits would be $551,459. Thus, he would have "bought" only 35 percent of his benefit (instead of the 63 percent shown for the realistic interest rate of 6 percent). This comparison at 4 percent interest would make it appear that everybody always gets a bargain under OASDI, an impossible situation! Conversely, using the unrealistically high interest rate of 8 percent—that is, unrealistic in comparison with the wage and CPI assumptions—would "show" that people would be getting poor buys under OASDI; the "bought" ratio for the man without an eligible wife would rise well above 100 percent (probably to about 130 percent).

Still another important factor is that in the foregoing examples, the graded schedule of OASI tax rates in the future was used for the new entrant considered. Such a new entrant coming in after 1976 would pay considerably higher rates according to the tax schedule in the present law. The comparison might have been made on the basis of a level tax rate of 5.10 percent, the ultimate OASI employee rate in the December 1973 amendments. Then, the taxes would accumulate, at 6 percent interest, to $377,455 at age 65 in 2020, and the proportion of the benefit "bought" would be 72 percent for the man without an eligible wife and 40 percent for the man with a wife (as against 63 percent and 35 percent, respectively, under the tax schedule in the law).

But, as indicated previously, it seems likely that the scheduled ultimate tax rate is too low. The 1974 official actuarial cost estimates indicate that the ultimate OASI employee tax rate will have to be about 7.7 percent, instead of 5.1 percent. On this basis, the taxes would accumulate, at 6 percent interest, to $509,490 at age 65 in 2020, and the proportion of the benefit "bought" would be 109 percent for the man without an eligible wife and 61 percent for the man with an eligible wife.

This discussion of actuarially purchasable amounts as compared with actual benefits under OASDI can be summarized by saying that precise conclusions cannot be drawn in all respects.

It is, however, obvious that those retiring in the early years, and even decades, of operation have received significant "actuarial bargains" whether only their own taxes are considered or whether the combined employer-employee taxes are considered. Such "bargains" have been greatest in relative terms for the lower paid and for those with eligible dependents, but in monetary terms more of a "windfall" has gone to the higher paid (and also to those with eligible dependents).

When the long-range situation is considered for current younger workers and for new entrants, the situation is less clear. If only the employee tax is considered—as the author believes is the proper procedure—the younger workers receive their money's worth in average benefit protection and, in fact, somewhat more than this (i.e., they derive some of their benefit protection from the pooled employer taxes). However, if only high-salaried younger workers are considered, there is probably about a standoff—that is, on the average, their taxes approximately "purchase" their benefits.

PART III

Medicare

Part II examined the OASDI portion of the social security program in the United States. Part III will complete this picture by providing the same treatment to the health care provisions of Medicare. Part III begins with a description of the basic principles and present provisions of the Medicare program, and then traces the development of Medicare and explains the financing basis of the program. This is followed by a description of some of the possible future developments in Medicare. Finally, a separate chapter provides actuarial and statistical information for both OASDI and Medicare.

chapter 6

Basic Principles and Present
Provisions of Medicare System

The Medicare program, which was originally officially designated as Health Insurance for the Aged but is now termed Health Insurance for the Aged and Disabled, consists of two separate plans—hospital insurance (HI) and supplementary medical insurance (SMI). In popular usage, these plans are often referred to as Part A and Part B. The Medicare portion of the Social Security Act (Title XVIII) is divided into three parts, the first dealing solely with HI, the second dealing solely with SMI, and the third dealing with provisions common to both.

Just as was done in Chapter 2 in connection with the OASDI system, this chapter will consider the Medicare program under several broad headings: eligibility conditions, benefit provisions, reimbursement bases, and financing provisions. Not only will the present provisions as of the beginning of 1975 be described, but also reasons will be given as to why they were adopted.

The development of the Medicare system is presented in Chapter 7, and its financing principles are examined in Chapter 8. Appendix C includes a summary of the provisions of both parts of the Medicare program. Then, Chapter 9 is devoted to the consideration of possible future changes in Medicare.

BASIC PRINCIPLES OF MEDICARE SYSTEM

There are a number of basic principles of the Medicare system which, more or less, parallel those of the OASDI system, although there are important differences. Among those which will be discussed are the following: (1) the basic nature of the program, (2) benefits being based on presumptive need, (3) relationship with the floor-of-protection concept, (4) nonearnings related nature of the benefits, (5) relationship between individual equity and social adequacy, and (6) self-supporting contributory nature. Just as was the case in connection with the OASDI system, there is not complete agreement by all persons with these principles.

The HI program clearly meets the usual definitions of social insurance (see Appendix A). HI can be characterized as a program that has the following characteristics:

1. Administered by a government agency.
2. Financed by compulsory contributions (taxes) from the protected persons and their employers (except as to certain older persons at the start of the program, whose benefits are financed from general revenues and a small number of persons aged 65 or over who voluntarily buy into the program at self-supporting premium rates).
3. Provides benefits as a matter of right, without any means or needs test, on the basis of satisfying specified eligibility conditions as to age and length of coverage.

On the other hand, SMI does not meet the usual definitions of social insurance, although it may be so categorized by some individuals. Perhaps a better way of designating the SMI program is to call it a voluntary individual insurance program with government subsidy that is underwritten and administered by the government using private carriers to assist with the administration. SMI is a program under which each eligible individual, in effect, elects whether he wishes to participate and pay a premium in partial financial support of the program. If he so elects, then the federal government pays a matching amount at least equal to the enrollee's premium. SMI has some of the characteristics of social insurance, such as a broad pooling of the risk, administration by a government agency, and establishment by legislative action, but it lacks the compulsory-participation basis that is one of the prime characteristics of social insurance. Some might argue that an element of compulsory coverage is present in the "actuarial bargain" basis of the premium rate, due to the government subsidization thereof.

SMI differs significantly from private individual insurance in that the premium payment with respect to the protected person is not the actuarial equivalent of his benefit protection. This is the reason for the matching government contribution, which meets at least half the cost. This basis balances out the different risk levels involved as between persons aged 65 and over, who have differing insurance costs because of their variations in age and state of health, but for virtually all of whom the actuarial value of the protection is more than half of the total cost (i.e., more than the enrollee premium). Similarly, the matching government contribution with respect to the disabled who are protected by the Medicare program meets an even larger proportion of the cost, since this is necessary because of the higher average cost for this group and its greater nonhomogeneity than the aged group.

It would not have been possible to have this voluntary plan financed only on the basis of a uniform premium from all participants (or even separate rates for the aged and the disabled), because then antiselection would have entered in—the highest cost risks would have tended to participate, and the lowest cost risks would have tended to stay out. If a self-supporting premium rate were desired, a snowballing effect would have occurred. With each increase in the rates, those in good health would consider dropping out, and many would do so. Accordingly, it is necessary to have some second-party financial participation. Since no employer contributions could be involved in a current-risk plan applicable to retired persons, the only remaining course of action is for the government to participate in the financing.

With the participants being required to pay no more than half the cost of the program, it is a good buy for even the lowest cost risks involved—such as the person just beyond age 65 who is in good health. Under these circumstances, it is a good buy—not only when considered on a lifetime basis, but also (and necessarily) when considered on a year-by-year term insurance basis. From a purely practical approach, it would be unreasonable to establish a program like this that would provide lifetime protection at an attractive premium rate, but that could be purchased at less cost on a term insurance basis from other sources during the first few years after age 65. Under such circumstances, many short-sighted persons might adopt the latter course until they could enroll under SMI only at a greatly increased premium rate, and then bring strong pressure to bear for letting them come into the governmental system at the standard premium rate.

Certain medical expenses are excluded from coverage under both HI and SMI. The services must be for diagnosis or treatment of an illness or injury or for improvement of the functioning of a malformed body member. Accordingly, routine physical examinations, prescribing and furnishing of eyeglasses (except after a cataract operation) and hearing aids, routine dental work, and innoculations are not covered. Also excluded are services paid for by a governmental agency, such as the Veterans Administration; services for which there is no legal obligation, such as chest X rays provided by voluntary health agencies without charge; services required as a result of war; and services for cosmetic purposes (except to repair the results of an accident), for custodial care, or for personal comfort purposes.

Another major exclusion is for services covered by a workmen's compensation law, which, of course, is not too likely a situation for persons aged 65 and over and also for the recently covered category of disabled persons on the cash benefits roll for at least two years. Such workmen's compensation exclusion would be much more important if younger beneficiaries or shorter duration disability beneficiaries were covered under Medicare. If Medicare pays for such services first, and it is later determined that a workmen's compensation program has liability, the latter must reimburse Medicare for the benefits which it paid.

Medicare benefit coverage is generally restricted to services rendered in the United States, including American Samoa, Guam, Puerto Rico, and the Virgin Islands. However, under certain circumstances, benefits are available for services rendered in Canada and Mexico; these provisions will be described later in the separate sections on HI and SMI, since they differ as between these two programs.

HOSPITAL INSURANCE PROVISIONS

This section will first discuss the eligibility conditions for the hospital insurance (HI) portion of the Medicare program. After that, the benefit provisions, the provisions for reimbursement of the providers of medical services, and the financing will in turn be discussed.

Eligibility Conditions

The HI benefits are available to all persons aged 65 or over who are "entitled" to monthly cash benefits under either OASDI or the railroad retirement system (RR) and to all disabled beneficiaries under those programs (namely, disabled workers, disabled widows and widowers aged 50 and over,[1] and adult children aged 18 and over of retired, disabled, or deceased insured workers who were disabled before age 22) after they have been on the benefit roll for at least two years.

A special type of catastrophic coverage applies with respect to persons with chronic kidney disease who, regardless of age, are considered for Medicare purposes to be eligible as though they were disabled persons on the cash-benefits roll if they are (*a*) fully or currently insured on their own earnings record, or (*b*) entitled to monthly benefits, or (*c*) the spouse or dependent child of a fully or currently insured worker or of a person entitled to monthly benefits. Such kidney cases do not have the two-year waiting period that disability beneficiaries have, but rather HI coverage begins in the third month after the month in which renal dialysis began or, if earlier, in the month in which the transplant occurs. Such protection is only available for the person with the kidney disease and not for other members of the family. It is important to note that this special type of coverage is available for the afflicted family member of a worker who is actively employed at customary earnings. The term "dependent child" is not defined in the law, but it is interpreted as meaning the same as for monthly OASDI benefits.

HI benefits are also available to noninsured persons who were over age 65 when the program began operations in July 1966 and to such persons who attained age 65 in the first few years thereafter, and, beginning in July 1973, to uninsured persons aged 65 or over who voluntarily enroll and pay a premium rate that meets the entire cost of their protection. The group initially blanketed in receives the benefit protection on a "free" basis.

The term *entitled* when used in connection with OASDI and RR benefits has a technical meaning that is important to understand. Entitlement merely means attainment of the required age, possession of either the necessary insured status conditions or relationship to a person who meets such conditions, and filing of a claim. Thus, it is not necessary that the entitled individual actually receive the monthly benefits in order to be eligible for HI benefits. In other words, a person

---

[1] Equitably, a widow or widower becoming disabled at ages 60–64, whose OASDI cash benefit is the same as though not disabled, can qualify for Medicare eligibility after two years of being in a disabled status that would have resulted in entitlement to OASDI benefit if the person had been aged 50–59.

(or his eligible dependent) may have HI protection even though he is fully employed at high earnings, under which circumstances the OASDI earnings test prevents receipt of OASDI monthly benefits.

HI benefit protection is available for dependents and survivors of insured workers only if they are at least 65 years old (except when such dependents have chronic kidney disease, in which case—as mentioned above—no age requirement is present). Furthermore, as to such a wife, the insured worker must be at least age 62, and he must be entitled to benefits (by filing for them, even though he is not retired, or not yet age 65). Because of the usual differential in age between husband and wife, there will be many instances of insured male workers who are aged 65 or over (and thus have HI protection), but whose wives are under age 65 and do not have HI protection.

Eligibility for HI benefits ceases when entitlement to OASDI monthly benefits terminates. In the vast majority of the cases of persons aged 65 and over, termination of the various OASDI benefits that yield eligibility to HI protection ceases only upon death. It may be noted that although an OASDI monthly benefit is not payable for the month of death of the beneficiary, HI benefit protection extends up through the date of death. If a disabled beneficiary recovers from his disability, his HI protection terminates at the end of the last month for which he is entitled to cash benefits (which will be three months beyond the actual month of recovery). Those who are eligible as a result of chronic kidney disease have their protection terminated after the 12th month after the month in which the transplant occurred or dialysis ceased.

As a transitional matter, HI benefit protection was made available to virtually all persons who were aged 65 and over when the system began operation and to those near that age at that time even though they are not "insured" under either the OASDI system or the RR system. The cost of the benefits and the related administrative expenses for this transitional noninsured group is met from general revenues of the federal government, rather than from the taxes of workers and employers, as is the case for the cost for the insured persons.

Specifically, except for certain individuals covered under the federal employees health benefits program and certain short-residence aliens, individuals who attained age 65 before 1968 are entitled to HI benefit protection without regard to their insured status under OASDI or RR. In order to avoid the abrupt change that would have occurred if those attaining age 65 before 1968 were insured for HI without any quarters of coverage, but those attaining age 65 in 1968 were required to have 17 quarters of coverage (14 quarters for women), a special transitional provision was introduced. Under this provision, a non-insured individual who attains age 65 after 1967 must have at least 3 quarters of coverage for each year after 1966 and before the year of attaining age 65. Thus, an individual who became age 65 in 1968 had to have at least 3 quarters of coverage, whereas the requirement for OASDI monthly benefits for such an individual was 17 quarters of coverage for men and 14 quarters of coverage for women. A court decision in 1973 seemed to have rendered the restrictions applicable to short-residence aliens invalid, as long as they were admitted as residents.

Since this requirement increases at the rate of 3 quarters per year, while the requirement for OASDI monthly benefits increases at only 1 quarter per year, this transitional HI provision for noninsured persons washes out. For women attaining age 65 in 1974 or after and for men attaining age 65 in 1975 or after, the requirement for OASDI benefits is at least as easy to meet as the special requirement for HI benefits for transitionally noninsured persons.

A special voluntary HI system financed on a premium-payment basis has been established for individuals aged 65 and over who do not qualify for HI benefits as either insured or noninsured persons, effective July 1, 1973. The benefit protection is the same as under the regular program. Coverage election is on an individual basis and is made under provisions corresponding with those for SMI. Such voluntary HI coverage is possible only when SMI coverage has also been elected.

Benefit Provisions

The basic benefit principle under the HI system is to provide hospital and posthospital services to the beneficiaries after certain deductible and cost-sharing amounts are paid by them, rather than providing specified indemnity benefits and leaving it up to the beneficiary to pay the difference between the charges and the benefits. In this respect, HI is patterned along the lines of Blue Cross benefits, instead of those found in the more usual insurance company plans.

Three separate types of benefits are provided under HI—inpatient hospital services, posthospital skilled nursing facility services (which, before 1973, were termed extended care facility services), and post-hospital home health services. The most important of these is the inpatient hospital benefit, with the other two benefits and certain portions of SMI being designed to reduce hospital utilization. For example, if inpatient hospital services are made available at relatively little financial cost to the individual, but diagnostic services by hospitals on an outpatient basis are not covered, significant use of hospital inpatient services might be made solely because of the lower cost to the individual (but at considerably increased cost to the insurance system). Accordingly, the insurance system might operate more economically by providing the outpatient diagnostic benefit directly than if beneficiaries utilize an inpatient benefit to obtain the diagnostic services indirectly. Such diagnostic benefits are covered under SMI.

HI covered services are generally available only from hospitals and other providers of services that are located in the United States. As used here, the United States includes American Samoa, Guam, Puerto Rico, and the Virgin Islands. One exception is in the case of an emergency illness occurring in the United States where the individual is taken to a hospital in Canada or Mexico because it is more accessible than the nearest suitable hospital in the United States. Another exception is for any type of hospitalization with respect to those whose U.S. residence is more accessible to a foreign hospital than it is to a United States one. The vast majority of the cases where these two exceptions are applicable occur in the northernmost parts of the New England states. Yet another exception relates to emergency hospitalization in Canada while traveling from Alaska to another state.

An individual is entitled to inpatient hospital benefits for the first 90 days in a spell of illness and for an additional "lifetime reserve" of 60 days, which can be used on an elective basis by the beneficiary at any time after exhaustion of the 90 days. The term *spell of illness* is defined as the period beginning on the first day for which he receives these benefits and terminating after he has had a period of 60 consecutive days during which he has not been an inpatient in a hospital or a skilled nursing facility.

As an example of how spells of illness are determined, consider an individual eligible for HI benefits who attains age 65 in April 1974. Suppose that he enters a hospital on October 1, 1974. His spell of illness begins at that time. If he leaves the hospital on October 10, 1974, and does not then enter a skilled nursing facility, his spell of illness will continue for 60 days thereafter—until December 10, 1974. If he enters a hospital before the latter date, his spell of illness will continue for

60 days after his subsequent discharge, and so on. Once the spell of illness is ended, a new one begins only when he again enters a hospital.

Inpatient Hospital Services. The inpatient hospital services that are covered under HI consist of room and board, general nursing services, general medical social services, use of operating room and similar facilities, drugs, medical supplies and appliances, diagnostic and laboratory tests, and therapeutic services (such as physical therapy). Excluded are the services of private-duty nurses, the excess cost of a private room over a semiprivate room (unless determined to be medically necessary), luxury items such as telephone and television, and services of physicians other than interns or residents in training under teaching programs and physicians engaged in administration, research, and education.

The services of radiologists, anesthesiologists, pathologists, and physiatrists in hospitals (the so-called hospital-based physicians) are not included under HI, although they are under SMI. The costs of an X ray, an anesthetic procedure, a laboratory test, or a physical therapy treatment furnished to an inpatient and billed by the hospital is subdivided into the amount attributable to the personal services of the physician involved and the remaining amount attributable to auxiliary personnel, supplies, and equipment. The latter part is covered by HI, and the former part is covered by SMI.

In order for a hospital to participate in the program, it must apply to do so and then meet certain requirements. In general, these requirements are the same as hospitals meet to qualify under some Blue Cross plans. In addition it must maintain a hospital utilization review plan and must comply with civil rights provisions established by other federal legislation. Also included as hospitals are Christian Science sanatoriums.

Utilization review is accomplished by a committee that must include physicians. This committee studies the admissions, the lengths of stay, and the services provided with respect to medical necessity and efficiency. Each case that lasts for an extended period must be approved by the committee as requiring further hospitalization, or benefits will terminate.

The beneficiary is covered for all inpatient hospital services, but he is required to make certain payments. First, there is an initial deductible, which initially was $40 in July 1966 through December 1968, was $44 in 1969, and then increased each year until being $84 in 1974. Such amount is $92 in 1975, and will increase in the future if hospital costs rise. Second, there is a daily cost-sharing charge for the 61st through the 90th day of the benefit period, determined as 25 percent of the initial deductible. Third, there is daily coinsurance equal to 50 percent of the initial deductible for lifetime reserve days used beyond the 90-day regular period. Fourth, the blood deductible requires the beneficiary to replace or to pay the cost of the first three pints of whole blood used in his treatment; its purpose is to encourage and stimulate the voluntary blood donor program, by replacement of the blood used by volunteers.

It is widely—and incorrectly—believed that the $40 figure for the initial deductible during 1966–68 was selected as being the cost of the first day's hospital care or as being the average cost of one day's care. Actually, this figure was selected somewhat empirically for cost and control purposes, although it happens to approximate what was expected to be the average daily cost under the program in the first year of operations.

A question might be raised as to why the inpatient hospital benefit protection covers only the first 90 days of hospitalization and up to an additional 60 days under some circumstances. It might be argued that there should be unlimited-duration protection, since one of the most important features of any insurance program is to cover catastrophic risks. On the other hand, many medical experts believe that, of the relatively few long-duration hospital cases, only a small proportion really should be in a hospital. Instead, lower cost forms of medical care, such as skilled nursing facilities and home health services furnished in the patient's residence, can provide what is needed. Thus, financial limitations placed on long-duration hospital cases can motivate patients toward more suitable forms of medical treatment.

The initial deductible has been criticized as being a deterrent to necessary hospitalization, which may be the case in some instances. On the other hand, it may have some effect in preventing overutilization, particularly as to short-duration cases where hospitalization is really not necessary (e.g., minor illnesses for which hospital care is more convenient to the patient, his family, or his doctor; administration of diagnostic tests; and parent-sitting, when the beneficiary's children take a short trip). The initial deductible is small enough that it does not present an unduly large financial barrier. Moreover, for those individuals who might find it to be a real barrier, Medicaid is available.

The possible future variation of the initial deductible and the cost-sharing amount for each day in the 61st to the 90th day in a spell of illness and for each day in the lifetime reserve of 60 additional days depends upon the future trend of hospitalization costs for insured persons. From the operations of the program, the average daily cost for covered inpatient hospital services for insured persons can be determined, disregarding the effect of the various cost-sharing payments.

Through 1968, the initial deductible remained fixed at $40. The amount for 1969 was determined by multiplying the initial figure by the ratio of the average daily cost for covered inpatient hospital services with respect to insured persons for 1967 ($43.03) to that for 1966 ($37.95). The result for the initial deductible was rounded to the nearest multiple of $4 and was $44.

The initial deductibles for years subsequent to 1969 were determined in similar manner and were as follows: $52 for 1970; $60 for 1971; $68 for 1972; $72 for 1973; $84 for 1974; and $92 for 1975. It is interesting to note that the determination made for 1973 actually yielded a figure of $76, but a rather strange (and possibly of doubtful legality) ruling of the Price Commission prevented the increase to the actuarially determined amount. Since no further preventive action was taken, the initial deductible for 1974 showed a sharp increase, since it moved, in essence, from the $76 base, rather from $72, to $84.

It is interesting to note that the Price Commission took no action at all in late 1972 (when it prevented the full increase in the HI initial deductible) with regard to the increase in the "cost" of OASDI and HI that was to take place in 1973. An employee with earnings of at least $10,800 in both 1972 and 1973 had his social security taxes increased from $468.00 to $631.80, or by 35 percent. For a similar self-employed person, the corresponding figures were $675 and $864, an increase of 28 percent. The same situation also prevailed for persons with lower earnings; for employees with wages of $9,000 or less the increase was 13 percent.

Consider a few examples of how the foregoing provisions for inpatient hospital benefits actually work out. If Mr. A was hospitalized in 1974 for the first time since he became age 65, his spell of illness would commence then and would continue until he had been out of a hospital and skilled nursing facility for at least 60 consecutive days. He would be liable for the $84 initial deductible (unless his stay was very brief, and the hospital's charges were less than this).

If Mr. A went in and out of the hospital several times but did not end his spell of illness, he would have only the one $84 initial deductible to pay, although after he had had a total of 60 days of hospitalization, he would have to pay the cost-sharing amount of $21 for each of the next 30 days of hospitalization. If he continued in the same spell of illness and had a cumulative total of more than 90 days of hospitalization, he could draw on his lifetime-reserve days (and pay the cost-sharing amount of $42 per day).

It should be noted that the various cost-sharing payments are dependent on when the spell of illness began, and not on the period when services are received.

Under certain circumstances, it is to the individual's financial advantage to remain within the same spell of illness, because he then has only the one initial deductible. This situation is reversed, however, for individuals with long hospitalization stays who have daily cost-sharing amounts to pay and then a complete cessation of benefit protection after 90 days of hospitalization (except for the lifetime-reserve days). For example, an individual with two hospital stays of 10 days each in a calendar year is financially better off if these occur within one spell of illness, whereas an individual with two 40-day hospital stays in a particular year is better off if these occur in separate spells.

Certain special conditions apply to services rendered in psychiatric hospitals. If an individual is a patient of such a hospital on the first day that he is eligible for benefits, the 90-day benefit period and the 60 lifetime-reserve days as applicable to the hospitalization for mental illness in that spell of illness will be reduced by the number of days of hospitalization in the preceding 150 days. A further restriction applies to psychiatric inpatient hospital services. During the individual's lifetime, HI benefits are available with respect to a maximum of 190 days of such care. Both limitations were introduced so as to provide some safeguard in those cases where these hospital services are utilized primarily for custodial or domiciliary care, but where sufficient medical services are being provided so that administrative determination that the services should not be covered would be difficult.

Benefits can be provided in nonparticipating hospitals in the United States if the situation is an emergency, but sometimes in these cases the benefits may be at a reduced level. If the hospital will not accept reimbursement on a reasonable-cost basis, then the beneficiary is reimbursed at the rate of 60 percent of room-and-board charges and 80 percent of ancillary charges, less the usual cost-sharing amounts.

Skilled Nursing Facility Services.   Many hospital patients—and especially those aged 65 and over—reach a stage in their illness where they no longer require the intensive and costly care furnished by hospitals, and yet they are not capable of returning to their homes. In recent years, there has been a growing tendency to have an intermediate facility for such cases. Some of these have been part of a hospital, such as a convalescent wing. In other instances, these have been completely separate organizations, designated as extended care facilities or skilled nursing homes (as distinguished from ordinary nursing homes that almost wholly provide only custodial or domiciliary care).

Before HI was enacted, some Blue Cross and insurance company plans provided benefits for services in extended care facilities and skilled nursing homes. This was done, hopefully, to decrease the unnecessary use of hospital services, as well as to provide benefits for another type of health care. Some experts believe that the total cost of hospital services and skilled nursing facility services may be less when both are covered than the total cost would be if only hospital services were covered. Other experts, however, believe that this will not be the case, although better medical care will be provided. In certain instances, however, SNF benefits are used (at little or no cost to the beneficiary) when, with a little personal effort on the part of the beneficiary's family, he could be well taken care of at home. The HI program has greatly accelerated the use of these intermediate facilities, and there will likely be a strong trend in this direction in the future.

Although there is great logic in the concept of an intermediate facility between the intensive care provided by hospitals and the care that can be furnished at home, new problems are created by this coverage. Frequently, and especially for persons of advanced age, it is difficult to draw a clear distinction between the need for SNF services and the need for custodial care with a limited amount of nursing care. The intended distinction is based on the level of care and medical supervision required by the patient and not the diagnosis, the patient's condition, or the degree of functional limitation. For example, a cardiac patient who has no serious associated illnesses but who requires only the assistance of an aide in feeding, dressing, and bathing is considered as being in need of only custodial care. On the other hand, a cardiac patient who requires a trained medical person in adjusting digitalis dosage, in maintaining proper fluid balance, and in constantly watching for signs of decompensation is considered as needing SNF care.

Custodial care is not covered under HI for either inpatient hospital services or for SNF services (nor was it covered by previously existing insurance or benefit programs, because it is not medical care). Accordingly, strong pressures will often be exerted to make it appear that SNF care is needed, since it involves obtaining needed personal care in a high-quality institution, without substantial cost. Moreover, many facilities provide both SNF care and domiciliary care, so that there is the difficulty in identifying which is being furnished in an individual case.

One might wonder why custodial or domiciliary care in a skilled nursing home is not covered under HI when some medical services are necessary and are provided. Probably the major reasons are the high cost involved because the use of such services could be largely at the choice of the beneficiary (and so it could be called an uninsurable risk) and the difficulty (even impossibility) of distinguishing this care from strictly hotel services. It is recognized widely that there are many instances where older people need this kind of service, and then high, and even catastrophic, cost burdens fall on these individuals or on others who must support them, unless public assistance is sought and is available. However, if benefits for this risk were provided as an "insurance right," many would use them who now are adequately (and perhaps even better—at least from a psychological standpoint) taken care of by sons, daughters, or other persons.

The SNF services covered closely parallel the similar inpatient hospital services. Included are room and board in a semiprivate room, general nursing care, medical social services, physical and other types of therapy, drugs furnished by the SNF, and supplies and appliances. Similarly, physician services are not covered except those performed by interns or residents in training of a hospital with which the SNF has a transfer agreement.

In order to obtain SNF benefits, the individual must have been hospitalized for at least 3 consecutive days, and he must be admitted to the SNF within 14 days after discharge from the hospital. Furthermore, he must need medical services in the SNF which can only be provided there.

The hospitalization requirement in order to be eligible for SNF benefits was introduced so as to assure that an individual's treatment in the SNF is for causes that would otherwise have required the more expensive care of a hospital and, in fact, to assure that it is medical care that is being furnished, not custodial care.

The SNF benefit provisions, too, are based on the spell of illness concept. The first 20 days of SNF care in a spell of illness are provided without cost to the individual. The following 80 days of SNF care have a cost-sharing provision of one eighth of the initial deductible per day. The SNF cost-sharing will, on the average, represent about one third to one half the SNF charges and will be somewhat more than the cost of living at home. Accordingly, it may serve as a significant preventative of overutilization.

Special provisions apply to those using Christian Science sanatoriums for SNF services. The benefits then are available for a maximum of only 30 days in a spell of illness, and the cost-sharing applies to all days.

Home Health Services. In certain instances, patients of a hospital or SNF may have progressed to the stage where they could be cared for at home with a certain minimal amount of services, which are generally referred to as visiting nurse services or home health services. These will generally be at a significantly lower cost to the insurance plan than if the individual stayed in the hospital or SNF, as he might do if it would be less costly for him because of the home health services not being covered. Furthermore, from a medical standpoint it is probably better for the patient to be at home instead of in an institution. It is required, however, that these services be provided by organizations meeting certain requirements as to professional standards, that the level of care furnished be necessary from a medical standpoint, and that, as a practical matter, such care cannot be furnished in another setting of lower cost nature (such as a physician's office or a hospital outpatient department).

The HI program provides for coverage of a wide range of home health services to homebound cases after hospitalization. (Home health services that are furnished when qualifying hospitalization has not occurred are covered under SMI.) These HH services include not only visiting nurse services but also physical, occupational, and speech therapy, medical social services, part-time services of a home health aide (not solely for housekeeping purposes), medical supplies and appliances (but not drugs), services of interns and residents in training of hospitals when the HH agency is affiliated therewith, and outpatient hospital, SNF, and rehabilitation center services arranged for by the HH agency that necessitate using equipment that cannot readily be brought to the patient's home.

The HH benefits under HI have no cost-sharing provisions. Just as in the case of the SNF benefits, there is the requirement that the individual must have been hospitalized for at least three qualifying days, and that the HH plan is established within 14 days after discharge from the hospital (or from an SNF if the individual received such benefits).

A maximum of 100 HH services are provided within the period before the next spell of illness begins. A further maximum is that home health services are not covered if they are furnished more than a year after the most recent qualifying discharge from a hospital or SNF. Actually, the law uses the term *visits* in lieu of *services*. A visit consists of one specific service furnished to the individual. Thus, more than one service can be furnished on a particular visit of a team of technicians (such as nursing care provided by one member and speech therapy provided by another member).

Reimbursement Provisions

Under HI, the institutional providers of services consist of hospitals, skilled nursing facilities, and home health service agencies. The law provides that reimbursement to these institutions should be on a reasonable cost basis (or on the basis of customary charges, if these are lower, which is only rarely the case). In essence, this means that the reimbursement will be on a nonprofit basis. The fact that usually no profits are allowed in the amount reimbursed is relatively unimportant in the hospital area since about 95 percent of all short-stay hospital beds are in nonprofit or government hospitals. Similarly, virtually all home health services agencies are of a nonproprietary nature. On the other hand, a substantial proportion of skilled nursing facilities are operated on a proprietary basis.

The reasonable-cost reimbursement approach had been more or less followed by Blue Cross in previous years, with certain approximations being made in actual practice to measure costs. Naturally, all types of indirect expense such as a share of interest on loans, bad debts, costs of research not paid for by other sources, and net expense of operating nursing schools are included, as well as the usual direct expenses associated with inpatient care. The general principle prevails that HI is to pay no more, and no less, than the actual cost of providing care for its beneficiaries. This approach differs from that applicable to private-paying patients, who pay charges that may bear no specific relationship to the actual costs involved.

It was widely considered, upon the enactment of Medicare, that HI would be a great financial boon to hospitals. Previously, many had received less than full costs from medically indigent patients, and those aged 65 and over made up a very large proportion of this category. In some instances, near-indigent patients did not pay their bills, or paid only part of them. In instances where public welfare agencies took over responsibility for the bills of indigent persons, limited welfare funds resulted in less than adequate payments to hospitals. The hospitals were forced to take these low reimbursements, a preferable situation as compared with the possibility of getting less from the patients themselves. Now, under Medicare, hospitals are assured of getting full reasonable costs with respect to patients aged 65 and over, according to the intent of the law.

Representatives of hospitals have argued that despite their generally nonprofit nature, a profit (or plus) factor must be made available. Otherwise, they assert, funds will not be available for replacement of capital assets or for future expansion. In answer to this argument, it should be pointed out that this need should be met by proper usage of depreciation funding and, as in the past, by fund raising from the general public, governmental grants, and loans (interest on which is considered a reasonable cost under HI). Moreover, if all hospitals are given a profit override, this would result in the undesirable situation of some hospitals that should not expand having available large sums that would not be needed. Furthermore, if the plus factor is a uniform percentage, the procedure will encourage inefficiency and high costs by giving a larger override under such circumstances.

The reimbursement principles developed by the federal government initially consisted of a 2 percent supplement on the determined reasonable costs. Effective July 1, 1969, this 2 percent factor was eliminated, on the grounds that, by this time, hospital cost-accounting systems should have been sufficiently refined so that all costs were being adequately recognized. The hospitals urged a change in the reimbursement principles to a basis that would give more equitable treatment to hospitals (e.g., by recognizing the alleged higher per capita nursing costs for persons aged 65 and over). As a result, about half of the 2 percent factor was restored by building an "excess nursing cost for the aged" differential into the reimbursement formula.

The owners of proprietary institutions receive a reasonable return on their investment capital, although not necessarily on their net equity. They obtain, in the reimbursement computations, a rate of return on their net investment capital equal to 1½ times the trust-fund interest rate, which is the rate on currently acquired special issues.

Reimbursement of institutional providers of medical services on a cost basis had been widely criticized as promoting inefficiency—or, at least, as not encouraging efficiency. This criticism has been particularly prevalent in recent years, when hospital costs have risen rapidly. Reimbursement on a cost-plus basis is even more susceptible to this criticism. Accordingly, it has been suggested that hospitals should be given financial rewards when they operate extremely efficiently—and, conversely, should be financially penalized when their operations are inefficient.

In theory, this system of rewards and sanctions sounds very logical and desirable. There is, however, the difficulty of measuring efficiency of operation. Simple statistical measures such as average daily cost or average duration of stays are not valid as between different hospitals because of differences in the characteristics of the patient loads. Even more important is the matter of basic philosophy and purpose. If all hospitals were of a proprietary nature, then rewards and sanctions would provide strong incentives to increased efficiency. However, since the vast majority are operated on a nonprofit basis, the granting of rewards to be spent in any way the hospital wishes (or the invoking of penalties, which must be recovered somehow) is anomalous.

Up to this point, the discussion of reimbursement has implied that hospitals receive payments only after a bill has been rendered for each individual patient. Such procedure is often followed for private patients, whether paying out of their own pockets or through an insurance company plan. It was possible from the inception of the program until mid-1973 for hospitals to obtain HI interim reimbursement so as to be, more or less, on an accrual basis, and the vast majority of hospitals did so. This procedure was stopped on the grounds that the performance of the fiscal intermediaries and the hospitals had reached such a high level of efficiency and speed that it was no longer necessary, and so in most cases reimbursement could properly be on a rendered-bill basis. Another reason that this was done was to improve the current budgetary situation of the federal government by having a one-time "gain" when outgo was temporarily reduced or suspended. Such action should be viewed in the light of the discussion on social security and the unified budget in Chapter 4.

The implementing of the reasonable-cost reimbursement provisions for hospitals involves many complicated cost-accounting problems for such matters as depreciation and allocating costs by departments and services. The charges that hospitals make to their bill-paying patients usually differ widely from determined costs, both as to levels and as to patterns.

The reimbursement principles for skilled nursing facilities and home health agencies are similar to those for hospitals. In fact, the reimbursement procedure is relatively much simpler for these facilities, because of their lesser scope of operations. Furthermore, the home health agencies have no problems in regard to deductible or cost-sharing provisions under HI. Similarly, the skilled nursing facilities have no problem with an initial-deductible provision, and the cost-sharing from the 21st through the 100th day creates no difficulties because invariably the reasonable costs of operation amount to more than this.

Special reimbursement provisions are applicable to health maintenance organizations (which, generally speaking, are group practice prepayment plans). HMOs may choose to receive, instead of actual costs, a single combined per capita payment for both HI and SMI for each of their Medicare members. This payment cannot exceed the current per capita such cost in the given geographical area, as actuarially determined with appropriate adjustment to reflect the particular demographic structure of the HMO. Thus, the HMO can make a "profit" on the arrangement, dependent upon its relative efficiency, which will be used to provide greater benefit protection for its Medicare members. Such profit is limited to half of the first 20 percent of the excess of the per capita cost of Medicare in the geographical area as actuarially determined applicable to such HMO over its actual cost. On the contrary, if the HMO has bad operating experience, it may have a loss under this procedure, as compared to what would have occurred under the cost basis.

Thus, in essence, the HMO is a risk bearer under this approach. The supporters of the HMO method of delivering health care have long asserted that great savings are possible through this approach. Accordingly, they believe that over an extended period, there is no likelihood of anything but profits (i.e., larger benefit protection for members) under this procedure. In actual practice, HMOs have not used this approach in many cases, because of its complexity, preferring instead the reasonable-cost basis.

Financing Provisions

The HI benefits and the accompanying administrative expenses are paid out of the Hospital Insurance Trust Fund. The income to this trust fund is derived basically from payroll taxes from covered workers and employers and from the investment earnings of the trust fund. The cost for the noninsured persons aged 65 and over during the initial stages of the program is met from the General Fund of the Treasury (i.e., from general revenues) by payments which flow through the trust fund, with appropriate interest adjustment for any timing differences. The premium payments by the noninsured persons who were not blanketed-in initially on a "free" basis and who elect to come in on a voluntary, self-supporting premium basis go into the trust fund too.

The tax rates are applied to the earned income of the covered workers up to the earnings base, which is the same as for OASDI (see Chapter 2). In fact, the OASDI and HI taxes are assessed and collected together. Again as with OASDI, the employer and employee HI tax rates are the same. But, differing from OASDI, the self-employed HI rate is the same as the employee rate, instead of being somewhat higher. These HI tax rates are shown in Table 6.1.

TABLE 6.1

Hospital Insurance Tax Rates

Calendar Year	Combined Employer-Employee Rate	Self-Employed Rate
1974–77	1.80%	0.90%
1978–80	2.20	1.10
1981–85	2.70	1.35
1986 and after	3.00	1.50

As indicated previously, the tax schedule in the law is intended to provide sufficient income to finance the program adequately over the next 25 years. As will be discussed in more detail in Chapters 8 and 10, the official actuarial cost estimates made in 1974 indicated a small actuarial surplus, 0.02 percent of taxable payroll. Accordingly, this criterion is met, although in some previous years this had not been the case because of the rapidly rising hospital costs.

The current favorable estimated actuarial situation results from the increases in the tax rates which were made in past years to take into account the experience as to hospital costs and the increases in the earnings base in 1973 and 1974, which were far larger than the rise in the general earnings level or the price level. With regard to the latter point, unlike the situation in OASDI, increases in the earnings base produce only additional income to the system, and not additional benefit liability.

The standard premium rate for those voluntarily covered was set at $33 per month for the year beginning July 1973. The rate for subsequent years will be $33 multiplied by the ratio of the inpatient hospital deductible for the calendar year in which the premium year begins to such deductible promulgated for 1973,[2] with rounding to the nearest whole dollar. The rate so determined for the year beginning July 1974 was promulgated by the Secretary of Health, Education, and Welfare to be $36, while that for the year beginning July 1975 is $40.[3] Just as in the case of the SMI premium basis, persons enrolling late in the voluntary HI program must pay an extra premium (10 percent increase for each full year of delay).

The assets of the HI Trust Fund are invested in exactly the same manner as are those of the two OASDI Trust Funds (see Chapter 2).

SUPPLEMENTARY MEDICAL INSURANCE PROVISIONS

This section will first discuss the eligibility and enrollment conditions for the supplementary medical insurance portion of the Medicare program. Then, the benefit provisions, the provisions for reimbursement of the providers of medical services, and the financing will successively be considered.

Eligibility Conditions

The basic coverage principle of the SMI program is that of individual voluntary participation. Basically, the program provides indemnity coverage for certain nonhospital medical expenses for persons aged 65 and over and for certain disabled persons (the same as are covered for HI benefits). The program is financed on a sharing basis by the individual and by the federal government out of general revenues, with the government paying at least half of the cost.

SMI is patterned after indemnity plans sold by insurance companies

---

[2] For these purposes, the initial deductible that is used as the base is taken from the 1973 determination made according to the provisions of the law, $76—and not at $72, the amount that was promulgated for 1973 at the insistence of the Price Commission (as discussed earlier in this chapter).

[3] It is interesting to note that the three dates for rate promulgations under the Medicare program are different—the third quarter of the year for the HI cost-sharing amounts, the fourth quarter of the year for the voluntary HI premium rate, and December for the SMI premium rate.

and thus has a basic point of difference from the traditional service-type plans of Blue Shield, which provide full coverage only when the individual falls below the prescribed income limit. In the same way, SMI with its indemnity-type approach differs from the basis of HI, which provides service-type benefits, although the services are not furnished by the government.

With certain minor exceptions, any person aged 65 or over in the United States can participate in the SMI program. All persons aged 65 or over who participate in the voluntary HI program must enroll in SMI. The exceptions are aliens who have not been lawfully admitted for permanent residence (such as officials of foreign embassies or of international organizations) and aliens so admitted who have not resided continuously in the United States during the five years preceding application for enrollment. The disabled persons who can participate in SMI are those disability beneficiaries under OASDI and RR (including the chronic kidney cases) who have HI protection, and not disabled persons in general. Persons who have been convicted of subversive activities are precluded from receiving SMI benefits. A lower court decision, *Diaz* v. *Weinberger*, 361 F. Supp 1 (USDC S.D. Fla., June 1973), held the requirement as to alien residence conditions to be unconstitutional. The court enjoined its enforcement, pending revision or reversal of the ruling on appeal; the appeal of the government is still pending.

The general basis of enrollment in SMI is that such action should be taken at about the time of attaining age 65 or, for the disabled, at about the time of first eligibility. Individuals who attain age 65 or who are disability beneficiaries have initial enrollment periods of seven months that are centered around the month of attainment of age 65 or, for disability beneficiaries, the month of first eligibility for SMI benefits (i.e., after having been on the cash benefits roll for two years). Any person who is entitled to HI benefits is deemed to have enrolled for SMI in the first three months of the initial enrollment period, although he can opt-out then. In such cases and in other cases where the election for SMI is made in the three months before such month, benefit protection (and premium payment) starts with the month of attainment of age 65. If election is made in such month, protection starts with the next month. If election is made in the month following such month, protection begins with the second following month, while if enrollment occurs in the second or third month following such month, protection begins with the third month after enrollment.

If an individual fails to enroll in his initial enrollment period, he can enroll only during a general enrollment period. General enrollment periods occur in the first three months of every calendar year. Persons who do not enroll in this initial enrollment period but who do so later in a general enrollment period are subject to two penalties or disadvantages. First, the benefit protection does not begin until the following July 1. Second, an increased premium rate over that for persons who enroll in their initial enrollment period may be payable (described in detail later).

An individual may withdraw from SMI by election at any time, effective as of the end of the following calendar quarter. An individual's coverage can also be terminated for nonpayment of premiums, which is possible only for persons who are not on the OASDI or RR monthly benefits roll, or who are on the roll but are not receiving benefits regularly because of being employed and subject to the retirement test. To put it another way, persons who make direct payment of premiums may at any time stop paying premiums and thus have their benefit coverage terminated. A grace period of not more than 90 days for payment of the SMI premiums is provided before coverage lapses.

If an individual's SMI coverage is terminated, he can reenter the program only by an election during a general enrollment period, but an increased premium rate may be payable. If an individual's coverage is terminated a second time, he can never enroll again.

The foregoing coverage rules are strict. This is necessary in order that antiselection against the system should not occur. Otherwise, many individuals attaining age 65 and in good health would not elect to participate in SMI and pay the standard premium rate if they could easily enroll in the future at the same rate when the need for medical care became more apparent.

Benefit Provisions

SMI, in supplementing HI, focuses principally upon insurance with respect to physician services. In addition to physician services, coverage also applies to a maximum of 100 home health services during a calendar year and to certain other specified medical and health services. The home health services under SMI are the same as those available under HI, except that previous hospitalization is not required.

These other medical and health services covered by SMI include a broad array of miscellaneous items such as: diagnostic tests; X rays and similar types of therapy; surgical dressings; splints used for bone fractures; drugs given incidentally as part of a physician's services which cannot be self-administered (e.g., local anesthetics); rental of medical equipment (e.g., iron lungs, oxygen tanks and tents, hospital beds, and wheel chairs) or purchase thereof if more economical ambulance service (subject to limitations, such as being to, or from the nearest hospital); various prosthetic devices; artificial limbs; physical and speech therapy services; podiatrist services (but only for services other than routine foot care); and certain chiropractic services (limited to treatment of the spine, when verifiable by X ray showing subluxation). Also covered are certain inpatient hospital services (such as X-ray and laboratory services) that would normally be covered by HI (and that would have been covered under SMI if furnished on an outpatient basis) but were not so covered because the individual had exhausted his benefits (or was not covered under HI). Blood received in a hospital outpatient department, a physician's office, or a clinic is an SMI covered expense, but only with respect to blood in excess of the first three pints a year (thus paralleling the HI blood-deductible provision).

The physician services that are covered include those of doctors of medicine and doctors of osteopathy, whether performed in hospital, office, home, or elsewhere. Not covered are any services for regular dental care, prescribing eyeglasses, immunizations, and routine physical examinations (but note that it may be difficult at times to distinguish between a physical examination and a diagnosis for an ill-defined ailment). The services of dentists are also covered, but only for surgery related to the jaw or any facial bone.

The most important "other medical and health services" not covered by SMI are eyeglasses, dentures, hearing aids, and out-of-hospital prescription drugs. Some might question why there are these various exclusions. Most of them have been instituted because of cost reasons and the difficulty to control utilization (or prevent costly overutilization). Probably the most concern has been over the exclusion of routine physical examination, which many experts advocate, although others question whether these are really desirable on a universal routine, regular basis. Such preventive medical care has its merits, but there is also a question of priorities. Consider the cost aspects if the more than 20 million SMI beneficiaries had regular annual comprehensive physical examinations at a cost of several hundred dollars each.

The coverage of out-of-hospital prescription drugs has also received widespread attention. Not only is this a costly benefit to provide—and one which would be subject to widespread overutilization if little direct cost were involved—but also there would be great administrative problems if all prescriptions were covered (there being about 400 million prescriptions each year for SMI beneficiaries). Most prescriptions cost only a few dollars and, except for the small proportion of persons who have large numbers of prescriptions, can readily be budgeted out of current income.

The services under SMI must be performed within the United States, including not only the 50 states and the District of Columbia, but also American Samoa, Guam, Puerto Rico, and the Virgin Islands; physician services and ambulance services are covered in Canada and Mexico when the case involves hospitalization, and this is covered by HI.

Although SMI is patterned closely after indemnity health insurance plans of the comprehensive type, it differs significantly in that with three minor exceptions, there is no maximum limitation on the benefits provided for covered services rendered in a particular calendar year. A maximum of 100 visits per calendar year is provided for home health services. No more than $100 per year of services of independent physical therapists are covered. A special maximum applies to psychiatric services provided by physicians out of hospitals.

Only 62½ percent of incurred expenses for such psychiatric disorders is considered as an incurred expense; and in any event, no more than $500 of such total expense in a calendar year is taken into account. This special limitation was introduced because previous insurance experience indicated that some cost-controlling element is necessary in this area, where a considerable part of the usage frequently depends on the personal wishes of the individual, especially if he has to pay only a small portion of the cost. No special limitations apply to psychiatric services furnished to hospital inpatients.

The SMI program has a different procedure for reimbursing the beneficiary for physician services than most Blue Shield plans and indemnity health insurance plans with fee schedules. Most Blue Shield plans are on a full-service basis for those with incomes below the prescribed limits and a fee-schedule indemnity basis for all other persons. Some insurance company indemnity plans, such as major medical insurance, operate without a fee schedule—namely, on a "reasonable and customary charges" basis, like a few Blue Shield plans. Under SMI, reimbursement for these services is determined on a "reasonable charges" basis.

Insofar as the beneficiary is concerned, the proportion of his costs for other medical services covered by SMI is determined from the reasonable charges of the institutional suppliers thereof. On the other hand, reimbursement to such suppliers under SMI which are hospitals, skilled nursing facilities, and home health agencies is on the basis of "reasonable costs," as is also the case under HI. All other institutional suppliers, such as independent laboratories (which make various diagnostic tests), ambulance services, and renters of medical equipment, are remunerated on a reasonable charges basis.

Insofar as the individual is concerned, it may be said in general that the SMI program provides for reimbursement of 80 percent of the reasonable charges of physicians for incurred services and of institutional providers for other services covered, after he has paid an initial deductible of $60 per calendar year (but with certain carry-over provisions from the previous year's deductible, which will be discussed later). In other words, he must annually pay the first $60 and then 20 percent of the remaining amount of reasonable charges. Until 1973, this initial deductible was fixed at $50. But it is not on a dynamic basis (i.e., varying with unit cost under the program as is the case with the the HI initial deductible and the related daily coinsurance amounts).

Exceptions to this reimbursement basis apply in the case of pathology and radiology services rendered by physicians to hospital inpatients and home health services. Neither the $60 deductible nor the 20 percent cost sharing is applicable to such pathology and radiology services; this change was made for administrative reasons, since the "professional component" charges for services of this type are relatively small, and the patient has no direct personal contact with the physician involved. The 20 percent cost sharing does not apply to the home health benefits, so that once the $60 initial deductible has been met (possibly by other services, such as physician charges), these services are available without cost to the beneficiary, as is also the case for the HH benefits under HI.

First, consider the procedures involved and the protection provided with respect to physician services other than those for out-of-hospital psychiatric services. For example, Mr. C has physician bills of $330 (including $20 for pathology services when he was an inpatient in a hospital) during a calendar year. These are all considered by the insurance carrier representing the SMI program to be reasonable charges. Then, the benefit protection that he has is $220—$20 (for pathology) plus $200 (80 percent of the excess of the $310 of total charges exclusive of pathology charges over the $60 deductible)—and so his out-of-pocket costs are the remaining $110. In the event that, in this case, the physician services totaled $520 because Mr. C is wealthy (or for other reasons) and was billed accordingly, the reasonable charges would still be determined as $330, and SMI would still pay only the $220, with him being responsible for the remaining $300.

Two procedures are available as to the manner in which the beneficiary receives the benefit protection. If the doctor accepts an assignment from the SMI program, and thereby agrees to bill for no more than "reasonable charges," he will be paid directly by SMI whatever amount is payable—that is, after taking into account the deductible and coinsurance applicable. Then, the physician may collect the balance of the bill from the patient. This procedure can have distinct financial advantages to the physician, because he can then be certain to collect at least an amount equal to the SMI benefit, even though the patient does not pay the balance of the bill due (for the cost-sharing provisions).

The other procedure is used when the doctor will not accept an assignment—and the American Medical Association has urged its members to follow this course of action. Under this procedure, the beneficiary need only present an itemized bill from his doctor in order to obtain the SMI benefit, which is based on the "reasonable charges" for the services rendered (as determined under the program). It is then up to the doctor to see that he is paid, including any excess of his actual charges over the determined "reasonable charges."

Many doctors have taken a position against accepting assignments because of their strong views against dealing directly with the federal government and having their fees be dictated by it. This is so even though they do not intend to charge more than the reasonable charges for the vast majority of their SMI patients and thus have no great financial incentive (and perhaps even a financial disincentive) not to follow the assignment procedure.

It may be recalled that insurance-company health insurance plans use an assignment method, but on a different basis. At the request of the insured person, the company pays the doctor whatever benefit is determined to be due (based on the charges being reasonable and customary), and this amount is considered merely as a payment on the account due, without any restraint being placed on the doctor to accept total payment of no more than reasonable charges.

Finally, one might raise the question as to why the assignment method under SMI was developed in its original form. Many persons influential in the development of the program believed that otherwise some physicians would increase their normal charges to the patient because he was relieved by Medicare from having to pay much of what he had previously been accustomed to pay and that, as a *quid pro quo* for assignment (and thus certainty of some payment), the doctor should agree to limit his charges to the patient to the difference between the reasonable charges and the SMI benefit payable.

Next, take into consideration the effect of the special limitations on out-of-hospital psychiatric services. If Mr. D had no medical expenses during a year other than $300 of such psychiatric services, then there would be considered as an SMI incurred expense 62½ percent thereof (assuming that the charges were considered to be reasonable), or $187.50. After taking into account the $60 deductible, SMI would provide benefits of $102.

If Mr. E had had $500 or more out-of-hospital psychiatric expenses and no other physician expense, only $312.50 would be considered as incurred expenses. After taking into account the $60 deductible, SMI would pay benefits of $202. If Mr. E had had other physician services of $60 or more and then had $500 or more of such psychiatric services, his benefits with respect to the latter would amount to $250 (80 percent of $312.50). In general, if the $60 deductible is met by other than out-of-hospital psychiatric services, then the reimbursement for such expenses is at the rate of 50 percent thereof (80 percent of 62½ percent), up to a maximum reimbursement of $250 per year.

With respect to the various nonphysician medical services and supplies covered by SMI that are furnished by institutional providers, the beneficiary is insured on a reasonable-charges basis. As indicated previously, some of these providers are reimbursed on a reasonable-charges basis, while others are reimbursed on a reasonable-cost basis. This means that the beneficiary must pay 20 percent of the reasonable charges for these services after the $60 deductible has been met in the year (whether by these charges, by physician charges, or by a combination of both). The reasonable charges—just as in the case of physician charges—can, of course, not exceed the customary charges for the particular services or supplies.

Many private health insurance policies contain "carry-over deductible" provisions. These are provided from an equity viewpoint, so as to give fair treatment to persons who had relatively small expenses in most of a year, but had an illness that began toward the close of that year. Specifically, under SMI, the $60 deductible for a particular calendar year is reduced by any expenses incurred in the last three months of the preceding year that were applied toward the deductible then.

As an example of how this carry-over provision works, consider Mr. G who has no SMI medical expenses in the first nine months of 1973, but who then has a serious illness with medical expenses running well beyond $60 in the last three months of the year. Not only does Mr. G have benefits for 1973 of 80 percent of the reasonable charges in excess of $60, but also his $60 deductible for 1974 is already satisfied.

Reimbursement Provisions

Services furnished by institutional providers are reimbursed under SMI on a reasonable-cost basis, except the professional component thereof (generally with respect to pathologists and radiologists), which is billed separately on a reasonable-charges basis. The procedure followed is exactly the same as under HI.

Payments to insured persons with regard to physician fees or to physicians in assignment cases are made on a reasonable-charges basis that is determined relative to both the particular doctor's customary charges and the adjusted prevailing fees for similar services in the particular geographic area. This does not mean that each physician must operate under a fixed fee schedule that applies either nationwide or in the particular locale, or even rigidly to himself. Rather, for a given procedure he may have a range of charges that, in order to be at the level that is fully reimbursable, must be consistent both with his customary charges to non-Medicare patients and with the adjusted general level of charges prevailing in the community. The range so allowed will permit reasonable variation, so as to reflect the particular circumstances of each case (i.e., the relative difficulties involved).

This profile is used to develop the "customary and prevailing charge" screen, with which actual bills are compared (generally by electronic data-processing equipment) to test whether they meet the reasonable-charges requirement. Such screen also has built into it the adjusted prevailing charges in the area for each particular service.

Health insurance plans as operated by insurance companies and other types of insurers, including some Blue Cross plans, had previously used (and still use) a somewhat similar concept when fee schedules were not contained, for example, major medical plans. (Most Blue Shield plans do not operate on this basis, since in essence they use fee schedules for reimbursement purposes.) The administration of such plans is carried out on a very broad and flexible basis. Fees are questioned only if they are obviously out of line. It is believed by the insurers that this rough-and-ready procedure is both efficient and sufficient to operate a sound program that is equitable to both the physicians and to the insured persons (in the resulting premium rates that have to be charged). It is also believed that too close a surveillance of fees is both administratively expensive and irritating to the physicians, without achieving any significantly greater savings in cost than under the looser method actually used.

Under the administration of the SMI program, a different and more detailed and complex procedure is followed. A so-called profile is built up for each doctor, showing his charges for various procedures. Then, bills are compared with this profile to determine whether they are reasonable charges. Of course, in developing the profile originally, its reasonableness would be determined in relation to the charges of other doctors in the same area. Specialists having certain skills are, of course, entitled to have a higher charge structure.

The customary charge of a particular physician for a given service is determined by statistical methods. This procedure is done by regulations, since the law does not provide specifically in this respect. The reasonable charge is based on the median charge made for the particular service by the physician.

When a physician changes his fee structure, the SMI program naturally recognizes this in determining the reasonable charge according to the customary charge criterion. The question arises as to when the changed fee structure becomes "customary." Changes in charges are not recognized as soon as they are made. Rather, such changes have a built-in lag of about 18 months on the average. Originally, this lag was the result of regulations, but the 1972 legislation legitimatized it for the future.

At first glance, this lag element in the determination of customary charges seems logical, as well as beneficial, to the SMI program by holding down its cost and possibly also by discouraging increases in physician fees. Some questions, however, have been raised about this. When a physician posts a new schedule of fees, to be effective at a certain future date, why should not his accepted customary charges also change simultaneously? Also, will such a procedure cause physicians to increase their fees somewhat sooner, so as to have the same overall effect as if increases were recognized simultaneously?

Under the procedure of failing to recognize fee increases immediately when they occur, it is true that the cost of the SMI program may be lower than under simultaneous-recognition procedures. But, at the same time, some of this cost falls on the enrollees, who must pay the increases in fees in full (except when the physician accepts the assignment procedure and therefore must absorb the difference during the lag period).

The law requires that for any physician, the reasonable charge for a service cannot be higher than either his customary charge or the adjusted prevailing charge in the locality. The adjusted prevailing charges are determined from what might be called the prevailing charges in the 12-month period July 1972 through June 1973 as adjusted for subsequent years by an economic index reflecting general earnings levels and the costs of operation of a physician's office. Actually, the prevailing charges for the 12-month base period were not really those current then, but rather had about an 18-month lag built into them. On that basis, the prevailing charge in a locality was the 75th percentile level of charges for the particular service. During the last few years, when wage and price controls were in effect, the Cost of Living Council imposed overriding control limits, such as a maximum increase of 2½ percent per year.

The procedure of the 18-month lag and the 75th percentile are now prescribed by law, as a result of the 1972 legislation. Before then, they were effectuated solely by regulation, and this procedure seemed to some to be contrary to the law, or at least to its intent. The original philosophy of SMI was that those aged 65 and over should no longer be second-class citizens insofar as medical bills were concerned, by paying lower, charity rates. Instead, with the aid of SMI, they would be able to pay the regular fees. But now with the lags introduced in the past and the economic-index adjustment for the future, this will no longer be the case, and the SMI beneficiaries will be charged lower fees than the remainder of the population (on assignment cases) or will pay substantially more than SMI had originally promised (in nonassignment cases).

The effect of the economic-index adjustment, as it operates in the future, will be to result eventually in a flat, uniform fee schedule in each locality. This will occur because physicians' customary fees will probably rise more rapidly than the adjusted prevailing-charges screen (which no longer will reflect actual prevailing fee levels, but rather will be well below). As a result, after some time, all physicians will be on the adjusted prevailing-charges basis.

Financing Provisions

The SMI benefits and the accompanying administrative expenses are paid out of the Supplementary Medical Insurance Trust Fund. The income to this trust fund is derived solely from premium payments from the enrollees, the matching payments from the General Fund of the Treasury, and the investment earnings of the trust fund.

The standard premium rate and the actuarial rates for enrollees aged 65 and over and for disabled enrollees are determined annually (in December, for the 12-month period beginning the next July) by the Secretary of Health, Education, and Welfare by appropriate actuarial methods. More details on such determinations and on the past experience will be presented in Chapter 8. Although in the past the government has shared the cost of the SMI program equally with the enrollees, this will not be so after 1973. Instead, the government will meet more than half the cost, because it will pay the excess cost for the disabled enrollees (first covered in July 1973) over that for the aged enrollees and because, in the future, the standard premium rate will not be permitted to rise more rapidly than the level of OASDI benefits.

Persons who enroll 12 or more months after first eligibility pay an additional 10 percent for each full 12 months of nonparticipation, with the monthly premium rate being rounded to the nearest 10 cents. Those who drop out of SMI and later reenroll are similarly charged an extra premium rate based on the intervening months of nonparticipation.

The standard premium rate, payable by both aged and disabled enrollees who elect to participate as soon as they are eligible (or within 12 months thereof), has been promulgated at $6.70 a month for the 12-month period beginning July 1974.

For the 12-month period beginning July 1973, the government paid matching amounts for each enrollee equal to the enrollee premium rate for those aged 65 and over. For the disabled enrollees, the government matching amount was equal to twice the actuarial rate for the disabled (which was $14.50 for this period) minus the standard premium rate ($6.30)—that is, a government amount of $22.70.

For the 12-month period beginning July 1974, the standard premium rate is $6.70, which represents an increase of 6.3 percent over the previous rate and is thus well below the 11 percent ceiling based on the increase in the cash benefits from June 1973 to June 1974 (based on the law as of December 1973). Accordingly, the government paid the same amount for enrollees aged 65 and over. The actuarial rate promulgated for disabled enrollees was $18 so that the government payment with respect to them was $29.30 per month.

Due to a technical error in the law (to be discussed in more detail in Chapter 8), the premium rate for the 12-month period beginning July 1975, as promulgated in December 1974, did not change as compared with that in effect during the previous 12 months. This was because the level of cash benefits for June 1975, as based on the law in effect in December 1974 and the conditions then prevailing, was the same as it had been for June 1974. As a result, since the actuarial rate for enrollees aged 65 and over was promulgated at $7.50, the government payment increased to $8.30 per month for them (2 times $7.50, minus $6.70). Likewise, the actuarial rate promulgated for disabled enrollees was $18.50, so that the government payment with respect to them was $30.30 per month (2 times $18.50, minus $6.70).

The increase in the actuarial rate for those aged 65 or over was 11.9 percent, while that for the disabled was only 2.8 percent. The smaller increase for the disabled was not the result of experience, but rather it was believed that the previous rate of $18.00 had been somewhat too high (very little actual experience for the disabled is, as yet, available for actuarial analysis).

Legislation was in process in March 1975 that would correct this technical error in the law. If this is enacted, the standard premium rate for the year beginning July 1975 will be increased to $7.40 per month. The corresponding government cost for those aged 65 and over will then be $7.60, while for the disabled it will be $29.60.

The assets of the SMI Trust Fund are invested in exactly the same manner as are those of the HI Trust Fund—that is, the same as is done for the two OASDI Trust Funds (see Chapter 2).

ADMINISTRATION OF MEDICARE

The administration of the Medicare program differs considerably from that of the OASDI program. The latter is almost entirely administered by the federal government, the only exception being the initial determination of disability. On the other hand, much of the administration of Medicare is done by private organizations. This was required by Congress in order that there would be less likelihood of interference with the practice of medicine by the government.

The administration of HI involves the Social Security Administration of the Department of Health, Education, and Welfare in several ways—maintaining the earnings records from which eligibility is determined, giving eligible persons information about the program and their individual utilization records, developing regulations for reimbursement of providers of services, reviewing and providing the funds for such reimbursements, and maintaining the individual records of utilization of services. The Treasury Department collects the HI taxes (along with the OASDI taxes) and administers the trust fund operations.

There are separate boards of trustees for the HI and SMI Trust Funds, although with exactly the same membership (and also the same as for the OASDI Trust Funds). The duties and functions of these two boards of trustees are the same as for the OASDI Trust Funds (see Chapter 2), the only difference being that the required estimates of the operations in the annual report are to be for only the next three years for the two Medicare Trust Funds, instead of for the next five years.[4]

Virtually all the direct relations with the providers of services under HI (hospitals, skilled nursing facilities, and home health agencies) are handled by fiscal intermediaries. Each provider is permitted to select its own intermediary, subject to the approval of the qualifications of such intermediary by the Social Security Administration. A provider can elect to deal directly with the SSA. However, only a few, mostly governmental hospitals, have chosen to do so. The fiscal intermediary reviews the operations of the provider and obtains from it the necessary financial reports, in line with the provisions of law and the directives of the SSA. The fiscal intermediary obtains funds from the HI Trust Fund, on approval of the SSA, and passes these along to the providers. Most providers have selected the Blue Cross Association as their fiscal intermediary, although some insurance companies serve in this capacity too (especially for skilled nursing

---

[4] The shorter period was selected probably because the SMI financing depends on a premium rate promulgated annually and thus not readily forecastable for long periods, with the same procedure being followed for HI for the sake of consistency.

facilities). The providers have their costs for administrative expenses reimbursed from the HI Trust Fund.

The SSA is involved in the administration of SMI in maintaining the records of premium payments and utilization of services, giving eligible persons information, developing the regulations, and providing the funds for reimbursement purposes. The Treasury Department provides the necessary financial services in connection with the operation of the SMI Trust Fund. The premium payments are largely collected by the deduction method—from OASDI benefit checks, from railroad retirement benefit checks (for all persons receiving such benefits, regardless if also getting OASDI), and from civil service retirement annuity checks (if not receiving OASDI or RR). In all other cases, SMI enrollees pay the premiums directly to the SSA, usually quarterly in advance, although it is possible to do so monthly.

Unlike HI, all relations with the providers of services under SMI must go through a third party and not deal directly with the federal government. The SSA designates carriers for each geographical area—usually an entire state, but in some instances only part of a state. These carriers are Blue Shield plans in the majority of cases, although a significant number of areas are assigned to insurance companies and, in a few instances, other organizations similar to Blue Shield.

The carriers have a large hand in the actual administration of SMI. They maintain the enrollee utilization records and inform the enrollees about them. The carriers also determine reasonable charges and pay the benefits (to the physicians in assignment cases and to the enrollees in other cases) for all providers in their area. The only exceptions to this are for RR beneficiaries, who deal with a single national carrier and for providers who are reimbursed on a reasonable-cost basis, who deal with their HI fiscal intermediary. The administrative expenses of the carriers are reimbursed by the SMI Trust Fund.

The law contains many controls on the operation of the program that affect the quantity, quality, and cost of covered health services. Insofar as the operation of hospitals is concerned, these include such matters as not paying costs for capital expenditures which have been disapproved by state or local health facility plans, not paying costs which are excessive as compared with similar services in comparable facilities in the locality, and requiring annual operating budgets and capital-expenditure plans.

Utilization review committees must be established by hospitals and skilled nursing facilities. Such a committee consists of either staff physicians (and possibly also including other professional personnel) or of a similar outside group established by the local medical society (or in absence of other action, named by HEW). Its functions are to review (possibly on a sample basis) admissions, durations of stay, and professional services rendered with regard to medical necessity and efficiency and with a view to the provision that limits beneficiary liability when a claim is disallowed (so that efficient functioning of this committee is necessary to prevent liability falling on the institution).

Professional standards review organizations (PSROs) must be established in localities. They consist of substantial numbers of physicians (300 or more) and have the responsibility for review of services covered under both Medicare and Medicaid to assure that they were medically necessary and provided in accordance with professional standards. Such groups have no responsibility in the reasonable-charges area. The PSROs are organized by physician-sponsored groups (such as local medical societies), but in the absence of a satisfactory PSRO in a locality, HEW will designate a qualified group. Some physicians are greatly concerned about the PSRO concept, which was introduced in the 1972 legislation, since they feel that it casts aspersions on their professional ability and work, and since it will be cumbersome, administratively expensive, and generally nonproductive. Moreover, they point out that they would not object to *peer* review, but they are strongly opposed to medical review by nonphysician personnel who, in their belief, are not professionally qualified to pass on their work.

chapter 7

Development of
Medicare System

This chapter will trace the beginning of the Medicare system from the early efforts at the turn of the century to establish broad governmental health insurance programs through the battle during 1950–65 to enact Medicare legislation for persons 65 and over.[1] Then, the significant amendments made to the Medicare program subsequent to its enactment in 1965 will be discussed. Finally, description will be given as to the Medicare provisions in legislation passed by both the House and the Senate in 1973 but not finally enacted, since this is a good indication of possible future changes, and as to legislative proposals made in early 1975 by the Advisory Council on Social Security and by President Ford. The chapter concludes with an historical summary of the various promulgated Medicare elements.

EARLY LEGISLATIVE EFFORTS

Germany established a governmental health insurance program in the 1800s, and a number of other European countries also did so in the next few years. These were relatively limited plans and applied gen-

---

[1] For more details on these historical matters, see Robert J. Myers, *Medicare* (Richard D. Irwin, Inc., 1970), Chapters 1–3.

erally only to manual workers and lower paid salaried employees. Some Americans studied this movement with great interest and approval.

The first national advocacy of governmental health insurance in the United States was a plank in the platform of the Socialist party in the early 1900s. Subsequently, when former President Theodore Roosevelt founded the Progressive Party before the 1912 elections, a plank supporting national health insurance was included in its program. The American Association for Labor Legislation (which ceased operations in the early 1940s) had a most important role in the legislative movement for health insurance, particularly in the period beginning in 1912 and ending somewhat after the termination of World War I.

The AALL, at its inception, was interested primarily in the promotion of state workmen's compensation laws that would provide both medical care and cash payments for workers suffering industrial injuries or diseases. In this respect, it was extremely successful.

With this first success as encouragement, the AALL turned its attention to the establishment of separate state programs of medical care and cash benefits on an earnings-related basis similar to workmen's compensation, but with broader application. The AALL prepared model bills and attempted to get them enacted by state legislatures. Success, however, was minimal, with little more than bills being introduced and hearings being held. The few instances where the bills came to a vote resulted in rejection. With the advent of World War I, activity in this area came to a virtual standstill and was not renewed afterward. The opposition to the AALL bills came not only from business and insurance groups but also from the national labor movement. In the beginning, the American Medical Association was favorably inclined, but it soon changed position.

After World War I, those favoring governmental health insurance regrouped their forces and made preparations for a new campaign. During the 1920s, their efforts were concentrated on laying the groundwork through studies of the matter, such as those of the Committee on the Costs of Medical Care. Then, in 1934–35, when the Committee on Economic Security (formed by President Franklin D. Roosevelt) was developing the proposals that became the Social Security Act, the proponents sought to have health insurance included with old-age insurance and unemployment insurance.

In part because of urgency and in part because of the controversial nature of the subject and the strong opposition involved, no legislative proposal in the health insurance area was made by COES or by President Roosevelt in his recommendations to Congress. Also involved was the possibility that any such proposal would be declared unconstitutional and might then even pull down with it the companion old-age benefits and unemployment compensation proposals that were made. Instead, the need for further studies on health insurance was cited by the COES report.

An interesting sidelight of the 1935 legislation that became the Social Security Act was that initially the section that pertained to the duties of the Social Security Board referred to making studies and recommendations in various fields of social insurance, including health insurance. The reference to this controversial subject was stricken out in the course of the legislative action. However, since the final language in regard to studies and recommendations in the social insurance field contained the phrase "related subjects," the Social Security Board never felt any hesitancy about making extensive studies in the health insurance area.

Even though there was powerful opposition to compulsory health insurance in 1935, one important shift in camps had been made since the 1910s and early 1920s. The American Federation of Labor had, in the meantime, changed its early views of opposition to most forms of social insurance. This position was not revised formally until a few years after the passage of the Social Security Act. In considerable part, this was probably because of the effects of the depression that began in 1930 and the different attitude of AFL President William Green as compared with that of his predecessor, Samuel Gompers.

Legislative Proposals between 1935 and 1950

When President Franklin D. Roosevelt signed the Social Security Act in 1935, he made clear his feelings that this legislation was only the cornerstone of a much more extensive program. Under the "study" provisions of the act, the staff of the Social Security Board continued the research and investigation made by the COES on national health insurance.

The Interdepartmental Committee to Coordinate Health and Welfare Activities was established by President Roosevelt directly after the Social Security Act became law. Its recommendations were presented to a National Health Conference in 1938, which brought together a large group of persons who were interested in this subject.

The committee reports recommended, among other things, social insurance provisions for temporary disability benefits on the pattern of state unemployment insurance programs and for permanent disability benefits under the national old-age benefits program. Also, it was proposed that federal grants should be made available to state programs providing medical care for the needy—both those receiving cash public assistance payments and those who were medically indigent. It was also recommended that the states, with federal financial and technical assistance, should establish plans to meet medical costs on a pre-payment basis. Such plans would be financed, at the state level, from general taxes and/or contributions from the covered persons.

The National Health Conference discussed these recommendations in depth. In general, there was complete agreement on the broad principle of improving the nation's health, but there were differences of opinion on the methods for doing so and especially as to how the costs should be financed.

Following the conference, somewhat amended versions of the inter-departmental committee recommendations were embodied in a bill introduced in 1939 by Senator Wagner (Democrat). This was the first major bill outlining a broad federal health program. This bill included, among other major proposals, federal grants-in-aid to the states for medical care programs, whether through insurance, public medical services, or combinations, as the state might decide. The categories of persons to be protected and the services to be covered were described in a very broad and general manner and were not specifically detailed.

Extensive hearings on the Wagner Bill were held. This became the first national legislative sounding on health insurance, bringing to the front the support of major consumer groups and the opposition of the medical profession. A report in favor of the bill was filed, but in view of the opposition the bill was not brought to a vote. The importance of this was twofold: it revived national interest in health insurance, which had been laid aside during the legislative progress of the Social Security Act; and it demonstrated that the compromise of a federal-state grant-in-aid pattern did not result in acceptance.

With the failure of the Wagner Bill to win support for the state-by-state approach (with federal grants), the executive branch gave up this pattern. Instead, encouraged by the successful establishment and operation of the *national* social insurance system of old-age and survivors insurance in 1937–40, the executive branch concentrated thereafter on national proposals for health insurance linked with that system.

These proposals became identified widely as the Wagner-Murray-Dingell Bills (after the two Democratic Senators and the Democratic Representative who sponsored the legislation). The first of these proposals was made in 1943, and bills along these lines were introduced at various times in the 1940s and 1950s. These bills closely followed general recommendations made by the executive branch, but they were never endorsed officially by either President Roosevelt or President Truman.

These proposals included programs to provide protection against a considerable part of the expense of hospital and medical services for all workers (including retired workers) and their eligible dependents—not merely for those workers then covered by the OASI program, but also agricultural and domestic workers, self-employed persons, and the like. President Truman expressed support of these general principles, even though he did not endorse the specific bills.

The Wagner-Murray-Dingell proposal included virtually all medical services, except for the exclusion of drugs (other than unusually expensive prescriptions). Administration would be on a state-by-state basis through state agencies (acting as agents) that would contract with providers of care and fix the rates of payment. Physicians would elect whether they wanted to be reimbursed on fee-for-service, capitation, or salary. However, the total amounts available for reimbursement would be fixed in accordance with what was available through the financing mechanism of the system and would be equivalent in the aggregate, regardless of whichever method was selected by the physicians. The hospitals and other institutional providers of services would be paid on a negotiated cost-reimbursement basis.

The financing provisions of the Wagner-Murray-Dingell proposal were somewhat vague, because the bills were introduced as health measures, rather than as tax measures. This legislative procedure apparently was adopted so that the bills would be referred to committees that would be more favorably disposed toward the legislation. The implication was that the financing would be on a percentage-of-payroll basis. A sum equal to 1 percent of taxable wages would be authorized as an initial reserve. A continuing total contribution of 3 percent would be required each year thereafter, plus a further 1 percent (only 0.5 percent for the first three years) for financing dental and home nursing services. Hearings on the Wagner-Murray-Dingell Bills were held for several years, but the legislation never came to the floor of either the House or the Senate for a vote.

An approach taken by a wide variety of bills in the 1940s, mostly introduced by Republican members of Congress, was to encourage voluntary health insurance by giving exemptions or credits for such premiums for federal income tax purposes.

A completely different approach was taken by Senator Taft—perhaps the leading Republican member of Congress in 1946—as an answer to the Wagner-Murray-Dingell Bills. The Taft Bill would have provided federal financial support for state programs for the medically indigent. Thus, it might be said that this proposal was the first to establish the format to be used in the later Medicaid program.

Legislative Action in 1951–64

The 14-year period 1951–64 saw great activity in the field of proposals for medical care benefits under social insurance and under public assistance. In the early part of the period, the activity was centered around the development and discussion of social-insurance proposals, primarily for persons aged 65 and over. Later, in the middle of the period, medical care services under public assistance were significantly expanded, in part because those who opposed the social insurance approach supported public assistance measures as "counterfires." Thus, the Kerr-Mills Act of 1960, establishing the program of medical assistance for the aged was enacted, and was the first legislation passed in the format that would later emerge as Medicaid.

Beginning in 1960, efforts to enact a social insurance program of hospital benefits were stepped up through a series of bills known as the King-Anderson Bills (named after the Democratic House and Senate sponsors). The subject never came to a vote in the House of Representatives, but rather it was decisively rejected several times by the Ways and Means Committee. On the other hand, several record votes on the matter were held in the Senate, and each time the margin of defeat became less. The basic natures of the various benefit proposals that were considered over the years were similar, but minor changes were made from time to time in an effort to answer some of the opposition arguments and thus win support.

Finally, in 1964, the Senate passed, by a close vote, an amendment providing hospital insurance benefits for persons aged 65 and over, but the House would not agree to any compromise position, and the legislation died in conference when the session adjourned for the presidential election.

Over the period, the financing provided in the various proposals was increased significantly—from a combined employer-employee contribution rate of about 0.5 percent of taxable payroll for the earliest proposal to somewhat more than 0.75 percent for the last proposal. This increase was due in part to the continuing rapid increases in hospital costs over the period and in part to the adoption of more conservative assumptions in the underlying cost estimates.

ENACTMENT OF MEDICARE

The deadlock that occurred in connection with the 1964 legislation left the battle lines clearly drawn in the impending presidential campaign between President Johnson and his Republican opponent, Senator Goldwater. The latter had taken a strong position against the King-Anderson Bill and similar proposals during the 1964 Senate debate. In the actual campaign, however, this issue was not particularly stressed but, rather, others such as the Vietnam War took precedence.

The results of the election were such that the complexion of the House of Representatives changed considerably. It appeared to most political analysts that the temper of the House was clearly in the direction of passage of some type of legislation providing hospital benefits under social security for persons aged 65 and over. And, of course, the Senate, which had favored such a proposal in the 1964 legislative activities, had a composition in 1965 that was even more favorably disposed in this direction.

Administration Proposal in 1965

President Johnson decided to make the hospital insurance (HI) proposal his major legislative goal in 1965. It was contained in identical bills introduced by Congressman King (H.R.1) and Senator Anderson (S.1).

The King-Anderson Bill of 1965 provided for 60 days of hospital benefits within a benefit period, with a flat deductible equal in amount to approximately the expected nationwide average daily hospital cost under the program initially, subject to variation in the future. A maximum of 60 days for the post-hospital extended-care facility benefits was provided. Also provided were 240 home health services visits during a calendar year and outpatient diagnostic services during a 30-day period in excess of a deductible equal to half the inpatient hospital deductible.

The benefits would be available not only for insured persons under

OASDI and under the railroad retirement system but also on a transitional basis for virtually all noninsured persons in the country (excluding only active and retired federal employees eligible for health benefits under their own plan, certain short-residence aliens, and members of subversive organizations). The 1964 Social Security Advisory Council recommended HI for the disabled, but this was not included.

The financing was at a significantly higher level than the legislative proposals of previous years. In large part, this was the result of the views of Chairman Mills of the House Ways and Means Committee because of his concern that the program should be soundly financed under conservative cost assumptions. The combined tax rate for OASDI and HI would be allocated between the two programs.

The allocation to HI, as to the combined employer-employee rate, would be 0.6 percent of taxable payroll for 1966, 0.76 percent for the next two years, and 0.9 percent thereafter. The lower rate for the first year reflected the fact that taxes would be collected for the entire year, but that benefits would be paid only for the last six months. The intermediate step for the next two years was established on the grounds that it would be desirable from an economic standpoint to have such a graduated basis so that the total tax collections for these years would be as low as possible (and yet meet the program costs), and any fiscal-drag effects would thus be lessened. The maximum taxable earnings base would be increased to $5,600.

Other Proposals in 1965

Although the political atmosphere seemed such that it was virtually certain that hospital benefits associated with the OASDI system would be enacted, other proposals were made to the Congress. In part, these were made for the purpose of showing that although the sponsors had been opposed to the compulsory hospital insurance approach and still were, they nonetheless were interested in solving the problem of health benefits for persons aged 65 and over, but through different means.

One approach was sponsored by Representative Byrnes, the ranking Republican member of the House Ways and Means Committee. His bill provided a full range of health benefits—rather than merely hospital and related benefits as did the King-Anderson Bill—with certain deductibles and coinsurance. The benefits under this proposal were closely modeled after the high-option indemnity plan of health benefits available for federal government employees of all ages (including also the retired). The financing was through individual monthly premium payments aged 65 and over who elected to be covered.

Although the same benefit protection would have been available for all protected persons under the Byrnes Bill, the premium rate would vary directly with the size of the OASDI or railroad retirement monthly benefit that the individual was receiving or was eligible to receive. Persons not receiving such a benefit would pay the maximum premium possible (i.e., based on the maximum OASDI benefit). Specifically, the monthly premium payment equaled 10 percent of the minimum benefit, plus 5 percent of so much of the monthly benefit as exceeded the minimum benefit (so that it would have varied from approximately $4 to $9 for a single person and from $5 to $12 for a married couple). It was estimated that the premium payments from the beneficiaries would meet about one third of the cost. The remainder of the cost would come from general revenues.

Another approach, sponsored by the American Medical Association in its last-ditch fight against the enactment of a health benefits plan associated with social insurance, was contained in bills introduced by Democratic Representative Herlong and Republican Representative Curtis. This proposal—popularly referred to as Eldercare—essentially would have expanded the medical assistance for the aged program (MAA). It would have permitted the development of private health insurance that would be fully paid by MAA for low-income persons and would be on a partial-payment basis for those somewhat above the maximum income limits for "free" coverage. No uniform program of health benefits would have been prescribed or required for the states that wished to participate. This bill also would have liberalized the MAA program in a number of respects, by easing the means test requirements and by providing increased federal financial participation.

Action of House of Representatives in 1965

Early in 1965, the House Ways and Means Committee held executive sessions on the various proposals for health benefits for persons aged 65 and over. Chairman Mills had become convinced that the mood of the membership of the House was such that a bill providing some form of health benefits was called for and that such a bill could be developed on a sound basis. In order to get a broad base of support, he proposed that the new bill to be written by the committee should incorporate the essential features of all three major pending proposals. This politically logical approach took virtually everybody by surprise, including the sponsors of the three separate approaches.

Actually, many ardent sponsors of health benefits provided through social insurance were greatly pleased by the much broader approach than merely hospital insurance, since their real desire was comprehensive medical care through social insurance for persons aged 65 and over—and, in fact, whenever possible for the entire population. The results, therefore, were much more sweeping than they had ever dreamed possible, although they had some regrets about the voluntary nature of SMI and about its being financed by the participants, rather than through payroll taxes. On the other hand, some advocates of a national health service viewed the item-by-item approach of Medicare without enthusiasm; they feared that it might inhibit the future growth of comprehensive, unified health services.

The three separate health benefits proposals were incorporated by the Ways and Means Committee in the following manner: An HI program would be established with provisions paralleling closely those of the King-Anderson Bill, but with significantly different financing provisions. In addition, a supplementary voluntary program covering physician services and certain other medical costs would be established. The benefit provisions were similar to those of the Byrnes Bill, except that the hospital and related benefits were carved out (since they were provided in the separate HI system). This new program would be available on the basis of individual voluntary election and would be financed by uniform premium rates from the beneficiaries and an equal matching contribution from general revenues.

The voluntary nature of SMI, and the requirement that it be administered with a third party (carriers) between physicians and the government, evolved because of the strong views of the AMA, which were recognized by the committee even though it did not support the proposal. The AMA had always taken a position against any health insurance plan affecting physicians that was financed through payroll taxes and was compulsory for the participants, on the grounds that this involved governmental control and was socialized medicine. The basis adopted for SMI thus avoided these criticisms.

Finally, as the third part of the combination of the several health benefits proposals, a medical assistance program (Medicaid) would be established by broadening the existing MAA program to provide more liberal eligibility conditions and federal matching (and also to extend it beyond the aged category to younger persons). These provisions were taken to some extent from the AMA's Eldercare proposal, but they went far beyond it, especially by including younger persons.

The HI benefit provisions adopted by the committee differed from those of the administration proposal in the following major respects:

1. Post-hospital extended care benefits would be available for a maximum of 20 days per spell of illness, plus two additional days for each unused day of hospital benefits up to a maximum of 80 additional days. Furthermore, a prior stay of three days in a hospital would be required.
2. The outpatient diagnostic benefits would be changed so that the period to which the deductible applied would be 20 days in the same hospital, rather than 30 days in all hospitals. Furthermore, any deductible paid for this benefit would be credited against the hospital deductible.
3. The home health services benefits would be limited to 100 visits and would be available only after hospitalization.
4. The services of certain medical specialists in hospitals (radiologists, anesthesiologists, pathologists, and physiatrists) would be covered under SMI rather than HI.
5. A deductible would be introduced with respect to the first three pints of whole blood furnished in a spell of illness.

The HI program would be financed by a long-range increasing tax schedule and by increasing the maximum taxable earnings base to $5,600 for 1966–70 and $6,600 thereafter (as compared with the level $5,600 in the Administration proposal). The combined employer-employee rate would begin at 0.7 percent in 1966, and would then increase to 1 percent in 1967–71, 1.1 percent in 1973–75, 1.2 percent in 1976–79, 1.4 percent in 1980–86, and 1.6 percent thereafter. These rates would be levied on the same earnings base as OASDI. Unlike any previous proposals, the self-employed would pay only half the combined employer-employee rate. The cost of the benefits for the uninsured group would be borne by general revenues.

The SMI program would cover physician services, home health services regardless of prior hospitalization (up to a maximum of 100 visits per year), and various other medical and health services, such as diagnostic tests, therapy treatments, ambulance services, surgical dressings, and medical equipment. An annual deductible of $50 and

20 percent coinsurance on the part of the participant would be applicable. Special limitations would be provided on outpatient psychiatric care (in essence, 50 percent coinsurance and maximum reimbursement of $250 per year).

SMI would be financed by premiums of $3 a month from the participants, with equal matching amounts from general revenues. The premium rate could be adjusted in the future (after 1967) as experience indicated and would be higher for individuals who did not enter the program when they were first eligible to do so, with strict requirements as to such late enrollments and as to reenrollments.

The House adopted the provisions of the Ways and Means Committee bill without change.

Action of Senate in 1965

The Senate Finance Committee approved the provisions for both HI and SMI in substantially the same form as the House bill. The HI benefit provisions of the Finance Committee bill differed from those of the House bill in the following major respects:

1. The hospital benefits would be available for an additional 60 days, with coinsurance of $10 per day (automatically adjusted in the future, with changes in hospitalization costs).
2. The outpatient diagnostic benefits would have 20 percent coinsurance (so as to parallel the treatment of such services when covered outside of a hospital under SMI).
3. The post-hospital extended care benefits would be available for a maximum of 100 days per spell of illness in all cases, but there would be coinsurance of $5 per day (automatically adjusted in the future with changes in hospitalization costs) for each day after 20 days.
4. The home health services benefits would have a maximum of 175 visits per year.
5. The services of certain medical specialists in hospitals (discussed previously) would be covered under HI, as in the King-Anderson Bill.

The HI program, as modified by the Finance Committee, would be financed by a revised contribution schedule and by an earnings base of $6,600 for all years after 1965. Somewhat higher rates would be provided in the later years of operation than in the House bill, because of the increased cost involved in the benefit changes discussed previously. The HI tax rates before 1971 would not be increased. The combined employer-employee rates after 1970 would be 0.1 percent higher than in the House bill.

The provision as to the coverage of railroad workers was changed so that, in essence, the maximum taxable wage base under the railroad retirement system would have to be equivalent to that under OASDI; otherwise, the HI program would not be administered in any way by the Railroad Retirement Board.

The SMI benefit provisions of the Finance Committee bill differed from those of the House bill principally only in the manner indicated in the previous discussion of the changes in the HI program. The SMI provisions were not changed significantly during the Senate debate, but the following important changes were made in the HI provisions:

1. There would be no limit on the number of hospital days covered (but with coinsurance after 60 days).
2. The requirement of prior hospitalization for the home health service benefits would be eliminated.
3. The tax schedule would be increased to finance these changes. The combined employer-employee rates would be 0.1 percent higher than under the Finance Committee bill during 1973–86.

Action of Conference Committee in 1965

The two versions of the bill contained health benefit provisions that did not differ greatly, and so it was a relatively simple matter to obtain agreement. The Senate provisions for HI were followed, except as follows:

1. The maximum number of hospital days per spell of illness would be 90 (with daily coinsurance after 60 days).
2. Prior hospitalization would be required for the home health services benefits.
3. The maximum number of home health services visits would be 100 in a one-year period.
4. The services of the medical specialists would not be covered (but rather would be under SMI).
5. The tax schedule of the House bill was adopted as being sufficient to support the benefit provisions, while the taxable earnings base of $6,600 in all future years in the Senate bill was adopted (see Table 7.1).

TABLE 7.1

Combined Employer-Employee Hospital Insurance Tax Rates
and Maximum Taxable Earnings Bases under Various Acts

Period	1965 Act	1967 Act	Mid-1972 Act*	End-1972 Act*	Present Law
		Combined Employer-Employee Tax Rate			
1966...................	0.7%	0.7%	0.7%	0.7%	0.7%
1967...................	1.0	1.0	1.0	1.0	1.0
1968–72..............	1.0	1.2	1.2	1.2	1.2
1973...................	1.1	1.3	1.8	2.0	2.0
1974–75..............	1.1	1.3	1.8	2.0	1.8
1976–77..............	1.2	1.4	1.8	2.0	1.8
1978–80†.............	1.2	1.4	2.0	2.5	2.2
1981–85†.............	1.4	1.6	2.0	2.7	2.7
1986 and after†........	1.6	1.8	2.4‡	2.9	3.0
		Taxable Earnings Base			
1966–67..............	$6,600	$6,600	$ 6,600	$ 6,600	$ 6,600
1968–71..............	6,600	7,800	7,800	7,800	7,800
1972.................	6,600	7,800	9,000§	9,000	9,000
1973.................	6,600	7,800	10,800	10,800	10,800
1974.................	6,600	7,800	12,000	12,000	13,200
1975 and after.........	6,600	7,800	‖	‖	‖

* The tax schedule in this act never went into effect, being superceded by the schedule in the amendments enacted later in 1972 and by the amendments enacted in 1973, which increased the earnings base from $12,000 to $13,200. (See next column.)
† For 1965 and 1967 Acts, these periods are 1978–79, 1980–86, and 1987 and after, respectively.
‡ 2.2 percent for 1986–92.
§ Based on 1971 Act.
‖ Automatically adjusted according to changes in earnings levels.

Both bodies readily accepted the bill as modified by the conference agreement. President Johnson signed the measure, which was one of the major triumphs in the achievement of his legislative goals for 1965.

CHANGES IN MEDICARE SINCE 1965

As might be expected in legislation of the nature and complexity of Medicare, changes in the original program have been proposed, discussed, and enacted. These changes have occurred in both the hospital insurance and supplementary medical insurance provisions, and in the persons covered or eligible for Medicare benefits. Many of the changes were effective during the Johnson administration, but they have continued through the Nixon administration.

Considerations and Actions during Johnson Administration

President Johnson, as indicated, placed great emphasis upon medical care legislation. After passage of Medicare, this emphasis did not subside, and many changes were proposed by the administration. Substantial revisions in Medicare were proposed in 1967, and some of these were enacted.

Consideration of Medicare for the Disabled in 1967. In 1967, the administration proposed Medicare benefits for disability beneficiaries who were eligible for cash benefits—disabled workers (but not their eligible dependents), disabled child beneficiaries aged 18 or over (children of retired, disabled, and deceased insured workers), and disabled widows.

The additional cost to the HI program would be met by increasing the earnings base from $6,600 to $7,800 in 1968–70, $9,000 in 1971–73, and $10,800 in 1974 and after. The SMI benefits for the disabled would be financed by premium payments from the enrollees at the same rate as paid by those aged 65 and over and by equal matching government contributions.

The bill written by the House Ways and Means Committee did not contain any provisions for extending Medicare to disabled beneficiaries. However, it provided for the establishment of an advisory council to be named by the Secretary of Health, Education, and Welfare to study this subject during 1968 (as did also the final legislation). The administration's proposal in 1967 to include disabled beneficiaries within Medicare was not accepted, primarily because of financing problems.

During the legislative considerations, data became available from a survey of OASDI disabled beneficiaries, and these showed that such persons have hospital and medical costs that are probably about two and a half to three times as high on a per capital basis as persons aged 65 and over. The use of these new data caused a significant increase in the estimated cost of both the HI and SMI benefits for disabled beneficiaries. The increased cost would have required a significant rise in the HI tax rates in order to finance the benefits for disability beneficiaries.

Each way that the increased cost of covering the disabled under SMI could be met within the premium-government contribution basis seemed to be unacceptable. If the costs were spread over all beneficiaries (the aged and the disabled), with equal government matching, then it would seem unfair for the aged to pay more than before and receive no more protection than otherwise.

If the disabled were charged a special higher premium rate that would be sufficient, together with an equal government contribution just as for the aged, the rate would be so high that many would not believe themselves able to afford it. More importantly, because of the diversity of physical conditions among the disabled, the protection for many would not be worth the premium charged. Accordingly, many would not enroll, so that a vicious circle of antiselection and rapidly rising per capita costs would occur.

The only other solution would be to charge the disabled the same premium rate as the aged, but to have a much higher government contribution for the former than for the latter. This procedure would destroy the equal-matching principle (by a considerable amount) and so was unacceptable to the Ways and Means Committee.

As a result, Medicare benefits for the disabled were not included in the 1967 legislation.

Other HI Legislative Action in 1967.   The developing experience during 1966–67 indicated that hospital costs had risen much more rapidly since enactment of Medicare than had originally been estimated. Accordingly, additional financing seemed necessary.

The 1967 administration bill also contained other changes in HI. The taxable earnings base was changed in the same manner as was proposed for OASDI, as mentioned in Chapter 3. This bill contained the following other important HI provisions:

1. The outpatient diagnostic benefits would be transferred to SMI. The original complicated, although logical, provisions that coordinated this benefit with HI had proved extremely difficult to administer.
2. The cost reimbursement would be reduced if capital expenditures made by the provider of services were contrary to state planning recommendations.
3. The professional (i.e., physician) component of pathology and radiology services furnished to hospital inpatients would be transferred from SMI to HI (and would not be subject to cost-sharing, other than the overall HI initial deductible).

The House bill took the following action with regard to HI:

1. The outpatient diagnostic benefits would be transferred to SMI.
2. The maximum duration of hospital benefits in a spell of illness would be increased from 90 days to 120 days, with the additional 30 days being subject to daily cost-sharing equal to half the initial deductible.
3. The tax rate would be increased for all years after 1968 by 0.1 percent for each party (employers, employees, and self-employed), and the earnings base would be $7,800 for all future years.

The major changes made by the Senate bill as compared with the House bill were as follows:

1. In lieu of increasing the maximum duration of hospital benefits from 90 days to 120 days (with daily cost-sharing equal to half the initial deductible), a "lifetime reserve" of 60 days, with daily cost sharing equal to one fourth of the initial deductible, would be provided.
2. Tax rates would be 0.1 percent higher for each party in 1968, the same in 1969–75, and lower in 1976 and after (such decrease being 0.15 percent in 1987 and after). Such decrease would be possible because of the higher earnings bases than in the House bill (namely, the same as in the administration bill).

The Conference Committee resolved the differences between the two versions of the bill in the following manner:

1. The additional hospital days in the lifetime reserve were subject to daily cost-sharing equal to half the initial deductible.
2. Tax rates were increased for all years after 1967 by 0.1 percent for each party, and the earnings base was $7,800 for all future years (see Table 7.1).

Other SMI Legislative Action in 1967. The 1967 administration bill contained certain changes in the benefit provisions of the SMI program as follows:

1. HI outpatient diagnostic benefits (relating to the nonprofessional component of such services) would be transferred to SMI (the professional component thereof had always been included in SMI).
2. The professional component of pathology and radiology service furnished to hospital inpatients would be transferred to HI.
3. Certain nonroutine podiatrist services would be covered.

The only significant SMI benefit changes that were made in the House bill were as follows:

1. Transfer of the outpatient diagnostic benefits from HI.
2. Making the cost-sharing provisions inapplicable to the professional component of pathology and radiology services furnished to hospital inpatients.

The Senate bill added the following benefit provisions:

1. Services of chiropractors and certain nonroutine services of optometrists would be covered.
2. Physical therapy benefits furnished outside of hospitals would be covered on a much broader basis.
3. Services of clinical psychologists would be covered (even though not referred by a physician and billed through him—the latter services being covered under previous law).

During the course of the Senate debate, Senator Montoya (Democrat) offered an amendment to include an out-of-hospital prescription drug benefit in SMI. A $25 annual deductible would be applied to charges for drugs. Then, individuals would be reimbursed directly on excess charges, with the reimbursement amount being based on the wholesale cost of the least expensive generic equivalent plus a pharmacist's professional fee (and not on actual charges, unless lower). The latter provision would thus have the effect of producing some cost-sharing. The sponsor of the proposal estimated that its cost would be $1 per month (divided equally between the enrollee and the government), while the Social Security Administration estimated the cost at $3.20. The amendment was defeated by a relatively close vote.

The final bill followed the provisions of the House bill, except that the physical therapy provision was retained, and a revision of the enrollment and premium-rate procedures that were added by the Senate Finance Committee was included. Under the final bill, general enrollment periods are to be held annually, instead of biennially. Also, enrollees are allowed to withdraw without waiting until an enrollment period occurs.

Under the initial legislation, the premium rate was established at $3 per month for July 1966 through December 1967 (see Table 7.2). The standard premium rate for persons enrolling in the earliest possible enrollment period for the succeeding two-year period was to be promul-

TABLE 7.2

Standard Supplementary Medical Insurance Monthly Premium
Rates in Various Periods

Period	Rate	How Determined
July 1966–December 1967	$3.00	1965 Act
January 1968–March 1968	3.00	1967 Act
April 1968–June 1969	4.00	Promulgated
July 1969–June 1970	4.00	Promulgated
July 1970–June 1971	5.30	Promulgated
July 1971–June 1972	5.60	Promulgated
July 1972–June 1973	5.80	Promulgated
July 1973–June 1974	6.30	Promulgated†
July 1974–June 1975	6.70	Promulgated
July 1975–June 1976	6.70*	Promulgated

* Law does not permit an increase because the OASDI cash-benefit level for June 1975 (as known in December 1974) was the same as in June 1974. This resulted from a technical error in the law, as discussed later in this chapter. Legislation in process in March 1975 would correct this error and would result in the premium rate rising to $7.40.

† Actually, because of action of the Price Commission, the rate was frozen at $5.80 for July 1973 and $6.10 for August 1973.

gated by the Secretary of Health, Education, and Welfare before October 1967. However, since the 1967 legislation was still pending in September and there was no possibility of its final enactment then, and since it contained significant changes in the program, a "quickie" bill was passed to make the promulgation applicable for April 1968 and thereafter (continuing the $3 rate until then). Under the final bill, the standard premium rate is determined annually—initially for April 1968 through June 1969, but then for 12-month periods beginning with July 1969.

Advisory Council on Health Insurance for the Disabled. At the end of 1968, the Advisory Council on Health Insurance for the Disabled made a number of sweeping recommendations. First, Medicare coverage should be made available not only to disability beneficiaries but also to insured workers who are disabled for at least three months. Not only would the waiting period for cash benefits not be required, but also the prognosis of the disability lasting for at least 12 months or until prior death would not be required. Further, for persons aged 55 or over, the definition of disability would be more lenient—by requiring disability only such that the person is unable to engage in substantial gainful activity in his regular work, rather than for any substantial gainful employment. This would produce an administrative nightmare by having more liberal conditions for the short-range Medicare benefits than for the long-range cash benefits.

Second, the Council recommended combining HI and SMI for the disabled for financing purposes, with the cost being met half by equal employer-employee contributions (the self-employed rate continuing equal to the employee rate) and half by a government subsidy.

Final Legislative Proposals of the Johnson Administration. Just before going out of office in January 1969, the Johnson administration made a number of sweeping recommendations for legislation to change the Medicare program. These proposals included: (1) extending HI and SMI to disabled beneficiaries, with a liberalized basis of disability eligibility; (2) combining HI and SMI, so that both would be financed by payroll taxes but with half the cost being met by a government subsidy; and (3) inclusion of out-of-hospital drug benefits under HI for so-called maintenance drugs (important in the treatment of chronic diseases). No specific recommendations were made as to how these expansions would be financed.

Considerations and Actions during Nixon Administration

The changeover from the Johnson administration to the Nixon administration did not have a substantial impact upon the flow of changes in the Medicare program. The administration continued to recommend legislative changes, and Congress continued to amend the program.

Initial Legislative Proposals of Nixon Administration. New actuarial cost estimates for the HI program were made in late 1968 and then again a year later. Each showed significantly higher costs than had previously been estimated. Accordingly, when the Nixon administration made social security recommendations in late 1969 (essentially to update the OASDI benefit provisions), it also made provision for meeting the financing problems of HI. This would be done in three ways. First, the ultimate combined employer-employee tax rate of 1.8 percent scheduled for 1987 and after (0.9 percent for self-employed persons) would be moved up to 1971 and held level thereafter. Second, the maximum taxable earnings base of $7,800 per year would be increased to $9,000. Third, for 1974 (and each second year thereafter), the earnings base would be subject to automatic increase, depending on changes in the level of earnings in covered employment.

There were no changes proposed in HI benefit provisions. However, the Nixon administration recommended certain legislative changes in the HI program (applicable also to the Medicaid program) to achieve more effective cost controls. Such measures would include requirements for better planning of medical facilities and would permit better control of some serious abuses, particularly in utilization of services.

Legislative Action in 1970–72. Beginning in 1970, Congress gave thorough consideration to extensive legislation modifying OASDI and Medicare. An omnibus bill containing many important changes in Medicare failed to win enactment in 1970 because insufficient time remained in the session to reconcile the many differences between the House and Senate versions. The various Medicare provisions were carried over into the legislation considered in 1971–72 and enacted in late 1972 (H.R.1 introduced by Chairman Mills).

While the omnibus bill was being considered in 1971, a "quickie" bill increasing OASDI benefits indirectly helped to lessen the long-range financing problems of HI by increasing the earnings base to $9,000 for 1972 and after. Another such "quickie" bill in mid-1972, in addition to increasing cash benefits, also remedied the financing problems of the HI system (at least, according to the current actuarial cost estimates) by increasing the earnings base to $10,800 for 1973 and $12,000 for 1974, with automatic adjustments thereafter based on changes in wage levels and by a new tax schedule (see Table 7.1). That schedule, however, never went into effect because it was superceded by the schedule in the omnibus bill enacted later in the year.

The initiative in developing the Medicare provisions in the legislation enacted in 1972 was largely taken by Congress, although the Nixon administration did not object to any of the changes. The administration, however, did propose that SMI should be financed by payroll taxes (as had the Johnson administration), thus indirectly increasing the level of cash benefits for persons aged 65 and over; under this proposal, the government contribution would have been eliminated (whereas the Johnson administration proposal would have increased it). Neither the House nor the Senate gave any support to this approach, and it was not included in any version of the legislation.

The legislation finally enacted in 1972 contained the following major provisions affecting both HI and SMI (with an indication of whether the provision originated in the House or the Senate):

1. Coverage of disabled beneficiaries on the roll for at least two years (House).

2. Coverage of insured workers and dependents with chronic kidney disease (Senate).
3. Antiduplication provisions with federal employees health benefits program effective in 1975, unless that program is changed so as to coordinate with Medicare (House).
4. Extension of coverage of services rendered outside the United States (Senate).
5. Special reimbursement provisions for health maintenance organizations (House).
6. Establishment of professional standards review organizations (Senate).
7. Several changes tightening cost controls and utilization (both bodies).

The 1972 legislation also made the following major changes affecting the HI program only (with an indication of which body originated it):

1. Liberalized definition of skilled nursing facility services (Senate).
2. Voluntary coverage for persons aged 65 or over, with full cost paid by enrollees (House).
3. Revised tax schedule to meet long-range imbalance for the previous program and to meet the cost for including the disabled; see Table 7.1 (both bodies).
4. Increase in taxable earnings base and automatic adjustment thereof in the future in accordance with changes in the level of wages in covered employment; see Table 7.1 (House).
5. Beneficiary relieved of liability when claim previously paid is disallowed if he is without fault (i.e., he did not know that services were not covered, and the provider of services was at fault); this will increase the direct cost of the program to some extent, but such higher cost should be more than offset by the closer scrutiny that utilization review committees will give so that the liability does not then fall on the institution (Senate).

It is also important to consider the provisions which were adopted by one body but were rejected in conference, since these often come up for consideration later. Such HI provisions were as follows (with an indication of which body passed the provision):

1. Daily cost-sharing for hospital services in the 31st to 60th days equal to one eighth of the initial deductible (House).

2. Increase in lifetime reserve days from 60 days to 120 days (House).
3. Reduction in daily cost-sharing for lifetime reserve days from half of the initial deductible to one quarter thereof (Senate).
4. Coverage of specifically named out-of-hospital prescription drugs used for specified chronic conditions, subject to a $1 cost-sharing payment per prescription—to be covered under HI, anomalously (Senate).
5. Voluntary HI coverage for OASDI and RR beneficiaries aged 60–64, on a cost basis (Senate).

The final 1972 legislation contained the following major SMI-only changes (with an indication of the originating body):

1. Initial deductible increased from $50 to $60 per year (House).
2. Coverage of disabled beneficiaries on the roll for at least two years (House).
3. Coverage made automatic for persons newly eligible (if under HI), with option to elect out (House).
4. Elimination of limitation that persons must enroll within three years of first eligibility (House).
5. Certain chiropractor services covered (Senate).
6. Speech pathologist services covered (Senate).
7. Limited independent physical therapist services covered (House).
8. Coinsurance for home health services benefits eliminated (Senate).
9. Premium-rate basis for persons aged 65 and over changed, so that increase in rate cannot exceed rise in cash-benefits level (House).
10. Railroad Retirement Board to collect premiums for all persons receiving RR benefits, even though also receiving OASDI benefits (House).
11. More restrictive basis for physician reimbursement—prevailing-charge screen at 75th percentile and adjusted in future by economic index, rather than actual prevailing charges (House).
12. More flexible reimbursement procedures for durable medical equipment to encourage purchase of used items (Senate).

Several SMI provisions added by the Senate were not included in the final 1972 legislation as follows:

1. Voluntary SMI coverage for OASDI and RR beneficiaries aged 60–64, on a cost basis (with no government contribution).

2. Coverage of clinical psychologist services when furnished by an independent practitioner.
3. Coverage of outpatient rehabilitation services.

In 1970, when the legislation became deadlocked and died at the close of the session, the Senate bill contained a provision for a payroll-tax-supported program of catastrophic medical insurance for insured workers and their dependents under age 65. This was sponsored by Chairman Long of the Finance Committee and, during subsequent periods, has been strongly urged by him. This provision would apply as follows:

1. Hospital costs for days in excess of 60 per year per individual would be covered, with a daily cost-sharing amount equal to one fourth of the HI initial deductible.
2. Costs for services covered by SMI would be covered after the family expenses in a year had exceeded $2,000, and there would then be 20 percent coinsurance. The $2,000 limit would be adjusted in future years according to changes in the physician-fee levels considered in preparing the Consumer Price Index.
3. There would be carryover deductibles under both the hospital and medical benefits provisions for expenses incurred (or hospital days) but not reimbursed in the last calendar quarter of a year.
4. The cost of this proposal would be met by payroll taxes on the earnings covered by OASDI and HI. The combined employer-employee tax rate would be 0.6 percent the first three years, 0.7 percent the next five years, and 1.8 percent thereafter, with the self-employed paying half this amount.

1973 Legislative Proposals of Nixon Administration.   In early 1973, the Nixon administration proposed several changes in the cost-sharing provisions of the Medicare program that would reduce federal expenditures—and thus increase individuals' expenditures (except in some long-duration hospital cases). Specifically, under the proposal, the HI cost sharing would be changed to an initial deductible of the first day's room and board charge in the particular hospital and then 10 percent coinsurance on all other charges thereafter. Likewise, the SMI cost sharing would be changed by increasing the initial deductible from $60 to $85 (which was the same relative to physician fees as $50 was in 1966) and the coinsurance rate from 20 percent to 25 percent. These would have resulted in cost reductions of $1.3 billion in the first full year of operation.

Although these proposals are quite reasonable and logical, and would have made good sense if they had been adopted originally, they represented a significant deliberalization. Accordingly, they received virtually no support in Congress (in fact, no member would even introduce a bill containing them!), and they seemed most unlikely of adoption. In fact, the Senate voted a "sense of the Congress" provision in a bill unrelated to social security that these recommendations of the President should be withdrawn; the provision, however, was deleted in the conference with the House.

The only legislative action taken in 1973 that affected the Medicare program was that in the July amendments which increased the maximum taxable earnings base for 1974 to $12,600, but this was overridden by the December amendments which further increased such base to $13,200 and also readjusted the tax schedule by lowering it in the early years and raising it in the later years (see Table 7.1).

LEGISLATION PASSED IN 1973 BUT NOT ENACTED

As brought out in Chapter 3, significant changes in the social security program were contained in legislation which passed the Senate in November 1973, but was not finally enacted. These proposed changes are of interest in connection with possible future legislative activity.

The only important Medicare provision proposed by the Senate Finance Committee, from a cost standpoint, was the inclusion of outpatient occupational therapy as an SMI benefit, paralleling physical therapy and speech pathology services. However, on the floor of the Senate the following significant provisions were added:

1. Certain named maintenance drugs for certain specified conditions would be covered under HI, with a cost-sharing payment from the beneficiary of $1 per prescription. The pharmacy would be reimbursed on the basis of the wholesale cost plus a professional fee minus the cost-sharing payment, but not in excess of the usual charge minus the cost-sharing payment.
2. The HI in-patient deductible would continue in 1974 at the 1973 level of $72, and increases for 1975 and after would be based on the $72 figure; the deductible actually rose to $84 in 1974.

3. The number of lifetime reserve days under HI would be increased from 60 to 120 days, and the daily coinsurance therefor would be reduced from 50 percent of the HI initial deductible to 25 percent thereof.

4. The definition of "spell of illness" under HI would be liberalized so that it would also end after the individual had been in an SNF for 180 days and had not received skilled nursing care or rehabilitative services. This can provide benefits in a new spell of illness when the individual involved had used up his maximum days of benefits in the previous spell of illness.

5. Coverage under both HI and SMI would be extended to the disabled spouse under age 65 of an individual who is covered under Medicare as a disability beneficiary.

6. Benefits for home health services under HI would no longer require prior hospitalization and would be paid for a maximum of 100 visits per calender year, instead of per spell of illness.

7. Coverage under both HI and SMI would be extended on a voluntary basis to persons aged 60–64 who are eligible for OASDI benefits (whether or not in receipt of them) and to persons aged 60–64 who are spouses of individuals covered under Medicare. The cost would be borne entirely by the enrollee under the same conditions as are applicable to voluntary HI enrollees aged 65 or over.

8. Additional financing of an increase in the combined employer-employee HI tax of 0.1 percent would be provided. Such financing was included with the amendment providing coverage for maintenance drugs and would, on a long-range basis, meet about 70 percent of the estimated cost thereof. No additional financing was provided for the other changes involving increased cost—items 2–6; these had an estimated long-range cost of about 0.1 percent of payroll.

1975 LEGISLATIVE PROPOSALS
OF FORD ADMINISTRATION

In early 1975, President Ford made several legislative proposals with regard to the Medicare program. In part, these were made to reduce costs, because of the budgetary situation of the federal government, although they also improved the extent of catastrophic protection. These proposals were somewhat like those made by the Nixon administration in 1973. Specifically, it was proposed that the cost-sharing provisions under both HI and SMI would be changed.

As to HI, the daily coinsurance for hospital days after the 60th one and for SNF days would be replaced by a straight 10-percent co-insurance on all charges over the initial deductible, but with maximum cost-sharing of $750 per spell of illness. Based on the 1975 cost-sharing provisions and on an average hospital charge of $100 per day, this proposal would result in higher costs to the beneficiary for stays of 88 days or less, and vice versa.

As to SMI, the deductible would be increased from year to year in accordance with increases in OASDI benefits, which would reflect changes in medical costs. To some extent, this procedure is followed in the determination of the SMI premium rate. Also, a maximum of $750 would be established for the amount of cost-sharing which the beneficiary would be required to pay for any calendar year. With the current $60 deductible, this maximum would be operative after recognized charges reach $3,510 for a year.

As was the case with the proposal of the Nixon administration in 1973, there was considerable logic in this proposal, but its reception by Congress was quite negative. At some point, however, it seems possible that the catastrophic portion, the $750 limits, might be pulled out from the proposal and adopted independently.

1974 ADVISORY COUNCIL ON SOCIAL SECURITY

As was mentioned in Chapter 3, the 1974 Advisory Council on Social Security had an extremely short time to accomplish its assignment. As a result of the financing problems of the OASDI system, it devoted almost all of its work to that program and practically none to the Medicare program. The council also stated that any recommendations that it might make as to the benefit structure of Medicare might soon be outdated by broader modifications of that program which would result if any of the current proposals for national health insurance were enacted.

The council made, indirectly, one important recommendation about the financing of HI, as described in Chapter 3, namely to gradually phase its financing from the payroll tax to general revenues. Primarily, this was done to solve the financing problems of OASDI, although it was argued that this would be logical because HI benefits are not earnings-related, as are the HI taxes that covered workers pay. (But note that this runs counter to the arguments about the regressivity of the Social Security taxes, since with uniform benefits and percentage-of-earnings taxes, much less regressivity is present than under OASDI, with its earnings-related benefits).

As mentioned previously, several council members opposed this change and instead recommended that the financial problems of OASDI be solved by higher tax rates and that the financing of HI be accomplished as under present law, by direct payroll taxes. President Ford, too, opposed this shift in the method of financing HI.

One member of the council, a representative from the National Council of Senior Citizens, also opposed the eventual complete financing of HI from general revenues. He took the position that this would destroy the "earned rights" nature of the program. However, he did take the position that a government subsidy to finance one-third of the cost of the program would be desirable.

When dealing with the financing of HI, the council neglected to mention whether its recommendation that, under OASDI, the self-employed should have a tax rate equal to 1½ times the employee rate would also apply to HI, at least as long as the payroll tax was used thereunder.

The council stated its finding that the long-range financing of the HI system and the short-range financing of the SMI system were in an actuarially sound position. The one member of the council who is an actuary dissented with regard to this view as to HI on the grounds that the council had not investigated this matter sufficiently to make such an unequivocal statement.

PROMULGATED MEDICARE ELEMENTS

Three important elements of the Medicare program are determined by promulgation of the Secretary of Health, Education, and Welfare, rather than by congressional action. These are the SMI standard premium rate, the HI initial deductible (upon which all other HI cost-sharing provisions are based), and the HI premium for voluntary enrollees who are not eligible as a result of insured status. Table 7.2 has presented the various SMI premium rates which have been promulgated in the past. Table 7.3 shows the amounts of the HI cost-sharing amounts that have been in effect in the past and currently, while Table 7.4 shows the corresponding voluntary HI premium rates.

TABLE 7.3

HI Cost-Sharing Provisions in Various Periods

| | | Hospital Daily | | |
Period	Initial Deductible	61st to 70th Days	Lifetime Reserve	SNF Daily after 20 Days
July 1966– December 1968*.........	$40	$10	$20†	$ 5.00
1969....................	44	11	22	5.50
1970....................	52	13	26	6.50
1971....................	60	15	30	7.50
1972....................	68	17	34	8.50
1973‡..................	72	18	36	9.00
1974....................	84	21	42	10.50
1975....................	92	23	46	11.50

* Determined by legislation; all other amounts promulgated by Secretary of Health, Education, and Welfare.

† Benefit first available in 1968.

‡ The amounts determined in accordance with the provisions of the law were $76, $19, $38, and $9.50, respectively, but a ruling of the Price Commission prevented these increases and allowed instead the amounts shown above.

TABLE 7.4

Standard Voluntary HI Monthly Premium Rates in Various Periods

Period	Rate
July 1973–June 1974*........................	$33.00
July 1974–June 1975........................	36.00
July 1975–June 1976........................	40.00

* Determined by legislation; all other rates promulgated by Secretary of Health, Education, and Welfare.

chapter 8

Medicare Financing Principles and Provisions

The two separate portions of Medicare, hospital insurance and supplementary medical insurance, have quite different characteristics, especially as to eligibility provisions. For this reason, the basic financing principles underlying HI and SMI are completely different. On a long-run basis, HI is financed by payroll taxes levied on employed and self-employed persons in covered work and on employers, while SMI is financed by premium payments of those currently being protected and by matching contributions from general revenues.

Under HI the vast majority of the persons paying taxes at any given time do not have immediate benefit protection if the need for hospitalization should occur at that time. Instead, it may be said that the HI contributors are accumulating earnings credits that may entitle them and their eligible dependents to HI benefit protection when they reach age 65, or earlier if they become disabled. Of course, there are some contributors who are aged 65 or over, or whose eligible dependent is of this age, so that there are instances where simultaneous tax payment and benefit protection exist. Conversely, under SMI, protection is always concurrent with premium payment and is on an individual basis, rather than on a family basis, since it never applies to one family member merely because another is covered.

HI FINANCING PRINCIPLES

The general financing principle of the HI system is that it should be completely self-supporting as to both benefit payments and administrative expenses by the taxes received from insured persons covered by the program and from employers. This principle does not require that there should be a fixed, level tax rate prescribed in the law for all future years, but rather that there be a schedule of rates which, over a long-range future period, will accomplish this result. Such financing also consists of interest earnings obtained by investing the available assets. The only exception to this general principle is in the case of noninsured persons who meet the necessary eligibility requirements, whose costs are met from general revenues, and of other noninsured persons who elect coverage on a voluntary, self-supporting premium basis.

The persons who are subject to HI taxes on their earnings are the same as those under the old-age, survivors, and disability insurance system, plus those under the railroad retirement system.

Individual Equity Concept

Under OASDI, when an individual contributes more, it is generally the case that his monthly benefit will be higher, either because of higher earnings or because of greater continuity of employment. Under HI, there is an entirely different principle, because the same benefits are provided for all who meet the eligibility requirements, regardless of their earnings level or their length of contributions in excess of the minimum period required.

The status of married women workers under HI is worthy of note. Under OASDI, a married woman who has covered employment of her own receives, in essence, whichever benefit is the larger—that from her own earnings or that from her husband's earnings. In many instances, she will receive only the latter, so that it may be argued that she does not obtain anything from her own taxes, other than the lump-sum death payment available from her own earnings record. On the other hand, there are many instances where her own earnings record produces benefit rights or additional benefit rights, such as when her own benefit is larger than that derived from her husband's earnings record or when she claims benefits before her husband retires from full-time substantial employment.

Under HI, if a woman has benefit eligibility from her husband's earnings record, having such eligibility on her own record will rarely be of any additional value. The only exceptions are if she is much older than her husband and reaches age 65 before he is aged 62 or if they are divorced and their marriage lasted less than 20 years. However, a female worker must pay the HI taxes even if she will be entitled to HI benefits through her husband.

If HI operated on the same financing principles as private insurance, one could well raise several critical questions. First, why should individuals contribute for more than the minimum period required for eligibility? Second, why should married women be required to contribute at all? Third, what is the advantage to a high-paid employee of paying larger taxes than a low-paid worker? Fourth, for those with maximum taxable earnings, what benefit will accrue to them if the taxable earnings base is increased? In all these cases, no additional benefit protection is generated by the additional taxes.

The answer to the foregoing questions is simply that social insurance in general—and HI in particular—is (and must be) guided largely by social-adequacy principles rather than individual-equity ones. In fact, as may be seen from the foregoing discussion, the social-adequacy principle is even stronger in HI than in OASDI.

It can be argued that any individual-equity comparisons and considerations should be made for OASDI and HI combined, and not for HI separately. Under these circumstances, the value of the HI protection can be regarded as a uniform, flat benefit for all persons. Even so, it is difficult to show that the young high-paid employee gets his money's worth under the combined OASDI and HI systems (although this is true when considering OASDI alone). However, for the *average* young employee the "money's worth" criterion is met for the combination of the OASDI and HI systems.

Financing and Investment Procedures

Insofar as the HI system is concerned, the financing principle of self-support from contributions and investment earnings is effectuated by the provisions of the law that establish a long-range tax schedule. These rates will, according to the best actuarial cost estimates available, provide sufficient income to support the program over a 25-year period. In addition, this financing is intended to be sufficient to leave a balance in the fund at the end of that time amounting to one year's outgo.

A separate trust fund is established for the HI program in the same manner as the OASDI trust funds. All receipts from taxes, investment earnings, and payments from the General Fund of the Treasury for the costs relating to noninsured persons flow into the HI Trust Fund. Likewise, all benefit payments to hospitals and other institutional providers of services and all administrative expenses, including those of the fiscal intermediaries, flow from it.

Allocation of Costs among Contributors

Ever since the OASDI system began operations in 1937, the taxes with respect to employees have been equally divided between the employer and the worker. There is no actuarial reason for this division; rather, it may be said that this procedure has aesthetic logic and appeal to the general public as being a fair sharing basis. It may be noted that in some foreign social insurance systems the share of the employer is more than 50 percent. When HI was established, the 50-50 allocation between employers and workers was adopted without question.

The situation for the self-employed is, however, different under HI than under OASDI. When this category was initially covered under OASDI (in 1951), a compromise basis was adopted for their tax rate, namely, 1½ times the employee rate. When the 1965 amendments were being considered, the projected self-employed rate under OASDI was thought by some to create a relatively heavy financial burden. Accordingly, a ceiling of 7 percent was then placed on the OASDI rate for the self-employed, and the HI rate for the self-employed was set at the employee rate for all years.

Self-Supporting Principle

Just as under OASDI, the HI program is intended to be on a self-supporting basis over the long range from the worker and employer taxes insofar as the benefit and administrative costs for insured persons are concerned. Thus, for this category, the tax schedule in the law is intended to provide sufficient funds, along with the interest earnings of the HI Trust Fund, to meet such costs over a 25-year period and to accumulate a trust fund balance at the end of the period equal to one year's outgo.

The benefit and administrative costs applicable to noninsured persons is met from the General Fund of the Treasury by periodic payments in reimbursement to the HI Trust Fund. The delay involved in making such payments is recognized by appropriate interest-adjustment payments in addition to the regular ones.

HI FINANCING PROVISIONS

Tax Rates

The HI program is financed by an increasing schedule of rates that are applicable to earnings in covered employment up to the maximum earnings base, which is the same as for OASDI (see Table 8.1 which

TABLE 8.1

HI and OASDI Tax Rates under Present Law

Period	HI Rate*	Combined HI and OASDI Rate	
		Employer-Employee	Self-Employed
1966	0.35%	8.4%	6.15%
1967	0.50	8.8	6.40
1968	0.60	8.8	6.40
1969–70	0.60	9.6	6.90
1971–72	0.60	10.4	7.50
1973	1.00	11.7	8.00
1974–77	0.90	11.7	7.90
1978–80	1.10	12.1	8.10
1981–85	1.35	12.6	8.35
1986–2010	1.50	12.9	8.50
2011 and after	1.50	14.9	8.50

* Same rate for employer, employee, and self-employed.

also shows the combination of these and the OASDI tax rates for purposes of comparison). The same tax rate is payable by employers, employees, and the self-employed under HI.

The tax schedule for HI is on a gradually increasing basis, just as OASDI has been in the past. The reason for this is to match up income and outgo approximately, so that current-cost financing occurs.

The HI tax rate increases gradually over the next decade and a half —unlike the OASDI rate, which remains virtually level then—because of the assumed significant increases in hospital costs, both in absolute terms and, more importantly, relative to the general earnings level.

The HI tax rate is scheduled to be level after 1985, since it is based on only a 25-year projection period. It is likely that, due to the abrupt change in the age structure of the population, a much higher HI tax rate after 2010 will be necessary on this account, as also seen in the OASDI tax schedule. This matter is discussed in more detail in Chapter 4.

Determination of Premium Rates for Voluntary Coverage

The 1972 amendments provided for voluntary individual coverage of noninsured persons who were not blanketed-in on a "free" basis under the original 1965 law (generally, persons who had attained age 65 before 1968, plus the small number of persons who attained age 65 before 1975 and had some quarters of coverage but not enough to be fully insured). Such voluntary-coverage persons pay a premium rate which is expected to meet the full cost of the benefit protection and the accompanying administrative costs. Persons enrolling late pay an extra premium over the standard rate, computed in exactly the same manner as is done under SMI (as will be described later in this chapter).

The standard premium rate was established at $33 per month for July 1973 through June 1974 by the 1972 legislation. This was based on actuarial estimates of what the cost for this small nontypical group would be. The law also provides that this rate shall be automatically adjusted for future periods in accordance with the changes in hospital costs for persons covered under the program. Specifically, the rate for subsequent years will be $33 multiplied by the ratio of the inpatient hospital deductible for the calender year in which the premium year commences to $76 (the deductible that the provisions of the law resulted in for 1973, although the actual deductible then was $72 due to an unusual ruling of the Price Commission, as discussed in Chapter 6), rounded to the nearest whole dollar. The rate so determined for the year beginning July 1974 was $36, while that for the following year is $40.

Interrelationship of HI and Railroad Retirement

Employment covered by the railroad retirement system is considered as covered employment for HI purposes. Persons aged 65 and over and disabled persons who are RR beneficiaries and whose railroad earnings would have made them eligible for OASDI monthly benefits if such earnings had been covered under OASDI are eligible for exactly the same HI benefits and in the same manner as are OASDI beneficiaries, with one minor exception. RR beneficiaries are also eligible for HI benefits in Canada, this provision being included because certain services for United States railroads operating in Canada (and generally performed by Canadian residents) are covered under RR, and so equity dictates this be done.

The law provides that the Railroad Retirement Board is to collect the HI taxes from railroad employers and employees and is then to turn them over to the HI Trust Fund only if the maximum taxable earnings base under the RR system is essentially the same as that under HI. Otherwise, the HI taxes with respect to railroad employees are to be collected by the Internal Revenue Service in the same manner as is followed for employment covered by OASDI.

In years prior to the enactment of Medicare, the RR maximum taxable earnings base was usually higher than that under OASDI. The increase in the OASDI annual base from $4,800 to $6,600 as a result of the social security amendments of 1965 would have reversed this situation for 1966. However, an amendment to the Railroad Retirement Act later on in 1965 established the RR earnings base automatically at whatever the OASDI base will be, and so the Railroad Retirement Board will always collect the HI taxes simultaneously with the RR taxes.

One minor difference with respect to HI taxes for railroad employees is worthy of note. The RR earnings base has always been on a monthly basis, as contrasted with the annual basis for OASDI. Under a $13,200 annual base, for example (i.e., $1,100 monthly for RR), this makes a difference only for individuals who earn more than $1,100 in some months of the year, but less in other months. Under the RR basis, the covered wages in the year in these cases will be lower than on the OASDI basis. The law provides that the RR system must turn over to the HI Trust Fund the amount that would have been collected under the "annual earnings base" basis applicable to OASDI, so that the RR system must make up this small difference out of its other funds. Similarly, the RR system must bear the additional cost of the special Canadian HI benefits.

The actual operation of the financial interchange provisions between the RR system and HI are carried out on an annual basis, rather than currently as the taxes are collected. The taxes with respect to each fiscal year (running from July 1 to June 30), after allowing for the difference in earnings-base concepts, are determined shortly after the close of the fiscal year. From this amount there is first deducted the additional administrative expenses of the Railroad Retirement Board in collecting the taxes. Then, there is added an amount representing the interest that the HI Trust Fund would have earned on these net taxes if it had received them at the time that they were paid to the RR system. The result is then transferred to the HI Trust Fund.

SMI FINANCING PRINCIPLES

The underlying financing principle of SMI is quite simple. The participants pay premiums on what might be said to be a term insurance basis, with the premiums intended to meet part of the cost of the program (no more than half), and the federal government paying the remainder out of general revenues. The premium rate can be changed at annual intervals, by promulgation of the Secretary of Health, Education, and Welfare.[1] This provision is unique among the financing provisions of the various social security programs, because it is the only instance where action other than by Congress can change financing rates.

Such an approach seemed necessary and desirable at the start of the program because of the short-range nature of the financing provisions and because of the volatile nature of the benefit costs, which were not at that time reliably predictable over a moderate period of years in the future. Now that the program has been in operation for several years, it would be possible to develop an increasing schedule of premium rates for future years that could be put in the law, thus placing the responsibility on Congress (as is the case for HI and OASDI).

Premium Rate Basis

The standard premium rate is applicable to all persons regardless of age, sex, or physical condition who enroll in the program at the first possible time. Late entrants usually must pay a somewhat higher

---

[1] The original law provided for biennial redeterminations—to be effective for two-year periods beginning January 1968 and each succeeding second January. The 1967 amendments changed this, on a permanent basis, to one-year periods beginning July 1969 and each succeeding July.

premium rate so as to offset the antiselection that is likely to result in these cases.

A uniform premium rate for all participants was desired when the program was initiated for persons aged 65 and over. Since the program is a purely voluntary one, it would have been impossible to develop an adequate premium rate based on financing solely from the participants, because of the "vicious circle of antiselection." Specifically, any rate established would be too high, on an actuarial basis, for the younger and healthier participants, especially if they considered the rate only on a term insurance basis, rather than on a lifetime basis. As a result, these individuals would tend not to join the plan (or would soon drop out of it), and the premium rate would have to be increased. This snowballing procedure would likely go on and on, so that eventually the plan would have few participants and very high per capita costs.

The solution, therefore, was to have a government contribution or subsidy, so that the plan would be financially attractive to all possible participants, not only on a lifetime basis but also on a short-term basis. Studies indicated that if a certain average premium rate was applicable to the entire population aged 65 and over, then a premium rate of half this amount would be somewhat less than the value of the benefit protection for the youngest members of this age group who are in reasonably good health. Accordingly, if the participants pay half the cost, all of them will be getting a good actuarial buy on a current-insurance basis.

Further, those who are the lowest cost risks will inevitably become higher cost risks as they become older. Therefore, viewed on a long-term basis, this 50–50 sharing of the cost results in the SMI program being attractive financially to virtually all potential participants. The only exceptions are those with religious principles against the treatment of illness by physicians and those who have free, or virtually free, medical care provided in other manners, such as veterans with service-connected disabilities or retired members of the uniformed services.

The intial law provided that the monthly standard premium rate should, for any particular premium period, be such that income therefrom would equal half the estimated cost for benefits and related administrative expenses, including an appropriate allowance for contingencies. The premium rate is rounded to the nearest 10 cents. The 1972 amendments provided that, effective for fiscal year 1974, such "half the estimated cost" would be termed the actuarial rate (sometimes referred to as the "adequate actuarial rate") for persons aged 65 and over, and the standard premium rate will be derived therefrom (as described hereafter); such actuarial rate is not subject to being rounded to the nearest 10 cents.

Since the premium rate does not vary by geographical regions or by urban-rural residence, although medical costs do so vary, there is somewhat of a reverse income redistribution than usually occurs in social welfare programs. Specifically, the cost of the program, on a relative per capita basis, is higher in the high-income areas than in the low-income ones if only the factor of fee levels is considered, and utilization rates are ignored. This means, in essence, that when considered on this basis, the high-income areas receive proportionately more of the government contribution.

When SMI coverage for disabled beneficiaries was first considered, it was believed that their per capita cost would approximate that for persons aged 65 and over. This belief was not based on any data, but rather on intuitive reasoning (namely, that the disabled are merely prematurely superannuated). However, a survey of OASDI beneficiaries refuted this by indicating a per capita cost more than twice as high for the disabled as for the aged.

This presented a dilemma from a financing standpoint. If the disabled paid half their own cost, the premium rate would be very high, and many of the lower cost risks might not participate, thus starting a circle of antiselection. Another possibility was to determine an average premium rate for the aged and disabled *combined* and to charge all participants 50 percent thereof. This had the obvious disadvantage of the aged paying more than otherwise would be the case if only they were covered, and thus they would apparently be paying part of the cost for the disabled. Yet another possibility was to charge the disabled the same premium rate as the aged, and have the government pay more than half the cost for them. This had the disadvantage of destroying the 50-50 matching basis between the participants and the government.

When the disabled were covered under SMI by the 1972 amendments, effective July 1973, the last-mentioned financing basis was adopted. The 50-50 matching basis for the aged was, at the same time, changed (as will be discussed hereafter), so that it no longer appeared undesirable to have the government pay more than half the cost for the disabled (in practice, likely about 80 percent or more).

The SMI premium rate for the aged has been increased significantly since the program began operations in 1966. These increases occurred principally because of liberalizations in the benefit provisions and because of the rising medical prices, which increased more rapidly than the general cost of living and, until 1972, more than the level of OASDI benefits. This produced a high level of dissatisfaction among the beneficiaries.

As a result, the 1972 amendments changed the basis for the determination of the standard premium rate. Now, the percentage increase in the standard premium rate that is promulgated in December (for the year beginning the following July) cannot exceed the percentage increase in the OASDI cash benefits level from the previous June to what will be payable for the following June according to the law in effect at the time of the promulgation. The OASDI cash benefits level is determined by the primary insurance amount applicable to an average monthly wage of $750. As before, the standard premium rate cannot exceed the actuarial rate for enrollees aged 65 and over.

As a result of this change, SMI enrollees aged 65 or over will, in the future, very likely pay somewhat less than half the cost of the program, and the government will pay the balance. Correspondingly, SMI enrollees under age 65 who are disabled, in paying the same premium rate as the aged, will meet far less than half their cost, on the average, because their aggregate per capita cost is higher than for the aged. As a result, for all enrollees combined, the government contribution will, on the average, always exceed the enrollee standard premium rate.

It is possible that the proportion of the estimated cost borne by enrollees aged 65 and over can increase from one year to the next (but, of course, can never exceed 50 percent). This can occur in the unusual circumstances that the level of OASDI cash benefits rises more rapidly than SMI costs (which, incidentally, has been occurring recently with the significant OASDI benefit increases and the strict governmental price controls on physician fees). For example, let it be assumed that in a certain year, the actuarial rate for the aged is $8, and the standard premium rate is $7.50, which meets 47 percent of the cost of the program. Suppose that for the next year, the actuarial rate is $8.20, and the rise in cash benefits is 15 percent. Then, the new standard premium rate could be increased to $8.20, meeting half the cost of the program since the limit based on the rise of the OASDI cash-benefits level would not prevent this (115 percent of $7.50 is $8.63).

The law requires that for information purposes, the actuarial rate for disabled enrollees should be promulgated at the same time the standard premium rate and the actuarial rate for enrollees aged 65 and over are promulgated. Such actuarial rate for disabled enrollees is used to determine the government contributions with respect to such enrollees.

Mathematically speaking, the per capita government cost, which is determined separately for aged and disabled enrollees, is the excess of twice the actuarial rate over the standard premium rate, for those enrolling on a timely basis and with the appropriate increased adjustments on both items for late entrants.

The amendments enacted in December 1973 were concerned primarily with increasing the level of cash benefits under OASDI. In doing so, they changed the automatic-adjustment provisions to become operative for June of each year, beginning 1975, rather than January of each year. Inadvertently, this created a serious anomaly under SMI. If in the future only the automatic-adjustment provisions are applicable in increasing OASDI benefits, then it will *never* be possible for an increased premium rate under SMI to be promulgated!

The reason that this result occurs is that the promulgation made in a given December cannot increase the premium rate by a greater percentage than benefits for the next June, according to the law then in effect, will be increased over the level for the previous June, when the most recent automatic adjustment will have been made. Such increase in benefits for the previous June will carry through the succeeding months until an automatic adjustment for that following June will be promulgated, which will not be done until April. Thus, in each December, the OASDI benefit level for the next June will appear to be the same as it was for the previous June—even though an increase for that next June may later occur—and so no increase in the premium rate can ever be made.

The solution to this undoubtedly unintended result is quite simple. The comparison of the OASDI benefit levels should be made each December—as between the preceding May and the next May. In early 1975, Congressman Rostenkowski introduced legislation to correct this error. This would be effective for the premium rate already promulgated for the year beginning July 1975. Accordingly, the rate promulgated in December 1974 may be changed.

Financing and Investment Procedures

The premiums are collected from the enrollees in several ways, with the primary method being by deduction from OASDI or RR monthly benefits. The premium collections are deposited in the SMI Trust Fund, as are the contributions from the federal government. Specifically, the government contributions amount to the enrollee premiums (including any additional premiums because of late enrollment) multiplied by the ratio of (1) twice the actuarial rate minus the standard premium rate, to (2) the standard premium rate. This is done separately for enrollees aged 65 and over and for disabled enrollees. The intent of the law is that the government contributions should be placed in the SMI Trust Fund simultaneously with the participant premiums. If this is not done, then, in accordance with a provision in the 1967 amendments, interest in an appropriate amount is paid to the trust fund by the General Treasury.

Benefit payments are disbursed from this trust fund, generally through the designated carriers, as are also the administrative expenses of both the various government agencies involved and the carriers. Any assets of the SMI Trust Fund not needed as a cash working balance are invested in the same manner as for the OASDI and HI Trust Funds.

When the HI system was inaugurated, a contingency margin in its financing in the initial years arose from the fact that payroll taxes were collected six months in advance of the first availability of benefits. It did not seem expedient to follow this procedure in SMI—collecting premiums well in advance of when benefit protection began—but rather premiums were made first payable at the beginning of the first month of operation. Although some funds would be accumulated—because of the effects of the $50 initial deductible and of the natural lag in filing claims and in adjudication—it was believed essential that there should be some additional financial backstop.

Accordingly, the original law authorized an appropriation from general revenues to be made available to serve as a contingency reserve and to be drawn upon only if needed for payment of expenditures under the program. The amount of this authorization was set at six months of contributions of the per capita federal matching amount applicable in 1966–67 (i.e., $18) times the estimated 19 million persons eligible to participate in the program when it would begin operations on July 1, 1966, or roughly $342 million. In actual practice, only $100 million was appropriated initially, although the remainder could have been appropriated if needed. None of this was actually used, because the experience—at least on a cash basis—was close enough to the level anticipated by the financing provided so as not to require it.

The law provided that any part of the contingency reserve actually used must be repaid, without interest, by the SMI Trust Fund at some later date. The provision for a contingency reserve lapsed at the end of 1969. A sufficient contingency reserve is intended to be provided in the future through the provision that the premium rates promulgated should be sufficient both to pay the necessary costs of the program and for this purpose.

The underlying principle of SMI is that the standard premium rate and the government contributions determined therefrom for each fiscal year should be sufficient, on an incurred-cost basis, to meet the benefit cost and administrative expenses for such year. In theory, the balance in the SMI Trust Fund at the end of a fiscal year should be at least equal to the incurred but unpaid benefits then outstanding (and the related administrative expenses) as a result of medical services previously furnished. Such lag results both from delay in filing claims and from the time necessary to adjudicate and pay claims. Such a requirement of reserves being at least equal to incurred but unpaid liabilities is applicable to insurance companies in the health insurance field, as a result of state regulatory laws; if it is not met in the aggregate, the company would be declared insolvent.

No such legal solvency requirement applies to SMI. Rather, it can continue to operate as long as it has sufficient cash resources to operate on a cash-flow basis. Such situation has been present in the past, even though the premium rates have been inadequate on an incurred-cost basis. Thus, at any point in time in the past operation of the system, the balance of the SMI Trust Fund has been less than the outstanding liability for incurred but unpaid benefits (specific data on this matter are given in the appendix to this chapter).

SMI FINANCING PROVISIONS

Determination of Premium Rates

The original law provided that the standard premium rate for July 1966 to December 1967 should be $3 per month. An amendment in 1967 extended this period for three months. A later amendment in 1967 provided that the subsequent new rate should be determined for the period April 1968 through June 1969. This rate was promulgated in December 1967 at $4 per month. The increase was due to the liberalized benefits provided by the 1967 amendments, the small inadequacy in the initial premium rate, and the anticipated future increases in physician fees and in utilization of covered services.

When the Secretary of Health, Education, and Welfare, Wilbur J. Cohen, made the promulgation required by law in December 1968, he held the standard premium rate at $4 per month for fiscal year 1970 (July 1969 through June 1970). This action was taken despite the recommendation of the chief actuary of the Social Security Administration that the rate should, at the least, be $4.40—and preferably $4.50. More details as to the reasons why this action was taken, and how it was justified, are given in the appendix to this chapter.

In December 1969, the new Secretary of Health, Education, and Welfare, Robert H. Finch, promulgated the standard premium rate for fiscal year 1971 at the actuarially determined amount of $5.30 per month. The Nixon administration announced that the existing $4 rate was providing inadequate financing and that half of the $1.30 increase resulted for this reason. The remainder took into account future recognizable increases in physician fees and in other covered services, increases in utilization, the changes in the per capita costs due to change in the mix of services and providers, and the need to build up the trust fund so that it can meet any unforeseen contingencies.

The subsequent promulgated standard premium rates—$5.60 for fiscal year 1972, $5.80 for fiscal year 1973, $6.30 for fiscal year 1974, and $6.70 for fiscal year 1975—also were based on the actuarially determined amounts. The increases reflected the anticipated future changes in charges for covered services and in the pattern of services used and, for 1974, the benefit liberalizations in the 1972 amendments (after adjustment for the reduction in cost due to increasing the amount of the initial deductible).

The new provision resulting from the 1972 amendments that limits the increase in the premium rate to no more than the increase in the OASDI cash-benefits level had no effect in the promulgation for fiscal year 1974, because the benefits increased by 20 percent from June 1972 to June 1973, while the promulgated actuarial rate for persons aged 65 and over of $6.30 was an increase of only 9 percent. Accordingly, the promulgated standard premium rate for fiscal year 1974 was $6.30. At the same time, the promulgated actuarial rate for disabled enrollees under age 65 was $14.50.

However, in June 1973, the Price Commission took the similar, unusual action that it had done in connection with the HI initial deductible (as discussed previously in this chapter) and froze the premium rate at $5.80. This was done only for the month of July and the first 12 days of August (so that the rate for that month was $6.10 —12 days at $5.80 and 19 days at $6.30 averaging this amount). This caused great administrative difficulties (and expense), because the millions of OASDI monthly benefit checks for June (which contained the deduction for the July SMI premium) had already been prepared with the $6.30 rate being deducted, and the same thing was done for the July checks. The correction could not be made until the November checks, which were thus at a higher rate than the two surrounding months, thus causing confusion for the beneficiaries. The net result of these small reductions in individual premiums was a refund of about $14 million in the aggregate. At the same time, to make up for this loss of income as against the actuarial rate, there was an increase of this amount in the government contribution. Also, there were significantly higher administrative expenses, which in fact represented a sizable proportion of the premium refunds!

For the remainder of fiscal 1974, the government payment for those aged 65 and over was the same as the enrollee premium rate, while for disabled enrollees the government contribution of $22.70 per capita per month (for persons enrolling in a timely manner) met 78 percent of their cost. Or, to put it another way, for that year the total government contribution with respect to enrollees aged 65 and over was exactly the same as the aggregate enrollee premiums. For disabled enrollees, the total government contribution was 4.3 times as large as the aggregate enrollee premiums (actually, $29.00 minus $6.30, divided by $6.30).

The $6.30 premium rate would have been maintained for fiscal year 1975 if no benefit increase applicable to June 1974 had been enacted before January 1974, since the benefit level would then have remained unchanged from June 1973 to June 1974, and so no increase in the rate would have been permitted by the law. The December 1973 amendments, however, provided an 11 percent benefit increase effective for June 1974, so that the standard premium rate for fiscal year 1975 could be increased from the $6.30 rate for fiscal year 1974 to as much as $7 (after rounding to the nearest 10 cents), but, of course, to no more than the actuarial rate for persons aged 65 and over. The actuarial rate that was determined was only $6.70, so that the limitation did not have effect. The promulgated actuarial rate for disabled enrollees was $18.

As a result, the government contribution for persons aged 65 and over for fiscal year 1975 is the same as the enrollee premium rate. At the same time, the government contribution of $29.30 per month for disabled enrollees (enrolling timely)—4.4 times the enrollee premium —represents 81 percent of their cost.

The situation for fiscal year 1976 is somewhat different. For the first time, the enrollee standard premium rate for the aged (which continues at $6.70 per month) is lower than half the total cost— namely, only 45 percent thereof, since the per capita government contribution is $8.30 per month. The government contribution with respect to disabled enrollees is $30.30 per month, or 82 percent of their total cost.

As discussed earlier in this chapter, the $6.70 premium rate was continued for fiscal year 1976 because of a technical error. However, legislation was in process in early 1975 to correct this error, both for fiscal year 1976 and for the future. If this is enacted, the premium rate for the year beginning July 1975 will be increased from $6.70 to $7.40 per month.

The limitation of the increase to the relative one for OASDI benefits would first be applicable. This is because the promulgated actuarial rate of $7.50 for persons aged 65 and over is in excess of this standard (the 11 percent increase of OASDI benefits when applied to $6.70 yields $7.44, which must be rounded to $7.40). Such an increase of $.70 in the premium rate, which seems equitable and consistent, would result in aggregate premium increases of about $200 million for the year, and a corresponding reduction in the cost to the General Treasury.

The general enrollment periods, during which individuals may elect to enter SMI after previously having refused, are established so that such persons will know about any higher premium rate that might be set for the period when their coverage begins. Thus, the promulgation of the rate is made in December of each year, and the next three months constitute the general enrollment period.

The higher premium rate payable by those who enter in a general enrollment period which is subsequent to their initial enrollment opportunity is based upon the number of months between the close of the individual's initial period and the close of the period in which he actually did enroll. For each full 12 months so involved, the standard premium rate is increased by 10 percent, with the premium rate actually payable being then rounded to the nearest 10 cents.

The 10 percent increase factor was not scientifically determined as an exact offset to the higher costs anticipated for the delayed-enroll-ment group. Rather, it was arbitrarily set at this figure to recognize, at least partially, this factor. No adequate data were available for making a precise determination of the amount needed for true actuarial equivalence. Also, it was hoped that a charge of this magnitude would strongly encourage enrollment as soon as eligibility is present.

Some examples of how these increased premium rates are determined might be helpful. Suppose that Mr. A attains age 65 in March 1975, but does not enroll in SMI in his initial period (December 1974 through June 1975). If he then enrolls in the general enrollment period that occurs in January through March 1977, there will have been 21 months between the end of his initial period and the end of the general period in which he enrolled. Accordingly, his increased premium rate during his entire future period of continuous participation will be 10 percent higher than the standard premium.

As another example, suppose that Mr. B attains age 65 in July 1975, but does not elect to participate in SMI in his initial enrollment period, which ends in October 1975. If he changes his mind and decides to enter SMI in the general enrollment period that occurs in the first quarter of 1976, only five months are involved in the determination of his premium rate (namely, November 1975 through March 1976), so that he does not have any increase and thus pays only the standard rate. Nonetheless, the possible antiselection due to his late entry is recog-nized, because the effective date of his coverage is delayed until July 1976.

An increased premium rate also is applicable for individuals who terminate coverage, but who reenter during a subsequent general en-rollment period. Only one such reentry is permitted. Under these circumstances, the increased premium rate is based on the months after the effective month of termination and up through the last month of the general enrollment period of reentry. Such months are added to any months that were used as a basis for determining an increased premium rate when the individual first enrolled.

For example, Mr. A has an increased premium rate of 10 percent above the standard premium rate because he had a period of 21 months involved between the end of his initial period and the end of the gen-eral period in which he elected to participate. Suppose that in the first quarter of 1979, Mr. A decides to terminate (effective at the end of June 1979). Then, in the general enrollment period in the first quarter of 1983, he decides to reenter the program (effective July

1983). His total months to be considered for purposes of the increased premium rate are then 66 (the original 21 months, plus the additional 45 months). Accordingly, his premium rate will be the standard rate increased by 50 percent.

Collection of Premiums

The enrollee premiums are payable monthly in advance. Wherever possible they are deducted from monthly benefit payments under the OASDI, railroad retirement, or civil service retirement systems (except in some cases where the individual is also receiving public assistance). In nondeduction cases, a grace period of up to 90 days is allowed.

The procedure is relatively simple for OASDI and RR beneficiaries who are receiving benefits regularly from month to month—that is, they are not affected by the earnings test. Under these circumstances, the SMI premium for a particular month is merely deducted from the monthly benefit check for the previous month, which is sent to the beneficiary just after the end of such month. When an individual is receiving both OASDI and RR benefits, the procedure, following changes made by the 1972 amendments, is to deduct the premium from the RR benefit.

Although federal employees under the Civil Service Retirement Act are not covered by OASDI and HI with respect to such employment, they may participate in SMI. Under these circumstances, the premiums are deducted from their CSR annuity if they are not also receiving an OASDI or RR benefit, in which case the premiums are deducted from the latter. Also, if the spouse of the CSR annuitant is under SMI, the spouse's premiums may be deducted from the annuity if the annuitant agrees. The same deduction procedure is also applicable to certain small retirement systems administered by the Civil Service Commission.

An exception occurs in regard to automatic deduction of SMI premiums from monthly benefit checks under OASDI, RR, and CSR. State public assistance agencies are permitted to "buy in" for certain such aged and disabled recipients, including recipients under the federal supplemental security income program who are eligible for Medicaid, by so electing on a mass enrollment basis. Under such circumstances, the state may make arrangements so that the SMI premiums will not be deducted from such benefits. This procedure simplifies administration for the public assistance agency since it need not reimburse the recipient for the cost of the SMI premium in cases that would otherwise involve automatic benefit deduction. On the other hand, the administration is made somewhat more complex for OASDI, RR, and CSR, since there will be cases transferring back and forth from the automatic-deduction procedure as they go on and off of public assistance.

States may also buy into SMI for medically indigent persons who are eligible for SMI, those whose income is just slightly higher than the income limit for cash assistance payments and who thus are eligible under the Medicaid program. The state must pay the entire enrollee premium for the medically indigent, without any matching or financial participation from the federal government (other than the matching applicable to all enrollees). This is unlike the situation for cash assistance recipients (whether under SSI alone or under both SSI and a state supplementary plan) where the usual federal Medicaid matching applies to the enrollee premium that the state initially pays.

APPENDIX

HI and SMI Cost Estimates

LONG-RANGE HI COST ESTIMATES

Principal Elements and Factors

There is a somewhat greater *relative* range of probable costs for HI benefits than for the OASDI monthly cash benefits that have been provided for over 35 years. When the HI program was under consideration, data were incomplete or unavailable for some of the many cost aspects and factors underlying these benefits as they would be provided under a social insurance system. Also, service benefits quite obviously do not have costs as readily determinable as cash benefits that are directly related to covered earnings. However, it should be recognized that, similarly, when the present OASDI cash benefits program was inaugurated in 1935, little was known about many of the factors entering into the actuarial cost estimates. Then, as later for health benefits, assumptions had to be made on the basis of the data available, using the best possible actuarial judgment.

From a cost standpoint, the major proposed HI benefit was coverage of the cost of hospital care. A great amount of data was available in regard to the use of hospital services by aged persons. However, little of such data related to the hospitalization that would occur and to the actual cost of providing such care under the conditions resulting from the availability of a hospital insurance program that would pay for almost the full cost of services for this population.

Thus, despite the availability of much data, precise estimates of the cost of the HI proposals were not possible because of the many biases in the data and the many adjustments required—for which data were lacking to form a guide, such as the extent of changes in hospital utilization that might occur after enactment with respect to persons who have not had insurance in the past, but who would have benefit coverage under the provisions of the proposals.

The important elements in making HI cost estimates are as follows:

1. The number of persons eligible for benefits, by age and sex, in all future years (obtained from the OASDI cost estimates).
2. The average number of days of utilization of hospital or skilled nursing facility services per year per eligible (or, for home health benefits, the average number of visits per year per eligible), by age and sex. (Note that disabled beneficiaries, although younger than old-age beneficiaries, have much higher utilization, even though utilization increases with age for the latter.)
3. The average reimbursable unit cost of each type of covered service, by age and sex (after allowance is made for the effect of any cost-sharing provisions).

The benefit costs are estimated by merely summing the products of items 1, 2, and 3 for each age-sex group for any particular year. The administrative expenses are determined as a percentage of the benefit payments. The tax income is determined in the same manner as is done for OASDI.

Knowing the actual utilization experience under the past operation of the program does not fully solve the cost estimating problems for this factor. Still remaining is the question of whether utilization will rise as people become more familiar with the protection offered by the program or as there is more general tendency to use hospitals to care for acute or terminal cases, especially when the direct cost to the beneficiary is low.

Another important cost-estimating problem is that the estimated cost of the HI program can vary greatly when only small changes are made in the assumptions as to future trends in hospital costs. For example, if hospital costs are assumed to increase at 7 percent per year for 25 years, the cost of the program in this period would be about 65 percent higher than if such increases were at a rate of 3 percent.

The long-range OASDI actuarial cost estimates made before 1971 assumed that earnings would be level in the future. This assumption meant that costs of the cash benefits relative to payroll would not be affected by any rising earnings trend that might develop, because it was assumed that the benefit structure, including the maximum earnings base that is creditable toward benefits and that is subject to taxes, would be adjusted to keep pace with the rising earnings.

When earnings levels rose in the past (increasing both benefit outgo and tax income—the latter more than the former, because of the weighted benefit formula), this factor was recognized in subsequent OASDI cost estimates. Any resulting net reduction in cost was thus made available for the financing of the program, including proposed benefit liberalizations. Changes financed entirely in this manner tended to keep the system up to date.

For purposes of consistency with the procedure for the OASDI cost estimates, the early HI estimates (before 1965) were based on such a level-earnings assumption. With such an assumption, it is sufficient for the purposes of long-range cost estimates merely to analyze possible future trends in hospitalization costs relative to covered earnings. Accordingly, any study of past experience of hospitalization costs should be made on this relative basis. The actual experience in years before the enactment of Medicare indicated, in general, that hospitalization costs had risen much more rapidly than the general earnings level, with the differential being in the neighborhood of 3 to 4 percent on an annual basis.

One of the uncertainties in the cost estimates for the proposed hospital benefits—and one that still remains in making cost estimates currently—was how long and to what extent this tendency of hospital costs to rise more rapidly than the general earnings level would continue in the future, and whether or not it might, in the long run, be counterbalanced by a trend in the opposite direction. One of the factors to be considered was the relatively low wages of hospital employees. These wage levels had been catching up with the general level of earnings and might obviously be expected to catch up completely at some future date and then level off, rather than to increase indefinitely at a more rapid rate than earnings generally. Another factor to consider is the development of new medical techniques and procedures, with their resultant increased expense.

In connection with the latter factor, there are possible counterbalancing factors insofar as the overall cost of the program is concerned. The higher costs involved for more refined and extensive treatments may be offset by better general health conditions (so that, in the long run, less hospitalization is needed), by the development of out-of-hospital facilities (with resulting lower overall costs when these services are used instead of hospitals), and by shorter durations of hospitalization and lower expense for curative treatments as a result of preventive measures. Also, it is possible that at some time in the future, the productivity of hospital personnel will increase significantly, so that, as in other fields of economic activity, prices will increase less rapidly than earnings.

For more than three decades, however, hospital costs have been increasing at a rate somewhat more than double that of earnings. Several reasons why this trend may continue for some time in the future are: (1) the acceleration of medical research and the accompanying discovery and use of new, and generally more expensive, techniques; (2) the increasing levels of skills required by hospital technicians and the accompanying more rapid rise in earnings for such persons; and (3) making the most advanced high-quality medical techniques available to all.

In making HI cost estimates, it might be assumed that in the immediate future, the costs of hospitalization would rise more rapidly than the general earnings level, but that the reverse trend would occur over the long range. Such a result could occur, because it is generally the case that earnings rise more rapidly than prices. A more conservative approach, however, is to assume that hospital costs will increase more rapidly than earnings for several years and that thereafter these two elements will rise at the same rate.

Alternatively, it might be assumed that hospital costs eventually will increase at a *lower* rate than the general earnings level. This assumption can be rationalized on the basis that, in general, prices do not increase as rapidly as earnings, because of increased productivity. Following this line of reasoning, it is possible that this could ultimately occur in the case of hospitalization costs, although there is the offsetting element of the increasing cost of product improvement (in this instance, more complex medical procedures). Such an assumption was recommended by the 1963–64 Advisory Council, but in connection with later legislation it was assumed that the ultimate rate of increase for hospital costs would be the same as for earnings in covered employment.

The major problem in making actuarial cost estimates for HI on a level-earnings assumption was that, unlike the situation for the OASDI monthly benefits, an unfavorable cost result is shown when total earnings levels rise, unless the provisions of the system are kept up to date (insofar as the maximum taxable earnings base and the dollar amounts of the deductibles are concerned). The reason for this is that there is the fundamental actuarial assumption that hospital costs will rise at the same rate over the long run as the total earnings level. However, the tax income rises less rapidly than the total earnings level, since it depends on the taxable earnings level, which is dampened because of the effect of the earnings base. For example, in 1974 the $13,200 earnings base resulted in only 85.7 percent of the total payroll in employment covered by OASDI and HI being subject to tax. Thus, a 1 percent increase in total earnings would produce an increase of only about 0.86 percent in taxable earnings and, accordingly, in tax income.

Accordingly, it is necessary in the HI actuarial cost estimates to assume either that earnings levels will be unchanged in the future or that wages will continue to rise and the system kept up to date insofar as the earnings base and the deductibles are concerned.

The assumption that the earnings base would be kept up to date with increases in the earnings level can be realized if Congress takes the necessary action to raise this base from time to time. Still another possibility—and what is now actually the case—is to have the earnings base on a dynamic basis by being automatically adjusted for changes in wage levels.

The cost estimates for HI made in recent years have assumed that earnings levels would increase in the future (at an annual rate of about 5 percent). Similarly, it has been assumed that over the 25-year period in the cost estimate, hospital daily costs would rise somewhat more rapidly (with a 2 percent ultimate differential in the main estimate, but with the effect of alternative higher differentials also being studied).

An important factor in connection with the actuarial analysis of HI is the cost interrelationship between the several types of benefits provided. For example, if hospital benefits were provided, but skilled nursing facility care were not, there would tend to be more utilization of the hospital benefits because an individual would be likely to stay longer in a hospital (at little or no cost to him) rather than to enter a skilled nursing facility operating at lower costs, but with the full cost to be paid by him. Similarly, if there were no outpatient hospital diagnostic benefits provided, and there were no deductible in the hospital benefits, there would be a financial incentive for an individual to enter a hospital (with resulting higher cost to the program) to obtain these services without cost to himself.

Likewise, the availability of home health services can reduce hospital stays in certain cases. Otherwise, an individual might enter a hospital or stay in it longer if, in doing so, it would cost him less personally than in obtaining home health services. On the other hand, the home health services, when available, will undoubtedly be utilized by many persons who would not otherwise have been in hospitals. In the same way, the presence (or absence) of a deductible provision for one benefit can influence not only the cost of that benefit but also the costs of other types of benefits.

Another important factor is the length of the period over which the cost estimates are made. Originally, for the sake of consistency, the HI cost estimates were made over the same period as the OASDI ones (into perpetuity, until the cost estimates made in 1964; since then, 75 years). Beginning in 1965, the HI cost estimates have been made for a future period of only 25 years, since longer estimates did not seem feasible in light of the many changes in medical practices and services that may occur in the future. On the other hand, it did not seem prudent to make the estimates over such a short period as three to five years, because this would not adequately portray the long-range upward cost trend that is almost certain to result from the rising trend of both hospital costs and number of eligible persons, and possibly utilization as well.

The long-range progress of the HI Trust Fund is developed from the estimated taxes, benefit payments, and administrative expenses in exactly the same manner as is done for OASDI. More details as to the methodology and assumptions used in making the HI cost estimates may be found in the annual reports of the board of trustees of the HI Trust Fund.

Determination of Tax Schedule

The actuarial status of the HI program is determined and measured in the same manner as is done for OASDI. The average costs (formerly, the level costs) of the benefits, administrative expenses, and taxes at the scheduled rates are determined. Then, taking into account the value of the existing fund, the actuarial balance between income and outgo is determined.

If there is not close actuarial balance, the tax schedule can be adjusted accordingly (by legislation). The general financing theory for HI is to have an increasing tax schedule in the 25-year valuation period considered, so as to meet the rising cost (primarily due to hospital costs increasing more rapidly than the general earnings level, but also due to the proportion of eligibles to covered workers increasing) on a current-cost financing basis.

Table 10.10 in Chapter 10 presents data on such valuations for HI in previous years, while Table 4.3 in Chapter 4 shows these results for certain recent years in terms of dollars on a present-value basis.

SHORT-RANGE SMI COST ESTIMATES

Principal Elements and Factors

As discussed previously, the supplementary medical insurance program had been considered for only a relatively short time before it was enacted—in contrast to the long period during which hospital insurance was a national issue. Only a relatively small amount of data was available for persons aged 65 and over with regard to insurance programs of this type. In this respect, considerably more difficulties existed in making actuarial cost estimates for SMI than for any of the other programs.

The cost estimate used in determining the initial premium rate specified in the 1965 legislation was based, insofar as assumptions for utilization of services were concerned, on data from the experience of the Connecticut-65 program (which was an insurance company-operated mass enrollment comprehensive health benefits plan for persons aged 65 or over and which terminated when Medicare went into operation). Subsequent cost estimates were based on the experience under SMI as it evolved.

The important elements in making SMI benefit cost estimates are as follows:

1. The number of persons who will be enrolled.
2. The average annual per capita cost of the benefits, on an accrual or incurred-cost basis.

Since SMI involves projecting the premium rate for only a short period, there is not the same difficulty involved as in the HI cost estimates, where future trends of hospital costs have to be assumed for many years into the future. Nonetheless, an important part in making the SMI estimates is to derive suitable assumptions as to increases in physician fees and other covered charges in the period covered by the cost determination of the premium rate. Allowance also has to be made for the secular trend of increasing utilization of medical services.

The true indication of the cost of a program such as SMI must be measured on an accrual basis, rather than on a cash basis. This is necessary so as to match up properly the costs incurred in a period with the premiums applicable to that period. The premium rate is to be determined in this manner, but estimates of the operation of the trust fund must be prepared on a cash basis, so as to show the actual assets that will develop.

This involves still another difficulty—namely, estimating the extent of the lag that will result. The relevant factors involved are the delay in presentation of bills by physicians to patients or to the carriers who administer the program, the subsequent delay in the submission of bills by patients to the carriers (especially considering the effect of the initial deductible), and the administrative lag involved in adjudicating the claims.

One element that arose in connection with the initial SMI cost estimates was estimating the participation in this voluntary plan. No pertinent experience existed that could be used as a guide in this respect. If participation would be at a relatively low level, it would be possible that there would be a very considerable degree of anti-selection. In other words, it would be likely that, under such circumstances, only the worst risks would elect to participate, and the per capita cost would turn out to be much higher than anticipated. However, the fact that the federal government would pay half the cost made the program attractive, so that even the lowest cost groups would find it advantageous to participate.

Because of these uncertainties as to extent of participation, it seemed advisable in the initial cost estimates to assume a range in the estimated participation rate of the eligible population aged 65 and over. The low estimate assumed 80 percent, while the high estimate assumed 95 percent. Even in the former case, the participation assumed seemed adequate so that no antiselection of any serious magnitude could be expected. Previous experience under group health insurance had indicated that participation of at least 75 percent is adequate protection against antiselection. In subsequent estimates, the actual enrollment experience (beginning at 92 percent in 1966 and increasing to 96 percent currently) was an accurate guide in making the assumption for this element for the future.

Unlike HI, the cost estimates for SMI do not involve the development of the enrolled population by age-sex groups, with corresponding annual per capita benefit costs. However, such a subdivision is made for the category aged 65 and over and for the newly covered disabled category, since the costs are so different for these two groups. Experience data are available by age and sex for enrollees aged 65 and over, but this is not utilized for the cost estimates since the change in the age-sex composition of this group from one year to the next is relatively small and thus would have little effect on the estimate.

In making an SMI cost estimate for a near-future year, the average annual per capita costs experienced in the most recent past years are projected ahead. Such projection is based on trends experienced to date and estimated for the near future as to unit costs and utilization of covered services. The effect of the initial deductible must be considered, too, since it results in a particular increase in unit costs and/or utilization producing more than a corresponding increase in the per capita benefit costs. For example, if an individual has covered costs of $200 in one year, his SMI reimbursement is $112; if his costs the next year increase 20 percent (to $240), his reimbursement is $144, or 29 percent higher.

More details as to the methodology and assumptions used in making the SMI cost estimates may be found in the annual reports of the board of trustees of the SMI Trust Fund.

Determination of Premium Rate and Government Share

As was discussed in this chapter, the standard premium rate payable both by enrollees aged 65 or over and by disabled enrollees is based on the so-called actuarial rate for enrollees aged 65 or over. Such actuarial rate for any given fiscal year is merely $\frac{1}{12}$th of the estimated projected annual per capita benefit cost for that year (on an incurred-cost basis) increased by the corresponding estimated applicable administrative expenses and by a small margin for contingencies. The actuarial rate for disabled enrollees, which is used in determining the government contribution for this group, is similarly estimated.

chapter 9

Possible Future Development of the Medicare Program

In considering the possible future changes in, and development of, the Medicare program, two distinct phases occur. The first phase deals with the existing Medicare program as it might be expanded in terms of services provided and in terms of covering more categories of social security beneficiaries, or as its financing might be changed. Special attention will be paid to proposals that have been made by the executive branch or that were passed by one House of Congress, even though they were not finally enacted.

Then, going well beyond this, the various national health benefit proposals which are pending currently will be considered. One such proposal would be to apply Medicare to the entire population (as is contained, to a considerable extent, in legislation sponsored by Senator Javits).

EXPANSION OF MEDICARE PROGRAM

The present Medicare program applies only to persons aged 65 and over, to disabled social security and railroad retirement beneficiaries who have been on the benefit roll for at least two years, and to persons with chronic kidney disease who are insured under either OASDI or RR, or are dependents of such persons. Expansion of the program to more types of beneficiaries has frequently been proposed.

Probably the most logical extension to other beneficiaries would be to disabled beneficiaries who are on the roll for less than two years. This limit was set largely, although not entirely, on cost grounds. It would seem desirable, however, that there should always be some requirement as to length of time on the roll because of the difficulty arising due to the lag in adjudicating disability claims. Thus, for example, disabled-worker beneficiaries may not have their claim finally adjudicated by the time that the waiting period for disability benefits (which, in effect, averages 6½ months) has ended and thus will not know whether their disability will be deemed severe enough to meet the definition. Under such circumstances, they would not then know whether they are currently covered for Medicare benefits. Accordingly, so that beneficiaries will know where they stand as to Medicare protection, it seems desirable to retain some requirement as to length of time on the cash-benefits roll.

Extension of the Medicare program might also be urged for all other types of social security beneficiaries, such as retired workers between ages 62 and 65, and to dependents of retired and disabled beneficiaries regardless of their ages. Also, Medicare coverage might be urged for young survivor beneficiaries, although many of these already have reasonably adequate health insurance as a result of the employment of the widowed mother. The Senate version of the 1972 amendments contained a provision extending the voluntary HI system for persons aged 65 and over, which was enacted in this legislation, to OASDI and RR beneficiaries aged 60–64 on the basis that such individuals would pay premiums equal to the full cost of their protection under both HI and SMI. This provision, however, was deleted in the conference committee between the House and Senate.

In early 1975, great interest and concern developed for the many workers who had become unemployed and thereby no longer had health insurance through their employer's plan. Senator Bentsen proposed that HI be extended to apply to workers receiving unemployment insurance benefits and their families, with the cost to be met by the general treasury. This proposal was criticized on the grounds that HI is not suitable for short-term coverage and that this approach could lead to Medicare coverage for all workers.

Senator Kennedy proposed to handle this problem, although supposedly for a temporary period, by continuing each such worker's previous health insurance plan, with the cost met by the general treasury. On the other hand, the Rostenkowski Bill, which was proposed in April, would require the employer to continue his health insurance plan to workers receiving UI benefits and to pay such cost in the same manner as when they were employed. The Rostenkowski Bill would be applicable on a permanent basis. Since all groups—such as the AFL-CIO, the AMA, and insurance carriers—favored action in this general area, it seemed likely that some such legislation would be enacted in 1975.

The 1972 legislation covered one catastrophic-cost group, those with chronic kidney disease. It might be urged in the future that categories with similar diseases or medical costs should be covered, such as those in need of open-heart surgery or organ transplants.

Relatively few medical services are not covered by Medicare. Of these, it is unlikely that private-duty nursing services will be covered. These no longer seem to be medically necessary due to the widespread availability of intensive care units, covered by HI. Nor is it likely that HI will cover the additional cost of private room occupancy, covered now only when medically necessary.

There has been considerable public pressure for liberalization of the skilled nursing facility benefits under HI. This has been a problem area because of the difficulty of separating the recuperative and convalescent services for acute conditions which had required prior hospitalization from the services involved in preventive and supportive matters or in domiciliary and custodial care for chronic conditions. Many individuals would like to have a broadening of the concepts involved in the strict, limited basis provided in the Medicare law, even to the extent of covering all SNF services regardless of prior hospitalization or acute medical condition. The same changes have also been urged for the home health benefits under both HI and SMI.

The greatest pressure for expansion of covered medical service under SMI is for the coverage of out-of-hospital prescription drugs. Under some proposals, all such drugs would be covered after a small cost-sharing payment (perhaps $1) for each prescription. This would involve huge and expensive administrative machinery, since more than 400 million claims per year would need to be handled. Other proposals in this area involve a relatively large annual deductible (such as $100 or $200), and then 20 percent cost sharing thereafter. The latter type of coverage is advocated on both "insurance" grounds (no need to cover the relatively small expenditures involved for those who have only occasional use for such drugs) and the administrative grounds of not handling such huge numbers of small claims.

Such coverage could be effected under either SMI or HI. The coverage would be financed under SMI with an increase in the premium rate and the matching government contribution, and under HI with increased payroll taxes. Since what is involved is an out-of-hospital benefit, it would seem more logical for coverage to be under SMI.

Proposals have been made that only certain types of prescription drugs should be covered, such as the so-called maintenance drugs, which are normally prescribed for chronic conditions. The Senate version of the 1972 amendments contained such a provision. In this case, certain specified drugs for treatment of 13 named conditions (such as diabetes, cancer, and chronic cardiovascular disease) would be covered under HI, after a $1 cost-sharing payment by the beneficiary. The drugs were selected on the basis that they would be easy to administer and that they would be used predominantly by persons with large recurring expenses for them. This provision, however, was deleted in the conference committee between the House and Senate.

Still others argue for expansion of SMI coverage into the areas of annual physical examinations, eyeglasses, and dental care (including dentures). The advocates of coverage of annual physical examinations make much of the point that prevention of illness is better and more efficient than subsequent cure. On the other hand, some experts argue against the indiscriminate use of annual physical examinations because they do not detect very much hidden illness. Moreover, the cost of a comprehensive annual physical examination for each of the more than 20 million persons now under Medicare would be very high. The furnishing of such examinations would severely tax the capabilities of the health care delivery system and would make unavailable adequate health care for acute conditions for the entire population that would otherwise be possible. The coverage of eyeglasses and dental care would involve significant cost and utilization problems.

Other proposals which have been made are of a relatively minor nature, often merely to simplify the program. For example, the maximum limit of 100 home health visits per year under SMI could be eliminated, since very few persons are affected by it and since no similar maximum applies to physician visits. Also, the provision for lifetime reserve days under HI causes problems because of its elective basis, and it could easily, with only slight additional cost, be applied on an automatic basis for each spell of illness. In this connection, however, the House version of the 1972 amendments would have moved in the other direction by increasing the number of such days from 60 to 120. However, this provision was deleted in the Senate.

A suggestion has been made in a study in the Department of Health, Education, and Welfare[1] that expansion of Medicare benefit protection to such features as out-of-hospital prescription drugs and more catastrophic coverage should be accompanied—and thus partially financed—by increased cost sharing along the lines of the ill-fated proposal made by the Nixon administration in early 1973.

The same study also suggested that physician reimbursement under SMI should be further restricted by limiting the charges of participating physicians to the so-called customary charge recognized by Medicare, so that in nonassignment cases the physician cannot charge the patient the excess of his *actual* customary charge over the recognized "customary" charge, as is now possible. The result could be that many physicians would cease to participate if their charges were controlled in this way. In any event, this might tend to make Medicare beneficiaries look even more like second-class citizens, with "charity" medical fees by government fiat.

Another proposal to restrict further physician reimbursement would limit the benefit payment on the so-called reasonable-charges basis only to doctors who agree to take all their Medicare patients on an assignment basis.[2] All other physicians would have to be only on the nonassignment basis, with the beneficiary being reimbursed on a flat fee schedule that would be at a lower level than that arising under the assignment basis. Thus, the pressure would be on doctors to be "participating physicians," since otherwise they might not always be paid their bills. And likewise, pressure would be exerted on physicians to "participate" by their patients, since they would be given lower benefit protection when their doctor did not do so.

REVISED FINANCING OF MEDICARE PROGRAM

A number of proposals have been made for changing the financing basis of Medicare, both the direct financing applicable to those with

---

[1] See "Health Program Memorandum, Fiscal Year 1975 Budget," p. S14480, *Congressional Record*, July 24, 1973.

[2] See "Let's Not Multiply Medicare's Mistakes," *Medical Economics*, January 7, 1974.

current or prospective protection (taxes and premiums) and the indirect financing through the cost-sharing provisions applicable to those who obtain medical services.

Those individuals embracing the expansionist philosophy would prefer to remove as much "evident" financing as possible. They would eliminate the SMI premiums payable by the enrollees and shift the cost burden to the payroll tax and to government subsidies. They would also shift part of the cost of the HI program to general revenues, by a government subsidy of perhaps one third of the cost. Further, they believe that the various cost-sharing provisions should be eliminated or lowered to eliminate the cost barriers to urgently needed medical care.

The Nixon administration, during 1969–72, proposed that the SMI premium payments by the enrollees should be eliminated, and the cost shifted to payroll taxes. The Congress considered this during the course of the legislation enacted then, but apparently was not sympathetic to this idea, since it applied the premium approach to the new category of disabled beneficiaries as well as maintaining it for the aged.

In 1973, the Nixon Administration proposed increasing the cost-sharing provisions under Medicare. The HI provisions would be an initial deductible of the first day's average room-and-board charges in the particular hospital and 10 percent coinsurance on all other charges thereafter. This basis would produce larger cost-sharing for the vast majority of cases, although smaller for a few long-duration cases. The SMI provisions would involve an annual deductible of $85 (instead of the $60 legislated in the 1972 amendments) and 25 percent coinsurance (instead of 20 percent). The $85 figure represents what the original $50 amount applicable in 1966 would have been in 1974 if it had been adjusted to reflect changes in the level of cash benefits (a figure of about $75 would have resulted if the increase had been based on changes in physician fees). Moreover, the $85 initial deductible proposed would be changed in the future in accordance with changes in cash-benefits levels. This proposal, although being logical in many ways (especially if the program had started off in this manner), met with strong opposition from congressmen of both parties and was not adopted.

The House version of the 1972 amendments would have introduced daily cost-sharing under HI for the 31st through 60th days of hospitalization at a rate of one eighth of the initial deductible (i.e., if applicable in 1973, at $9 per day); this provision was deleted in the Senate. At the same time, the Senate version of this legislation would have reduced the daily cost-sharing for the lifetime reserve days from one half of the initial deductible to one quarter thereof; this provision was not agreed to by the House and was deleted in conference.

In early 1975, President Ford proposed changes in the Medicare program somewhat paralleling those made earlier by President Nixon. More cost-sharing would be introduced, although this would be partially offset by catastrophic protection such that the maximum annual cost-sharing per capita would be $750 under each part of Medicare. Again, this proposal met with no enthusiasm on the part of Congress.

It would seem desirable that the initial-deductible amount under SMI should be automatically adjusted for changes in physician fees in the future—just as is done under HI (on the basis of hospitalization costs).

NATIONAL HEALTH BENEFIT PROPOSALS

Those holding the expansionist philosophy of social security feel quite strongly that all residents of the United States should receive high-quality medical care under governmental auspices. For the last 50 years, they have been trying to achieve this goal—either by direct action or by a gradual approach, whichever gives promise of being successful.

When national health insurance was not included in the proposals of President Franklin D. Roosevelt that led to the enactment of the Social Security Act, the expansionists next tried to have such a program enacted separately in the 1940s (the several Wagner-Murray-Dingell Bills). These failed to gain favorable consideration by Congress because the attention of the nation was focused on World War II, and then later because of the phenomenal growth of private insurance (Blue Cross–Blue Shield and insurance companies). The expansionists next focused on the Achilles' heel of private health insurance—the population aged 65 and over, who were sparsely protected. And so there came the numerous proposals for this age group which led to the enactment of Medicare in 1965.

The next step by the expansionists came as a result of the inflation arising from the Viet Nam War. A hue and cry of "crisis" was raised by the expansionists in the late 1960s and early 1970s.[3] They saw a need for the complete tearing down of the existing health care delivery system to solve the situation of rising health care costs which have risen much more in absolute dollar terms than other prices or, much more significantly, have risen at about the same rate as the general wage level.

As a result of these efforts by the expansionists and the concern of the general public over rising health care costs, various organizations developed their own proposals in this area. Because the term "national health insurance" (NHI) seems to have such an appeal—unlike "socialized medicine"—most of these proposals have been so designated. In actuality, many of them should be termed "national health benefits" proposals, since NHI really means a program under which virtually all health care for practically the entire population is financed through the federal government. "Socialized medicine" may be defined as one extreme of NHI—namely, when virtually all health care for practically the entire population is not only financed by the government, but also is provided through government-owned facilities by salaried employees of the government.

Several of the current proposals are truly NHI, but most are not. None of the proposals of an NHI nature are socialized medicine, but they could readily develop into that form of health care delivery.

Now to be considered are the major entries in the national health legislation field as they were in 1974–75. This will be done alphabetically, giving a brief description of each plan, its cost, and its likely impact on the medical profession.

The American Hospital Association has developed a general proposal, which it calls Ameriplan, that would require individuals under age 65 to have private insurance for their basic health protection, with a governmental plan for catastrophic costs. The aged and the medically indigent would be completely protected under governmental plans. An underlying feature of the AHA proposal would be the vir-

---

[3] For more details as to why the claim of "crisis" was (and is) an exaggeration, see (1) Harry Schwartz, *The Case for American Medicine: A Realistic Look at Our Health Care System* (New York: David McKay, Co., Inc., 1972); (2) Marvin H. Edwards, *Hazardous to Your Health* (New York: Arlington House, Inc., 1972); and (3) Robert J. Myers, "Fallacies Expounded by Advocates of National Health Insurance," *New York Medicine*, November 1971. For views on the other side, see (1) Edward M. Kennedy: *In Critical Condition: The Crisis in America's Health Care* (New York: Simon and Schuster, 1972); and (2) Abraham Ribicoff: *The American Medical Machine* (New York: Saturday Review Press, 1972).

tual requirement that all medical care be furnished by so-called health care corporations, which would be nonprofit community-based organizations that would likely be run essentially by hospitals. This proposal would have a significant impact on the manner in which medical care is provided and on the practices of physicians.

The AHA proposal was never put into legislative form, although a bill introduced by Congressman Ullman, which has AHA support, bears certain similarities to it. However, there is no requirement in this bill that all medical care be furnished by health care corporations, although this is strongly encouraged by federal subsidization of 10 percent of the insurance premium cost when such organizations are used. No cost estimates have been made public for this proposal by its sponsors. (In 1975, Mr. Ullman succeeded Mr. Mills as chairman of the House Ways and Means Committee.)

The American Medical Association in 1974 proposed the Medicredit plan, contained in the Fulton-Broyhill Bill. The general concept of this proposal is to give credits against personal income taxes for the premium costs of qualified private health insurance plans or policies for persons under age 65. Such tax credits would be a proportion of the premiums paid, varying inversely with income, from 100 percent for low-income persons to 10 percent for high-income persons. Actually, because the present medical-expenses deduction could not be used if these tax credits are used, the tax credit washes out for higher income persons.

In order to qualify under the Medicredit proposal, a health insurance policy would have to provide quite comprehensive protection, including catastrophic coverage, with only relatively small cost-sharing requirements on the part of the individual. The cost of the Medicredit proposal to the federal government would be about $14 billion per year initially if it were widely used. There are, however, cost offsets of about $2 billion annually to both the federal government and to the states as a result of elimination of the Medicaid program. Interestingly, the Department of Health, Education, and Welfare has set a much lower cost on this proposal (about $8 billion per year). This lower cost resulted under the theory that it would not be used widely by middle-income persons.

The Medicredit proposal would have relatively little effect on the manner in which health care is provided, although the AMA has stated that this is a separable issue and that it has certain suggestions in other areas which it makes in other proposals.

In 1975, the AMA drastically revised its proposal. The tax credit basis would no longer be used for the vast majority of persons, but rather there would be an employer-mandated plan for employees, with the employer responsible for at least 65 percent of the cost. The self-employed would still have the tax credit approach, as would also the unemployed and nonemployed. The new proposal is thus quite similar to the 1973–74 Nixon plan, to be discussed later.

The Research and Policy Committee of the Committee for Economic Development proposed a plan in 1973 under which employers would be required to provide health insurance policies, to be financed jointly by the employers and employees, which would meet certain minimum standards, including catastrophic coverage. Those not covered by such employer plans or by Medicare would be protected under federally sponsored community trusteeships, which would furnish the same basic coverage as under the employer plans. This part of the program would be financed primarily by the federal government, with the participants paying cost-sharing amounts for services related to income status. Persons with sizable incomes not under an employer plan (such as the self-employed) could contract-out of the community trusteeships by purchasing an adequate equivalent private policy. Medicaid would continue in operation to meet the residual, catastrophic needs above the standard plans.

The Health Insurance Association of America has sponsored a plan which it calls Healthcare, which is supported by other insurance business organizations. This proposal has been introduced in the McIntyre-Burleson Bill. It would encourage voluntary health insurance on the part of employer-employee plans and voluntary plans for other individuals, as well as state plans for the indigent. The benefit structure of all three of these types of plans would be the same and would ultimately provide a comprehensive range of benefits, which would be phased in over a period of several years in the future. Catastrophic coverage, however, would be provided for persons who incur more than $5,000 of medical expenses (whether or not covered by insurance) within 12 consecutive months. This part of the HIAA plan was first contained in its 1973 version (previous ones strongly opposing catastrophic coverage). Employers would be encouraged to upgrade their plans to meet the minimum standards, because otherwise they would not be able to take their entire health insurance costs as business expenses for income tax purposes.

The cost to the federal government for the Healthcare proposal would be probably about $10 billion per year, primarily for furnishing protection to indigent persons and for the various planning provisions and loans and grants provisions in the bill. State governments would, however, have cost reductions of about $3 billion annually due to the larger federal financial participation in the proposal than under the present Medicaid program. This proposal would have some effect on the manner in which health care is provided, because of its encouragement of ambulatory health centers and HMOs.

Senator Javits has introduced a bill which would, in essence, extend the Medicare program to persons of all ages and would expand the benefit protection provided by including such items as physical examinations, dental care for young people, and out-of-hospital prescription drugs for chronic conditions. The Javits Bill would have a cost of about $40 billion per year initially and would be financed from payroll taxes and from a government subsidy of one third of the cost. Much of this cost would reflect a decrease in costs not paid directly through the private sector. This proposal would probably have a very significant effect on physicians because fees would be determined by the government, since there would no longer be available the yardstick of customary and prevailing fees for persons not under the program.

Senator Kennedy, and Congresswoman Griffiths in 1973 introduced the most sweeping proposal of all, a plan that was developed by the Committee for National Health Insurance and that is supported by the AFL-CIO, which is termed Health Security. In essence, the Kennedy-Griffiths Bill would result in virtually all medical care for persons of all ages being financed through a governmental system under which about 13 percent of the cost would be met by worker payroll taxes and taxes on unearned income, 37 percent by employer payroll taxes, and the remainder by a government subsidy. The total cost to the federal government would be in the neighborhood of $90 billion in 1976, so that very sizable tax burdens would be involved. About $10 billion of this federal cost would be a shifting of expenditures from the present Medicare and Medicaid programs, which would be abolished. State and local governments would have reduced expenditures of about $5 billion annually as a result of the elimination of Medicaid. It must be remembered, however, that a considerable part of the remainder of the cost would come from a shifting of costs from what is now being done in the private sector. The sponsors of the legislation, however, assert that the gross cost will be only $76 billion in 1976.

The Kennedy-Griffiths proposal is established in such a manner that physicians would virtually be forced into group practice on an institutional basis, since the solo practitioner might receive quite reduced income from the program if the anticipated financing is not sufficient (because the bill provides that they would be the last ones to be paid) and since beneficiaries receive less benefit protection if not in a group plan (because then only maintenance drugs, not all, would be provided). Some supporters of this bill assert that they are not in favor of socialized medicine—in the sense that physicians would become government employees or else employees of organizations which are rather strictly controlled by the government—but this could possibly inevitably result from its operations. Quite obviously, this plan would have the greatest impact on the status of physicians.

When this proposal was reintroduced in 1975, it was designated as the Kennedy-Corman Bill, since Congresswoman Griffiths had retired from Congress, and Congressman Corman took her place as sponsor in the House. Under this new version, the tax rates are 3½ percent on employers on their total payroll, 1 percent on employees with a maximum taxable wage base equal to 1½ times the OASDI base, 2½ percent on the self-employed with the same base as employees, and 2½ percent on unearned income. The unearned income, however, is taxed only up to the excess of the employee earnings base over what is taxed as an employee or a self-employed person; further, there is an exemption of the first $3,000 of unearned income for persons aged 60 and over.

Senator Long, Chairman of the Senate Finance Committee, has for some time favored a purely catastrophic health insurance proposal, financed from payroll taxes applicable to persons under age 65. Such a proposal was added to social security legislation in 1970 that was not finally enacted because of lack of time for a conference between the House and Senate on differing versions of the legislation. The Long proposal would cover, with certain cost-sharing, hospitalization in excess of 60 days per year per person and physician and related expenses in excess of $2,000 per year per family. This proposal was once again strongly advocated by Senator Long in late 1973, with the support of Senator Ribicoff and a majority of the members of the Senate Finance Committee. The proposal would have an annual cost initially of about $3 billion per year. Its impact on the manner in which medical services are provided would be relatively minimal. In addition, the Long-Ribicoff Bill would extend the protection furnished by the Medicaid program, at an initial cost of about $5½ billion a year.

The Long-Ribicoff Bill for catastrophic health insurance was strongly opposed by both those who want a broad comprehensive program such as would be established under the Kennedy-Griffiths Bill and those who advocate health insurance protection being provided completely through the private sector. Such opposition occurred, however, for completely opposite reasons.

The expansionists fear that passage of a catastrophic bill will greatly diminish the pressure for a broader program. The private-sector supporters fear that any catastrophic program supported by payroll taxes will be gradually liberalized, by people being willing to pay just a little more in order to obtain more benefits, until it develops, or degenerates, into a broad, comprehensive plan.

Senator Ribicoff in supporting only a catastrophic plan at this time has stated his belief that the country is not ready yet, either philosophically or administratively, for a broad comprehensive NHI plan.[4] Further, he expressed his belief that we should proceed in the national health area on a step-by-step basis. Such an approach is what those who oppose this proposal on the grounds that it will expand ultimately to a Kennedy-Griffiths basis believe will happen. On the other hand, those who support the Kennedy-Griffiths Bill either do not think that this will occur, or else they believe that it will take too long.

An interesting development in connection with catastrophic health insurance occurred in January 1975 when Rhode Island initiated such a plan. Out-of-pocket medical costs will be reimbursed for a family after they have surpassed an amount that varies depending upon whether it has a qualified health insurance policy, as follows:

	Deductible Is Larger of	
Health Insurance Policy	Amount	Percent of Income
None.............................	$5,000	50%
Qualified policy, but not major medical...	1,250	25
Qualified policy, with major medical.....	500	10

A qualified policy under the Rhode Island plan, for example, must provide 120 hospital days and 120 in-hospital physician visits with no cost-sharing and in-hospital maternity care with a $150 deductible. The major medical requirement is satisfied by a policy with a $100 per person annual deductible (only two per family) and 20 percent co-insurance. For persons covered by Medicare, the deductible is $5,000 or

[4] See "National Health Insurance; The U.S. Isn't Ready for It!" an interview with Sen. Abraham Ribicoff, *Medical Economics*, July 8, 1974.

50 percent of income, if larger, when no supplemental health insurance is carried and a $500 deductible when there is a supplemental policy which fills in all the Medicare cost-sharing (a $1,000 deductible for a supplemental policy that is not this comprehensive). Although specific provisions are expressed for qualification of a policy, one that has somewhat different ones of at least equivalent actuarial value also can qualify.

The Rhode Island catastrophic health insurance plan is administered through private insurers and is financed from general revenues of the state. This plan could well be the model for a national program.

Other proposals for catastrophic health insurance under governmental auspices take a different approach. For example, a bill sponsored by Senator Brock in 1975 would provide such protection to the entire population, with financing from general revenues. The Brock Bill quite simply would pay for 85 percent of all health care costs in excess of 15 percent of a family's income, as defined for income tax purposes.

Chairman Mills of the House Ways and Means Committee, in conjunction with Senator Kennedy, introduced a bill in early 1974 that somewhat paralleled the 1974 version of the Nixon administration proposal insofar as the benefit protection is concerned (described hereafter). However, the Mills-Kennedy Bill would provide somewhat larger benefits for persons under age 65 (by having somewhat lower initial deductibles and also lower limits on when catastrophic coverage begins) and would leave unchanged the Medicare program. The major difference, and a most significant one, between the two proposals is in connection with the financing and administration. The Mills- Kennedy Bill would be financed by payroll taxes (with no government subsidy) and administered by carriers as under Medicare, whereas the administration proposal would be on an employer-mandated basis, with the financing and administration being completely in the private sector.

It will be observed that the Mills-Kennedy Bill is a substantial departure from the Kennedy-Griffiths Bill. Although Senator Kennedy thus significantly shifted his approach, most of the supporters of his original proposal did not change their views and instead strongly criticized the new bill. This bill was not reintroduced in 1975.

President Nixon, in 1971–72, made an extensive proposal in the national health field, including significant encouragement of the Health Maintenance Organization approach. This proposal was contained in a bill introduced by Senator Bennett and also, in slightly modified form, in a bill introduced by Congressman Byrnes. This plan was termed National Health Insurance Partnership. Under this proposal, employers would be required to establish private health insurance plans meeting certain specifications, financed in part by the employees (no more than 25 percent). Although employers should be required to establish such a plan, individual employees could opt-out.

In addition, a federally operated health insurance plan, with some-what lower benefit protection than would be required under the mandated employer plans, would be provided for low-income families with children. Such a plan would be financed predominantly from general revenues, although with certain cost-sharing payments and with certain premiums being paid by covered persons who are above the lowest income level, but yet not above the maximum income limit.

The Nixon proposal would have an annual cost of about $3 billion per year initially insofar as the federal government is concerned and correspondingly of about $10 billion per year for private plans as they are established or liberalized to meet the minimum requirements. It would have relatively little impact on the health care delivery system, other than for its very significant encouragement of the HMO ap-proach.

In early 1974, the Nixon administration proposed a considerable revision of its original plan. The same general approach of an employer-mandated basis for employed persons was taken, but the differentiation in benefits as between the employed and the eligible medically indigent was dropped. For those under age 65, the required minimum benefit standard would be a per capita annual deductible of $150 ($300 per family) with 25 percent coinsurance; further, catastrophic coverage would be provided, since no family would be required to have cost sharing of more than $1,500 in a year (after which the plan would meet the entire cost). Low-income persons and families would have lower deductibles and catastrophic limits.

The 1974 Nixon administration proposal would drastically change the Medicare program. All disabled persons under age 65 would cease to be covered under Medicare and instead would be under the pro-gram for the medically indigent. The HI and SMI programs would be combined (but an enrollee premium would still be required, and there would be an annual deductible of $100 per person with 20 per-cent coinsurance and with maximum required cost-sharing of $500 per year per person and $1,000 per family. However, this cost-sharing (both the deductible and the catastrophic limit) would be lower for persons with low incomes—as is the case for most persons aged 65 and over. Such an approach raises a significant question of philosophy. Should a social insurance program have a means test incorporated in it?

Some time after the proposal of the Nixon administration had been introduced, two others were put forward—the Mills-Kennedy Bill (as discussed previously) and one by the Chamber of Commerce of the United States. The latter plan was incorporated in a bill introduced by Senator Fannin; it paralleled the Nixon proposal but would provide a somewhat lower level of benefit protection.

When President Ford took office in August 1974, following President Nixon's resignation, he urged prompt enactment of a national health bill along the lines of what the Nixon administration had proposed. In 1975, President Ford seemed to continue to favor this approach. He urged, however, that because of the business recession and the budgetary situation no action should be taken on any national health proposals in 1975.

In August 1974, Chairman Mills sought to obtain a consensus on a national health bill from his committee. He suggested a compromise which moved further away from his previous position in the bill that he jointly sponsored with Senator Kennedy by dropping the approach of a national program supported by payroll taxes and administered by the federal government. Instead, he put forth for consideration a basic plan to be financed and operated in the private sector (as in the Nixon approach), a payroll-tax-supported catastrophic plan (as in the Long approach), and replacement of Medicaid on a national "insurance" approach.

The committee staff, at the direction of Chairman Mills, had developed this proposal which was stated as not being the recommendation of anybody.[5] Apparently, it was hoped that this proposal might obtain a consensus of view among the advocates of the several previously developed proposals. It is worthwhile considering this plan in some detail because it might represent the starting point for legislative activity after 1974.

The staff proposal incorporated three separate plans, as well as revising the Medicare program (and resulting in the Medicaid program having only a residual role to play). These were the employer health

---

[5] This proposal is described in a committee print, "A National Health Insurance Proposal," Committee on Ways and Means, House of Representatives, August 19, 1974.

insurance plan, the alternate health care insurance plan, and the catastrophic health insurance plan.

The employer plan would require all employers (including state and local governments, but not the federal government) to provide for their employees a health insurance plan that would meet certain minimum benefit standards. Such plans could be with an insurer, such as Blue Cross–Blue Shield or an insurance company, or could be self-insured. The employer would be required to pay at least 65 percent of the cost for the first three years and then 75 percent. Employers who have relatively high costs—in excess of 3 percent of payroll—would have part of such excess cost subsidized by the federal government, 75 percent in the first year, grading down each successive year until being phased out in the sixth year.

The range of benefits required under the employer plan would be very comprehensive, including, in general, all services covered by Medicare, plus out-of-hospital prescription drugs and dental, vision, and hearing services for children under age 13. No duration limits would apply except for skilled nursing facility services (100 days per year) and mental illness cases (60 hospital days per year and an annual dollar limitation for outpatient services based on the average cost of 15 visits to a private practitioner, but double that amount for treatment at a comprehensive community care center). As to cost-sharing payments, there would be: an annual deductible of $150 per person, but no further payment therefor after three members of the family had met the deductible; a separate annual deductible of $50 per person for out-of-hospital prescription drugs; coinsurance of 25 percent after the deductible; and annual cost sharing for a family not to exceed $1,000. The maximum amount of benefits payable for a year would be $6,000, since the catastrophic plan would take over then.

The alternate plan under the staff proposal would be available to all persons not covered by the employer plan and would be operated on a state-by-state basis. Persons on public assistance would be required to join, but it would be optional for others. This plan would have the same benefits as the employer plan. The financing would be from premiums paid by the enrollees and from federal and state subsidies. The standard premium rate, varying only as between one-person families and other families, would be 125 percent of the average premium in the state under the employer plan. Low-income people—with annual family income of less than $2,400 for one person, increasing $400 for each additional member to a maximum of $4,800—would be exempt from both the premium charge and all cost-sharing payments. Persons above these income limits would be phased in by paying premiums equal to 8 percent of their income in excess of the limit and by having maximum cost sharing of 25 percent of such excess income.

The catastrophic plan under the staff proposal would apply to virtually the entire population under age 65. The principal exclusion would be persons not under the employer plan who did not choose to join the alternate plan. This plan would be operated in the same manner as Medicare is now. It would be financed by percentage tax rates on all income, including unearned income, social insurance benefits, and public assistance payments, up to $20,000 of annual income of the individual or, in the case of a married couple, that of the husband and wife combined. The tax rates would be: ¼ percent for the employee on his wages and ¾ percent for the employer, on the first $20,000 of annual wages of each employee; ½ percent for the self-employed; ½ percent on unearned income; and ¾ percent on public assistance payments, paid by the federal government for SSI and by the states for AFDC. Persons under age 18 and persons aged 65 or over would not be taxed on unearned income or social insurance benefits. The benefits of the plan for a family would be payment for all costs of covered medical services exceeding $6,000 per year.

The Medicare program would be revised under the Ways and Means staff proposal so as to be at least as favorable as the coverage provided under the other plans. Specifically, the limit on hospital days covered would be removed, out-of-hospital prescription drugs would be covered, maximum annual cost-sharing of $1,000 per family would be provided, and lower cost sharing would be applicable to low-income persons. At the same time, the disabled beneficiaries under age 65 and the chronic kidney disease cases now covered would no longer be covered, since they would be under either the employer or alternate plans. The program would be financed by percentage tax rates on the same income as is taxed for the catastrophic plan (rates not specified).

Under all three Ways and Means staff proposals, institutional providers of services would be reimbursed on a prospective basis, such that they would receive their costs, and possibly even a reward for efficient operation, or vice versa. Physicians would be reimbursed only if they agreed to accept payment according to a fee schedule developed for geographic areas and based on 1973 average fees adjusted for economic changes subsequently; services rendered by nonparticipating physicians would not be covered. In all instances, providers of services would receive full payment from the program, which in turn would collect the cost-sharing amounts from the beneficiaries.

The Committee on Ways and Means, however, could not come to any clear-cut decision on the matter because it was divided in several ways. By a tie vote, it rejected the AMA's Medicredit proposal, the Fulton-Broyhill Bill. And it also turned down the insurance industry's proposal, the McIntyre-Burleson Bill, by a one-vote margin. At the same time, Chairman Mills was only able to obtain approval for parts of his suggested compromise by slim margins, so he dropped the whole matter for the current session since there did not seem to be sufficient time left to obtain a solid majority of the committee in favor of any specific proposal. This impasse resulted from the split of the committee membership into three apparently irreconcilable factions who could not compromise their differences—conservatives favoring the Medicredit approach, liberals favoring the original Kennedy-Griffiths approach, and the middle group favoring the Nixon approach. Most members, however, seemed to favor some sort of catastrophic protection. As a result, no further legislative activity on this subject occurred in 1974.

An interesting development in Hawaii may give an indication of how a national health benefits program on an employer-mandated basis could be accomplished. In mid-1974, the Hawaii Prepaid Health Care Law took effect. Under this plan, all private employers must provide health care benefits for their employees. This can be done through an insurance company, Blue Cross–Blue Shield, or an HMO. The benefits must include 120 inpatient hospital days per year, surgical and medical benefits, diagnostic benefits, and maternity benefits.

The Hawaii plan is financed by both employer and employee contributions. The employee pays 1½ percent of his wages, but not more than half the cost; while the employer pays the balance of the cost. Employers of less than 8 workers can have a subsidy of their cost in excess of 1½ percent of payroll, to the extent that such excess exceeds 5 percent of their pre-tax net income from their business.

chapter 10

Actuarial Cost Estimates and
Analysis and Statistical
Information for OASDI and
Medicare

The foregoing chapters have described the provisions of the OASDI
and Medicare systems, the methods of making actuarial cost estimates
therefor, and the general concepts underlying these cost estimates. In
this chapter, there will be presented the results of these actuarial cost
estimates so that the subject may be seen in actual practice, as well
as in theory. Then data on the general operations of the program will
be given, as well as illustrative information on the amount of survivor
insurance in force under OASDI.[1]

Data with respect to the actuarial cost estimates will be presented
for several of the recent legislative actions. The estimates for both sets
of the 1972 amendments will be discussed in detail because of the vast
changes in the benefit provisions made then and because of the different
approach adopted as to actuarial methodology and financing. Consideration will then be given to the cost estimates made for the December 1973 amendments, which, in essence, overrode the amendments
made in July 1973, at the time of their enactment. Finally, the cost

---

[1] The data presented here are taken from various official published sources
(such as the trustees reports and congressional committee reports) or else have
been obtained directly from the Office of the Actuary, Social Security Administration.

estimates for that same legislation that were made later in the 1974 Trustees Report will be discussed.

Because of the considerable number of tables presenting statistical data in this chapter, all tables appear as an appendix to the chapter text.

ACTUARIAL COST ESTIMATES MADE AT ENACTMENT OF 1972 AMENDMENTS

Table 10.1 presents the estimated average cost, as percentages of taxable payroll, of OASDI benefits by type, according to the official estimates made for the 1972 amendments at the time of their enactment.[2] Also shown are comparable data for administrative expenses and for the effect of the existing trust fund at that time. In the OASI portion of the system, the primary benefits (for retired workers) represented 70 percent of the total benefit cost; wife's benefits were 5 percent; widow's benefits were 15 percent; and survivor benefits for younger persons were 10 percent. Benefit costs for disabled workers were 80 percent of the total cost for the DI program.

Table 10.2 shows the estimated cost of OASI, DI, and HI, separately, as percentages of taxable payroll for selected future years, as well as the average long-range costs.

The OASI costs were estimated to rise slowly but steadily until 1990, as the population aged 62 and over grows (in both absolute and relative terms) and as an increasing proportion of this age group becomes eligible for benefits. The OASI cost was shown as leveling off in the two decades following 1990; this was the result of the changing population structure, since then the aged population will be largely composed of the cohorts born in the 1930s, when the birth rate was relatively low. But after 2010 the cost rises sharply (by about 20–30 percent) as the survivors of the larger numbers of births in years after the end of World War II reach retirement age. The ultimate cost is about one third larger than the cost in the near future.

The DI costs were estimated to rise somewhat more rapidly in the next 30 years than the OASI ones, since the DI system will reach relative maturity much more rapidly. The increase in DI costs is shown to be relatively small after the year 2010. The ultimate DI cost is about 25 percent larger than the cost in the near future.

The OASDI cost data shown in Table 10.2 are based on the official

---

[2] The term "1972 amendments" as used here means the amendments of October 30, 1972, so that the effect of the amendments of July 1, 1972, is also included.

dynamic economic assumptions used by the Social Security Administration—namely, that, over the long range, wages will increase by 5 percent per year, and prices will increase by 2¾ percent per year (plus a contingency margin of ⅜ percent per year up to 2010). Subsequently, data will be presented to show the effect of variations in these economic assumptions.

The HI costs were estimated to increase steadily over the future years to almost 3 percent of taxable payroll by 1995. This results largely because of the assumption that hospital costs will continue to rise more rapidly than earnings in covered employment. The HI cost estimates are carried out for only 25 years in the future—as against 75 years for the OASDI estimates. It seems very likely that higher HI tax rates will be needed after the turn of the century than are now scheduled, at least because of the higher proportion of aged persons in the population.

Table 10.3 presents the estimated future progress of the OASI Trust Fund in the near future as it was estimated that it would develop under the 1972 amendments. Table 10.4 shows corresponding information for the DI Trust Fund. The OASI Trust Fund is shown as rising from $36 billion at the end of 1972 to $52 billion at the end of 1977, with the increases after 1973 being at annual rates of about 10 percent. Comparing the fund balance under OASI at the beginning of the year with the outgo in the year, the ratio for 1973 was 75 percent, and 73 percent for 1974, but it then increased to 77 percent for 1977. Thus, the recommendation of the 1970–72 Advisory Council that the fund balance should approximately equal the next year's outgo and should not be less than 75 percent thereof was followed, but just barely.

The DI Trust Fund was estimated to increase from $7.5 billion at the end of 1972 to $9.3 billion at the end of 1977, again with annual increases of about 10 percent after 1973. The ratio of the fund balance at the beginning of the year to the year's outgo was 122 percent for 1973 and 107 percent for 1977. Thus, the 75 percent rule was readily met for the DI Trust Fund. When the two funds are considered together, the test ratios were 81 percent for 1972 and 80 percent for 1977.

Unlike previous procedure, no long-range cost estimates as to the operations of the trust fund for OASDI (or HI either) in terms of dollars were presented at the time of the 1972 amendments. Apparently, this course of action was taken because of the dynamic economic assumptions used, since the resulting figures would thus have been very large—and perhaps unduly alarming to some. Nonetheless, it would seem desirable to have such figures available, with proper qualifying statements, for informational purposes.

Tables 10.5 and 10.6 show the progress of the fund over the short range for the two Medicare trust funds, as estimated at the time of enactment of the October 1972 amendments. As a result of the increased financing provided by these amendments, the HI Trust Fund would grow rapidly during the period—from $2.6 billion for 1973 to $12.9 billion for 1978. The ratio of the trust fund balance at the beginning of the year to the year's outgo also rose rapidly—from 30 percent for 1972 to 79 percent for 1976.

The future course of the SMI Trust Fund depends on the "adequate actuarial rates" promulgated. The estimate shown in Table 10.6 assumes relatively small increases in such rates (and thus in the benefit experience). The trust fund balance would roughly triple during 1972–77, rising from $600 million to $1.8 billion. The ratio of the fund balance at the beginning of the year to the year's outgo increased from 20 percent for 1973 to 28 percent for 1977. This ratio for this program need not be as much as 100 percent or even 75 percent, as is the recommended rule for OASDI and HI, since it is financed on a year-by-year incurred-cost basis, rather than on a long-range basis. Rather, such ratio should be about 25–30 percent in order that the fund balance should approximate the incurred but unpaid claims at any time. It may be noted, however, that none of the parties concerned with the financing of the program—Congress, the executive branch, and advisory councils—have ever addressed themselves specifically to this matter of the desirable level of the SMI Trust Fund.

Congress has, since the 1950 amendments, consistently enunciated the principle that, according to the intermediate-cost estimates, the OASDI and HI programs should be self-supporting from contributions of covered workers and their employers. Of course, it would be only by coincidence that an exact balance would result. Generally, there has been a small deficiency in comparing the level cost of the benefits with the level equivalent of the contributions, under the intermediate-cost estimate. The situation under the 1972 Act, as of the time of its enactment, is indicated in Table 10.7 (in percentages of taxable payroll).

Congress has quite properly considered that the long-range actuarial cost estimates are not precise and that a reasonable range of variation may be present. Accordingly, the principle has been established that the OASDI and HI systems are considered to be actuarially sound if they are in reasonably close actuarial balance (provided that the year-by-year projections indicate that the balance in each trust fund will never become negative or, in other words, that there will always be money available to pay the benefits). Congress—or at least the congressional committees that deal with OASDI and HI legislation—has used a "rule of thumb" that this condition is satisfied.

This rule initially set a maximum on the actuarial imbalance of 0.30 percent of taxable payroll for OASDI (0.25 percent for OASI alone). This limit was reduced to 0.10 percent in 1965, when the period over which the estimates were made was reduced from an infinite one to 75 years. In the consideration of the 1973 amendments, the congressional committees decided that the limit might be as much as 0.50 percent, or about 5 percent of the average long-range cost of the system.

The corresponding limit for the HI program has been set at 0.10 percent of taxable payroll.

Table 10.8 presents an historical summary of the actuarial balance of the combined OASDI program over all past years, while Table 10.9 gives corresponding data for OASI and DI separately (for 1956 and after, when DI first was operating). Table 10.10 shows such data for the HI program.

The actuarial balance of OASDI was invariably maintained within the limits considered acceptable in the past (or else such balance was achieved in the next amendatory legislation—for example, for OASI in the 1954 Act). However, in 1973, a much larger deficiency than was previously considered acceptable was allowed in the legislation of that year, and the subsequent estimates in the 1974 Trustees Report showed a much worse situation (the causes for which will be discussed subsequently).

The DI program showed a steadily increasing estimated level cost after 1960, rising from about 0.4 percent of payroll to 1.6 percent of payroll for the 1973 amendments at the time they were enacted. In part, this was because of liberalization of its benefit provisions in 1958 and 1960, but later because of its developing adverse experience. However, these increasing-cost elements were taken into account at the several times when legislation was enacted thereafter, and the system was maintained in close actuarial balance. The latest estimates indicate a significant imbalance, and thus there is a need for still further financing to be legislated.

To summarize the long-range cost situation of the DI system as indicated by the various official actuarial cost estimates over the years, there have been six different times when higher disability assumptions had to be made because of the adverse experience developing (1964, 1966, 1969, 1972, 1973, and 1974). Largely as a result, the tax allocation from the combined employer-employee rate rose from 0.5 percent of payroll initially to 1.15 percent for 1974–77, and 1.7 percent ultimately under current law. Part of this increase is due to certain benefit liberalizations in the DI program, and part is due to an expansion in the general OASDI benefit level, but most of it is due to the adverse disability experience.

In similar manner, the estimated level or average benefit cost of the HI program has increased significantly since the program was enacted in 1965, rising from about 1.2 percent of payroll to 2.2 percent for the estimates made in 1971–72 and then to 2.6 percent for the latest estimates (the latter increase being due to the extension of the program to disabled beneficiaries). The rising trend in the late 1960s occurred primarily because the estimates initially underestimated both the extent of hospital utilization which occurred and the rising trend of hospital costs.

It should especially be noted that part of the estimated increase in cost of HI was dampened in the 1969 estimates when a basic change in the cost-estimating procedure was instituted. Previously, the very conservative assumption had been made that the maximum taxable earnings base would remain unchanged in the future at the level prevailing at the time the estimate was made. This was assumed despite the fact that increasing-earnings assumptions were made in connection with the projected future trend of hospital costs. Thus, it might be said that these assumptions were inconsistent and resulted in an overstatement of costs. However, this was done in order to have a margin of safety, and also, to some degree, because changes in the earnings base were under the jurisdiction of Congress, not the actuaries.

In 1969, it was decided to shift the methodology and to assume that the earnings base would increase in the future to the same extent as the assumed increases in earnings. This was done, in part, to recognize that sufficient operating experience had accumulated so that a better fix on costs could be obtained and thus the need for an arbitrarily obtained margin of safety was lessened. Also, it appeared very likely that automatic-adjustment provisions applicable to the earnings base would soon be enacted (as they were in 1972). The net effect was to show a lower level cost of about 0.7 percent of taxable payroll.

As a result of the rapidly rising hospital costs after 1965, as will be analyzed in more detail later in this chapter, and as a result of the somewhat higher hospital utilization actually experienced as compared with the initial assumptions, the actuarial balance of the program deteriorated during 1966–72. However, as hospital costs tended to stabilize during the price controls of the early 1970s and as the financing provisions were strengthened through increases in the tax rates and the earnings base, the estimated balance was brought to "acceptable" levels in 1972–74. This favorable situation was particularly due to the earnings base being raised so much more rapidly than the general level of earnings in 1973 and 1974. Such action produces more tax income without increasing benefit amounts (unlike the situation under OASDI).

ACTUARIAL COST ESTIMATES MADE AT ENACTMENT OF 1973 AMENDMENTS

Table 10.11 shows the estimated cost of OASI, DI, and HI benefits, separately, as percentages of taxable payroll for selected future years, as well as the average long-range costs for the program as it was amended in December 1973, according to the estimates made when the legislation was enacted. The trends of these costs are about the same as those shown for the program as it was after the 1972 amendments, but as to OASDI the figures are at a somewhat higher level (as a result of the changes in economic conditions in 1972–73 being less favorable than had been assumed).

Table 10.12 shows the corresponding estimated future progress of the combined OASI and DI Trust Funds in the near future. Such fund is shown as increasing from $44 billion at the end of 1973 to $52 billion at the end of 1977 and $54 billion at the end of 1978, with the annual increases being about $2 billion, or about 4 percent relatively. It will be noted that the trust fund growth is much less than under the October 1972 amendments, when the corresponding 1977 figure was $61 billion. Comparing the fund balance with outgo in the next year, the ratio for 1973 is 72 percent, and it then decreases to 62 percent for 1977, a ratio well below the minimum standard of 75 percent recommended by the Advisory Council of 1970–72.

Table 10.13 shows the progress of the HI Trust Fund under the December 1973 amendments over the short range as estimated at the time of enactment of the legislation (no such estimate was made for the SMI Trust Fund). The trust fund balance increases from $6.3 billion at the end of 1973 to $14.9 billion at the end of 1978. These figures are little different from those developed at the time of the October 1972 amendments (see Table 10.5). The ratio of the trust fund balance to the next year's outgo rises steadily over the period—from 64 percent for 1973 to 72 percent for 1977 (or a higher ratio than for OASDI).

ACTUARIAL COST ESTIMATES MADE
SUBSEQUENT TO 1973

As has traditionally been the case, continual reexamination of the actuarial cost estimates is made in the light of developing experience. New cost estimates which were developed in 1974 (presented in the reports of the board of trustees) indicated that the actuarial status of the OASDI program had deteriorated considerably over that previously estimated. This has been shown by Tables 10.8 and 10.9 (in percentages of taxable payroll).

These new cost estimates utilized revised assumptions as to a number of factors. The economic assumptions over the long range were annual increases of 5 percent in earnings and 3 percent in the CPI. In balance, these long-range assumptions had about the same effect as those used previously when taken in combination with the assumed safety margin, which was eliminated in the 1974 cost estimates. Over the short range, the earnings assumptions were an 8.5 percent increase for 1975, grading down to 7.6 percent for 1977 and then 5.5 percent for 1978–80 and 5.0 percent thereafter. The corresponding assumed CPI increases were 5.7 percent for 1975, grading down to 3.0 percent for 1978 and thereafter.

An alternative set of economic assumptions, which were somewhat more pessimistic and probably more realistic, were used for an alternate short-range estimate. The earnings increases assumed were 9.3 percent for 1975, grading down to 7.5 percent in 1978 and 6.0 percent in 1979–80. The CPI increases assumed were 7.1 percent in 1975, grading down to 4.0 percent in 1979–80.

The effect of these new assumptions on the estimated cost of the OASDI system is shown in Table 10.14. About 75 percent of the resulting higher cost arose on account of the revised demographic assumptions, particularly the much lower fertility rates used, which reflected the recent actual experience for this element. Specifically, it was assumed that the total fertility rate would increase slowly from its current lower-than-replacement level to the replacement level of 2.1 children being borne, on the average, by each woman.[3] Previously, fertility had been assumed to decline slowly in the future, but to be always above the replacement level. The 1975 trustees report showed a further rise in the OASDI deficiency, to 5.32 percent of payroll.

The 1974 HI cost estimates, which show the HI system to be in close actuarial balance, are based on the assumption that the annual rate of increase in hospital costs will exceed the annual rate of increase in earnings in covered employment.

It is assumed that taxable earnings will increase at the rates assumed in the OASDI cost estimates. At the same time, it is assumed that per capita hospital costs will increase 13.1 percent in 1975, and then grade down to 11.2 percent in 1980 and 8.5 percent in 1985 and after. To the extent that the experience does not follow these assumptions, the cost of HI will be similarly affected.

The actuarial cost estimates for HI as presented in the 1974 Trustees Report also contained two alternative estimates that were based on different assumptions as to the future trend of per capita hospital costs. Under the high-cost assumptions that the 1975 increase rate would be 14.0 percent and the ultimate rate would be 9.0 percent, the average cost increases from 2.63 percent of taxable payroll to 3.29 percent, resulting in an actuarial imbalance of 0.64 percent. Similarly, under the low-cost assumptions that the 1975 increase rate would be only 10.5 percent and the ultimate rate would be 7.5 percent, the average cost drops to 2.50 percent of payroll, providing an actuarial surplus of 0.15 percent.

The reasonableness of the economic assumptions used in the actuarial cost estimates for OASDI and the effect of alternative ones on the resulting financial status has been discussed in Chapter 4, in particular in connection with Table 4.3. From that discussion, it may be seen that the future experience as to economic conditions can have a great effect on both the dollar figures and the percentage-of-payroll figures presented here.

Table 10.15 shows the estimated average cost, as percentages of taxable payroll, of OASDI benefits by type for the program as it was at the end of 1974, according to the official cost estimates in the 1974

---

[3] The total fertility rate is the average number of children that a newly born girl baby will have during the course of her lifetime. Such a rate of 2.1 means that, considering mortality and the sex ratio at birth, the population will just replace itself.

Trustees Report. The subdivision of the costs as between the different beneficiary categories is virtually the same as was previously the case in connection with the 1972 amendments, as discussed previously, even though the absolute level is significantly higher.

The estimated average cost of the HI program, expressed as percentages of taxable payroll, is subdivided as follows:

Persons aged 65 and over...........................	2.11%
Disabled persons.................................	0.35
Persons with chronic kidney disease.................	0.01
Total benefits...............................	2.47%
Administrative expenses...........................	0.05%
Effect of size of fund*	+0.11
Total cost..................................	2.63%

* This item represents the effect of the trust fund being less or greater than one year's outgo.

The subdivision of the total benefit cost of 2.47 percent of taxable payroll as between types of benefit is as follows: hospital, 2.41 percent; skilled nursing facility, 0.05 percent; and home health care, 0.01 percent.

In the same manner, Table 10.16 presents the estimated cost of OASI, DI, and HI, separately, as percentages of taxable payroll for selected future years, as well as the average long-range costs. The OASI cost is estimated to rise from the 1973 level of 8.70 percent of taxable payroll to about 9½ percent in 1990 and then level off for the next 15 years before beginning a very significant increase to about 15½ percent in the year 2030 and subsequently. The ultimate level is thus about 80 percent higher than that prevailing in 1973.

The DI cost is estimated to increase steadily over the years until leveling off in about the year 2010 and thereafter. The ultimate cost of about 2.2 percent of taxable payroll is about 60 percent higher than the 1973 cost.

The estimated HI cost rises relatively rapidly over the 25-year period considered in the cost estimate. The 1995 cost of 3.45 percent of taxable payroll is 2½ times as high as the actual 1973 cost, in part due to assumed rising hospital costs and in part due to the benefits for disabled beneficiaries going into effect only in the middle of 1973.

Table 10.17 presents the estimated short-range future progress of the OASI Trust Fund according to the 1974 estimates, while Table 10.18 gives corresponding data for the DI Trust Fund. The OASI

Trust Fund increases only slowly during 1974–78, rising from $36.5 billion to $37.2 billion. At the same time, the DI Trust Fund decreases from $8.0 billion to $6.8 billion. Thus, the two funds combined are virtually level during the next four years.

The ratio of the fund balance at the beginning of the year to the expenditures during the year is estimated to decrease from 67 percent for OASI in 1974 to 46 percent in 1978. For DI, the corresponding ratios are 110 percent in 1974 and 61 percent in 1978. For OASI and DI combined, these ratios are 72 percent in 1974 and 48 percent in 1978. Thus, the recommendation of the 1970–72 Advisory Council that this ratio should be about 100 percent, but not less than 75 percent, has been violated. If it were desired to raise the tax rates sufficiently in 1975 and after so that a ratio of 75 percent would be achieved for 1978, then an increase in the combined employer-employee rate of 1 percent would be necessary.

One might wonder what are the short-range and medium-range effects of the long-range OASDI financial deficit of almost 3 percent of taxable payroll. Consider the situation under the basis that all the assumptions in the official cost estimates presented in the 1974 Trustees Report turn out to be exactly correct, even what are, in the author's opinion, the unrealistic economic assumptions, and that the benefit structure and the financing provisions will not be changed despite their long-range instability, again most unlikely. Both the OASI and DI Trust Funds would have ample resources to meet their benefit obligations for at least a decade. But after then, serious financing problems would arise, with the necessity for higher tax rates, although not greatly increased, largely due to the trough or plateau occurring in the 1990s as to the OASDI costs as a result of the leveling off of the population aged 65 and over.

Tables 10.19 and 10.20 present the short-range progress of the fund for the two Medicare trust funds according to the 1974 estimates. Despite the reduction in the HI tax rates for 1974–80 in the 1973 amendments, which was offset to a considerable extent by the increased taxable earnings base,[4] the HI Trust Fund is shown to increase rapidly after 1974. The balance at the end of 1978 is estimated at $21.6 billion, or somewhat more than twice as large as at the end of 1974; the large increase in 1978 results from the significant increase in the HI tax rate for that year. This trend is quite in contrast with the level

---

[4] Unlike OASDI, an increase in the earnings base for HI has no effect on benefit costs, but rather only produces higher tax income.

trend estimated for the OASI and DI Trust Funds. The ratio of the fund balance at the beginning of the year to the year's outgo was 72 percent for 1974 and rose to 107 percent for 1978. Thus, unlike the situation for the OASI and DI Trust Funds, the trust fund ratio for HI, according to this estimate, conforms with the recommendations of the 1970–72 Advisory Council. In fact, for 1978 it is shown as being somewhat above the middle of the acceptable range of 75–125 percent, and for 1979 it will be close to the top.

It should be noted, however, that the assumptions underlying the 1974 HI cost estimates are based on relatively small projected increases in hospital costs. The experience in this respect since price controls were removed in early 1974 is not favorable. As a result, the HI Trust Fund may not have the favorable experience shown in Table 10.19.

The progress of the SMI Trust Fund shown in Table 10.20 is based on the enrollee standard premium rate being frozen at the $6.70 figure applicable in fiscal year 1974. As was brought out in Chapter 6, this illogical result will occur because of the technical error in the 1973 amendments, as long as OASDI benefits increase only as a result of the automatic-adjustment provisions and not through ad hoc legislative changes.

The government contribution was equal to the enrollee premiums in periods before July 1973, on an accrual basis, although sometimes being slightly different than this on a cash basis. For 1974, the ratio of the government contribution to the enrollee premiums was 123 percent, due to the higher matching ratio for disabled enrollees than for aged ones, for whom equal matching then prevailed. This ratio increases steadily over the period, until for 1978 it is 241 percent, or, in other words, the government contribution then bears 71 percent of the total cost.

The balance in the SMI Trust Fund is estimated to increase from $1.3 billion at the end of 1974 to $2.4 billion at the end of 1978, or almost twice as large. The ratio of the fund balance at the beginning of 1974 to that year's outgo is 29 percent. This ratio increases to 32 percent for 1978 according to this estimate. As indicated previously, this ratio need not be as high as the level of 75–125 percent deemed desirable for OASI, DI, and HI, but rather seems to be satisfactory if at or somewhat above 25–30 percent.

Details of the actuarial balances of the OASI, DI, and HI programs, according to the 1974 estimates, are presented in Table 10.21. The actuarial deficits shown for OASI and DI represent a relative deficiency of 21 percent as measured against their total costs in each case, or, conversely, 27 percent of their tax income.

The Senate Finance Committee appointed a Panel on Social Security Financing in 1974, consisting of actuaries and economists. This panel made somewhat different assumptions than those contained in the official cost estimates for OASDI made earlier in the year. The long-range economic assumptions were annual increases of 6 percent in wages and 4 percent in prices. Lower fertility rates were assumed for the near future, although the replacement rate of 2.1 was assumed for the year 2010 and thereafter. The panel also assumed lower mortality rates, especially after the year 2000.

All changes in assumptions made by the Senate Finance panel were in the direction of higher estimated costs. The resulting estimated OASDI current costs and the long-range average deficit relative to the financing provided by the present schedule of tax rates, as compared with those in the 1974 official cost estimates, were as follows (in terms of percentages of taxable payroll):

Year	Official Estimate	Panel Estimate
1990	11.0%	11.5%
2010	12.7	14.6
2030	17.6	23.3
2045	17.9	24.7
Average cost	13.9	16.9
Average deficit	3.0	6.0

Thus, the estimate of the panel resulted in a doubling of the estimated deficit of the OASDI program as against that shown in the 1974 official cost estimates. Such increase in the deficit tended to be concentrated in the years following 2000.

All of the foregoing discussion of the deficit in OASDI is based on the foundation of the 1974 official cost estimates. An increase in the deficit will occur, on an immediate basis, as a result of the automatic adjustment of benefits for June 1975. This will result in an increase of 8.0 percent in the general benefit level, whereas the 1974 official cost estimate assumed that such increase would be only 4.4 percent. The net effect of this factor alone is to increase the long-range deficit by about 0.5 percent of taxable payroll. A further increase in the deficit of about 0.1 percent of taxable payroll resulted from the 1975 Supreme

Court decision providing equal benefit treatment for men and women.

In February 1975, the Social Security Administration released part of the 1975 official actuarial cost estimates, which will be included in the 1975 Trustees Report. These will show a larger deficit than 3 percent of taxable payroll. Such result will be caused not only by the effect of the automatic adjustment of benefits for June 1975, but also by changes in assumptions as to fertility rates and wage-price increases.

These 1975 official cost estimates also show that a serious short-range financing problem is likely. This results from changes in the economic assumptions as to wage and price increases in the next few years as compared with what had been assumed previously, so as to recognize the current inflationary situation. Specifically, it is assumed that the general benefit increase will be 9.2 percent for June 1976, decreasing to 6.9 percent for 1977, 5.7 percent for 1978, 4.4 percent for 1979, and 4.0 percent for 1980. At the same time, the general wage level is assumed to increase by about 10 percent per year during 1976–79 and by 7 percent in 1980.

The results under these 1975 official cost estimates are that the OASI Trust Fund decreases from $37.8 billion at the end of 1974 to $36.0 billion at the end of 1975. Then, with annual decreases of about $6 billion, its balance drops to $4.1 billion at the end of 1980 and is exhausted the next year. At the same time, the DI Trust Fund of $8.1 billion at the end of 1974 declines by about $2 billion per year until being exhausted in 1979. The detailed estimates are as in the following table (in billions):

Calendar	OASI Trust Fund			DI Trust Fund		
Year	Income	Outgo	Balance	Income	Outgo	Balance
1974........	$54.7	$53.4	$37.8	$ 7.4	$ 7.2	$8.1
1975........	59.0	60.7	36.0	8.0	8.8	7.3
1976........	64.9	69.4	31.5	8.7	10.2	5.8
1977........	72.5	78.7	25.3	9.6	11.7	3.7
1978........	80.2	87.2	18.3	11.1	13.1	1.6
1979........	88.5	95.6	11.1	12.2	14.5	−0.7
1980........	97.0	104.0	4.1	13.3	15.8	−3.3

This short-range problem of rapidly decreasing trust fund balances could be solved by increasing the combined employer-employee tax rate by 1 percent, effective in 1976. Under such circumstances, the trust funds would maintain their current absolute levels and, in fact, would increase a little. However, their sizes relative to annual outgo would fall to somewhat less than 50 percent and would thus be far below the minimum standard recommended by the 1970–72 Advisory Council. No change in this standard was proposed by the 1974 Advisory Council.

EFFECT OF VARYING ECONOMIC ASSUMPTIONS FOR OASDI COST ESTIMATES

Now that automatic-adjustment provisions are incorporated in the OASDI system, dynamic economic assumptions as to future earnings changes and future price level changes (which determine the benefit level) are used in the actuarial cost estimates. These assumptions are extremely important, and, in fact, the results are very sensitive for what appear to be small differences therein. This, in essence, is due to their compounding nature over the long periods of years involved in the cost estimates.

The official cost estimates in 1972 used the assumptions over the long range of 5 percent annual increases in earnings and 2¾ percent annual increases in prices (plus, in essence, an additional ⅜ percent per year until 2010). In 1974, this approach was changed slightly, with the long-range assumptions being 5 percent for earnings and 3 percent for prices in all years after 1980 and with grading-in from the present situation to 1980. The validity of these assumptions over the long range has been discussed in Chapter 4. Here, there will be presented illustrative data to show the effect of varying these assumptions as they are involved in the 1974 cost estimates.[5]

Table 10.22 presents the "current cost" of the OASDI program expressed as a percentage of taxable payroll for selected years and the long-range "average cost" for the program according to the 1974 cost estimates.

The "current cost" represents the total outgo for benefit payments and administrative expenses in the year, plus the amount needed to maintain the trust fund balance at a level of one year's outgo, as measured against effective taxable payroll. The long-range "average cost" is merely the arithmetic average of the 75 "current costs" (with-

---

[5] Also see Geoffrey N. Calvert, *New Realistic Projections of Social Security Benefits and Taxes* (New York: Alexander and Alexander, Inc., December 1973) for an analysis of this matter.

out any discounting for interest over the time period) for 1974 through 2048.

The figures in Table 10.22 are grouped according to the difference between the assumed rate of increase in wages and that for prices. Thus, the first line is the official "central" assumptions, with a 2 percent difference (reflecting the assumed rate of productivity increase), and the next two lines of the group also have such a 2 percent difference. The second group has a 3 percent difference, while the third group has a 1 percent difference.

It will be seen that the year-by-year cost figures are about the same for the next 25 years for a particular difference between the assumed rates of increase of wages and prices, but that the cost is significantly higher as such difference decreases, and vice versa. For a given difference between wage and price increase rates, the cost is somewhat higher when such increases are larger. Actually, stability of the cost figures tends to be achieved somewhat more on a ratio basis than on an absolute difference basis.

In the first 25 years, the current-cost figures do not spread out greatly as between the various sets of economic assumptions. Such costs do not differ greatly from the scheduled level combined employer-employee OASDI tax rate of 9.9 percent *if the differential between wages and prices is 2 percent.* Under such circumstances, a 1 percent higher tax rate would suffice to finance adequately the system for this period. But a lower differential would mean that much higher tax rates would be needed within a few years from now. The other side of the coin, however, is that, at the same time, the program would be getting out of control insofar as the relationship of benefits to recent earnings is concerned, as was discussed in Chapter 2.

After 25 years, the current-cost figures spread out much more, for any particular differential between wages and prices as the level of such elements changes. For example, in the year 2010, just before the combined employer-employee tax rate scheduled under present law rises from 9.9 percent to 11.9 percent, the current cost is 12.7 percent under the central assumptions of 5 percent and 3 percent increases in wages and prices, respectively, but 14.0 percent for the 6 and 4 percent assumptions, and 11.8 percent for the 4 and 2 percent ones.

In the ultimate situation, for the year 2045, the problem is magnified. The current cost under the central assumptions is 6.0 percent higher than the tax rate, a clear indication of the magnitude of the financing problem involved as disclosed in the 1974 official cost estimates. For the 6 and 4 percent assumptions, the deficiency is 9.5 percent of taxable payroll. On the other hand, the 4 and 2 percent assumptions show a deficiency of only 3.0 percent of taxable payroll.

If the differential between wages and prices is as much as 3 percentage points, which seems most unlikely to occur, the presently scheduled OASDI tax rates would be adequate to finance the system. In fact, under the 5 and 2 percent assumptions, a continuation of the present 9.9 percent rate for the entire 75-year period, without the necessity of the scheduled increase in 2011, would be close to being sufficient. However, it is unlikely that the program would remain unchanged under either of these sets of economic conditions, since then the relative level of the benefits would deteriorate, again as was discussed in Chapter 2.

Table 10.23 gives the long-range average costs for a wider variety of sets of economic assumptions than were shown in Table 10.22. Under static economic assumptions (no increases assumed in either earnings or prices), the average cost is estimated at 18.0 percent of taxable payroll, or 4.1 percent of payroll above the official cost estimate (30 percent relatively) and 7.1 percent of payroll above the average equivalent of the tax schedule (65 percent relatively).

Table 10.24 rearranges the data in Table 10.23 according to certain constant differentials between the assumed rates of increase of wages and prices, while Table 10.25 does the same for such rates of increase having a 2 to 1 ratio. The data in these two tables more clearly demonstrate some of the points brought out in the preceding discussion.

In recapitulation, then, the drastic and sensitive effect of the economic assumptions is clearly evident. When the spread between wages and prices is assumed to be large, the current costs over the years are low. But if the difference is small, then sharply rising costs—even catastrophically rising ones—result. For example, when wages and prices rise at the same rate over the long run (say, 5 percent or more), the ultimate current cost can be close to 50 percent of payroll, and the average long-range cost can be over 30 percent of payroll. The other side of the coin of this situation is, of course, that the benefit level is extremely high, producing benefit amounts generally well in excess of final pay.

What is the cure for the situation of runaway costs (and, correspondingly, benefit levels) under the operation of the automatic-adjustment provisions if the spread between wages and prices is much smaller than in the official cost estimates? It seems very likely that in the future such spread will be much smaller than it has been in the past, which experience was directly extrapolated for the future. The reasons that the spread will likely be less (i.e., lower productivity) are many—changed life-style desires by many, scarcity of raw materials, concern over ecology, more service industries, and so forth. The possible solutions to this problem were discussed in Chapters 3 and 5.

Alternative estimates were also made in 1974 to show the effects of varying the demographic assumptions as to future fertility rates.

The official cost estimates, which used the long-range economic assumptions of annual increases in wages of 5 percent and in the CPI of 3 percent, also assumed that the ultimate total fertility rate, in the year 2005 and after, would be at the replacement level of 2.1. This would mean that zero population growth (ZPG) conditions would then prevail insofar as fertility is concerned and that, accordingly, the total population would eventually, after some decades, level off. It was also assumed that fertility in the 25 years before 2005 would gradually phase in from the present level of a rate of about 1.9 to the ultimate rate of 2.1. These assumptions seem quite reasonable, because over the long run it would seem that the population of the country would neither decline to extinction nor increase to an infinite size.

Alternative ultimate total fertility rate assumptions of 1.9 and 2.3 were made, keeping all other assumptions the same. The long-range average cost was estimated at 14.64 percent of taxable payroll for the 1.9 fertility rate and at 13.27 percent for the 2.3 rate, as compared with the cost of 13.89 percent in the official cost estimate. These are differences of only about 5 percent relatively, so that it can be seen that the variability of this factor does not have nearly as great an effect on costs of the OASDI program as do economic factors.

Moreover, as might be anticipated, the current costs under the three fertility assumptions are virtually identical for the next 20 years and then begin to diverge. Such costs for the year 2045 are 19.91 percent of taxable payroll for the low fertility assumption and 16.15 percent for the high fertility assumption, as against 17.87 percent for the official estimate.

PAST OPERATIONS

Considerable financial and statistical data are published in the monthly issues and the annual statistical supplements of the *Social Security Bulletin.* The Social Security Administration also publishes an

Annual Handbook of Old-Age and Survivors Insurance Statistics that gives detailed information on the earnings of covered workers and annual issues of Medicare data in several volumes; unfortunately for purposes of use and analysis, these volumes are usually three or four years behind time. This agency also prepares extensive tabulations of detailed data on claims awards and benefits in current payment status. The board of trustees of the OASI and DI Trust Funds issues an annual report giving details on past operations of the funds, investment activities, and estimates of future operations. Similar reports are issued for both the HI and SMI programs. This section will give certain summary data on the operations of OASDI and Medicare since their establishment, since this may prove helpful in understanding the program.

Data on OASDI Coverage and Benefits Experience

Table 10.26 present information on the number of workers covered by the program (i.e., in employment yielding earnings on which contributions are payable), on the number of covered employers, on the number of persons who have insured status (regardless of whether currently in covered employment), and on the amount of earnings in covered employment (both total and taxable, after the effect of the earnings base). The number of covered workers is shown on the basis of the number with covered employment at any time during the year. The number actively at work in an average week during the year (disregarding, however, the effect of the maximum taxable earnings base, which results in many persons not having their wages taxable toward the end of the year) is, of course, lower. Some 20 percent more persons are in covered employment during a calendar year than at a given time in the year as a result of the movement in and out of the covered labor force.

The total number of persons who possess insured status, either fully or currently, is about 20 percent larger than those working in the year, which gives an indication of the extent of turnover of employment and the maintenance of benefit protection after employment has ceased. Those with disability insured status represent only about 68 percent of the total insured population, reflecting the effect of the more stringent requirement as to recency of employment. The sharp rise in the number of persons with disability insured status from 1968 to 1969 resulted from the liberalized conditions made applicable in February 1968 for persons aged 30 and under.

The proportion of the total covered earnings that was taxable decreased steadily from about 92 percent in the late 1930s and early 1940s to 80 percent in 1950 (since the earnings base was held fixed at $3,000, while earnings steadily rose). The increase in the base to $3,600 for 1951 caused this proportion to rise to 85 percent for wages, but the inclusion of the self-employed in the coverage of the system then resulted in an overall proportion of 81 percent. In the succeeding years, this ratio remained at about 80 percent as the base was regularly increased to match the rise in the general earnings level. Of course, between changes in the base, the ratio declined until the increased base became effective. For example, the ratio fell from 79.3 percent in 1959 (the first year that the $4,800 base was in effect) to 71.3 percent in 1965 (the last year for the $4,800 base), and then it rose to 80.0 percent in 1966 (when the base became $6,600).

This stability in the relative size of the earnings base was destroyed by the 1972 and 1973 amendments. The base legislated for 1974 was $13,200 as compared with $10,800 in 1973, and $9,000 in 1972. As a result, the proportion of the total covered payroll that was taxable increased to 81.8 percent for 1973 and to an estimated 85.8 percent for 1974, which ratio will be maintained relatively constant in the future as a result of the automatic-adjustment provisions. If the earnings base had been kept at the same relative level in 1974 at which it had been in 1951–72, it would have been $11,100 instead of $13,200.

In 1951–72 the proportion of all persons with covered earnings at least as high as the maximum amount taxable (and creditable for benefit purposes) generally varied between 25 and 35 percent. This proportion decreased to 20 percent in 1973 and then to 14 percent in 1974, as a result of the base then being increased more rapidly than the general earnings level rose. The corresponding proportions for men who worked in all 4 quarters of the year were about 45 to 55 percent in 1951–72 and then dropped to 40 percent for 1973 and 28 percent for 1974. For 4-quarter women workers, these proportions were about 10 to 15 percent in 1951–72 and then decreased to 6 percent in 1973 and 2 percent in 1974. When the program began in the late 1930s, the earnings base was relatively high, $3,000, and these proportions were only 3 percent for all workers, 7 percent for 4-quarter men and ½ percent for 4-quarter women.

Table 10.27 shows the number of monthly beneficiaries in current payment status at the end of each year, the number of deaths for which lump-sum payments were awarded each year, and the average old-age benefit (for only the retired worker, without considering supplements for dependents).

The data for beneficiaries in current payment status are on an accounting basis rather than an accrual basis. Some persons are included who should not be, such as terminations or suspensions because of employment that were reported late. Others are omitted who properly should be included, such as reinstatements to the roll when termination of employment was reported late or, more importantly, awards in process of adjudication and claims that will be filed subsequently. In the latter two cases, payments will actually be made for the particular month, even though the persons are not shown in the statistics to be in current payment status then. In balance, the data for benefits in current payment status understate the number of persons for whom payments in respect to the particular month are made, such payments being made at the beginning of the next month or in subsequent months.

The number of monthly beneficiaries has increased steadily over the years, reaching 30.9 million at the end of 1974. At that time, 20.0 million beneficiaries were aged 65 or over, representing 64.9 percent of all beneficiaries and 88.5 percent of the total population in the country at these ages. The only major beneficiary category that has not shared in such increasing trend is the transitional noninsured one, a closed group of persons who are at least age 72, which has declined from a peak of 729,000 at the end of 1966 to 278,000 at the end of 1974. As to the 11.5 percent of the population aged 65 or over who are not receiving OASDI benefits, almost half of them could receive such benefits if they or their spouses were to retire from substantial employment.

The number of deceased workers with respect to whom lump-sum death payments are made has been about 1¼ million in the last six years. This represents about two thirds of all the deaths in the country.

The average old-age benefit for a retired worker alone in current payment status at the end of 1974 was $188 per month. It should be noted that this figure is not truly representative of the benefits payable to retired workers who have been in the system continuously for many years and who retire at age 65 or over. Such average benefit, first awarded at the end of 1974, was about $227 per month for male workers and $188 for female workers.

A substantial number of persons living outside the United States receive OASDI monthly benefits, either based on their own earnings record or as dependents or survivors. At the end of 1973, there were

276,000 foreign beneficiaries, or 0.92 percent of the total, living in 119 countries. Their benefits were somewhat lower, on the average, so that the benefit payments abroad were only 0.80 percent of the total payments. About 37 percent of the beneficiaries living abroad are United States citizens, and another 11 percent are entitled on the earnings record of a citizen although not citizens themselves. These foreign beneficiaries were highly concentrated in a few countries; about 53 percent were in Canada, Italy, Mexico, and the Philippines, roughly the same number in each of these nations.

About 55 percent of the retired workers receiving OASDI benefits at the end of 1974 had first claimed early-retirement benefits before age 65 and were thus receiving actuarially reduced benefits. This proportion was 46 percent for male workers and 65 percent for female workers.

At the beginning of 1975, 50 percent of all persons aged 62–64 who had fully insured status were actually receiving OASDI primary benefits. Such proportion was higher for women than for men, 56 percent versus 44 percent, and it had risen steadily in the past, being only 35 percent in 1963 (when the effect of men being able to claim benefits before age 65, as a result of the 1961 amendments, was first fully apparent). Next, considering persons aged 65–71, where the earnings test is applicable, 84 percent of the fully insured at the start of 1975 were on the benefit roll, about the same proportion for both men and women. This proportion had been as low as 61 percent in 1955, 76 percent in 1960, and 80 percent in 1965.

The average benefit for those who had actuarially reduced benefits in current payment status at the end of 1974 was about 16 percent lower, for both men and women, than for those who first claimed benefits at age 65 or over. Somewhat more than half of this differential is due to the actuarial reduction, and the remainder is due to the generally lower earnings of those who retire early.

The foregoing data indicating the very considerable extent of early retirement under OASDI are very significant. With such a trend continuing in the future, pressure will possibly grow for a reduction in the normal retirement age at which unreduced benefits are payable.

Table 10.28 gives a distribution of the 28.5 million monthly beneficiaries in current payment status at the end of 1972[6] by category, so as to indicate the relative importance of a number of the major and

---

[6] The latest date for which such detailed data were published at the beginning of 1975.

minor beneficiary categories. Retired workers aged 62 and over represent about 50 percent of the total beneficiaries; about 55 percent of the retired workers are men; and 10 percent of the retired workers are under age 65. Rather surprisingly, the eligible children of retired workers number about four per hundred primary beneficiaries, and about 35 percent of such children are aged 18 or over (about equally divided between those in school and those disabled, primarily due to mental causes). The smallest beneficiary categories at the end of 1972 were dependent husbands, dependent widowers, and male dependent parents; the category of grandchildren, added by the 1972 amendments, is expectedly very small, only 137 such beneficiaries at the end of 1973.

Table 10.29 presents data for the more important family groups, showing the numbers of families and beneficiaries in current payment status at the end of 1972[7] and the corresponding average family benefits. The average benefit for a retired worker with no eligible dependents was $157 per month, while that for a worker with an eligible spouse was $191, or 73 percent larger. This difference results not only from the effect of the wife's benefit but also because men have higher primary benefits, on the average, than women (as well as the fact that married men tend to have larger primary benefits than other men). The average benefits for wives (and widows, too) tend to be artificially low, because when women receive such benefits and also primary benefits based on their own earnings record, only the excess of the former over the latter is shown. Benefits currently being awarded were somewhat larger than those in current payment status— by about $3.50 for primary benefits. In considering the figures, it should be kept in mind that the general benefit level at the beginning of 1975 was 11 percent higher than at the end of 1972.

The average benefits for disabled workers at the end of 1972 were significantly higher than for old-age beneficiaries because the qualifying requirements for disability benefits eliminate many irregularly employed persons, who nonetheless at age 62 can qualify for old-age benefits. For example, a person who worked for six years during World War II and not at all since then would not be eligible for disability benefits if disabled currently, but if attaining age 65 now, could qualify for the minimum monthly old-age benefit. Also, the average old-age benefit is pulled down because about half of such beneficiaries are receiving reduced benefits because of early retirement.

---

[7] Ibid.

The relatively high size of the benefits for young-survivor families at the end of 1972 was noteworthy. For example, the average monthly benefit for a widowed mother and two or more children was $378 at the end of 1972, and at the end of 1974 it was about $425. These payments fulfill a real social purpose that is often not recognized, since the public generally considers only the old-age aspects of the program. It is also noteworthy that among the survivor families with children, 189,000 are those of deceased female workers, or 12 percent of the total.

Data on Medicare Coverage and Benefits Experience

Table 10.30 shows the numbers of persons eligible for benefits under HI and SMI at various past dates. Virtually all persons aged 65 and over were covered automatically by HI when it went into operation in July 1966. The 200,000 not covered consisted primarily of persons covered by the federal employees health benefits program and a few short-term nonresident aliens. The number covered by HI increased from 18.9 million in mid-1966 to 21.5 million in mid-1974. As of July 1, 1974, only about 1.2 million of the persons aged 65 or over eligible for HI benefits were from the uninsured, blanketed-in group, which had originally numbered 3.0 million. On the same date, the number of uninsured persons aged 65 or over who had voluntarily opted to participate in HI on a basis of paying premiums supposed to meet the full cost was about 10,000. The number of persons aged 65 and over who elected to enroll in SMI increased from 17.7 million at the start of the program in 1966 to about 21.0 million in mid-1974.

Disabled beneficiaries who have been on the benefit roll for at least two years are automatically covered for HI benefits and are eligible to enroll under SMI. When such persons were first protected, in July 1973, about 1.74 million were under HI, and of these, about 1.58 million were under SMI. About 80 percent of these disabled persons were disabled workers, 16 percent were disabled child beneficiaries aged 18 or over, and 4 percent were disabled widow and widower beneficiaries. In addition, about 9,300 persons with chronic kidney disease were deemed to be disabled and eligible for Medicare benefits in July 1973.

The vast majority of persons eligible to enroll in SMI did so. Considering only the eligibles within the 50 states and the District of Columbia, 93.6 percent of those eligibles aged 65 and over as of July

1966 actually enrolled.[8] At the present time, this proportion has increased to 96.5 percent.

A somewhat lower proportion of the eligible disability beneficiaries has enrolled in SMI, namely, 91.4 percent when the program began operations in July 1973. This lower participation results entirely from the experience for disabled workers since the proportion for the disabled widow and disabled child categories is about the same as for the aged. Only 90.1 percent of the eligible disabled workers elected SMI; this lower participation probably reflected the fact that many such persons had health care available without cost from the Veterans Administration since they were veterans or had continuing private health insurance coverage from their previous employment or from their spouse's current employment.

Data on the utilization of Medicare services has been made available with a considerable lag. Perhaps this is because of the greater complexity of statistics on health care services as compared with OASDI benefits data. The following data and the accompanying analysis relate almost entirely to the experience for persons aged 65 and over, since little data are available as to benefit experience since mid-1973, when disabled beneficiaries were first covered.

In recent years, about 25 percent of the beneficiaries received HI benefits in the course of a year. The corresponding figure for SMI was 35 percent in 1967, the first full calendar year of operation; it then increased to about 47 percent in 1972 and was about 50 percent in 1974. This increasing trend over the years was the result of the initial deductible being more readily met as medical prices rise.[9] The inpatient hospital admissions represented about 300 per thousand eligible persons per year at the inception of the program, and increased to 313 in 1972, with an apparently level trend since then.[10] The corresponding rate for skilled nursing facilities was about 25 per thousand in 1967–69, and then it decreased to about 20 per thousand as a result of tightening, administratively, the requirements to be met for this benefit. The average duration of hospitalization per admission was about 13.5 days in

---

[8] Persons in outlying areas such as Puerto Rico are not as likely to enroll in SMI because medical care is much less costly there. Even more so, persons in foreign countries who are OASDI beneficiaries are not likely to enroll in SMI because they have no benefit protection while residing there.

[9] The increase in the deductible from $50 to $60 in 1973 naturally temporarily reversed this trend.

[10] Such admission rates are higher than the proportions of persons receiving HI benefits because of some persons admitted more than once during a year.

1966–68, but it decreased thereafter to about 11.5 days in 1973. Early data for the disabled beneficiaries indicate a slightly lower duration of hospitalization than for the aged.

Hospital benefits represent the vast majority of the benefits paid under the HI program. Home health benefits have never been more than 1.0 percent of the total, and in recent years have been only about 0.7 percent. Likewise, SNF benefits are currently only about 3 percent of the total, although they were as much as 8–9 percent in 1967–69.

The HI program paid about 80 percent of the hospital charges of the covered individuals, on the average, in 1966–68. Since then, this proportion decreased, until for 1971 and since, it has been about 76 percent. This decreasing trend was largely the result of the reduction in the average duration of hospitalization, since then the effect of the initial deductible is relatively greater. The current 24 percent remainder reflects the effect of the cost-sharing provisions (about one third of the differential), noncovered services such as the additional cost of private room or television, and the excess of charges over the reimbursement of the HI program on a cost basis.

SMI benefit outgo consists predominantly of physician benefits. Such proportion, however, has been decreasing over the years, from about 95 percent initially to 84 percent in 1974. At the same time, outpatient hospital services have played an increasing role, rising from only 2 percent to 10 percent. The foregoing trend reflects both the increasing usage of outpatient hospital services and the more rapidly rising cost of such services since they have not been controlled as much by Medicare as have physician fees. Home health services and independent laboratory services each account for about 1 percent of the total SMI costs, and the remaining 4 percent is for other services, such as ambulances, rental of medical equipment, and prosthetic devices. Benefits for the services of surgeons represent about 42 percent of the physician benefits. The early experience for the disabled beneficiaries indicates a much larger proportion of the outgo being for outpatient hospital services (35 percent) and a lower proportion for physician services (60 percent) than is the case for the aged.

The SMI program has, in all years, paid about 73 percent of the cost of medical services furnished to enrollees who had at least enough such costs to meet the initial deductible.[11] The 27 percent remainder

---

[11] As used here, "cost" means the amount determined as "reasonable charges," except for outpatient hospital and home health services, for which the basis is the actual billing.

arises because of the effect of the initial deductible and the subsequent 20 percent coinsurance.

Considerably different experience under Medicare occurs as between the various states. In fiscal year 1972, the hospital admission rate for the system as a whole was 313 per thousand persons per year. Some 17 states had rates which were at least 10 percent higher than the national average, while only eight states were that much below such average. The states with high rates were all in the west north central states, the south central states, or the mountain states, all of which are relatively sparsely populated. The highest rates were 456 for North Dakota, 431 for Montana, and between 390 and 399 for Arkansas, Mississippi, and Oklahoma. The states with low rates were all in the northeastern region plus Alaska, namely, Connecticut, Delaware, Maryland, New Jersey, New York, Pennsylvania, and Rhode Island. The lowest rates were 233 for Maryland, 241 for New Jersey, and 252 for New York.

HI benefits paid in fiscal year 1972 averaged $291 per person eligible for benefits. Some 14 states had per capita averages which were at least 20 percent lower than the national average, while only eight states were that much above the average. The states with low averages were mostly in the southeastern, south central, or mountain regions, plus Alaska. The lowest averages were $169 for Alaska, $186 for South Carolina, and between $200 and $210 for Arkansas, Idaho, Utah, and Wyoming. The states with high averages were in the northeastern region (District of Columbia, Massachusetts, New York, Rhode Island, and Vermont), plus California, Colorado, and Nevada. The highest average was $486 for the District of Columbia and $390 for Vermont, with the others generally being about $350–360. In general, some correlation was present as between HI benefit outgo per capita and average HI taxes per covered worker.

SMI benefits paid in fiscal year 1972 averaged $112 per enrollee, as against the enrollee premium at the standard rate amounting to $67.20 then. Some 11 states had per capita averages which were at least 25 percent below the national average, while only five states were that much above the average. The states with low averages were predominantly rural ones, scattered throughout the country. The lowest averages were in Iowa, Indiana, South Carolina, South Dakota, and Wyoming, all of which had averages falling within the range of $66 to $76. The states with high averages were high income ones. The highest average was $237 for the District of Columbia, followed by

California with $170, and Florida, Hawaii, and New York, all at about $150.

The interesting feature that can be observed about the SMI experience is that, in general, the per capita costs for the low-income sections of the country are lower than for the high-income ones. This can be viewed as meaning that the government contributions are not equally spread on a per capita basis over all sections of the nation, but, rather, are devoted to a greater extent to the high-income states. This is the reverse of the usual result under federal grant programs, where the low-income states generally receive proportionately more as a result of a weighted matching formula. This result under SMI is not necessarily inequitable or preferential, since the sources of general revenues tend to be more concentrated in the wealthier states.

Physicians and certain suppliers of health services (independent laboratories, ambulance services, and medical supply stores) have their choice of two reimbursement methods under SMI. They can either bill the patient directly or else take an assignment and accept for reimbursement purposes whatever amount the Medicare system decides is the "reasonable" charge. For purposes of analysis of the experience in this area, it is appropriate to disregard claims from hospital-based physicians and group practice prepayment plans, because such claims are, by definition, considered in the assignment category. The resulting net assignment rate is indicative of physician and supplier satisfaction with SMI reimbursement methods and, conversely, of how many beneficiaries are spared from administrative participation in the program.

The net assignment rate based on number of claims rose from 58.8 percent in 1968 to 61.5 percent in 1969. Then, such rate decreased to 60.8 percent in 1970, 58.5 percent in 1971, 54.9 percent in 1972, and 52.7 percent in 1973. A factor tending to make the rate high, which was probably effective in the beginning, was the greater assurance of the physician receiving payment and the simpler administration involved. In recent years, however, these elements were apparently more than offset by physician dissatisfaction with SMI reimbursement bases as these were gradually tightened and moved further and further away from true customary and prevailing charges.

Another indication of the extent of the gradual restrictions that were introduced in recognizing physicians' customary and prevailing charges can be seen from the proportion of assigned physician claims which are reduced because of determinations as to reasonable charges by the Medicare system. Such reduction rate, on the basis of number of bills, was 22 percent in mid-1969 and then increased steadily to 45 percent from mid-1971 through mid-1972, and then increased further until, at the end of 1973, it was 59 percent. The reduction rate for nonassigned claims is even higher, being 63.5 percent at the end of 1972, as against 51.5 percent for assigned claims. It should be noted that this statistic is somewhat misleading because it relates to bills on which a reduction was made in at least one of the several charges for services there reported; the proportion of reductions would be significantly lower if it were based on the separate charges for each service rendered.

The cost of the HI program depends to a considerable extent on the trend of the average daily per capital hospital cost experienced. This per capita cost is obtained by dividing the total reported hospital costs incurred in a year by the total reported inpatient days for the year. This per capita cost with respect to insured beneficiaries (i.e., not including those blanketed-in at the start of the program) is used in the automatic adjustments of the HI cost-sharing provisions. Such rates actually experienced in the past have been as follows:

Year	Per Capita Cost	Increase over Previous Year
1966*	$37.92	—
1967	43.03	13.5% (18.0%)†
1968	49.34	14.7
1969	55.70	12.9
1970	63.14	13.4
1971	72.21	14.4
1972	79.07	9.5
1973	85.77	8.5

* The 1966 rate is for only the last six months of the year. The rate actually used in the determinations of the cost-sharing provisions in 1966–70 differed by a cent or two from this figure, which is based on final data.

† Annualized rate of increase, taking into account that 1966 figure relates only to last six months of year.

It will be observed that these rates of increase for 1967–71 are considerably higher than those assumed for the future in the 1974 HI cost estimates.

Further indication of general hospital cost trends relative to those for wages and prices can be seen from Table 10.31, which shows such data for the years immediately preceding the enactment of Medicare as well as subsequent ones. This table also gives similar data for physician fees, which are a principal component of the cost of the SMI program.

Over the past two decades, hospital costs have increased far more rapidly than the general price level, the general wage level, or physician fees. In fact, on the average, hospital costs rose about twice as fast as either wages or physician fees, and this was equally true in the last eight years, when all elements increased greatly, as it was previously when the economy was more stable. In other words, as yet, no diminution in the large differential increase of hospital costs over other economic elements is evident.

The large increases in hospital costs after 1965 that are shown in Table 10.31 were, of course, the major reason why the cost estimates made for the HI program when it was enacted were too low and, as a result, additional financing was required. If the trend that actually occurred in the general price level or the general wage level after 1965 had been known then, the trend of hospital costs could have been well estimated, and the appropriate financing could more nearly have been provided in the initial legislation.

During the same period, although physician fees increased more rapidly than the general price level, they rose at only the same rate as general wages, and this was equally the case in both halves of the period. This analysis thus refutes the commonly held belief that "there is a crisis existing in health care delivery because physician fees have risen exorbitantly since Medicare was enacted." It certainly seems not unreasonable that physician fees should rise in a parallel manner to wages generally.

The more rapidly increasing trend of physician fees than had been thought likely had its effect on the SMI financial experience. Another factor, of course, was somewhat higher actual utilization of services. The following data compare the actual costs on a per capita monthly basis for benefits and administrative expenses, on an incurred-cost basis, for the different premium-payment periods with the actual premium rate applicable plus the equal matching government contribution:

Period	Actual Cost	Premium Rate Plus Government Contribution	Ratio of Column (2) to Column (1)
July 1966–December 1967...........	$ 6.44	$ 6.00	93.2%
January–March 1968*..............	8.22	6.00	73.0
April 1968–June 1969..............	8.56	8.00	93.5
July 1969–June 1970...............	9.12	8.00	87.7
July 1970–June 1971...............	9.84	10.60	107.7
July 1971–June 1972...............	10.86	11.20	103.1
July 1972–June 1973...............	11.04	11.60	105.1
July 1973–June 1974...............	12.12	12.60	104.0

* The original $3 premium rate was applicable for only 18 months, but this rate was extended for three months by legislation in 1967. Thus, it is not appropriate to measure the actuarial determination for this period as against the actual experience.

The initial premium rate of $3 for July 1966 through December 1967 turned out to be too low by 7 percent, even though it had been estimated when the legislation was enacted that it contained a safety margin averaging about 10 percent. The $4 premium rate promulgated for April 1968 through June 1969 was deficient by about 6½ percent, but freezing it at this level for fiscal year 1970 resulted in a 12 percent deficiency. Thereafter, the promulgated rates were somewhat more than adequate, by amounts of about 5 percent relatively. Such course of action was followed so as to build up the trust fund to a more adequate and responsible level after the catastrophic financial experience in fiscal year 1970.

Data on Operations of Trust Funds

Table 10.32 shows the past progress of the OASI Trust Fund. Tax income has grown steadily over the years—as a result of the increasing labor force, increases in coverage by legislative enactments, rising general earnings levels, the increasing tax schedule, and the raising of the maximum taxable earnings base by legislative enactments. Benefit payments, too, have risen steadily and significantly over the years as a result of the gradual maturing of the system and as a result of the various factors that affected the rise in the tax income.

Although tax income was considerably higher than benefit outgo in the early years of operation, these two elements were closely in balance during the period 1954–65. However, beginning in 1966 tax income exceeded benefit outgo in every year. The level trend in 1954–65 was, in part, due to the desires of the economic planners to avoid a growth in the trust fund as being a "fiscal drag." Similarly, the rising trend in 1966–74 was to the liking of the economic planners since this served as a brake on inflation (through a tax which is more popular than most taxes).

Measuring the trust fund balance at the end of the year in relation to outgo for benefits (including the RR financial interchange) and administrative expenses for the following year gives a good indication of its relative size. In the mid-1950s, this ratio was about 4. By the mid-1960s, it had fallen to about 1, and this level was maintained until 1970. After then, as discussed previously in this chapter, this ratio decreased as the benefit level was expanded, and it was only 0.75 as of the beginning of 1973, 0.67 at the beginning of 1974, and an estimated 0.60 at the beginning of 1975.

Administrative expenses have risen for the same reasons that tax income and benefit outgo have grown. In most years, these administrative expenses were only 2 to 3 percent of benefit outgo, and in the latest years this ratio has fallen to about 1½ percent.

The OASI Trust Fund (and, correspondingly, the interest earnings thereon) grew steadily until it reached a peak of $22.5 billion at the end of 1956. The trust fund balance then slowly decreased to a low of $18.2 billion at the end of 1965, but it has subsequently increased steadily, until it reached $36.5 billion at the end of 1973 and then $37.8 billion at the end of 1974. The decline during the 1960s was greeted with enthusiasm by the economic planners who then feared deflation and viewed trust fund growth as a fiscal drag. These same persons approved the increase in the trust fund balances after 1965 as desirable, since this tended to be antiinflationary (and, too, the OASDI taxes are more popular with the general public than other taxes!).

Table 10.33 gives similar information for the DI portion of the program. The trust fund balance grew slowly but steadily from its inception in 1957 until reaching a peak of $2.4 billion in 1961 and then declined slowly to a low of $1.6 billion in 1965. The amendatory legislation of that year and subsequent higher allocations to DI have caused the balance to increase rapidly since then—to $7.9 billion at the end of 1973 and $8.1 billion at the end of 1974. The DI Trust Fund leveled off in 1974, despite the increased allocation to it and the higher taxable earnings base, as a result of the worsening benefit experience.

Administrative expenses for the DI Trust Fund have naturally been higher than for OASDI (because of the problems involved in determining disability) and were about 5 percent of the benefit outgo in 1965–72, but only about 3 percent in 1973–74. This sharp decrease is, in part, due to the much higher level of benefit outgo resulting from more beneficiaries and higher benefit amounts. Conceivably, such relatively lower administrative costs could be due to the reduced emphasis on federal supervision of the disability determinations, which, in turn, could possibly result in higher benefit costs.

The past operations of the HI Trust Fund are presented in Table 10.34. The trust fund balance increased from its inception in 1966 to $3.2 billion in 1970, with a small decrease for 1971–72, when the tax rate was insufficient on a long-range basis. The corrective action in this respect taken in the 1972 amendments resulted in a sharp increase in the year-end balance, to $6.5 billion in 1973 and $9.1 billion in 1974. Administrative expenses have been about 3 to 3½ percent of benefit outgo.

Table 10.35 shows the operations of the SMI Trust Fund since it began in 1966. Its balance rose to about $400 million in 1967–68 and then fell precipitously to only $57 million in mid-1970 (as a result of the grossly inadequate premium rate promulgated for fiscal year 1970 in 1968, as discussed in Chapter 8). Since then, adequate premium rates have been promulgated, and the experience has been favorable, so that the trust fund balance has steadily increased and was $1.1 billion at the end of 1973 and $1.5 billion at the end of 1974.

The administrative expenses of the SMI program have represented about 12½ percent of the benefit outgo in recent years. This considerably higher ratio than for HI is due in part to the fact that SMI must handle many relatively small benefit payments and in part to the "overadministration" of the program required by the Social Security Administration.

As has been indicated in Chapter 4, the financing of SMI is on a different basis than OASI, DI, or HI, since it is on a year-by-year incurred-cost basis, rather than on a long-range basis. Thus, the financial status of SMI is best measured by comparing the fund on hand at the close of a fiscal year, which is the end of the period to which a particular premium rate is applicable, with the benefits incurred but unpaid then, plus the administrative expenses applicable thereto. Table 10.36 presents such data for various dates back to June 30, 1967, along with estimates as to what may be the case for 1975.

The incurred deficit for SMI increased steadily from the inception of the program in 1966 until it reached $370 million on June 30, 1969.

This was the result of the slightly inadequate premium rates, both in the initial law and subsequently promulgated, as was discussed earlier in this chapter. Then in the next year, the deficit soared to $690 million as the trust fund was almost exhausted, which was the result of the politically inspired freezing of the premium rate for fiscal year 1970. Thereafter, adequate premium rates have been promulgated, and the deficit has been reduced gradually. In 1974–75, the deficit was only about $200 million, or only 14 percent relative to the outstanding liabilities.

Up through the end of 1974, the total OASDI payments to beneficiaries amounted to the staggering sum of $454 billion dollars. The corresponding figures for HI and SMI were $47 billion and $17 billion, respectively. Although OASDI benefits have been payable for the last 35 years, 89 percent of them have been made in the last 15 years and 49 percent in the last 5 years. This is an indication of both the maturing of the system and the effect of inflationary conditions.

As indicated previously, most of the assets of these trust funds are invested in securities of the federal government. On June 30, 1974, the $37.9 billion of assets of the OASI Trust Fund were distributed as follows:[12] cash balance, $149 million; marketable treasury notes and bonds (maturing in 1975–98, at coupon rates ranging from 3 to 8.5 percent), $2.5 billion; obligations of federally sponsored agencies (maturing in 1982–88, at coupon rates of 5.1 to 6.45 percent), $555 million; nonmarketable treasury bonds (maturing in 1980, at a coupon rate of 2.75 percent), $1.1 billion; and special issues (maturing in 1975–89, with coupon rates varying from $2\frac{5}{8}$ to $7\frac{5}{8}$ percent), $33.6 billion. Similarly, the $8.3 billion of assets of the DI Trust Fund were then distributed as follows: cash balance, $61 million; marketable treasury notes and bonds (maturing in 1975–98, at coupon rates ranging from $3\frac{1}{2}$ to 8 percent), $315 million; and special issues (maturing in 1974–80, at coupon rates ranging from $3\frac{7}{8}$ to $7\frac{5}{8}$ percent), $7.9 billion.

The $7.9 billion of assets of the HI Trust Fund as of June 30, 1974, were invested as follows: cash balance, $70 million; obligations of federally sponsored agencies, $50 million (maturing in 1982, at a coupon rate of 5.2 percent); and special issues (maturing in 1977–89, with coupon rates ranging from $5\frac{5}{8}$ to $7\frac{5}{8}$ percent), $7.8 billion. The $1.3 billion of assets of the SMI Trust Fund were invested in the fol-

---

[12] Analyses of the investments of the trust funds is best made as of June 30, since investments made during each fiscal year are in short-term certificates that are redeemed and reinvested on June 30.

lowing manner: cash balance, $45 million; and special issues (maturing in 1978–89, with coupon rates ranging from 5¾ to 7⅝ percent), $1.2 billion.

The average interest rate on the investments of each of the trust funds as of June 30, 1974 was 6.1 percent for OASI, 6.5 percent for DI, 7.0 percent for HI, and 6.8 percent for SMI. The rate for the OASI Trust Fund was relatively low because it contains many investments purchased years ago when interest rates were far below recent levels. Similarly, the rates for the Medicare trust funds are the highest because they had most of their growth since 1970. It is interesting to note the increase in the average year-end interest rate of the investments of the OASI Trust Fund over the years—from about 2.2 percent in 1943–51 to 2.5 percent in 1956, 3.0 percent in 1963, 4.0 percent in 1968, 5.2 percent in 1970, and 6.0 percent in 1973.

The interest rate applicable to new special issues for the four trust funds has fluctuated greatly in recent years, ranging from a low of 5¼ percent in April 1971 to a high of 7½ percent in August 1973, with the customary rate being about 6½ to 7 percent. It rose from 2⅝ percent in June 1960 to about 5 percent during 1966–68 and then increased to a level of somewhat over 7 percent in 1970. Following this, the rate fell to a level of about 6 percent during 1971–72 and then rose to about 6½ percent during 1973 and to over 7½ percent in mid-1974. By December 1974, the rate had fallen back to 7⅜ percent. The highest rates attained were 7⅞ percent in February 1970 and July 1974, and 8 percent in August 1974.

Amount of Life Insurance under OASDI

An interesting concept is the estimated amount of life insurance in force as survivor benefits under OASDI.

Such amount of life insurance in force as survivor benefits is defined as the total for all insured workers of (*a*) the lump-sum death payment and (*b*) the present value, at a specified interest rate, of the monthly survivor benefits available if death of the insured worker occurred at the valuation date. In other words, the concept represents the total life insurance protection currently available to all insured workers, as distinct from the total liability that will be entered into, on their behalf, in any given year. This is similar to the concept in private life insurance of totaling the face amounts of all policies in force, even though it is obviously recognized that by no means all insured persons will die at any one moment of time (or even within any particular year).

The estimates developed are "net" estimates in the sense that the amounts of insurance are adjusted to allow for the effect of employment by survivor beneficiaries on the benefits payable to them and to allow for possible "forfeiture" of part or all of the benefits payable to widows in cases where they have earned old-age benefits in their own right (i.e., based on their own earnings credits).

Table 10.37 presents an historical series of figures as to the amount of life insurance in force as survivor benefits under OASDI from 1940 up to the present time. It will be noted that the higher the interest rate used, the lower is the amount of insurance in force (because of the greater discounting of future payments).

In an analysis such as this, it is quite proper to use an interest rate in the neighborhood of 3 percent, as representing a "real" interest rate—that is, substantially on a net basis after taking into account the inflation element. Or, to put it another way, a relatively low interest rate (considering the high interest rates currently), in essence, takes into account, and counterbalances, any possible future benefit increases that may be made due to general price and wage inflation. Thus, under the automatic-adjustment provisions of the 1972 Act, it seems realistic to use a 6 percent interest rate.

The amount of life insurance in force as survivor benefits increased from only about $40 billion in 1940 to about $190 billion in 1951 and then to about $680 billion in 1966 and $2.0 trillion in 1974. There was a sharp increase in the amount of such life insurance in force as a result of the 1967 Act, under which survivor benefits were made available to female insured workers on a much more liberal basis (by requiring only the same insured status conditions as for men, instead of requiring either proof of dependency or recent attachment to covered employment). The 1974 figure does not reflect the increase in insurance in force as a result of the Supreme Court decision in 1975 requiring equal treatment for widowers as compared with widows; this would produce about a 10 percent increase.

It may be of interest to make a comparison of life insurance in force as survivor benefits under OASDI with life insurance in force in private insurance companies. Such a comparison is not entirely valid, because of the numerous variable factors affecting benefit receipt under the social security program, nor is it especially meaningful, because of the different natures of the types of insurance (e.g., most of the survivor insurance under OASDI is on young lives, who have relatively small probabilities of death, whereas under private insurance much of the protection is on middle-aged and older lives).

In any event, keeping in mind these differences and qualifications, it is interesting to note that over the years, the amount of life insurance in force as survivor benefits under OASDI has closely paralleled the life insurance in force in private insurance companies in the United States. Until the last few years, when OASDI has been significantly expanded, the private insurance coverage ran somewhat ahead, but now the reverse is the case.

For example, at the beginning of 1974, private insurance in force amounted to $1.78 trillion,[13] as compared to $2.04 trillion under OASDI, while at the beginning of 1970, private insurance in force amounted to $1.28 trillion, as compared with $1.10 trillion under OASDI. In 1960 the corresponding figures were $542 billion for private insurance and $503 billion under OASDI, while for 1951 (after the 1950 Act had updated the social security program) the corresponding figures were $234 billion for private insurance and $170 billion under OASDI. In 1940 the comparison was not nearly as close—namely, about $112 billion under private insurance and $37 billion under OASDI.

---

[13] From *Life Insurance Fact Book, 1974* (New York, Institute of Life Insurance).

APPENDIX

Tabulated Data on Actuarial Cost Estimates and Statistics for OASDI and Medicare

TABLE 10.1

Estimated Average Cost of OASDI Benefit Payments, Administrative Expenses, and Interest Earnings on Existing Trust Fund as Percentage of Taxable Payroll,* by Type of Benefit
(estimate made at time of enactment of 1972 amendments)

Item	OASI	DI
Primary benefits	6.30%	1.03%
Wife's benefits	0.48	0.05
Widow's benefits	1.34	†
Parent's benefits	0.01	†
Child's benefits	0.75	0.17
Mother's benefits	0.13	†
Lump-sum death payments	0.06	†
Total benefits	9.07%	1.25%
Administrative expenses	0.16	0.06
RR financial interchange‡	0.06	0.00
Existing fund‡	0.03	0.00
Net total average cost	9.32%	1.31%

  * Including adjustment to reflect the lower tax rate for the self-employed as compared with the combined employer-employee rate, and similar adjustments.
  † This type of benefit is not payable under this program.
  ‡ This item is taken as an addition (or offset, as the case may be) to the benefit and administrative expense cost. The trust fund item represents the effect of the trust fund being less or greater than one year's outgo.

TABLE 10.2

Estimated Cost of OASDI and HI Benefits and Administrative Expenses* as Percentage of Taxable Payroll†
(estimate made at time of enactment of 1972 amendments)

Calendar Year	OASI	DI	OASDI	HI
1980.................	8.14%	1.15%	9.29%	2.50%
1985.................	8.20	1.16	9.36	2.65
1990.................	8.56	1.15	9.71	2.86
1995.................	8.26	1.15	9.41	2.99
2000.................	8.00	1.20	9.20	n.a.
2005.................	7.95	1.31	9.26	n.a.
2010.................	8.50	1.41	9.91	n.a.
2020.................	10.15	1.43	11.58	n.a.
2030.................	10.86	1.39	12.25	n.a.
2045.................	10.94	1.45	12.39	n.a.
Average cost‡.........	9.32	1.31	10.63	2.61

* Including amounts to maintain the trust fund balance at a level of about one year's outgo.

† Taking into account the lower tax rate for the self-employed, as compared with the combined employer-employee rate, and similar adjustments.

‡ Arithmetic average of the year-by-year costs for OASDI for 1973–2046 and for HI for 1973–1997, adjusted for the trust fund ratio at the end of 1972.

n.a. = not available.

Note: The actual cost for 1972 as a percentage of taxable payroll was 6.46 percent for OASI, 0.55 percent for DI, and 1.26 percent for HI.

TABLE 10.3

Estimated Progress of OASI Trust Fund under 1972 Amendments
(in millions)

Calendar Year	Taxes*	Benefit Payments†	Administrative Expenses	Railroad Retirement Financial Interchange‡	Interest on Fund	Fund at End of Year
1972.....	$38,685	$37,117	$623	$ 725	$1,818	$35,827
1973.....	46,458	46,039	641	805	1,868	36,668
1974.....	51,927	48,443	659	961	2,015	40,547
1975.....	56,055	53,032	690	1,015	2,273	44,138
1976.....	59,102	55,707	717	1,020	2,514	48,310
1977.....	63,934	61,303	750	1,036	2,702	51,857

* Includes reimbursement from the General Fund for additional cost of noncontributory credit for military service (about $140 million in 1972–75 and about $230 million in 1976–77) and for payments to noninsured persons aged 72 and over (decreasing from $337 million in 1972 to $229 million in 1977).

† Includes payments for vocational rehabilitation services (about $5 million a year).

‡ Payment from the trust fund to the Railroad Retirement Account. Interest payment adjustments between the two systems are included in the Interest column.

Note: Estimate made at time of enactment of 1972 amendments.

TABLE 10.4

Estimated Progress of DI Trust Fund under 1972 Amendments (in millions)

Calendar Year	Taxes*	Benefit Payments†	Administrative Expenses	Railroad Retirement Financial Interchange‡	Interest on Fund	Fund at End of Year
1972	$5,240	$4,526	$221	$24	$420	$7,534
1973	5,961	5,905	236	24	443	7,773
1974	6,635	6,367	248	32	468	8,229
1975	7,180	7,003	261	30	497	8,612
1976	7,599	7,387	274	27	519	9,042
1977	8,224	8,131	288	29	527	9,345

* Includes reimbursement from the General Fund for additional cost of noncontributory credit for military service (about $50 million in 1972–75 and about $100 million in 1976–77).

† Includes payments for vocational rehabilitation services (increasing from $34 million in 1972 to $93 million in 1977).

‡ Payment from the trust fund to the Railroad Retirement Account. Interest payment adjustments between the two systems are included in the interest column.

Note: Estimate made at time of enactment of 1972 amendments.

TABLE 10.5

Estimated Progress of HI Trust Fund under 1972 Amendments (in millions)

Calendar Year	Taxes*	Payment from General Fund†	Benefit Payments	Administrative Expenses	Interest on Fund	Fund at End of Year
1972	$ 5,689	$468	$ 6,615	$165	$147	$ 2,558
1973	10,491	556	8,222	203	213	5,393
1974	11,989	582	10,084	248	371	8,003
1975	12,950	585	11,468	287	513	10,296
1976	13,543	585	12,986	325	625	11,838
1977	14,769	576	14,603	365	702	12,917

* Includes transfers from Railroad Retirement Account with respect to railroad workers covered by HI and reimbursements from the General Fund for additional cost of noncontributory credit for military service (about $50 million a year).

† For noninsured persons blanketed-in.

Note: Estimate made at time of enactment of 1972 amendments.

TABLE 10.6

Estimated Progress of SMI Trust Fund under 1972 Amendments
(in millions)

Calendar Year	Enrollee Premiums	Government Contribution	Benefit Payments	Administrative Expenses	Interest on Fund	Fund at End of Year
1972..........	$1,392	$1,406	$2,340	$330	$31	$ 609
1973..........	1,561	1,619	2,629	369	42	833
1974..........	1,725	2,155	3,267	456	55	1,045
1975..........	1,788	2,569	3,715	502	67	1,252
1976..........	1,852	3,023	4,153	564	80	1,490
1977..........	1,915	3,519	4,629	636	94	1,753

Note: Estimate made at time of enactment of 1972 amendments.

TABLE 10.7

Actuarial Balance of OASDI and HI Systems as of Time of
Enactment of 1972 Amendments, as Percentages of
Taxable Payroll

Level Equivalent*	OASI	DI	HI
1. Benefit costs†...................	9.13%	1.25%	2.55%
2. Administrative expenses.........	0.16	0.06	0.06
3. Taxes‡.......................	9.31	1.32	2.63
4. Existing fund§.................	−0.03	0.00	0.00
5. Actuarial balance‖.............	−0.01	+0.01	+0.02

* Valuation as of the beginning of 1973.
† Including effect of railroad retirement financial interchange transactions.
‡ Adjusted to reflect the lower tax rate for the self-employed as compared with combined employer-employee rate and other factors.
§ This represents the effect of the fund being greater (or less) than one year's outgo.
‖ The sum of items 3 and 4, minus the sum of items 1 and 2. A negative figure indicates the extent of lack of actuarial balance.

TABLE 10.8

Actuarial Balance of Combined OASDI* Program under Various Acts for Various Estimates on an Intermediate-Cost Basis

Legislation	Date of Estimate	Level or Average Equivalent†		
		Benefit Costs‡	Contributions	Actuarial Balance§
1935 Act....................	1935	5.36%	5.36%	0.00%
1939 Act....................	1939	5.22	5.30	+0.08
1939 Act‖	1950	4.45	3.98	−0.47
1950 Act....................	1950	6.20	6.10	−0.10
1950 Act....................	1952	5.49	5.90	+0.41
1952 Act....................	1952	6.00	5.90	−0.10
1952 Act....................	1954	6.62	6.05	−0.57
1954 Act....................	1954	7.50	7.12	−0.38
1954 Act....................	1956	7.45	7.29	−0.16
1956 Act....................	1956	7.85	7.72	−0.13
1956 Act....................	1958	8.25	7.83	−0.42
1958 Act....................	1958	8.76	8.52	−0.24
1958 Act....................	1960	8.73	8.68	−0.05
1960 Act....................	1960	8.98	8.68	−0.30
1961 Act....................	1961	9.35	9.05	−0.30
1961 Act (perpetuity).........	1964	9.36	9.12	−0.24
1961 Act (75 years)...........	1964	9.09	9.10	+0.01
1965 Act....................	1965	9.49	9.42	−0.07
1965 Act....................	1966	8.76	9.50	+0.74
1967 Act....................	1967	9.72	9.73	+0.01
1967 Act....................	1969	8.72	9.88	+1.16
1969 Act....................	1969	9.96	9.88	−0.08
1969 Act....................	1970	9.60	9.94	+0.34
1971 Act....................	1971	10.27	10.17	−0.10
1971 Act (level earnings)......	1972	10.16	10.21	+0.05
1971 Act (dynamic)..........	1972	8.96	10.29	+1.33
July 1972 Act...............	1972	9.77	9.84	+0.07
October 1972 Act............	1972	10.63	10.63	0.00
October 1972 Act............	1973	10.95	10.63	−0.32
December 1973 Act..........	1973	11.39	10.88	−0.51
December 1973 Act..........	1974	13.89	10.91	−2.98

* The DI program was inaugurated in the 1956 Act, so that all figures for previous legislation are for the OASI program only.

† Expressed as a percentage of taxable payroll.

‡ Including adjustments (*a*) to reflect the lower contribution rate for the self-employed as compared with the combined employer-employee rate, (*b*) for the interest earnings on the existing trust fund, (*c*) for administrative expense costs, (*d*) for railroad retirement financial interchange transactions, and (*e*) for reimbursement of military wage credit costs.

§ A negative figure indicates the extent of lack of actuarial balance. A positive figure indicates more than sufficient financing, according to the particular estimate.

‖ As amended during the 1940s, the major change being the revision of the contribution schedule (as of the beginning of 1950, the ultimate combined employer-employee rate scheduled was only 4 percent).

Note: The figures for the 1950 Act and for the 1952 Act according to the 1952 estimates have been revised, as compared with those presented originally, so as to place them on a comparable basis with the later figures (since these figures as previously presented did not include an adjustment to reflect the lower contribution rate for the self-employed as compared with the combined employer-employee rate).

TABLE 10.9

Actuarial Balance of OASI and DI Programs under Various Acts for Various Estimates on an Intermediate-Cost Basis

Legislation	Date of Estimate	Old-Age and Survivors Insurance* Level or Average Equivalent†			Disability Insurance* Level or Average Equivalent†		
		Benefit Costs‡	Contributions	Actuarial Balance§	Benefit Costs‡	Contributions	Actuarial Balance§
1956 Act............	1956	7.43%	7.23%	−0.20%	0.42%	0.49%	+0.07%
1956 Act............	1958	7.90	7.33	−0.57	0.35	0.50	+0.15
1958 Act............	1958	8.27	8.02	−0.25	0.49	0.50	+0.01
1958 Act............	1960	8.38	8.18	−0.20	0.35	0.50	+0.15
1960 Act............	1960	8.42	8.18	−0.24	0.56	0.50	−0.06
1961 Act............	1961	8.79	8.55	−0.24	0.56	0.50	−0.06
1961 Act (perpetuity).	1964	8.72	8.62	−0.10	0.64	0.50	−0.14
1961 Act (75 years)...	1964	8.46	8.60	+0.14	0.63	0.50	−0.13
1965 Act............	1965	8.82	8.72	−0.10	0.67	0.70	+0.03
1965 Act............	1966	7.91	8.80	+0.89	0.85	0.70	−0.15
1967 Act............	1967	8.77	8.78	+0.01	0.95	0.95	0.00
1967 Act............	1969	7.76	8.93	+1.17	0.96	0.95	−0.01
1969 Act............	1969	8.86	8.78	−0.08	1.10	1.10	0.00
1969 Act............	1970	8.55	8.84	+0.29	1.05	1.10	+0.05
1971 Act............	1971	9.13	9.07	−0.06	1.14	1.10	−0.04
1971 Act (level earnings)..........	1972	8.98	9.11	+0.13	1.18	1.10	−0.08
1971 Act (dynamic)..	1972	7.81	9.19	+1.38	1.15	1.10	−0.05
July 1972 Act.......	1972	8.51	8.60	+0.09	1.26	1.24	−0.02
October 1972 Act....	1972	9.32	9.31	−0.01	1.31	1.32	+0.01
October 1972 Act....	1973	9.41	9.32	−0.09	1.54	1.31	−0.23
December 1973 Act...	1973	9.81	9.38	−0.43	1.58	1.50	−0.08
December 1973 Act...	1974	11.97	9.39	−2.58	1.92	1.52	−0.40

* The DI program was inaugurated in the 1956 Act; data for OASI for previous years may be found in Table 10.8.

† Expressed as a percentage of taxable payroll.

‡ Including adjustments (a) to reflect the lower contribution rate for the self-employed as compared with the combined employer-employee rate, (b) for the interest earnings on the existing trust fund, (c) for administrative expense costs, (d) for railroad retirement financial interchange transactions, and (e) for reimbursement of military wage credit costs.

§ A negative figure indicates the extent of lack of actuarial balance. A positive figure indicates more than sufficient financing, according to the particular estimate.

TABLE 10.10

Actuarial Balance of HI Program under Various Acts for Various Estimates on an Intermediate-Cost Basis

Legislation	Date of Estimate	Level or Average Equivalent*		
		Benefit Costs†	Contributions	Actuarial Balance‡
1965 Act	1965	1.23%	1.23%	0.00%
1965 Act	1966	1.54	1.23	−0.31
1967 Act	1967	1.38	1.41	+0.03
1967 Act	1968	1.79	1.50	−0.29
1969 Act	1969	2.76	1.52	−1.24
1969 Act	1969§	2.04	1.56	−0.48
1969 Act	1970	2.09	1.56	−0.53
1971 Act	1971	2.20	1.58	−0.62
1971 Act	1972	2.21	1.60	−0.61
July 1972 Act	1972	2.09	2.10	+0.01
October 1972 Act	1972	2.61	2.63	+0.02
October 1972 Act	1973	2.67	2.63	−0.04
December 1973 Act	1973	2.61	2.61	0.00
December 1973 Act	1974	2.63	2.65	+0.02

* Expressed as a percentage of taxable payroll.
† Including adjustments (a) to reflect the lower contribution rate for the self-employed as compared with the combined employer-employee rate, (b) for the interest earnings on the existing trust fund, (c) for administrative expense costs, (d) for railroad retirement financial interchange transactions, and (e) for reimbursement of military wage credit costs.
‡ A negative figure indicates the extent of lack of actuarial balance. A positive figure indicates more than sufficient financing, according to the particular estimate.
§ This estimate and the subsequent ones assume that the maximum taxable earnings base will be kept up to date in the future with the rises in earnings assumed in projecting hospital costs. The preceding estimates had assumed that such base would remain unchanged in the future at the level prescribed in the law in existence at the date of the estimate.

TABLE 10.11

Estimated Cost of OASDI and HI Benefits and Administrative
Expenses* as Percentage of Taxable Payroll†
(estimate made at time of enactment of December 1973
amendments)

Calendar Year	OASI	DI	OASDI	HI
1980	8.92%	1.26%	10.18%	2.31%
1985	8.97	1.29	10.26	2.59
1990	9.11	1.32	10.43	2.92
1995	8.83	1.37	10.20	3.18
2000	8.47	1.47	9.94	n.a.
2005	8.42	1.62	10.04	n.a.
2010	8.92	1.75	10.67	n.a.
2020	10.48	1.77	12.25	n.a.
2030	11.25	1.73	12.98	n.a.
2045	11.36	1.80	13.16	n.a.
Average cost‡	9.81	1.58	11.39	2.61

* Including amounts to maintain the trust fund balance at a level of about one year's outgo.
† Taking into account lower tax rates for the self-employed, as compared with combined employer-employee rate.
‡ Arithmetic average of the year-by-year costs for 1973–2046 for OASDI and for 1973–97 for HI, adjusted for the trust fund ratio at end of 1972.
n.a. = not available.

TABLE 10.12

Estimated Progress of Combined OASI and DI Trust Funds
under December 1973 Amendments, According to Estimate Made
at Time of Enactment
(in billions)

Calendar Year	Net Income*	Net Disbursements†	Net Increase in Fund	Fund at End of Year
1973	$54.8	$53.4	$1.4	$44.2
1974	63.1	61.2	1.9	46.1
1975	68.5	67.6	0.8	46.9
1976	74.8	73.1	1.7	48.6
1977	80.9	77.8	3.1	51.7
1978	85.5	83.7	1.9	53.6

* Taxes, interest on fund, and reimbursements from the General Fund for additional cost of noncontributory credit for military service wage credits and of payments to noninsured persons aged 72 and over.
† Benefit payments, administrative expenses, and railroad retirement financial interchange.

TABLE 10.13

Estimated Progress of HI Trust Fund under December 1973 Amendments, According to Estimate Made at Time of Enactment (in billions)

Calendar Year	Net Income*	Net Disburse-ments†	Net Increase in Fund	Fund at End of Year
1973	$11.4	$ 8.1	$3.4	$ 6.3
1974	12.1	9.8	2.3	8.6
1975	13.1	11.5	1.5	10.1
1976	14.3	13.0	1.2	11.3
1977	15.4	14.7	0.7	12.0
1978	19.4	16.6	2.8	14.9

* Taxes, railroad retirement financial interchange, contributions from general fund (for noninsured persons blanketed-in), and interest on fund.
† Benefit payments and administrative expenses.

TABLE 10.14

Changes in OASDI Long-Range Actuarial Balance as Percentage of Taxable Payroll* as Result of 1974 Cost Estimates, by Type of Assumption

Assumption	OASI	DI	OASDI
Actuarial balance under previous estimate	−0.43%	−0.08%	−0.51%
Retirement rates	−0.14%	—	−0.14%
Disability rates	—	−0.21%	−0.21
Fertility and mortality assumptions	−1.79	−0.08	−1.87
Economic assumptions	−0.18	−0.01	−0.19
All others	−0.04	−0.02	−0.06
Total effect	−2.15%	−0.32%	−2.47%
Actuarial balance under 1974 estimate	−2.58%	−0.40%	−2.98%

* Taking into account the lower tax rate for the self-employed, as compared with the combined employer-employee rate, and similar adjustments.

TABLE 10.15

Estimated Average Cost of OASDI Benefit Payments, Administrative Expenses, and Interest Earnings on Existing Trust Fund as Percentage of Taxable Payroll,* by Type of Benefit
(estimate based on data presented in 1974 Trustees Report)

Item	OASI	DI
Primary benefits..............	8.52%	1.59%
Wife's benefits..............	0.58	0.09
Widow's benefits..............	1.54	†
Parent's benefits..............	0.01	†
Child's benefits..............	0.71	0.15
Mother's benefits..............	0.22	†
Lump-sum death payments..........	0.07	†
Total benefits..............	11.65%	1.83%
Administrative expenses............	0.21	0.09
RR financial interchange‡..........	+0.07	0.00
Existing fund‡..............	+0.04	0.00
Net total average cost............	11.97%	1.92%

* Including adjustment to reflect the lower tax rate for the self-employed as compared with the combined employer-employee rate, and similar adjustments.
† This type of benefit is not payable under this program.
‡ This item is taken as an addition (or offset, as the case may be) to the benefit and administrative expense cost. The trust fund item represents the effect of the trust fund being less or greater than one year's outgo.

TABLE 10.16

Estimated Cost of OASDI and HI Benefits and Administrative Expenses* as Percentage of Taxable Payroll†
(estimate presented in 1974 Trustees Report)

Calendar Year	OASI	DI	OASDI	HI
1985..............	9.00%	1.44%	10.44%	2.48%
1990..............	9.52	1.51	11.03	2.94
1995..............	9.64	1.61	11.25	3.45
2000..............	9.54	1.77	11.31	n.a.
2005..............	9.72	1.97	11.69	n.a.
2010..............	10.56	2.13	12.69	n.a.
2020..............	13.47	2.24	15.71	n.a.
2030..............	15.46	2.14	17.60	n.a.
2045..............	15.53	2.33	17.86	n.a.
Average cost‡..........	11.97	1.92	13.89	2.63

* Including amounts to maintain the trust fund balance at a level of about one year's outgo.
† Taking into account the lower tax rate for the self-employed, as compared with the combined employer-employee rate, and similar adjustments.
‡ Arithmetic average of the year-by-year costs for 1974–2045 for OASDI and for 1974–98 for HI, adjusted for the trust fund ratio at the end of 1973.
n.a. = not available.
Note: The actual cost for 1973 as a percentage of taxable payroll was 8.70 percent for OASI, 1.11 percent for DI, and 1.37 percent for HI.

TABLE 10.17

Progress of OASI Trust Fund under 1973 Amendments, According to Estimates in 1974 Trustees Report

(in millions)

Calendar Year	Taxes*	Benefit Payments†	Adminis-trative Expenses	Railroad Retirement Financial Interchange‡	Interest on Fund	Fund at End of Year
1974............	$52,162	$52,409	$813	$ 909	$2,028	$36,546
1975............	59,063	58,912	817	1,006	2,079	36,953
1976............	65,753	65,532	872	1,084	2,081	37,299
1977............	72,990	72,567	927	1,171	2,077	37,601
1978............	79,509	79,689	979	1,268	2,092	37,266

* Includes reimbursement from the General Fund for additional cost of noncontributory wage credits for military service (about $140 million per year in 1974–75 and about $290 million per year in 1976–78) and for payments to non-insured persons aged 72 and over (decreasing from $307 million in 1973 to $205 million in 1978).

† Includes payments for vocational rehabilitation services (about $6 million per year).

‡ Payment from the trust fund to the Railroad Retirement Account. Interest payment adjustments between the two systems are included in the interest column.

Note: Two slightly different cost estimates were prepared, varying by economic assumptions. The one shown here is based on the more pessimistic, and probably more likely, assumptions.

TABLE 10.18

Progress of DI Trust Fund under 1973 Amendments, According to Estimates in 1974 Trustees Report

(in millions)

Calendar Year	Taxes*	Benefit Payments†	Adminis-trative Expenses	Railroad Retirement Financial Interchange‡	Interest on Fund	Fund at End of Year
1974............	$ 6,792	$ 6,957	$200	$22	$487	$8,029
1975............	7,773	8,046	241	20	492	7,987
1976............	8,661	9,120	256	14	475	7,733
1977............	9,608	10,285	274	15	440	7,207
1978............	10,963	11,454	288	18	415	6,825

* Includes reimbursement from the General Fund for additional cost of noncontributory wage credits for military service (about $60 million per year in 1974–75 and $95 million per year in 1976–78).

† Includes payments for vocational rehabilitation services (increasing from $67 million in 1974 to $131 million in 1978).

‡ Payment from the trust fund to the Railroad Retirement Account. Interest payment adjustments between the two systems are included in the interest column.

Note: Two slightly different cost estimates were prepared, varying by economic assumptions. The one shown here is based on the more pessimistic, and probably more likely, assumptions.

TABLE 10.19

Progress of HI Trust Fund under 1973 Amendments, According to Estimates in 1974 Trustees Report (in millions)

Calendar Year	Taxes*	Payment from General Fund†	Benefit Payments	Administrative Expenses	Interest on Fund	Fund at End of Year
1974............	$10,841	$478	$ 8,686	$330	$ 440	$ 9,210
1975............	11,998	479	10,250	346	592	11,683
1976............	13,284	479	11,709	371	734	14,100
1977............	14,648	471	13,269	397	873	16,426
1978............	19,046	456	14,999	422	1,091	21,598

* Includes transfers from Railroad Retirement Account with respect to railroad workers covered by HI ($125 million in 1974, increasing to $165 million in 1978), reimbursements from the General Fund for additional cost of non-contributory wage credits for military service ($48 million in 1974–78), and premiums for voluntary enrollees (about $5 million per year).

† For noninsured persons blanketed-in.

TABLE 10.20

Progress of SMI Trust Fund under 1973 Amendments, According to Estimates in 1974 Trustees Report (in millions)

Calendar Year	Enrollee Premiums	Government Contributions	Benefit Payments	Administrative Expenses	Interest on Fund	Fund at End of Year
1974.........	$1,764	$2,168	$3,331	$442	$ 71	$1,341
1975.........	1,864	2,666	3,925	464	85	1,567
1976.........	1,903	3,347	4,587	509	99	1,820
1977.........	1,941	4,035	5,262	556	114	2,092
1978.........	1,979	4,765	5,954	603	131	2,410

TABLE 10.21

Actuarial Balance of OASDI and HI Systems under 1973 Amendments, as Percentages of Taxable Payroll, According to Estimates in 1974 Trustees Report

	Level Equivalent*	OASI	DI	HI
1.	Benefit costs†.....................	11.72%	1.83%	2.48%
2.	Administrative expenses.............	0.21	0.09	0.06
3.	Taxes‡............................	9.39	1.52	2.65
4.	Existing fund§.....................	−0.04	0.00	−0.09
5.	Actuarial balance‖	−2.58	−0.40	+0.02

* Valuation as of the beginning of 1974.

† Including effect of railroad retirement financial interchange (0.04 percent for OASI and negligible for DI; not applicable to HI, because benefits are paid by HI Trust Fund, and taxes are transferred in full).

‡ Adjusted to reflect the lower tax rate for the self-employed as compared with combined employer-employee rate.

§ This represents the effect of the fund being greater or less than one year's outgo.

‖ The sum of items 3 and 4, minus the sum of items 1 and 2. A negative figure indicates the extent of lack of actuarial balance.

TABLE 10.22

Current Costs and Long-Range Average Costs of OASDI System for Various Dynamic Economic Assumptions, According to 1974 Estimates (costs expressed as percentages of effective taxable payroll)*

Assumed Annual Increase in—		Current Cost					Long-Range Average Cost
Earnings	Prices	1974	1990	2000	2010	2045	
5%	3%	10.67%	11.03%	11.31%	12.69%	17.86%	13.89%
6	4	10.76	11.50	12.15	14.03	21.42	15.58
4	2	10.67	10.93	10.91	11.79	14.94	12.71
5	2	10.67	9.76	9.07	9.28	10.35	10.06
6	3	10.64	9.65	9.29	9.88	12.40	10.86
4	3	10.67	12.36	13.60	16.17	26.80	18.15
5	4	10.80	13.14	14.81	18.11	32.11	20.59

* Cost includes benefit outgo, administrative expenses, and amounts needed to maintain the trust fund balance at a level of one year's outgo.
Note: These data differ slightly from the corresponding data presented in the 1974 Trustees Report, because of subsequent revisions.

TABLE 10.23

Long-Range Average Costs of OASDI System for Various Dynamic Economic Assumptions, According to 1974 Estimates (cost expressed as percentages of effective taxable payroll)*

Assumed Annual Increase in—		Average Cost	Assumed Annual Increase in—		Average Cost
Earnings	Prices		Earnings	Prices	
7%	3½%	10.30%	4%	1%	9.16%
7	4	12.21	4	2	12.71
7	5	17.05	4	3	18.15
7	6	24.67	4	4	27.88
7	7	36.54			
			3	0	8.27
6	3	10.86	3	1	11.46
6	4	15.58	3	1½	13.92
6	5	22.30	3	2	16.45
6	6	33.37	3	3	24.25
5	2	10.06	2	1	15.17
5	2½	11.66			
5	3	13.89	0	0	18.03
5	4	20.59			
5	5	30.63			

* Cost includes benefit outgo, administrative expenses, and amounts needed to maintain the trust fund balance at a level of one year's outgo.
Note: These data differ slightly from the corresponding data presented in the 1974 Trustees Report because of subsequent revisions.

TABLE 10.24

Long-Range Average Costs of OASDI System for Various Economic Assumptions Having Constant Differences, According to 1974 Estimates
(costs expressed as percentages of effective taxable payroll)*

Assumed Annual Increase in—			
Earnings	Prices	Average Cost	Ratio of Average Cost to That for 7 Percent Earnings Increase
Earnings-Increase Differential of 3 Percent			
7%	4%	12.21%	100%
6	3	10.86	89
5	2	10.06	82
4	1	9.16	75
3	0	8.27	68
Earnings-Increase Differential of 2 Percent			
7%	5%	17.05%	100%
6	4	15.58	91
5	3	13.89	81
4	2	12.71	75
3	1	11.46	67
Earnings-Increase Differential of 1 Percent			
7%	6%	24.67%	100%
6	5	22.30	90
5	4	20.59	83
4	3	18.15	74
3	2	16.45	67
2	1	15.17	61
No Earnings-Increase Differential			
7%	7%	36.54%	100%
6	6	33.37	91
5	5	30.63	84
4	4	27.88	76
3	3	24.25	66
0	0	18.03	49

* Cost includes benefit outgo, administrative expenses, and amounts needed to maintain the trust fund balance at a level of one year's outgo.
Note: These data differ slightly from the corresponding data presented in the 1974 Trustees Report because of subsequent revisions.

TABLE 10.25

Long-Range Average Costs of OASDI System for Various Economic Assumptions Having Uniform Relative Differences, According to 1974 Estimates
(costs expressed as percentages of effective taxable payroll)*

Assumed Annual Increase in—		Average Cost	Ratio of Average Cost to That for 7 Percent Earnings Increase
Earnings	*Prices*		
Earnings Increase Twice as Fast as Prices			
7%	3½%	10.30%	100%
6	3	10.86	105
5	2½	11.66	113
4	2	12.71	123
3	1½	13.92	135
2	1	15.17	147

* Cost includes benefit outgo, administrative expenses, and amounts needed to maintain the trust fund balance at a level of one year's outgo.

Note: These data differ slightly from the corresponding data presented in the 1974 Trustees Report because of subsequent revisions.

TABLE 10.26

Covered Workers, Covered Employers, Insured Persons, and
Covered Earnings under OASDI and HI, 1937–73
(in millions of persons and billions of dollars)

Year	Covered Workers in Year*	Covered Employers in Year	Insured Persons		Covered Earnings§		
			Total†	Disability‡	Total	Taxable	Percent Taxable
1937.........	32.9	2.42	‖	‖	$ 32.2	$ 29.6	92.0%
1938.........	31.8	2.24	‖	‖	28.5	26.5	93.0
1939.........	33.8	2.37	‖	‖	32.2	29.7	92.3
1940.........	35.4	2.50	22.9	‖	35.7	33.0	92.4
1941.........	41.0	2.65	24.9	‖	45.5	41.8	92.0
1942.........	46.4	2.66	27.5	‖	58.2	52.9	90.9
1943.........	47.7	2.39	31.2	‖	69.7	62.4	89.6
1944.........	46.3	2.47	34.9	‖	73.3	64.4	87.8
1945.........	46.4	2.61	38.6	‖	71.6	62.9	88.0
1946.........	48.8	3.02	40.3	‖	79.3	69.1	87.2
1947.........	48.9	3.25	41.8	‖	92.4	78.4	84.8
1948.........	49.0	3.30	43.4	‖	102.3	84.1	82.3
1949.........	46.8	3.32	44.8	‖	100.0	81.8	81.8
1950.........	48.3	3.34	45.7	‖	109.8	87.5	79.7
1951.........	58.1	4.44	59.8	‖	148.9	120.8	81.1
1952.........	59.6	4.45	62.8	‖	159.9	128.6	80.5
1953.........	60.8	4.35	68.2	‖	173.0	135.9	78.5
1954.........	59.6	4.35	71.0	‖	171.9	133.5	77.7
1955.........	65.2	5.05	70.6	31.9	196.1	157.5	80.3
1956.........	67.6	5.10	71.4	35.4	216.8	170.7	78.8
1957.........	70.6	5.10	74.3	37.2	233.9	181.4	77.5
1958.........	69.8	5.10	77.0	38.4	236.5	180.7	76.4
1959.........	71.7	5.20	78.9	43.4	255.0	202.3	79.3
1960.........	72.5	5.27	79.7	46.4	265.2	207.0	78.0
1961.........	72.8	5.32	85.4	48.5	270.9	209.6	77.4
1962.........	74.3	5.37	89.1	50.5	289.0	219.1	75.8
1963.........	75.5	5.45	90.4	51.5	302.3	225.5	74.6
1964.........	77.4	5.51	92.0	52.3	324.5	236.4	72.8
1965.........	80.7	5.59	93.6	53.3	351.7	250.7	71.3
1966.........	84.6	5.54	95.8	55.0	390.7	312.6	80.0
1967.........	87.0	5.52	98.3	55.7	422.3	330.0	78.1
1968.........	89.4	5.47	101.2	56.9	460.0	375.9	81.7
1969.........	92.1	5.42	104.0	70.1	502.0	401.3	79.9
1970.........	92.8	5.38	106.9	72.4	532.0	415.5	78.1
1971.........	93.0	5.40	109.8	74.5	559.2	429.3	76.8
1972.........	95.7	5.70	112.2	76.1	600.5	483.5	78.4
1973.........	98.7	5.80	114.8	78.1	677.5	553.9	81.8

* Workers (including self-employed persons in 1951 and after, and persons in the armed forces in 1957 and after) with earnings in covered employment (see note §). Data for "average" are for a typical week in March, June, September, and December.

† Persons who are either fully or currently insured at beginning of year, including retired persons (for 1973, only 1.6 million persons were currently insured but not fully insured).

‡ Persons who would be eligible for a "disability freeze" if they met the definition of disability; excludes all persons aged 65 and over, and all persons aged 62 to 64 who are entitled to old-age benefits.

§ Total earnings in covered employment represents the total earnings of persons in the specified employments covered by the program, where such earnings are subject to the taxes (or would be except for the effect of the maximum taxable earnings base).

‖ Not applicable under law then in effect.

Note: Coverage under the railroad retirement system is not included in the data.

TABLE 10.27

Beneficiaries and Average Old-Age Benefits, 1940–74

(beneficiaries and average old-age benefit as of end of year; beneficiaries and lump-sum payments in thousands)

Year	Old-Age (retired worker)	Monthly Beneficiaries					Total	Lump-Sum Death Payments*	Average Old-Age Benefit†
		Dependents of Old-Age Beneficiaries	Disabled Workers	Dependents of Disabled Workers	Survivors	Transitional Non-insured			
1940	112	36	—	—	74	—	222	61	$ 22.60
1945	518	173	—	—	597	—	1,288	179	24.19
1950	1,771	555	—	—	1,152	—	3,477	200	43.86
1955	4,474	1,314	—	—	2,173	—	7,961	567	61.90
1960	8,061	2,538	455	232	3,558	—	14,845	779	74.04
1961	8,925	2,730	618	409	3,813	—	16,495	813	75.65
1962	9,738	2,938	741	534	4,102	—	18,053	865	76.19
1963	10,263	3,000	827	625	4,320	—	19,035	969	76.88
1964	10,669	3,028	894	669	4,540	—	19,800	1,011	77.57
1965	11,101	3,076	988	751	4,951	—	20,867	990	83.92
1966	11,658	3,144	1,097	873	5,360	634	22,767	1,060	84.35
1967	12,019	3,159	1,194	948	5,659	729	23,707	1,134	85.37
1968	12,421	3,167	1,295	1,040	5,963	676	24,562	1,159	98.86
1969	12,824	3,168	1,394	1,093	6,229	603	25,312	1,222	100.40
1970	13,352	3,215	1,493	1,172	6,469	534	26,235	1,220	118.10
1971	13,925	3,263	1,648	1,282	6,700	472	27,289	1,252	132.16
1972	14,455	3,308	1,824	1,427	6,919	412	28,345	1,290	161.97
1973	15,364	3,429	2,017	1,544	7,160	358	29,872	1,299	166.42
1974	15,958	3,451	2,237	1,675	7,254	278	30,854	1,285	188.21

* Represents number of deceased workers for whom claim was awarded in the year.
† Including effect of actuarial reduction for retirement at ages 62 to 64 (for women, beginning in 1956; for men, beginning in 1961).

TABLE 10.28

OASDI Monthly Beneficiaries in Current Payment Status
at End of 1972, by Category

Category	Number
Retired workers	14,555,475
Men, aged 62–64	689,588
Men, aged 65 and over	7,541,259
Women, aged 62–64	750,602
Women, aged 65 and over	5,574,026
Wives of retired workers	2,726,732
Aged 62 and over*	2,548,097
Under age 65, with children	178,635
Husbands of retired workers (aged 62 or over)	7,967
Children of retired workers	580,001
Under age 18	367,794
Aged 18–21, in school	105,425
Aged 18 or over, disabled	106,782
Disabled workers (under age 65)	1,832,916
Men	1,300,284
Women	532,632
Wives of disabled workers	349,613
Aged 62 and over*	50,671
Under age 65, with children	298,942
Husbands of disabled workers (aged 62 or over)	526
Children of disabled workers	1,088,431
Under age 18	968,587
Aged 18–21, in school	102,260
Aged 18 or over, disabled	17,584
Widows, aged 60 or over	3,442,595
Disabled widows, aged 50–61	64,015
Widowers, aged 60 or over	3,015
Disabled widowers, aged 50–61	152
Parents	26,055
Men, aged 62 or over	1,234
Women, aged 62 or over	24,821
Widowed mothers†	540,965
Children of deceased workers	2,847,201
Under age 18	2,239,764
Aged 18–21, in school	426,796
Aged 18 or over, disabled	180,641
Transitional noninsured, aged 72 or over	410,369
Men	56,754
Women	353,615

* Does not include a few wives aged 62–64 with children, who are included in the next category.

† Under age 60, except in unusual circumstances.

TABLE 10.29

Number of OASDI Families and Beneficiaries in Current Payment Status and Average Monthly Benefit, for Selected Family Groups at End of 1972

Family Classification	Families (thousands)	Beneficiaries (thousands)	Average Family Benefit
Retired-Worker Families			
Worker only	11,653	11,653	$157
Men	5,364	5,364	177
Women	6,288	6,288	140
Worker and spouse aged 62 or over	2,518	5,034	272
Worker, wife, and children	218	799	310
Worker and children	174	390	259
Disabled-Worker Families			
Worker only	1,287	1,287	$175
Men	821	821	188
Women	467	467	152
Worker and wife aged 62 or over	52	104	274
Worker, wife, and children	298	1,338	361
Worker and children	198	542	295
Survivor Families			
Widow or widower only	3,439	3,439	$138
Parents only	25	26	121
Widowed mother and one child	191	379	290
Widowed mother and two or more children	350	1,394	378
One child alone	568	568	133
Two children alone	208	416	265
Three or more children alone	152	555	171
Transitional Noninsured, Aged 72 or Over			
Total	402	410	$ 58
Men	49	57	58
Women	354	354	58
Total Families			
Total*	21,803	28,481	—

* Total slightly exceeds sum of individual items above because some minor family classifications are not shown (e.g., remarried widow, and widow [aged 61 or over] or widower with children). Total does not quite agree with data in Table 10.27 for certain technical reasons.

TABLE 10.30

Persons Eligible for Benefits under HI and SMI at Various Dates
(all figures for numbers of persons in thousands)

As of *July 1 of—*	*Persons Aged 65 and over*		*Disabled Beneficiaries*	
	HI*	*SMI*	*HI*	*SMI*
1966............	18,900	17,725	†	†
1967............	19,200	17,840	†	†
1968............	19,510	18,755	†	†
1969............	19,788	19,186	†	†
1970............	20,102	19,585	†	†
1971............	20,428	19,898	†	†
1972............	20,744	20,282	†	†
1973............	21,103	20,700‡	1,740‡	1,580‡
1974............	21,455	21,000‡	1,850‡	1,710‡

* Does not include beneficiaries permanently residing outside the United States, since they do not have any real benefit coverage under HI.

† Medicare was not then applicable to disabled beneficiaries.

‡ Preliminary estimate.

TABLE 10.31

Average Annual Rates of Increase in Hospital Costs and Physician Fees in Comparison with Rates of Increase of Price and Wages

Year	Increase over Previous Year			
	Hospital Costs	Physician Fees	Prices	Wages
1956................	4.5%	3.1%	1.4%	6.3%
1957................	7.7	4.3	3.5	3.7
1958................	8.6	3.4	2.8	2.3
1959................	6.8	3.3	0.8	5.0
1960................	6.8	2.5	1.6	3.3
1961................	8.5	2.6	1.1	1.4
1962................	5.3	2.9	1.1	4.7
1963................	5.6	2.2	1.2	2.9
1964................	7.0	2.5	1.3	4.6
1965................	7.9	3.6	1.7	2.5
1966................	7.6	5.8	2.9	5.5
1967................	13.3	7.1	2.9	5.7
1968................	12.8	5.6	4.2	6.4
1969................	15.2	6.9	5.4	6.6
1970................	14.7	7.5	5.9	5.4
1971................	13.2	6.9	4.3	5.1
1972................	13.7	3.1	3.3	6.6
1973................	8.6	3.3	6.2	7.5
1974................	11.2	9.1	11.0	8.0
Average for 1956–65.......	6.9	3.0	1.7	3.7
Average for 1966–74.......	12.2	6.1	5.1	6.3

Sources of data:
1. Hospital costs—based on data from American Hospital Association with regard to total hospital expense per patient day (for 1963 and after, based on adjusted data that allow for outpatient expenses); data are for fiscal years generally ending in September or June of year shown.
2. Physician fees—physician's fee component of the Consumer Price Index.
3. Prices—Consumer Price Index (for all items).
4. Wages—average of estimated total wages in covered employment (i.e., without regard to the effects of the taxable earnings base), excluding self-employment earnings.

TABLE 10.32

Progress of OASI Trust Fund, 1937–74
(in millions)

Year	Taxes*	Benefit Payments†	Adminis-trative Expenses‡	Railroad Financial Inter-change§	Interest on Fund	Fund at End of Year‖
1937..........	$ 765	$ 1	—	—	$ 2	$ 766
1938..........	360	10	—	—	15	1,132
1939..........	580	14	—	—	27	1,724
1940..........	325	35	$ 26	—	43	2,031
1941..........	789	88	26	—	56	2,762
1942..........	1,012	131	28	—	72	3,688
1943..........	1,239	166	29	—	88	4,820
1944..........	1,316	209	29	—	107	6,005
1945..........	1,285	274	30	—	134	7,121
1946..........	1,295	378	40	—	152	8,150
1947..........	1,558	466	46	—	164	9,360
1948..........	1,688	556	51	—	281	10,722
1949..........	1,670	667	54	—	146	11,816
1950..........	2,671	961	61	—	257	13,721
1951..........	3,367	1,885	81	—	417	15,540
1952..........	3,819	2,194	88	—	365	17,442
1953..........	3,945	3,006	88	—	414	18,707
1954..........	5,163	3,670	92	+$ 21	447	20,576
1955..........	5,713	4,968	119	+ 7	454	21,663
1956..........	6,172	5,715	132	+ 5	526	22,519
1957..........	6,825	7,347	162	+ 2	556	22,393
1958..........	7,566	8,327	194	− 124	552	21,864
1959..........	8,052	9,842	184	− 282	532	20,141
1960..........	10,866	10,677	203	− 318	516	20,324
1961..........	11,285	11,862	239	− 332	548	19,725
1962..........	12,059	13,356	256	− 361	526	18,337
1963..........	14,541	14,217	281	− 423	521	18,480
1964..........	15,689	14,914	296	− 403	569	19,125
1965..........	16,017	16,737	328	− 436	593	18,235
1966..........	20,658	18,267	256	− 444	644	20,570
1967..........	23,216	19,468	406	− 508	818	24,222
1968..........	24,101	22,643	476	− 438	939	25,704
1969..........	28,389	24,210	474	− 491	1,165	30,082
1970..........	30,705	28,798	471	− 579	1,515	32,454
1971..........	34,211	33,415	514	− 613	1,667	33,789
1972..........	38,256	37,124	674	− 724	1,794	35,318
1973..........	46,416	45,745	647	− 783	1,928	36,487
1974..........	52,528	51,623	865	− 909	2,159	37,777

* The figures for 1937–40 embody certain artificial, nonsignificant fluctuations because of the method of making appropriations then. Also includes transfers from the General Fund for military service wage credits (small amounts in 1946–51 and moderate amounts in 1966–73—with $140 million in 1974) and for reimbursement of costs of transitional noninsured benefits (beginning in 1968; with a level of about $300 million per year in 1969–74).

† Beginning in 1966, includes a very small amount of expenditures for rehabilitation services (about $5 million in 1974).

‡ No figures are shown for 1937–39, since then the estimated administrative expenses were deducted from the estimated tax receipts to yield the net contributions. The figures for 1957 and subsequent years embody certain artificial, nonsignificant fluctuations because of the method of reimbursements between the trust funds.

§ A positive figure indicates payment to the trust fund from the Railroad Retirement Account, and a negative figure indicates the reverse.

‖ Not including amounts in the Railroad Retirement Account to the credit of this trust fund. In millions, these amount to $377 in 1953, $284 in 1954, $163 in 1955, $60 in 1956, and nothing thereafter.

TABLE 10.33

Progress of DI Trust Fund, 1957–74
(in millions)

Year	Taxes	Benefit Pay- ments*	Adminis- trative Expenses†	Railroad Financial Inter- change‡	Interest on Fund	Fund at End of Year
1957............	$ 702	$ 57	$ 3	—	$ 7	$ 649
1958............	966	249	12	—	25	1,379
1959............	891	457	50	+$22	40	1,825
1960............	1,010	568	36	+ 5	53	2,289
1961............	1,038	887	64	− 5	66	2,437
1962............	1,046	1,105	66	− 11	68	2,368
1963............	1,099	1,210	68	− 20	66	2,235
1964............	1,154	1,309	79	− 20	64	2,047
1965............	1,188	1,573	90	− 24	59	1,606
1966............	2,022	1,784	137	− 25	58	1,739
1967............	2,302	1,950	109	− 31	78	2,029
1968............	3,348	2,310	127	− 20	116	3,025
1969............	3,615	2,557	138	− 21	177	4,100
1970............	4,497	3,085	164	− 10	277	5,614
1971............	4,670	3,782	205	− 13	361	6,645
1972............	5,158	4,502	233	− 24	414	7,457
1973............	5,984	5,764	190	− 20	458	7,927
1974............	6,880	6,957	217	− 22	500	8,109

* Beginning in 1966, includes a small amount of expenditures for rehabilitation services ($54 million in 1974).
† The figures for 1957 and subsequent years embody certain artificial, nonsignificant fluctuations because of the method of reimbursements between the trust funds. Also includes transfers from the General Fund for military service wage credits (small amounts in 1966–74—with $52 million in 1974).
‡ A positive figure indicates payment to the trust fund from the Railroad Retirement Account, and a negative figure indicates the reverse.

TABLE 10.34

Progress of HI Trust Fund, 1966–74
(in millions)

Year	Taxes*	Payments from General Fund†	Benefit Payments	Adminis- trative Expenses	Interest on Fund	Fund at End of Year
1966.........	$ 1,901	$ 26	$ 891	$107	$ 31	$ 944
1967.........	3,250	301	3,353	77	51	1,073
1968.........	4,246	1,022	4,179	99	74	2,083
1969.........	4,607	617	4,739	118	116	2,505
1970.........	5,020	863	5,124	157	161	3,202
1971.........	5,097	503	5,751	149	195	3,034
1972.........	5,779	381	6,319	184	182	2,935
1973.........	10,090	451	7,057	232	281	6,467
1974.........	11,029	471	9,101	271	523	9,119

* Includes transfers from the general fund for military service wage credits (about $11 million per year in 1966–70 and $48 million per year in 1971–74). Also includes the transfer from the RR Account of the HI taxes with respect to railroad workers ($48 million in 1974) and the premiums for voluntary enrollees ($5 million in 1974).
† For the benefit costs and related administrative expenses with respect to noninsured persons eligible for HI benefits.

TABLE 10.35

Progress of SMI Trust Fund, 1966–74
(in millions)

Year	Enrollee Premiums	Payments from General Fund	Benefit Payments	Administrative Expenses	Interest on Fund	Fund at End of Year
1966.......	$ 322	—	$ 128	$ 74	$ 2	$ 122
1967.......	640	$ 933	1,197	110	24	412
1968.......	832	858	1,518	183	21	421
1969.......	914	907	1,865	196	18	199
1970.......	1,096	1,093	1,975	238	12	188*
1971.......	1,302	1,313	2,117	260	24	450
1972.......	1,382	1,389	2,325	290	37	643
1973.......	1,550	1,705	2,526	318	57	1,111
1974.......	1,804	2,225	3,318	410	95	1,506

* The fund balance fell to a minimum of $57 million on June 30, 1970.

TABLE 10.36

Deficit in SMI Program on Incurred Cost Basis, as of July 1 of Various Years
(dollar figures in millions)

Year	Benefits Incurred but Unpaid	Administrative Expenses for Such Benefits	Total Liabilities*	Assets on Hand†	Deficit	Ratio of Assets to Liabilities
1967..........	$ 515	$ 55	$ 572	$ 512	$ 60	90%
1968..........	625	63	690	398	292	58
1969..........	679	75	758	388	370	51
1970..........	681	82	767	77	690	10
1971..........	727	95	826	318	508	38
1972..........	750	98	852	484	368	57
1973..........	839	128	971	746	225	77
1974‡.........	1,184	154	1,342	1,155	187	86
1975‡.........	1,368	178	1,551	1,332	219	86

* Includes a small amount of premiums collected in advance and government contributions with respect thereto.
† Includes a small amount of premiums dues and uncollected and government contributions due and unpaid.
‡ Projected estimates, shown in 1974 Trustees Report.

TABLE 10.37

**Estimated Amount of Life Insurance
in Force as Survivor Benefit under OASDI,
as of Beginning of Year
(in billions)**

Year	Act Valued	Interest Rate	Amount of Insurance
1940.....................	1939	3%	$ 37
1951.....................	1950	3	170
1953.....................	1952	3	298
1955.....................	1954	3	345
1957.....................	1956	3	416
1959.....................	1958	3	460
1961.....................	1960	3	547
1962.....................	1961	3	585
1966.....................	1961	3	685
1966.....................	1961	3½	655
1966.....................	1965	3½	700
1968.....................	1967	3½	930
1970.....................	1969	3½	1,100
1972.....................	1971	3½	1,310
1973.....................	1972	6	1,760*
1974.....................	1973	6	2,040*

 * Also includes the effect of the automatic-adjustment provisions (an assumed
2¾ percent annual increase in benefit amounts).

PART IV

Allied Programs

The social security program examined in Parts II and III does not satisfy all of the economic security needs of persons in the United States. Additional programs designed to fulfill specific security needs have been adopted.

Part IV will look at the importance of and changing patterns of security provided by public assistance programs. Part IV also includes a description of the separate railroad retirement system, the important programs of unemployment insurance and workmen's compensation, and the existing cash sickness programs. The final chapter in Part IV describes the special programs designed for federal, state, and local employees and for veterans of military service.

chapter 11

Public Assistance Programs
before and under the Social
Security Act

The social security programs in the United States dealing with the long-range risks have been shaped by long-standing traditions and developments. As a young country with abundant natural resources, the United States offered rich opportunities to most of the millions of immigrants and their descendants. In such a pioneer country, there was naturally a widespread general belief that anyone—no matter how poor his start—could get full security and even wealth for himself and his children through his own efforts.

Before the enactment of the Social Security Act in 1935, there was no social insurance covering the general risks of old-age, disability, and survivor protection, nor were there many private pension plans which provided protection against these risks. The various workmen's compensation systems, established under state legislation, covered the risks of disability and survivorship, but only for occupational injury and, in some cases, disease. Retirement and disability pensions under organized, definite plans were provided by governmental action only for most federal employees and many state and local government employees; these plans provided only limited survivor benefits in the form of lump-sum refunds of contributions or elective joint-and-survivor pensions. On the other hand, a number of public assistance programs had been developed under state and local auspices before 1935.

PUBLIC ASSISTANCE PROGRAMS BEFORE THE SOCIAL SECURITY ACT

From colonial times, local communities were responsible for aiding the needy. So-called "paupers" sometimes received public help in the form of food and fuel. At other times, they were cared for in poor-houses. Such aid was frequently given grudgingly, with the feeling being widespread that people who needed continued help from the community were shiftless and lazy. As the country developed, how-ever, the realization spread that certain groups of people could do relatively little to support themselves and might need help for a long period—such as the aged, the widows and orphans, and those disabled to such an extent that they could not work.

Shortly after the turn of the century, a series of state commissions investigated the situation of aged persons, and a number of organiza-tions began to urge legislation on behalf of the needy aged. Until after World War I, the only permanent provision for the needy aged in nearly all states was in so-called "almshouses" or "poor farms." On the whole, this was an extremely unsatisfactory method of caring for the problem. Not only were conditions unsatisfactory in regard to food, physical surroundings, and intermingling of the aged with the mentally defective and the chronically ill, but the cost was relatively high due to inefficient management.

The first effective legislation for old-age assistance was enacted by Alaska in 1915. Arizona had passed an old-age assistance and aid-to-dependent-children law earlier that year, but it was declared un-constitutional. The Alaskan law was quite restricted, since it applied only to aged persons (65 for men and 60 for women) who had been in the territory since 1906.

Then, beginning in 1923 (with Montana, Nevada, and Pennsyl-vania), a growing number of states enacted and put into force old-age assistance plans, so that there were 18 by the beginning of 1931 and 30 by the beginning of 1935. Most of these plans had a minimum age of either 65 or 70, and had both residence and citizenship requirements of 10 or 15 years. Also, other requirements were rather strict, so that persons were ineligible if financially able children or near relatives were present. Liens on assets of the recipients were frequently imposed so as to provide repayment of any assistance furnished. Initially, the plans were usually financed and administered wholly by counties. Whether a program was established was usually optional with the county, so that the extent of the assistance varied widely within each state.

In the area of survivor protection for orphaned children, so-called "mothers' pensions" or "mothers' aid" was available by law in nearly all states by 1935. The first such laws were in Illinois and Missouri (1911). In many instances, however, the financing was provided by local governments, so that it was not actually available throughout all local units. The vast majority of the recipients were cases where the father had died, although assistance was furnished in certain cases of desertion, divorce, or incapacity. In general, unlike old-age assistance, the residence requirement was relatively short (usually only one or two years at most).

The only available public assistance for disabled persons on an organized basis was in respect to the blind, a category which naturally attracts great public sympathy and recognition. In 1935, 27 states had blind pension laws that, on the whole, were similar to the old-age pension laws, although somewhat more liberal in regard to such matters as residence and other requirements. Some states also carried out extensive service programs for the blind, such as vocational training workshops and employment services. Other disabled persons were cared for by general public relief (of a rather spotty nature) and by private charity.

The Great Depression of the early 1930s swept away millions of jobs. As a result, many persons used up their accumulated savings and even lost their homes. In addition, others lost their savings in bank and business failures. Many states had great difficulty in continuing to finance both general relief and the special types of assistance discussed previously. The federal government first made loans to the states for these purposes and later made outright grants, as well as establishing direct federal emergency relief programs.

A very considerable public demand developed for long-range, rather than emergency, measures in these areas. Such pressures were especially heightened by the popular appeal of the so-called "Townsend Plan," which was proposed both to help the aged and to cure the depression. Under this plan, $200 a month (which, incidentally, at that time was about twice the earnings of the average full-time worker) would be paid to all persons aged 60 and over, regardless of whether need existed, under the condition that it would all be spent within a month. The plan would have been financed by a 2 percent general transactions tax (although most estimates indicated that such a tax would have produced totally inadequate revenue). A number of similar general pension proposals were propounded in the same period—such as the "$30 every Thursday" plan. The political pressure for these plans was, to a considerable extent, responsible for the passage of the public assistance and old-age insurance provisions of the Social Security Act, since many political conservatives viewed the latter as by far the better alternative.

PUBLIC ASSISTANCE PROGRAMS UNDER THE SOCIAL SECURITY ACT

In 1934, President Roosevelt established a special committee to study all matters relating to economic security. This group recommended far-sweeping legislation in many areas, including public assistance and social insurance covering the risk of old-age protection. Some of these proposals were enacted by Congress as the Social Security Act of 1935. This law authorized federal grants to states to pay part of the costs of aid to aged persons, blind people, and needy children. In 1950 a fourth program was added—aid to the permanently and totally disabled. In 1960 a fifth program was inaugurated—medical assistance for the aged (MAA), which was intended for persons aged 65 and over not on old-age assistance (OAA) who have sufficient financial resources to meet their usual needs but not any heavy medical expenses. In 1965 the MAA program and the federal matching for medical vendor payments for other public assistance categories than OAA were combined into the new medical assistance program (popularly referred to as Medicaid), although states were permitted either to continue the former programs until 1970 or to adopt the new program immediately.[1] Over the years to 1974, these public assistance programs improved and expanded but, on the whole, maintained the same general philosophy and characteristics. In 1956, provision of services to promote self-support or self-care became an explicit federal legislative objective. But then in 1974, the character of the three adult cash-payments programs was considerably changed when they were federalized, being then termed the supplemental security income program (SSI).

---

[1] For more details on the history and provisions of the Medicaid program, see Robert J. Myers, *Medicare* (Homewood, Ill: Richard D. Irwin, Inc., 1970).

The state public assistance programs had a number of common characteristics, which are still applicable to the aid to families with dependent children program (AFDC). Persons aided must be needy, according to the definition of need established by the state. Each state is free to decide whether it wishes to take part in the program, but if it does, it must have its plan approved by the federal government as meeting certain general requirements set forth in the law. The programs relate only to the specific categories indicated, and the so-called "general assistance" programs operated by most states for other types of needy persons are not participated in at all by the federal government.

Among the general requirements that must be met for all public assistance programs for which federal grants are available are the following:

1. The plan must operate throughout the entire state.
2. The states must at least share the costs with the local government (many states pay the entire amount).
3. A single state agency must administer the program or supervise its administration.
4. The assistance must be paid in cash except for vendor medical service payments.
5. Opportunity for fair hearing and appeal must be provided.
6. All income and resources must be taken into consideration, other than for certain small exceptions.
7. Administration must be proper and efficient (and with employees hired under a merit system basis), subject to federal review.

Special requirements related to each of the programs. For old-age assistance the minimum age requirement was 65, although a state could make payments to younger persons entirely from its own funds (but in actual practice, only one state did so). Similarly, aid to permanently and totally disabled persons could be paid, with federal financial participation, only to persons aged 18 and over under a definition of disability established by the state; the same was also true for aid to the blind. For aid to families with dependent children, the state can make payments with federal participation for children up to but not including age 18 and, as a result of amendments in the mid-1960s, also at ages 18 to 21 if regularly attending school.

Medical assistance covers all categorical assistance recipients and all other persons who are medically needy and who, except for the amount of their income and assets, could qualify for categorical public assistance. The age limit for children is, however, age 21 even if a lower age applies for cash assistance. All other medically needy children may also, at the option of the state, be included. The MA program could be accepted by each state during 1966–69, or it could continue under previous provisions. After 1969, however, the only federal funds available to states for medical care costs under public assistance are under MA. In conjunction with the supplemental security income program for cash payments to the adult categories, which became effective in 1974, the state can have the federal government make eligibility determinations for Medicaid benefits with respect to all persons receiving SSI. Such procedure has the "advantage" to the state that then the federal government pays the administrative costs—another move away from the "new federalism" philosophy of moving power away from the federal government to the states. At the inception of the SSI program, 25 states accepted this "offer."

Medical assistance programs are required to furnish certain services —physician, inpatient hospital, outpatient hospital, laboratory, X ray, and home health services, as well as nursing home care for those over age 21, and early and periodic screening and diagnostic treatment for those under age 21. Most other medical services (such as drugs, dental care, and eyeglasses) can be included, for federal matching purposes, at the option of the state. A state can also buy in to the supplementary medical insurance portion of the Medicare program (as was discussed in Chapter 8).

Originally, certain provisions were contained in the medical assistance program that required the states to expand them continually. Due to the very sharply increasing costs of the program, these have been eliminated. For example, the 1972 amendments struck out the requirements that states must make efforts in the direction of broadening the scope of services and liberalizing eligibility requirements and that states could not reduce aggregate expenditures for their share of the program's cost from one year to the next. Also, this legislation permitted states to introduce cost-sharing provisions for optional services for cash-assistance recipients and for all services for the medically indigent. Further, the states were required to charge premiums, graded by income of the recipient, for the medically indigent, if they are included in the plan. In 1974, this requirement was removed, because of administrative difficulties it has caused, although states may charge such premiums.

According to the Social Security Act, states may not have any "length-of-residence" requirement for the medical assistance program. The requirement for the aid to families with dependent children program may not exceed one year for children over a year old. For the other three programs, it may not be more than five years out of the nine preceding years, including continuous residence for the last year. Likewise, under the law, citizenship may be required by the state, but no duration of citizenship can be required. In the past, many states had considerably less stringent residence and citizenship requirements (or none at all), and the federal government participated completely in the financing in all such cases. The Supreme Court, however, has ruled that all these residence and citizenship requirements are unconstitutional.

Originally, the aid to families with dependent children program was focused primarily on the problem of child support in families where the father had died. Over the years, however, as the social insurance systems met most of the problem in this area, this program expanded into caring for needy families where the father was otherwise absent from the home (divorce or desertion, including absence of the father in cases of illegitimate children) or disabled. In 1950 the law was changed so that one adult caretaker in the family could be included as a recipient; in 1962 a further change made both parents eligible to be recipients. Legislation in 1961 permitted payments to be made when the father is present but is unemployed and cannot find work. This was to be effective only for the 14-month period beginning in May 1961, but was made effective for another five years by legislation in 1962. This legislation also changed the name of the program from aid to dependent children (in recognition of its expanded scope) to "Aid and Services to Needy Families with Children"—known more popularly as "Aid to Families with Dependent Children" (AFDC). Later, the provision applicable to unemployed fathers was made permanent.

The 1967 amendments inaugurated a new public assistance program with federal financial participation, emergency assistance for needy families with children. Temporary emergency assistance is available for a maximum of 30 days in a 12-month period for children under age 21 and their families. This assistance can be in any form—money, medical aid, clothing, food, and payment of rent or utilities. The federal government pays half of the cost in all states.

States must consider other income and resources in determining the extent of need for public assistance. There must be considered both cash and noncash gifts from relatives, earnings from employment, pensions (including social insurance benefits), and assets (such as homeownership, savings accounts, and life insurance). Certain reserves of a reasonable nature are permitted. Thus, assistance is not refused or payments reduced because of possessing small amounts of savings or life insurance.

Blind persons were granted certain special privileges. For a number of years before 1974, when the new supplemental security income program became effective, the first $85 per month of earned income plus half of any additional earned income had to be completely disregarded in considering need. Also, then, state programs were allowed to provide for disregard of the first $20 of monthly earned income of OAA and APTD recipients and 50 percent of the next $60 of such income in considering need. In addition, states could permit APTD recipients undergoing vocational rehabilitation to have all their earnings disregarded during the first three years thereof. Under the AFDC program, the state was permitted to provide for disregard of the total earned income of any child recipient who is attending school and does not have a full-time job; for any other child, the first $30 of monthly earnings could be disregarded, plus one third of any additional earnings.

The states were also allowed to disregard small amounts of other income in determining the need of recipients—$7.50 per month for the three adult categories and $5 per month per family for AFDC. States were permitted to place liens on assets of recipients (such as homes) so as to recover later the amounts spent for cash assistance, but this cannot be done under the medical assistance program.

State participation in the public assistance programs for which federal funds were available developed rapidly, and virtually all states had old-age assistance, aid to the blind, and aid to families with dependent children programs within a few years after 1935. Likewise, following the inception of the aid to the permanently and totally disabled program in 1950, states gradually adopted such plans. At the end of 1973, all states and other jurisdictions had old-age assistance, aid to families with dependent children, and aid to the blind programs, while all except Nevada had aid to the permanently and totally disabled plans. The participation of the states in the medical assistance program grew rather rapidly after its inauguration in 1965, until at the end of 1974 all states except Arizona had such programs. About half of the states were participating in the emergency assistance program for needy families with children at the end of 1974.

FOOD STAMP PROGRAM

A new form of public assistance in the United States was instituted in 1964, when the Food Stamp Act was signed into law. In the preceding three years, this program had been tested by several pilot projects. Previously, and for many years, there had been relatively narrow programs of this type that were primarily concerned with the distribution of surplus foods of particular types to low-income or destitute people.

In 1973 the food stamp program was significantly changed by mandating that it should be expanded to all parts of the country on a virtually uniform basis. In the last few years, the program has grown, almost unnoticed, to a very large size, and it has potentialities of even further growth.

The food stamp program is operated on a county-by-county basis within each state. The state welfare agency administers the program, with overall supervision by the U.S. Department of Agriculture. Until the 1973 legislation, whether a county participated in the program was at its own option, but now all areas must participate unless the state involved demonstrates that this would be impossible or impractical. In the past, a number of counties did not participate for various reasons, such as political philosophy or a belief that they were better off under a surplus foods distribution basis.

The entire cost of the benefit payments is met by the federal government from general revenues. The federal government also pays part of the administrative expenses; currently, the federal share is 50 percent.

The general approach of the food stamp program is quite simple— low-income persons can purchase food stamps (actually in the form of coupons) of specified amounts at a discount, and these can be used like cash to purchase almost any type of food item from about 180,000 participating stores. Housebound people over age 60 can use these coupons to pay for meals-on-wheels services. They may also be used to purchase plants and seeds used to produce food for personal consumption. Unlike some public assistance programs, there is no needs test on the basis of an investigation of the actual needs of each individual case. Rather, there is a mathematically structured net income and assets test, which generally produces the same result for identical cases as to these two elements without regard to differing needs.

Public assistance families are eligible for food stamps without regard to income and assets. Usually, any applicable cost therefor may be deducted from their public assistance payment, at their option. Other families, to be eligible, must meet certain conditions. The assets cannot exceed $1,500, except for families with more than one person which include at least one person aged 60 or over, in which case it is $3,000. Certain assets, such as the home, furniture, clothing, life insurance policies, and an automobile, are not counted as assets.

The family income, after certain deductions, must not exceed the following amounts:[2]

Family Size	Monthly Net Income
1	$194
2	280
3	406
4	513
5	606
6	700
7	793
8*	886

* $73 for each additional member.

The deductions are: all income taxes, OASDHI taxes, pension plan contributions, union dues, medical costs when over $10 a month, child care costs when needed for employment, education costs, and housing cost in excess of 30 percent of family income minus all the preceding deductions.

It is significant to note that these income standards have changed since mid-1971, in line with generally rising family income levels, including those of social security beneficiaries. Such changes are made by the Secretary of Agriculture, in consultation with the Secretary of HEW, when the amounts of food coupon allocations are changed. At the end of 1974, the average social security benefit for both a single person and a married couple happened to be at about the same level as the food stamp income standards. This means that even considering that many social security beneficiaries have other income than their benefits, a large proportion of them are eligible for food stamps. Also, it would appear that with the payments under the supplemental security income program (discussed subsequently) then having an effective level of $166 per month for a single person (including the $20 disregard of other income) and $239 for a couple, all SSI recipients are eligible for food stamps, except those in California, Massachusetts, Nevada,

---

[2] These amounts apply only in the 48 continental states and are applicable at the beginning of 1975. Alaska, Hawaii, Guam, Puerto Rico, and the Virgin Islands have separate standards because of differing income levels and food costs.

New York, and Wisconsin, which elected to provide the bonus value of food stamps in cash.

Under certain circumstances, food stamps are given without any charge to victims of disasters. These can either be general disasters, such as hurricanes, floods, or earthquakes, or individual ones, such as destruction of the home by fire.

Another eligibility requirement is that all able-bodied family members aged 18–64 must be registered for work at the state employment service and must accept suitable job offers, unless employed, caring for dependent children or incapacitated adults, or attending school.

The amount of free coupons depends upon both the size of the family and its monthly income, after deductions, in the form of regular income of all sorts. The total amount of coupons, both "free" and purchased, varies by family size and is supposed to supply the recipients with a low-priced nutritionally adequate diet.[3] For persons with very low incomes (less than $20 a month for one- and two-person families and $30 for larger ones, a not very likely situation considering all the public support programs in existence),[4] "free" or "bonus" coupons in the following amounts were given for various family sizes, as of the beginning of 1975:

Family Size	Food Coupons
1	$ 46
2	84
3	122
4	154
5	182
6	210
7	238
8*	266

* $22 for each additional member.

These amounts are based on the economy food plan, developed by the U.S. Department of Agriculture, which is a low-priced, nutritionally adequate diet. The amounts are automatically adjusted semiannually to reflect changes in the food component of the Consumer Price Index.

---

[3] But note that the recipients are quite free to purchase any type of food that they wish. Nothing prevents them from buying filet mignon instead of equally nutritious stew beef, or fresh strawberries in midwinter, or excessive amounts of calorie-laden cakes, cookies, and soft drinks.

[4] Certain categories could have little or no income, however, such as "hippies" or college students living on their own. Quite obviously, the requirement of registering for work could readily be made ineffective if the person did not really want to work.

Unlike the automatics under OASDI, there can be downward movements as well as upward ones.

The amount required to be paid for food coupons depends upon the size of the family monthly income after deductions. Such purchase requirements are determined from a table with net income grouped by intervals. In general, for those above the "completely free" category, the charge in the beginning of 1975 was about $3 (actually, varying between $2 and $4) for each additional $10 of monthly net income above the "free" limit, being slightly more in terms of dollars, but less relative to total food coupon allotments, for larger families. For example, for monthly net income of $160 (the middle of an income interval), the monthly purchase requirements were: $33, or 72 percent of the total coupon value, for a one-person family; $38, or 45 percent, for a two-person family; and then increasing gradually to $45, or 17 percent, for an eight-person family.

Illustrative monthly purchase requirements for certain family sizes for several selected net incomes were as follows in the beginning of 1975:

	Family Size				
Monthly Net Income	*1*	*2*	*3*	*4*	*8*
$ 20– 29.99	$ 1	$ 1	—	—	—
30– 39.99	4	4	$ 4	$ 4	$ 5
70– 79.99	12	15	16	16	19
130–139.99	27	32	33	34	39
170–189.99	36	44	46	47	51
250–269.99	*	64	70	71	75
450–479.99	*	*	*	130	135
870–886.00	*	*	*	*	226

* Not eligible.

The corresponding "free" coupons for the foregoing cases were as follows:

	Family Size				
Monthly Net Income	*1*	*2*	*3*	*4*	*8*
$ 20– 29.99	$45	$83	$122	$154	$266
30– 39.99	42	80	118	150	261
70– 79.99	34	69	106	138	247
130–139.99	19	52	89	120	227
170–189.99	10	40	76	107	215
250–269.99	*	20	52	83	191
450–479.99	*	*	*	24	131
870–886.00	*	*	*	*	40

* Not eligible.

The law provides that the purchase requirement shall not exceed 30 percent of the net income of the family and that there shall be no purchase requirement for one- and two-person families with net income of less than $20 per month and for larger families with net income of less than $30 per month. For one-person families who have purchase requirements, such requirement varies from about 5 percent at the lowest income levels up to about 20 percent for the highest eligible incomes. For larger families, these proportions of purchase requirement to net income are higher and, in fact, are the 30-percent maximum in a few cases—for example for 8-person families, for net incomes of $110 and over—and almost this percentage for somewhat smaller families at the same income level.

It may be noted that the benefit schedule contains sharp, inequitable breaking points. A few cents of additional income, if reported, can increase the purchase requirement by as much as $9, although usually by only $2 to $6. Even more sizable, however, is the situation for persons near the maximum allowable income. Those just below this point receive "free" coupons ranging from $10 worth for one-person families and $20 for two-person families to $24 for four-person families and up to $40 for eight-person families; here, a slight additional amount of income could result in a substantial financial loss.

In December 1974, the Ford administration announced its intention to increase the purchase requirements, effective for March 1975. Under this change, all recipients would be required to pay a uniform 30 percent of net income for the food stamps, except for those who, by law, are eligible for completely free stamps. This uniform 30 percent rate, which is the maximum permitted by the law, contrasts with the varying proportions then in effect, which ranged from 5 percent to 30 percent. The result of this change would have been to eliminate for eligibility or to sharply reduce the free coupons for many persons, including virtually all SSI recipients.

The proposed change was made for federal budgetary purposes and would reduce the cost of the program by about $650 million a year. Congress, however, overwhelmingly enacted legislation to prevent this change and to retain the basis applicable at the beginning of 1975 for the entire year.

A family, other than one on public assistance which has its purchase requirement deducted from the welfare check, can purchase the stamps twice a month (weekly in some states) and can elect to purchase any 25 percent multiple of the full allotment.

In many instances, because of the large number of eligibles, the determination of eligibility and of the income level is done on a rather sketchy or "simplified" basis without extensive field investigation. Thus, abuse is much more likely than under the cash assistance programs, where case workers visit the home and conduct intensive investigations of income, assets, and needs. This is so at least to the extent that people can understate their incomes and/or their assets by not reporting those which are not too readily observable or can report the presence of fictitious or nonpresent family members.

One statement of the purposes of the food stamp program is as follows:

1. To help low-income families buy better foods and more foods, to have more satisfying and better balanced meals, to select the foods they want.
2. To increase business for food outlets in a city or county, and thus help other business too.[5]

This statement seeks to appeal politically to large groups, both those who want to help the poor and those who want to help agriculture and business. It, of course, ignores the taxpayer who must foot the bill for the program, which is financed from general revenues of the federal government.

The preamble of the Food Stamp Act of 1954 states these purposes somewhat differently: "To strengthen the agricultural economy; to help to achieve a fuller and more effective use of food abundances; to provide for improved levels of nutrition among low-income households through a cooperative Federal-State program of food assistance to be operated through normal channels of trade."

The net result of the food stamp program is, in actuality, quite different from the foregoing stated purposes. It seems reasonable to conclude that many participants under this program do not really purchase more food than they would otherwise have done. After all, food is a necessity for life, and, despite the grandiose stated purposes of the program resulting in better diets, it seems likely that the free coupons really are often only a substitute for money that would otherwise have been spent. It is possible, too, that either the coupons themselves or food bought with food stamps can be sold to other persons for cash, since there are no effective controls to prevent this. In some cases,

---

[5] From *Pamphlet No 16*, Social Services Administration, Maryland Department of Employment and Social Services, July 1973.

clearly, food stamps may help families purchase more food, and perhaps even better food, than would otherwise have been possible.

To the extent that the food stamps thus represent increased cash income to the recipients, the program is really a significant public assistance program that benefits low-income persons. To a very real extent, it has some of the characteristics of negative income tax proposals or guaranteed income plans, such as the supplemental security income program, to be discussed next. Proposals have been made to extend this general approach of indirectly giving cash to low-income persons, including the working poor, on a gradually phasing-out basis by having it also apply in the area of housing costs. Programs such as this can have a vast effect in the field of economic security, both the public and private sectors thereof.

Expenditures for "free" coupons have risen rapidly over recent years. They amounted to only $577 million in fiscal year 1970, but by 1974 they had increased to $2.8 billion and were continuing to rise. The estimated outgo for fiscal year 1975 is $3.8 billion, with 15 million recipients in a typical month and about 20 to 22 million different persons in the course of a year. It is estimated that only about half of those eligible actually participate. However, if all eligibles participated, the cost would by no means double, because those who do not participate undoubtedly would have to pay a larger proportion of the allotment than those now participating. In mid-1973, participants paid, on the average, for 45 percent of the total value of the food coupons received, and their payments represented about 23 percent of their net incomes as computed for purposes of this program.

SUPPLEMENTAL SECURITY INCOME PROGRAM

Public Law 92–603, enacted October 30, 1972, which also contained significant changes in the social insurance programs, resulted in the inauguration, in 1974, of an entirely new type of economic security program—namely, the supplemental security income program (SSI). On the surface, this new program appears to be only an equitable and logical revamping of the previous public assistance programs for the three adult categories (aged, blind, and disabled) and shifting the administration from the states to the federal government. However, SSI introduces a brand new philosophy, since it can quite properly be termed to be a guaranteed-annual-income plan for certain categories of the population, which some might argue should be extended to everybody. SSI could be classified as a demogrant program, rather than a social assistance one as are the other public assistance programs. The reason for this is that SSI is universally available, and the payments are mathematically determined essentially only on the basis of the individual's income.

Before going into detail as to what SSI is and how it may possibly develop and affect other public and private economic security programs, it is important to note that it results in more federal responsibilities and diminished state and local responsibilities. Although President Nixon supported the resulting increased federalization, this change is in contrast with his frequently stated philosophy of moving power down from the federal level to the state and local level.

The SSI program replaces the federal-state public assistance programs of aid to the aged, blind, and disabled, except in Guam, Puerto Rico, and the Virgin Islands. Instead, there will be a new, wholly federal plan for these cash-assistance programs. The social services for these adult categories will continue as federal-state programs, as will also the cash-assistance and social service programs for families with dependent children.

The definitions of what constitute disability and blindness, which were formerly at the discretion of each state, are standardized, so as to be the same as under OASDI. A savings clause applies to existing recipients when SSI begins for those who had previously qualified under public assistance with a less strict definition.

SSI initially provided a guaranteed minimum income for these adult categories of $140 per month for an individual and 50 percent more ($210) for a couple.[6] Beginning in July 1974, these amounts were increased to $146 and $219, as a result of legislation enacted in December 1973. There thus was some indication of congressional intent to keep SSI payments up to date with changes in the cost of living.

Legislation enacted in August 1974, which was initially proposed by President Nixon, introduced an automatic-adjustment provision into SSI very closely paralleling that used under OASDI. Specifically, whenever OASDI benefits are automatically adjusted for June of a given year (first possible for 1975), the SSI payment amounts will be increased by the same percentage, with the monthly amounts resulting being rounded to the next even 10 cents. However, unlike the situation

---

[6] Actually, the 1972 legislation provided for a basic amount of $130, but this was increased, before the program went into operation, to $140 by legislation in July 1973.

under OASDI, an ad hoc increase in the SSI payment amounts will not prevent the automatics for SSI from being operative.

As a result of these automatic-adjustment provisions, the SSI payment level rose by 8.0 percent to $157.70/$236.60 for June 1975. Just as in the case of OASDI, President Ford had recommended in January 1975 that this increase should be held to 5 percent, but Congress did not do so.

A so-called "essential person" in the family of an SSI recipient, who was recognized under a state program in December 1973 in the determination of need (typically, a spouse under age 65 of an SSI recipient over age 65), is also eligible for SSI (as a result of the legislation in July 1973).

A number of "income disregards" are contained in the program, none of which are subject to the foregoing automatic-adjustment provision. Perhaps the most important is the disregard of $20 per month per family of income from such sources as OASDI, railroad retirement, other pensions, earnings, and investments—in fact, any income except payments based on need. Since virtually the entire population aged 65 and over has some such nonneed-related income, this really meant a guaranteed monthly income of $160 for an individual and $230 for a couple in almost all cases initially, $166/$239 for June 1974 to May 1975, and about $178/$257 for June 1975 and after.

A special exception to this guaranteed-income feature is that individuals in an institution whose care is being paid by Medicaid are eligible under SSI for only $25 per month, less any other income that is countable. As a result, OASDI beneficiaries who are so institutionalized will not receive any SSI payment, because the OASDI benefit will always be large enough to eliminate it.

Another important income disregard is with respect to earned income. The first $65 per month is disregarded, plus 50 percent of the remainder of the earnings (actually, administered on a quarterly basis). Blind persons have a further disregard of income equal to the reasonable expenses of earning income and of the income necessary for the fulfillment of a plan for achieving self-support. Blind persons on the assistance roll at the beginning of the plan will receive certain additional income disregards, so that they will not be disadvantaged under SSI as compared with previous public assistance provisions. Also disregarded is nominal nonearned income received on an irregular basis (if at a rate of $20 or less per month).

In addition to the income disregards, SSI also has certain resource exemptions. In order to receive SSI, resources cannot exceed $1,500 for an individual and $2,250 for a couple. However, in determining resources, certain items are excluded—the home, household goods, personal effects, an automobile, and property needed for self-support, if these are found to be reasonable. Also, if life insurance policies have a face amount of $1,500 or less for an individual, their cash values are not counted as assets. A savings clause applies for current recipients under public assistance programs where the state had permitted higher resource limits.

States may pay supplements to SSI, with the federal government administering such payments if the state so desires, and then the federal government pays the administrative expenses—a great attraction to hand this responsibility over to the federal government. For persons on the public assistance rolls in December 1973, states *must* supplement SSI so that no decrease in payments will occur; if a state does not do so, then it will be cut off from federal Medicaid matching funds. The state is permitted to require a residence period for these supplementary payments. Texas is not affected by this mandatory requirement because its constitution prevents compliance; it does not have voluntary supplementary payments. Sixteen states, mostly southern ones, elected mandatory supplementation only.

A savings clause provides for federal payment of any excess of the costs of the state supplemental payments over what the state had been paying in 1972 as its share of the cost of the adult assistance programs if the same total payment level is maintained. In determining such total payment level to be maintained, an upward adjustment is included to reflect the effect of the elimination of food stamps for SSI recipients. The bonus value of such food stamps (generally, $10 per month per recipient) must also be included in the determination of whether the level of payments in December 1973 is being maintained.

As of the end of 1974, all but 17 states had signed agreements with the federal government to have it administer the mandatory state supplements at federal expense. These tend to be the largest states since they encompass over 80 percent of all persons who will receive state supplements. Of the 16 states with mandatory supplementary programs, all but three chose federal administration. For the states with both mandatory and optional supplementation, 16 (and the District of Columbia) chose federal administration of both programs, 14 chose state administration of both programs, and three chose federal administration of the mandatory supplementation and state administration of the optional supplementation.

In the initial 1972 legislation, SSI recipients were not to be eligible for food stamps. It was anticipated that in many states, the new SSI payment level would exceed the former public assistance level plus the bonus value of the food stamps. In the other states where this would not be the case, it was hoped that the loss of the food stamps would be compensated by state supplements, as described later. As an incentive for states to take such action, the bonus value of the food stamps would be included in determining the federal payments toward the cost of the supplements.

In the actual experience, only five states (California, Massachusetts, Nevada, New York, and Wisconsin) have "cashed out" or replaced the food stamps by increased supplements. Accordingly, the December 31, 1973, amendments to the Social Security Act (containing the 7 and 11 percent OASDI benefit increases) also provided for a delay of six months, until July 1974, in instituting this elimination of food stamps in the other states. Legislation in July 1974 extended this deadline until July 1975.

In the past, states have been required to cover all cash assistance recipients under Medicaid. They will not be required to so cover newly eligible SSI recipients.

The SSI program clearly has certain attractive and desirable features. SSI will provide desirable equitable treatment of adult public assistance recipients in the few states where payments previously were clearly inadequate. The Social Security Administration will administer SSI, with certain safeguards to keep it separate from the OASDI system. The result should be a reduction in administrative expenses, particularly since much of the investigation of individual income, resources, and needs will not be necessary as before. SSI will eliminate much of the stigma that is now attached to receiving public assistance. This may be considered either good or bad, depending upon one's philosophy. Certainly too much stigma is undesirable, but nonetheless it does seem best if individuals take more pride in receiving benefits based on their own direct efforts than on means-test payments.

Significantly, in making the adult public assistance programs more equitable and adequate, SSI was estimated to almost double the number of persons on the roll—from 3.2 million to 6.2 million (the latter figure being exclusive of about 500,000 institutionalized persons who are eligible for at most $25 a month and 125,000 "essential persons" whose presence results in an increase in the SSI payment). The additional cost for SSI as compared with the previous program was estimated at $2.0 billion a year at the $140/$210 payment rates, a 77 percent increase.

One thing that may result from SSI is that individuals will often dispose of their excess income and assets in order to qualify for SSI, since these will really not be doing them any good. For example, if an aged individual has $4,000 in a savings account producing $15 of monthly income, and if he has an OASDI benefit of $100, he will not be eligible for SSI, even though his monthly income is less than $158. Such a person can become eligible for SSI, however, by spending or giving away $2,500 of his bank account, and therefore satisfying the maximum asset requirement for eligibility—assuming no other non-qualified resources. Thus, SSI can have a serious effect on private savings for persons at the lower and middle economic levels.

Persons with moderate or low OASDI benefits—say, $160 per month or less (the average benefit for a single person aged 65 or over is about $195)—and no other income might well wonder whether it was worthwhile being covered by social security (and paying its taxes) when this produces extra income of at most only $20 per month over what SSI would have paid anyhow. As a result, many low-income workers—such as domestic employees, migrant farm workers, and subsistence farmers—might wish to avoid coverage (which is not too difficult to do).

On the other hand, it can be said that one of the good features of SSI is that economic-security protection will be provided in all cases for low-income workers. Many such workers are not now covered by OASDI in all their employment, and therefore qualify for a relatively low benefit. SSI will increase the level of income for these individuals.

The real danger of SSI lies in what it could potentially do if its benefit level were substantially increased. One excellent control on the reasonableness of the level of OASDI benefits over the past has been that this program is fully financed by the contributions (i.e., taxes) of workers and employers. As a result, any proposals to increase the benefit level must carry with them concommitant increases in payroll taxes. Under SSI, however, with its general-revenues financing, proposals can easily (and painlessly) be made to raise what some would consider its "grossly inadequate" level. For example, it might be difficult for Congress to vote down a proposal to raise SSI payments to, say, $300 per month for an individual and $450 for a couple. If this were done, and if only a $20 OASDI disregard were continued, the vast majority of prospective OASDI beneficiaries would see little reason for the continuance of OASDI with its heavy payroll taxes. They would argue that SSI by itself would do almost as well and would apparently be "paid for by somebody else."

Only the future will tell what the new SSI program will do. Will it only result in desirable equity and adequacy in dealing with the low-income aged, blind, and disabled? Or will it be a sleeping giant which, when aroused, will produce undesirable results by destroying or diminishing both the OASDI program and private economic-security measures?

At the end of 1974, Secretary of Health, Education, and Welfare Caspar W. Weinberger submitted a proposal for a negative income tax to President Ford. Although the details of the plan were not made public, it was supposed to be of such a magnitude that it would replace all existing welfare and public assistance programs. Cash grants would be payable not only to those now receiving assistance, but also to the so-called working poor, whether or not children are present (as is required under the FAP proposal). President Ford rejected this proposal as being too costly at the present time, when there are such serious economic problems facing the nation.

FINANCING OF STATE PUBLIC ASSISTANCE PROGRAMS

The federal government originally participated in the financing of the payments to recipients on a 50–50 basis up to a specified maximum on individual payments for old-age assistance and aid to the blind, and on a lower basis for aid to dependent children. Over the years the federal matching proportion has risen, as also has the individual matchable maximum, which was changed in 1958 to a maximum on the overall average payment. Also in 1958, the principle was introduced of varying part of the grant, depending upon the average per capita income of the state; 50–50 matching continued to apply to three jurisdictions of the United States included in the program (Guam, Puerto Rico, and the Virgin Islands), with further limitations on the total dollar amounts of federal grants in a year.

The federal matching proportion is defined as the percentage or percentages prescribed by law that are applied to the total *matchable* assistance payments. Under the basis of individual matchable maximums that originally applied, any payments made to individuals in excess of prescribed dollar amounts were excluded from the total *matchable* assistance payments to which the federal matching proportion applied. For example, under old-age assistance, initially the federal matching proportion was 50 percent, and the individual matchable maximum was $30 per month. The federal grant to be paid for a month was obtained by multiplying 50 percent by the total assistance payments, excluding any amounts paid to individuals in excess of $30.

After 1958, the matchable portion of the total assistance payments under the cash-assistance programs was based on the overall average payment, which is, of course, a more liberal procedure insofar as the states are concerned. For example, for the old-age assistance program under the 1958 Act, the *matchable* assistance payments were the total payments if the statewide average payment was $65 or less (regardless of the fact that some individuals might have had a payment of more than $65), or $65 times the number of recipients if the statewide average was more than $65.

In 1960, additional federal financing was provided for medical care given to old-age assistance recipients through vendor payments made directly to the suppliers of medical care. For example, in 1964 the basis was as follows: (1) for states with average total grants (cash and medical vendor) *above* the maximum matchable under the regular formula, there was variable-grant matching on the smallest of (*a*) the excess of the average total grant over the maximum matchable, (*b*) the average medical vendor payment, or (*c*) $15; and (2) for states with average total grants *below* the maximum matchable, there was an extra 15 percent, from federal funds, on the first $15 of average medical vendor payment. If the latter method produced a more favorable result for a state with average total grant *above* the maximum matchable, it was used.

As a result of the 1962 amendments, similar additional federal financing for medical vendor payments was available for the aid to the blind and aid to the permanently and totally disabled programs if the state combined them with the old-age assistance program into a unified one.

Such combining could also be advantageous in that the average payment for matching purposes was determined for all three programs combined so that under some circumstances, more of the total payments will be matchable for federal funds. For example, if a state's average payment for aid to the blind was in excess of $70, not all of it was matchable. But if the programs were combined, lower average payments for OAA and APTD might have brought down the overall average to $70 or less, so that all payments under all programs were matchable. At the beginning of 1973, a total of 19 states had made such a combination of programs.

The federal share of the administrative cost of the public assistance program is 50 percent, except that the matching proportion is 75 percent in respect to social services that will help recipients achieve greater self-support and family stability (90 percent for family planning services). The federal share is 75 percent for compensation of professional medical personnel, 90 percent for the cost of designing, developing, and installing mechanized claims processing and information retrieval systems (75 percent for the cost of their subsequent operation), and 100 percent of the survey and inspection costs of skilled nursing facilities and intermediate care facilities.

The development of the federal financing basis for cash payments under the state public assistance programs is summarized in Table 11.1. The federal matching ratios under the current variable-grant procedure are explained by the following formula, where P is the federal grant percentage applicable to the upper portion of the average payment in the state (i.e., above $18 for the aid to families with dependent children program), and N and S are the national and state per capita incomes:

$$P = 100 - 50 \cdot \frac{S^2}{N^2} \quad \text{and} \quad 50 \le P \le 65$$

except that for medical vendor payments for medical assistance the formula is:

$$P = 100 - 45 \cdot \frac{S^2}{N^2} \quad \text{and} \quad 50 \le P \le 83$$

Thus, the federal matching ratio for a state with the same average per capita income as for the nation as a whole is 50 percent for the variable-grant portion of the cash-payment programs and 55 percent for Medicaid. For most above-average income states, the 50 percent minimum applies for Medicaid, and only the lowest income state is affected by the 83 percent maximum. In November 1974, President Ford proposed that in order to reduce federal spending, the 50 percent minimum should be reduced to 40 percent.

TABLE 11.1

Maximum Matchable Amounts and Federal Matching Proportions for Cash Payments under Public Assistance under Various Laws*

Law	Maximum Matchable Individual Payment†	Federal Matching Proportion‡
Old-Age Assistance, Aid to Blind, and Aid to Disabled§		
1935 Act	$30	½
1939 Act	40	½
1946 Act	45	⅔ of first $15 + ½ of remainder
1948 and 1950 Acts	50	¾ of first $20 + ½ of remainder
1952 and 1954 Acts	55	⅘ of first $25 + ½ of remainder
1956 Act	60	⅘ of first $30 + ½ of remainder‖
1958 Act	None	⅘ of first $30 + variable grant (ranging between 50 percent and 65 percent) on next $35
1960 Act	None	Same as 1958 Act, plus, for OAA only, an additional amount on first $12 of average medical vendor payment (see text)
1961 Act	None	Maximum for average medical vendor payment raised to $15, and first bracket of formula extended to $31
1962 Act	None	29/35 of first $35 + variable grant (ranging between 50 percent and 65 percent) on next $35
1965 Act#	None	31/37 of first $37 + variable grant (ranging between 50 percent and 65 percent) on next $38
Aid to Families with Dependent Children		
1935 Act	$18 and $12	⅓
1939 Act	18 and 12	½
1946 Act	24 and 15	⅔ of first $9 + ½ of remainder
1948 and 1950 Acts	27 and 18	¾ of first $12 + ½ of remainder
1952 and 1954 Acts	30 and 21	⅘ of first $15 + ½ of remainder
1956 Act	32 and 23	14/17 of first $17 + ½ of remainder‖
1958 Act	None	14/17 of first $17 + variable grant (ranging between 50 percent and 65 percent) on next $13
1965 Act#	None	⅚ of first $18 + variable grant (ranging between 50 percent and 65 percent) on next $14

* Not applicable to Puerto Rico and the Virgin Islands (included for the first time in the 1950 Act), and Guam (included for the first time in the 1958 Act), for which jurisdictions there is 50–50 matching, within certain dollar limits.

† Per month. For aid to families with dependent children, first figure is applicable to first child (and beginning with 1950 Act, to one adult in the family and with 1962 Act, to two such adults), while second figure is applicable to all other children.

‡ Dollar figures relate to average matchable payment (for AFDC, averaged over all child recipients for 1946 and 1948 Acts, and overall child and adult caretaker recipients for later acts).

§ Aid to permanently and totally disabled was introduced in the 1950 Act. All these programs were discontinued, for the 50 states and D.C., when the SSI program went into effect in 1974.

‖ Also, federal matching was made available for medical vendor payments up to a maximum of $6 for adults and $3 for children (averaged overall recipients). This provision was eliminated in 1958.

In lieu of these formulas, the state can elect to have unified matching for all the cash-payment programs and Medicaid combined (see text).

Some examples of how the regular federal matching formulas work out for illustrative cases may be helpful. First, consider the variable-grant factor P. If a state has the same per capita income as the national average (i.e., $S = N$), P will be 50 percent. Similarly, if the average per capita income of the state is higher than the national average, then P will also be 50 percent because of the minimum provision. On the other hand, if a state has a per capita income that is 80 percent of the national average, then P will be reduced to 65 percent because of the maximum provision, since the formula produces 68 percent ($100 - 50 \times 0.64$).

The matching formulas for the cash payments have been, over the year, of a weighted nature. States with low average payments receive a relatively larger federal matching ratio than do states with high average payments. Generally, but not always, the size of the average payment is correlated with the per capita income in the state, so that the poorer states tend to be given relatively larger federal financial participation. Thus, under the present formula for the AFDC category, if the average monthly payment is $18 or less, the federal financial share is 83.3 percent of the total cost. As the average payment increases beyond $18, this proportion decreases, more for high-income states than for low ones. For example, for a state with an average payment of $32 (the highest on which full federal matching occurs), the federal share is 68.7 percent for above-average-income states and 75.3 percent for the lowest income states (those with per capita income of less than 83.3 percent of the national average).

From the time of the beginning of the MAA program until 1970, the federal matching basis for vendor medical payments generally was on a more liberal basis than for the cash-assistance payments. In some instances, the matching basis was very complicated so as to assure that all states would be treated as favorably (or more favorably, generally) as if the vendor medical payments had, instead, been cash payments.

As an alternative to the federal matching basis for the cash-payment assistance programs (OAA, AB, APTD, and AFDC) shown under the "1965 Act" sections of Table 11.1, a state could have chosen to have the federal financing apply on a unified basis to all payments to recipients combined (i.e., both cash and Medicaid). Under these circumstances, the generally more liberal formula for vendor medical payments is applied to the total payments. This unified basis was used by more than 30 states in 1973, the ones that had the larger average payments and generally higher-than-average per capita incomes. It may still be used for the combination of AFDC and Medicaid.

The alternative unified basis was advantageous to such states because the maximum on the average payment above which no federal matching occurs was not applicable and because the matching ratio under the regular formula was only 50 percent in the second step. For example, considering only the AFDC category, for a state with above-average per capita income, the aggregate federal matching ratio under the regular basis is 68.7 percent if the average grant is $32 and only 50 percent if such average grant is $44 and 40 percent if it is $55 (since no federal matching applies beyond the $32 point). On the other hand, under the alternative unified basis, the federal matching ratio would always be 50 percent for the highest income states (and 55 percent even for a state with a per capita income equal to the national average).

Under the federal matching formula for cash payments, as it applies for the period from July 1973 through June 1975, 15 of the 51 jurisdictions (the 50 states and the District of Columbia) have a federal matching proportion of 50 percent (as, by law, do Guam, Puerto Rico, and the Virgin Islands), while 15 have the maximum proportion of 65 percent, leaving only 21 falling between 50 and 65 percent. It should be noted, however, that many states do not use this formula for their matching for cash assistance, but instead use the Medicaid formula. Similarly, under the federal matching formula for medical vendor payments (and for the unified-program basis described previously), 13 states have the minimum proportion of 50 percent, and no state has the maximum proportion of 83 percent (the highest proportion being 80.55 percent for Mississippi, which in previous years had been at the 83 percent level).

PROPOSAL FOR FAMILY ASSISTANCE PLAN

For a number of years, there has been considerable public dissatisfaction with the aid to families with dependent children program. The criticisms came from all sides of the spectrum of political views.

Conservatives criticized the ever-growing recipient roll and the large costs. They asserted that many persons avoided work and had many children in order to receive public assistance, which became a way of life for them.

Liberals, on the other hand, criticized the program as not being at a high enough level. Thereby, the children involved were penalized since they would not be properly cared for and educated and would thus continue in the vicious circle of poverty and relief.

Still others criticized AFDC because it was inequitable to the so-called "working poor," who could frequently have a lower total income by working than if their family were on welfare. In other words, some people asserted that fathers would often do better economically for their families by deserting the home and thus make the mother and children eligible for AFDC.

In an attempt to solve this very serious problem, President Nixon in 1969 proposed an entirely new, unique approach, the so-called family assistance plan (FAP). This program, just as SSI, can be categorized as a demogrant plan. It can also properly be called a guaranteed-income plan, although its sponsors vigorously denied this.

The FAP would eliminate AFDC and instead would provide a basic payment to families with children amounting to $500 per year for each of the first two members, plus $300 per year for each additional member. Thus, for a family of four the basic annual payment would be $1,600. In order to be eligible, the family could not have more than $1,500 in resources, not counting the home, household goods, and personal effects.

The FAP payment would be reduced on a dollar-for-dollar basis for all income, with certain exceptions. The most important exceptions were 50 percent of unearned income (including OASDI survivor benefits) and the first $720 of annual earned income, plus 50 percent of the remainder of earned income. Other exceptions included earnings of a student, inconsequential or irregular income, income offsetting child care costs while training or working, public assistance or private charity, and the value of food stamps, which represent a significant net benefit because they are sold to eligible low-income persons at only a fraction of their store value.

The earned-income exclusion, of course, was intended to encourage individuals receiving FAP to become employed and hopefully to increase their earning capacity so as to go off the roll. At least, it would provide more equitable treatment for the working poor.

The Committee on Ways and Means of the House of Representatives approved FAP in principle in 1970, although making several significant changes. Perhaps the most important of these changes was the elimination of the exclusion from countable income against the FAP payment of 50 percent of unearned income. Specifically, this would mean that OASDI survivor benefits would be fully deductible from

FAP payments. Also a number of changes were made that would tighten up the program and encourage training and employment of FAP recipients. A detailed account of this version of FAP and the arguments in favor of it can be found in the committee report on the bill.[7]

The House of Representatives passed this bill in 1970. The Senate Committee on Finance, however, was unenthusiastic about FAP, and the legislation died with the end of the 91st Congress in 1970.

In 1971 the Nixon administration urged the enactment of FAP. The House Committee on Ways and Means approved the proposal with certain modifications. Several different provisions were contained in the 1971 version as compared with the original one. First, the program was divided into two parts. In families with at least one employable person, the program would be called "Opportunities for Families" and would be administered by the Department of Labor. For families with no employable person, the program would be termed "Family Assistance" and would be administered by the Department of Health, Education, and Welfare. Considerable emphasis would be placed on training and registration for employment among the former group, but both groups would receive cash payments under the same conditions.

The eligibility conditions and the payment amounts under the 1971 version did not differ greatly in effect from those in the 1970 version adopted by the House of Representatives. One difference was that the payments were at the rate of $800 per year for each of the first two family members, $400 for each of the next three members, $300 for the next two members, and $200 for the 8th member, and no benefit for additional members. This produced a payment of $2,400 per year for a family of four and a maximum payment for a family of eight or more of $3,600 per year. At first glance, it would seem that the 1971 proposal was at a considerably higher level than the 1970 one. But the apparent increase was largely offset by the fact that the families under this program could no longer receive food stamps.

The other important difference was that the proportion of earnings in excess of $720 per year that was not countable as a reduction against the payment under the program was reduced from 50 percent thereof to 33⅓ percent. Further details and arguments in favor of

---

[7] House Report No. 91–904, "Report on H.R. 16311, The Family Assistance Act of 1970," March 11, 1970.

this proposal are contained in the committee report on the legislation.[8]

Once again, the House of Representatives passed the proposal, but the Senate Committee on Finance did not react favorably. Instead, during the remainder of 1971 and most of 1972, this committee developed a substitute proposal which it termed "Guaranteed Job Opportunity for Families" (which was more popularly known as "workfare"). The emphasis of this program would be to provide jobs, under a new agency, the Governmental Work Administration, for those able to work—at a rate of pay of $1.50 an hour for a maximum of 32 hours a week. Also provided would be wage supplements for persons employed in private industry at wages of $1.50 to $2 per hour and a work bonus equal to 10 percent of wages covered under OASDI up to a maximum bonus of $400 a year (with reductions in the bonus as the annual family income rises above $4,000). This so-called work bonus, which can be viewed as a negative income tax or even a refund of virtually the entire employer-employee OASDI and HI taxes, was included for a 1-year "temporary" period in tax-reduction legislation enacted in April 1974 (but applicable to *all* earned income, not merely OASDI earnings).

AFDC would continue to be available under the Senate Committee on Finance proposal for families where there was no person deemed able to work (essentially families headed by a mother with a child under age 6). Further details of this proposal and arguments in favor of it, and against the provisions in the House bill, are contained in the committee report on the legislation.[9] When the legislation came to the floor of the Senate, no agreement could be reached on either the House version or the Finance Committee version of the proposal, and the entire subject was dropped.

One reason that no agreement or compromise could be obtained was the lateness in the session. But far more important were the philosophical differences. Many liberals were opposed because they thought that the payment level was far too low, with some supporters of the general idea urging payments of $6,500 a year for a family of four, instead of the $2,400 in the bill. On the other hand, conservatives

---

[8] House Report No. 92-231, "Report on H.R. 1, to Amend the Social Security Act to Replace the Existing Federal-State Public Assistance Programs with a Federal Program of Adult Assistance and a Federal Program of Benefits to Low-Income Families with Children with Incentives and Requirements for Employment and Training to Improve the Capacity for Employment of Members of Such Families," May 26, 1971.

[9] Senate Report No. 92-1230, "Report on H.R. 1," September 26, 1972.

opposed the plan because of its cost (and the likely much higher costs as the payment level was subject to upward pressures politically) and because it "would solve the problem of the burgeoning AFDC relief rolls by doubling them, from about 10 million persons to 19 million." It was also claimed by some that the Nixon administration no longer was enthusiastic about the proposal and accordingly did not exert significant efforts for a compromise to be reached.

As a result of these fruitless and exhausting efforts to enact FAP legislation in 1969–72, many of its supporters lost enthusiasm. Thereafter, neither the Nixon administration nor any members of Congress made significant proposals in this area subsequent to 1972.

APPENDIX

Cost Estimates and Operational Data for Public Assistance Programs

COST ESTIMATES FOR PUBLIC ASSISTANCE PROGRAMS

In most instances, cost estimates for the various public assistance programs are made only on a very short-range basis, such as for the first full year of future operations. Such estimates are merely a simple statistical (usually linear) projection of past trends, but take into account any legislative changes affecting numbers of persons eligible and amount of individual payments. One of the complex problems frequently involved is the matter of cost estimates for each of the separate states and jurisdictions, especially determining the effect of an increase in the federal financial sharing, thus making a judgment as to whether additional federal money will cause the state to (1) withdraw some of its own money, (2) maintain its own appropriations, or (3) put up additional funds so as to take advantage of any federal "bargains."

At certain times, long-range cost estimates for the old-age assistance programs have been made, since it is particularly subject to long-range trends that can be estimated—such as the growth in the total aged population and the increasing role of OASDI. In fact, before the enactment of the Social Security Act, long-range projections of OAA costs were made under the alternative hypotheses of whether or not there would be an old-age benefit program under contributory social insurance.

Long-range cost estimates for OAA have been made on a rather rough estimating basis that is largely based on population projections, OASDI beneficiary projections, and dependency assumptions (along with the assumption that average payments will remain level). Thus, in essence, the total aged population is subdivided into two groups, those eligible for OASDI and the remainder. Then, separate dependency ratios are applied to each group; these ratios are based on actual experience (including analysis for the non-OASDI group of those with other income, such as government employee pensions and veterans' pensions) and on judgment of future trends in these factors.

Cost estimates for the new supplementary security income program have also been made on only a very short-range basis. The data utilized have been from census studies and from the past operations of the adult categories of the public assistance program and of OASDI. A major problem in the cost estimating is the extent to which people will adjust or manipulate their incomes and assets in order to qualify for SSI. Another such problem is the extent of nonfiling by persons eligible for SSI (particularly those eligible for relatively small residual payments).

EXPERIENCE DATA FOR PUBLIC ASSISTANCE PROGRAMS

Actual Operational Data for State Programs

Table 11.2 shows, for selected years from 1936 to 1974, the number of recipients under each of the four federal-state cash public assistance programs and under SSI, the average and total payments to recipients. The data in this section were obtained from various publications of the

TABLE 11.2

Number of Recipients and Payments to Recipients under
Federal-State Cash Public Assistance Programs, 1936–73

Number of Recipients, December (in thousands)

Year	OAA*	AFDC* Children	AFDC* Adults	AB*	APTD*	Total
1936..............	1,108	404	142	45	†	1,699
1940..............	2,070	895	327	73	†	3,365
1945..............	2,056	701	242	71	†	3,070
1950..............	2,786	1,661	572	97	69	5,185
1955..............	2,538	1,661	531	104	241	5,075
1960..............	2,305	2,370	703	107	369	5,854
1965..............	2,087	3,316	1,080	85	557	7,125
1970..............	2,082	7,033	2,626	81	935	12,757
1971..............	2,024	7,707	2,946	80	1,068	13,825
1972..............	1,934	7,984	3,081	80	1,168	14,246
1973..............	1,820	7,812	3,002	78	1,275	13,987
1974#.............	2,477	7,884	3,120	80	1,736	15,297

Total Payments to Recipients (in millions)

Year	OAA	AFDC‡	AB	APTD	Total
1936..............	$ 156	$ 50	$ 13	†	$ 219
1940..............	473	133	22	†	628
1945..............	726	149	27	†	902
1950..............	1,454	547	53	$ 8	2,062
1955..............	1,488	612	68	135	2,303
1960..............	1,626	994	86	236	2,942
1965..............	1,594	1,644	77	417	3,732
1970..............	1,866	4,857	97	976	7,796
1971..............	1,920	6,230	101	1,185	9,436
1972..............	1,894	7,020	105	1,393	10,412
1973..............	1,743	7,212	104	1,610	10,669
1974#.............	2,525	7,917	131	2,624	13,197

Average Payments to Recipients, December

Year	OAA	AFDC§	AB	APTD
1936..............	$18.50	$ 29.85	$ 26.10	†
1940..............	20.25	32.40	25.35	†
1945..............	30.90	52.05	33.50	†
1950..............	43.05	71.45	46.00	$ 44.10
1955..............	50.05	85.50	55.55	48.75
1960..............	58.90	108.35	67.45	56.15
1965..............	63.10	136.95	81.35	66.50
1970..............	77.65	187.95	104.35	97.65
1971..............	77.50	190.90	106.50	102.25
1972..............	80.00	191.20	112.85	106.10
1973..............	76.15	195.20	112.00	109.75
1974#.............	86.75	217.55	136.10	142.00

* OAA: old-age assistance; AFDC: aid to families with dependent children; AB: aid to the blind; APTD: aid to the permanently and totally disabled.
† Program not in operation.
‡ Amounts include emergency assistance payments.
§ Amounts are average payment per family.
# For 1974, the data shown for OAA, AB, and APTD are for the federal SSI program and for state supplementation under both federally-administered and state-administered programs (for the latter, data are not included for a few states that did not report).

Social Security Administration and the Social and Rehabilitation Service, Department of Health, Education, and Welfare.

The number of old-age assistance recipients rose rapidly from 1937 to 1940 and then remained more or less level during World War II. After that, there was a further rise, until a peak was reached in 1950. Since then, there has been a gradual decline as the effect of the OASDI program became more significant.

The number of recipients under aid to families with dependent children increased significantly over the years as the nature of the program was broadened. The growth since 1965 has been especially notable, an increase of about 140 percent in the number of children on the roll, although there was a leveling-off in 1971–74. This trend occurred largely because of the increased national emphasis and concern over poverty and the growing awareness of low-income persons about how they could utilize the program.

During the more than two decades of operation of aid to the permanently and totally disabled, the number of recipients rose steadily and did not level off, despite the effect of the disability benefits under the OASDI program. The number of recipients of aid to the blind increased to somewhat more than 100,000 in 1955–60, but since then it fell off to a level of about 80,000 in recent years. In the late 1930s, about 40 percent of the child recipients of AFDC (approximately 350,000) were on the roll because of death of the father, while in 25 percent of the cases the father was incapacitated and in 35 percent he was absent from the home. In 1973, only 4 percent (or 307,000 which is slightly below the level of the 1930s) were death cases, 10 percent were incapacity cases, 81 percent were "absence" cases, 4 percent were in the new "unemployment" category, and the remaining 1 percent were stepfather or motherless cases.

In the early days of the public assistance program, the bulk of the recipients were OAA ones, but in 1974 AFDC recipients represented about 75 percent of the total. This changed distribution has caused much public dissatisfaction with the welfare programs.

The total payments to recipients under the various programs have, in general, increased steadily over the years—due to the rising recipient roll under most programs, the rising general price level, and the broader scope of the programs. The total payments increased from about $200 million in 1936 to $13.2 billion in 1974. About 60 percent of the 1974 payments were under AFDC, with 19 percent under OAA, 20 percent under APTD, and 1 percent under AB. In 1936, OAA was

71 percent, and AFDC was 23 percent. The 1974 proportions for OAA and APTD were somewhat higher than in 1973, as a result of the new SSI program, which made payments to more persons and at a higher level. Correspondingly, the AFDC proportion fell from 68 percent in 1973 to 60 percent in 1974.

The average payment per recipient has risen significantly over the years under all programs. In part, this trend has reflected changes in the cost of living; but in part, it is due to increasing adequacy of the assistance payments. Between 1936 and 1973, the average payment quadrupled under OAA and AB, and rose sixfold under AFDC. At the end of 1973, the average monthly payment under OAA was $76, while the average payment per family under AFDC was $195 (representing, however, an average of $57 per recipient). The average monthly payments under the APTD and AB programs were considerably higher than for OAA—namely, $110 and $112, respectively, at the end of 1973—primarily because relatively more in the latter program received OASDI, and then the public assistance payment was only a supplementary one.

Payments under the program for emergency assistance to needy families with children increased from $2 million in its first year of operation, 1968, to $64 million in 1974. In December 1974, about 32,000 families were given such assistance, averaging $179 per family.

Table 11.3 presents data on medical vendor payments under state plans where federal matching is provided. Only total payments data are shown, since numbers of cases and average payments are not too meaningful. Total payments have risen meteorically, from virtually nothing in 1951 (although then and previously, some amounts for medical care were included in the cash payments) to $11.5 billion in 1974. Part of this increase was due to rapidly escalating medical care prices, but most was due to increased scope of services made available and greater utilization of services.

The federal share of the cost of payments under the public assistance programs is shown in Table 11.4 for various selected past years. It was somewhat less than 50 percent in the early years of operation, which was in part due to the effect of nonmatchable payments (with respect to individual payments in excess of the prescribed individual matchable maximums) and in part due to the relatively low matching ratio then for AFDC.

The federal share of OAA rose over the years as the matching formula was liberalized and, in recent periods, has been as high as 65

TABLE 11.3

Medical Vendor Payments under Federal-State Public
Assistance Programs, 1951–74 (in millions)

Year	Medical Assistance*	Medical Assistance for the Aged	Other†	Total
1951	—	—	$ 57	$ 57
1955	—	—	163	163
1960	—	$ 5	415	420
1965	—	586	774	1,360
1966	$1,194	293	436	1,923
1967	2,511	64	232	2,807
1968	3,792	65	172	4,029
1969	4,584	59	178	4,821
1970	5,923	—	—	5,923
1971	7,481	—	—	7,481
1972	8,708	—	—	8,708
1973	9,707	—	—	9,707
1974	11,501	—	—	11,501

* Includes payments to intermediate-care facilities (which payments before 1972 were counted as cash payments, but are included in this category for all years).
† Medical vendor payments with respect to recipients under the cash-assistance programs; first applicable for October 1950.

TABLE 11.4

Proportion of Cost of Public Assistance Payments under
Federal-State Programs Met by Federal Government, 1937–73

Fiscal Year*	Program†					
	OAA	AFDC	AB	APTD	MA	Total
1937	48.8%	20.5%	31.1%	—	—	42.8%
1940	49.0	32.7	27.4	—	—	44.9
1945	47.8	35.0	36.9	—	—	45.4
1950	54.9	43.7	43.0	—	—	51.7
1955	55.7	57.4	49.3	50.4%	—	55.6
1960	58.7	59.8	49.1	56.5	—	58.6
1965	64.8	55.5	47.4	56.0	51.8%	58.8
1970	64.6	53.6	57.5	54.9	50.9	54.5
1971	62.3	53.2	57.4	55.7	52.4	54.2
1972	62.2	53.8	57.2	54.0	51.2	53.5
1973	63.2	55.2	59.0	56.6	54.9	55.9

* Twelve-month period ending June 30 of year shown.
† OAA: old-age assistance; AFDC: aid to families with dependent children; AB: aid to the blind; APTD: aid to the permanently and totally disabled; MA: medical assistance (includes medical assistance for the aged before 1971 and payments to intermediate-care facilities for 1969 and after).

percent (although lower in 1971–73, 62 percent, since many states have shifted over to the Medicaid formula, which has lower federal matching percentages—but this is more than offset by then not having a dollar-average matching limit). The same general trend was present for the other two adult categories, although the federal ratios were somewhat lower, due to the use of the Medicaid formula by many states or else due to the generally higher payment level (so that there were relatively more nonmatchable amounts where the statewide average was in excess of the overall average matchable payment as prescribed in federal law).

The federal matching proportion was relatively low for Medicaid (and its predecessor, MAA) before 1973, because the higher income states participated most heavily then, and they had only 50 percent ratios. For example, even in fiscal year 1973, 62 percent of the total payments under the program were concentrated in California, Illinois, Massachusetts, Michigan, New York, Pennsylvania, and Texas (38 percent in California and New York alone). Then, in fiscal year 1973, the overall federal matching proportion increased significantly (from 51.2 percent to 54.9 percent) as lower income states increased their participation.

Total payments to recipients under the new SSI program, plus those under the state supplements, amounted to $5,280 million in 1974. Of this amount, $3,857 million was paid by the federal government for SSI, $1,285 million was paid through the SSI system for federally administered state supplements, and $138 million was paid in state supplements through state-administered plans. Thus, the federal cost was 73 percent of the grand total, or well above the 60 percent for the three adult categories combined for 1973.

In addition to the various federal-state programs of public assistance, all states have general assistance programs that are financed wholly by state and/or local funds. These plans provide assistance for cases that do not fall within the federal-state categorical assistance programs, but they vary widely as to scope and adequacy. The number of cases under general assistance was as high as 1½ million in the late 1930s, but decreased rapidly during World War II and since then has generally fluctuated between 300,000 and 500,000. The total annual payments under general assistance (including medical vendor payments) were close to $500 million in the late 1930s, then fell to about $100 million in the middle 1940s, rose to about $450 million in 1959–61, then fell to about $350 million in 1966, and subsequently rose until in 1974 they were about $930 million. At the end of 1974, the average cash payment per case was $140 per month, representing $96 per recipient. At that time, there were 586,000 cases on the roll, involving 855,000 recipients.

Estimated and Actual Operational Data for SSI

The SSI program will result in drastically different experience than prevailed under the three adult public assistance programs which it replaces. Many persons not previously receiving public assistance will be eligible for SSI. On the other hand, some persons previously receiving public assistance under the three adult programs will not be eligible for SSI, but they will continue to receive public assistance under supplementary state plans that have standards higher than SSI.

About 6.2 million persons were originally estimated to be eligible for either SSI (whether with or without a state supplementary payment) or a supplementary state plan alone.[10] This represented a 94 percent increase over the estimated number of persons receiving adult public assistance just before SSI went into effect (3.2 million). Not included in the 6.2 million figure were about 125,000 "essential persons" (mostly spouses under age 65 of recipients aged 65 or over) with respect to whom the SSI payment to the eligible recipient is increased and 500,000 institutionalized persons for whom a payment of at most $25 a month is available.

Considering only those aged 65 and over, it was estimated that 4.9 million persons (or 23 percent of the population aged 65 and over in the 50 states and the District of Columbia) would be eligible in January 1974 for SSI or a state supplementary payment. Of these 4.9 million persons, 1.6 million would be eligible for only SSI, 2.2 million for both SSI and a state supplement, and 1.1 million for only a state supplement. The proportions of those receiving assistance who would also be receiving OASDI benefits were estimated as follows:

Category	Proportion
Total recipients	77%
SSI recipients	71
SSI only	72
Both SSI and state supplement	71
State supplement only	96

---

[10] Estimates in this section are based on data from "Supplemental Security Income: The Aged Eligible," by Thomas G. Staples, *Social Security Bulletin*, Vol. 36, No. 7 (July 1973), as modified by the author to reflect the effect of the amendments enacted in July 1973.

The fact that virtually all "state supplement only" cases are also OASDI beneficiaries is explained by the fact that these cases are where the countable income (nearly always inclusive of OASDI) is above the SSI standard.

The estimated 3.8 million persons eligible for SSI, whether with or without a state supplement include 2.7 million, or 71 percent, who are OASDI beneficiaries, and these represent about 14 percent of total OASDI beneficiaries aged 65 or over.

The foregoing SSI estimates allow neither for any eligibles not claiming benefits nor for persons "adjusting" their income or assets so as to become eligible for benefits. For this reason, the estimates may be too high in the early months of operation, but too low subsequently.

The actual experience in 1974 was very much lower than the initial estimates. At year-end, the total recipients receiving either SSI or a supplementary state payment only amounted to 4.3 million—2.5 million aged 65 or over, 80,000 blind, and 1.7 million disabled. Included are those receiving supplementary state payments but not SSI under state-administered plans; such plans are in only 17 states, which have only an estimated 20 percent of those receiving state supplementation.

As compared with the last month that the state OAA plans operated (December 1973), the number of both aged and disabled recipients receiving SSI or state supplementation increased about 36 percent in the first year of SSI, while the blind category remained at about the same level (see Table 11.5). Total payments rose from an annual rate of $3.46 billion in 1973 to $5.28 billion in 1974, or by 53 percent. Most of this increase was due to the inauguration of SSI, although some would have occurred anyway due to the inflationary conditions.

The average payments to recipients increased significantly, although this average might actually have decreased. The higher SSI payments to those formerly on the state public assistance rolls might have been offset by the likely smaller residual SSI payments for new recipients. However, not nearly as many new persons came on the SSI rolls at the start as was expected, or as will likely be the case in the future when the availability of SSI in residual cases is better known.

The actual 4.3 million recipients under SSI and the state supplementary payments at the end of 1974 were 31 percent lower than the estimate of 6.2 million. This discrepancy was caused by the aged category, where the actual number was 2.5 million, as compared with the estimate of 4.9 million. The number of OASDI beneficiaries among the 2.5 million recipients aged 65 and over was about 1.8 million, or 72

TABLE 11.5

**Comparison of Experience under Public Assistance Programs for
Adult Categories in 1973 and under SSI in 1974**

Category	Public Assistance, December 1973	SSI and State Supplements, December 1974			Increase in 1974
		Federally Administered	State Administered*	Total	
		Number of Recipients (thousands)			
Aged..........	1,820	2,286	192	2,478	36%
Blind..........	78	74	6	80	3
Disabled.......	1,275	1,636	100	1,736	36
Total.....	3,173	3,997	298	4,294	35
		Average Payment			
Aged..........	$ 76.15	$ 91.06	$34.59	$ 86.75	14%
Blind..........	112.00	140.57	54.49	136.12	22
Disabled.......	109.75	141.98	40.14	141.98	29
Total.....	$ 90.51	$112.83	$36.85	$107.61	19

Amount of Payments (millions)

	Public Assistance, 1973	SSI and State Supplements, 1974				Increase in 1974
		Federally Administered		State Administered*	Total	
		SSI	State Supplements			
Aged..........	$1,743	$1,794	$ 642	$ 89	$2,525	45%
Blind.........	104	92	35	4	131	26
Disabled.......	1,610	1,971	608	45	2,624	63
Total....	$3,457	$3,857	$1,285	$138	$5,280	53

* Data are not included for a few states that did not report.

percent of the total recipients and 8.9 percent of the total OASDI beneficiaries aged 65 and over.

In September 1974, the proportions of recipients under SSI and the state supplementary payments which were federally-administered who were also OASDI beneficiaries were 73 percent for the aged, 37 percent for the blind, and 30 percent for the disabled. The average OASDI benefit for these cases was $115 for the aged, $123 for the blind, and $126 for the disabled.

Table 11.6 presents data on the operations of the SSI program and the federally-administered supplements for the third quarter of 1974 by category and the type of payments. The proportions of those receiving SSI who also had a state supplement were 30 percent for the aged, 40 percent for the blind, and 42 percent for the disabled. Those

TABLE 11.6

Numbers of Recipients and Average Monthly Payments under SSI and State Supplements for Federally Administered Payments, July–September 1974

Type of Payment	Category			
	Aged	Blind	Disabled	Total
		Number of Persons (thousands)		
SSI only....................	1,361	41	827	2,229
SSI and state supplement....	576	27	606	1,209
State supplement only........	229	6	87	322
Total................	2,166	74	1,520	3,760
		Average Monthly Payment		
SSI*......................	$ 78.67	$114.27	$123.30	$ 97.98
State supplements†..........	67.34	90.50	76.87	72.15
Total................	$ 95.40	$145.20	$151.29	$118.97

* Average for persons receiving SSI.
† Average for persons receiving supplements.

with state supplements only represented the following percentages of the SSI recipients: aged, 12 percent; blind, 9 percent; and disabled, 6 percent. The average monthly SSI payment was relatively low for the aged, $78.67 as compared with the maximum possible rates of $146 for single persons and $109.50 per person for a couple, because such a high proportion were also receiving OASDI.

In summary, then, the initial months of operation of SSI have shown significant increases in average payments to recipients, but with a smaller rise in the numbers of persons involved. It still seems likely that the rolls will grow steadily and significantly in the future as eligible persons with small incomes who can receive residual SSI become aware of their rights and then file for benefits.

INTERRELATIONSHIP BETWEEN PUBLIC ASSISTANCE AND SOCIAL INSURANCE PROGRAMS

General Interrelationship Principles

The descriptions of the public assistance and social insurance provisions of the Social Security Act indicate that although these programs are completely separate as to content, nonetheless there is a certain close relationship between them, in that they cover generally the same risks, except that AFDC protects a wide variety of children besides orphans. The general theory has been that it is desirable to have social insurance programs instead of public assistance programs. The reasons for this are, on the whole, based on their different natures.

Social insurance programs have benefits payable as a matter of right on the basis of a specific earnings record and in amounts that are precisely calculated according to the earnings record. On the other hand, public assistance programs have the basis of needs being in-dividually determined after consideration of the individual's income, assets, and possible financial support from relatives, with the amount of the payment possibly varying from time to time due to changes in the individual's financial condition and in general economic conditions (and, in some instances, due to changes in the state's financial position). Nonetheless, there has been the belief that public assistance programs are necessary for individuals who do not qualify for social insurance benefits or whose benefits are insufficient to meet their needs.

The view has been expressed that the dividing line between social insurance and public assistance is not so definite as it would seem to be at first glance. In connection with pension benefits, the eligibility con-ditions under OASDI are quite liberal as to required length of par-ticipation in the system (and these conditions have been significantly liberalized over the years). As a result, the proportion of the OASDI benefit that has been "actuarially purchased" by the direct contribu-tions or taxes of those retiring in the early decades of operation has been relatively low—from less than 1 percent in some instances to at most about 20 percent. Accordingly, it has been argued from this standpoint that there is really relatively little difference between those who have barely met the OASDI eligibility requirements and receive "insurance benefits" and those who have not met these conditions and receive public assistance payments (or nothing). Following this argu-ment further, it accordingly has been proposed that all retired aged persons should be eligible for at least minimum OASDI benefits.

Since the Social Security Act of 1935 provided social insurance benefits only for the risk of old-age retirement, and since it provided for immediate public assistance provisions for the aged, for children, and for the blind, it was only natural that the public assistance pro-grams began rather full-scale operations more or less immediately. The vast majority of the states that did not already have public assistance programs proceeded to establish them in the first few years after 1935, particularly so for OAA. At the same time, the effectiveness of the social insurance program was relatively slow in developing, despite the addition of benefits for dependents and survivors in the 1939 amendments, because of the "insured status" requirements, because no monthly benefits were payable until 1940, and because no disability benefits were available until the 1956 amendments.

There has been a rather widespread view that the social insurance program (the OASDI system) was intended to replace eventually the public assistance program, or at least the most important part of it (from a cost standpoint)—namely, OAA. On the basis of this belief, there have appeared from time to time statements of concern that so many persons were on the OAA rolls. (With the addition of the SSI program in 1974, the number of persons aged 65 and over who receive public assistance will be increased substantially.) In actual fact, this was never the case because it was always the intention that the social insurance program should gradually assume more and more of the burden from the public assistance program, but that the latter would always have a significant, although minor, role—and such has been the case under OAA, although there will be somewhat of a reversal under SSI.

It may be argued that the only way the public assistance programs—particularly SSI—could be eliminated would be if the benefits under the social insurance program were at such a high level that the minimum needs of all persons could be satisfied. If this were done, then the OASDI benefit level would be so high that the need for private individual and group provisions in this area would be significantly reduced, if not virtually eliminated.

As a general criterion, it might be argued that there should be a public assistance system to supplement the social insurance program for the relatively small minority of cases where essential needs are not met through the social insurance benefits. The proportion of social insurance beneficiaries who receive public assistance might be considered a criterion. Correspondingly, this would also serve as an indication of the relative adequacy of the social insurance benefits. So long as this proportion did not exceed 10 percent under OAA, it might have been considered that there was a proper balance between the two programs. Of course, with the different concept of SSI, the situation is entirely changed.

The foregoing discussion, although in general terms, has been primarily focused on the relationship between OAA and OASDI. There are similar relationships, although not so close, between OASDI and the other three public assistance programs providing cash payments directly to recipients for general needs. The availability of survivor benefits for orphaned children and their widowed mothers under OASDI naturally has an impact on the AFDC program, although over the years the latter has become more concerned with needy children whose paternal source of support has been missing because of desertion, separation, or divorce, mother being unmarried, disability, or unemployment. Part of this shift in emphasis has been due to the availability of survivor protection from the OASDI system, and part has been due to the decreasing number of orphans in the country (as a result of rapidly declining mortality among persons in the parenthood years). In the early years of operation of the AFDC program, about 40 percent of the recipients were orphans, whereas currently this proportion is only about 4 percent; in absolute numbers, the decline was from about 350,000 to 280,000.

Similarly, there is a relationship between OASDI and the public assistance programs for the blind and the disabled. Again, there is not complete correspondence because, at least in certain states, the definitions of disability and blindness are not so strict as under OASDI. Nonetheless, far more recipients would now be under these public assistance programs if it were not for the existence of OASDI.

Although the foregoing discussion considered only the relationship between OASDI and the public assistance programs, it is obvious that similar relationships exist between the latter and other social insurance programs and private employer programs. For example, the existence of the railroad retirement system and of the various pension and other fringe benefit plans for private employees and for employees of federal, state, and local governments naturally has had a significant effect in holding down the public assistance rolls. Some individuals, of course, receive benefits both under the foregoing programs and under public assistance, although probably relatively less frequently than is the case for OASDI beneficiaries, since the benefits under these systems are generally at a higher level than OASDI. Similarly, the various programs of pensions and compensation for veterans of military service have an effect on public assistance because all such payments must be taken into account by the latter in determining need.

Data in Regard to Interrelationship of Public Assistance and OASDI

The number of OAA recipients was about 2.0 million at the beginning of the 1940s. Following World War II, it rose gradually to a peak of 2.8 million in 1950. At the same time, the number of OASDI beneficiaries aged 65 and over grew gradually as the roll built up during the 1940s, and it exceeded the number of OAA recipients for the first time in the early part of 1951. The number of OAA recipients had begun to decline slowly at the end of 1950, because of the liberalized insured status provisions for OASDI introduced then that brought a considerable number of individuals on the roll (and also, to some extent, because of the increase in the general benefit level as a result of that legislation). In fact, in subsequent years, as a result of extension of OASDI coverage and additional liberalizations in the OASDI insured status provisions and benefit computation procedures, OAA rolls were further decreased. Some of these declines occurred immediately when the liberalized OASDI provisions became effective, since many individuals who thereby became eligible for OASDI benefits were removed from the OAA roll. Others were not removed, although they had their OAA payment reduced in recognition of the new OASDI benefit. As a result, the OAA roll declined steadily, so that by mid-1973 there were 19 million OASDI beneficiaries aged 65 and over, or 10 times as many as the number of OAA recipients (1.9 million).

Over the years, a growing number of individuals aged 65 and over have been receiving both OASDI benefits and OAA payments, although this number seems to have reached a peak in 1971–72 and since then has declined somewhat (possibly because of the relatively large increases legislated in the OASDI benefit level). Table 11.7 shows the estimated number of such concurrent recipients for June in various selected past years.

The proportion of OASDI beneficiaries receiving OAA has been only about 7 percent in recent years. When these data are examined by age, it is found that the proportion tends to be higher for the older beneficiaries. This might be expected for several reasons. First, these older persons frequently have lower OASDI benefits because their benefits are based on the lower earnings of the past; the several benefit increases that applied to existing beneficiaries, as well as to future ones, did not entirely compensate for this factor. Second, in some cases, these persons have greater needs because of medical expenses. Third, these persons are less apt to have other resources because of such factors as having used them up over the period of their retirement, having passed through the depression of the 1930s immediately before retirement so that there was more difficulty in accumulating assets for their

TABLE 11.7

Persons Receiving Both OASDI and OAA Payments,
as of February of Selected Years

Year	Estimated Number of Concurrent Recipients (thousands)	Concurrent Recipients as Percentage of—	
		OASDI Beneficiaries Aged 65 and over	OAA Recipients
1940	5	7.6%	0.3%
1945	49	7.6	2.4
1950	276	13.8	10.0
1955	487	7.9	19.1
1960	669	6.6	28.1
1965	944	6.9	43.9
1967	1,096	7.0	53.2
1970	1,243	7.4	60.4
1971	1,277	7.3	62.1
1972	1,276	7.1	63.0
1973	1,189	6.4	62.4

Source: Social and Rehabilitation Service, Department of Health, Education, and Welfare.

retirement, and the much smaller availability of private pension plans in the past.

Quite naturally, in the early 1940s, few OAA recipients were also receiving OASDI because it was difficult for most of the then-aged population to so qualify. But, over the years, this proportion increased, until by the mid-1960s, about half of the OAA roll was made up of concurrent recipients. In the last few years, this proportion has increased to almost two thirds. Eventually, almost all those aged 65 and over receiving either SSI or supplementary state assistance payments will also be OASDI (or RR) beneficiaries.

Another important comparison between these two programs is the relationship between OASDI beneficiaries aged 65 and over, OAA recipients, and total population aged 65 and over. Table 11.8 summarizes these relationships as of June of certain past years.

Since 1950 the relative proportion of the aged population receiving OASDI benefits has increased by five times, while the proportion receiving OAA has decreased by about 60 percent. At the same time, the proportion receiving either or both has increased by about 140 percent. In addition to the 91 percent receiving OAA or OASDI in 1974,

TABLE 11.8

Proportion of Aged Population Receiving OASDI and OAA Payments, as of June of Selected Years

Year	OASDI	OAA	OASDI or OAA, or Both
		Percentage of Population Aged 65 and over Receiving	
1936	—	8.1%	8.1%
1938	—	19.4	19.4
1940	0.7%	21.7	22.3
1945	6.2	19.4	25.1
1950	17.0	22.6	37.4
1955	40.5	17.5	54.5
1960	62.4	14.1	72.3
1965	75.2	11.7	81.5
1967	82.8	10.9	87.8
1969	83.4	10.2	87.6
1970	83.9	10.1	87.8
1971	84.7	9.9	88.4
1972	85.7	9.6	89.4
1973	87.0	8.6	90.0
1974	87.7	10.4	90.6

Source: Social Security Administration, except 1974 estimated by author.

another 5 percent of the population aged 65 or over is eligible for OASDI benefits but is not receiving them because of continuation of employment. Thus, virtually the entire population aged 65 or over currently is receiving OASDI or SSI or is eligible for OASDI but not receiving benefits because of substantial employment earnings. The remaining 4 percent of the aged population consists largely of persons receiving only RR, civil service retirement, or state and local government employee pensions.

The interrelationship between OASDI and the various public assistance programs is shown in Table 11.9, according to the most recent surveys made.

The relatively smaller proportions of concurrent recipients in relation to the assistance roll for the other programs than prevails for OAA reflect several factors. For the blind and disabled, the assistance rolls are made up of many persons who have been in this condition for years and possibly never could have qualified under OASDI even if its

TABLE 11.9

Comparison of Concurrent OASDI and Public Assistance Recipients

Programs	Number of Concurrent Recipients (thousands)	Concurrent Recipients as Percentage of—	
		OASDI Beneficiaries	PA Recipients
OAA and OASDI aged 65 and over*	1,189.0	6.4%	62.4%
AFDC families with orphans and OASDI child-survivor families†	51.0	3.5	2.2
APTD and OASDI‡	207.1	12.2	23.9
AB and OASDI‡	27.0	1.6	34.3

* As of February 1973.
† As of January 1971. These data are based on numbers of *families*. The concurrent families are contrasted with *all* OASDI families with a survivor child beneficiary and with *all* AFDC families (regardless of whether containing an orphan).
‡ As of June, 1970. OASDI base figures represent total of disabled workers and disabled child beneficiaries; concurrent recipients compared to this base include PA recipients aged 65 or over (about 3.4 percent of all APTD recipients were aged 65 or over and thus could not have received disabled-worker OASDI benefits; for AB, the corresponding proportion was 36.0 percent).

coverage had been available, although the proportions of concurrent recipients on the PA rolls have been increasing over the years (having been only 8.6 percent for APTD and 18.1 percent for AB in 1961). In some instances the assistance definitions are not as strict. For the children, causes of dependency other than orphanhood are taken into account under the public assistance program.

Data on concurrent receipt of SSI and OASDI benefits is shown in Table 11.10, as of June 1974. About 70 percent of those aged 65 and over on the SSI roll were also receiving OASDI benefits; in the future, this proportion will increase toward 100 percent as virtually all such

TABLE 11.10

Concurrent Receipt of SSI and OASDI Benefits, June 1974

Reason for Eligibility	Number of Persons (thousands)		Proportion with OASDI	Average OASDI Benefit
	With SSI	With Both SSI and OASDI		
Aged	2,093	1,463	70%	$115
Blind	73	26	36	122
Disabled	1,418	391	28	124
Total	3,584	1,880	52	117

Source: *Social Security Bulletin*, December 1974.

persons will become eligible for OASDI. The corresponding proportions for the blind and disabled are much lower, since many previously on the public assistance rolls, who were taken over by SSI, either had no work record or had a lower degree of disability than required under OASDI. Naturally, because of the provisions of SSI, the average OASDI benefit of concurrent recipients was relatively low—not much above the minimum OASDI benefit of $93.80, before reduction for early retirement.

chapter 12

Railroad Retirement System

The OASDI system, as indicated previously, covers virtually all non-governmental wage employment in the United States except for railroad employees, who are covered by the railroad retirement system. As will be indicated hereafter, this separate system is coordinated closely in many ways with OASDI, and its general structure is quite similar, although the retirement benefit level is significantly higher. It may be said that the railroad retirement system is a social insurance program, although it has certain of the characteristics of a large multi-employer private pension plan. It is administered by the Railroad Retirement Board, with headquarters in Chicago and about 100 local offices throughout the country, in conjunction with certain other benefit programs for railroad employees that will be described in subsequent chapters (namely, unemployment insurance and cash sickness and maternity benefits).

EARLY PENSION DEVELOPMENTS

Most of the large railroads established private pension plans for their employees before 1930, in most instances in the early 1900s. This was the result, at least in part, of the strongly unionized nature of this industry. Naturally, these plans differed from one railroad to another, but it can be said that they generally possessed common characteristics, as follows:

1. The plans were noncontributory.
2. The plans were financed on a "pay-as-you-go" basis.
3. Benefits were not vested and were only payable if the employee was in active service at the time of reaching retirement age (relatively long service was usually required for eligibility).
4. Pensions were computed as a given percentage (usually 1 percent) of final-average salary (usually over the last 10 years) per year of service.
5. Disability pensions were provided, but not survivor benefits.
6. The minimum retirement age was generally 65, but as high as 70 in some plans.

In the early 1930s, due to the effects of the depression, combined with a lack of funding, many railroads had difficulty in maintaining their pension payments. In fact, in a number of instances, reductions of 10 percent or more were instituted, which, of course, disturbed the covered individuals. Railroad workers were also dissatisfied with the existing pension setup because those who might be laid off (or go out on strike) feared that their break in service might result in complete loss of the pensions they anticipated.

Before 1930, various railroad labor organizations, particularly those of the "operating employees," were active in establishing their own pension plans. In some instances, participation was on a voluntary basis, while in other cases the plans were financed on a compulsory assessment basis as mutual benefit societies. These plans, on the whole, did not have successful financial operations. Some of them are still in existence, although they have ceased to be in the pension field, but instead are providing insurance (death, disability, and endowment) on a "legal reserve" basis.

INITIAL GOVERNMENTAL ACTION

As a result of these difficulties in the early 1930s, the railroad labor organizations made efforts to secure federal legislation in this field that would establish an industrywide pension plan under governmental administration. In 1934, such a law was passed, but it was declared unconstitutional by the Supreme Court for a number of reasons beyond the general matter of whether such a pension plan was constitutional. These reasons included certain features of the particular plan, such as giving prior-service credit for all persons who had ever worked for a railroad regardless of their current employment status, and provisions that meant virtually compulsory retirement at age 65.

Following the successful attempt of the railroad employers to have the 1934 Act declared unconstitutional, the railroad labor organizations attempted to get new legislation enacted that would meet or bypass the objections of the Supreme Court. It was hoped that this would be accomplished by completely separating the benefit and tax provisions by having two separate acts (as was, to some extent, done in the original Social Security Act, which was under consideration at the same time), by partially eliminating the compulsory retirement provisions (the 1937 amendments completely eliminated such provisions), and by providing equal employer and employee contributions (instead of the employer contribution being two thirds of the total— possibly to recognize greater employer responsibility for prior-service liability—as under the 1934 act).

At the same time that this legislation was in process, the Social Security Act was in the legislative mill. In fact, it was enacted some two weeks before the Railroad Retirement Act of 1935. Thus, for this brief period, railroad workers were covered under the initial old-age benefits program in the same way as all other commercial and industrial workers, but they were excluded thereafter.

Immediately, the constitutionality of the second Railroad Retirement Act was challenged. In part, it too was declared unconstitutional by a lower court (namely, as to the tax provisions). In an effort to clarify the confused situation, President Roosevelt called a conference of railroad labor and management.

A compromise was worked out under which the railroads agreed not to challenge the constitutionality of the program, provided that certain changes were made (as was done by amendments in 1937). An important concession made to railroad employers was that all pensioners under their existing private pension plans (numbering almost 50,000) would be taken over by the railroad retirement system, and the payments to them would be met from the general financing of the system. This was of great financial assistance to several of the largest railroads which had sizable, steadily increasing pension rolls that they were financing on a current-cost basis. In turn, railroad labor agreed that the program would be on a 50–50 financing basis *for all time to come* (as contrasted with the 1934 legislation, under which the employers paid two thirds of the cost). This situation was changed in 1966, when a supplemental annuity program financed entirely by the employers was instituted and, even more significantly, in 1973, when the equal-matching basis for employer-employee taxes to the regular program was abandoned. Since 1937, there has been no challenge of the constitutionality of the railroad retirement system, and while it has been amended from time to time, its basic characteristic as a social insurance plan for a single nationwide industry has been retained.

RETIREMENT AND DISABILITY BENEFIT PROVISIONS

The coverage provisions of the railroad retirement system are relatively clear-cut, since it covers all railroad employment in the country, including that with railroad labor organizations, REA Express, and the various consolidated railroad terminal stations. Coverage is restricted entirely to the United States, except for certain employment in Canada for a U.S. carrier. Coverage does not apply to local or interurban electric street railways unless they are part of a general railroad system. Likewise, coverage does not apply to certain railroad facilities operated by mining and manufacturing industries within the confines of their plants. There are certain borderline areas, such as the "captive" railroads of steel companies. However, because of the limited number of railroad employers, questions as to whether borderline employment is covered by RR or OASDI have been relatively easily worked out.

The original effective Railroad Retirement Act (as applicable in 1937) provided for a contributory old-age and disability pension plan. There were no survivor benefits other than a provision guaranteeing that total benefits paid would at least equal the employee contributions, plus an implied allowance for interest, and other than the availability on an elective basis of actuarially computed joint-and-survivor annuities, requiring a reduction in the employee's benefit to provide possible survivor benefits. The basic amount of the pension was determined from a formula that followed the general pattern of those under private pension plans, except that it was graded to give relatively higher pensions for those with low earnings.

The original formula was 2 percent of the first $50 of average monthly wage, plus 1½ percent of the next $100 of average monthly wage, plus 1 percent of the next $150 of average monthly wage, all multiplied by the number of years of creditable service.

The maximum creditable wage was $300 per month, the same as the maximum taxable wage. Unlike OASDI, and because of the availability of good employment records for all past years due to the regulated nature of this industry, credit was given for all service before the enactment date for individuals who were in an "employment relation" at that time. Service after age 65 was not creditable—a slight continuation of the policy in the previous legislation that was declared unconstitutional to encourage retirement at that age. If any prior service would be used in computing the pension, the total service credited could not exceed 30 years (so that until 1967, no more than 30 years could be used in the benefit computations). Under the original act the maximum benefit initially payable was thus $120 a month, and this maximum was to be effective for all retirements in the first 30 years of operation.

The average salary used in the benefit formula is, in essence, a "when employed" average one, computed over the months of actual service, with the average wage applicable for service before 1937 generally being the average during months of service in 1924–31. This basis has been continued unchanged over the years, unlike the situation under OASDI, where the average wage has tended more toward a final-average basis because of the several new-start and dropout provisions introduced (which have the effect of eliminating optionally all earnings before 1951, which were generally low). However, changes in earnings levels since the 1930s have, to some extent, been recognized by changes in the benefit factors, as a result of several amendments. The 1974 amendments, however, while continuing this average-wage basis, split it up into two portions—before 1975 and from 1975 on.

The monthly benefits were payable upon retirement at age 65 or after. Early retirement between ages 60 and 65 was permitted for those with at least 30 years of service if they took a permanent reduction in their benefit of $\frac{1}{180}$th for each month under age 65, which is close to the true "actuarial" factor for nondisabled lives. This is the same factor currently used under OASDI for retirement between ages 62 and 65. Persons withdrawing before age 65 who were not eligible for an immediate benefit received a deferred benefit beginning at age 65, regardless of their length of service. In order to receive the retirement benefits, the individual was required to relinquish all rights to railroad employment, so that thereafter he had relatively little likelihood of working for a railroad. Then, the benefit was payable so long as he did not work for any railroad or, if he had last worked for another employer before retiring, for that particular employer.

Monthly benefits were also payable upon permanent and total disability if the individual had at least 30 years of service, or if he was aged 60–64.

The original Railroad Retirement Act of 1937 was financed by equal taxes from the employer and the employee on the first $300 of earnings during a month (note that this monthly basis produces a different result than the annual basis under OASDI, even when the annual base under the latter is 12 times the RR monthly base—as has generally been the case beginning in 1951). The initial combined employer-employee tax rate was 5½ percent for 1937–39 and was scheduled to rise by ½ percent steps every three years until it reached a maximum of 7½ percent in 1949. All taxes went into—and all benefits and administrative expenses were paid from—the Railroad Retirement Account. The investments of this account were to be in special issue government obligations, bearing an interest rate of 3 percent, or in any other government bonds bearing at least this rate. This investment procedure was maintained until 1963, and almost all investments in that period were in these special 3 percent obligations.

Amendments of 1946

The first major legislative changes in the RR system occurred in 1946. The principal change was the introduction of monthly survivor benefits paralleling those under the OASDI system, which had been in effect since 1940, and which undoubtedly exerted pressure for the inclusion of this type of protection in the RR system. One of the most important features of the survivor benefits is that they are virtually completely coordinated with OASDI. The earnings credits under the two systems are combined in determining benefits eligibility and amounts. The only previous coordination between the two systems had been a provision guaranteeing that RR employee benefits would always be at least as large as those under OASDI, but this provision never became effective, although a provision with similar effect was introduced in 1947 and is now operative (in fact, on a 110 percent guarantee basis before the 1974 Act, but currently on the 100-percent basis).

The survivor benefits based on the combined earnings record are payable by RR if the worker had a "current connection" at the time of death or retirement (generally meaning that he had at least 12 months of service in the preceding 30 months, not counting as part of this period any months when not employed at all). Later legislation added a requirement of 10 years of railroad service. Otherwise, the railroad earnings are transferred to the OASDI system, and benefits are computed in exactly the same manner as though such earnings had been obtained in OASDI covered employment.

When the survivor benefits are payable by RR, the basic benefit formula is similar to that of the OASDI system as it was under the 1939 OASDI amendments, except that it was at a somewhat higher level. This formula was 40 percent of the first $75 of average monthly remuneration (instead of the first $50, as under OASDI), plus 10 percent of the remainder, all increased by 1 percent for each year with earnings of at least $200 (the benefit factors of 40 percent and 10 percent were increased several times in subsequent legislation and before the 1974 Act were 52.4 and 12.8 percent). Average remuneration for survivor benefits was computed in the same way as under OASDI— namely, the average covered wage over the working lifetime after 1936.

An alternative compution was provided for a closed group of retired employees (retired before 1948 with at least 10 years of service at any time). This group was given an insured status for survivor benefits regardless of their employment history after 1936. For this group, if a higher result was obtained from the "when employed" average wage concept used for retirement and disability benefits, which is based on the average during the actual months of service (regardless of whether before or after 1937), this result was utilized instead. The latter alternative applied in many cases of persons who retired in the early years of the system, particularly before 1940.

Another interesting feature was the introduction of a type of "disability freeze" provision at the inception of the RR survivor benefit program (not provided under OASDI until 1954).

The survivor benefits were payable to the same categories of beneficiaries as was then the case under OASDI and in the same proportions of the basic benefit (three fourths for the widow—either aged 65 and over or with orphan children—and one half for children and parents). The provision as to "guaranteed return of contributions" was eliminated, since this did not appear to be necessary when monthly survivor benefits were available. In general, over the years, as the OASDI survivor beneficiary categories have been liberalized, so also have those under RR (except as will be noted hereafter).

The 1946 amendments made several other significant benefit changes, such as liberalizing the disability provisions and eliminating the actuarial reduction in the retirement benefit for the relatively few women workers who retire at ages 60 to 64 with 30 years of service. Permanent and total disability benefits were made available after 10 years of service, instead of 30 years, and at ages 60 to 64 regardless of service (and with no actuarial reduction). In addition, benefits for occupational disability were made available for those with either 20 years of service, or at ages 60 to 64 regardless of years of service. The disability benefits are computed by the same formula as the age retirement benefits. The benefits for permanent and total disability are available even though the individual may have been separated from railroad service for a considerable period of time, but the benefits for occupational disability require a current connection.

The tax schedule was increased in order to meet the additional costs of the foregoing benefit liberalizations and in order to meet the estimated deficiency for the previous benefit provisions. The rates previously scheduled for the combined employer-employee contributions had been 7 percent until 1949 and then 7½ percent. The new schedule provided a rate of 11½ percent until 1949, then 12 percent for 1949–51, and 12½ percent for 1952 and thereafter.

Amendments of 1948

In order to recognize in part the increases in the cost of living and in earnings levels since the 1930s, legislation in 1948 increased the factors in the benefit formula for retirement and disability benefits by 20 percent relatively (but left unchanged the bands of wages to which the factors applied). The carriers agreed to this liberalization as part of a package that included the reduction of the employer-paid tax for unemployment insurance from 3 percent to ½ percent. The survivor-benefit provisions were not changed, except that the "guaranteed return of contributions" provision, which had been eliminated in 1946 when monthly survivor benefits were introduced, was reinstated. Despite the benefit liberalizations, no change was made in the financing provisions.

Amendments of 1951

Spurred on by the important 1950 amendments to the OASDI system, which significantly liberalized benefit amounts and beneficiary categories, the railroad retirement system was substantially amended in 1951.

The survivor beneficiary categories and benefit amounts were broadened to parallel the OASDI changes. Survivor-benefit amounts were increased by one third by changing the proportions applied to the basic benefit, which continued to be computed by the same formula and on the basis of average lifetime earnings back to 1937 (unlike OASDI, which went over to a new benefit formula, with a "new-start" average wage).

In addition, benefits were provided for wives of retired workers aged 65 and over, on the basis of 50 percent of the employee's benefit, but with a dollar maximum. Initially, this maximum was $40, but in 1955 it was made equal to the highest amount payable as a wife's benefit under OASDI for that month (increased to 110 percent of such OASDI maximum in 1959). No child's benefits were provided for retired workers except as, in essence, would arise from the "social security minimum guarantee" provision, described hereafter.

At the same time, retirement and disability benefits were increased by a further 15 percent in the same manner as in the 1948 amendments —by increasing the benefit factors. A minor change—but one that is of interest from the standpoint of the philosophy of the program and of the economy generally—was the elimination of the provision that service after age 65 was not creditable for retirement benefit purposes.

These amendments also introduced the provisions for the financial interchange with the OASDI system, which has been discussed in Chapter 4. In conjunction with this, several other changes were made. One of these was to make ineligible for RR monthly benefits all workers who have less than 10 years of railroad service and transfer of their railroad wages to the OASDI system for benefit purposes (except that the "guaranteed return of RR contributions" provision still applies, although certain OASDI benefit payments are offset against it).

Another coordinating provision with OASDI was the "social security minimum guarantee," under which any benefit payable by RR will be at least as large as would have resulted under OASDI. When a person is eligible for benefits under both programs, the guarantee relates only to the RR benefit being larger than the additional OASDI benefit that would have resulted if the railroad earnings had been OASDI earnings. It is through this guarantee provision that recognition is given in some cases to children of retired workers, when such children would have received OASDI benefits if that system had been paying the retirement benefit. Under the 1959 amendments, this guarantee is a "110 percent of OASDI" provision, as will be discussed later.

These amendments contained a number of provisions that prevented duplicate payment of benefits under RR and OASDI. Subsequent legislation eliminated many of these restrictions, so that, for example, it would be possible for an individual to receive full retirement and disability benefits under both programs and for a woman to receive full RR widow's benefits (from her husband's railroad work record) and also full retirement benefits from OASDI and/or RR (on the basis of her own earnings). On the other hand, there can be no duplication of survivor benefits between the two systems on the basis of the earnings records of a particular individual, since these are always combined. The 1974 Act eliminated the possibility of dual benefits for service after 1974.

Despite the above liberalizations, no changes were made in the financing provisions of the system, other than those resulting indirectly from the financial interchange provisions, which were estimated by the Railroad Retirement Board to provide some gain to its system.

Amendments of 1954–63

Amendments to the Railroad Retirement Act were made several times during 1954–63. Primarily, these had the purpose of increasing benefit amounts, adjusting the survivor and supplementary benefits to reflect changes in the corresponding OASDI provisions, increasing the minimum guarantee provision relative to social security benefits payable on the same wage record from 100 percent thereof to 110 percent, and revising the financial basis of the program. The 110-percent guarantee as applicable to survivor benefits was increased to 130 percent by the 1974 Act and was reduced to 100 percent for other benefits.

The maximum monthly earnings base, from which both benefits and contributions are determined, was increased from the original $300 to $350 for service after June 1954; to $400 for service after May 1959; and to $450 for service after October 1963. The first two of these changes tended to correspond (except for effective dates) with those made in the OASDI annual earnings base.

The general level of retirement and disability benefits was increased by raising the basic factors in the benefit formula by 10 percent in 1956 and again in 1959. Over the years the method of computing the average wage for use in the benefit formula has remained substantially unchanged; technically, the average wage so determined is defined as the "average monthly compensation." Similarly, the bands of wages to which the factors are applied have also remained fixed, except for extension of the top band to reflect the higher earnings base. The 1974 Act, however, radically changed the benefit computation procedure for service after 1974.

The tax schedule was increased by the 1959 amendments in order to meet the additional costs arising from benefit liberalizations made then and previously and to recognize the higher cost of the program due to its unfavorable experience. The combined employer-employee rate was increased from 12½ to 13½ percent for 1960–61, to 14½ percent for 1962–64, and to the OASDI rate plus 9 percent for 1965 and after.

The general qualification provisions for retirement and disability benefits have been unchanged in recent years, except that—to conform with the 1961 changes in OASDI—men aged 62–64 with less than 30 years of service can obtain retirement benefits with an actuarial reduction. This had previously been the case for men aged 60–64 with at least 30 years of service. In 1973 the actuarial reduction procedure was eliminated for the 30-year category.

The foregoing discussion has omitted reference to a number of RR provisions which are of moderate importance. These include the special earnings test provision for disability and survivor beneficiaries and the special provisions for crediting military service wage credits. The latter produce considerable complications in regard to financing, since they are interconnected with the financial interchange provisions with OASDI. Also, no mention has been made of the special provisions applicable to the closed group of pensioners taken over from the railroad private plans in 1937 (now almost extinct). This group has shared in the several general benefit increases and in the availability of survivor benefits.

Amendments in Retirement and Disability Benefit Provisions in 1965–73

Legislation enacted in 1965 provided that the maximum taxable earnings base under RR would always be the same as under OASDI (except for being on a monthly basis instead of an annual one). This was done to achieve uniformity for the HI taxes under the two systems (see Chapter 7). At the same time, the tax schedule was changed to include the HI rates. The resulting combined employer-employee rate was 15.9 percent for 1966, increasing gradually to 19.8 percent in 1973–75, and then ultimately to 20.3 percent in 1987 and after.

Legislation in 1966 provided for a new retirement program for railroad workers in addition to the regular RR benefits, the so-called supplemental annuity system, which will be discussed in a subsequent section. Also provided was a 7 percent across-the-board increase in the general level of the regular benefits (to match the similar increase then effective for OASDI), but a partial reduction was made for those receiving OASDI benefits (dual beneficiaries). Similar increases to match OASDI benefit increases were made in 1968 (approximately 10 percent), 1970 (15 percent), 1971 (10 percent), and 1972 (20 percent). All such increases were the same percentage as under OASDI, except for 1968 (when the OASDI increase was 13 percent), the theory then being to give RR beneficiaries about the same *dollar* increase in benefits as they would have received with the same wage record under OASDI. The 1966, 1968, and 1970 amendments provided for some offset against the increase resulting from applying the percentage to the RR benefit for those also receiving OASDI benefits; the offset was the amount of the increase in the OASDI benefit. No such offset was applicable in the 1971 and 1972 legislation.

The 1970, 1971, and 1972 increases were termed "temporary," because of the financing problems of the RR system. Quite obviously, both political and humane considerations dictate that these increases cannot be taken away from the beneficiaries. The deadlines for the "temporary" increases originally established have been extended several times, finally until December 31, 1974. They were made permanent as part of the 1974 Act.

Because of the financial problems of the RR system in keeping up with OASDI—RR is a more mature, high-cost system and thus has more difficulty in raising the benefit level—the 1970 legislation provided for a Commission on Railroad Retirement to study the matter (a subsequent section discusses its findings). The 1971 legislation increasing benefits was enacted before the commission had completed its report, and the corresponding 1972 legislation was enacted shortly after the report's completion (and such legislative action was taken without any regard to the commission's recommendations). The 1972 legislation further provided that railway labor and management should together develop a plan to finance adequately the RR system (since they could not agree on the commission's proposals) and submit it to Congress by March 1, 1973.

The 1972 legislation was passed over the veto of President Nixon, who objected to the benefit increases on the grounds that they further weakened the financial status of the system. The President, however, favored RR beneficiaries getting the same dollar increase as OASDI beneficiaries with the same earnings records, as the Commission on Railroad Retirement had recommended.

The cumulative result of the nine general benefit increases enacted through 1972—20 percent in 1948, 15 percent in 1951, 10 percent in both 1956 and 1959, 7 percent in 1966, approximately 10 percent in 1968, 15 percent in 1970, 10 percent in 1971, and 20 percent in 1972— has been an overall increase of about 198 percent in the benefit level. The benefit formula, resulting from the cumulative multiplication of these increases, on an approximate basis, was thus 5.96 percent of the first $50 of average monthly compensation, 4.47 percent of the next $100, and 2.98 percent of the excess over $150, all multiplied by the number of years of creditable service. For average monthly compensation in excess of $150, this can be expressed as 2.98 percent of AMC plus $2.98, all multiplied by years of service. Although these benefit factors seem to be very large, it should be kept in mind that a partial explanation thereof is that they are applied to a career average wage. The 1974 Act completely changed the method of computing retirement-benefit amounts and eliminated the foregoing formula with respect to service after 1974.

Legislation enacted in 1973 provided that any across-the-board increase in OASDI benefits in 1973–74 would apply also to RR beneficiaries. The basis, paralleling that used in 1968, was to give an increase in the RR benefit equal to the percentage increase in the general level of OASDI benefits applied to the theoretical OASDI benefit based on combined RR and OASDI earnings (without regard to the fact that a dual OASDI-RR beneficiary would also receive an increase on his OASDI benefit). Thus, the 7 and 11 percent OASDI benefit increase legislated in 1973 (effective for March and June 1974) was applicable to RR benefits in this manner.

The 1973 legislation also provided that male workers with at least 30 years of service can retire at ages 60–64 without the actuarial reduction previously applicable. This basis had been available for female workers since 1946. No additional financing was provided for this liberalization, for the "temporary" general benefit increases, or for the resulting overall actuarial deficiency of the system.[1]

---

[1] In one version of the legislation, the total tax rate would have been increased by 7.5 percent (no allocation as between employer and employee specified), which would have provided sufficient financing on a current-cost basis for a number of years, although not enough over the long run. This provision, however, was dropped in the final version of the legislation.

The historical 50–50 split of the total tax rate between employers and employees was significantly altered in the 1973 legislation. Beginning in October 1973, railroad workers pay only the same rate as employees under OASDI and HI, and the railroad employers will pay the balance of the scheduled RR total rate. This follows the usual pattern in private pension plans in the mass-production industries, where the workers pay only the OASDI and HI taxes, and the employer pays all the cost of the private plan, plus the employer OASDI and HI taxes. At the same time, the employers are permitted to shift their increased cost directly to freight shippers without delay by the rate-setting authority of the Interstate Commerce Commission.

At first glance, it might be thought that this change in the proportion of the RR tax paid by the employees was a great financial gain for them. Such change was the result of collective bargaining, and Congress enacted the necessary legislation merely because both parties involved were in agreement. But, in fact, another element must be considered.

The increase in the cash wages in the railroad industry which was bargained for at the same time was less than might have been expected from the general trend of earnings, and by about the amount of the additional RR tax (4¾ percent) that the employers agreed to pay. Accordingly, the employer cost is about the same as it would have been if a "normal" wage increase had been given, and the employee take-home pay is also about the same, although some savings in income tax results. This raises once again the long-standing question of who really pays the cost of pension plans, whether nominally contributory or non-contributory.

Further, the 1973 amendments established a railroad labor-management committee whose function was to make recommendations as to restructuring RR so as to assure its long-range actuarial soundness. This committee, in a sense, was a continuation of the one established in the 1972 legislation, whose recommendations underlay the 1973 amendments. It was required to report by April 1, 1974; the legislative results of its recommendations are discussed subsequently.

Amendments in Supplementary and Survivor
Benefit Provisions in 1965–73

Important changes in the survivor-benefit provisions were also made in 1965–73. Certain changes were made to conform with liberalizations in the OASDI system (or, in some instances, in advance thereof) such as including as eligible children those disabled continuously since before age 22, and lowering the age requirements for widows, widowers, and dependent parents. In the latter category, the minimum age was reduced from 65 to 60 in 1954, whereas under OASDI the reduction was to age 62 for women in 1956 and for men in 1961, and then for widows to age 60 in 1965 and for widowers to age 60 in 1972.

The basic survivor-benefit formula was increased by 10 percent in 1956 and by approximately another 10 percent in 1959, and another 7 percent in 1966. The same general nature was, however, maintained since it is based on the average monthly wage over the potential working lifetime after 1963 (counting in as zeros any periods of nonemployment), except for the closed group described earlier, for whom the average wage on which the annuity was based is used if it is larger. Thus, the RR survivor-benefit formula still did not have the "new-start" characteristics of the OASDI average wage method. However, the OASDI new start is frequently introduced to comply with the RR social security minimum guarantee. This method of computing survivor benefits was eliminated by the 1974 Act.

This basic survivor-benefit formula has been increased four times since its inception in 1946 (by 33⅓ percent as to the beneficiary proportions and by two 10 percents and a 7 percent as to the benefit factors), with a net cumulative effect of about a 72 percent increase. The formula before the 1970 Act was 52.4 percent of the first $75 of average monthly wage, plus 12.8 percent of the remainder, all increased by 1 percent for each year after 1936 with at least $200 of earnings. The full basic amount arising under this formula is payable to the widow—either aged 60 and over or with eligible children—while 66⅔ percent is payable to each other survivor beneficiary. For widow's benefits, there is a minimum guarantee provision that it shall not be less than the wife's benefit which was being paid at the time of death of the husband (if such was the case). About 6 percent of the widow's benefits were affected by this spouse-minimum at the end of 1972. The "temporary" benefit increases enacted in 1970–72 also applied to survivor benefits, so that the formula for the basic amount had an effective factor of about 80 percent of the first $75 of average monthly wage, plus 20 percent of the remainder.

In considering survivor-benefit amounts and also benefits for dependents of retired workers and disabled workers, it is most important to keep in mind the effect of the social security minimum guarantee.

In actual practice, the special survivor-benefit formula of the railroad retirement system, described just previously, was not used in the majority of cases, since the minimum guarantee provision usually produces a larger benefit. For example, at the beginning of 1973, about 70 percent of all benefits to widows aged 60 and over were payable under the minimum guarantee provision. The corresponding proportions for survivor cases involving orphan children and their mothers on the roll was 92 percent and 97 percent, respectively.

Until the 1959 amendments, this provision guaranteed that the benefits would be at least equal to those under OASDI, but thereafter the minimum guarantee was set to yield at least 10 percent more. This 10 percent differential is also applicable to the guarantee provision as it relates to retirement and disability benefits and to the maximum wife's benefit. This "110 percent guarantee" was argued for on the basis of the RR taxes being so much higher than the OASDI ones.

In addition to monthly survivor benefits and a "guaranteed return of contributions" benefit, RR provided a lump-sum death payment for workers dying with a current connection and leaving no survivor immediately eligible for monthly benefits (unlike OASDI, where the lump-sum payment has, since the 1951 amendments, been 10 times the basic amount (resulting from the survivor-benefit formula), which is generally much higher than the OASDI maximum lump-sum death payment of $255. These two death-benefits provisions were drastically changed by the 1974 Act.

The supplementary benefit payable to the wife of a retired worker has been changed to keep pace with the various OASDI liberalizations. In 1959 the age limit was lowered from 65 to 62, with an actuarial reduction to parallel the corresponding change made under OASDI in 1956. At the same time, women workers with less than 30 years of service, but at least 10 years, were permitted to retire at ages 62 to 64 with an actuarial reduction.

The introduction of supplementary benefits for dependents of disabled worker beneficiaries under OASDI and the availability of such supplementary benefits for early retirement beneficiaries under OASDI did not result in a corresponding *direct* change in RR. When a retired or disabled worker under RR reaches age 65, his wife then becomes eligible for a benefit. These OASDI changes, however, had an *indirect* effect on RR through the "social security minimum guarantee" provision. For example, an RR disability beneficiary could have received more than the amount of his benefit as computed by the benefit formula if 110 percent of the benefit that his earnings record would produce under the OASDI system, including supplementary benefits for his eligible dependents, was larger.

COMMISSION ON RAILROAD RETIREMENT

The 1970 RR legislation established the Commission on Railroad Retirement to make a comprehensive study of RR and its financing, including the desirability of its partial or complete merger with OASDI. The commission was composed of five members—three named by the President (one representing labor and one representing management), one by the president pro tempore of the Senate, and one by the Speaker of the House. The commission was supposed to report by July 1, 1971, but it was granted a year's delay.

The major recommendations of the commission—one public member dissenting—were as follows:

1. The railroad retirement system should be restructured into two separate tiers of benefits. Tier one should provide regular social security benefits, financed and paid under the social security laws, and represented by a separate social security check. In relation to tier one, the Railroad Retirement Board should function as a social security claims agent and payment center for claims-taking, adjudications, and certification for payment of social security benefits for railroad beneficiaries in accordance with policies set by the Social Security Administration. Tier two should be a completely separate supplementary retirement plan administered by the Railroad Retirement Board under Federal law, structured to fit with and augment social security and to float on top of tier one.

2. Legally-vested rights of railroad workers and railroad retirement beneficiaries to benefits based on social-security-covered non-railroad service should be guaranteed, but future accrual of these dual benefits should be stopped.

3. A firm financial plan should be adopted forthwith to finance the second tier of supplementary benefits through the Railroad Retirement Account on an assured, fully self-supporting basis by contributions from the railroad community through the crisis period of the next 20 to 30 years and then beyond.

4. The benefit formulas and provisions of the system should be restructured and revised to assure that the overall benefits in the future continue to bear a reasonable relationship to wages in a dynamic economy and to make benefits more equitable among the various groups of beneficiaries.[2]

---

[2] "The Railroad Retirement System: Its Coming Crisis," Report of the Commission on Railroad Retirement, June 30, 1972, House Document No. 92-350, p. 3.

The commission also recommended that if a further OASDI benefit increase were enacted (such as the 20 percent one pending in June 1972), the basis for increasing RR benefits should be on the same pass-through basis as was used in the 1968 legislation, and as was incorporated in the 1973 legislation as to benefit increases which might be enacted in 1973–74.

The dissenting public member was opposed to eliminating dual benefits, was in favor of reducing the employee tax rate to the level of the OASDI rate, and did not agree with the estimates that showed the system to be in a dangerous financial condition over the long range.

The labor member, although concurring in the two-tier approach, urged that the employees should contribute at only the OASDI tax rate (plus, of course, the tax for HI), with the employers paying the balance of the cost (as was done in the 1973 amendments) and that the employers should pay all the cost of the second tier.

The commission's report and the supporting staff papers were a monumental (and costly and time consuming) effort, consisting of about 2,430 pages. It can be criticized, however, for the fact that although it contained a vast quantity of extensive, interesting research, its conclusions were only in terms of general principles. Specifically, no concrete plans were suggested for the second tier and, even more importantly, for the necessary transition from the present plan to the first tier. The commission also did not take the practical approach of proposing a "second line of defense" in case Congress did not look with favor on such a drastic overhauling of RR.[3]

AMENDMENTS IN 1974[4]

The railroad labor-management negotiating committee to which the 1973 legislation gave the responsibility of making recommendations to restructure RR so as to assure its long-range actuarial soundness came forth with a proposal in April 1974. This proposal was enacted

---

[3] For an incisive critique of the commission's report, see A. M. Niessen's review thereof in *Transactions*, Society of Actuaries, 1972, p. 520.

[4] For a complete account of the development, rationale, and details of these amendments, see "Restructuring of the Railroad Retirement System," Report of the Committee on Labor and Public Welfare, Senate Report No. 93–1163, September 23, 1974. No change in the bill to which this report was applicable was made on the Senate floor, and the House accepted the Senate version without going to conference.

into law in October 1974, after a few changes, which will be discussed hereafter.

The measure was passed initially by both the House and the Senate by overwhelming votes (343 to 10 and 86 to 1, respectively). However, President Ford vetoed the bill on the grounds that the financing of the RR system should not be accomplished by payments from the General Fund of the Treasury, that the revised investment procedure for the RR Account was inequitable, and that the revised benefit structure was too complex and would create administrative and public-explanation problems. As might be expected from the size of the initial votes, the veto was easily overridden by both the House and the Senate (by votes of 360 to 12 and 72 to 1, respectively).

The new law changes the benefit structure of the RR system in a number of respects. The two-tier approach proposed by the Commission on Railroad Retirement is followed to a certain extent, but there are certain significant deviations therefrom. It might be said that the two-tier basis was adopted essentially in substance, although not in form. Also, certain other features were added that were not proposed by the commission.

Two major benefit liberalizations were provided in the 1974 Act. First, the vast majority of survivor benefits are increased by changing the "110 percent of OASDI" minimum guarantee to a 130 percent one. Second, spouse annuities, previously payable only when the insured worker was age 65 or over, are now available on a full-rate basis for spouses at age 60 if the insured worker is at least age 60 and has had at least 30 years of service, and on a reduced basis, like under OASDI, for spouses at ages 62 and over (or at any age if an eligible child is present) if the insured worker is at least age 62. The reduction factors, however, are somewhat smaller than under OASDI, resulting in a 20 percent reduction at age 62 instead of 25 percent. The liberalized spouse benefits are only available for retirements after June 1974.

Two major cost-reduction changes were made, as well as several minor ones. The basic benefit formula for retirement annuities had gradually gone out of control in the past and would become more so in the future, producing benefit amounts relatively much larger than present retirants receive. This had come about as a result of the various benefit increases which had been made to parallel OASDI increases. The changes in the benefit formula had been made improperly, by only increasing the factors and not adding on new bands of wages with a low benefit factor when the wage base was increased, as was

done in OASDI. Furthermore, just as for OASDI, the future development of the benefit formula in the light of possible economic changes
would probably intensify the problem.

The second major cost-reduction change was to eliminate dual
benefits with respect to future service and also with respect to persons
who were not vested in such rights at the beginning of 1975. By
"vested" is meant that under previous existing law, individuals would
have qualified separately for *both* OASDI and RR benefits at retirement if they had had no further employment after 1974 or, if earlier,
after the last year in which they had railroad employment. This elimination is accomplished by permitting the dual benefit from OASDI,
but subtracting that amount from the first component of the RR benefit, as will be discussed subsequently.

In other words, such a person, in order to be vested, must have had
10 years of railroad service before 1975, and he must have had sufficient
OASDI coverage before 1975 or, if earlier, before the end of the year
of his last railroad employment to have been fully insured when he
would attain age 62 with no further employment after 1974 or, if
earlier, the last year of railroad service. The use of the end of 1974 as
a determining point for the measurement of OASDI vesting is extended
to certain other categories than those who had railroad service in
1974—namely, to those with 25 years of railroad service before 1975
and to those with a current connection either at the end of 1974 or
at retirement.

A basic principle of changing the benefit computation method was
that nothing should be taken away from the benefit rights that had
been earned to date. Rather, any changes made would affect only
service after 1974.

Retirement Benefit Amounts

Now, the specific form of the retirement benefit formula as it is
under the 1974 Act will be considered. Such formula is extremely
complex and difficult to explain as to present employees but is considerably simpler for new entrants.

First, as to new entrants, there would be the following four components in the monthly benefit:

1. The OASDI benefit, which would be based on combined RR and
    OASDI earnings, and no dual benefits would be payable.
2. $4, times years of RR service after 1974.

3. One-half percent of average monthly RR earnings after 1974, times years of RR service after 1974.
4. For those with at least 25 years of service and a current connection with RR, a supplemental annuity of $23 for 25 years of service, increasing to $43 for 30 or more years.[5]

As to the effect of cost-of-living changes on the amounts of the benefits, the OASDI benefit component would be increased in the same manner as an OASDI benefit based solely on OASDI earnings. The second and third components would be increased before retirement by 65 percent[6] of the increase in the CPI after September 1976 up to retirement, but not more than the increase up to September 1980 for retirements in 1981 or after; the exact procedure is described in the appendix to this chapter. These two components would be increased after retirement by 32½ percent of the increase in the CPI, with such increases to be effective in June of only the four years 1977 through 1980. The fourth component, the supplemental annuity, would not be subject to cost-of-living adjustments either before or after retirement.

Next, as to persons with service before 1975, additional monthly past-service benefits would be paid, consisting of the following three components:

1. An RR benefit computed under the prior law on the basis of service before 1975, minus an OASDI primary benefit computed as of the end of 1974, using 18 computation years, based only on RR wages before 1975.
2. $1.50 for each of the first 10 years of service before 1975 and $1 for each such additional year (but only applicable if some service is performed after 1974).
3. For vested individuals, a "windfall dual benefit" consisting of the excess of (*a*) the OASDI primary benefit which the individual would receive under the law in effect at the end of 1974 on the basis of his RR wages before 1975, plus (*b*) such an OASDI benefit

---

[5] In essence, these are the same as the previous supplemental annuities of $45 to $70, since the regular annuity of those with a supplemental annuity had not been increased as much as that of other persons under various past amendments, so as to reflect the presence of the supplemental annuity. The supplemental annuity provisions are discussed subsequently.

[6] It is interesting to note that this 65 percent factor appeared in the collective bargaining agreement between the United Steelworkers of America and the three major aluminum companies made in February 1974.

based on his OASDI earnings before 1975 or his determining point for vesting purposes, if earlier, over (c) such an OASDI benefit based on his combined RR and OASDI earnings before 1975 or before such earlier determining point.

As to the effect of cost-of-living changes on the amounts of the past-service benefits, the first component would be subject to the 65 percent CPI adjustment before retirement for the limited period involved. The third component, the windfall dual benefit, would be adjusted in exactly the same manner as OASDI benefits are increased after 1974 under the automatic-adjustment provisions (exclusive of what would happen under any ad hoc increases that Congress might legislate).

After retirement, the first component would be adjusted by 32½ percent of the CPI increase for the limited period involved, as is done for the future-service benefits, other than the supplemental annuity. However, the other two components would not be so adjusted.

Persons whose annuities begin to accrue after 1974, but before 1983, are guaranteed that their total family benefit, exclusive of their OASDI benefit but inclusive of the supplemental annuity, shall not be less than what would have been payable under the prior law. It is likely that this guarantee will have little effect, both because of the new flat-dollar benefit for each year of service before 1975 and because of the likely CPI benefit increases in the future.

A limitation on total family benefits was introduced by the 1974 Act. Such monthly benefits as of initial award cannot exceed the larger of $1,200 or the maximum amount determined from 100 percent of such portion of the "final average monthly compensation" as is less than half of the current maximum taxable wage base in the year of annuity accrual (year of retirement), plus 80 percent of the remainder of such average compensation. The term "final average monthly compensation" means the average monthly wage in the highest 2 years out of the last 10 years. For example, if the final average monthly compensation of an individual retiring at some future date is $1,400, and the current earnings base is $1,600 a month, then this limitation would amount to $1,280 a month (100 percent of $800, plus 80 percent of $600). This limitation will probably only rarely affect benefit amounts.

Persons on the roll at the end of 1974 would continue to receive the same benefit amount as previously. However, their benefit would be divided into an OASDI component (after taking into consideration any OASDI benefit which they are receiving on the basis of OASDI earnings) and the residual. The former would be increased in the future for changes in the CPI to the same extent as OASDI benefits are; the latter would be increased by the 32½ percent procedure.

The minimum guarantee provision as it relates to RR benefits for the employee relative to what the same wage record would have produced under OASDI was reduced from the 110 percent basis previously applicable to a 100 percent basis. This provision had had little effect in the past and will have even less in the future.

Spouse Benefit Amounts

Spouse's annuities would, in general, be 50 percent of each component of the employee's annuity except for the supplemental annuity, but subject to reductions for being under age 65 at claim or, as to the OASDI component, for OASDI benefits on the spouse's own earnings record.[7] As a special exception, the foregoing offset applicable to the OASDI component will not apply where the spouse's earnings record was under RR. The overall maximum on the spouse's annuity (including the OASDI component thereof) previously present continues—namely, that it cannot exceed 110 percent of the highest wife's benefit payable at the time to anybody under OASDI.

Frozen windfall dual spouse's benefits are provided if the employee is vested under both OASDI and RR in the same manner as described previously, or if at the end of 1974 the employee has 10 years of service under RR and the spouse is then vested under OASDI. The amount of this dual benefit is the smaller of (*a*) the OASDI benefit at age 65 based on the spouse's earnings record before 1975, or (*b*) the OASDI wife's (or husband's) benefit at age 65 based on the employee's RR and OASDI earnings before 1975, but in any case not less than (*c*) 50 percent of the employee's frozen dual benefit, if any. When the employee's determining point for vesting is before 1974, such point is used instead of 1974 for computing the spouse's OASDI benefit. The computations are made on the basis of the law in effect at the end of 1974.

---

[7] When the spouse receives unreduced benefits at age 60–64, because the employee retired at age 60 or over with at least 30 years of service, the full benefit payable at age 65 on the spouse's earnings record is considered for offset purposes in connection with the OASDI component.

The cost-of-living adjustments for spouse's annuities are made in the same manner as is done for employee annuities.

Survivor-Benefit Amounts

The 1974 Act eliminated the regular RR survivor-benefit formula and increased the "110 percent of OASDI" minimum guarantee to 130 percent. It will be remembered that the regular formula had little effect due to the 110 percent guarantee, so that its elimination when the latter was increased to 130 percent was logical. In applying this minimum guarantee, a special feature is applicable to widows and dependent widowers who first claimed benefits at ages 60–61 and to such disabled beneficiaries when they attain age 60. In such cases, they are considered to be age 62 for purposes of determining the OASDI reduction factor for claiming benefits before age 65. The guarantee that the widow's benefit shall not be less than any spouse annuity received before widowhood is continued.

Frozen windfall dual widow's (and widower's) benefits are provided if the employee has 10 years of service before 1975, and if the spouse was then vested under OASDI on the basis of her own earnings record. The amount of this dual benefit is the sum of (*a*) the RR widow's benefit at age 65 computed under the former regular RR benefit formula for RR and OASDI earnings before 1975, and (*b*) the OASDI benefit at age 65 based on the widow's OASDI earnings before 1975 using the benefit formula in effect at the end of 1974, minus (*c*) 130 percent of the widow's OASDI benefit based on both RR and OASDI earnings before 1975 using the benefit formula in effect at the end of 1974.

Other Benefit Changes

The amount of the residual lump-sum death benefit, which in essence is a guarantee of return of employee taxes plus some interest, would be frozen at its size at the end of 1974. This action merely reflects the fact that since October 1973, the employee taxes have been at the OASDI rates rather than the higher level previously applicable. Accordingly, since no such refund guarantee is present under OASDI, it does not seem necessary for RR in the future.

The regular lump-sum death benefit previously available under RR will be continued for employees with a current connection who had at least 10 years of service before 1975, but its amount will be frozen at the level at which it was at the end of 1974. All other employees would have only the OASDI lump-sum death payment.

The 1974 Act contains a general provision that would make any future liberalizations of OASDI eligibility conditions equally applicable to RR. This would not, however, affect previously existing differences, such as with regard to divorced wives and children of retired workers.

BENEFIT AMOUNTS BEFORE AND AFTER 1974 AMENDMENTS

Table 12.1 gives illustrative monthly benefits for age retirements when no actuarial reduction applies, exclusive of any supplemental annuity (discussed in a subsequent section) for the program as it was before the 1974 amendments. It is worthwhile to present these data so as to show the effect of the significant changes made by the 1974 amendments. It is important to note that the figures presented for the lower average monthly compensations are meaningful since such average is computed on a career-average basis extending back to the beginning of the employee's working lifetime (with certain special provisions for service before 1937).

The figures for "retired worker only" with the supplementary annuity not payable also apply for disability retirements, except that the presence of eligible dependents might produce larger amounts under the "social security minimum guarantee" provision. In the actual experience, the social security minimum guarantee does not apply in many cases; for benefits in current-payment status in mid-1973, it had effect in only 3.1 percent of the age retirements and 14.0 percent of the disability retirements.

Similarly, Table 12.2 gives illustrative monthly survivor benefits for the program as it was before the 1974 amendments. It will be observed that the railroad survivor benefit formula applies in only a few cases—for low-paid workers. The 110 percent social security minimum provision is otherwise generally applicable. Here, too, the figures for the lower average wages are meaningful because such average is computed on a past career-average basis, back to 1937.

It is interesting to note the relatively high levels of benefits that can be obtained by recent retirements. Consider a male employee who retired at age 65 on July 1, 1974, with maximum creditable wages in all years since the system began in 1937 and who was never covered under

TABLE 12.1

Illustrative Amounts of Regular Employee Annuities under Railroad Retirement, under Law in Effect Prior to 1974 Amendments (amounts payable for June 1974 and thereafter)

Average Monthly Compensation	10 Years of Service		20 Years of Service	30 Years of Service		40 Years of Service	
	O/M Applies*	O/M Does Not Apply*		S/A Payable†	S/A Not Payable†	S/A Payable†	S/A Not Payable†
			Retired Worker Only				
$ 100.....	$133	$108	$163	$161	$170	$205	$218
200.....	189	118	200	265	281	343	363
300.....	236	155	263	351	372	456	481
400.....	285	191	327	436	463	565	590
600.....	378	267	457	608	633	765	799
800.....	445	333	573	760	786	964	999
1,100.....	516	438	739	997	1,023	1,272	1,306
			Retired Worker and Spouse Aged 65 or Over				
$ 100.....	$199	$163	$244	$ 246	$ 255	$ 314	$ 326
200.....	283	177	300	406	422	525	545
300.....	354	232	395	537	558	697	722
400.....	427	287	491	668	695	823	848
600.....	568	400	686	866	891	1,023	1,057
800.....	668	499	831	1,018	1,044	1,222	1,257
1,100.....	774	657	997	1,255	1,281	1,530	1,564

* Overall minimum (O/M) in principle equal to 110 percent of the benefit or of the additional benefit which OASDI would have paid on the basis of the railroad service involved. Generally, the O/M does not apply to cases where the RR beneficiary is also receiving OASDI.

† S/A denotes supplemental annuity. This benefit is available only to retired employees with 25 or more years of service and cannot begin before attainment of age 65. S/A is $45 for 25 years, increasing to $70 for 30 or more years; S/A is not included in above figures. Whenever S/A is payable, the regular annuity is somewhat reduced, as shown here.

Note 1: The amounts shown include the special "pass-through" increase provided for in the July 1973 amendments. For purposes of computing this increase and for purposes of computing the O/M, the average monthly wage as defined under OASDI was taken to equal the AMC. In actuality, the two averages differ by considerable amounts.

Note 2: For spouses annuities, the 1976 maximum of $258 was used. The maximum amounts before 1976 are $188.50 for 1973; $203.30 to $225.70 for 1974; and $247 for 1975. The 1975 amounts do not allow for possible increases caused by automatic adjustments in OASDI benefits.

Note 3: Some of the AMCs in the upper range will not be possible for a number of years. As of June 1974, the maximum AMCs possible are $657 for 10 years of service; $518 for 20 years; $445 for 30 years; and $416 for 38 years (40 years of creditable service will become possible in June 1976).

Source: Office of Chief Actuary, Railroad Retirement Board.

OASDI. His regular RR benefit was $559.75 per month, and his supplemental annuity of $70 increased this to $629.75. If he had a wife aged 65 or over, a further benefit of $225.70 was payable, making total benefit income of $850.45.

The average monthly compensation on which the above regular RR benefit is based is only $416 (low because of its career-average nature). The better comparison of the benefit level is with the final

TABLE 12.2

Illustrative Amounts of Monthly Survivor Benefits
under Railroad Retirement, under Law in Effect
Prior to 1974 Amendments
(amounts payable for June 1974 and thereafter)

*Average Monthly Remuneration**	*Age at Beginning of Annuity*				*Years with Earnings of $200 or More*			
	60–62	63	64	65	10	20	30	40
	Aged Widow				*Widowed Mother with Two Children*			
$ 100............	$110	$118	$125	$133	$216†	$231†	$246†	$261†
200............	156	167	178	189	286†	306†	326†	345†
300............	196	209	222	236	387	387	406†	406†
400............	236	253	269	285	520	520	520	520
600............	314	335	357	378	670	670	670	670
800............	369	394	420	445	779	779	779	779
1,100............	428	457	487	516	903	903	903	903

* Based on combined earnings under RR and OASDI and computed under the OASDI formula, but without regard to the new-start and dropout provisions.

† Railroad formula (basic amount) applies.

Note: Except when indicated otherwise, all amounts were computed under the 110 percent social security minimum formula. The average monthly wage was assumed to be the same as the average monthly remuneration, although in practice these two averages may differ by considerable amounts The highest AMR possible in June 1974 is $690. The amounts shown relate to cases where no concurrent OASDI benefits are payable and the "spouse annuity minimum" was disregarded. All figures are rounded to nearest dollar.

Source: Office of Chief Actuary, Railroad Retirement Board.

wage ($1,100 per month), and even then the total family benefit was 77 percent of wage. This family benefit may also be contrasted with what would be paid under OASDI under similar circumstances— $457.40, or only 54 percent as much (but this would quite possibly be supplemented by a private pension).

Tables 12.3 and 12.4 present data on illustrative benefits under the 1974 Act for persons entering RR service after 1974. These data are prepared under the assumption of static economic conditions in the future and, therefore, have some limitations as to their meaningfulness. This is especially so because the automatic adjustments for increases in the CPI that are applicable to components other than the OASDI one do not recognize the full change in the CPI and, moreover, are supposed to be applicable only for four years. No data are shown for very low earnings levels since these would not often be applicable in the strongly organized railroad industry; even the data for averages of less than $800 per month are not very meaningful.

TABLE 12.3

Illustrative Amounts of Total Employee Annuities under Railroad Retirement for Entrants after 1974, under 1974 Amendments, Based on Law in Effect in January 1975

Average Monthly Compensation	Period of Railroad Service					
	10 Years	20 Years	25 Years	30 Years	35 Years	40 Years
	Retired Worker Only					
$ 400............	$319	$379	$432	$482	$512	$542
600............	414	484	542	587	632	667
800............	485	565	628	688	728	768
1,000............	539	629	697	762	807	852
1,175............	583	682	754	823	873	922
	Retired Worker and Spouse Aged 65 or Over					
$ 400............	$479	$569	$ 637	$ 702	$ 747	$ 792
600............	621	726	802	863	898	933
800............	727	831	894	954	994	1,034
1,000............	805	895	963	1,028	1,073	1,118
1,175............	849	948	1,020	1,089	1,139	1,188

Note: These figures are based on the following assumptions:
1. Employee retires at age 65.
2. Cost-of-living adjustments are not included.
3. Employee with 25 or more years of service receives supplemental annuity.
4. Spouse does not have an OASDI benefit based on her own earnings record.
5. Figures rounded to nearest dollar.
6. In cases where worker has less than 35 years of RR service, he has equivalent coverage under OASDI.

TABLE 12.4

Illustrative Amounts of Monthly Survivor Benefits under Railroad Retirement for Entrants after 1974, under 1974 Amendments, Based on Law in Effect in January 1975

Average Monthly Wage	Age of Widow at Beginning of Annuity				Widowed Mother with—	
	60–62	63	64	65	One Child	Two or More Children
$ 400.......	$279	$298	$318	$337	$505	$ 614
600.......	371	396	422	447	671	791
800.......	436	466	496	526	789	921
1,000.......	484	517	551	584	876	1,022
1,175.......	522	558	594	629	944	1,101

Note: These figures are based on the following assumptions:
1. Cost-of-living adjustments are not included.
2. Survivor beneficiary does not have a benefit based on her own earnings record under OASDI.
3. Figures rounded to nearest dollar.
4. Effect of "spouse annuity minimum" is disregarded.
5. Deceased employee assumed to have stated average wage, as defined under OASDI, from RR and OASDI earnings combined.

The retirement benefits available for future retirants are at a relatively high level and approach full pay, especially when an eligible wife is present, for workers at the typical normal earnings levels of $800 per month or more. In most cases, the spouse's annuity is at the $266.20 maximum based on 110 percent of the OASDI wife's benefit for an AMW of $1,175.

Although the retirement benefits are at a relatively high level, in essence representing the sum of an OASDI benefit and a staff pension plan benefit, and thus involve high costs, they are lower than would have resulted under previous law. For example, persons at the highest creditable earnings with long service would have received total benefits of considerably more than their gross pay, especially including wife's benefits. If they also had OASDI dual benefits, the situation would be even more aggravated. However, under present law, such total benefits would rarely exceed total pay under the static economic assumptions used in Table 12.3, and there would be no possibility of OASDI dual benefits.

The level of survivor benefits shown in Table 12.4 is, of course, relatively high because of the effect of being 30 percent higher than the OASDI level.

PRESENT FINANCING PROVISIONS

The financing provisions were not changed following the 1946 amendments until the 1959 amendments (other than for raising the earnings base and for introducing financial interchange provisions with OASDI), despite several significant benefit liberalizations. Of course, during that time the tax rate increased according to the schedule in the law. In 1959 the combined employer-employee tax rate was increased from 12½ percent to the following schedule: 13½ percent through 1961, 14½ percent for 1962–64, and for years after 1964 to 14½ percent plus the excess of the then current OASDI rate over 5½ percent, which was the OASDI rate scheduled for 1960–64 under the social security amendments of 1956 (although, as it turned out, the actual rates for that period were different from this). To put it another way, the RR tax rates for years after 1964 would, under the 1959 legislation, be the OASDI rates plus 9 percent—that is, 14½ percent, plus OASDI rate, minus 5½ percent, equals 9 percent plus the OASDI rate.

Railroad retirement legislation in 1965–66 provided that the HI tax for the Medicare program would also be included in the RR tax and that the basic RR tax rate would be increased from 14½ percent to 15 percent in 1965. As a result, the combined employer-employee tax rate under RR after 1968 is 9½ percent plus the then prevailing OASDI and HI rates. Under the OASDI and HI tax schedule in the 1973 social security amendments, the combined employer-employee RR tax rates are scheduled at 21.2 percent for 1973–77, 21.6 percent for 1978–80, 22.1 percent for 1981–85, 22.4 percent for 1986–2010, and 24.4 percent for 2011 and after. As mentioned previously, the 1973 amendments provided that railroad employees would, in the future, pay the same tax rates as employees under OASDI. Thus, the railroad employers will pay amounts matching the employee taxes *plus* a tax rate of 9½ percent.

The 1963 amendments had the primary purpose of improving the financial position of the system, which had had a long-range actuarial deficiency of 1.79 percent of taxable payroll. This was accomplished (a reduction of the deficit to only 0.41 percent) by raising the taxable wage base from $400 a month to $450 and by having a more favorable basis for the special-issue investments of the RR Account. Under the new basis, the rate for such new investments is the average market yield rate, at the time of issue, on all interest-bearing obligations of the United States government having at least three years to maturity, rounded to the nearest ⅛ percent and with a minimum of 3 percent. This is substantially the same procedure as is followed for the OASDI trust funds, except that a 3 percent minimum is given to the account. Further, all special-issue investments of the account on the enactment date were converted to the new interest basis, which at that time pro-duced a rate of 4 percent. In 1970 a further change favorable to RR was made—basing the interest rate for special issues on the average market rate for notes of the United States government having at least three years to go until maturity. This produced a higher result, be-cause of the elimination of long-term bonds from consideration (which generally, unlike short-term notes, by law have a ceiling on the interest rate payable).

The 1974 Act made substantial changes in the RR financing pro-visions. A government subsidy was introduced to pay for the cost of the windfall dual benefits that had arisen as a result of persons being covered under both RR and OASDI in years before 1975. Such wind-fall dual benefits were eliminated by the 1974 Act with respect to service in the future.

The joint labor-management committee that had been assigned the task of coming up with a solution for the financial difficulties of RR had recommended that such cost should be borne by OASDI. Congress, however, believed that this would not be proper and that, instead, it should be borne by the General Fund of the Treasury. The rationale for this action, rather than having the cost be met by the employers and the employees, was that it was the fault of Congress in liberalizing OASDI benefits and providing corresponding increases under RR and in repealing restrictions on dual benefits that had originally been contained in RR. Of course, in actual practice such changes in RR were often made because of the pressures therefor of the railroad labor organizations, often over management's objections.

The specific operation of this government subsidy is that equal annual appropriations are to be made for the 25-year period beginning with fiscal year 1976. Such appropriations are intended to meet the total costs incurred as the result of the windfall dual benefits payable in the future, even after the year 2000. Since an estimate is involved in this procedure, the annual amount will be changed from time to time in the future, but with the same ending date for these payments, so as to reflect actual experience. Current estimates of such an amount are $285 million a year, making total payments of $7.1 billion.

Another important change in the financing provisions is that in the future the investments of the RR Account will be under the authority of the RR Board, rather than the Secretary of the Treasury. Accordingly, investments in special issues can be redeemed whenever the board decides, and this will, of course, always be done when current market yields are higher than the coupon rates on special issues obtained in the past. But if the opposite situation occurs, the special issues obviously would continue to be held. President Ford, in his veto of this legislation, pointed out that such an investment procedure was unfair and improper because it was a "heads I win, tails you lose" arrangement. The RR Board would also have flexibility about investing in other than special issues if a greater rate of return could be obtained, although in these instances there would not be the advantage of redemption at par if interest rates rise, as can be done for special issues.

Although the 1974 Act gives quite discriminatory treatment to RR with regard to investment operations, this advantage is entirely taken away for the next 25 years, since interest income under such investment policy provisions in excess of that which would have occurred under the provisions in effect previously, which were very similar to those for OASDI, is to be deducted from the government subsidy for the windfall dual benefits. It is currently estimated that the net appropriations for such benefits would thereby be reduced from $285 million a year to $250 million a year. As a result, it would appear that the net effect for both RR and the General Fund of the Treasury is about the same as if the revised investment procedure had not been enacted, at least until the year 2000.

Another financing change made by the 1974 Act was in connection with the taxes paid by employees in years when they work under both RR and OASDI. After 1974, the maximum tax liability for employees will be that based on the maximum taxable wage base, with refunds being available on the income tax return when combined RR-OASDI earnings exceed such base. Employees with past service who are not vested for windfall dual benefits will also be eligible for similar refunds for years before 1975, payable at the time a claim is awarded on their earnings record. Vested employees will not be so eligible because their separate RR and OASDI earnings will produce separate benefits.

As was indicated previously, the form of the supplemental annuities was considerably changed for new awards after 1974, with apparently much lower benefit amounts. In actual fact, however, the substance is still the same because of the simultaneous elimination of certain offsets against the regular RR annuities for those with supplemental annuities. The special tax on employers on the basis of cents-per-hour that finances the supplemental annuities would be continued as though the full $45 to $70 supplemental annuites were payable. The portion of these taxes necessary to pay the supplemental annuities at the level of $23 to $43 established in the 1974 Act for such annuities which begin after 1974 will be appropriated to the RR Supplemental Account, with the remainder of such taxes going to the RR Account.

The Senate committee report on the 1974 Act includes a statement from the chief negotiator for the railroad employers making a commitment to the effect that all future RR benefits liberalizations, other than those occurring as a result of OASDI amendments, will be financed entirely by the employers. Although this does not have the effect of law, it has a very strong precedental force. Similarly, it would seem to be implied strongly that any actuarial deficiency present at the enactment of this legislation or arising from future experience being different than the assumptions in the current actuarial cost estimates will be entirely the responsibility of the railroad employers.

Under the proposal of the labor-management negotiating committee, the cash-flow difficulties of RR would have been lessened some-what by putting the financial interchange with OASDI on an accrual basis, rather than on a deferred-payment basis with approximately a one-year lag. This procedure, which is roughly what is done for the HI portion of the financial interchange, would, of course, have ab-solutely no long-range actuarial effect. It would, however, bolster the RR Account by about $1 billion for all future years, and have exactly the opposite effect for the OASDI Trust Funds.

Congress, upon the urging of the Nixon administration, did not adopt this accrual approach for the financial interchange, although its validity was not denied. The reasons given for such action were the current financial difficulties of OASDI and the fact that its trust fund balances were estimated to be relatively level in the near future, and this change would produce a significant decline.

SUPPLEMENTAL ANNUITY SYSTEM

In 1966 a new system of supplemental annuities was enacted on top of the regular RR benefits. This program applied only to persons retiring at age 65 or over whose regular benefits were awarded after June 1966 and who have at least 25 years of service and a current con-nection (as defined earlier in this chapter). It provided benefits for only the retired worker, in the flat monthly amount of $45 for 25 years of service, increasing by $5 per year of service to a maximum of $70. Such amount is, however, reduced by the amount of any private railroad pension financed by the railroad employer. This procedure was established so that employers who had established private pension plans in the past would not be disadvantaged as against those who had not done so. Initially, the system was to be only "temporary," but in 1970 it was made permanent.

Under the original legislation, the supplemental annuity program was financed entirely by the employer—an indirect breaking of the 1937 labor-management agreement for there always to be 50–50 financing of governmental retirement benefit programs for railroad workers. However, this approach was not at all unreasonable in view of the fact that private pension plans in the mass industries, particularly collectively bargained ones, are almost always entirely paid for by the employer. The financing was not based on a percentage payroll tax but, rather, on a tax of 2 cents per hour per employee. Employers with private pension plans could deduct from the amount of tax due any pension payments, up to the amount of the supplemental annuity that they made to pensioners eligible for supplemental annuities. This financing was estimated to be sufficient to meet the cost for at least the first four years of the "temporary" five-year period for which the plan was to be effective. However, higher retirements than expected and lower employment had an adverse effect, and by the end of 1969 the special fund established for this program became exhausted.

This resulted in legislation in 1970 that made the program permanent and that provided for financing on a pay-as-you-go basis, with the Railroad Retirement Board to promulgate the cents-per-hour tax rate on a quarterly basis. Such rate was 6 cents during April–June, 1970; then 7 cents for July–December 1970, 6 cents for 1971 and the first half of 1972, and 7½ cents thereafter through 1974, and then 8½ cents. This legislation also authorized a loan from the RR Account to meet part of the outgo for supplemental benefits payable in early 1970. Such a loan was made, but was subsequently repaid.

The 1970 legislation also restricted the benefit eligibility conditions by *requiring* retirement within a certain time after age 65, or else the supplemental annuity would be permanently forfeited. This was done on a graded basis so that those attaining age 65 in 1974 and thereafter must retire from railroad employment by the end of the month following the month in which they attain age 65. In this sense, a full circle has been completed, since the original 1934 Act (declared unconstitutional) also had a compulsory retirement feature, which was dropped in the 1935 Act.

The 1974 Act changed the supplemental annuity program in several respects. These annuities are now available at age 60 for employees with at least 30 years of service, although they are not compelled to retire until age 65 in order to be eligible. As was indicated previously, the benefit amounts appear to have been changed from the $45 to $70 range previously applicable to a $23 to $43 range. In fact, however, the same net result still prevails, as a result of eliminating certain reductions which had previously been made in the regular RR annuities. It is significant to note that automatic adjustments for changes in the CPI are not applicable to these supplemental annuities, so that to a certain extent they are tending to "wither away" as economic conditions change.

In connection with the financing of the supplemental annuity program, the benefit liberalization mentioned previously will, of course, mean a higher cents-per-hour tax rate. Also, as mentioned earlier, the receipts from this tax will be divided between the RR Supplemental Account and the RR Account to reflect that, in actuality, part of the supplemental annuity is merely being paid with the regular RR benefit. It appears likely that the tax rate for supplemental annuities will be increased in the future and will probably rise to at least 14 cents per hour by 1985. In the long run, however, as the "retirement wave" rolls along, the tax rate will drop, eventually to somewhat less than the present level.

An interesting feature of the supplemental annuities is that, unlike OASDI and regular RR benefits, they are subject to federal income tax. For this reason, the revised, lower basis for new retirants after 1974, which resulted in a shift of part of the supplemental annuity to the regular RR annuity, was favorable to them from the basis of net income after taxes.

APPENDIX

Operational Data and Actuarial Basis for Railroad Retirement System

DATA ON OPERATIONS OF RR SYSTEM

The total number of workers with any covered employment in the RR system during the course of the year was about 730,000 in 1974. The average monthly employment in the railroad industry rose from about 1.2 million in the late 1930s to a peak of 1.7 million during World War II. It then declined slowly to about 1.4 million during the early 1950s and then steadily to only 594,000 in 1974, or 81 percent of the total with wages in the year. A considerable number of railroad workers also have employment covered by OASDI; for example, of those with RR service in 1969, about 85 percent had had some OASDI coverage in 1969 or before (29 percent had such dual coverage in 1969 alone), and 17 percent were permanently fully insured under OASDI.

The total wages in the railroad industry were about $8.4 billion in 1974, of which only about $7.3 billion, or 87 percent, was taxable (within the $1,100 monthly earnings base then applicable). The annual taxable payroll increased from about $2.2 billion in the late 1930s to a maximum of about $5.0 billion in 1948–57 (fluctuating in this period generally between $4.9 and $5.1 billion), despite the fact that the general earnings level was steadily rising. Following 1957 the taxable payroll declined by almost 20 percent, to $4.0 billion in 1962–63, but the subsequent increases in the earnings base had the effect of increasing it thereafter, until it was at a level of about $5.0 billion in 1968–71. The taxable payroll increased to $5.35 billion in 1972, $6.26 billion in 1973, and is estimated to be $7.3 billion in 1974, such rises resulting primarily from the increases in the maximum taxable earnings base. Rises in wage rates in the past years have largely been offset by the declining employment and, in many years, by the effect of the earnings base remaining unchanged.

Benefit payments under RR increased from about $100 million per year in the early years of operation to $2.74 billion in 1974 (plus $93 million in supplemental annuities). Administrative expenses in 1974 were about $25 million, or 1 percent of benefit outgo. Tax income was under $200 million per year in the early years of operation and grew steadily to around $600 million per year in 1951–63 (the declining *total* payroll during this decade was, on the whole, offset by rising tax rates and higher earnings bases), and then gradually to about $1.0 billion in 1969–72 (due largely to increased tax rates, including those for HI, which are transferred entirely to the HI Trust Fund, and to higher earnings bases) and sharply to $1.3 billion in 1973 and $1.5 billion in 1974 (due to increases in the taxable wage base).

The RR Account received interest income of $257 million in 1974. This, together with the tax income, was $1,120 million less than the outgo for benefits and administrative expenses. This difference was largely met by the payments from the OASDI system under the financial interchange provisions ($931 million from OASDI, less $132 million to HI).

The total assets of the RR Account as of June 30, 1974 on a cash basis amounted to $4.3 billion,[8] most of which was invested in special issues bearing interest at rates of $5\frac{3}{4}$ to 8 percent (net amount of $3.66 billion) and in public issues bearing interest at rates of 3 to $7\frac{1}{2}$ percent ($839 million), with a negative cash balance of $213 million. The average interest rate on all assets combined was 6.6 percent.

At the end of 1959 the RUI Account was exhausted, and legislation permitted it to borrow from the RR Account (with appropriate interest being paid). The balance owed to the RR Account grew and reached a maximum of $335 million in early 1964, but it was then gradually reduced and finally eliminated in the second half of 1973. Similarly, when the supplemental annuity program experienced financial problems at the end of 1969, its account received legislative authority to borrow from the RR Account. Thus, in March 1970, the RR supplemental account borrowed $25 million, which it repaid with interest a year later.

The RR Account has been relatively level in the past decade. It increased from $3.8 billion at the end of 1963 to $4.4 billion at the end of 1970 and declined to $4.0 billion at the end of 1972, $3.8 billion at the end of 1973, and $3.6 billion at the end of 1974.[9]

Over the years, the current financing of RR (on an income-outgo basis) has been greatly aided by the financial interchange with OASDI. The cumulative effect of the financial interchange through June 30, 1974, was net income to RR of $11.9 billion (including interest). Since the RR Account then was only $4.4 billion, it can readily be seen that without this source of income, RR would have been bankrupt (on a cash basis) some years ago. It is estimated that the financial interchange will produce a flow of funds to RR from OASDI for about four decades, but that then there will be a reversal of small magnitude.[10]

The number of worker beneficiaries (both age and disability) increased from about 150,000 in the late 1930s to 420,000 at the end of

---

[8] The assets at midyear are larger than those at the beginning of the year because of the substantial financial interchange payment made by OASDI in the first half of each year. For example, such balance was $3.8 billion at the beginning of 1974 and $3.6 billion at the end of 1974.

[9] These figures are on a cash basis. On an accrual basis, they would be about $1.2 billion higher currently (largely because of the financial interchange with OASDI).

[10] For more details, see "The Financial Interchange and Its Cumulative Effects on the Railroad Retirement Account," *Actuarial Note No. 8-73*, Railroad Retirement Board, September 1973.

1963 (including only about 400 of the original closed group of pensioners taken over from the railroad private pension plans) and to 457,000 at the end of 1974 (only 36 pensioners). The 457,000 annuitants included 40,000 disabled annuitants under age 65. At the end of 1974, there were also on the benefit roll 210,000 wives and 336,000 survivor beneficiaries (294,000 widows, 34,000 children, 7,000 widowed mothers, and 300 parents). Thus the total number of monthly beneficiaries at the end of 1974 was 1,003,000, or about 69 percent higher than the number of covered workers during a typical month of 1974. About 44 percent of the beneficiaries at the end of 1974 were also receiving OASDI benefits (40 percent for retired employees, 64 percent for wives, 41 percent for aged widows, but only 3 percent for young survivor beneficiaries). The proportion of dual beneficiaries has been increasing steadily over the years; for example, being only about 25 percent in 1972.

The average monthly benefits payable at the end of 1974 were as follows: age annuitants (and disability annuitants) aged 65 or over, $297; disability annuitants under age 65, $334; widows aged 60 or over, $185; widowed mothers, $219; and children, $157.

In 1974 the supplemental annuity system received $94 million in taxes and $3 million in interest, while paying out $93 million in benefits and only $600,000 in administrative expenses. The RR Supplemental Account had a balance of $38 million at the end of 1974 and at that time was paying benefits averaging $66 to 210,000 annuitants.

ACTUARIAL BASIS OF RR SYSTEM

The original RR Act required that actuarial valuations should be made at intervals of not less than three years. The actual work is done by the chief actuary of the Railroad Retirement Board, with the results being reviewed by an Actuarial Advisory Committee, established in accordance with law. This committee is composed of three designated actuaries, of whom two are appointed by the Board (one upon the recommendation of the employers and the other upon the recommendation of the labor unions), and the other is designated by the Secretary of the Treasury. This committee also is empowered to make recommendations as to actuarial methods, and it takes note of the financial situation of the system.

The valuations are carried out according to standard pension fund procedures (except for being on an open-end basis that considers new entrants into the indefinite future), with the results being presented in the form of a balance sheet. Thus, indication is given as to the sufficiency or insufficiency of the tax schedule in the law and the amount of any such differential. In the past, a single estimate was prepared, rather than a range showing possible low-cost and high-cost estimates, and no year-by-year projections were given.

The twelfth actuarial valuation was made as of the end of 1971, but it took into account the effect of all pertinent legislation enacted in 1972 (but not the significant OASDI and RR amendments in 1973). This valuation was made on three alternative bases:

1. Assuming static economic conditions in the future as to prices and wages and, alternatively, interest rates of 3 percent and 5.75 percent, and assuming that the three "temporary" benefit increases legislated in 1970–72 would be made permanent.
2. The same static economic assumptions and the assumption that the "temporary" increases would really be so (which basis was stated to be highly unrealistic, although it was necessary for illustrative purposes).
3. Assuming dynamic economic assumptions (annual rates of increase of 2¾ percent in prices and 5 percent in wages, which was the same as currently used in the OASDI cost estimates), 5.75 percent interest, and dynamic adjustment of the RR benefit formula and taxable wage base in the future in the same manner as is done under OASDI.

The two static valuations covered an infinite future period (as had previous ones), while the dynamic one was limited to the next 75 years.

One of the most crucial factors in regard to the cost of RR is what the taxable payroll will be in future years. As indicated previously, there has been a very substantial decrease in railroad employment in the past. In this respect, the financial interchange provisions with OASDI have a very strong cushioning effect, but nonetheless the use of a considerably lower payroll assumption results in significantly higher costs expressed as percentages of taxable payroll. The twelfth valuation assumed that the future equivalent-level payroll would be determined from current pay levels (after adjustment for the effect of the higher earnings base applicable in 1974) and from an assumed decline in railroad employment (persons with any creditable wages in the year) from 730,000 in 1972 to 465,000 in the early 1980s and thereafter. The result was an equivalent level annual taxable payroll of $5.55 billion under the static economic assumptions (versus the actual taxable payroll of about $6.1 billion in 1973 under a $10,800 base).

The basic part of the twelfth valuation is based on static economic conditions, 5 ¾ percent interest, and the assumption that the "temporary" benefit increases will be permanent, and was made as of the end of 1971 (but including legislative changes through June 1973). The level cost of the future benefit payments for present beneficiaries, present workers, and new entrants combined was estimated at 43.4 percent of taxable payroll, before taking into account the estimated level equivalent of the net gain from the financial interchange provision (12.6 percent of taxable payroll). Administrative expenses were estimated at 0.4 percent of taxable payroll. Accordingly, the net cost of the benefits and administrative expenses was 31.2 percent of taxable payroll. Part of this cost is to be met from future interest earnings of the existing fund, which have a level equivalent of 5.5 percent of taxable payroll. The level equivalent of the graded tax schedule was 19.4 percent of taxable payroll, so that the actuarial imbalance as of the end of 1971 was 6.3 percent of taxable payroll. As of June 30, 1973, this imbalance was 6.85 percent.

Table 12.5 presents data on the basic valuation made in the twelfth valuation and on four alternative ones. The first alternative shows the effect of using a 3 percent interest rate (which is reasonable for static assumptions) instead of 5 ¾ percent in the static assumptions valuation—namely, a significantly higher actuarial deficiency. The second alternative assumes that the three "temporary" benefit increases legislated will not be made permanent. Under these circumstances the program would be adequately financed by the existing tax schedule, but the underlying assumption is completely unrealistic (as the actuarial report well recognizes).

The two other alternative valuations, which assume dynamic economic conditions, likewise show the dire financial situation of RR. Under all the alternatives except the unrealistic one that assumes the three legislated "temporary" benefit increases will really be temporary, the RR Account would be exhausted in 1980 or 1981, and the pay-as-you-go tax rate (employer and employee combined) would then be about 32 percent of taxable payroll. Such rate would be somewhat lower after 1995, because the financial crunch for RR comes primarily in the next two decades, when the survivors of the high employment of the past make up such a large retirement roll "wave." This may be

TABLE 12.5

Actuarial Balances and Years of Exhaustion of Railroad Retirement Account under Various Alternatives in Twelfth Valuation

Valuation	Economic Assumptions*	Interest Rate	"Temporary" Increases in Benefits Made Permanent	Actuarial Balance†	Year of Exhaustion of Account	Current-Cost Tax Rate Needed after Exhaustion
Basic.........	Static	5¾%	Yes	− 6.85%	1981	32%
Alternative 1..	Static	3	Yes	−10.85	1980	32
Alternative 2..	Static	5¾	No	+ 2.5	None	n.a.
Alternative 3..	Dynamic (2¾%/5%)	5¾	Yes	‡	1981	30
Alternative 4..	Dynamic (3½%/5%)	5¾	Yes	‡	1980	32

* Under dynamic assumptions, figures in parentheses refer to assumed increases in prices and wages, respectively.
† In terms of level-equivalent percentage of taxable payroll. As of June 30, 1973.
‡ Not given.
Source: A. M. Niessen, "Twelfth Actuarial Valuation of the Assets and Liabilities under the Railroad Retirement Acts as of December 31, 1971," Railroad Retirement Board, August 1973.
n.a. = not available.

compared with the tax rate scheduled in the law for that period of 19.1 percent (exclusive of the HI portion of the tax).

Calculations made by the Railroad Retirement Board subsequent to the twelfth valuation have shown the situation under the static valuation at 5¾ percent interest on the basis that the "temporary" benefit increases are permanent and with the effect of the July 1973 OASDI and RR amendments. The net result of these OASDI amendments was an increase in the actuarial deficiency of 0.59 percent of taxable payroll. The RR amendments (providing full benefits at age 60 for male workers with 30 or more years of service) produced a further increase in cost of 1.22 percent of taxable payroll. Thus, the total increase in the actuarial deficiency was 1.81 percent of taxable payroll, and the resulting total actuarial deficiency became 8.66 percent of taxable payroll, or 45 percent of the level equivalent of the tax schedule (excluding the HI portion thereof). Truly, the RR system then faced a financial crisis of major order—both over the long range and in the immediate future (since, under the then-existing law, the RR Account would be exhausted within a decade, and then the necessary tax rates—even on a current-cost basis—would be staggering).

The twelfth valuation also examined the status of the supplementary annuity program. It was estimated that the tax rate would have to be increased gradually from the present 8½ cents per hour to 12¾ cents in 1985, but that ultimately it would decrease to less than 5 cents.

After considering the effects of the OASDI amendments of December 1973 (increasing the benefit level by 11 percent for June 1974, instead of the 5.9 percent according to the amendments of July 1973, and raising the taxable earnings base for 1974 from $12,600 to $13,200), the total actuarial deficiency increased from 8.66 percent to 9.05 percent of taxable payroll.

The 1974 amendments largely remedied the financial crisis of the RR system. Despite the serious financial imbalance at the time, benefits were liberalized in certain respects (for example, supplemental annuities made available at age 60 with 30 years of service, increased survivor benefits, and unreduced wife's benefits at age 60 for workers with 30 years of service). This cost increase, which had a level cost of 2.78 percent of taxable payroll exclusive of the cost for liberalizing the supplemental annuities, was more than offset by the reduction in the retirement benefit amounts that would be payable in the long-distant future (a savings of 3.43 percent of payroll) and by the elimination of dual-benefits accruals in the future (a savings of 3.80 percent of payroll). The financing was greatly helped by the payment of the cost of windfall past-service dual benefits in the future by the General Fund of the Treasury and by the revised interest basis for the investments of the RR Account (a combined effect of 3.64 percent of payroll). The net result was an estimated actuarial deficiency for the RR system of only 0.96 percent of taxable payroll on a level basis. Thus, the long-range financing problem was largely solved, although the deficiency is still of a significant amount.

Table 12.6 presents data on the projected operations of the combined regular and supplemental programs for the next 25 years. From a short-range standpoint, the cash-flow problems of the next two decades have also been largely solved. There could, however, be difficulties in the 1990s when the fund balance is estimated to reach a minimum of only about $100 million before rising again in the subsequent years, when the retirement roll "wave" due to the high employment of bygone years has ebbed. Such cash-flow problem would be dissipated if the financial interchange provision between OASDI and RR were put on an accrual basis, as was proposed initially in connection with the 1974 legislation.

TABLE 12.6
Projection of RR Fund under 1974 Amendments, Static Conditions
(in millions)

Calendar Year	Benefit Outgo*	RR Tax Income†	Supplemental Annuity Taxes	Financial Interchange‡	Windfall Reimbursement§	Fund at End of Year‖
1975.........	$3,135	$1,230	$110	$1,145	$250	$3,810
1976.........	3,135	1,190	115	1,180	250	3,700
1977.........	3,120	1,155	120	1,185	250	3,565
1978.........	3,105	1,120	125	1,190	250	3,400
1979.........	3,095	1,100	125	1,190	250	3,205
1980.........	3,075	1,075	130	1,190	250	2,985
1981.........	3,055	1,055	130	1,175	250	2,725
1982.........	3,040	1,055	135	1,160	250	2,450
1983.........	3,025	1,055	135	1,140	250	2,150
1984.........	3,005	1,055	135	1,115	250	1,820
1985.........	2,970	1,055	140	1,095	250	1,490
1990.........	2,580	1,055	130	1,030	250	360
1995.........	2,145	1,055	115	755	250	100
2000.........	1,790	1,055	80	540	250	625

* All benefits derived from both RR and OASDI earnings, including supplemental annuity and windfall amounts, less any concurrent benefits based on OASDI wages only.

† From regular RR tax rate.

‡ OASDI benefits on combined earnings, less OASDI taxes on railroad earnings, less concurrent benefits based on OASDI wages only.

§ Amount needed to finance the entire windfall liability by level payments over a 25-year period. Each payment is reduced by a level amount of an estimated $35 million, derived from the excess interest earned under the provisions of the 1974 Act as compared with the interest under the previous law.

‖ Includes the combined regular and supplemental accounts. The fund begins with $3,900 million at the end of 1974. The interest rate used to estimate the interest receipts begins at approximately the level anticipated under the investment policy of the 1974 Act and decreases eventually to 5¾%. The development of the fund balances includes the effect of both interest receipts and administrative expenses.

Source: Railroad Retirement Board.

OPERATION OF AUTOMATIC-ADJUSTMENT PROVISIONS

The 1974 Act provided for automatic adjustment of certain parts of the new basic future service RR benefit formula provided in that legislation to reflect changes in the CPI prior to retirement.

Initially, this basic formula, on a monthly basis, is $4.00N + (0.005) \cdot N \cdot W$, where N is the years of service after 1974 and W is the average monthly compensation after 1974. For retirements in 1978 and after, the amount so derived is increased by $4.00(0.65C)N$, where C is the increase in the CPI from September 1976 to the September before either the year of retirement or 1980, whichever is earlier. There is also a further increase amounting to

$$(.005)N\left[(.65)C \cdot W_{1980} - (W_{1980} - W_{1976})\right],$$

if this amount is not negative, where W_{1980} is the average monthly compensation after 1974, disregarding any compensation after 1980 which is in excess of the maximum taxable wage base in 1980, and W_{1976} similarly relates to 1976.

The foregoing complicated procedure is done in an attempt to update the formula for changes in economic conditions, although only for a temporary four-year period. Before 1981, however, there may well be further collective bargaining on this matter. The adjustment procedure for the flat-dollar part of the benefit formula is straight-forward; the use of only 65 percent of the CPI increase resulted from the collective bargaining involved in the labor-management negotiations. The complicated expression for the adjustment of the percentage-of-wage part of the benefit formula arose from the refinement of deducting (1) the gross increase in the basic benefit from this part of the formula that results from a higher wage base from (2) the increase that results from the 65 percent of the CPI change.

chapter 13

Unemployment Insurance
Programs

Before the passage of the Social Security Act in 1935, formalized protection against the risk of unemployment in the form of cash benefits was relatively sparse. There had been a number of nongovernmental plans sponsored by labor unions and also by individual employers, largely in the form of a minimum guarantee of a certain amount of employment per year. In the 1950s, several supplemental unemployment benefit plans (SUB) were established by collective bargaining in some of the mass-production industries (steel and automobile, primarily).

The first governmental unemployment insurance program was enacted by Wisconsin in 1932 and served as a forerunner for the unemployment insurance provisions of the Social Security Act, even though it did not come into full operation until after the latter was enacted. Interestingly enough, however, the Wisconsin provisions were, and still are, significantly different from those of the vast majority of the state plans now in operation.

The high unemployment prevalent in the early 1930s gave great impetus to the inclusion of unemployment insurance provisions in the Social Security Act of 1935, even though these provisions related to persons with current employment and then potential subsequent unemployment in the future, and not to those currently unemployed when the legislation was being enacted. The early terminology of this branch of social insurance was "unemployment compensation" rather than "unemployment insurance," which was used because of what were believed to be constitutional problems. Just as with OASDI, the benefit provisions and the contribution (or tax) provisions were two separate titles of the law.

Although there was much discussion about having unemployment insurance (UI) be a national program administered by the federal government, as is OASDI, this path was not taken; rather, it was decided to have separate state plans. This has resulted in variations among the states, and a lack of the uniformity that would have been possible under a national system.

For constitutional reasons, the federal government could not compel the states to establish unemployment insurance systems. In actual practice, however, this was accomplished by the so-called "tax offset" procedure. By July 1937, all states, Alaska, Hawaii, and the District of Columbia had enacted laws establishing UI programs. Puerto Rico did likewise on its own in the 1950s, and came under the federal-state system as a result of the 1960 amendments to the Social Security Act; the Virgin Islands also enacted an unemployment insurance system in 1961, but it is not included in the federal-state UI program.

The tax offset procedure worked in the following manner. A federal unemployment tax was imposed on all employers in industry and commerce who had eight or more employees on at least one day in each of 20 different weeks in a year. However, employers could be relieved of paying as much as 90 percent of this tax if they made contributions under an approved state UI system. Accordingly, a state that taxed employers to pay for UI did not put the employer at a disadvantage in competing with similar businesses in other states. If a state did not establish a UI system, employers in that state still would have to pay the full federal unemployment tax, and yet no benefits would be payable to unemployed workers. Moreover, employers in states with UI systems might pay less in total (i.e., the sum of the reduced federal tax and the tax for the state UI system) because of the merit-rating or experience-rating provisions included in an approved UI system. These provisions could result in a lower state tax rate than the amount of waived federal tax if the UI costs are low for the particular employer (and which only rarely result in a higher rate for employers with poor experience). The tax offset is an obvious and apparent reason why all the states established UI systems.

Another incentive existed for states to set up UI systems. The Social Security Act also authorized grants to states to meet the necessary and proper costs of administering UI systems. Although not explicitly stated in the law, the source of these grants was the residual federal unemployment tax collected that remained after waiving 90 percent of the employer tax for employers in states with approved UI systems.

PROVISIONS OF ORIGINAL FEDERAL LAW

The federal unemployment tax originally applied to all employers in industry and commerce (including railroads) who had eight or more employees in at least 20 different weeks of the year. States could— and many did—have broader coverage than this. The tax was at a rate of 1 percent for 1936, 2 percent for 1937, and 3 percent for 1938 and thereafter, and was levied on the entire payroll of the employer. No employee contributions were required, although a few states provided for them.

This graded tax schedule was introduced in order that the economy should not be seriously affected by the sudden impact of a 3 percent tax. Unemployment benefits were to be payable only after a certain period (generally, not until 1938), so as to permit earnings records to be developed and so as to permit the building-up of a fund. However, extensive funds were thus not immediately needed, and so a level high tax rate was not required from the start.

An employer could offset 90 percent of the foregoing federal tax if the state UI system to which he contributed had a basic rate of at least this amount. In actual practice, all states so provided. Furthermore, the employer would have this 90 percent offset—or, in other words, pay only 10 percent of the federal tax—if under the merit-rating provisions of the state plan he was excused from paying the normal rate as a result of his unemployment experience. In some plans, these provisions can excuse the employer completely from paying any tax to the state UI system. Initially, many states did not have experience-rating provisions, but interstate economic pressures and competition soon resulted in all states doing so. Accordingly, beginning in 1938, employers paid a federal tax of 0.3 percent of covered payroll that went into the General Treasury, but in actuality was used in large part for the administrative grants to the state UI systems.

There are various requirements that state UI systems must meet to be "approved" under the federal law. The most important of these are as follows:

1. All taxes collected must be deposited in the Unemployment Trust Fund in the United States Treasury. This fund is invested as a whole, but each state has a separate account to which are credited its deposits and its share of investment income. The state UI system may withdraw money from its account at any time, but only for the purpose of paying benefits or refunding taxes that were improperly paid. The assets of the Unemployment Trust Fund may be invested only in United States Government securities in the same way as is applicable for the OASDI trust funds, except that the interest rate on special issues is based on the average coupon rate on all interest-bearing obligations of the United States (the same basis as for OASDI before the 1956 amendments).

2. Unemployment benefits must be paid through public employment offices or other approved agencies.

3. The UI system must have methods of administration that will assure full payment of benefits when due.

4. Beneficiaries must have a right of appeal of the decisions of the state UI system.

5. Benefits cannot be denied because a claimant refuses to accept a job under certain conditions, so that established standards as to prevailing wages, working conditions, and union affiliations are protected.

It will be seen that the above requirements of federal law are intended to assure that an approved state UI system is fairly administered. The state itself, however, determines the appropriate benefit provisions —qualification period, waiting period, duration of benefits, and amount of benefits. Similarly, the state can decide to cover additional categories of workers over those prescribed by federal law, and can also establish the basis for tax rates, including the form of merit rating.

AMENDMENTS TO FEDERAL LAW

The UI provisions of the federal law have been amended a number of times since the original program was enacted in 1935, although the changes made were not usually as significant as those made in OASDI over the years. In 1938, legislation removed railroad employers from coverage of the system by establishing a separate UI program for railroad workers (described in a subsequent section). In 1939, effective for that year, the unemployment tax was made applicable only to the first $3,000 of annual wages of each worker, rather than to the total payroll. This then conformed with the basis under the OASDI system, although subsequently the UI base was not increased at times when the OASDI base was raised.

Beginning in 1955, employees of the federal government were brought under the coverage of the UI program. This was accomplished by such employees being compensated under the UI provisions of the state in which they were employed and by the federal government reimbursing the state systems for the cost of unemployment benefits paid to former federal employees on the basis of their federal employment. In 1958, similar coverage was provided for unemployed ex-servicemen. These benefits are paid in accordance with the provision of the state in which the claim is filed, with the previous wage history being based on length of service at an earning rate determined from a schedule according to final military pay (the state merely acts as the agent of the federal government and is fully reimbursed for its expenditures).

Beginning in 1956, the coverage to which the federal unemployment tax applied was changed from employers of eight or more on 20 different days in a year to such employers with four or more employees on 20 days. By that time, however, most of the states had already covered such smaller employers by their own actions.

Over the years, the funds allocated for administration to the state UI systems had, in the aggregate, been somewhat less than the receipts under the Federal Unemployment Tax Act. As a result, pressure arose to make such "windfall income" to the federal government available to the states.

One way this was done was by a legislative change in 1954 that provided for federal assistance (in the form of loans) to states with low UI reserves; legislation along these general lines had been enacted in 1944, but never became effective. It was provided that after a $200-million total cash reserve had been built up for the purpose of making loans to states for payment of benefits (and, under certain conditions, payment of administrative expenses), any excess of collections from the Federal Unemployment Tax Act over (1) grants to states for administrative expenses and (2) federal administrative expenses should be turned over to the state UI systems. These loans are on a no-interest basis. However, equitably, any interest earnings on the state account in the Unemployment Trust Fund of a state that has an outstanding loan is not credited to that state, except for earnings on such portion of the account as exceeds the loan. In determining whether the $200-million limit has been reached, there are not counted the amounts of any loans outstanding. Furthermore, any repayment of loans that would bring the balance over $200 million is permitted. The foregoing financial arrangement was only prospective and did not take into account the past excess collections.

In 1958, certain temporary provisions were enacted to provide extended unemployment benefits for those who had exhausted their rights under the state UI systems. The cost of these additional benefits was met by interest-free loans to the state UI systems from the General Treasury. Only about one third of the states (generally the larger industrial ones) utilized these provisions.

In 1960 the following important changes were made in the UI program:

1. The net portion of the federal unemployment tax (the remainder of the federal tax could be offset by credit for taxes paid under a state UI plan) was increased from 0.3 percent to 0.4 percent (since the tax offset for those covered by a qualified state plan remained at the 2.7 percent rate that had been in effect since 1938), applied to the first $3,000 of annual covered wages. This increase was needed because of rising operational costs which, by then, were about equal to the receipts of the residual federal tax.
2. The proceeds of this higher federal tax, after covering the administrative expenses of the employment security program, were available to build up a larger fund for loans to states whose reserves had become depleted. The maximum limitation on the cash size of the loan fund was increased from the $200 million under the previous law to the higher of $550 million or 0.4 percent of total wages subject to state UI taxes. Also, the conditions relating to eligibility for and repayment of loans were tightened.
3. Improvements were made in the arrangements for financing the administrative costs of the program by building up a revolving fund of $250 million for such expenditures.
4. Coverage was extended to some 60,000 to 70,000 additional employees—those working in federal reserve banks, federal credit unions, and commercial and industrial activities of nonprofit institutions.
5. Puerto Rico was brought into the program.

In 1961, temporary provisions for extended unemployment benefits were again legislated. Each unemployed worker would receive benefits for an additional number of weeks equal to 50 percent of those provided by the state program under which he had received benefits, but subject to a 39-week maximum on the "regular" and extended benefits combined. These extended unemployment benefits (including those paid beyond 26 weeks under the permanent "regular" benefit provisions) would be applicable to persons exhausting their regular benefits in the 21-month period beginning July 1960. These benefits would be paid automatically (without change in state systems being necessary) through the state systems, financed entirely from federal funds that would be obtained by increasing, temporarily for 1962–63, the tax rate from 3.1 to 3.5 percent, with the net portion retained by the federal government being raised from 0.4 to 0.8 percent. It was estimated that this temporary additional tax would finance the additional extended benefits.

In 1963 the experience under the extended-benefits provisions indicated that its financing was more than adequate. Accordingly, the gross tax rate was reduced from 3.5 to 3.35 percent for 1963, so that the remaining net rate was 0.65 percent. In 1964 the gross rate returned to 3.1 percent, with the net rate being 0.4 percent.

The 1970 amendments broadened the coverage of UI by removing the four-employee requirement, so that all firms are included as long as they have at least one employee who meets the wage-service requirement (one employee or more in each of 20 weeks in a year, or quarterly payroll of at least $1,500). Also covered under UI are certain categories which have been covered for some time as employees under OASDI (persons who are not considered employees under common law, such as certain agent-drivers and outside salesmen;[1] certain agricultural processing workers; and U.S. citizens employed abroad by a U.S. employer). This legislation also required the state programs to extend coverage to state hospitals and universities and to nonprofit institutions in the charitable, educational, and scientific fields other than churches and schools below the university level. Such nonprofit coverage is not subject to the federal UI tax, and the employers so involved may "contract-out" by reimbursing the state system on an

---

[1] But note that other groups of noncommon-law employees covered as employees under OASDI are not covered under UI—namely, persons who work in their homes on materials furnished by others and full-time life insurance salesmen.

"actual cost" basis for the benefits actually paid to its exemployees, rather than paying the applicable state UI tax rate. Since most such organizations have little unemployment that they create, many of them have chosen the contracting-out route.

The 1970 amendments further provided that retroactive to the beginning of the year, the gross tax rate would be increased from 3.1 percent to 3.2 percent, with the net tax rate being 0.5 percent. The same legislation also increased the taxable wage base—from the $3,000 which had been in effect since 1939 to $4,200, effective in 1972. It was remarkable that the $3,000 base had been unchanged for over three decades in the face of the great increases in wages during that time.

In addition, the 1970 legislation initiated a permanent extended-benefits program, which states had to adopt before 1972 (or lose the tax-offset privilege). This was financed half by the above-mentioned increase in the net UI tax rate for 1970–71 and by 10 percent of the net federal UI tax receipts thereafter (i.e., based on a 0.05 percent tax rate) and half from the state's UI fund. These benefit provisions are described in more detail later.

In 1971, because of continued high unemployment, the duration for which benefits would be available in states with continuous high unemployment was increased on a *temporary* basis (until September 1972)—in essence, by allowing a further 13 weeks of "emergency" benefits after both regular and extended benefits are paid. This was extended for six months by legislation in 1972. The temporary emergency benefits under the 1971 law were financed out of general funds of the federal government, although these may be repaid (without interest) in the future if all the various federal accounts in the unemployment trust fund reach their statutory maximums. The 1972 law provided for financing these emergency benefits for the period July 1972 through March 1973 from the Extended Unemployment Compensation Account, whose income was augmented by a legislated increase in the net federal tax rate—from 0.50 percent to 0.58 percent—instead of half from this account (through the net federal tax rate) and half from the state UI funds as is the case for the permanent extended benefits. This increased tax rate for 1973 was payable by employers in all states even though their state did not have high enough unemployment to have the emergency-benefit provisions apply or did not agree to participate in this program.

Because of the continuous high level of unemployment in some states, further legislation in 1972 removed *temporarily* (until July

1973) one of the restrictions against the extended benefits being able to go into effect in particular states (described in more detail later). This provision was extended for six months by legislation in 1973.

From time to time, there have been proposals that the federal law should include certain minimum benefit standards (in regard to maximum duration of benefits, amount of benefits, and so forth). However, no legislative action along these lines has occurred. For example, an administration bill introduced in 1963 included the following provisions:

1. The net federal tax rate would be raised from 0.4 to 0.7 percent —to finance equalization grants of two thirds of the excess benefit costs of states whose benefit costs (under a plan with approved provisions as to benefits) exceed 2.7 percent of taxable wages and to finance a new program of federal unemployment adjustment benefits for those who had had a long-employment record and had exhausted their state benefits—payable at the same rate and for a period of 13 to 26 weeks.
2. Weekly benefit amounts, to meet approval for equalization grants, and to give full credit toward the federal tax for state unemployment taxes, would have to be at least 50 percent of the worker's average wage, up to a maximum benefit amount of at least 66⅔ percent of the average covered wage in the state (lower proportions permitted until 1970). In 1965 the Senate passed a bill containing benefit standards (but not equalization grants). The House, however, did not accept this change, and the proposal died.

In 1973, President Nixon proposed several important changes in the UI program. First, the maximum benefit should be 66.6 percent of the average weekly wage in the state; only four jurisdictions (Arkansas, District of Columbia, Hawaii, and Utah) met this standard at that time. Second, farm workers should be covered. Third, employees on strike should not be able to receive benefits (New York and Rhode Island permit this). Congress did not act in 1973 on these proposals.

In early 1974, President Nixon renewed his request for enactment of these proposals and added several further ones as a result of the energy crisis and the accompanying unemployment. Further, it was proposed that the conditions for the provision of extended benefits during periods of high unemployment should be temporarily liberalized. In addition, extended benefits for an additional 13 weeks would be available in all states, making a total of 26 weeks of extended benefits in states where the permanent extended benefits provision had been triggered by high unemployment (such provision is described in more detail later). Also, 26 weeks of benefits should be available to workers not covered by UI (such as farm workers, domestic workers, and state and local government employees), with benefit amounts and eligibility conditions based on state laws and with the cost met by the federal government.

In October 1974, in recognition of the high rate of unemployment, President Ford proposed a program of temporary unemployment assistance, and also a program of work projects. The unemployment assistance benefits, which would be made through the state programs at their benefit rates, would be completely financed by the federal government. Such benefits would be available only after the national unemployment rate averaged at least 6.0 percent for three consecutive months; actually, it reached this level in October 1974. The program would cease, as to new beneficiaries, at the end of 1975.

Such proposed unemployment assistance benefits would be paid for an additional 13 weeks to those who had exhausted their benefit rights under the state UI programs. They would also be paid for 26 weeks to other workers who had a significant attachment to the labor force even though not covered under UI. In either case, benefits would be available only with respect to workers who last worked in an area with substantial unemployment.

Congress enacted these proposals at the end of 1974. The payments for an additional 13 weeks to those who had exhausted their regular and extended UI benefits are designated as emergency benefits. In the same legislation, the national trigger for payment of extended benefits was reduced, for 1975–76, from 4.5 percent to 4.0 percent. The legislation also provided for waiving the 120 percent requirement for operation of state extended-benefit "on" triggers until 1977.

Then in April 1975, in connection with tax reduction legislation, the maximum duration of emergency benefits was increased to 26 weeks. As a result, the overall maximum benefit duration could be as much as 65 weeks. Such change is effective only until June 30, 1975, but as has happened in the past, "temporary" provisions often later become permanent.

FEDERAL FINANCING PROVISIONS

Table 13.1 presents the UI tax rates and wage bases which have been in effect over the years.

TABLE 13.1

Unemployment Insurance Tax Rates and Wage Bases

Period	Wage Base	Federal Tax Rate (on employers)	
		Gross	Net*
1936............	None	1.00%	0.10%
1937............	None	2.00	0.20
1938............	None	3.00	0.30
1939–60.........	$3,000	3.00	0.30
1961............	3,000	3.10	0.40
1962............	3,000	3.50	0.80
1963............	3,000	3.35	0.65
1964–69.........	3,000	3.10	0.40
1970–71.........	3,000	3.20	0.50
1972............	4,200	3.20	0.50
1973............	4,200	3.28	0.58
1974 and after..........	4,200	3.20	0.50

* Rate payable if state has a qualified UI program.

The federal unemployment tax was, for many years, collected annually, after the end of the calendar year (unlike OASDI, under which most employers pay the taxes monthly and submit detailed reports quarterly). Now, however, it is collected quarterly.

The federal law does not require a tax on employees but, on the other hand, does not prevent this. In the beginning, nine states had employee contributions. Now, only two of these states (Alabama and New Jersey) plus Alaska provide for employee contributions, and in Alabama they are payable only when the fund is low. In two states (New Jersey and Rhode Island), the employee contributions that were originally established for unemployment insurance purposes were changed over and used for purposes of temporary disability benefits (see Chapter 15).

In general, the theory underlying the financing almost entirely by employers—as compared with the joint contributory nature of OASDI and railroad retirement—has been that unemployment which is compensable is rarely the "fault" of the employee and is frequently the "fault" of the employer (although often actually being due to general economic conditions).

It is interesting that as a practical matter, many representatives of labor now regret that UI is not a joint contributory system because, under such circumstances, they would have much more influence in legislative modification of the UI system (both federal and state). As the situation is now, they have much less influence than under the joint contributory OASDI system. Under UI, the legislators tend to feel that the labor unions do not have an important stake, since "the employer pays the entire bill."

Considering the federal requirements, it was possible for state UI programs to be established without experience-rating provisions (described in the next section). In the beginning, a number of plans did so and thus devoted the full 2.7 percent tax (in 1938 and thereafter) to UI purposes. However, the states without experience-rating provisions rapidly adopted them, and now all jurisdictions except Puerto Rico follow this procedure. In part, this was because of the large funds that were built up, since unemployment was relatively low after the systems really began operating in the early 1940s. In part, this was due to interstate economic competition with states that had considerably lower average UI contribution rates because of the experience-rating provisions. Alaska had experience-rating provisions until 1955, when they were eliminated as one step to solve the financial difficulties of its UI system; in 1960, they were readopted.

All funds collected by the state UI systems (and by the railroad UI system) must be deposited in the Unemployment Trust Fund in the United States Treasury. Each system has a separate account (see subsequent section for description of special accounts for the railroad UI system). Disbursements are made from these state accounts to pay benefits (each UI system draws lump sums as needed and then pays the benefits individually, maintaining a small cash working balance) and to refund any taxes that were erroneously collected.

There are three general accounts in the Unemployment Trust Fund. The Employment Security Administration Account provides a reserve fund to help finance current administrative expenses, primarily needed as a result of the uneven flow of the net tax income during the year, as against the more or less regular flow of the administrative expense reimbursements.

Prior to legislation enacted in 1963, federal appropriations for grants to the states for administering the UI program were limited by specified annual dollar maximums (for all state systems combined). Now, there is a flexible basis for determining the amount of this ceiling—namely, 95 percent of the estimated receipts from the net tax rate after deducting the rate which goes for financing the extended benefits (e.g., for 1974 and after, 0.5 percent minus 0.05 percent, or 0.45 percent).

Advances to state UI systems with depleted accounts are made from the Unemployment Account, repayable without any interest charge. Such advances are made only in amounts necessary to pay benefits during the current month of advance, after taking into consideration available assets and income to be received by the state account. If a state UI system does not repay the advance within about 23 months, the credits that employers in such state can obtain against the federal unemployment tax (a credit of 2.7 percent) are successively reduced for each year of delay (with further reductions if subsequently the state UI system does not collect, in the aggregate, at least as much as a flat 2.7 percent tax rate would provide). The increased federal unemployment tax in such cases is applied to reduce the state's loan.

The Extended Unemployment Compensation Account is first credited with 10 percent of the tax receipts (20 percent in 1970–71 and an additional 0.08 percent of payroll in 1973 for financing the temporary emergency benefits), until it reaches the larger of $750 million or ⅛ percent of the total payroll in covered employment (the $750 million will apply for about five years, since the latter basis goes into effect only when such payroll exceeds $600 billion, and in 1974 that payroll was only about $480 billion). The remainder of the net federal tax is credited to the Administration Account until it reaches its statutory maximum of 40 percent of the total of the annual state administrative expenses (before July 1972, this maximum was fixed at $250 million). After this level is reached, the excess is transferred to the Extended Unemployment Compensation Account, until it reaches its prescribed maximum.

The Unemployment Account does not receive any funds from the receipts of the net federal tax until the Extended Unemployment Compensation Account and the Administration Account are at their prescribed maximum levels. Then, the Unemployment Account (exclusive of outstanding noninterest-bearing loans to systems with depleted reserves) is built up to a maximum of the larger of $550 million or ⅛ percent of the total payroll in covered employment. Since such total payroll has been, in 1973 and subsequently, in excess of the "breaking point" of $440 billion, the $550 million limit no longer will be applicable.

Under previous law, the Unemployment Account had precedence on the net federal UI taxes over the Administration Account until, as of any June 30, it reached a maximum of the larger of $550 million or 0.4 percent of taxable wages in the previous calendar year (the latter limit having been applicable since the mid-1960s). At the time of change in the funding basis of the several UI accounts in mid-1972, the Unemployment Account had a balance of $550 million.

Interest from investments is credited to the state and other accounts in the Unemployment Trust Fund. Although there are a number of separate accounts (as described previously), their investment experience is on a pooled basis. The investments must all be in federal government securities, just as is the case with the OASDI Trust Funds. The interest basis on special issues of the Unemployment Trust Fund is that which prevailed for the OASDI Trust Funds during 1940–56 (namely, the average coupon interest rate on all interest-bearing obligations of the United States government).

ADMINISTRATION OF THE PROGRAM

Initially, the Social Security Board was responsible for administering the aspects of the UI program that related to the federal government, such as determining whether the state UI programs meet the federal requirements and making the grants for administrative expenses were concerned. Subsequently, this responsibility was transferred to the Bureau of Employment Security in the Department of Labor, which is also involved with the public employment service offices. It is because of the latter function that it was decided to transfer this branch of social insurance away from the federal agency that deals with the remainder of the programs established by the Social Security Act.

Each state has an employment security agency that administers the UI program. Some of these are in the department of labor of the state, although most are independent agencies within the state government. The collection of the federal unemployment tax and the investment of the Unemployment Trust Fund have always been a responsibility of the U.S. Department of the Treasury.

COVERAGE PROVISION CHARACTERISTICS
OF STATE PLANS

As indicated previously, the federal law requires that certain coverage provisions be contained in the state UI systems (hereafter, this term denotes not only the systems of the 50 states but also those of the District of Columbia and Puerto Rico), but many go beyond the federal requirements. About 60 percent of the states have adopted the federal definition of employer and do not go beyond it. On the other hand, about 15 percent of the states have the broadest possible coverage by including all employers (just as does OASDI). The remainder of the states have requirements of less than 20 weeks or quarterly payrolls of less than $1,500 (such as using a 13-week requirement or a $225 requirement).

Almost all states exclude farm and domestic workers; employees of charitable, religious, and educational nonprofit organizations who are not required to be covered by federal law; and self-employed persons, although there are certain minor instances where such coverage exists. Probably the only major coverage provided that is not required by federal law is in connection with state and local government employees, in which area most states provide coverage to some categories of these workers.

BENEFIT PROVISION CHARACTERISTICS OF STATE SYSTEMS

As indicated previously, the states have great latitude in establishing the benefit provisions for their UI systems. In fact, it can well be said that no two state systems are anywhere near identical. The following discussion will consider in turn the eligibility requirements, disqualification conditions, waiting periods, maximum durations, and benefit computations. The discussion will relate essentially to current "permanent" provisions, and will not deal with any "temporary extended unemployment" provisions, which have been described previously. Some indication, however, will be given as to historical developments.

Eligibility Provisions

Initial eligibility for unemployment benefits depends upon having a certain amount of covered wages and/or a certain period of covered employment with a certain average wage within a base period. In all systems, this has the effect of requiring a certain amount of earnings in the base period (generally ranging from $300 to $800). In a few instances, the requirement is a flat amount (such as $600); in most instances, it is a multiple of the weekly benefit for which the individual will qualify (such as 30 times the weekly benefit amount) or a multiple of the high-quarter wage (such as $1\frac{1}{2}$ times). A number of states also require that wages must be received in at least 2 quarters of the base period.

Base periods for measuring eligibility for benefits are 52 weeks. These are on a uniform calendar year basis in one state, but in the other states they vary with each individual, depending upon the quarter when he first becomes unemployed. Generally, in such cases, the individual base period is the 4-calendar-quarter period beginning before the quarter preceding the quarter in which he is first unemployed (e.g., if unemployment begins in February 1975, the base period would be October 1973 through September 1974). The reason for the lag between the base period and the beginning of the period of unemployment, the "benefit year," is to permit sufficient time to have elapsed for wage data to be available for the adjudication process.

Disqualification Provisions

Benefits are available only if the individual is able to work and is available for work, as evidenced by registration at a public employment office. A few states, however, permit beneficiaries to continue to be considered eligible even though they become ill after being unemployed and are not able to work. Even though the individual is able to work, he is not necessarily deemed ineligible for benefits if work is available.

In general, the beneficiary is not compelled to take work that differs greatly from his previous employment or that involves unusually unsuitable conditions, such as being at a considerable distance from his residence or being at unusually inconvenient hours. In fact, on this point, it may be noted that the basic philosophy of unemployment insurance is to provide a carry-over period during which an individual can attempt to obtain suitable employment comparable with that in which he has had experience and for which he is trained, rather than forcing him to accept any type of remunerative employment. Most states require that an individual should not only be registered at a public employment office but also should be actively seeking work.

Beneficiaries otherwise eligible may be disqualified for a number of reasons connected with their previous employment, such as voluntary separation, involuntary separation for misconduct, and unemployment due to labor disputes. A disqualification also may be imposed for refusal of suitable work. In some instances, disqualification means a postponement of benefits for a number of weeks, while in other cases, it means a complete cancellation of benefit rights.

If the worker voluntarily quits without good cause, there is always disqualification (ranging from a few weeks to full disqualification). In almost all states, disqualification because of a labor dispute lasts as long as the dispute does.

Special disqualification provisions apply to students who are attending school and to women who are unable to work because of pregnancy or marital obligations (such as a change of residence because of the husband's employment).

Under some state systems, disqualification or reduction of unemployment benefits occurs when certain types of income are received. Duplication of UI benefits under the various systems is not generally permitted (see later discussion about interstate claims). In some states, but by no means in all, such reduction for other income applies to OASDI benefit, workmen's compensation payments, private pensions, and dismissal payments from the employer. Almost all states permit simultaneous payment of unemployment benefits under UI plans and supplemental unemployment benefits under collective-bargaining agreements.

Waiting Period

All but nine states require a waiting period of one week of total unemployment before benefits are payable. In 11 of the states with such a waiting period, retroactive benefits for the waiting period are paid if the benefit period runs for a certain length (usually about five weeks). The remaining states have no waiting period. In the early years of operation of the program, these waiting periods generally were two or three weeks, primarily to be conservative insofar as costs and possible malingering were concerned.

Maximum Duration of Benefits

Eight states have a uniform figure for the maximum duration of benefits for all eligible claimants (generally 26 weeks). All the other states have a maximum duration, but vary it among the beneficiaries according to such factors as the beneficiary's wages in his base period or his weeks of employment in his base period (for example, maximum benefits of one third of his base period wages or maximum duration of 75 percent of his number of weeks of qualifying employment in the base period, but in each case subject to a 26-week maximum). In the latter type of systems a maximum duration is either specified or automatically results. As a result, almost all states have a maximum potential duration of benefits of 26 weeks or more, with a few states going as high as 30–36 weeks. The programs that have variable maximum duration provisions have minimum durations which are either specified or result (in most instances, from 12–15 weeks).

The foregoing discussion does not take into account the special provisions for extending the maximum duration for those who have exhausted their regular benefits when unemployment reaches specified levels.

In the early years of the state plans the maximum durations were considerably shorter—often only 10–15 weeks. As experience developed, it was found that longer maximum durations were financially possible, and they were gradually increased.

Duration of Extended Benefits

So-called extended benefits are paid under a state system after the regular benefit duration has been reached if there is high unemployment in either the nation or the state. These provisions are financed equally from federal funds (from the residual tax rate) and state funds (from its UI taxes). This permanent program was enacted in 1970, effective for October. Temporary programs of this nature were enacted in 1958 (effective for persons exhausting their regular benefits after June 1957, for payments through March 1959) and again in 1961 (effective for persons exhausting their regular benefits in July 1960 to March 1962). The 1958 program merely provided interest-free loans to states that provided for extended benefits beyond their normal durations, but only about one third of the states utilized this provision. The 1961 program was made available on a "free" basis (since it was financed by an increase in the federal net UI tax) and so was utilized by all states.

An extended-benefits period for a state goes into effect three weeks after there is either a national "on" indicator or a state "on" indicator. It ends three weeks after there is an "off" indicator both nationally and in the state, but it must run at least 13 weeks.

A national "on" indicator occurs after three consecutive months in each of which the nationwide insured unemployment rate (seasonally adjusted) is 4.5 percent or more. It should be noted that such rate is based on insured workers who are unemployed and on the average covered employment in the last 12 months and is thus significantly lower than the unemployment rate for the general labor force. The indicator goes "off" after three consecutive months in each of which such rate is less than 4.5 percent. The nationwide insured unemployment rate since October 1970, when the program began, and through December 1973 was 4.5 percent or more in only January–March 1971 and January–February 1972, so that the national indicator did go "on" only once during that period. It rose above 4.5 percent again in November 1974 and was above that level for the next four months, being 6.68 percent in February 1975. As a result, the indicator went "on" in January 1975. It will likely remain "on" for some months, since unemployment was then high and would apparently continue to be so. Also, the law had been changed "temporarily" for 1975–76 to set the limiting point for the indicator at 4.0 percent, instead of 4.5 percent.

A state "on" indicator occurs when, for a 13-week period, its insured unemployment rate is both at least 4.0 percent and at least 20 percent greater than such rate in the corresponding period of the last two years. However, the "on" indicator is not effective if the previous extended-benefit period had ended less than 14 weeks ago. The state indicator goes "off" when such unemployment rate either falls below 4.0 percent or is less than 20 percent above the rate in each of the corresponding periods in the last two years.

The extended benefits are paid at the same rate as the regular benefits, with eligibility for them being based on state law. Their maximum duration is 50 percent of the regular benefits that had been received (including dependents' benefits) or 13 weeks, whichever is less. However, in no event can the combined duration of regular and extended benefits exceed 39 weeks. This would appear to be an incentive for states to establish the duration of regular benefits at 26 weeks, no more and no less.

A few states have wholly state-financed extended-benefits provisions applicable during periods of high unemployment. Since these generally are supplementary to the federal-state extended benefits, they are not of much significance.

The maximum possible duration of benefits was increased *temporarily* by legislation enacted in 1971 that provided for "emergency" benefits, and this was continued by legislation in 1972, but was then allowed to expire. The provision, in essence, gave another 13 weeks of benefits beyond the 39 weeks resulting under the regular and extended benefits. It was effective from the end of January 1972 through March 1973 (but only for persons entitled to benefits before January 1973) in states that agreed to participate (about 20 states did so). Such additional 13 weeks of benefits was provided again by the 1974 amendments.

Since the rate of insured unemployment in several states had remained relatively high for several years, further legislation in 1972 removed *temporarily* the requirement for extended benefits that a state indicator would go "off" if the state's insured unemployment rate for a 13-consecutive-week period is less than 20 percent above such rate in each of the corresponding periods in the last two years. This was effective at each state's option (about 10 states were potentially affected and about half of them had actually utilized this provision) for October 1972 through June 1973. Legislation in 1973 and 1974 extended the termination date to April 30, 1975, and at the same time removed the requirement as it applies to the "on" trigger for that period. Legislation enacted at the end of 1974 further extended this waiver of the 20-percent limiting value until the end of 1976.

Computation of Benefit Amounts

The weekly benefit amount depends upon past covered wages, within certain minimum and maximum limits. Most UI systems base benefits on the calendar quarter in the base period during which wages were highest, since this is supposed to reflect most nearly the worker's typical full-time earnings. In order to achieve a benefit of 50 percent of full-time earnings, the benefit amount is computed at a fraction of such high-quarter wages—frequently 1/26th, but in some plans 1/25th, or even a larger fraction, in order to give some recognition that even in the highest earnings quarter, individuals may not be employed full time. A number of states use a weighted schedule so as to give a higher proportion to lower paid workers (yielding, for example, 1/20th of high-quarter wages for those with the lowest earnings and 1/25th for those with the highest earnings).

The states that do not use the high-quarter method utilize two other approaches—the annual wage formula and the average weekly wage formula. Under the annual wage formula, the weekly benefit is a percentage of annual wages that varies inversely with wage levels (e.g., 2.0 percent of annual wages for the lowest wage groups, down to 1.1 percent for the highest wage groups). Under the average weekly wage formula, the benefit is generally 50 percent of the average weekly wage (usually computed on a "while substantially working" basis during the base period).

An overriding factor in the computation of benefit amounts by these methods is the existence of significant minimum and maximum benefit provisions. Most states prescribe a minimum of about $10–$20 per week. The maximum provisions are probably even more important in their effect on the actual operations of the program. These vary considerably among the states, ranging from a low of $60 to a high of $127 (without considering dependents allowances, discussed subsequently). In the vast majority of the systems the range is from $70 to $90. In about half the states, the maximum benefit provision is on a flexible basis, being a prescribed proportion (generally 50 percent) of the average wage of all covered workers in some previous period. It is, of course, possible that such average wage, or even the prescribed proportion of it, can exceed the maximum taxable wage base.

When a worker is only partially unemployed, all states provide for reduced benefits. The definition of partial unemployment is usually based on having earnings of less than the benefit amount or of less than the benefit amount plus a nominal sum, such as $10 per week. Similarly, the amount of the partial benefit is usually the weekly benefit amount less the wages actually earned in excess of a nominal allowance (such as $5 or $10 a week).

The benefit computation methods have been gradually liberalized over the years. The basis of determining "typical full-time earnings" has been changed on the basis of operating experience so as to increase benefit adequacy. The minimums and maximums have been increased over the years, both to reflect rising price and wage levels and to utilize the generally favorable operating experience.

Dependents Benefits

Eleven states increase the unemployment benefits by providing dependents allowances. The definition of "dependent" in four states includes only children under age 18, or older if unable to work. In the other states, the nonworking wife or husband (and, in some states, parents and brothers and sisters) are considered as dependents. In some states the amount per dependent is a flat sum (such as $5 per week). In other states, the allowance per dependent decreases with increasing size of family. The dependents allowances are subject to certain maximum provisions, generally in dollars (either directly specified, or indirectly by limiting the number of eligible dependents) or as a proportion of the basic benefit amount.

Dependents allowances were not generally contained in the initial laws, but they were added in the early years of operations. The amounts of these benefits have been increased somewhat over the years, although not as much as changes in the price and wage levels. Moreover, there has been no significant tendency for these benefits to be provided by most UI systems.

INTERSTATE PROVISION CHARACTERISTICS OF STATE PLANS

Many covered workers are employed in several states during the course of their lifetimes—and even often within the same year. Problems can arise if the worker becomes unemployed within a few months after taking up employment in a new state because he then may not have sufficient coverage in that state to qualify for benefits. Even if he can qualify, the amount of his benefit might be very low and might be payable for a relatively short duration.

In order to recognize and solve this problem, a vast network of interstate agreements was developed by the various UI systems before 1970, although this was not by any means complete. The 1970 amendments required the states to participate in arrangements for combining the wage record when the claimant has earnings in more than one state. The earnings records in the various states in which the worker had been employed are combined in the determination of benefit eligibility, amounts, duration, and so forth (except in the rare instances that this might be disadvantageous to him—as, for example, by changing the relationship between high-quarter wages and total wages in the year). The cost of the benefits in such cases is shared among the various states involved.

Generally, the state in which the claim is filed is liable for payment of unemployment benefits; and if the claimant had covered wages in that state, its law governs the benefit amount and conditions.

When a beneficiary moves away from the state that is paying his benefits, his new state of residence generally will continue to pay the benefit and to check on his availability for work. But this is done by the new state only as the agent of the UI system that determined the benefit (and, of course, then on a completely reimbursable basis).

FINANCING PROVISION CHARACTERISTICS
OF STATE PLANS

In 1975, in all but six states, the employer tax is based on the same maximum wage base as the federal tax, although a few states had a higher base than the federal one. The base was $4,800 in Minnesota and New Jersey, $5,000 in Oregon, $6,600 in Washington, $7,300 in Hawaii, and $10,000 in Alaska. Also, Hawaii, New Jersey, North Dakota, and Washington have automatic-adjustment provisions, with the base being a certain percentage of a recent state average wage. For example, such percentage is 90 percent for Hawaii, 70 percent for North Dakota (but not less than the federal base, which is currently applicable), and 75 percent for Washington (but subject to no increase if the UI fund balance is 4.5 percent or more of total payrolls).

Before 1972, when the federal requirement as to the base was increased from the original $3,000 to $4,200, quite a few states had bases above the federal requirement. For example, in 1970, 22 states had such a base (mostly, $3,600).

EXPERIENCE-RATING PROVISIONS

The experience-rating provisions are very complex.[2] In general, the state UI system can employ such provisions only after the system has been in operation for three years. On the other hand, new employers can have such provisions applicable to them, on the basis of their own experience, after one year, and, as a result of the 1970 legislation, can have a rate as low as 1 percent for their first year if the state so allows. The experience rating can be based entirely on the experience of the particular employer, or it can be based on both the experience of the particular employer and the pooled experience of all employers. The reasons why there are differences in the tax rates as between employers are either to give an incentive for employment stabilization or to allocate unemployment costs, or a combination of these two elements.

The different systems of experience rating can be roughly classified into five categories, namely, reserve ratio, benefit ratio, benefit-wage ratio, payroll decline, and compensable separations formulas. Some states have combinations of these categories. About two thirds of the

---

[2] For an excellent discussion of this subject, see Denis R. J. George, "Experience Rating Unemployment Insurance," *Proceedings*, Canadian Institute of Actuaries, vol. 4, 1974.

UI systems (32) use the reserve ratio formula method. Only one UI system (Connecticut) used the compensable separation formula method, and it has ceased to do so. The benefit ratio method is used by ten states, the benefit-wage ratio method by five states, and the payroll decline method by four states. Only the Puerto Rico plan has no experience rating, although at times in the past, during periods of high unemployment and thus high UI costs, some states temporarily abandoned their experience rating. For example, in 1962, Oregon, Rhode Island, Washington, and West Virginia did so and assigned a uniform rate of 2.7 percent to all employers.

Under the reserve ratio formula, the cumulative excess of contributions paid by each employer over the benefits paid to his former workers is carried forward and is compared with his payroll, averaged over a period of years (usually the last three years), to give a reserve ratio. A schedule of reduced tax rates (and usually of increased rates as well) is established for various reserve ratios, with such rates being inversely proportional to such ratios. For example, the employer may have to pay the full rate (the amount creditable against the federal tax) if his reserve ratio is less than 5 percent of payroll. In most systems, a very low ratio (or a negative one) results in an employer paying more than the "full rate" (and up to as much as 1 percent of payroll in excess thereof). Then, for reserve ratios in excess of 5 percent, the rate might drop off by 0.2 percent for each increase of 0.5 percent in the reserve ratio until a minimum tax rate of 0.5 percent is reached (in many states, the lowest rate is 0.1 percent; in other states, no tax at all is required for the most favorable experience). In a number of states, there are several different schedules of tax rates for various reserve ratios, depending upon the overall status of the state's UI account; the more favorable the latter is, the lower is the general level of the schedule.

The benefit ratio formula considers only the ratio of benefit payments to former employees of the particular employer as against his taxable payroll, using only the experience (as to both benefits and payrolls) in a recent period, such as the last three years. A schedule of tax rates is established such that each employer's rate will approximate his benefit ratio, and, accordingly, the aggregate statewide result will approximate the benefit ratio for the entire system. In addition, certain minimum and maximum rates are established. In certain systems, there are several schedules, depending upon the financial status of the state UI account.

The benefit-wage ratio formula compares what are termed the "benefit wages" (wages of unemployment beneficiaries of the particular employer) with the employer's total taxable wages both for recent years. This procedure thus takes into account the incidence of unemployment and the unemployment benefit level, but it does not consider the duration of unemployment of the particular employer's former workers. The ratio for a particular employer is, in essence, contrasted with that for the entire state UI system. A schedule is developed so that an employer with the same ratio as the statewide average will pay a tax rate that if paid by all employers, would supply sufficient income to meet the total benefits payable under the system. An employer with a higher ratio would pay a proportionately higher rate, and vice versa, but with certain minimum and maximum rates being established. It might be said that the theory of this method is that no account is taken of the duration of unemployment because this is no "fault" of the particular employer.

Under the payroll variation plan, the benefit experience is not considered, but rather the relative variations in the payroll from year to year or from quarter to quarter. Under this method, as under the previous one, an overall state tax rate is decided upon, and either lower or higher rates are assigned on the basis of the variation in payroll for the particular employer being less or greater than the overall experience in the state.

The compensable separations formula is similar to the benefit-wage ratio method in that the primary factor is the number of former workers of the particular employer who have drawn unemployment benefits. The number of separations multiplied by the weekly benefit (rather than the beneficiaries' wages) is compared with the employer's total payroll, both over a period of several years. The resulting ratio is then compared with the average ratio under the state UI plan. Those employers having such average ratio receive the average tax rate, those with higher ratios receive higher tax rates, and those with lower ratios receive lower tax rates. The overall average tax rate for the state depends on the relation of its account to the total taxable payroll covered by the system (the lower the ratio, the higher is the statewide average tax rate).

Many complicated administrative problems arise under the experience-rating provisions, and these have been handled by various complex procedures. Among such problems are the transfers of the experience of one employer to that of a successor employer, charging of benefits when a worker has been employed by several employers, interest problems, and the like. In addition, the experience-rating schedules sometimes produce anomalous borderline situations when the experience ratios are very close to a boundary point. Under such circumstances, employers are often permitted to make voluntary contributions to change their ratios and thus obtain lower future contribution rates.

Many arguments have been raised pro and con experience rating in UI. Those opposed point out that in social insurance the risks should be spread broadly and that high unemployment for a particular employer may not be his "fault" but rather that of the economy as a whole or due to the nature of his particular business. On the other hand, those favoring experience rating point out that individual employers can stabilize employment if financially encouraged to do so by this procedure and that industries with high UI costs should be obliged to bear their real share of the cost and not have others do so. In any event, by the very nature of interstate business competition, if some states have experience rating, the others will be forced to do so too, since otherwise their employers will be at a tax disadvantage.

RAILROAD UNEMPLOYMENT INSURANCE SYSTEM

When the UI program began operations in 1936 (as to collection of taxes and accumulation of creditable earnings records—benefits not being payable until 1938 or 1939, except in Wisconsin), railroad workers were covered under the various state plans in the same manner as other industrial and commercial workers. However, after the Railroad Retirement Act had been established on a firm basis, and agreement had been reached that no challenge to its constitutionality would be made (see Chapter 12), the railroad labor unions successfully obtained legislation to establish a separate national unemployment insurance system for railroad workers. In part, this was argued for on the basis of the considerable number of railroad workers with interstate employment, although a major factor probably was the desire to obtain a higher level of benefit protection.

Accordingly, in 1939 a separate railroad UI system was established, to be administered by the Railroad Retirement Board. This agency not only pays the benefits but also collects the taxes for this program, instead of having the Treasury Department do so (as is the case for RR). The constitutionality of this program was never challenged by the railroad employers, probably because they would have to be covered under some UI system anyhow.

The RUI system is different in many ways from the state UI systems. The benefit provisions, on the whole, were more liberal than those of the state systems in the early years of operation. In recent years, however, as the railroad industry experienced decreasing employment (and thus RUI costs rose) and since the RUI benefit provisions did not change as greatly as did the state ones, the RUI benefits became more comparable with those under the state plans. The RUI maximum benefit is now somewhat lower than under the state systems (but almost all railroad workers get the maximum, so that the RUI average benefit is higher than in most state plans). With respect to disqualification provisions and extended-benefit provisions, RUI continues to be more liberal than most state systems.

RUI is financed completely by employer taxes that are not individually experience rated. The taxes were, until November 1963, based on the same amount of wages that are taxable and creditable under the railroad retirement system—namely, $300 a month initially (through June 1954); $350 a month for July 1954 through June 1959; and $400 a month for July 1959 and thereafter (not changed in November 1963 when the RR wage base was increased to $450 or for subsequent increases). The total amount of these taxes in essence goes to the RUI system to be used for benefit payments and administration (or, in other words, there is no tax offset device, as in the state UI systems).

Until the 1948 amendments, the RUI tax rate was 3 percent for all employers, but following that legislation, a variable-rate structure was introduced. The rate depends on the size of the fund, and all employers are charged the same rate. This tax, which finances both the UI benefits and the temporary disability benefits (which were inaugurated by the 1946 legislation; see Chapter 15), was set at ½ percent if the balance in the RUI Account on September 30 of the previous year was $450 million or more (as it was at the time of the 1946 legislation). The rate increased by ½ percent for each $50 million less than the $450-million limit, until it reached a maximum of 3 percent if such balance was less than $250 million. The basis was changed in 1959—in part to reflect adverse experience and in part to recognize liberalized benefits instituted then—and the tax schedule was as shown in Table 13.2.

When the 1959 legislation was enacted, the determining balance was under $300 million, so that the maximum rate applied, as it has in

TABLE 13.2

Railroad Unemployment Insurance Tax
Rates under 1959 Amendments

Balance (rounded down, disregarding fractional millions)	Rate
$450 million or more................	1½%
$400–449 million....................	2
$350–399 million....................	2½
$300–349 million....................	3
Under $300 million..................	3¾

all subsequent years. Legislation in 1961 which provided for extended benefits on a temporary basis (paralleling the federal action in this area) increased the tax rate to 4 percent for 1962–63. The 1963 legislation increased the 3¾ percent rate permanently to 4 percent, effective in 1964, where it has since remained.

In connection with the 1968 legislation that established extended benefits for sickness, a yearly transfer of funds from the RR Account to the RUI Account was established. Its purpose was to reimburse the latter account for the estimated savings in disability annuities resulting from payment of extended cash sickness benefits.

The RUI Account, which actually consists of two separate accounts, one for benefits and the other for administrative expenses, with the latter receiving an amount equal to ¼ percent of taxable payroll, is pooled with the various state UI and other accounts in the Unemployment Trust Fund. The investments of all accounts are pooled, and the resulting investment income is prorated. Because of financial difficulties of RUI, legislation in 1959 permits the RUI Account to borrow money from the RR Account when it does not have sufficient funds to pay benefits. Such loans bear interest at the average interest rate earned by special issues of the RR Account.

The RUI benefits, as amended a short time after the program started, were payable with what amounted to a one-week waiting period. Actually, benefits for the initial period of unemployment were payable on the basis of days of unemployment in a 14-day period in excess of 7 days (not counting Sundays and holidays as days of unemployment unless they were preceded and followed by days of unemployment). For subsequent two-week periods of unemployment, benefits were paid for days of unemployment in excess of four days. The 1959 legislation, in essence, eliminated any waiting period by providing that days of unemployment in all two-week periods in excess of four days are compensable (counting all Saturdays and Sundays as days of unemployment).

Under the 1940 legislation, unemployment benefits were payable for a uniform maximum period of about 20 weeks, with a uniform benefit year beginning July 1. This was raised to 26 weeks in 1946. The 1959 legislation provided 13 weeks of additional benefits for those with 10–14 years of railroad service and 26 additional weeks for those with 15 or more years of railroad service. In addition, *temporary* extended unemployment benefits for those with less than 10 years of railroad service were provided by legislation in 1959, parallel to that described previously for workers under the state UI programs. In 1961, legislation provided extended benefits for all workers (limited to 195 times the daily benefit rate), financed by an additional ¼ percent employer tax for 1962–63. The 1959 extended benefits were paid out of the funds in the account.

Qualification for RUI benefits is determined in a simple manner. The individual must have a certain amount of creditable earnings in the base year, which is the calendar year preceding the benefit year, which begins July 1. Initially, this amount of creditable earnings was $300, but over the years—paralleling the rise in the general earnings level—it was increased to $750 in the 1963 amendments and to $1,000 in the 1968 amendments. The 1963 amendments also introduced a further qualifying condition for new entrants into the system, who must also have seven months of service in the base year. These qualifying requirements are generally stricter than those under the state plans.

Disqualification provisions under RUI are generally less severe than under the state systems. For example, unlike almost all state plans, RUI pays benefits to those on strike if the strike is not in violation of the Railway Labor Act or the rules and practices of the labor organizations.

The RUI daily benefit rate is determined in a simple manner. The initial law provided a schedule of rates varying with total creditable earnings (i.e., not counting any monthly wages in excess of the monthly earnings base) in the base year. The current schedule, adopted in 1968, is as shown in Table 13.3.

An alternative method of computation of the daily benefit rate was introduced in the 1951 amendments. This rate was 50 percent of the daily rate of pay for a worker's last railroad job in his base year, if this

TABLE 13.3

Railroad Unemployment Insurance Benefit
Rates Based on Earnings in Base Year

Creditable Earnings in Base Year	Daily Benefit Rate
$1,000–1,299	$ 8.00
1,300–1,599	8.50
1,600–1,899	9.00
1,900–2,199	9.50
2,200–2,499	10.00
2,500–2,799	10.50
2,800–3,099	11.00
3,100–3,499	11.50
3,500–3,999	12.00
4,000 or more	12.70

gave a more favorable result, but in no case could the result exceed the highest one in the benefit schedule. The 1959 legislation liberalized this alternative so that it would be on a 60 percent basis.

On the basis of the benefit schedule, the maximum benefit for a full two-week period of unemployment is $127, or $63.50 per week. This was well above most state UI systems as of 1960, when only one system paid more than this when no dependents were present, and only six systems paid more when dependents were present. However, by 1975, almost all states had liberalized their programs, while RUI had not been changed in this respect, so that RUI held a very low relative position, with only five states having a smaller maximum.

In early 1975, legislation was in progress in Congress that would raise the benefit level significantly, more than doubling it. Also, the benefit level would be automatically adjusted in the future. The financing would be substantially increased by raising the maximum taxable wage base of $400 per month to the same as under the railroad retirement program ($1,175 in 1975). Also, that relationship would be maintained in the future as the RR base rose parallel to that under OASDI, as automatically adjusted.

The RUI benefit rate, when derived from this schedule, can be relatively high in relation to previous earnings. For example, if an individual has average creditable wages of about $900 a month in the base year, his monthly rate of unemployment benefits would be about $279 (since there are about 22 benefit days in a month), or 31 percent of pay. The weighted nature of the benefit schedule results in higher ratios for lower paid workers, but, as a matter of fact, considering the current pay structure in the railroad industry, relatively few persons fall in the middle and lower portions of the benefit table, where there are such high ratios of benefit to average wage. For example, in the unusual case of a worker who earns $300 per month throughout the base year, the daily benefit would be $12 (computed from the benefit schedule, since the "60 percent method" produces only $8.31), which is equivalent to about $264 on a monthly basis, or 88 percent of wages.

A somewhat different picture results when workers with sporadic earnings histories are considered. For instance, consider the unlikely case of an individual who works for four months each year at $300 per month and is unemployed the other eight months. He receives each year $1,200 in wages and $1,080 in unemployment benefits (13 benefit periods of five days each at a daily benefit rate of $8.31 from the "60 percent method," since the benefit schedule yields only $8 per day).

The operations of the RUI system have been affected by the trend in railroad employment (as described in Chapter 12 in connection with the railroad retirement system, which has the same coverage). The number of unemployment beneficiaries (receiving benefits at any time during the year) fell from a level of about 160,000 in benefit years[3] 1940 and 1941 to only 5,000 per year in the middle of World War II, and then rose to levels of 150,000 to 300,000 in most postwar years up through 1963–64 (a high of 470,000 in 1950). Since then, the number of unemployment beneficiaries has fluctuated widely—from about 80,000 in benefit years 1967 and 1970 to 316,000 in 1971. The high years in this period are due to the large numbers eligible for benefits as a result of brief major strikes. Removing this element would result in levels of about 100,000 beneficiaries annually.

The number of beneficiaries per 100 eligibles in the postwar period has been as low as eight and as high as 28 (in 1961). In recent years, this ratio has generally ranged from 10 to 15 percent. For the benefit year 1972, the eligibles (with at least $1,000 of wages in the base year, and more restrictive conditions for new entrants) represented 87 percent of those with any wages in the base year (1970).

About 90 percent of these eligibles had at least $4,000 of wages in 1970, so that it is not too surprising that 99 percent of them had the

---

[3] Generally speaking, a benefit year covers a fiscal year period; for example, fiscal year 1975 is July 1974 through June 1975

maximum daily benefit rate of $12.70 (considering also that the alternative method of benefit computation almost always produces this rate if the earnings schedule does not). As a result, the average daily benefit (payable for five days per week of unemployment) was $12.67 in benefit year 1972. Over the years, this average grew steadily from $2.25 in 1940—as a result of wage increases and liberalizations in the law. Such average benefit remained at a level of about $12.65 in 1973–74.

The average weekly benefit payable under RUI was $63 in all years during 1969–73. It represented 39 percent of average weekly earnings in the railroad industry in 1969, but only 26 percent in 1973. At the same time, the average weekly benefit under the state plans increased from $46 to $59, and the average benefit relative to average earnings stayed relatively level at about 38 percent. These trends for RUI give clear evidence as to why the amendatory legislation in process in early 1975, as mentioned previously, was being advocated.

The average number of days of unemployment (including the two days per week that are not compensable) per beneficiary has been about 60–70 per year recently, although it was as high as 125 in benefit year 1959. Benefit exhaustions in recent years have occurred in about 10 percent of the cases (as high as 33 percent in 1959).

Unemployment benefit disbursements were about $15 million per year before World War II, less than $1 million per year during World War II, and then gradually increasing amounts—$20–$50 million in the lowest years and peaks of about $110 million in benefit year 1950, $150 million in 1955, and $237 million in 1959. The benefit outgo was about $40 million per year in 1965–71, $80 million in 1972, and $20 million per year in 1973–74.

Tax receipts were about $125 million per year until the experience rating (for the system as a whole) became effective in 1948. Then, the receipts (for both UI and cash sickness benefits) fell off to only about $25 million per year, since they were at the ½ percent rate. Following fiscal 1955, they rose as the tax rate was increased when the fund fell—to 1½ percent for 1956, 2 percent for 1957, 2½ percent for 1958, 3 percent for the first five months of 1959, then 3¾ percent, and finally 4 percent beginning in 1962. From fiscal 1960 through fiscal 1967, tax receipts were about $150 million per year. Thereafter, they have decreased slowly, since the taxable payroll declined due to lower employment (which was not offset by higher wage rates, because the maximum taxable earnings base remained at the relatively low level of

$4,800). In 1972–74, the annual tax receipts have been only about $110 million.

Currently, payments from the RR Account to the RUI Account for disability annuities that it did not have to pay because RUI was paying cash sickness benefits are about $5 million per year.

Benefit payments from the RUI Account (for both unemployment and sickness) substantially exceeded tax income in fiscal years 1949 through 1963, but the reverse has usually been the case subsequently. In each year of fiscal year 1969 through 1971, benefit outgo was only about 75–80 percent of tax income, but in fiscal year 1972 it was 106 percent, and in fiscal years 1973 and 1974 it fell to 65 and 45 percent, respectively. This benefit outgo was $93 million in fiscal year 1970, $95 million in 1971, $120 million in 1972, $73 million in 1973, and $51 million in 1974.

Administrative expenses of RUI have been running at about $7 million per year (for UI and cash sickness benefits), or about 4 to 10 percent of benefit outgo, depending on the level thereof.

As a result of the foregoing trends, the RUI Account built up to a peak of about $970 million in fiscal 1948 and then declined, until it was virtually exhausted in fiscal 1960. From then on, this account had to borrow from the RR Account. In November 1963, this debt reached a peak of $327 million, but it subsequently declined, since the 1963 amendments strengthened the RUI financing. Finally, in September 1973, this debt was extinguished, and in December 1973, the RUI Account had a small positive balance, $39 million, while one year later it was $100 million.

APPENDIX

Cost-Estimating Procedures and Operational Data for Unemployment Insurance System

ACTUARIAL COST-ESTIMATING PROCEDURES AND TECHNIQUES

The actuarial methodology for making cost estimates for unemployment insurance is considerably different from that for long-range benefit programs, such as OASDI (as described in the appendix to Chapter 4). Probably the most important reason for such differences is the differing basic nature of the programs. While the UI program, in its entirety, is permanent, the wage-loss protection afforded to each individual worker is comparable to protection provided under one-year renewable term insurance, since both the prior employment needed to acquire eligibility and the duration of benefits that may become payable are limited.

While the probability of unemployment can vary greatly from year to year, the statutory limitations on eligibility, weekly benefit amount, duration, et cetera, tend to limit the range of costs. Cost estimates are prepared in two forms: (1) short-range estimates covering a period of one or two years in the immediate future, and (2) long-range estimates that may extend over an economic cycle of 7 to 10 years. These estimates are used to evaluate the impact of statutory changes in eligibility, weekly benefit amount, duration, et cetera, so as to appraise the adequacy of accumulated reserves and to test the sufficiency of employer tax rates that are produced under experience-rating formulas.

Significant refinements in both cost methods and assumptions have been made over the years. This has occurred as the patterns and features of both the unemployment insurance laws and their operational and administrative consequences have become more clearly defined, and as more information and understanding have been acquired with respect to the economic factors related to the labor market, wage levels, employment and unemployment generally, and that portion (or segment) which is covered under the UI laws. Much of this knowledge has been acquired largely as the result of the accumulation and analysis of large volumes of controlled statistical data which emerged from the unemployment insurance programs. Simultaneously, improvements and refinements in the field of economic measurement, with respect to both the collection and the interpretation of economic statistics, have aided the development of methodology for making cost estimates for unemployment insurance.

In the early 1930s, cost estimates were, of necessity, based largely on hypothetical or mathematical models, due largely to the absence of sufficient statistical experience data. These models were constructed from the very limited census-type data then available on the accessions and separations from the labor work force. Initially, these estimates were used to determine benefit levels and eligibility rules that could be sustained by the predetermined contribution rate.

Only a small volume of benefit payments under the state unemployment insurance programs was made prior to 1939. With the commencement of war in Europe, rising employment in the United States resulted in increased tax revenues and in relatively low total benefit payments under unemployment insurance, reflecting the effects of a wartime economy. The effect of the war was to minimize the emphasis on cost methods and to invalidate the statistics that were then being accumulated for cost projections for the years following the termination of hostilities.

Cost-estimating methods in the years immediately following World War II were therefore restricted by the limited amount of valid data then available. Nevertheless, sufficient knowledge of the nature of unemployment insurance existed to initiate the collection of the types of data likely to be most useful in the preparation of cost estimates. As statistical data were accumulated in the years following 1950, and as postwar economic readjustments and changes became more clearly identifiable and measurable, the patterns of experience data relating to unemployment insurance have revealed an increasing degree of order and consistency. For example, it has been observed that the prevalence of unemployment is greater for older workers than for younger workers (the lower probability of becoming unemployed being more than counterbalanced by the longer duration of unemployment), and likewise greater for less skilled workers than for more skilled workers.

Furthermore, experience tables of continued compensable unemployment provide duration distributions for different types of claimants under different general levels of unemployment. Using such tools, it is possible to measure the effect that factors such as changes in the composition of the work force, age, sex, skills, and wage levels will have on unemployment insurance costs in states such as California, West Virginia, and Arizona, where measurable economic transitions are occurring.

In recent years, improvements in cost-estimating methods have been encouraged by the recognition of the need for adequate and dependable financing provisions in state laws and by the utilization of rapid data processing machinery to summarize the vast variety and detail of economic statistics and unemployment insurance experience data in a cognizable and relevant form. Perhaps the greatest handicap to thorough actuarial cost analysis of UI has been the fact that there are 52 different systems. No two of these systems have identical provisions (or even nearly identical ones). Accordingly, there cannot be the concentrated effort in obtaining statistics and in making cost analyses as is done in connection with the OASDI system.

STATISTICS OF OPERATION OF STATE SYSTEMS

Table 13.4 gives data indicating the coverage operations of the UI system. The number of covered workers almost tripled in the 36 years of operations—as a result of improved business conditions, growth of the population of the country, and extension of coverage by legislative action. The taxable payroll was about 10 times as large in 1973 as it was in 1938, because of the increase in the covered population, because of the rise in the general wage level, and because of the increase in the taxable earnings base that occurred in 1972. The taxable payroll increased by 40 percent from 1971 to 1972, with about three fourths of the rise being due to the higher taxable earnings base and the remainder being due to the higher general wage level, more covered workers as a result of the coverage extensions in the 1970 amendments, and higher general employment. The increase in the taxable payroll from 1972 to 1973 was 7 percent, due primarily to higher earnings levels.

TABLE 13.4

Covered Workers, Taxable Payroll, and Average Wages under State UI Systems for Selected Years

Year	Number of Covered Workers* (millions)	Taxable Payroll† (billions)	Proportion of Covered Payroll That Was Taxable	Average Weekly Wage‡
1938	19.9	$ 25.7	98.0%	$ 25.28
1940	23.1	30.1	92.8	27.02
1945	28.4	58.5	87.8	45.11
1950	32.9	81.5	79.1	60.31
1955	36.6	101.6	68.3	78.12
1960	40.2	119.2	61.1	93.30
1965	45.1	144.0	55.8	109.99
1970	52.2	182.7	47.7	141.09
1971	52.2	182.8	45.2	148.87
1972	56.6	236.3	51.7	155.30
1973	59.7	253.1	49.7	163.97

* In an average payroll period in a month.
† Under the state UI systems.
‡ Without regard to maximum taxable wage base.
Note: Data on covered federal government employees and members of the armed forces are not included here.
Source: *Handbook of Unemployment Insurance Data,* Manpower Administration, U.S. Department of Labor.

The average weekly wage in covered employment (without regard to the maximum taxable wage base) increased by 6½ times from 1938 to 1973. Because the maximum taxable wage base remained at $3,000 during 1939–71, not all the rise in wage levels was reflected in the trend of the taxable payroll. In 1940, about 7 percent of the total payroll in covered employment was not taxable; by 1971, this proportion had risen to 55 percent, although in 1972, as a result of the legislated increase in the tax base, it fell to 48 percent and in 1973 it rose to 50 percent. By states, the average total weekly wage in 1973 varied from a low of about $125–140 in some states, mostly southern ones, to a high of about $175–200 in some of the industrial northern and western states ($233 in Alaska).

Data on beneficiaries and on benefit amounts and durations are given in Table 13.5. The years are selected to include certain ones during which there were business recessions. The average duration of benefits

TABLE 13.5

Beneficiaries, Benefit Amounts, and Duration of Benefits*
under State UI Systems for Selected Years

Year	Number of First Payments† (millions)	Average Duration of Benefits (weeks)	Proportion Exhausting Benefits	Average Weekly Benefit	Benefit as Percentage of Wage‡
1940	5.2	9.8	51%	$10.56	39.1%
1944	0.5	7.7	20	15.90	35.9
1945	2.9	8.5	18	18.77	41.6
1950	5.2	13.0	30	20.76	34.4
1954	6.6	12.8	27	24.93	33.5
1955	4.5	12.4	26	25.04	32.1
1958	7.8	14.8	31	30.54	35.3
1960	6.8	12.7	26	32.87	35.2
1961	7.1	14.7	30	33.80	35.4
1962	6.1	13.1	27	34.56	34.9
1965	4.8	12.2	22	37.19	33.8
1969	4.2	11.4	20	46.17	34.4
1970	6.4	12.3	24	50.31	35.7
1971	6.6	14.4	31	54.35	36.5
1972	5.8	14.0	29	55.82	35.9
1973	5.3	13.4	28	59.00	36.0

* For regular benefits only (i.e., exclusive of extended benefits).
† The number of persons who received at least one weekly benefit in the year.
‡ Without regard to maximum taxable wage base.
Note: Data on covered federal government employees and members of the armed forces are not included here.
Source: *Handbook of Unemployment Insurance Data*, Manpower Administration, U.S. Department of Labor.

rose over the years up to 1950 as the maximum duration provisions were liberalized and was, of course, somewhat higher in years of poor business conditions. For the same reason, the proportion of beneficiaries exhausting their benefit rights has decreased, being recently as low as 20 percent in years of good business conditions (1951–53, 1956–57, and 1966–69) and about 30 percent in recession years (1950, 1958, 1961, and 1971–73). In 1973 the proportion of exhaustions varied widely by states, being as low as 15 percent in some to as much as 40 percent in others.

The average weekly benefit amount was six times as high in 1973 as in 1940 and generally represented about 35 percent of average total wages in all recent years. In 1973 this ratio was as high as 43 percent in some states and as low as 30 percent in others.

In 1973 the average duration of benefits, exclusive of extended benefits, varied widely—from nine weeks in a number of states to 16 weeks in other states.

The number of different persons who received UI benefits in the course of a year did not fluctuate greatly. As shown in Table 13.5, such number was about 5 to 7 million in all years in the past. The average number of persons receiving UI benefits in a week does, however, vary considerably over the years. Such average for December, for example, was somewhat less than 1.0 million in 1945, 1950, and 1968, but was as high as 2.0 million in 1960 and 1970. Then, beginning with the economic recession in 1974, this average increased, until in the early part of 1975, it was 5.7 million.

The permanent extended benefits resulting from the 1970 legislation were first available in October 1970. In 1971, 22 states paid extended benefits totaling $664 million (half from the state funds and half from federal general revenues). There were 1.4 million first payments in 1971 (or 21 percent of the regular first payments), and the average benefit duration was 9.2 weeks, with 51 percent exhausting their benefit rights; the average weekly benefit was $51.25 (or slightly less than the average for the regular benefits). The corresponding data for 1972, when all the states operated under this program because the national indicator was "on" for the first three months of the year, were: Total benefits of $482 million; 1.1 million first payments (19 percent of regular first payments); average duration of 8.5 weeks, with 49 percent exhausting benefit rights; and average weekly benefit of $52.40 (or, again, slightly lower than the average for regular benefits). In 1973 the national indicator was not "on" in any month, and only three states (Massachusetts, New Jersey, and Rhode Island) paid any benefits under this program: $141 million, of which about half came from the federal government, to 160,000 persons, of whom 85 percent exhausted their benefit rights, and average benefit duration of 8.9 weeks.

Table 13.6 gives data on the financial operations of the state UI systems for various selected years in the past that indicate the effects of

TABLE 13.6
Financial Operations of State UI Systems and Average Employer State UI Tax Rates for Selected Years
(all figures in millions, except for rates)

Year	Total Taxes	Benefit Payments	Interest Earnings	Funds at End of Year*	Average Employer Contribution Rate†
1936	$ 65	—	$ 1	$ 66	0.9%
1937	592	$ 2	8	664	1.8
1938	819	394	21	1,111	2.8
1939	825	429	32	1,538	2.7
1940	854	519	42	1,817	2.7
1943	1,325	80	82	4,716	2.1
1945	1,162	446	127	6,914	1.7
1948	1,000	790	155	7,603	1.2
1950	1,191	1,373	146	6,972	1.5
1951	1,493	840	158	7,782	1.6
1954	1,136	2,027	199	8,219	1.1
1955	1,209	1,350	185	8,264	1.2
1956	1,463	1,381	200	8,574	1.3
1957	1,544	1,734	220	8,662	1.3
1958	1,471	3,513	199	6,953	1.3
1959	1,956	2,279	178	6,892	1.7
1960	2,289	2,727	195	6,643	1.9
1961	2,450	3,423	176	5,802	2.1
1962	2,952	2,675	173	6,273	2.4
1963	3,019	2,775	194	6,648	2.3
1964	3,048	2,522	225	7,296	2.2
1965	3,053	2,166	266	8,357	2.1
1966	3,030	1,771	329	9,828	1.9
1967	2,678	2,092	398	10,778	1.6
1968	2,552	2,030	460	11,717	1.5
1969	2,545	2,126	536	12,638	1.4
1970	2,508	3,848	610	11,897	1.3
1971	2,637	4,957	527	9,703	1.4
1972	3,899	4,471	442	9,423	1.7
1973	5,000	4,008	519	10,934	2.0

* Includes balances not only in state accounts in Unemployment Trust Fund but also in their operating accounts for tax collections and benefit payments (the latter being relatively small as compared with the former). Does not include operations under permanent-extended benefits program, first operative in 1970 or under reimbursable accounts (state and local government employees, and employees of some nonprofit charitable, religious, and educational organizations).
† For state UI fund only. As percentage of taxable payroll.
Source: *Handbook of Unemployment Insurance Financial Data*, Manpower Administration, U.S. Department of Labor.

changes in economic conditions. It should be noted that the figures are for actual operations and do not agree completely with data for the operations of the Unemployment Trust Fund, because of slight differences in timing and reporting of financial transactions.

As would be anticipated, benefit outgo fluctuates considerably, whereas contributions vary much less widely. In the first decade of operations, benefit disbursements were generally less than half of tax income; but beginning in 1946, the opposite situation prevailed in all years except 1947–48, 1951–53, 1956, and 1962–69. In fact, in several years, benefit outgo was about twice as high as tax income. In 1974, as a business recession set in, benefit outgo rose and was about $6.0 billion for the year.

Interest income grew slowly until, during 1953–64, it averaged about $200 million a year. Then, after 1965, it gradually grew to $610 million in 1970 as the fund balance increased and as interest rates rose. In 1971–73, interest receipts fell as the fund balance dropped. The average interest rate on the investments of the Unemployment Trust Fund (and thus for the state accounts therein) ranged between 2 and 2½ percent during most of the early years of operation, but in 1960 and thereafter, it rose to about 5 percent.

As a result of the foregoing trends, the funds available to the state UI systems increased steadily after 1936 to a peak of almost $7 billion in 1945, and then remained more or less level until 1950. Thereafter, they increased to a level of between $8 and $9 billion in 1952–57. After 1957 the funds available slowly declined and at the end of 1961, they were only $5.8 billion. Then, the fund balance grew to a peak of $12.6 billion in 1969. It has subsequently fallen by 25 percent, to $9.4 billion at the end of 1972, as a result of moderate unemployment and low tax rates because of the experience rating based on the favorable financial situation in the last half of the 1960s. It then increased by $1.5 billion in 1973, as the higher tax rate in that year took effect but it fell by $300 million in 1974, to $10.6 billion at the end of the year. The high unemployment at that time made it appear likely that the balance would decrease significantly in 1975.

The average employer tax rate under the state UI systems, shown in Table 13.6, was 2.7 percent of taxable payroll during 1938–40, but then fell off sharply as experience rating took effect. This average rate reached a low of 1.2 percent in 1948, rose to 1.6 percent in 1951, and then fell to 1.1 percent in 1954. Thereafter, this rate steadily rose until it was 2.4 percent in 1962. Following 1962, the average rate dropped slowly to a low of 1.4 percent in 1969–71. In 1972 this rate increased slightly as the experience rating took account of the moderately higher unemployment in 1970–71, and increased further in 1973. This trend, of course, reflects the effect on the experience of changes in economic conditions. It should be noted that the average cost of 2.0 percent of *taxable* payroll for 1973 is only 1.0 percent when measured against *total* payroll.

An argument frequently advanced against experience rating, as it is generally practiced, is that it operates exactly inversely to what it should from an economic standpoint, since the rates will tend to be low during prosperous years and high during years of poor business conditions. It will be noted, however, that the net income will be positive in good years and negative in bad years.

It should be recognized that the foregoing figures do not include the employer tax that goes directly to the federal government, which was 0.3 percent for 1938–60, 0.4 percent for 1961–69 (except for the temporary additional 0.4 percent during 1962 and 0.25 percent in 1963), and 0.5 percent for 1970 and after (except for the temporary additional 0.08 percent in 1973).

The average employer tax rate to the state UI systems as measured against taxable payroll was 1.99 percent in 1973, but there was considerable variation by state. California, Massachusetts, New Jersey, Rhode Island, and Washington had by far the highest average rates (between 3.0 and 3.5 percent). On the other hand, seven states had an average rate of less than 1.0 percent and two states (Colorado and Virginia) had rates of about 0.4 percent.

The adequacy of the funds available for the various state UI systems varies significantly. One measure of adequacy is a comparison of the funds available at end of year as a percent of total payroll of covered employees in the year (not taxable payroll, since the freezing of the maximum taxable wage at $4,200 in most states has made this less meaningful. For 1973 this figure was 2.15 for all systems combined. It varied from a low of 0.1 in Washington and about 0.4 in Connecticut and Vermont to a high of 4.0 to 5.2 (Alaska, Georgia, Idaho, North Carolina, and South Carolina).

Perhaps the best measure of financial adequacy of the funds of the state UI systems is one that takes into account not merely the relative size of the funds, but also the variations among the states in their benefit experiences, reflecting both the provisions of the program and the economic situation of the particular state. Such a measure of adequacy that will measure the ability of the funds to finance recession costs is obtained by dividing (1) the ratio of the funds available on a given date to the total payroll in the last year by (2) the highest ratio in the last 10 years of annual costs to total annual payroll.

At the end of 1973, the resulting factor was 1.05 for the United States as a whole. Studies indicate that benefit costs in a recession have totaled about 1½ times the benefit cost during the highest year. In this connection, it may be noted that recessions have generally run about 18 months. Accordingly, a minimum factor of 1.5 is desirable. At the end of 1973, only 22 states had sufficient funds according to this measure. The jurisdictions with the highest factors measuring financial adequacy in this way had factors of 2.5 to 3.0 (Arizona, Georgia, South Carolina, South Dakota, and Virginia). The states with the lowest such factors had 0.5 or less (Connecticut, Maine, New Jersey, Rhode Island, Vermont, and Washington).

Before 1954, any excess of the net federal unemployment tax of 0.3 percent over the administrative expenses of the UI systems (primarily allocations to the state UI systems as reimbursement of their administrative expenses) remained in the General Treasury. Such excess was about one third of the total tax collections, or approximately $900 million in the aggregate. Beginning with the tax collections for 1954, any such excesses were credited first to the Federal Unemployment Account, until it attained a cash balance of $200 million, and then were allocated to the state accounts.

In its first three years of operation the Federal Unemployment Account built up to its specified maximum and made only a few loans, which were relatively small. Then, in fiscal years 1956–58, such excesses (which amounted to almost $140 million) were allocated to the state accounts. In fiscal year 1959, two large loans were made, and the balance in the account was virtually wiped out. In this and the following two years, there was also no longer a significant excess of federal tax collections over the administrative grants, so that the account could not be built up and made available for further loans. It was for this reason that the net federal tax was increased from 0.3 to 0.4 percent beginning in 1961, since otherwise there apparently would never have been sufficient new funds for this purpose.

Only six states have made effective loans from the Federal Unemployment Account since its inauguration in 1955—namely, Alaska, Connecticut, Michigan, Pennsylvania, Vermont, and Washington. Some repayment of these noninterest-bearing advances had been made, but in the middle of 1974, they were still outstanding, as follows: Connecticut, $62 million; Washington, $44 million; and Vermont, $3 million.

In fiscal year 1974, administrative expenses of the UI system (both state and federal expenses, including those for employment services activities) amounted to $902 million. This represented 17.5 percent of benefit payments during the year.

In the middle of 1974, the balance in the Unemployment Trust Fund was $12.5 billion. The vast bulk of this was credited to the state accounts ($10.9 billion). The Railroad Unemployment Insurance Account (for benefits) contained $66 million, and the Railroad UI Administrative Expense Account had $6 million. The balance in the Federal Unemployment Account (exclusive of outstanding loans) was $529 million, or slightly below the statutory maximum of about $635 million then prevailing (based on ⅛ percent of total payroll in covered employment in 1973). The balance in the Employment Security Administration Account was $762 million, or considerably above the statutory maximum, which was then about $330 million (40 percent of the annual administrative expenses of the state plans); this excess balance was transferred to the Extended Unemployment Compensation Account shortly after the middle of 1974.

The Extended Unemployment Compensation Account had a balance of $276 million in mid-1974. This was far below its statutory maximum of $750 million. Since its inception in October 1970 through June 1974, this account had received net transfers of $661 million from the General Fund of the Treasury and $937 million from the Employment Security Administration Account, while making transfers totaling $1,323 million to the state accounts for benefit payments purposes.

The assets of the Unemployment Trust Fund in the middle of 1974 were almost entirely invested in U.S. government securities (a cash balance of $416 million). Investments in public issues (at coupon rates of 2¾ to 8¾ percent) totaled $2.6 billion, while the remaining $9.5 billion was in one-year 6½ percent certificates that were special issues.

The special unemployment benefits that are paid to unemployed former federal employees and to ex-servicemen are administered by the state UI systems, but there is complete reimbursement by the General Treasury. With respect to federal employees, this cost was about $30 million a year in 1955–57 and about $40 to $60 million a year in 1958–69 and then increased to a level of about $125 million in 1972–73. The program for ex-servicemen began toward the end of 1958, and in 1959–65 the cost generally ranged between $80 and $100 million per year, but it then fell to about $40 million per year in 1966–67 and subsequently increased to $203 million in 1970, $356 million in 1971, $362 million in 1972, and $209 million in 1973, as a result of the war in Viet Nam.

chapter 14

Workmen's Compensation
Programs

One of the problems to emerge from the industrialization of our economy was the increasing financial loss suffered by workers who experienced job-related injuries, sickness, or death. The close personal relationships associated with an agrarian economy rapidly disappeared and were replaced with the more impersonal nature of industrial life. As workers became more and more dependent upon wages as the sole source of support for their families, an interruption of those wages created financial hardship. How was a worker to recover his loss? Where the cause of the loss was job-connected, the worker sought financial assistance from his employer, hopefully on a voluntary basis, but if not, then through the courts. Both ways proved to be inadequate for the worker.

During the early years of the 20th century, a new philosophy for meeting the financial problems of job-connected injuries emerged. The various states enacted so-called workmen's compensation legislation, designed to alleviate the inequities of the common-law and employers liability systems. This legislation is generally considered the earliest form of social insurance in the United States. Curiously, the name "workmen's compensation," which has had long usage in the English language, is not really a very accurate descriptive phrase. One would normally believe that it should refer to all remuneration of a worker, including wages. Currently, with the growth of the women's rights movement, there has been some effort to refer to workmen's compensation as "workers' compensation."

DEVELOPMENT OF WORKMEN'S COMPENSATION

Prior to the enactment of workmen's compensation laws, a well-established common-law principle held that an employer was responsible for injury or death of employees resulting from a negligent act by the employer. This may appear logical and equitable, but in practice did not work to the employee's benefit.

A disabled worker who sued his employer for damages had to prove his injuries were due to employer negligence. Not only was this a slow, costly, and uncertain legal process, but also one that proved to be inadequate in satisfying the worker's need. At common law, the employer could avoid liability for the worker's injury through the utilization of several defenses—contributory negligence of the worker, negligence of a fellow worker, or assumption of risk.

The defense of contributory negligence was always available in suits based upon negligence. In operation, it defeated a worker's claim for damages if he had in any way contributed, through his own negligence, to the occurrence of the injury. The second defense, negligence of a fellow worker, was an exception to a well-established tort doctrine which held a master responsible to third persons for injuries inflicted by his agents. The worker was not a third person stranger to the employment situation, and as such could not hold the employer responsible for injury caused by the negligence of a fellow worker. The assumption of risk defense in effect held that the hazards of an occupation were noncompensable. The application of the three common-law defenses often proved to be very effective in preventing recovery by the worker.

The relatively harsh conditions prevailing under common law with respect to work-connected injuries led to the so-called "employer liability" acts. Under these laws, the common-law defenses were weakened, especially fellow worker and assumption of risk. Employer liability laws brought about other changes, but what was not altered was the necessity for the worker to initiate a lawsuit against his employer. This meant that the costs and uncertainties of the legal system still persisted. Other legal remedies were urged to satisfy the problems of occupational injury.

In the early 1900s there was a strong movement to enact workmen's compensation laws, but the early efforts were unsuccessful because the laws were declared unconstitutional. Finally, in 1911, the first state workmen's compensation law which met the test of constitutionality was passed, and this set the pattern for all states to follow. It was 1948, however, before all states had enacted workmen's compensation legislation.

The basic concept of workmen's compensation laws establishes that the employer should assume the costs of occupational disabilities. The benefits provided to the employee are considered costs of production chargeable, to the extent possible, as a price factor. The laws relieve employers of liability from common-law suits involving negligence. This is replaced by a system of income and medical benefits to the worker for job-related injuries without regard to the establishment of fault. The injured worker agrees to accept the benefit prescribed by law on this no-fault basis as the sole remedy for his economic loss.

COVERAGE OF LAWS

Workmen's compensation laws are state laws, and as such vary from state to state. In addition, there are separate laws covering federal employees and covering private or public employees engaged in nationwide maritime work. Data are also available on the laws of the District of Columbia, Guam, Puerto Rico, and the Virgin Islands. A description of the laws in each of these jurisdictions is beyond the scope of this chapter. A more generalized approach is undertaken, with this section being a discussion of differentiating characteristics of the various state laws, and the following two sections containing a discussion of benefits.[1]

---

[1] For excellent and detailed descriptions of these laws as they currently exist, see *Analysis of Workmen's Compensation Laws*, issued annually by The Chamber of Commerce of the United States, Washington, D.C. (1974 edition) and *State Workmen's Compensation Laws*, Bulletin 161 (revised 1969), U.S. Department of Labor.

Types of Laws

Workmen's compensation laws are of two types, elective or compulsory. A compulsory law requires that each employer subject to the act accept the provisions of the law and provide the benefits prescribed. Forty-five states now have compulsory laws. This is an increase of 18 since 1970, and indicates a major trend from elective to compulsory laws.

Under elective laws, an employer, or an employee, may accept or reject the act. If an employer rejects the act, he typically loses the three common-law defenses. Where an employee rejects the act and the employer has accepted it, the employer normally retains the three common-law defenses. In actual practice, the vast majority of covered employers elect to comply with the workmen's compensation provisions. This could result from the fact that states with elective laws may require positive action on the part of the employer or employee to elect not to be covered by the provisions of the act. In other words, failure to elect not to be covered means acceptance or election to be covered. Another factor might be the desire to avoid abrogation of the common-law defenses. Practically, this means that all the laws approach the status of being "compulsory."

Funding Requirements

State workmen's compensation laws require that benefits as prescribed by law be available through some form of insurance secured by the employer. There are various methods of funding this insurance requirement. In six states there is an "exclusive" state fund. Under this approach, employers must obtain workmen's compensation requirements from the fund. The state functions as a monopoly in this arrangement. In these instances, the program can properly be classified as social insurance.

There is a "competitive" state fund in 12 states. Here, the state funds operate in competition with private insurance, and employers may select the insuring method they desire. Such programs are combinations of social insurance and employer-mandated programs. In the other 32 states, there is no state fund and employers utilize private insurance companies, so that this is entirely the employer-mandated approach.

The importance of insuring is the requirement that adequate resources are available to provide the benefits. Most states impose a penalty for failure to insure.

Self-insurance is permitted in 46 states. Of the four that do not permit it, three are exclusive-fund states. The requirement that adequate resources be available for benefit payments is facilitated under self-insurance by establishing certain safeguards, such as the posting of bonds or financial deposits. Another safeguard exists in that the successful self-insurance program operates best when an employer has a large spread of risks. Therefore, only large firms tend to utilize self-insurance.

Employments Covered

Workmen's compensation laws are further characterized by distinguishing the employments that are covered. A compulsory law does not necessarily mean that all employers are subject to the law. An additional inquiry must be made to determine the real extent of such classification. The first distinction is between private and public employment. A particular law may be classified as compulsory for private employments and elective for public, compulsory or elective for both, or elective for private and compulsory for public. In each case, reference must be made to the specific law to discover the general categories of employments that are covered.

A further determination of the applicability of the law can be found by examining the private employments that are exempted, or listed as exceptions to the law. A law will be compulsory as to all employments except those excluded. For instance, the majority of states exclude agricultural workers, although a growing number include farm workers when power machinery is used. Similarly, almost all states exclude domestic workers and casual employment. Most jurisdictions permit employees in an exempted class to be brought under coverage of the act through voluntary action of the employer. In some states such action must be concurred in by the employees.

Another significant type of exclusion from coverage is based on the size of a firm. The law may specify that employers are subject to the act only if they have a given number of employees. Most states with numerical exemptions have coverage limits that are usually between "two or more" and "five or more" employees, although two states have higher limits, with one having a limit of six or more and the other seven or more. The trend is toward lower limits, or the total elimination of such limit. Thirty-four states no longer have size-of-firm exclusions.

QUALIFYING FOR BENEFITS

A basic objective of workmen's compensation laws is to provide benefits to work-related accident victims, regardless of fault. The right of a worker to these benefits is defined in the laws of the various states. In essence, an employee in covered employment need show only that he has suffered an injury that is traceable to the employment.

Workmen's compensation applied originally only to the clearly definable matter of work-connected injuries. Occupational diseases were included within the scope of workmen's compensation gradually, either through court interpretation or by legislation. In most jurisdictions the worker is now eligible for benefits for disabling injuries and sickness. In practice, the term "injury" is interpreted broadly to mean disabling injury, nondisabling injury, or disease. Also, the reference to "accident" has been eliminated from many state laws, or interpreted broadly in others.

A considerable volume of litigation has been developed on the question of who is an "employee," particularly in the areas of independent contractors, but an interpretation is now fairly well established. The identification of covered employment was discussed in the previous section. "Traceable to employment" requires that there be a proper relationship between the employment and the injury. This requirement centers around an interpretation that injury "arise out of and in the course of employment." The courts have taken a fairly liberal view of what is "in the course of employment." The major issue today is agreement on an interpretation of "arising out of the employment." This has not been clearly defined.

The injured worker must satisfy the qualifications for benefits. Having done so, he is eligible for the benefits prescribed by law.

TYPES OF BENEFITS

Benefits under workmen's compensation programs are directed at the economic loss the injured workers suffer, the loss of earning power, and the increase in expenses to recover from the injury. This is translated in the laws as two types of benefits—cash benefits and medical service benefits. Some states also provide rehabilitation services benefits, along with additional cash maintenance benefits payable at such times.

Cash Benefits

The cash benefits include periodic payments to the injured worker during the disablement period, survivorship benefits payable in the event of fatal injuries, and lump-sum payments for burial expenses.

An occupational injury may cause a permanent or temporary loss of earning power, and a total or partial loss of such capacity. There are, therefore, four classifications of disability for cash benefits: (1) permanent total, (2) permanent partial, (3) temporary total, or (4) temporary partial. Each disability is analyzed from the standpoint of the extent of the disablement, total or partial; and from the standpoint of how long the disability will last, permanently or temporarily.

Most occupational injury cases involve total disability for a temporary period, after which the worker will have recovered and be able to return to work. When the worker has been determined to be permanently and totally disabled for any type of gainful employment, permanent total benefits are available.

If the permanent disablement is only of a partial nature, which may or may not lessen his future work ability, permanent partial benefits are payable. The cash benefit is in part compensation for the direct loss of income resulting from the injury, and in part to compensate for a possible future reduction in earning capacity. Permanent partial benefits are determined either on a "schedule" basis, for those injuries clearly measurable, such as loss of a member of the body; or on a "nonschedule" basis when measurement is not so clearly defined.

Death benefits, typically in the form of periodic payments, are available for various categories of survivors, including widows and children, and in some cases, dependent parents, brothers, and sisters. These benefits are available when the worker dies at the time of the accident, and also when death occurs during disability and is due to the occupational cause. In addition, lump-sum burial allowances are available.

Duration of Cash Benefits. Two factors affect the duration of weekly cash benefits: (1) when they begin, and (2) how long they continue. State statutes stipulate that a specific waiting period elapse before cash benefits are payable. The typical waiting period is seven days, with several states requiring three or five days. The waiting period is used to eliminate claims of short duration, thereby effecting a reduction in the total cost of the program, primarily from an administrative standpoint. The implication might be, however, that workers in an affluent society can absorb an interruption in income for a short period of time or that the employer, on a voluntary basis, will pay full wages then. The waiting period should also discourage absenteeism when a worker can be productive on the job.

The intent to limit cash benefits to those cases of more significant duration is emphasized by incorporating a retroactive provision in the law. This provision recovers the benefit lost because of a waiting period. If the disability continues for more than a certain length of time, a benefit will also be paid for a number of days equivalent to the waiting period. The number of days of continued disability required to qualify for the retroactive benefit varies considerably among the states, ranging from five days to six weeks. The more common lengths of time are 14 and 28 days. The intent to provide cash benefits only for disability of longer duration is further emphasized by the fact that several states specify that a waiting period applies only to temporary disability.

The duration of cash benefits is limited by either time or amount, and differs between permanent and temporary disabilities. Many states pay temporary total disability benefits for as long as the disability lasts. Some states prescribe a maximum duration in terms of weeks, ranging from 206 to 500 weeks. Other states limit the duration by specifying a maximum aggregate benefit payable, ranging from $10,750 to $65,000.

Permanent total disability benefits are payable for life in about 70 percent of the states. In other states, payments are limited in terms of weeks, 300 to 650, or aggregate benefits payable, $21,000 to $35,100. Permanent partial disability benefits are similarly limited in all states. For injuries falling under the schedule basis of classification, the maximum duration in almost all instances is fixed, varying with the severity of the disablement.

Survivor benefits are generally payable to the widow until remarriage and to children until a specified age. A few states allow commuted lump-sum amounts to be paid to a widow upon remarriage. A specified number of weeks may also be stated to limit the duration of survivor benefits. Burial allowances are normally paid as a lump-sum benefit.

Benefit Amounts. The basic amounts of the workmen's compensation benefits are determined from the injured worker's wage at the time of the accident or onset of the industrial disease. The determination of the wage to be used as such a base thus presents far less of a problem than for other social insurance benefits. An important limiting factor, however, is that maximum benefit provisions tend to hold down benefits determined as a percentage of wage. Over the years, these dollar maximums have been increased, but not nearly so rapidly as the general wage level has risen. Accordingly, in some instances the maximum benefit provision is so dominant that, to a considerable extent, a flat-benefit system is in effect.

The benefit rate as a percentage of wage for temporary total disability is most often 66⅔ percent, although 60 percent and 65 percent are also common. A few states vary the percentage according to the number of dependents. Other states recognize the presence of dependents by adding flat amounts for each of a limited number of dependents and by increasing the maximum benefit.

The maximum weekly benefit for temporary total disability, exclusive of any increase for dependents, ranges from as low as $56 to as high as $175, but most fall within the range of $60 to $110. About 15 states have "dynamic" maximum benefit provisions, which are typically based on 66⅔ percent of the "average wage" in the state.

Almost all states have minimum benefit provisions for temporary total disability. These are typically $10 to $30 per week, but considering present wage levels, generally have little application.

For permanent total disability, the "percentage-of-wage" benefit rate is generally the same as for temporary total disability. The same is also true as to the maximum benefit provisions.

For permanent partial disability, the benefit rates are generally the same as those for permanent total disability multiplied by the percentage of disability, except that sometimes no dependents' benefits are payable. However, for nonschedule injuries the percentage-of-wage rate is sometimes applied only to the difference between the wage before injury and that possible after injury. For schedule injuries the full benefit rate is payable, but only for the schedule period provided, which naturally will be shorter than for schedule permanent total disability cases.

The size of the monthly survivor benefits varies generally according to whether or not the widow has children, and then sometimes according to the number of children. For the widow alone, the benefit is sometimes at the same rate as the worker's permanent total disability benefit, but is often only one half or two thirds thereof. For a widow with children, the benefit is usually the same as the worker's permanent total disability benefit.

The lump-sum burial allowances range from $300 to $1,800.

Coordination with OASDI Benefits. An individual who suffers an occupational disease or injury and receives permanent total disability benefits under a workmen's compensation system frequently may also qualify for monthly disability benefits under OASDI. The same duplication of benefits may also occur for survivors of workers dying as a result of an occupational cause.

Under such circumstances, particularly when young children are present, total benefits under the two programs may, in the absence of nonduplication provisions, exceed previous earnings. For example, a young married worker with one child and with earnings of $800 a month could, without such a restriction, receive $765 a month in disability benefits payable from OASDI and $110 a week from one of the more liberal workmen's compensation systems if he is permanently and totally disabled as a result of an occupational cause. Thus, his total benefits would amount to $14,900 per year, or 155 percent of his previous wage, and he would not have much incentive to be rehabilitated and return to work.

When the OASDI disability benefits were established in 1956, such duplication of benefits was prevented (as to disability benefits, but not survivor benefits) by an offset of workmen's compensation benefits against the OASDI benefit. This provision, however, was eliminated in 1958. A provision for a combined "80 percent of wage" maximum on OASDI and workmen's compensation benefits was introduced into the OASDI system in 1965, insofar as disability benefits payable up to age 62 are concerned, but it is not applicable to disability benefits payable at ages 62–64, old-age benefits, and survivor benefits. (See Chapters 2 and 3.)

Workmen's compensation laws generally do not prevent this duplication. However, in Colorado, if an employee is receiving OASDI benefits for disability, the workmen's compensation benefit to the disabled worker may be reduced by 50 percent of such payments.

Medical Services Benefits

The basic format of the medical benefit is simply to furnish all the care medically indicated, without legal limitation to a specified time or amount. Only nine states limit medical care costs, either in terms of duration or as an aggregate amount, and some of these states permit extensions of benefits.

The waiting period found with cash benefits does not apply to medical benefits. The majority of work-related injuries are of short duration, so do not involve cash benefits, but account for substantial medical benefits. Nearly one third of all workmen's compensation benefits paid go for medical services.

As discussed in Chapter 6, when a person is eligible for medical care benefits under both Medicare and WC, the latter is basically liable.

Occupational Disease

Occupational disease perhaps should not be identified as a type of benefit. However, the various state laws afford separate and specific recognition to this category of coverage. Cash benefits generally are the same as for injury. Medical benefits may differ, as several states limit medical care in occupational disease cases.

Although workmen's compensation laws originally did not specify provisions for occupational diseases, all states now recognize responsibility for them. However, the extent of this recognition varies. Most states extend benefits to all diseases. Other states list the diseases subject to the provisions of the law, extend special provisions for particular diseases, or impose special restrictions on them. Of particular importance in virtually all states are the time limits on filing of claims and on eligibility for death benefits. These restrictions arise from the inherent nature of occupational disease disability.

Rehabilitation

The rehabilitation of a disabled worker can be one of the most beneficial objectives of workmen's compensation legislation. Unfortunately, the performance in this benefit area has not reached its potential. The idea of rehabilitation is now widely endorsed. Yet, many states make no provision for rehabilitation, and most of the others are not directed at the control problem.

The cash benefit to a totally and permanently disabled worker is a future financial commitment. Add the unlimited medical services cost to this cash benefit, and the total potential expenditure can be substantial. If the disabled worker can be rehabilitated and returned to a useful productive capacity, the cost savings in future benefits can more than offset the immediate additional cost of rehabilitation. Also, from a social viewpoint, it is more desirable to rehabilitate a disabled worker.

The rehabilitation benefit in most states merely directs the compensation agency to refer cases to federal or state vocational rehabilitation programs. However, many of these programs are already over-burdened with other caseloads. Several states also provide a maintenance allowance during the retraining period.

Another aspect of rehabilitation is the reluctance of the disabled worker to seek rehabilitation. He often sees in rehabilitation the possible forfeiture of his maximum cash benefit claim. This conflict between rehabilitation and cash benefits needs to be resolved. In fact, a greater total effort needs to be made before the potential benefits of rehabilitation will be realized.

Subsequent Injury

When a worker has had a work-connected injury involving the loss of one or more members of the body, he is in greater danger of being a permanent total disability case if he then suffers another industrial injury that otherwise would have been of only a partial nature. In other words, if a worker who had already lost one eye suffers the loss of the second eye in an industrial accident, he becomes a permanent total case rather than a permanent partial one, and is eligible for a greater aggregate cash benefit than that provided for scheduled injuries. Because of the potential increased cost of compensation benefits, an employer may be influenced to refuse employment to handicapped workers. As a result, almost all states have established "subsequent-injury" or "second-injury" funds. Some of these apply to all previous industrial injuries or diseases, rather than merely where there was a loss of a member of the body.

The function of the second-injury fund is to pay for the excess of the benefit cost when a pre-existing injury combines with a second one to produce disability greater than that caused by the latter alone. These state-operated funds are financed in several ways. Most of the 46 states with second-injury funds charge a fixed amount in each no-dependency death case. Other funds are financed through assessments on insurance carriers, self-insurers, or employers; legislative appropriations; charges against other than no-dependency death claims; and, in some "exclusive" fund states, by general pooling of the risk.

Subsequent-injury programs have not been as effective as might be expected. Employers are not fully aware of their existence, or perhaps do not understand their function, and therefore are still hesitant to hire the handicapped. Another factor is the continuation of restrictions or limitations in some laws which constrict their application. The future direction of subsequent-injury programs is still uncertain.

Federal Black Lung Benefits[2]

A federal program was established in 1969 to provide so-called "black lung" (pneumoconiosis) benefits to coal miners who are totally disabled from this occupational disease and to widows of miners whose death resulted from this cause. Specific legislation was enacted with respect to this disease because it is often very slow in coming on, and state workmen's compensation programs had not provided adequate coverage for it.

Monthly benefits are at uniform rates, varying only with the composition of the beneficiary family. The basic benefit amount is payable to a miner without any dependents and is taken at 50 percent of the prevailing level of workmen's compensation benefits under the Federal Employees' Compensation Act for a totally disabled federal employee at the entrance salary of grade GS-2, for which the benefit rate is 75 percent of salary. Beginning with October 1974, the basic black lung benefit was $187.40 per month.

A disabled beneficiary receives supplements to the basic benefit if he has a dependent wife and/or dependent children. Survivor benefits are paid to the widow and/or children or, in the absence of a surviving widow or child, benefits can be paid to dependent parents, brothers, or sisters. The basic benefit is payable when there is only one beneficiary or dependent in the family. With two eligibles in the family, the total benefit is 150 percent for the basic benefit, while it is 175 percent for three eligibles, and 200 percent for four or more eligibles.

There is a complete offset of any state workmen's compensation benefits against the black lung benefits, but this is of limited application because so few miners with this disease were receiving workmen's compensation payments. Originally, the black lung benefits were counted as workmen's compensation benefits in the "80 percent of wage" maximum on combined workmen's compensation and disability benefits under OASDI. Although about three quarters of the cases receive both types of benefits, this maximum affected less than

---

[2] For more details on this program, see "Black Lung Benefits: An Administrative Review," *Social Security Bulletin*, vol. 34, no. 10 (October 1971), and "The Black Lung Benefits Program: Two Years of Experience," Research and Statistics Note No. 21–1972, Social Security Administration.

10 percent of such dual cases. In 1972, however, this antiduplication provision was repealed.

Until mid-1973, this program was administered entirely by the Social Security Administration, with the cost for benefits and administration being borne by the General Fund of the Treasury. Beginning in July 1973 for miner claims, and in January 1974 for survivor claims, the administration of the program was assigned to the Department of Labor. However, if a state workmen's compensation law pays comparable benefits, the state plan has the jurisdiction. After 1981 the federal responsibility for new cases is terminated. For claims under the jurisdiction of the Department of Labor with entitlement date after 1973, the cost is to be borne by the coal mine operators.

FINANCING

The financing of workmen's compensation is somewhat unique among social insurance programs in that self-insurance and private insurance are both permitted, and in fact combine, to dominate the flow of funds for benefit payments.[3] Approximately three quarters of the total benefits are distributed through self-insurance programs and private insurers. The governmental "trust fund" is not a characteristic feature in workmen's compensation. Also, perhaps because of the role of private insurers, the contributions for workmen's compensation provisions are not called taxes but are referred to as premiums.

All employers subject to the workmen's compensation laws, with the exception of qualified self-insurers, purchase insurance from a private insurer or state fund. The premiums payable by the employer vary with the size of the firm and the risk involved. Premium rates are classified by occupational categories to yield manual rates representative of the hazards of a particular occupation. These rates are then applied to units of payroll to arrive at manual premiums. Then, based on the level of such premiums, they may be modified prospectively by the past experience of the particular employer, and they may be further modified on a retrospective basis through dividends or under a specific retrospective rating plan.

As an example of the manner in which these programs operate in some states, the firm that develops an annual premium of $750 or more is automatically experience rated. The actual past experience of an em-

---

[3] Similar provisions are found in some cash sickness programs. See Chapter 15.

ployer over a three-year span is modified somewhat and then compared with the expected experience for that occupational category. This will result in an adjustment of the manual premium upwards for poor relative experience or downward for good relative experience. If an employer's annual premium exceeds $1,000, he is eligible for an additional modification if he elects a retrospective rating plan. There are several such plans available, and their basic concept is to provide an adjustment in the premium based upon actual experience during the current policy period.

Experience rating is an attempt to provide "equity" in the financing of workmen's compensation. However, the majority of employers are not large enough to generate such a premium of $750. This means that smaller firms are not paying a premium related directly to their own experience, but are sharing, through a pooling process, in the losses of all similar firms. Although a small firm may have no workmen's compensation losses over a long period of time, the employer will pay the same premium as a firm of identical size and occupational categories, but with thousands of dollars of losses. For the small firm, then, equity is based solely on occupational classifications.

ADMINISTRATION

Workmen's compensation laws are state laws, and as such are administered by the states, generally by a commission or board created for this purpose. A few states still provide for court administration. An objective of workmen's compensation is the prompt delivery of benefits to work-connected injury victims. Sound administration plays a key role in meeting this objective. Many of the provisions relating to administration are directed at the process of claim filing and claim settlement.

Although variation is the basic descriptive word for administration of workmen's compensation among the 50 state jurisdictions, one method of claims settlement emerges as most predominant. This is the "by agreement" method, under which the assumption is made that the injured worker can agree with the settlement proposal of the employer or insurance carrier. Disputed cases would be settled by the administrative board or commission. Other methods of claim settlement include the hearing method and direct settlement. The hearing method would create the longest delays because a hearing would be needed to settle almost every claim. The direct settlement method would be the quickest process since noncontested cases would be paid directly upon notice of disability.

The expenses of administration are normally provided by general appropriations. Most states allocate the appropriation without assessment provisions. Other general-appropriation states charge an assessment against insurance carriers or self-insurers, normally as a percentage of premiums. States with special funds finance these through assessments against carriers and self-insurers, while Oregon charges the employer a percentage of his payroll.

FEDERAL INVOLVEMENT

The federal government has been taking a more active interest in workmen's compensation in recent years. Coordination with OASDI benefits and the black lung disease benefits have already been mentioned. Of greater interest are the federal Occupational Safety and Health Act of 1970 and the more recent National Commission on State Workmen's Compensation Laws.

Occupational Safety and Health Act

The major purpose of the Occupational Safety and Health Act is to provide workers with safe and healthful working conditions. Under this act, federal or approved state safety standards are being established and enforced. The basic premise for the establishment of standards is derived from the fact that employers should have a general duty to furnish employment free from recognized hazards. An employer who does not comply with established safety and health standards should be penalized.

To enforce the standards, federal safety inspectors are authorized to inspect the premises of any covered establishment. A written citation will be issued for each violation of standards discovered by the inspector. The employer is given a reasonable time to correct the situation, or to appeal the citation. An employee may also request an inspection if he believes that a violation of standards exists. Penalties for violations vary, with some more serious violations having a mandatory penalty up to $1,000. Failure to correct violations could result in a penalty up to $1,000 for each day beyond a prescribed time that the violation continues. Willful or repeated violations could result in penalties of $10,000, and in some cases, imprisonment.

It is perhaps too early to assess the effectiveness of the federal program, but the act has important implications for state workmen's compensation. In addition to the provisions mentioned, the act authorized a National Commission on State Workmen's Compensation Laws to evaluate state laws, and to report its findings and recommendations.

National Commission on State Workmen's Compensation Laws

On July 31, 1972, the National Commission on State Workmen's Compensation Laws issued its report, based on extensive public hearings and evaluations of available evidence. The commission concluded that the protection furnished by the various workmen's compensation programs was, in general, neither adequate nor equitable. The commission indicated that significant improvements are necessary if the system is to fulfill its potential.

The commission offered recommendations for improvement in workmen's compensation laws. Several of these were identified as "essential" recommendations, and are summarized as follows:

1. Coverage should be compulsory rather than elective, and there should be no exemptions of small firms or government employment. Coverage should apply to all types of workers, including many farmworkers and domestic employees.
2. All work-related diseases should be covered.
3. Weekly cash benefits should be at least two thirds of the gross wage, and the maximum weekly benefit should be at least 100 percent of the average weekly wage in the state.
4. Permanent total disability benefits and survivor benefits should extend for the duration of the risk (and not have arbitrary limits on the duration or the aggregate amount of benefits). Similarly, there should be no statutory limits as to duration or aggregate amount of medical services and physical rehabilitation.

Quite naturally, these changes would increase significantly the cost of the programs. If the recommended 1975 maximum weekly benefits are employed, such increases were estimated to be less than 10 percent in five states, between 10 and 29.9 percent in 19 states, between 30 and 49.9 percent in 21 states, and greater than 50 percent in the remaining five states. The overall range of increased cost was from 2.4 to 62.4 percent.

The commission also made a number of other recommendations that it deemed to be desirable, although not "essential." The most important of these were as follows:

1. The maximum weekly cash benefit should, by 1981, be 200 percent of the average wage in the state.
2. The weekly cash payment should eventually be 80 percent of the individual worker's *spendable* earnings (gross after deducting withholding and payroll taxes and work expenses, subject to the maximum-benefit provisions).
3. Survivor benefits should be at least 50 percent of the average wage in the state, as a minimum.
4. OASDI disability benefits should continue to be reduced as they now are when workmen's compensation benefits are payable. Survivor benefits under workmen's compensation should be reduced by OASDI survivor benefits (not now the case).
5. Permanent total disability benefits and survivor benefits should be automatically increased in accordance with changes in the wage level in the state.
6. All states should have second-injury funds.

The commission believed that states should continue to have primary responsibility for workmen's compensation and that they should be given the opportunity to renovate their laws before any federal mandatory standards should be adopted. The commission recommended that the states should have until mid-1975 to comply with its essential recommendations. If the state systems are still lagging, the commission recommended that Congress should then take action to establish standards.

The impact of the Occupational Safety and Health Act and the implications of the report of the National Commission on State Workmen's Compensation Laws provide strong evidence that the role of the federal government will no longer be passive in this branch of social security. The states have a clear challenge to improve the effective delivery of adequate benefits and to encourage safe and healthy working conditions.

In mid-1974, the chairman of the Senate Labor and Public Welfare Committee (Senator Williams) and the committee's ranking minority member (Senator Javits) sponsored legislation which would require the states to adopt the major recommendations of the commission; some states had already done so, but most had not. President Nixon proposed instead that the states should have more time to take action, and he appointed a task force to help the states make the changes on their own. Congress did not take any action on this matter in 1974.

Some students of the subject favor complete federalization of the program, rather than merely federal standards. Then, there would be uniform national provisions as to coverage, benefits, and financing, as well as federal administration. Under this approach, complete co-ordination with OASDI would be likely, as well as the program being administered by the Social Security Administration. Such unification of general pension provisions with work-connected benefits is found in the social insurance systems of a number of countries.

APPENDIX

Operational Data and Question of Superiority of Insurers

SOME FIGURES ON OPERATIONS

The number of persons protected by workmen's compensation programs in 1973 was about 66 million in an average week, or 86 percent of the number of persons in civilian wage and salary employment.[4] The annual payroll of covered workers was $563 billion, disregarding in this figure any maximum earnings limits in state laws that affect benefit amounts.

Total benefit payments in 1973—both in cash and for medical services—amounted to $5,064 million, including $1,045 million under the federal "black lung" program. The payments, exclusive of the black lung disease benefits, amounted to 0.71 percent of covered pay-

---

[4] The data analyzed in this section for 1973 are from Daniel N. Price, "Workmen's Compensation Payments and Costs, 1973," *Social Security Bulletin*, vol. 38, no. 1 (January 1975).

roll. Insurance companies paid out 62.6 percent of the total benefits, while 22.9 percent was paid by state funds and 14.5 percent through self-insurance. About 36 percent of the total benefits in 1973 was for medical expenses, as against 30 percent in 1972.

Although most cash benefit rates are about two thirds of pay, the effect of the dollar maximum provisions is to make the average effective proportion about 50–55 percent, although somewhat higher in states that pay dependents' benefits. Before 1940 the average effective proportion was much closer to two thirds of pay; but since then benefit liberalizations have not kept pace with the rising trend of earnings. In the late 1950s there was some "catching-up" in this respect, and again in the past few years.

The total cost to employers for workmen's compensation amounted to $6,722 million in 1973, or 1.19 percent of payroll. This cost has been increasing in recent years and was as low as 1.0 percent in the early 1960s. These costs, of course, vary greatly as between employers in different industries and in different states, depending on the relative liberality of the laws.

The 60 percent ratio of benefits paid to premiums paid (exclusive of the black lung benefits program) is, of course, misleading because no account is taken of increases in statutory reserves, dividends, and the fact that self-insurers generally finance on a current-cost basis (or else report that way). The proper method of analysis is on an "incurred losses to net premiums earned" basis. When this method is used, the loss ratio of insurance companies in 1973 was 68.8 percent, as against 69.1 percent for state funds.

Private Insurance versus State Funds

There is much controversy on the question of the relative superiority of insurance companies as against state funds in connection with workmen's compensation. The higher loss ratio (or, conversely, the lower retention ratio) of state funds is, at least in part, due to the following factors:

1. State funds pay lower taxes, or no taxes.
2. State funds tend to insure a larger proportion of the hazardous industry business. This theoretically implies a higher level of benefits, or that administrative expenses constitute a relatively lower proportion of premiums.

3. State funds do not provide extensive inspection and safety engineering services, and therefore devote smaller amounts to this expense.
4. Certain expenses are met from general state revenues rather than by the fund itself.

On the other hand, the state fund advocates assert that the major reason for the lower loss ratio for the insurance companies is the higher operating expenses of the companies, including high acquisition costs and commissions. There are many other arguments on both sides, including such questions as speed of claims settlement, equity of settlements, comparative security, and cost to the employer.

chapter 15

Cash Sickness Benefits
Programs

One branch of social insurance provides cash payments during short-term periods of sickness or illness, due either to disease or to injury, that are not caused by employment conditions. Under some circumstances, such payments are also made in a somewhat parallel fashion with respect to pregnancy of female workers. These benefits serve the primary purpose of compensating the worker for some of the wages he has lost because of the sickness. This branch, which may be termed "cash sickness benefits," is thus distinct from disability benefits (cash payments for long-term cases), medical care (services in kind), and workmen's compensation (both cash and service benefits for work-connected cases). In the United States, this branch is frequently referred to as temporary disability insurance (TDI).

In the United States, most of the protection in the area of cash sickness benefits is provided through private rather than governmental means. This is accomplished through (1) benefits provided under insurance company policies (both group and individual) that have been purchased at the volition of the employer alone, as a result of collective-bargaining procedures, or by the individual worker by his own action; and (2) benefits under formal sick-leave plans that are administered by the employer and that provide continuation of full pay (or in some instances, partial pay) for a certain period. Then, too, many employers, particularly those with few employees, continue the pay of sick employees on a discretionary basis (informal sick-leave plans). Furthermore, most workers have sufficient savings (in cash and in kind) so that they can readily meet the cost, in terms of lost wages, of short illness.

With respect to the latter point, it should be noted that cash sickness benefit plans under both social insurance and private plans (other than sick-leave plans) usually provide for an initial waiting period (often seven days) during which no benefits are paid. The purpose of this is primarily to avoid the relatively high administrative expense involved in adjudicating and paying the many claims that would occur for only a few days' illness. At the same time, workers can be expected to have accumulated sufficient means to be able to meet the income loss for the first few days of sickness. This is particularly true in a high-wage economy like the United States; in countries with relatively low wages, either a shorter or no waiting period is economically necessary.

Five states (California, Hawaii, New Jersey, New York, and Rhode Island) and Puerto Rico, which include about 27 percent of all industrial and commercial workers in the United States, have established cash sickness benefit systems. As will be brought out subsequently, the California and New York programs provide certain other benefits than cash sickness benefits. Unlike unemployment insurance, there was no federal legislation in this area that, in essence, compelled the states to establish such programs. Workers covered by the nationwide railroad retirement and railroad unemployment insurance systems are also covered for cash sickness benefits under the latter system (see Chapter 13).

The Rhode Island system was established in 1942, Hawaii and Puerto Rico in 1968, and the other four in 1946–49. In the initial legislative proposal underlying the 1950 amendments to the OASDI system, made by the Truman administration, there was a section that would have established a system of cash sickness benefits for all persons covered by OASDI—to be administered by the Social Security Administration in conjunction with the OASDI system. This proposal was quickly rejected by Congress (in House committee consideration).

The remainder of the chapter will deal solely with the seven governmentally established programs. The provisions of the systems as they now stand will be considered, as well as their historical development and some statistics of operation.

ADMINISTRATION

All systems except the New York one are administered, from a governmental standpoint, by the same agency that operates the corresponding unemployment insurance program. In New York, such administration is through the state workmen's compensation agency. As might be expected then, the provisions of the several programs bear a certain similarity with the primary program of the administering agency.

Rhode Island and the railroad plan are operated completely by the governmental agency (the so-called "monopolistic" basis). The other systems permit "contracting-out" through private plans established by employers, which may be either self-administered or insured with an insurance company. Such contracting-out is permitted in California only if the employees concur with the employer's action.

New York has a different situation, since there the employer is held liable for failure to make arrangements for the benefit protection, in a manner similar to workmen's compensation. New York has a competitive state fund from which the statutory benefit protection can be purchased (and, in addition, a special fund for paying sickness benefits to workers who have been unemployed for more than four weeks). Alternatively, the employer may self-insure, insure with an insurance carrier, or make an agreement with a union for a jointly administered fund.

In plans that are not operated completely by a governmental agency, the benefit protection of the private plans must at least equal that of the statutory benefits. In New York, this "equating" is done on the basis of the entire package of benefits (including any medical, surgical, and hospital benefits provided). Thus, in Hawaii and New York, the employer may provide either the statutory benefits or a "package" of benefits that is at least actuarially equivalent to the statutory benefits. The provisions of the alternative benefits are, however, required by regulation to be within certain specifications, and they are evaluated by detailed tables of credits so as to test their actuarial equivalence. In the other plans, equivalence must prevail for each benefit separately. In New Jersey and Puerto Rico, the contracted-out plan can be exactly the same as the statutory benefits, but in California it has to be more liberal in at least one respect.

When there is contracting-out, special problems arise in connection with persons becoming sick after separation from employment covered by a private plan (including those in noncovered employment when they become sick). As will be described later, benefit payments to such individuals are generally paid by the state fund, but are financed by levies on the private plans.

COVERAGE

In all systems except the New York one, the TDI coverage is essentially the same as for unemployment insurance, although in some instances TDI coverage is broader (and, in a few instances, narrower). In New York, coverage applies to all industrial and commercial employers who have one or more workers on at least 30 days of a calendar year (not the same as the workmen's compensation coverage provision); in addition, employers with four or more domestic workers on each of at least 30 days in a calendar year are covered. In California, certain agricultural workers are covered, and self-employed persons can be covered on a voluntary elective basis. In Hawaii and Puerto Rico, certain farm workers not under UI are covered under TDI. In Rhode Island, state employees are under UI, but not under TDI. Several states permit individuals to elect out of TDI on religious grounds.

BENEFIT PROVISIONS

The benefit provisions of TDI follow the general patterns established in other social insurance programs. These provisions will be considered from the standpoint of identifying the types of benefits, qualifying requirements, waiting periods, duration of benefits, and benefit amounts.

Types of Benefits

As indicated previously, the primary purpose of TDI is to provide some cash income during a worker's illness when he no longer has wages. In general, sickness is defined as the inability to perform customary work because of a physical or mental condition. Cash sickness benefits are generally not payable for illness arising from work-connected causes.

Disability due to pregnancy entitles the worker to benefits only in the Hawaii, New Jersey, Rhode Island (only a lump-sum payment, with $250 maximum), and railroad systems, except that in the other systems, unusual illness due to pregnancy is covered.

The California system provides benefits, in addition to the cash sickness benefits, in the form of extra payments while in a hospital or nursing home ($12 per day for 20 days within a benefit period). The Puerto Rican plan has a death benefit of $1,000 for death resulting from sickness or injury, if within six months of the inception of the illness.

Qualifying Requirements

Except for the New York system, the amount of qualifying employment required is generally the same or somewhat less than for unemployment insurance benefits (although much less in California— namely, only $300 of wages in the base year, whereas UI requires $750). The basis in New York is having covered employment in at least four consecutive weeks (extended coverage of four consecutive weeks applies after termination of such employment).

Waiting Period

Under the state plans, the waiting period before benefits begin is one week, or for California and Puerto Rico the date of hospitalization, if earlier. For partial weeks of sickness after the waiting period has been satisfied, the payment is usually on a pro rata basis (e.g., in Hawaii and New York, the daily benefit rate is the weekly amount divided by the individual's usual number of working days per week, and it is paid for the number of "usual working days" in the week that he was sick).

In the railroad system, for claimants who are sick for at least two weeks, the waiting period, when measured in terms of benefit receipt, is in essence reduced to about half a week, since seven days of benefits are paid for the initial two-week period, which represents 70 percent of the amount that is payable for subsequent two-week periods of complete sickness. If the individual is not sick for the entire initial 2-week period, he receives benefits only for days of sickness in excess of 7 days, including Saturdays and Sundays. In any subsequent 2-week period in the benefit year after the individual has had an initial period of sickness of at least 7 days, and if the individual is sick during the entire 14 days, then 10 days of benefits are paid (actually, for such subsequent periods, benefits are paid for all days of sickness after the first 4 days thereof, including Saturdays and Sundays, so that there is a

4-day waiting period before benefit payment begins). It is interesting to note that the waiting period for cash sickness benefits was not eliminated when this was done in 1959 for unemployment benefits.

In New York, an employer may provide an alternative package of benefits that contains a shorter waiting period than one week. Also, in this state the waiting period is eliminated for workers who have been unemployed for at least four weeks and get benefits from the special fund that is established for such purposes.

Maximum Duration of Benefits

In all six state programs, benefits may be drawn for a maximum of 26 weeks (in a benefit year or in a continuous sickness period, depending on the plan). In some states, the 26-week maximum applies to all eligibles (Hawaii and New York), while in the other states the maximum duration is lower (as little as six weeks in California) for those with low earnings in the base period—for example, in California and Puerto Rico, total benefits cannot exceed 50 percent of base-year wages. On the whole, this coordinates with the six-month effective waiting period for disability benefits under OASDI. When the railroad unemployment benefits were liberalized in 1959 by extending the uniform-maximum duration beyond 26 weeks for those with 10 or more years of service, this was not done for the cash sickness benefits. However, in 1968 the conditions were made the same for both programs—an additional 13 weeks for those with 10–14 years of railroad service and an additional 26 weeks for those with 15 or more years of railroad service (but only if under age 65).

A lower maximum duration of benefits in the case of pregnancy of an insured worker applies in New Jersey, eight weeks (four before and four after childbirth). In the railroad plan, before the 1968 amendments, there were special duration provisions (and also higher benefit rates) for maternity benefits; now, the same maximum durations apply for both cash sickness and unemployment benefits.

Benefit Amounts

In the New Jersey, Rhode Island, and railroad programs the benefit amounts are computed in exactly (or substantially) the same manner as are the unemployment benefits, although in Rhode Island the TDI maximum is lower than the UI one. In the California and Hawaii plans, the cash sickness benefits are computed in the same general manner as the unemployment benefits but are usually somewhat higher, even before considering the hospital supplements. Under the New York program, the benefit amount under the statutory coverage provisions is 50 percent of the average weekly wage during the eight weeks of covered employment before the illness began, with a minimum of $20 (or the average wage, if less) and a maximum of $95. In the Puerto Rico system, the cash sickness benefits for nonagricultural workers are computed in the same manner as the unemployment benefits for benefits of up to $50 per week, but high-paid workers may receive more (based on 1 percent of annual wages, up to a maximum benefit of $90); for agricultural workers, benefits are computed differently, being based on total annual wages, and are generally at a lower level, ranging from $7 to $30 per week.

The state plans have minimums for the weekly benefit amount, ranging from $7 for Puerto Rico to $25 for California (under the railroad plan, $40). The maximum weekly benefits are $63.50 under the railroad plan, $72 in Rhode Island, $95 in New York, $85 in New Jersey, $90 in Puerto Rico, $104 in Hawaii, and $119 in California.

FINANCING

In all six state plans, the employees make contributions for the cash sickness benefits, except for the Puerto Rican plan for agricultural workers, which is financed entirely by the government. On the other hand, under the railroad plan, the employer pays the entire cost (as part of a pooled contribution for both unemployment and cash sickness benefits—see Chapter 13). In Rhode Island and in California (for employers under the state plan), no employer contribution is payable. The contribution bases for 1975 for the state programs are shown in Table 15.1.

For contracted-out plans, the employer may collect the statutory employee contributions and then must meet the balance of the cost. In Hawaii and New York, the employees may be required to contribute more if sufficient additional benefit protection is provided. In California, the covered self-employed workers contribute at 1¼ percent on a flat amount of earnings in all cases ($2,850 per quarter).

That a major portion of the financing of the state cash sickness systems comes from employee contributions may be explained by the fact that in California, New Jersey, and Rhode Island, there were

Table 15.1

Contribution Bases for State Cash Sickness Benefit Systems, 1975

State	Maximum Taxable Earnings	Employer Rate	Employee Rate
California	$9,000 per year	—	1%
Hawaii	$7,300*	Balance of cost	½†
New Jersey	$4,800 per year	½%‡	½
New York	$60 per week	Balance of cost	½
Puerto Rico§	$9,000 per year	¼	¼
Rhode Island	$4,800 per year	—	1½

* 1.21 times state average weekly wage.
† But not more than 50 percent of the cost.
‡ Basic rate, which is experience rated (varying from 0.1 to 1.1 percent).
§ Plan for nonagricultural workers.

originally employee contributions for unemployment insurance that were diverted for this purpose. In fact, an amendment to the Social Security Act in 1946 permitted states to transfer accumulated unemployment insurance contributions of employees to any cash sickness benefit program that was established. Rhode Island took the entire $29 million so provided, since it needed funds in the late 1940s because of bad experience (before its law was tightened in regard to such matters as maternity benefits and duplication of cash sickness benefits with other benefits). New Jersey also took the entire amount available ($50 million), but is using it solely for its interest earnings, which go toward meeting the cost of cash sickness benefits for unemployed workers. California took only a token amount of what was available.

The sickness benefits paid to unemployed workers in the states where contracting-out is permitted are financed in different ways. In New Jersey, if the interest on the transferred employee unemployment insurance contributions is not sufficient for this purpose, there can be an assessment of up to 0.1 percent of taxable payroll against both the private plans and the general state fund. In California, the cost of sickness benefits for unemployed workers who were under contracted-out plans was formerly assessed individually against each plan in proportion to the beneficiaries' creditable wages thereunder. Now, a uniform rate of contribution is assigned against each plan—0.12 percent of taxable payroll. In Hawaii, an initial fund for this purpose was developed by a temporary general payroll tax; additional amounts needed later are to be raised by assessments against insurance carriers and self-insurers.

In New York, an interest-earning fund was developed by a special contribution rate of 0.1 percent on both employers and employees in the first half of 1950. If the interest of this fund is not sufficient to pay the cash sickness benefits to unemployed workers and to maintain at least a $12-million balance, a flat contribution rate can be assessed against all private plans and the "general" state fund.

DUPLICATION WITH OTHER BENEFITS

As indicated previously, all systems essentially do not permit duplication with workmen's compensation benefits. The railroad plan does not permit payment of benefits if sick leave (at either full or partial pay) is granted; it pays only the excess, if any, of the cash sickness benefit over any other social insurance benefit payable (such as OASDI, or state cash sickness or unemployment benefits), and it offsets any damage settlements received with respect to the worker's illness (not only for work-connected accidents, but also for any other injuries for which he is so compensated by a third party).

All state plans, except Rhode Island, limit the sickness benefits, so that, together with any other payment from the employer as sick leave, the total does not exceed previous earnings.

APPENDIX

Statistics of Operation

Complete data on the operation of the seven cash sickness systems are difficult to obtain, since they are not available in many respects for the contracted-out portions of those state programs, where this is permitted. Accordingly, some of the data presented here will be only for the portion of the program that is administered by government agencies. In the latter respect, the New York system (except the separate portion that is for unemployed workers) is considered to be a program with administration by private carriers.

Table 15.2 shows the number of persons covered by the programs for various years, subdivided by whether covered under a private plan or by one administered by a government agency. The coverage grew rapidly from 1945 to 1950 as new systems began operation. Since then, coverage has grown slowly as the labor force has risen and then, in 1969–70, when two new plans were established (Puerto Rico and Hawaii). The proportion of the coverage that is in private plans has decreased since 1953—from 57 percent then to 47 percent in 1973— although the absolute number in private plans has varied only slightly. The vast majority of the private-plan coverage is concentrated in New York, all of whose plan is considered to be in this category. The relative drop was due largely to the effect of significant shifts from private plans to government programs as benefits were liberalized under the state laws in California and New Jersey, sometimes without increases in contribution rates.

The proportion of the coverage that is under private plans in

TABLE 15.2

Workers in Employment Covered by Cash Sickness Benefit Programs, Average Monthly Number (in millions)

Year*	Private Plans†	Government Plans	Total
1950‡	2.09	3.43	5.52
1953‡	7.28	3.55	10.84
1955	7.03	3.72	10.75
1960	7.01	4.45	11.46
1965	6.63	6.29	12.92
1970‖	7.38	7.57	14.95
1971‖	7.25	7.57	14.82
1972‖	7.64	7.92	15.56
1973‖	7.46	8.30	15.76

* In July.

† Includes competitive state fund in New York.

‡ Does not include the New York program, which began paying benefits in July 1950.

§ First year for which data are available for the New York program.

‖ Data for Hawaii not available.

Source: Social Security Administration.

California decreased from 47 percent in 1955 to only 7 percent in 1973. Similarly, for New Jersey, the decline was from 62 percent to 34 percent. At the start of the Puerto Rico plan, about 55 percent of the coverage was under private plans, and it has remained at this since then. In the two states with long-established programs where there are both private plans and a state program (California and New Jersey), the average size of firms which have contracted out is much larger than that of those in the state program (about four or five times as large).

In 1973 the average weekly benefit amount under the government programs was about $54 in Rhode Island, $67 in New Jersey, $61 in the railroad plan, $77 in California (exclusive of hospital supplements), and $33 in Puerto Rico. In California, the average benefit under private plans was about 35 percent larger than under the governmental plan, while in Puerto Rico, it was about 60 percent larger.

The ratio of the average weekly number of beneficiaries to the average number of covered workers in 1973 was only 0.4 percent in Puerto Rico, 1.1 percent in New York, about 1.5 percent in New Jersey and in California, 1.9 percent in Rhode Island, and 1.3 percent in the railroad plan. The average duration of benefits per period paid was seven to nine weeks in most programs except the railroad plan (10 weeks), Puerto Rico (10 weeks), and New York (four weeks).

Table 15.3 gives the total benefit payments under both private plans and government plans for all systems combined. The total annual

TABLE 15.3

Benefit Payments* under
Cash Sickness Benefit Programs
(in millions)

Year	Private Plans†	Government Plans	Total*
1950.............	$ 56	$ 66	$122 (5)
1955.............	152	114	266 (21)
1960.............	225	187	412 (41)
1965.............	224	295	219 (52)
1970‡.............	348	438	786 (66)
1971‡.............	359	437	796 (71)
1972‡.............	373	436	809 (66)
1973‡.............	422	476	878 (70)

* Including hospital supplements in California and medical, surgical, and hospital benefits in New York; shown in parentheses in Total column.
† Includes competitive state fund in New York.
‡ Data for Hawaii not available.
Source: Social Security Administration.

benefits rose from $122 million in 1950 to about $800 million in recent years. This rise is attributable to the larger number of persons covered, to the higher general wage level, and to the liberalization of the benefit provisions. Corresponding information on contributions is not available.

More detailed information is available as to the operations of the programs that are completely under governmental auspices and the state-operated portions of the programs where there are both government and private programs. Table 15.4 summarizes such data for benefit payments, contributions, and fund balances. Contribution and fund data are not available for the railroad program because—as mentioned in Chapter 13—these operations are combined with unemployment insurance. In the early years of operation, the contributions under the state plans exceeded the benefit payments; but in the late 1950s and

TABLE 15.4

Benefit Payments, Contributions, and Funds Available under Cash Sickness Benefit Programs, Government Plans*

Year	Benefit Payments		Contributions, States†	Funds Available at End of Year, States†
	Railroad	States†		
	Amounts (in millions)			
1950.............	$ 29	$ 37	$ 48	$214
1955.............	52	61	64	272
1960.............	57	128	104	214
1965.............	41	251	257	149
1970*............	56	378	363	139
1971*............	45	387	388	164
1972*............	36	395	454	219
1973*............	28	443	446	259
	As Percentage of Taxable Payroll			
1950.............	0.62%	0.77%	1.00%	‡
1955.............	1.06	0.88	0.93	‡
1960.............	1.38	1.16	0.94	‡
1965.............	1.10	0.95	0.97	‡
1970*............	1.76	1.04	1.00	‡
1971*............	1.46	1.05	1.05	‡
1972*............	1.20	0.91	1.05	‡
1973*............	.95	1.06	1.07	‡

* Data for Hawaii not available; data for New York (special state fund for benefits for unemployed workers and competitive state fund) not included.
† Includes only California, New Jersey, Puerto Rico, and Rhode Island; includes hospital and other medical supplements.
‡ Not computed.
Source: Social Security Administration.

early 1960s, this was not the case, as benefit liberalizations became effective. The deficits were met by drawing on accumulated funds and by transferring certain employee contributions from the unemployment insurance program to this one. In recent years, benefit outgo and contribution income have been in close balance.

Quite obviously, the funds available for benefits are only of a contingency reserve nature, and at the end of 1973, they represented less than one-half year's benefit payments. For both the railroad program and the state programs, the benefit cost was about ¾ percent of taxable payroll in the early years of operation; but in recent years, it rose to about 1½ percent for the railroad plan, although dropping off to slightly under 1 percent in 1973, and to about 1 percent for state plans. The average contribution rate under the state programs has been about 1 percent of taxable payroll throughout the entire period of operation.

Because of the very low maximum taxable wage base in the railroad system, $4,800 on an annual basis, the cost of this program relative to taxable payroll is artificially high. For example, the benefit payments of $28 million in 1973 were 0.95 percent of taxable payroll, but if the tax base had been the same as for the Railroad Retirement system, the cost would have been only 0.45 percent. About the same experience developed in 1974, when the benefit payments were $30 million, or 1.01 percent of RUI taxable payroll and 0.41 percent of RR taxable payroll.

The decreasing trend of the cost of the railroad cash sickness benefits program in recent years has been the result of the benefit level remaining more or less constant while earnings have risen. Thus, there may have been less incentive to draw benefits. In early 1975, legislation was in progress in Congress that would raise the benefit level under both this program and RUI significantly (more than double) and would provide for its automatic adjustment in the future. This legislation would provide the necessary financing to meet the cost of the benefit liberalizations by increasing the tax base to the same as that under RR, and thus include automatic adjustment in the future as the general wage level rises.

Table 15.5 shows the operating experience of the various state funds in 1973. The benefit cost for California represented 1.05 percent of payroll, or about the same as the 1 percent contribution rate. Similarly, in New Jersey, there was also a close balance, the benefit cost being 1.19 percent versus an average contribution rate of 1.25 percent. On

TABLE 15.5

Benefit Payments, Contributions, and Funds Available
under Cash Sickness Benefit Programs, Government Plans,* by States, 1973
(in millions)

State	Benefit Payments	Adminis- trative Expenses	Contribu- tions	Excess of Contributions over Outgo†	Fund at End of Year
California............	$350.0	$14.0	$332.4	−$31.6	$138.5
New Jersey..	74.6	3.3	87.7	9.8	86.8
Puerto Rico.........	1.7	n.a.	6.9	5.2	24.7
Rhode Island........	16.4	1.2	19.2	1.6	8.5

* Data for Hawaii not available; data for New York (special state fund for benefits for unemployed workers and competitive state fund) not included.
† Note that at least part of any deficiency shown is offset by investment earnings of the fund.
n.a. = not available.

the other hand, in Rhode Island, the benefit cost of 1.42 percent was somewhat below the 1½ percent contribution rate. In the new Puerto Rican plan, benefit costs were only 0.2 percent as compared with the contribution rate of 1.0 percent then applicable; the low benefit cost perhaps occurred because the covered workers were not yet cognizant with the benefit provisions. Because of this favorable early experience, the combined employer-employee contribution rate was reduced to 0.5 percent in mid-1974.

Most of the discussion of the operation of the state programs has considered them as a whole, although the operations differ significantly by state. The Rhode Island program had certain financial difficulties in its early years of operation, but these were largely eliminated by several amendments that tightened up the program (such as restricting duplication with workmen's compensation benefits, and more restrictive conditions for maternity cases). For a number of years after 1960 the Rhode Island system consistently had benefit outgo in excess of contribution income (by about 20 percent), with the deficit being met by drawing down the fund. As a result, several years ago the contribution rate was increased from 1 percent to 1½ percent, and the fund balance has slowly, but steadily, risen.

On the other hand, the California system had considerable excesses of benefit costs over contributions in the late 1950s and early 1960s (roughly a 20 percent differential) that were met by transferring funds from the unemployment insurance system (representing past employee contributions). This type of deficit financing could, of course, occur for only a limited period because the monies available were from a "closed fund" that would have no further income in the future. During this time, the inadequate state-plan rate attracted many employers to shift away from their private plans to the "less costly" state plan. Beginning in 1965, the state-plan rates were increased, and income has been sufficient to meet the costs of the program and to increase the size of the fund. However, in both 1971 and 1972, a small deficit of income versus outgo appeared, but since then the fund balance has been growing.

The New Jersey plan had shown a steadily increasing balance in its fund for a number of years, because income had exceeded outgo, although the difference had been decreasing. In 1962, for the first time, benefits exceeded contributions by a significant margin. In subsequent years, benefit outgo exceeded contribution income, and the fund was drawn down. In 1971, contribution rates were increased, and then income and outgo were in close balance. In fact, since 1971, the fund balance has increased steadily, and the employee contribution rate was reduced from 0.75 percent to 0.50 percent in 1975.

The average contribution rate in 1973 for the state-operated funds in the four state plans for which information is available was slightly more than 1 percent of taxable payroll. California and Puerto Rico were close to 1 percent, but New Jersey was about 1.4 percent and Rhode Island was 1.5 percent.

Administrative expenses in the state-operated funds recently have averaged about 4½ percent of benefit outgo—4 percent in California, 5 percent in New Jersey, and 8 percent in Rhode Island.

chapter 16

Special Programs for Government Employees and Veterans

As in many countries throughout the world, the first governmental programs to provide various types of employee benefits in the United States were those for members of the military services and ex-servicemen (veterans). The next types of programs to be developed were benefit protection plans for civilian employees of the federal government and employees of state and local governments (often for police and firemen first). Because these governmental employee plans preceded general overall social insurance programs, they were continued in most cases without being coordinated with such systems.

This chapter, in rounding out the discussion of allied governmental programs separate from the general social insurance system established by OASDI and Medicare, will discuss the protection afforded to federal civilian employees, state and local employees, members of the armed forces, and veterans. A brief description of the actuarial funding methods for the civil service retirement system and other governmental employee plans was presented in the appendix to Chapter 4.

FEDERAL CIVILIAN EMPLOYEES

The economic security measures for civilian employees of the federal government are provided by a number of different programs applicable to this category of employees. Retirement, survivor, and disability protection for the vast majority of such employees arises under the civil service retirement system. Special retirement systems apply for certain small groups such as foreign service employees, the Tennessee Valley Authority, the Board of Governors of the Federal Reserve Bank, and the federal judiciary.

Medical care benefits for active and retired federal employees are furnished under the Federal Employees Health Benefits Act. Protection in the area of cash sickness benefits is provided by a sick leave system. Unemployment benefits are payable through the state UI systems. Benefits in case of work-connected injury or disease are available under the federal employees compensation program.

Civil Service Retirement System

Although a few private employers had established pension plans before 1920, the federal government, in then enacting the civil service retirement system (CSR), was a pioneer in this area. The program was originally a relatively modest one insofar as the benefit level was concerned. Also, it tended to emphasize a benefit structure for employees remaining in service until age or disability retirement, without providing for survivor pensions or for vested deferred pensions for those withdrawing from active service after a significant period of employment.

CSR is completely independent of OASDI, although logically it could have been integrated therewith when OASDI was initiated in 1937, just as private employers with pension plans were allowed to do. The logic has always been for coordination of CSR with OASDI, by providing coverage under the latter and adjusting the former accordingly. There are some probable underlying reasons why this logic has not prevailed. The leaders of federal government employee organizations have always opposed an extension of OASDI coverage to their membership and the coordination of CSR with OASDI. This opposition arose primarily because long-service career employees can enjoy an advantage by having CSR separate from OASDI, although this is not so for short-term ones. Career employees often can qualify for dual benefits thereby and thus have the windfall arising from the heavily weighted OASDI benefits for short periods of coverage and low covered earnings. Also, in cases of early retirement, say, at ages 55–59, persons can receive both CSR pensions and wages from nonfederal employment and, at the same time, be building up OASDI benefit rights.

Another possible reason for the opposition to coordination of CSR and OASDI by the leaders of the government employee organizations has been that their influence in the employee benefit area would be lessened. They would then have influence over the course of only the portion represented by the reduced coordinated CSR program.

Nonetheless, the OASDI program has had a considerable effect on CSR. The advocates of coordination pointed out some of the weaknesses in CSR and indicated how they could be solved through their proposals. However, the supporters of an autonomous and independent CSR program countered by expanding CSR. For example, the complete absence of any protection for persons withdrawing with substantial service before reaching retirement age was remedied by introducing a liberal vesting provision (full vesting after five years of service).

Similarly, the absence of adequate survivor protection in CSR (such as was introduced in OASDI in 1940) was remedied by providing for a full range of monthly survivor benefits for both active and retired employees. This included the availability of such benefits for widowed mothers with children after only 1½ years of service, so as to parallel the currently insured protection under OASDI.

The following is a brief description of CSR as it existed at the beginning of 1975. The aspects that will be considered are coverage, types of benefits, amounts of benefits, and financing.

Coverage. Virtually all federal civilian employees are covered under CSR. The only exceptions are those who are covered under certain small special systems (as mentioned previously) and the relatively few temporary employees. The latter category, except for very temporary workers such as census takers, are covered under OASDI. It is interesting to note that when the postal system was converted from a regular government department to an independent corporation, the employees continued to be covered under CSR. Members of Congress and employees of Congress are covered under CSR on an individual voluntary basis and have certain special benefit conditions, as will be indicated subsequently.

Types of Benefits. CSR provides retirement, disability, and survivor pensions and also lump-sum refunds for those separating from service who are not eligible for, or who do not choose, deferred vested pensions.

The retirement benefits are generally payable without any reduction for early retirement under several combinations of age and service, namely, age 55 with 30 years of service, age 60 with 20 years of service (for members of Congress, 10 years), and age 62 with five years of service. Retirement is compulsory at age 70 with 15 years of service, or at such later age when 15 years of service is attained. Special provisions apply to persons involuntarily separated from service without cause, namely, for those with 25 years of service, regardless of age at separation, and for those with 20 years of service and at least age 50. However, such involuntary separation pensions carry reductions of 2 percent for each year below age 55 (for members of Congress, the reduction is 1 percent for each year below age 60 down to age 55, and then the 2 percent factor applies).[1]

Special retirement conditions apply for certain occupational groups. Law enforcement officers and firefighters can retire on full annuity at age 50 with 20 years of service; beginning in 1979, retirement will be mandatory at age 55 with 20 years of service. Air traffic controllers can retire on full annuity and with a special guaranty of at least a 50 percent annuity rate, which normally requires 23¾ years of service, with either 25 years of service or at age 55 with 20 years of service; retirement will be mandatory at age 56 for those hired after this change was enacted in 1972.

Disability pensions are payable on a full basis for individuals who have at least five years of service. The definition of disability is much more liberal than that under OASDI, since it involves incapacity for performing the duties of the usual occupation, rather than any reasonable type of gainful employment.

Survivor pensions under CSR are payable to widows and children of active workers and also for all widowers of active workers; this is unlike OASDI, under which a dependency requirement is present for widower's benefits.[2] Also unlike OASDI, CSR has no age requirement for widow and widower pensions. In other words, they are paid regardless of age or presence of eligible children. Such widow and widower pensions cease on remarriage (except, as under OASDI, not for remarriages after age 60). Also unlike OASDI, duplication of CSR

---

[1] Such reductions are far smaller than the true actuarial reductions, which would be about 7 percent per year.

[2] This equal treatment of men and women as to survivor pensions is required of private pension plans by the Equal Employment Opportunities Act. But in March 1975, a Supreme Court decision apparently struck out this dependency requirement in OASDI.

pensions is permitted. For example, a woman can draw both a CSR widow pension and a CSR employee pension based on her own work. Further, as indicated previously, no restrictions prevent receipt of CSR when there is substantial employment with any other employer than the federal government.

Child-survivor pensions under CSR are payable under somewhat the the same conditions as under OASDI, except that the school attendance eligibility conditions extend up to the July 1 following attainment of age 22 if such birthday occurs in September to June.

The survivor-benefit protection under CSR after retirement is on an automatic basis only insofar as the child survivor pensions are concerned. Widow pensions and widower pensions without a dependency requirement are available only if the employee pensioner elects to take a reduction in his own pension.[3] Nonmarried retirants who wish to provide survivor benefits for a dependent with an insurable interest, such as a sister, can do so, with reductions that more closely approximate the true actuarial ones.

Amounts of Benefits. The amount of the basic employee pension is determined from the number of years of service and the average salary during the highest three consecutive years of service. The benefit formula for general employees is 1½ percent per year for the first five years of service, 1¾ percent per year for the next five years, and 2 percent per year thereafter up to a maximum pension of 80 percent (attained by 42 years of service).[4] An interesting feature of computing the length of service is that it includes both military service not included for a military pension and unused sick leave at time of retirement.

Higher benefit factors apply for certain special groups. Members of Congress and congressional employees have a 2½ percent benefit rate

---

[3] The reduction is quite nominal, however, being only 2½ percent of the first $300 of monthly pension and 10 percent for all pension above this amount—as against the true actuarial reductions for such protection probably averaging about 15 percent. Accordingly, the vast majority of persons eligible for this survivor protection take it. The election must be made at the time of retirement. It applies to marriages after retirement if the annuitant lives for at least one year after the marriage. The reduction is not applicable during periods of retirement when the annuitant is not married (e.g. after divorce or death of the wife).

[4] There is an alternative formula which has the purpose of giving more heavily weighted benefits for low-paid individuals (under $4,000 per year), but this has become virtually obsolete because its salary brackets were not changed as the general earnings level rose over the past two decades, and so few individuals are "low paid" for these purposes.

for all years of service except that the latter have a 2 percent benefit rate for military service in excess of 5 years. Law enforcement employees and firefighters have a 2½ percent rate for the first 20 years of service and a 2 percent rate for all subsequent years. An 80 percent maximum applies for all these categories.

Individuals withdrawing from service who are not eligible for an immediate pension may elect to receive a deferred pension at age 62 if they have at least five years of service. Such deferred pension is computed in the same manner as retirement pensions. No survivor protection exists during the interval of deferment, but once the pension is entered into, the same type of survivor protection applies as for retirements directly from service.

In lieu of a deferred pension, and in cases of less than five years of service, the withdrawing employee can receive a lump-sum refund of his CSR contributions. In a manner rather unusual for contributory pension plans, no interest is paid on the accumulated contributions making up these refunds, except, strangely enough, in those instances where the individual has at least one year of service but less than five years.

The amount of the disability pension is computed in exactly the same manner as for retirement pensions, except that a special minimum is applicable for those with short service, but with at least the five years required for eligibility purposes. This minimum is 40 percent of the high three-year average salary, unless the pension rate which the individual would obtain if he continued in service until age 60 is less than 40 percent, in which case such lower rate is applicable for the minimum. The minimum thus applies generally to disability cases with less than about 22 years of service.

The amount of the widow and widower pensions is 55 percent of the full pension for which the retired member was eligible (i.e., before any reduction on account of taking the survivor protection) or of the full disability pension for which the deceased employee would have been eligible if he had become disabled instead of dying in active service. The survivor pension in the case of nonmarried pensioners who have a beneficiary with an insurable interest is 50 percent of the *reduced* employee pension. Child survivor pensions, when a widowed mother is present, were established in 1969 as flat-dollar amounts of $75 per month per child, with a maximum for all children of $225 per month (or, if less, 60 percent of the high three-year average salary, which is rarely applicable). This flat-dollar amount is subject to automatic adjustment for changes in the cost of living, as described hereafter, and was $116 and $348, respectively at the beginning of 1975. In instances where the only survivors are children, the pension amounts are 20 percent higher (or, if less, 75 percent of average salary).

Legislation in 1974 provided that for persons not receiving other governmental benefits such as OASDI (or receiving such benefits in a lesser amount than the minimum PIA under OASDI), the CSR benefit will not be less than the minimum PIA under OASDI.

In 1962, automatic cost-of-living adjustments were introduced into the benefit structure of CSR. As amended in 1969, these adjustments, applicable to all types of pensions, are based on the percentage increase in the Consumer Price Index from the last previous base month to the highest month in a three-month period during each of which the percentage increase in the CPI was at least 3.0 percent. The pensions in force are then increased by such percentage increase in the CPI plus one additional percentage point. For example, if the CPI increases 3.6 percent, pensions are raised by 4.6 percent.

When the legislation initiating this provision for the 1 percent bonus was passed by the House, the additional 1 percent was "rationalized" on the grounds that approximately a three-month lag occurred between the CPI computation point and when benefits would actually be increased (so that, say, for a 4 percent annual rate of increase in the CPI, a 1 percent addition would be appropriate). However, when it was pointed out in the Senate consideration of the legislation that such adjustment need be on only a one-time basis to accomplish the desired result rather than each time that pensions were increased, the rationale was changed. The procedure was then "justified" on the grounds that retired persons should share to some extent in this manner for increased productivity in the country.

When the automatic-adjustment provisions were initiated, they had an unusual result for new retirants. Persons retiring just after the effective date of a benefit increase would receive significantly less than if they had retired just before then, even though they had acquired more service and had paid more contributions, since they would not receive the CPI increase then given. In 1973, this situation was remedied by the enactment of a "notch" provision, under which the pension will not be less than the sum of the pension based on the service and salary up to the date of the last previous CPI increase and the amount resulting from such increase. Now, the pension payable to new retirants is usually not less than what they would have received if they had retired just before the effective date of the last previous automatic adjustment.[5]

In January 1975, President Ford recommended to Congress that the automatic-adjustment provisions should not be allowed to increase benefits under CSR by more than 5 percent, just as he had proposed for OASDI and SSI and for several other federal employee programs described later in this chapter. Congress, however, did not see fit to enact the necessary legislation.

Additional voluntary contributions may be made under CSR, up to a maximum of 10 percent of salary. These accumulate at 3 percent interest and are used to purchase a cash-refund annuity at retirement (with the automatic-adjustment provisions not being applicable). The annuity purchase factors are arbitrary, being prescribed by law at $7 of annual annuity per $100 of accumulation at age 55 or under for a single-life annuity, with the factor increasing linearly for older ages to $10 at age 70. Joint-and-survivor annuities can also be elected, on the same basis as is applicable for the regular pensions of nonmarried beneficiaries. These voluntary annuities are not subject to the automatic CPI increases.

Although originally the voluntary system was an "actuarial bargain" because of the favorable purchase factors, this is no longer the case. Not only is the 3 percent interest rate during the accumulation period very low as compared with generally available rates, but also (again due to interest rates) the purchase factors are not especially favorable. As a result, relatively few people use this program; moreover, this was even the case in the past when it seemed to offer a "bargain."

An overall residual return-of-contributions provision applies such that if the total pension payments made with respect to a retirant and his survivors do not equal his total contributions, a refund of the difference is made to a named beneficiary. This provision is rarely ap-

---

[5] The only circumstances when this would not be so are when the pension payable for retirement just before the effective date of the last previous automatic adjustment would have been larger if computed under this notch provision as of the second (or even earlier) previous automatic adjustment than if computed as of the last such adjustment. Such a situation occurs when the final average salary remains the same over a period of years, and the CPI increase under the second previous adjustment more than offsets the effect of additional months of service to be used in the benefit formula. This situation currently prevails for members of Congress and employees at the highest grades. The remedy to this anomalous situation is simply to have the notch provision apply with respect to any previous adjustment date, not solely to the *last* one.

plicable, except in the case of deaths in active service who do not leave any eligible dependents. In most retirement cases, this guarantee runs out after about one to one-and-a-half years on the pension roll.

Financing. The CSR employee contribution rate currently is 7 percent, although it is 7½ percent for congressional employees, law enforcement officers and firefighters, and 8 percent for members of Congress—in *partial* recognition of their more liberal benefits. This rate has risen over the years from the 2½ percent rate that applied initially in 1920. The remainder of the cost of CSR (plus all administrative expenses) is borne by the federal government. On a level basis, CSR has a cost of about 25½ percent of payroll, not taking into account the cost of the automatic-adjustment provision. Thus, the level cost to the federal government is about 18½ percent of payroll, although this is not met on a current basis. Instead, the financing on the part of the federal government in the past has been rather sporadic.

Before 1929, no government payments were made to CSR, and in most subsequent years up to 1959 the government appropriations were considerably lower than the employee contributions. This approach was "justified" on the grounds that the fund was quite sizable and that the income from employee contributions was well in excess of the benefit outgo. Beginning in 1959 the federal government began to pay amounts equal to the employee contributions (as a budgetary responsibility of each agency separately),[6] but no payments from the General Treasury were made to meet the remainder of the overall cost of the program.

Beginning in 1971 a more responsible method of financing the government's share of the cost of CSR was adopted. In addition to the equal matching payments from each agency, the General Treasury began paying each year an increasing proportion of the annual interest on the unfunded accrued liability (and by 1980 will be paying all of that cost). Such unfunded accrued liability was $77.0 billion as of mid-1974, computed on a closed-group basis, which was equivalent to about 2.3 times the annual payroll of covered employees.[7] Further,

---

[6] As a result of this procedure, the administrative expenses of OASDI and Medicare, paid out of the trust funds, include the 7 percent agency share of CSR for employees of the Social Security Administration, but not any portion of anything that the General Treasury may pay.

[7] This accrued liability figure, as well as others quoted later in this chapter, are from "Statement of Liabilities and Other Financial Commitments of the U.S. Government as of June 30, 1974," Department of the Treasury, January 1975 (as required by Sec. 402, P.L. 89–809).

the General Treasury makes annual payments to amortize in level installments over a 30-year period any increase in the unfunded liability resulting from legislation enacted after October 20, 1969, which liberalizes benefits, adds new persons to the coverage, or (most importantly) increases the salary levels of covered persons. Thus ultimately, all other factors being unchanged, the cost of CSR will become stabilized and the General Treasury will be paying a level cost each year of about 16–20 percent of payroll, and each employing agency will be paying 7 percent.[8]

Operations. The CSR system is administered by the Civil Service Commission. Its assets are invested by the Treasury Department entirely in obligations of the federal government, with the investment procedures being exactly the same as under OASDI.

A few statistics of the operations of CSR may be of interest. As of June 30, 1974, about 2.7 million persons were in active service, at an annual payroll rate of about $34 billion. On the same date, there were 1,314,000 pensioners, of whom 941,000 were retired employees and the remaining 373,000 were survivors. The total employee contributions in fiscal year 1974 were $2.3 billion, and there was an equal matching amount from the various federal agencies, plus $2.5 billion from the General Fund of the Treasury. Interest income on the fund (which amounted to $34.2 billion at the end of the year) was $1.8 billion. Pension outgo during the year was $5.5 billion, and there were lump-sum refund payments of $0.2 billion. Thus, the fund grew by $3.2 billion during fiscal year 1974. All direct administrative expenses of CSR are paid from the fund and amounted to $9 million in fiscal 1974.

In 1972, 58 percent of CSR employee pensioners were also receiving OASDI benefits.[9] About 52 percent of the families getting a CSR survivor pension also received OASDI. Only 1 percent of the CSR beneficiaries also received public assistance. About 22 percent of the employee pensioners had employment income in 1972.

Retirement Systems for Other Federal Civilian Groups

Both the Tennessee Valley Authority and the Board of Governors of the Federal Reserve Bank have established pension plans for their

---

[8] For more details as to the financing and actuarial basis of CSR, see "Fiftieth Annual Report of the Board of Actuaries of the CSR System," House Document No. 93–97, January 3, 1973 (the latest such report available at the end of 1974).

[9] From "Survey of Income of Civil Service Annuitants," Committee Print No. 93–7, Committee on Post Office and Civil Service, House of Representatives, September 3, 1973.

employees. In both instances, OASDI coverage is applicable, and the supplementary pension plans are quite similar to those of private employers.

Employees of the State Department who are in the Foreign Service (about 6,000 persons) have a separate retirement system, which resembles CSR but has significantly more liberal provisions. For example, the pension rate is 2 percent for all years of service, the normal retirement age is 50 with 20 years of service, and extra service credit of 50 percent is given for service at designated posts. The employee contribution rate is the same 7 percent as under CSR, and the government meets the balance of the cost which, on a level basis, is at the staggering level of about 48 percent of payroll. Currently, the government is matching the employee contribution rate and is paying part of the interest on the unfunded accrued liability, just as under CSR. The benefit outgo of the system was about $40 million in fiscal year 1974, representing about 30 percent of payroll. Contribution and interest income was $75 million in fiscal year 1974 of which all but $4 million was contributions. The fund balance on June 30, 1974, was $104 million. As of June 30, 1974, the estimated unfunded liabilities amounted to $835 million, or about 6.3 times the annual payroll of the covered employees. Obviously, the future portends gradually rising costs and thus serious financing problems for this program.

Supreme Court justices and other federal judges have a special retirement system, with retirement at age 70 after 10 years of service, at age 65 with 15 years of service, or for disability. Their salary continues for life, and the retired pay increases just as the salary of active judges does (except for those who resign instead of retiring, in which case the amount remains fixed). Survivor protection can be obtained only by the judge electing to pay a 3 percent contribution rate that is payable on both active salary and retired pay. The widow pension is 1¼ percent of the judge's pay for each year of service, including congressional, military, and certain other federal service, with a maximum benefit of 37½ percent, and small additional uniform amounts are payable for children.[10]

Federal Employees Group Life Insurance Program

In 1954 the federal government instituted a group life insurance program for its civilian employees, available on an individual volun-

---

[10] Formerly, widows of Supreme Court justices had noncontributory pensions of $5,000 per year (later increased to $10,000 for widows on the roll).

tary-election basis. Currently, about 91 percent of the eligible employees have so elected; this low rate is due to the relatively high cost at the younger ages and the resultant nonparticipation of many in this category, especially young unmarried women. Such programs had been provided by private employers for their employees for many years, and generally at a somewhat higher participation level than under this program.

The amount of life insurance is approximately one year's salary, plus $2,000, with a minimum of $10,000 and a maximum of $45,000. Accidental death and dismemberment benefits which equal the face amount are also provided.

Although the benefits for active employees are not at a particularly high level (since private employers often provide two or three years' salary), the insurance protection after retirement is rather liberal, unlike the practice in such plans of private employers where coverage often ceases or is reduced to a small flat amount. The full amount continues until age 65 and is then reduced at a monthly rate of 2 percent until reaching 25 percent of the full amount, after which it remains level.

As with many group life insurance plans in private industry, the employees contribute during their active service, but not after retirement. The employees pay two thirds of the cost, and the government pays the remainder.[11] The employee contribution rate currently is about $9.25 a year per $1,000 of insurance, which is more than the usual *maximum* rate of $7.20 (often as little as half this for younger members) under similar plans of private employers. The high rate under this program is due to the fact that over half the cost is for the "free" post-retirement insurance. Employees of the postal service, which is a government corporation and which has collective bargaining applicable, have their contributions paid by their agency.

Employees have an option to purchase up to $10,000 of additional life insurance. This insurance is of the same form as the regular coverage. The employees pay premiums, graded by age at entry, which are payable until age 65 (or retirement, if later) and are intended to meet the full cost of the protection.

This program is underwritten by a consortium of about 360 life insurance companies. As a result, the conversion privileges for employees who separate from service before retirement can be readily provided.

---

[11] In connection with the administrative expenses of OASDI and Medicare, the trust funds are charged these costs.

In fiscal year 1974 the total employee contributions amounted to $306 million, and the cost to the federal government was $133 million. During the same period, total benefit payments were $373 million. At the end of the year, contingency reserves in the amount of $1.6 billion were held.

As of June 30, 1974, 2.5 million employees were covered for the regular life insurance, and 550,000 of them also had the optional insurance. At the same time, 790,000 annuitants had the "free" post-retirement insurance. The total insurance in force was $51 billion.

Federal Employees Health Benefits Program

In 1960 the federal government established a health insurance program for its employees and their dependents, again lagging somewhat behind what most large, progressive private employers had done for their employees. The benefit protection generally available has been quite comprehensive. On the other hand, the government's share of the cost under this program was initially quite low as compared with what private employers usually pay, although it has been increased recently.

Rather than a single uniform health benefits program, federal employees are offered a choice of carrier, some of which have a low option and a high option providing more comprehensive benefits (such as longer duration of hospital care or lower cost-sharing payments). All employees can choose between a governmentwide indemnity-type plan offered by a consortium of insurance companies and a governmentwide service-type plan offered by Blue Cross–Blue Shield. In addition, some 44 other plans are available to employees in certain occupations, unions, or geographical areas (such as the group practice prepayment plan, Group Health Association, in Washington, D.C.).

The scope of the benefit protection under the various plans is quite comprehensive. The differences between the low option and the high option in the various plans have been narrowed over the years, and about 85 percent of the employees now take the high option. The governmentwide Blues plan is not greatly different from the governmentwide insurance company plan, although the latter tends to have somewhat more cost sharing and more catastrophic protection.

Ever since the inception of this program, the same benefit protection has been available for retired employees as for active employees.[12] This is considerably different than most health insurance plans of

---

[12] Those retired at the inception of the plan were excluded, and instead have a separate program with much smaller benefit protection.

private employers which, before Medicare, had generally provided reduced benefit protection (if any) for pensioners.

Since federal employees are not under OASDI, their health insurance plan as applicable to persons aged 65 and over was not modified when Medicare was enacted (as invariably were health insurance plans of private employers). Of course, as indicated in Chapter 6, this situation was recognized by the Medicare provision which blanketed-in to HI all insured persons aged 65 and over before 1968 by excluding such persons who were already protected under the federal employee plan.

Nonetheless, there remain significant problems as to the interrelationship of the Medicare program and the federal employee health benefits program. As to HI, many federal employees acquire such benefit protection through private employment. Yet, because of the coordination-of-benefits provision in the federal employee plan, they receive relatively little additional benefit protection as a result of the HI benefits which they had "bought" by paying HI taxes.

Similarly, individuals covered under the federal employee health benefits plan are free to elect SMI coverage by paying the required premiums. But once again, the desirability of doing this is open to question. Although some additional benefit protection would thereby be received, the coordination-of-benefits provision cancels out much of the SMI protection. Under such circumstances, only persons who expect relatively high medical expenditures find it worthwhile to opt for SMI.

Because of these difficulties in the interrelationship of the two programs, Congress took action in the 1972 amendments to the Social Security Act. If the federal employee health benefits program is not amended before 1976 (originally 1975, but changed by 1974 legislation) to provide for its coordination with Medicare (including lower premium rates under the federal employee plan for those who have protection under Medicare), then Medicare will cease to pay benefits for services covered under the federal employee plan.

This program is financed by a flat monthly contribution by the federal government for each covered person, varying only as between single persons and persons with eligible dependents.[13] Thus, the covered individual who joins a plan with more comprehensive coverage or who

---

[13] Here, too, these employee-benefit costs are reflected in the administrative expenses of OASDI and Medicare by direct payment thereof for employees of the Social Security Administration from the trust funds.

takes the high option pays more out of his own pocket than if he takes lower benefit protection. Originally, the payment by the federal government was $2.82 per month for single persons and $6.76 per month for persons with covered dependents, which was one half the cost of the low option of the governmentwide indemnity-type plan; for plans with lower premiums, the government share was limited to one half. Currently, the government pays a uniform amount equal to 60 percent of the average of the premiums charged for the high option by the six plans with the highest number of persons covered, separately for single individuals and those with eligible dependents, subject to the government share not exceeding 75 percent of the total premium. Employees of the postal service have, as a result of collective bargaining, 65 percent of the cost paid by their employing agency, instead of 60 percent, and a maximum of 81¼ percent instead of 75 percent.

As of June 30, 1974, about 3.0 million employees and pensioners, plus 6.0 million of their dependents, were covered under this program. Rather surprisingly, only about 75 percent of those employees eligible to participate actually have elected to do so; some of those not electing to participate may have their health insurance protection from the plan of their spouse who is also employed. The total employee and pensioner contributions during fiscal year 1974 were $766 million, while the federal government paid $729 million, or 49 percent of the total cost. The total benefit payments amounted to $1,334 million, while the administrative expenses of the various plans were $69 million, or 5 percent of the benefit outgo. Total contingency and other reserves held by the various plans (actually maintained by both the plans and the Civil Service Commission) amounted to $247 million at the end of fiscal year 1974, representing about 2.2 months' benefit outgo.

Federal Employees Compensation Program

In 1908 the federal government established its own workmen's compensation program for its employees, leading the way for the various state systems. For many years, this program has provided significantly more liberal benefit protection than any of the state programs. Administration is entirely by the federal government, through the Department of Labor.

Temporary disability benefits are payable after a three-day waiting period, with a retroactive benefit for these three days after three weeks of disability. The benefit rate is two thirds of salary if no dependent is present, and three fourths otherwise. The term "dependent" includes spouses (regardless of actual dependency), eligible children as defined in CSR, and dependent parents. The maximum benefit is 75 percent of the highest salary (i.e., maximum increments for length of service) of the top regular civil service grade (GS-15); beginning with October 1974, this amounted to $519 per week. The minimum benefit is 75 percent of the entrance salary of the second grade (GS-2); beginning with October 1974, this amounted to $86 per week.

Permanent disability benefits are available on either a scheduled basis for such injuries as loss of a limb or as compensation for loss of earning capacity. Just as in the case of the temporary disability benefits, there is coordination with sick leave and CSR so that not more than full pay can be received.

Monthly survivor benefits are payable under this program. The benefit for a widow without an eligible child is at the rate of 50 percent of the final salary. The rate for a widow with one child is 60 percent, while it is 75 percent for the widow with more than one child. When children survive without a parent, the benefit varies with the number of children, being 40 percent for one child, 55 percent for two children, 70 percent for three children, and 75 percent for four or more children. These periodic survivor benefits are coordinated with those under CSR, since the choice must be made between one or the other; if CSR benefits are waived, then refund of the employee CSR contributions is available. Such survivor benefits are also available for *dependent* siblings, parents, grandparents, and grandchildren. A burial allowance of up to $800 is also provided.

Automatic-adjustment provisions apply to these benefits. The procedure is somewhat different than under CSR. The 1 percent bonus is not given, and no increase can be made until the beneficiary has been on the roll for at least one year before the effective date of the increase.

Medical care for work-connected injuries and diseases is provided through federal medical facilities, except in cases where these are not readily available, and then private facilities may be used. Legislation enacted in September 1974 also permits the injured employee to obtain physician services from a designated panel of private doctors.

As with other workmen's compensation programs in the United States, the entire cost is borne by the employer, the federal government. Each agency is assessed annually an amount equal to the benefits paid with respect to its employees. Thus, the financing is entirely on a current-cost basis, and there is no advance funding or reserves for the permanent disability or survivor cases. The estimated unfunded liabilities for future payments to those on the roll as of June 30, 1974, was $1.2 billion.

During fiscal year 1974, total benefit disbursements under this program amounted to $260 million. Of this, $42 million was for temporary disability cases, $153 million was for permanent disability cases, and $29 was for survivor benefits. The cost of the medical care was $35 million.

Sick Leave System

Federal employees are provided cash sickness benefits through a sick leave system of continuance of full pay for a certain period. Employees earn 13 days of sick leave each year, and this can be accumulated indefinitely if not used. Thus, an employee who has served for 25 years without using any sick leave will have accumulated leave of 325 working days, or roughly 1 ½ years. As mentioned previously, any unused sick leave at the time of retirement can be converted to additional service credit in computing the pension under CSR.

STATE AND LOCAL EMPLOYEES

Quite naturally, with the large number of state and local governmental units, there are many separate retirement systems for employees in this category. Many such plans were initiated decades ago, although others were brought into existence by the growing interest in economic security that produced OASDI and private pension plans generally.

The general pattern of these retirement systems is that the state has two separate systems for its employees—one for school teachers and the other for general employees. The state law enforcement officers either have a separate system or more liberal provisions within the general program.

Local governments (such as counties, cities, townships, and other tax districts) often have separate retirement systems, although in some instances their employees are covered by a state program. Some local governments, especially large cities, have separate retirement systems for teachers if they are not included in a statewide program. Almost invariably, local governments have separate retirement systems for police and for firemen, and these provide very liberal benefits (usually with very early retirement provisions, which are based solely on length of service, such as 20 or 25 years).

A wide divergence exists among the various state and local retirement systems as to whether or not they have elected OASDI coverage. In some such programs, there was strong support for having OASDI as the basic floor of protection and then to add a supplementary pension plan—or, in some cases, to modify downward the previously existing retirement system so as to coordinate it properly with OASDI. In a few instances, OASDI was merely added on top of the previous plan. In other instances, there was the equally strong view that OASDI coverage was not desirable and that the system should remain completely independent, at a level providing very substantial benefit protection. Of course, in many instances where state and local government employees did not have a retirement system, OASDI coverage was welcomed by the employees and the employing agency. About 55 percent of all state and local employees who have retirement system coverage also are under OASDI, while for those with no such coverage, about 80 percent are under OASDI.

In general, the benefit level under state and local retirement systems (including the effect of OASDI where present) is relatively high and, like CSR, liberal early retirement is possible with full benefits. Disability retirement is also possible on a liberal basis as to the definition of disability. Again, just as under CSR, many state and local retirement systems formerly provided little survivor protection, except in the form of joint-and-survivor annuities derived from actuarial reductions of the retirement pension. More recently, such survivor protection has been provided to a greater extent—either through OASDI coverage or through independent survivor benefits. Vesting provisions under these plans have been liberalized gradually over the years, although in many instances they are still applicable only for relatively long-service cases.

Most state and local retirement systems, other than many plans for police and firemen, are on a contributory basis. Employee contribution rates are usually at a level of 5–7 percent. Accordingly, the share of the cost met by the governmental agency involved is usually at least twice as large as the employee share. In police and firemen plans, with their very liberal benefit provisions, the cost of the governmental agency, when expressed in level terms, will often run to well over 50 percent of payroll.

Many state and local retirement systems are financed on an actuarial funding basis. Frequently, however, the funding payments have not been adequate, due to budgetary problems, and a substantial accrued liability has developed. Very frequently, the plans for police and firemen have not been funded, but have been on a pay-as-you-go basis. As a result, the costs appeared to be low for a number of decades, but have gradually built up to very high levels, and these cause increasingly difficult budgetary problems.

In those state and local plans where there has been considerable funding, the investments originally were bonds of various governmental units or of the United States. Over the years, however, this investment policy has shifted greatly, and now many such funds are invested to a considerable extent in corporate bonds and stocks.

State and local governments also provide other types of economic security programs for their employees. Sick leave provisions are quite common. Health insurance plans are provided for most such employees in the same manner as private employers, through Blue Cross–Blue Shield or insurance companies. Group life insurance is provided for many state and local government workers, although not to the extent as in private industry or the federal government. Long-term work-connected injury benefits are generally made available as part of the retirement system, often with larger benefit rates than for ordinary disability (particularly for police and firemen). Unemployment benefits are provided in some states through extending the UI program to these employees, at the option of the state.

In 1973, total payments made by retirement systems for state and local government employees totaled about $5.4 billion, consisting of $4.6 billion as age or service pensions, $350 million as disability pensions, $275 million as survivor pensions, and $235 million as survivor lump-sum payments.[14] The beneficiaries involved as of mid-1973 were 1,320,000 age or service pensioners, 95,000 disability pensioners, and 135,000 survivor pensioners. Many of these pensioners were also receiving OASDI benefits.

MEMBERS OF THE ARMED FORCES AND VETERANS

For obvious reasons, governments have always provided various forms of economic security for members of the military forces, and

---

[14] Data are from Research and Statistics Note No. 21–1974, Social Security Administraton.

the United States has been no exception. Pensions were payable to the veterans of the Revolutionary War and to their surviving widows. The same procedure was followed for all subsequent wars, although generally the pensions were not payable until some years after the end of the war (except for disabled veterans). For the earlier wars, the pensions were payable as a matter of right and did not involve any means test. However, for veterans of World War I and subsequent conflicts, the pensions are payable as a matter of right only for service-connected disability; in other instances, they are payable only in case of disability or after age 65, and then, only after a means test. Probably because of the existence of OASDI, relatively little pressure has been exerted toward extending pensions to the general cases where there is no service-connected disability and no need because of low income.

As has been discussed in Chapter 2, members of the military services are covered under OASDI and Medicare in exactly the same way as are most workers in the country. Their taxable wages are equivalent to their cash pay. Their creditable wages include the cash pay plus an additional $100 per month, regardless of rank, as an allowance for remuneration in kind. Such gratuitous wage credits, as well as those for military service before 1957, when regular contributory coverage first began, is financed completely by the federal government on an "excess cost" basis (rather than on a percentage-of-payroll basis). As a result, since a considerable part of military service employment will not be used in computing benefits, the cost to the government is relatively small for these gratuitous wage credits.[15]

Pension Benefits

In addition to OASDI coverage, members of the military services are protected by a noncontributory pension plan, which is operated on a completely pay-as-you-go basis from current appropriations and with no separate fund. This plan provides for retirement after 20 years of service regardless of age (but with the consent of the government, which is generally readily obtained) or unilaterally with 30 years of

---

[15] Such gratuitous wage credits are only infrequently of assistance in obtaining insured status, because this can so readily be achieved by the earnings credits from other employment. Similarly, the benefit amounts will frequently not be affected by the gratuitous credits, because of the dropout of low earnings before 1951 and before age 22.

service. Because of the regulations of the armed forces, retirement is compulsory at certain ages or lengths of service, depending upon grade. Retirement before 20 years of service is possible only in the case of disability (and even then the pension may not be payable, because a larger benefit would often be available from the Veterans Administration, as will be described subsequently). Military personnel are not covered by a separate system for work-connected causes, but rather such protection is provided by provisions built into the retirement system.

The amount of the pension (termed "retired pay") under the military retirement system is 2½ percent of final pay for each year of service up to a maximum of 30 years, except that in case of disability retirement, alternatively the amount is the percentage disability times the basic pay, with a maximum of 75 percent of pay.[16] Such pay, however, includes only the basic pay plus increments for service and does not include allowances for such items as quarters and subsistence or special pay, such as for flight or submarine duty. As a result, a person retiring with 30 or more years of service at a benefit rate of 75 percent usually has a pension amount which is very roughly about 50 percent of what his gross take-home pay had actually been. In actual practice, the average nondisability retirant receives about 46 percent of his gross take-home pay (basic pay plus cash allowances for quarters and subsistence).

The military retirement system has no vesting provisions for those with moderately long service, but with an insufficient number of years to qualify for immediate retirement. As a result, the large number of persons who serve only a few years in military service acquire no benefit rights, except for the fact that they have had OASDI coverage, which was one of the strong reasons why such coverage extension was legislated.

Survivor benefits are provided on an elective basis under the military retirement system for those who have retired and for those who are eligible to retire by reason of having at least 20 years of service, in a manner somewhat parallel to those under CSR. The benefit rate is 55 percent of the retired pay for the widowed spouse, regardless of age, and can be provided for surviving children, but with no payment for children when the widowed spouse is present (unlike the

---

[16] Use of the alternative disability formula is also advantageous from an income tax standpoint.

flat amounts under CSR). However, unlike CSR, these survivor benefits are integrated with those under OASDI under certain circumstances, namely, with respect to widow's and widower's benefits and widowed mother's benefits when exactly one child is present.[17]

Integration of survivor benefits is accomplished by reducing the military survivor benefit by the portion of the spouse's OASDI benefit which is attributable solely to military coverage under OASDI. If any benefits are payable under the dependency and indemnity compensation program, which is applicable to deaths in active service regardless of length of service and to deaths caused by service-connected causes and is described subsequently, the survivor pensions under the military retirement system are reduced thereby. A small reduction in the military pension is made to provide this survivor protection after retirement (2½ percent of the first $300 per month, plus 10 percent of the excess), similar to what is done under CSR, except that, when eligible children are included, a relatively small additional reduction is made. Just as under CSR, the retirant with no wife or child can elect to provide a survivor pension for any person with an insurable interest; the reduction factors, however, are different than under CSR for this category.

A gratuity is payable for all deaths in active service. The amount is equal to six months' pay, subject to a minimum of $800 and a maximum of $3,000.

Until 1972 the only survivor benefit protection under the military retirement system had been under a program that provided joint-and-survivor annuities on an actuarial equivalent basis (i.e., intended to be at no net cost to the federal government). This basis had been adopted, instead of the "actuarial bargain" basis under CSR, on the grounds that the military service pensions were on a noncontributory basis and thus not paid for by the participant (unlike CSR), and therefore the survivor protection should not be given at any additional cost to the federal government. The participation under this elective joint-and-survivor annuity program was relatively poor (being about 15 percent of those eligible to participate), probably because of what appeared to be the high cost involved (i.e., the absence of an actuarial bargain). As a result, pressure built up for the change to the present basis.

---

[17] Apparently, no such reduction applies for the case of a widowed mother with more than one child because the resulting amount of the two benefits seemed reasonable, especially since the OASDI maximum family benefit has such a strong effect for such families.

The military pensions are subject to automatic adjustment for changes in the cost of living. The procedure is the same as that under CSR except that a much smoother transitional procedure is followed for persons retiring between two effective dates of automatic adjustment.[18]

Before 1963, when the automatic-adjustment provisions were first enacted for the military retirement system, the approach taken was quite different. For many years, military pensions were, in essence, automatically adjusted for the changes in active-duty pay. This was done by basing the pension on the pay grade currently applicable to an individual of the same rank and length of service as the pensioner was when he retired. Then, for the period after 1957 and before the automatic-adjustment provisions were adopted in 1963, the military pensions were "uncoupled" from the pay structure; arbitrary percentage increases were given in the pensions when the general pay structure was changed (the pension increases being lower than the pay increases).

Normally, the adjustment of pensions in force by changes in the general salary level of the active members of the pension plan is more advantageous to the pensioners than adjustment for changes in the cost of living. This is so because wages generally rise more rapidly than prices.

However, for military personnel, it so happens that, during the 50 years preceding the change from adjusting pensions according to the pay level of active duty personnel, the trend of military pay had very closely paralleled the trend of the CPI. Thus, the same effect occurred then as if there had been automatic adjustment by the CPI. Moreover, there was not then the 1-percent bonus now present. Also, there was no provision preventing decreases in pensions when the CPI or pay went down; this actually occurred in the early 1930s when pensions were reduced.

For some years after the automatic adjustment of pensions in force was adopted in 1973, the military pay scale rose more rapidly than the price level. Thus, military pensioners were not as well off under the automatics as if their pensions had been tied to active duty pay. In the last year or two, however, the situation has been reversed.

Pensions as a matter of right, which are termed "veteran's compen-

---

[18] For more details, see Robert J. Myers and Marice C. Hart, "Automatic Cost-of-Living Adjustments in Federal Benefit Plans," *Pension and Welfare News*, March 1970.

sation," are paid to veterans with a service-connected disability who are not receiving pensions under the military retirement system. This program is administered by the Veterans Administration and is financed from current appropriations. The pension amounts vary by degree of disability, ranging from $32 per month for 10 percent disability to $325 at 90 percent disability and $584 for 100 percent disability. Very seriously disabled veterans, such as the blind or amputees, receive additional amounts that can bring the total to over $1,400 per month. Additional allowances are paid for dependents of those with at least 50 percent disability; these are computed as flat amounts, such as $36 for a wife with no children and $77 for a wife and two children, multiplied by percentage of disability.

Pensions are also paid for veterans with nonservice-connected disabilities or aged 65 or over, subject to an income and assets test. The pension is $143 per month if annual income is $300 or less, and it decreases slowly as income rises until gradually becoming nonexistent for an income of $2,700 or more.[19] If the veteran has a dependent, the full pension amount is $154 (plus $5 for each of the next two dependents) and gradually is decreased as income rises to the limiting point of $3,900. These benefit amounts are changed on an ad hoc basis, the last time having been in January 1974.

Survivor benefits for those dying in active service or as a result of service-connected causes are payable under the dependency and indemnity compensation program (DIC), administered by the Veterans Administration. These benefits are financed entirely by the federal government through current appropriations, with no separate fund.

The DIC benefits are paid as a matter of right to the surviving widow and children, but on a means test basis for surviving dependent parents. The amount of the widow's benefit depends on the rank of the deceased serviceman, ranging from $215 to $549 per month, and a flat additional amount of $26 per month is given for each eligible child (under age 18, or in school until age 23, or disabled). Eligible children with no widowed mother present receive larger flat amounts. Dependent parents also receive uniform benefits not related to the rank of the deceased serviceman, but they are reduced for income in excess

---

[19] Income includes all items except 10 percent of OASDI and other retirement benefits and either the spouse's earned income or up to $1,200 of her total income, whichever is larger. The reduction begins at 3 cents for each dollar of excess income, and the reduction rate gradually increases until becoming 8 cents per dollar at the upper eligible incomes.

of $800 per year. The amounts prior to reduction are $110 per month for one parent and $148 per month for two parents living together, and they gradually are reduced for "excess" income, being eliminated for incomes of $2,700 and above for one parent and $3,900 for two parents. The rates have been increased from time to time on an ad hoc basis.

Survivor pensions are payable in conjunction with the nonservice-connected pensions, also with an income and assets test. For a widow alone, the full amount is $96 per month, and this is reduced for income over $300 per year until gradually phasing out when income reaches $2,700. For a widow and one child, the full amount is $114 per month ($18 for each additional child), and the pension phases out at income of $3,900. When a widow is not present, the full amount for the first child is $44 per month. Under a special provision, if the deceased member was on the military retirement roll before March 20, 1974, the Department of Defense will build up the widow's VA pension by sufficient to make a total pension of $175 per month.

Medical Benefits

Active members of the military services receive full medical care at military installations. Retired members of the military services can also receive such medical services (with only nominal charges for subsistence); of course, if they are not located near a military medical installation, they may not choose to obtain such care. Dependents of active members and dependents of retired members can also receive medical services from military installations if sufficient facilities are available and, again, assuming that they live near such an installation. In other instances, such dependents can receive medical care benefits under a program which was originally entitled Medicare, until that attractive name was usurped by the social security program. The medical care program for dependents is insured by several private insurance organizations, each with a certain geographical jurisdiction.

Ex-servicemen (veterans) can obtain medical care from the federal government through the Veterans Administration in all cases where this is necessary for service-connected causes or for nonservice-connected causes for veterans who are service disabled, with a liberal interpretation. Medical care can also be received for nonservice-connected causes of illness under a means test (again, liberally interpreted and to a considerable extent based solely on the word of the individual). Such medical care is not available for dependents of veterans.

Life Insurance Benefits

Survivor protection in addition to that under OASDI, DIC, and the military pension system has been available since World War I for active members in the form of life insurance policies administered through the Veterans Administration. Later, when they become veterans, they can be covered under several life insurance programs administered through the Veterans Administration that are similar to policies of private insurance companies. Initially, the VA completely administered these programs, but since September 1965, new policies are administered by the private insurance business, and the VA only supervises the program. One insurance company is the primary insurer, and almost 600 other companies are in a reinsurance pool.

The maximum amount of insurance possible since mid-1974 is $20,000.[20] During active service, the insurance has always been on a term basis. Currently, the premium rate for those in active service is $0.17 per month per $1,000.[21] Coverage is automatic at the full $20,000 amount, unless the individual elects a lower amount (or even none).

Before 1965, following active service, the veteran could continue his term insurance, or he could convert it to other forms such as whole life and 20-payment life under policies administered entirely by the Veterans Administration. Provision for monthly total disability benefits can be obtained for an additional premium. Actuarially determined premium rates, dependent upon plan of insurance and age, are payable under these policies by the individual. Such policies are on a participating basis, with dividends being paid.[22] The federal government participates financially in these life insurance programs only by meeting the cost of administration and also the cost for any deaths which

---

[20] The maximum, exclusive of paid-up additions from dividends, is $10,000 for veterans of World Wars I and II and the Korean War and subsequently until 1970; beginning then, it was $15,000. Currently, virtually all eligibles partcipate in the program, and in almost all cases with maximum coverage.

[21] Reservists, who are covered only when on training duty, pay $0.10 per year per $1,000.

[22] Unlike the procedure followed by private life insurance companies, these dividends have not always been paid on the policy anniversary. At times, as President Ford directed for the 1975 dividends, they are paid in advance so as to "stimulate the economy."

occurred in service or afterward as a result of a service-connected cause (which is interpreted rather liberally). As a result, the cost for these insurance policies is relatively low. The funds of these programs are invested in government obligations, with the interest rates thereon being determined in somewhat the same manner as for the OASDI and Medicare trust funds.

Currently, following active service, the veteran can continue his insurance as a five-year nonrenewable term policy.[23] This is administered by the life insurance company serving as primary insurer for the policies of those in active service and with the same reinsurance pool. At the termination of the five-year period, the veteran has conversion privileges with any insurance company in the pool, as well as with a few additional companies.

Other Benefits

Cash sickness benefits are, of course, provided for members of the military services through continuation of pay. Unemployment benefits are provided for persons who leave the armed forces; this is done under the provisions of the various state UI programs, depending upon the residence of the ex-serviceman.

Data on Operations

In conclusion, a few statistics on the operations of the several benefit plans for military personnel and veterans will be presented. The military retirement system paid monthly benefits totaling $4.7 billion in 1973 to a monthly average of about 950,000 persons; 84 percent of these benefits were for service retirement, 15 percent for disability retirement, and only 1 percent for survivors. The vast majority of these pensioners were also receiving OASDI benefits or would do so when they attained age 65.

As mentioned previously, the military retirement system operates on a completely pay-as-you-go basis, with annual appropriations from the General Fund of the Treasury. The estimated unfunded liabilities for retired pay was $147 billion as of June 30, 1974.

---

[23] Before August 1974, this term policy was not available, but, rather, the veteran had only immediate conversion rights during the 120 days following separation or discharge from military service. Now, at the option of the veteran the new 5-year nonrenewable term policy becomes effective at the end of the 120 days.

As to veterans benefits, monthly pensions for both service-connected and nonservice-connected disability cases amounted to about $6.4 billion in 1973 and were paid to a monthly average of about 5.6 million persons, of whom 3.3 million were veterans and the remainder were survivors. About 69 percent of the veterans receiving benefits did so on a service-connected basis, and only about 11 percent of these had a disability rating of 70 percent or more. Despite the income test for nonservice-connected disability pensions and the almost universal receipt of OASDI benefits, the 1.0 million veterans receiving these pensions included about 700,000 who were aged 65 and over; this category, however, has been decreasing in recent years, despite the growing total aged population. Another 150,000 were aged 65 and over and receiving service-connected pensions.

These veterans benefits are paid from current appropriations, and no fund is present. The estimated *total* of compensation, pensions, and other benefit costs to be paid under these programs in the future was about $177 billion as of June 30, 1974.

The several life insurance programs operated by the Veterans Administration had a total of about 8.2 million persons with policies in force at the end of 1973, with a face amount of about $74.2 billion, of which $38.3 billion was with the commercial insurance pool and $35.9 billion was under programs administered by the VA. Total benefit payments in 1973 under programs administered by the VA was $606 million (inclusive of disability benefits, cash surrenders, and supplementary contract payments, but exclusive of dividends and amounts left with the program under settlement options), while total premium income was $422 million (net of dividends taken in cash), and total interest income was $434 million. The total assets of the programs administered by the VA as of the end of 1973 amounted to $9.3 billion, including $1.1 billion of policy loans.

PART V

Foreign Programs

Economic security programs developed in other countries both before and after the United States programs described in the preceding Parts of this book. The single chapter in Part V presents a comparative survey of social security programs in foreign countries.

chapter 17

Foreign Social Security Systems

The previous chapters have attempted to describe the social security program of the United States. To round out the picture, it may be worthwhile to give a brief description of social security systems of other countries. First, there will be a general discussion of similarities and differences, and then the general bases of the programs in several selected nations will be described (in order, by continents). Quite naturally, it would be impossible (within any reasonable space) to give a full discussion of all plans in all countries.

Strangely enough, many people in the United States believe that social security was an American invention and that most other countries do not have similar programs. Actually, although the phrase "social security," as it is currently used, was invented here and now has worldwide usage, the general basis of social security has been present in European and other economically well-developed countries for far longer and to a much greater extent than in the United States.

Insofar as social insurance is concerned, the beginning development was in Germany in the 1880s. It is said that Bismarck pushed this concept to combat the Socialists, by taking away one of their most potent points in arguing for a change in the economic system. By the early 1900s, most of the leading European countries had some types of social insurance programs. And by the time the United States had enacted old-age insurance and unemployment insurance in 1935, the European systems were quite broad and inclusive of many types of benefits, while programs were being prepared even in some economically underdeveloped countries. In the Americas, Chile led the field with an extensive system that began under legislation of 1924. Brazil, Ecuador, Peru, and Uruguay also inaugurated programs before the United States (or at about the same time). By now, all American nations have programs. Most developing countries throughout the world have social security systems, even if only in the planning stage.

What is a proper and adequate social security system for one country is obviously not necessarily satisfactory for another country. Much depends on economic, demographic, social, and even philosophical conditions.

A country with low earnings levels, with most people at bare subsistence levels and with little personal savings, more likely must have a benefit level that is relatively higher (in relation to wages) than an economically well-developed nation. This is so because otherwise the benefits, being so far below the subsistence level, would possess little economic significance. Likewise, in such an economically poor country, waiting periods for short-term benefits will often be short because people will not have the resources to tide them over longer periods.

The provision of medical care through social security systems (rather than in other ways) may, from a humanitarian standpoint, be much more necessary in economically poor countries. These nations may not have any other way of getting medical services to the populace in the immediate future than through governmental measures financed by social insurance contributions. On the other hand, in economically well-developed countries, much (if not all) of the needed medical care is often readily available to the vast majority of the population. This has been accomplished, over the years, through a wide variety of means such as prevailing individual resources, cooperative and commercial insurance carriers, voluntary organizations (which have developed hospitals, clinics, research facilities, and the like), and social insurance—all complemented by governmental action in certain broad areas such as public health services. In many such countries, some or all of the medical care has been provided through governmental social security programs that have combined, coordinated, and expanded the previously existing private measures.

It is common for an economically underdeveloped country, which generally is largely agricultural, to have a considerable amount of unemployment (especially underemployment). From a political standpoint, there is often great pressure to establish an unemployment insurance system in such nations—in the mistaken belief that this will solve the unemployment problem. Nothing, however, would be done for those who had little or no employment previously, because unemployment insurance benefits customarily require a past earnings record.

As a matter of fact, the establishment of an unemployment insurance system in an underdeveloped country might even make the unemployment problem worse, by resulting in less partial employment—or, in other words, freezing the work force into two groups, those with continuous full employment and those with no employment. Many employers would refuse to hire workers on a temporary basis if this would increase their unemployment insurance costs. Furthermore, the successful operation of an unemployment insurance system requires the existence of an effective employment service to provide jobs for unemployed workers. As a practical matter, very few developing countries have established unemployment insurance programs.

The demography of a country also can have a significant effect on the character of its social security system. When high mortality is present, the accompanying conditions seem to make it necessary or desirable that retirement ages for old-age pensions should be low. But those responsible for the planning and development of the system should bear in mind that mortality improvements are likely to come. The general populace, however, will likely be influenced in this respect by what had been the case in the past (as "evidenced" by the current age structure) and so will be difficult to convince about higher retirement ages.

In many economically underdeveloped countries, the family system still plays an important role. There, the aged and the infirm are taken care of by the younger, active members of the family. Any social benefits provided in such nations are often, because of the apparent desire of those concerned, large lump-sum payments under the so-called provident-fund plans, rather than periodic ones (which may have a much larger actuarial value). However, with growing industrialization and urbanization, such countries may have more need for the usual types of social security programs.

Social and philosophical views can also play an important role in defining the categories of dependents. The position of women in the social structure is especially significant. Thus, where women are relatively infrequently employed, the widows' pensions may be payable regardless of age at widowhood (and regardless of whether children are present). As to the upper age at which children are considered to be dependent, this may be relatively low for boys, but there may be no such limit for girls who do not marry. In many systems the categories of dependents are quite extensive, including not only spouses, children, and parents, but also grandchildren, grandparents, and brothers and sisters incapable of self-support.

COVERAGE

Great differences exist as to the categories of persons protected under the social security systems of various countries. It is the usual practice to have a separate system for government employees (and some of these have been in operation, in one form or other, for centuries, but in some countries these workers are covered by the general program (either with or without a supplementary plan of their own).

Some economically well-developed nations have "demogrant" programs, which cover all citizens (and in some instances, even all residents, but generally then with short residence requirements for short-term benefits and longer residence requirements for pensions). In other such countries, where there are social insurance systems, coverage extends to all, or virtually all, the employed labor force. In some of these programs, self-employed persons and high-salaried employees are excluded. Also, in some cases, there are separate systems for white-collar employees and for manual workers (and often, too, for self-employed persons, miners, railroad workers, seamen, and farmworkers). At times coverage is restricted, for practical or policy reasons, by not requiring contributions from very young workers or from workers beyond retirement age.

In economically developing countries, coverage is usually limited in one or more of several ways. Restrictions are based on factors such as occupation, size of firm, permanency of employment, geographical location, and so forth. Frequently, the law provides for extensive coverage but permits the administrative agency to put it into effect gradually by regulation. Moreover, in many instances, actual effective coverage is well below what is called for by the legislation and its implementation by administrative regulation. (It should not be forgotten that under OASDI, there are still certain difficulties in obtaining full coverage compliance, especially in the agricultural and domestic employment areas.) This incompleteness of coverage arises because of lack of knowledge of the requirements on the part of the employers and workers, and because of inadequate enforcement efforts by the authorities. In fact, in some cases, there is the attitude that the program is really just like private insurance so that if those who are supposed to be compulsorily covered do not wish to be covered, this is perfectly proper.

TYPES OF BENEFITS

In most countries the first form of social security was workmen's compensation, because of the employer's legal responsibility in many such cases. Now, all the economically well-developed countries and many of the other countries have systems that provide more branches of social security than is so in the United States. This is especially the case in regard to medical care benefits, cash sickness and maternity benefits, and family allowances. On the other hand, unemployment insurance is not widespread outside of the economically well-developed nations. This is also true as to social assistance programs providing cash payments to needy persons—whether or not supplementing social insurance systems.

Medical care benefits are provided in a diverse number of ways. In some countries, medical care is provided on a demogrant basis under a national health service. Generally, the social insurance institution or the responsible government agency directly finances the services, through social insurance taxes or contributions, and/or general revenues (sometimes with the covered person paying certain charges for services rendered, especially for medicines and appliances). In some cases the doctors are on salary, while in other systems they are paid on a capitation basis (an annual amount for each person to whom the doctor furnishes general practitioner services) or a fee-for-service basis. Similarly, in some systems the hospitals are owned by the social security organization or the government, while in others the services are purchased from hospitals operated by other organizations. A few systems provide only certain cash payments for medical costs, with the individual having to make up the balance of the charges (but with some control of fees). Usually, the same care is provided for dependents as for covered persons, but a few systems exclude dependents. Most systems furnish more or less complete medical care.

Systems that provide benefits for work-connected accidents almost always provide similar protection for industrial diseases, either all such diseases or certain specified ones.

BENEFIT LEVELS

In most countries the level of benefits in relation to the wage level is higher than in the United States. In large part, this is to be expected because, from a social adequacy standpoint, there necessarily must be relatively high benefits in nations where wages are often only sufficient to provide a minimum standard of subsistence, or little more.

In the United States, unlike many other countries, the social security benefits need be only the basic floor of protection on which additional protection is built by voluntary means (private pension plans, individual savings, homeownership, and the like). The foregoing statement should not be taken to imply that the social security benefits carry out the entire job of social protection in *all* other countries, because in many nations, much is done by private voluntary action. Generally, however, this portion of the benefit protection afforded is at a relatively lower level than in the United States.

In a few developing countries the current benefit level under pension provisions of social insurance is relatively low. This occurs because such systems are patterned after private insurance. The benefits are proportional to contributions paid or to length of covered employment, and the systems are still in their early years of operation. Eventually, the benefits called for under such plans will be relatively large, but this is not so now.

In most systems, benefits are increased when dependents are present. In a few systems, which are generally based to a considerable extent on individual equity principles, this practice is not followed. Sometimes, problems exist in defining dependents in countries where marriage and living arrangements are not very formalized for a large sector of the population. In certain countries, particularly those where the family system is very strong, and where women generally do not engage in paid employment, the definition of "dependent" may be very broad— including unmarried daughters, regardless of age; parents; grandparents; brothers; sisters; and grandchildren.

In a growing number of countries (generally, those most economically advanced), provision is made for automatically increasing the benefit level in accordance with changes in economic conditions. Such adjustments are usually made on the basis of price changes, but in a few instances on the basis of wage changes, so as to maintain the relative standard of living.

PENSIONABLE AGES

A wide spread occurs in the minimum pensionable ages under the old-age pension provisions of social security programs. Some countries go as low as age 50 (primarily those with high mortality, especially when it was very high in the recent past). On the other hand, a few countries (those with relatively low mortality) have such a minimum age above 65. Most countries set this age at between 60 and 65 (both inclusive). A few follow the OASDI practice of permitting earlier retirement with permanently reduced benefits. Some countries have the same retirement age for both men and women, whereas others have a lower age for women (usually by five years).

In some systems, old-age pensions are payable automatically upon claim, without a retirement requirement, upon attainment of the minimum pensionable age. Frequently, this results in a general practice by employers of compulsory retirement. In some instances the wages a pensioner may receive may be reduced because he may change jobs or work only part time. Other systems require retirement as a condition of benefit payment. Under such circumstances, the treatment differs as to whether or not the amount paid subsequently will be increased to reflect the deferment of retirement. In some instances, as in the OASDI system, the two procedures are merged—payment, regardless of retirement, is made when the individual attains a prescribed age somewhat higher than the minimum age.

Treatment also varies as to what is done when pensioners have earnings. Some systems (at least in theory) do not pay any benefits if this is so, or at least if this is so in connection with earnings from covered employment. Other systems permit a certain amount of earnings to be exempt, and further may have a graded benefits basis for higher amounts of earnings (as does OASDI).

Some systems pay pensions to widows regardless of age at widowhood. Other programs pay only while children are in the widow's care and then after a certain age, or if disabled. Sometimes, payment is continued to a widow regardless of her age if she was paid a pension because eligible children were present. In some systems, when pensions for life (or until remarriage) are not payable to a widow, a temporary pension is paid. In all cases where survivor pensions are paid, they are available at least to widows with children.

Generally speaking, the amount of the invalidity pension is the same as the old-age pension. Disability pensions of reduced amount are paid under some systems in cases of partial invalidity or in cases of disability preventing the following of the usual occupation. Sometimes supplements are paid for pensioners who are so disabled as to require an attendant.

FINANCING

The vast majority of social insurance programs are financed by contributions from workers and employers that are determined as a percentage of the earnings of the covered individuals, usually with some prescribed maximum earnings. In most such plans, the government is responsible for a certain proportion of the costs (or of the combined employer-employee contributions) or has a legal commitment for any residual cost or for any deficit occurring. A few social insurance systems have uniform contributions (in monetary terms) from all covered persons, possibly varying by sex and age (i.e., different for youth and adults); these generally also have flat benefits.

Social assistance programs are financed from general revenues, although at times, specially earmarked taxes are used. This is also true of many demogrant programs, although many of these are financed, in part, by direct contributions (of either flat amounts or percentages of income or earnings) of the participants and their employers. Such direct contributions are often waived for low-income persons.

In most countries, social insurance systems are financed by taxes or contributions (not necessarily equal) from three parties—the worker, the employer, and the government. A few systems have only worker and employer contributions, as under OASDI. Most Communist nations have only employer and government contributions. In other plans the employer contribution, as compared with the employee contribution, generally is within the range of being equal or being twice as large. The government contribution (when present) ranges from 10 to 50 percent of the combined employer-employee contribution, when it is expressed as a percentage of payroll. In some countries the social security system often has difficulty in getting the government to pay its "required" contribution.

Contributions related to earnings are determined either by applying the applicable percentage to the actual wages or to wage classes. They are collected, and the earnings record is developed, by either payroll-listing or stamp-book methods. In some systems a single combined contribution rate applies for all branches together (generally so for pensions, at least).

The combined level of contributions in systems with a broad span of benefits at high levels runs up to as much as 40 to 45 percent of payroll. Although this in itself is a heavy economic burden, there should be borne in mind the fact that, because of this high charge on production, the wages paid (or take-home pay) may be correspondingly lower (disregarding the income-tax effect[1]).

For example, the *net economic effect on production costs* of gross pay of 100 units, employee contribution of 15 units, and employer contribution of 20 units is no different than if there were no social security system, and the worker were paid 120 units. Under the foregoing circumstances, the worker would have to provide his own social benefit protection from the additional 35 units in his take-home pay. Likewise, when no contributions are collected from the worker, this does not necessarily mean that he is better off financially. In the foregoing example, with the same social security benefits, there would be no economic effect on any party concerned if the employee did not contribute, but his take-home was 85 units, and the employer contributed 35 units.

Also, it should be noted that the high cost of some social security systems results, to an appreciable extent, from the cost of the family allowance payments. In essence, this benefit may be viewed as a redistribution of current wages among workers with children and other workers.

When funds accumulate in a social security system, various investment procedures are followed. The pension systems of most countries that have had them for a long period are, more or less, on a "pay-as-you-go" basis and so have little accumulation of funds. This, of course,

---

[1] The income-tax effects can be disregarded in countries where such tax is levied on net pay after social-insurance contributions (probably the case in most countries). But this is not the situation for countries where income taxes are levied on gross pay, before social insurance contributions (as in the United States).

is also the case for programs providing short-range benefits. Some systems follow the OASDI practice of investing only in government securities. The more general practice, however, is to have provision in the law for a wide variety of investment areas, including private bonds and stocks, home mortgage loans (often only to covered workers), commercial mortgages, hospitals and clinics for the system, ownership and operation of commercial enterprises, and the like. Of course, not all systems go into all such areas.

ADMINISTRATION

In some countries the social security programs are administered by government departments, as is OASDI. Most social insurance systems, however, are administered by separate agencies that are established by law and have varying degrees of autonomy, although usually being subject to a certain degree of government supervision. Such institutions are governed by boards that are frequently composed of representatives of employers, employees, and the government. Because of their autonomous nature, these institutions often wield great financial power when large funds are accumulated, and then their role in economic development can be significant.

Some countries have a unified social security program administered by one agency. Generally, however, several institutions administer different programs—either by type of employment covered and/or by type of risk, although generally old-age, survivors, and disability pensions are administered as a unit.

Bilateral and multilateral conventions or treaties exist among many countries, particularly in Europe. These have the effect of guaranteeing equal treatment of aliens with citizens, payment of benefits outside the country, and pooling or transfer of service records or periods of residence to meet qualifying periods.

Sometimes a procedure termed "totalization" is used.[2] The countries agreeing to do this count the earnings record of the individual in other countries as part of his earnings record in the given country for purposes of determining benefit eligibility. Each country determines a theoretical benefit amount as though the entire earnings record had

---

[2] Provision for this under OASDI and Medicare was contained in legislation passed by the Senate in 1973, but not enacted (see Chapter 3). This part of the legislation was not controversial and is likely to be enacted sometime in the near future.

been established there. However, only a proportionate part, based on the proportion that his covered work in the particular country bears to his covered work in all countries, of the theoretical benefit is then payable, unless this produces a smaller benefit than results from only his earnings in the particular country. No transfer in funds between the several countries is involved. Combined with this is an agreement that social insurance contributions will not be assessed on the earnings of an alien worker by both the home country and the country of employment for the same work. In mid-1973, Italy and the United States signed a totalization agreement, but it cannot be effective until enabling legislation is enacted by the United States.

The International Labor Organization has several conventions in the field of social security, under which ratifying nations agree to meet certain standards in their systems. The United States has not ratified any of these social security conventions, partly because of constitutional reasons (in connection with programs operated in whole or in part by the states over which the federal government has no control and thus cannot "guarantee" that the provisions will continue ot meet the international standards).

BRIEF DESCRIPTIONS OF FOREIGN SYSTEMS

There will now be given relatively brief descriptions of the general characteristics of the social security programs in a number of countries throughout the world.[3] These have been selected either because of their importance or to indicate some of the different bases prevalent. The countries are taken up hereafter by geographical position, moving around the world in an easterly direction.

Canada

In Canada, flat-rate pensions on a demogrant basis (in general, limited to residents of 10 years or more) are paid to all persons aged 65 or over, with no supplement payable for a wife under age 65. These benefits are financed from general revenues, although they were initially financed through earmarked sales taxes, personal income taxes, and corporation income taxes.

---

[3] For further details of the systems of these and other countries, see "Social Security Programs throughout the World, 1973," Social Security Administration, U.S. Department of Health, Education, and Welfare, 1974.

Also, earnings-related pensions for old age, survivors, and disability are available in addition to the universal old-age pension. Initially, the retirement pensions were payable at ages 65–69 subject to a retirement test similar to that under OASDI, and at age 70 and over regardless of employment. In 1974, legislation was enacted eliminating the retirement test completely and also providing for completely equal treatment for men and women with regard to dependents and survivor benefits. Both the flat-rate and the earnings-related systems contain automatic-adjustment provisions for the benefits, based on the increase in the cost of living; originally, this had a 2 percent annual maximum, but in 1973 this was eliminated.

The pensions are financed by equal employer-employee payroll taxes on all types of employment except casual earnings, and except for voluntary individual opting out by persons in a religious sect that does not believe in private or public insurance (somewhat similar to the "Amish" provision in OASDI). The maximum taxable earnings base in 1975 is $7,400, and the first 10 percent thereof ($700) is not taxable, although it does count for benefit purposes. The earnings base is to be increased 12 ½ percent each year until it reaches the average earnings of all workers.

Quebec has a separate, generally identical plan to that in the remainder of Canada. Government employees have separate pension plans and receive benefits thereunder in addition to and coordinated with those under the general systems.

Family allowances for all children under age 18 are financed from general revenues. An allowance *averaging* $20 per month per child is paid. A province may vary the amount to be paid in accordance with age and/or family size, so long as the amount for each child is at least $12 and the average for all children is $20. The benefits of this program are also automatically adjusted for changes in the cost of living.

Unemployment insurance on a wage-related basis is operated by the federal government and is financed by employee contributions whose rate is set each year and is 1.4 percent for 1975, and employer contributions of 140 percent of the employee rate. There is provision for an experience-rating formula for the relative employer contribution rate, which may then vary between 100 and 200 percent of the employer rate, depending upon the unemployment experience of the employer, plus a government contribution equal to the additional benefit cost when the unemployment rate exceeds 4 percent and the cost for extended benefit periods for the long-term unemployed. This system also pays weekly benefits for temporary sickness and maternity up to 15 weeks. The maximum amount of earnings covered by the program is automatically adjusted for changes in the general level of wages.

The federal government pays the entire cost of a supplemental guaranteed income plan for persons aged 65 and over. Social assistance programs, administered by the provinces and municipalities, are provided for (1) the blind, (2) the totally and permanently disabled, (3) needy mothers who are deprived of the support of the breadwinner and who require assistance to maintain their children, and (4) other needy persons for whom the province applies a uniform means or eligibility test. The federal government pays for about half of the costs involved in these programs. The benefit amounts are automatically adjusted for changes in the cost of living.

Hospitalization benefits, including diagnostic services (on a service basis), and benefits for physician and laboratory services generally for the entire population, are provided under provincial systems that are "encouraged" by federal financial participation of about 50 percent of the total cost. In some provinces the plans are financed partially by general revenues (including sales taxes) and partially by flat-rate contributions or premiums from the persons protected or by cost-sharing provisions by the beneficiaries. In other provinces the entire cost is met from general revenues.

Work-connected injury benefits are financed entirely by employers, with administration by monopolistic provincial funds.

Mexico

The Mexican social insurance program provides wage-related benefits—old-age, disability, and survivor pensions; cash sickness and maternity benefits; and work-connected injury benefits in a single coordinated system—and medical care benefits on a service basis for both workers and dependents. The old-age pensions, payable on retirement at age 65 (reduced amounts for involuntary retirement at age 60) without supplement for a wife (widow's pension payable regardless of age), follow the individual-equity bases of requiring long qualifying periods and of being somewhat related to length of contributory service. The system applies only to regularly employed industrial and commercial workers (in most geographical areas) and to agricultural workers in large-scale operations in a few areas. The earnings-related contributions are paid by employers (all the cost of the work-connected benefits, varying by risk, plus about 60 percent of the other benefits), employees (25 percent of cost for other than work-connected benefits), and the government (15 percent of cost for other than work-connected benefits).

Panama

The social insurance program in Panama furnishes wage-related benefits—old-age, survivors, and disability pensions, and cash sickness and maternity benefits—and medical care benefits on a service basis for both workers and dependents. The old-age pensions, payable on retirement at age 60 for men and 55 for women, with flat supplement for wife and children (widow's pension payable regardless of age), are along individual equity bases. The system covers government workers and industrial and commercial workers, although until recently, the latter were covered only in selected areas. The earnings-related contributions are paid by employers, employees (somewhat lower rate than employers), and the government (less than 10 percent of employer-employee rate). Work-connected injury benefits are provided through private insurance companies.

Peru

For many years, two separate systems for private workers had been present in Peru—for salaried employees and for manual workers. Recently, these two plans were combined. Both systems provided old-age, survivor, and disability pensions; cash sickness and maternity benefits; and medical care benefits, primarily only for the worker, although gradually being extended to dependents (on a service basis generally, although salaried employees can elect indemnity benefits). Old-age pensions were on an individual equity basis for manual workers (payable at age 60, without retirement being required) and on a social adequacy basis for salaried employees (payable at age 60 for men and age 55 for women, with a retirement test). Both systems paid widows' pensions regardless of age. Under the new coordinated system, the benefits closely parallel those of the more liberal of the two previous plans. The earnings-related contributions for these benefits are paid by employers, by employees (at a somewhat lower rate than employers), and by the government (at a much lower rate than employees), with different rate structures for the two systems.

Benefits for work-connected causes are payable under a separate governmental system (formerly, through insurance companies), financed entirely by employer contributions.

Chile

There are two large general systems for private workers in Chile —for manual workers and low-earnings self-employed workers, and for salaried employees—and a number of smaller ones for special groups such as railroad workers, seamen, government employees, and the like. Almost all types of benefits are provided—old-age, disability, and survivor pensions; cash sickness and maternity benefits; work-connected injury benefits (with state fund); unemployment insurance; and family allowances (for all children under age 18, or under 23 if in school, or disabled).

Pension benefits are on an individual equity basis, with long qualifying periods, and are automatically adjusted for changes in prices (formerly for changes in wage level). Pensions are subject to a retirement test and are payable at age 65, without supplement for a wife (widow's pension payable regardless of age). In the salaried employee plan, pensions are also payable, regardless of age, after 35 years of contribution.

Contributions are earnings related. Employers pay the entire cost of work-connected injury benefits, 92 percent of the cost of family allowances, and about 68 percent of cost of all other benefits for salaried employees (who pay remainder of cost) and about 50 percent of cost for manual workers (remainder of cost shared about equally by workers and government). The government also pays special subsidies to help finance the automatic-adjustment provisions for benefits.

A national health service, separate from the foregoing systems, provides benefits to all persons (which is unique for Latin America, being similar to the British and Swedish programs). Cost-sharing provisions apply to salaried employees.

Great Britain

In Great Britain, demogrant programs for all residents (almost entirely financed from general revenues, with a small portion coming from direct contributions) are present for medical care benefits (small amount of cost sharing) and for flat-payment family allowances (for each child present under age 16—or under age 19 if in school or if an apprentice—except for the first such child, with lower payment for the second child than for the third and higher order children).[4]

Flat-rate periodic benefits, with eligibility based on the contribution record, are provided with respect to the following categories:

1. *Old-age and survivor pensions.* Old-age pensions are subject to a retirement test until age 70 for men and age 65 for women, and are increased for deferred retirement beyond age 65 for men and age 60 for women. A widow receives a pension if she has an eligible child in her care, or if she is aged 40 or over at widowhood, or when last child becomes ineligible.
2. *Cash sickness and maternity benefits.*
3. *Disability benefits.* Disability pensions are provided by paying invalidity benefits after 28 weeks of sickness at the same rate as cash sickness benefits, without restriction as to duration. In addition, an invalidity allowance is paid to individuals who become chronically sick, with the flat amount varying inversely with age at disablement.
4. *Unemployment benefits.*
5. *Work-connected injury benefits.*

Supplements are paid with respect to wives and children. The benefit amount is reduced for an incomplete contribution record. Government employees have a separate pension plan and receive benefits both thereunder and from the general flat-rate system (but for those entering employment after the establishment of the latter system, there is a partial offset of the general benefits against what is payable under the special system).

Periodic cash sickness and maternity benefits apply only to employees and self-employed. Periodic work-connected injury benefits (administered by the government) and unemployment benefits apply only to employees. Old-age and survivor pensions, flat-rate lump-sum death grants for insured persons and their dependents, and flat-rate lump-sum maternity grants for insured persons and their wives are available for all categories of insured persons.

The entire package of flat-rate benefits is financed by flat-rate contributions. With respect to employees, the employer contributes about 60 percent of the total employer-employee rate. Employees whose

<hr>

[4] For a very incisive analysis of the overall structure and accomplishments of the British program, see Sir John Walley, *Social Security: Another British Failure?* (London: Charles Knight, 1972).

employers have contracted out of the old-age benefits payable on an earnings-related basis (as will be discussed later) pay a slightly higher flat-rate contribution rate (by about 10 percent), as do also their employers. A small part of the contribution goes to assist in the financing of the National Health Service. The self-employed pay a contribution rate that is slightly less than the combined employer-employee rate, while nonemployed persons pay at a rate that is about two thirds of the combined employer-employee rate. The government makes a contribution equal to about 20 percent of the total direct contributions. Within each category, women (and, where applicable, their employers) pay about 15 percent lower contributions than men. These differentials by employment category and by sex reflect the different scopes of protection furnished. Married women (and certain widows receiving pensions) may elect not to contribute—either as employed persons (although their employer must contribute, regardless) or as self-employed or nonemployed persons. The financing of the program is on a "pay-as-you-go" basis.

For employees, supplements to the flat-rate benefits are added to old-age and survivor pensions, sickness benefits, and unemployment benefits on an earnings-related basis, with the amounts being computed by reference to earnings or earnings-related contributions. Contracting-out of private plans is permitted for old-age benefits (the plan for government employees is one of these contracted-out plans). These earnings-related benefits are financed by percentage-of-payroll contribution rates of 4¾ percent from both the employer and the employee, on earnings above a small exempt amount and up to a maximum earnings base. Where employees are contracted out for old-age benefits by the employer having an acceptable private plan, the contribution rates are lower.

There is also what can be called a general supplemental benefit program augmenting the social insurance programs, including a program to supplement the income of low-paid workers with children.

In 1975 the old-age and survivor benefits have been drastically altered. The flat-rate benefits will be continued (with annual adjustment when prices and wages change), but the earnings-related benefits will be discontinued as to future accruals. These flat-rate benefits will be financed by payroll taxes on earnings above a small exempt amount and up to a maximum earnings base. The standard contribution rate for the plan will be 5½ percent for employees (of which 0.4 percent is for the National Health Service) and 8½ percent for employers

(0.6 percent for NHS); married women and certain widows can elect not to participate (and then pay only 0.6 percent). Self-employed persons pay a flat-rate contribution plus a percentage contribution on a moderate range of earnings.

Beginning in 1975, employers were to have been required to establish an acceptable pension plan providing retirement and widow pensions or else participate in a government-operated "reserve pension" plan.[5] This plan was to have been financed by a contribution rate of 4 percent of payroll, of which ⅝ (2½ percent) is paid by the employer. The benefits were to have been determined on a money-purchase basis (with a certain amount being guaranteed and with additional "participating" payments if the experience is favorable). The financing was to have been on a full-reserve basis, and the investments to have been made in governmental or private securities or in property.

The proposal of the Labor Party was released in September 1974. Under British parliamentary procedure, it is likely to become law sometime in the future, unless a change in the government occurs, which does not seem likely. This proposal has the following features:

1. The flat-rate pensions, which the Labor Party had increased by about 30 percent (to £10 per week for a single person and £16 for a married couple; £1 equals about $2.40) when it took office, would be increased in the future in accordance with changes in the general earnings level.
2. An earnings-related pension plan would be established on top of the flat-rate plan. It would consider only future earnings, and the earnings record would be adjusted for changes in the general earnings level up to the time of retirement. This two-tier approach could also be considered as one involving a single pension calculated by a two-tier formula.
3. The earnings-related pensions would be based only on earnings above the amount of the flat-rate pension for a single person up to seven times that figure. The benefit rate would be 1¼ percent of average adjusted earnings per year of coverage, up to a maximum of 20 years. Thus, the ultimate benefit rate would be 25 percent.

---

[5] This plan was developed by the Conservative Party in 1973. But when the Labor Party took over in 1974, the plan was abolished, with the promise that a new proposal would be developed. The description of the reserve plan is given here because of its unique nature.

Persons with more than 20 years of adjusted earnings would use only the highest 20 years in computing the average. The ultimate level of combined flat-rate and earnings-related pensions would range, for a single person, from 100 percent of earnings at the bottom of the range to 36 percent at the top, and from 160 percent to 44 percent for a married couple. For a worker with average earnings, the benefit rates would be about 44 percent and 59 percent. It would be very unlikely that any individual would have earnings as low as to qualify at 100-percent benefit rate.

4. The earnings-related pensions would be increased by 6½ percent for each year of deferred retirement, beyond age 60 for women and age 65 for men.

5. Earnings-related pensions would be payable to widows and disabled workers, computed in similar manner to the old-age pensions and in the same amount.

6. The earnings-related pensions would be adjusted after award for changes in the cost of living.

7. The combination of the earnings-related and flat-rate pensions would be financed by contributions payable by employers and workers on total earnings up to the maximum amount of earnings creditable. The employer would pay about 60 percent of the total rate and the employee 40 percent, while there would be a government subsidy of about 18 percent of the combined employer-employee rate. The total contribution rate initially would be about 16½ percent, including 1 percent for the National Health Service.

8. Private pension plans could be the basis for contracting-out of the earnings-related plan. To do so, such plan must provide pensions at the rate of 1¼ percent of final salary or updated career-average salary. Such contracted-out pensions would be kept up to date with changes in the cost of living after retirement insofar as the portion thereof which would have occurred under the government plan; this updating would be paid for by the government. Those covered by a contracted-out plan and their employers will pay a lower contribution rate into the government plan, but only on their earnings above the bottom of the range of earnings considered for the earnings-related pensions.

It is interesting to note that the proposal of the Labor Party bears considerable resemblance to the Canada Pension Plan. The period of deferment until full pensions are payable is, however, twice as long.

France

A number of systems in France cover different risks and different categories of workers and self-employed persons. There is, however, a general system covering most nonagricultural workers. All systems provide a wide variety of benefits—old-age, survivor, and disability pensions; cash sickness and maternity benefits; medical care benefits (on a reimbursement basis, with cost sharing); work-connected injury benefits; unemployment benefits (on both an insurance and an assistance basis); and family allowances (relatively large payments for second and higher order children present—under age 16 or under age 20 if in school, when disabled, or if a girl working at home—with amount related to a standard average wage, and with higher amounts for third and higher order children).

Old-age pensions are payable without a retirement test from age 60, but the amount is significantly increased for deferment of claim (e.g., by 100 percent for claim at age 65 and by 200 percent at age 70). A supplement to the old-age pension is payable for the wife regardless of age, but a widow's pension is payable only at age 65, or at age 60 if disabled. Pension amounts are related to earnings or contributions paid, but are automatically adjusted annually to reflect changes in the general wage level. None of the cost of the general systems for nonagricultural workers and agricultural workers is borne by the government, except for unemployment assistance benefits, which are financed completely by the government, and a small part of the cost of medical care benefits. Employers under these general systems bear the entire cost for work-connected injury benefits (on an experience-rating basis) and for family allowances, and about 70 percent of the cost for the other benefits.

Netherlands

A system of old-age and survivor pensions covers all residents in the Netherlands and provides flat-rate pensions payable without a retirement test at age 65 (wife regardless of age). Survivor pensions of flat-rate amounts are payable for widows with children, or for widows alone if age 40 or over at husband's death or if disabled then. The pension amounts are automatically adjusted for changes in the general wage level. The pensions are financed by a percentage contribution on net income of individuals up to a certain limit (also automatically adjusted), with a small government contribution as national assistance for low-income persons. Wage-related disability pensions for employees in industry and commerce are provided by employer and employee payroll taxes (67 percent being paid by the employer).

Cash sickness and maternity benefits (of an earnings-related nature) and medical care benefits for workers and dependents (on a service basis, by about 100 approved sickness funds who contract with providers) are paid. The system covers all but high-paid workers and is financed by employer and employee wage-related contributions (the employer rate bearing about 70 percent of total cost). Employment injury cash benefits are included in the normal disability benefit provisions. Both the cash sickness and employment injury benefits have been merged in all their essentials with the general disability benefits.

Unemployment benefits (of a wage-related nature), varying by industry but with a basic national minimum plan, are financed by equal employer and employee wage-related contributions and by a small government contribution.

Family allowances of a flat amount per child are provided for children under age 16, or under age 27 if in school or disabled (the amount increasing by child order). These benefits are automatically adjusted for changes in the general wage level. They are payable with respect to all children of employees, pensioners, and low-income self-employed persons. All other residents can receive family allowance benefits for third and higher order children. These benefits are financed by employer percentage-of-payroll contributions, by percentage-of-income contributions (on the same income as for pensions) for the self-employed and nonemployed, and by the government for the benefits for first and second children of low-income self-employed.

Germany (West)

There are two large old-age, survivor, and disability pension systems in the Federal Republic of Germany—one for manual workers and the other for salaried employees (formerly, and for many years, those earning in excess of the maximum earnings base were completely excluded)—and several smaller ones (for miners, farmers, and government employees). The provisions of these two large systems are now the same, although for over 50 years they were different (the plan for salaried employees being more liberal).

The pensions are related directly to length of coverage and average lifetime earnings, but these earnings are automatically adjusted for changes in the general earnings level in the past; pensions in course of payment are similarly adjusted for current changes in the earnings level. The pensions are payable at age 65 without a retirement test (at age 60 if unemployed for one year, or if a woman with substantial recent employment) and do not have supplements for dependents, other than children (widow's pension payable regardless of age, but with smaller amount for healthy young widows with no children). Pensions are also payable at age 63 for those with at least 35 years of coverage (and with a retirement test). Persons eligible for such pensions at age 63 who continue working at ages 63–66 and do not elect to draw pensions, then receive an actuarially increased pension at age 67 (with no retirement test). The pension system is financed by equal employer-employee earnings-related contributions, with a government contribution of about 15 percent of the cost of the system.

The unemployment insurance system covers most workers, with earnings-related benefits; it is financed by equal employer-employee earnings-related contributions (the government finances an unemployment assistance program). Earnings-related cash sickness and maternity benefits and medical care benefits for workers and dependents (on a service basis, by private doctors and facilities under contract, with small cost sharing for some prescriptions) are provided, on a compulsory coverage basis, by about 2,000 separate sickness funds. These benefits are financed by roughly equal employer-employee earnings-related contributions. Employment injury benefits are provided in somewhat the same manner as in the United States for all workers (and also for some categories of self-employed persons), with the administration being through semipublic carriers.

Family allowances of a flat amount per child are provided for all children who are under age 18, or under age 25 if in school, or disabled, for second and higher order children with an income test applicable for the second child. The amount payable increases with the order of the child. These are financed entirely by the federal government.

Switzerland

An old-age, survivors, and disability pension system, patterned to some extent after OASDI, covers all residents of Switzerland. The pension amounts are related to the average income on which contributions were paid (and not to length of coverage, although related to the proportion of the potential period of contributions that contributions were actually paid), under a weighted benefit formula. Pensions are paid without a retirement test at age 65 for men and age 62 for women (for wife's supplement, age 45 or disabled; for widow alone, age 40). Employees, employers, and self-employed persons contribute on their entire earned income, without maximum limit. Nonemployed persons, other than wives and widows, also contribute on their income. Pensions are financed by equal employer-employee earnings-related contributions. Self-employed and nonemployed pay about 80 percent of the combined employer-employee rate—originally 100 percent—although a lower rate is applicable to low-income persons. There is a government contribution of about 20–25 percent of the cost of the old-age and survivor pensions and of one half of the disability pension cost (payable 75 percent by the federal government and 25 percent by the cantons).

Unemployment benefits are paid through about 200 separate funds (by region or industry). Membership in these funds is compulsory in most cantons for nonagricultural and nongovernmental employees who have less than a prescribed amount of earnings. Benefits are earnings-related and are financed primarily by employee contributions (but with government contributions in some cases), although in certain instances the employer pays part of the employee contribution.

Medical care benefits (on a service basis, with coinsurance, provided by doctors and facilities on contract) are provided through more than 800 separate funds, with membership being compulsory for all residents (other than those with large incomes) in some cantons and optional in others, with about 90 percent of the population being members. A few of these funds provide cash sickness and maternity benefits. The medical care benefits are financed primarily by contributions of the members, with small government contributions and, in some cases, with employer contributions under collective-bargaining agreements.

Employment injury benefits for all workers are provided in a manner similar to that in the United States, except that the carrier is a government agency. Associated with this system is a program for nonoccupational accidents, which is financed by employee contributions.

Family allowances (flat amounts) are paid under two types of public programs (many workers receive family allowances under collective-bargaining agreements). One, on a nationwide basis, pays a flat amount per child (under age 16, or under age 21 if in school, or disabled) for all children of farmworkers and of farmers in mountain regions with low incomes; it is financed by percentage-of-payroll contributions from employers of farmworkers and by government contributions. The other, on a cantonal basis (in all cantons) applies to other workers, including government employees, with varying provisions as to what children are eligible for payment and as to the amount of the allowance; the financing is entirely by employers.

Norway

The general old-age, disability, and survivor pension system in Norway is on a dual basis—flat-rate demogrants, with residence qualifications (with proportionate reduction for those with less than 40 years of residence), and an earnings-related system for persons with earned income, except those with very low earnings. Special supplementary systems apply for government employees, nurses, seamen, fishermen, forestry workers, and railroad workers. The old-age pensions are payable at age 67 (formerly age 70, until 1973), with flat-rate supplements for dependent spouses. The old-age pension is actuarially increased for deferment of retirement (at ages 68–70). Widow's and widower's pensions are payable under both flat-rate and earnings-related parts. The benefit provisions are automatically adjusted for changes in price and income level.

An unemployment insurance system covers almost all private employees, with wage-related benefits. Cash sickness and maternity benefits on an earnings-related basis are provided on a compulsory basis for all employees and self-employed persons. Medical care benefits (on an indemnity basis with coinsurance, generally) are provided on a compulsory basis for all residents. Employment injury benefits on a wage-related basis are available for all employees.

The pension, unemployment, cash sickness and maternity, medical care, and employment injury benefits are provided through a coordinated national insurance system. Until 1971, there were separate systems for each branch, but in the next two years they were coordinated. Now, the financing is on a pooled basis. The employees and self-employed pay a contribution rate on earnings and on total income as assessed for income tax up to a certain limit (which is automatically adjusted for changes in earnings levels), while employers contribute on total payroll. The employer contribution rate is about 1.75 times the employee rate on the average, while the self-employed rate is about twice the employee rate. The nonemployed, who are covered only for medical care benefits, have a contribution rate somewhat less than half of the employee rate. The government (national and local sharing equally) contributes an amount equal to about 17 percent of the total contributions of individuals and employers.

Family allowances are payable on a demogrant basis to all children present, under age 16. The payments are in the form of a flat amount per child, increasing with child order, and are financed entirely by the national government.

Sweden

In Sweden, demogrant programs provide old-age, disability, and survivor pensions for all citizens and family allowances for all residents (a flat payment for each child under 16, or under 19 if in school) financed entirely by the government. The pensions are flat amounts that vary automatically with the cost of living and are payable as a matter of right. A supplementary housing allowance, financed by local governments, depends on a means test. The old-age pension is payable at age 67 (with a supplement for the wife aged 60 to 66), with no retirement test; the pension may be paid at ages 63 to 66 with an actuarial reduction or may be deferred to ages 68 to 70 with an actuarial increase. A widow's pension is payable while the widow is caring for a child under age 18, or after age 50 (or from ages 35 to 49 at a reduced rate). These pensions are financed by the government (national and local); until 1974, about 30 percent of the financing came from a 5 percent tax on all income (up to a certain limit).

There is also a supplementary earnings-related pension plan that is optional for the self-employed and compulsory for employees earning over a fixed amount. Pension amounts are related to the long-term average of earnings above a certain amount and below an upper limit, but with automatic adjustment of past earnings to reflect changes in the price level (both before and after award of pension). The pensionable age is 67 (earlier and deferred retirement is possible, as in the case with the demogrants), with no retirement test and with no wife's supplement. Disability pensions (both total and partial) and survivor pensions are available in this earnings-related system. Contributions are paid by the employers and self-employed persons.

Unemployment benefits are available through a number of voluntary union funds (usually compulsory for union members), with financing by employees and with subsidies from the government.

Cash sickness and maternity benefits (primarily on an income-related basis, but with a small flat-rate basic amount) and medical care benefits (hospitalization on a service basis; physician and dental services on a coinsurance indemnity basis) are provided on a compulsory basis to all residents. These health benefits are financed by contributions of protected persons that are a percentage of their income, by a percentage payroll tax on employers, and by government subsidies. Work-connected injury benefits (coordinated with general sickness benefits, although more extensive) are provided on a compulsory basis through a government agency and are financed entirely by employer contributions of a uniform rate as a percentage of payroll (until recently, risk-related).

Soviet Union

Medical care (on a service basis by government doctors and facilities, with the person paying for out-of-hospital medicines) and family allowances are provided on a demogrant basis, financed entirely by the Soviet government. The family allowances are lump-sum payments for the birth of third and higher orders of children (size of payment increasing with order) and monthly payments with respect to fourth and higher birth orders of children while aged 1 to 4 (note that eligibility depends on birth order and not on the number of children present at the time of payment), with size of payment increasing with birth order.

Old-age, disability, and survivor pensions and cash sickness and maternity benefits are provided, on an earnings-related basis, for all workers in industry, commerce, government, and agriculture. Until recently, there was a separate, less liberal system for the 40 percent of the work force on collective farms, but now such workers are covered under the general system (but with lower minimum-benefit provisions). The pension amounts are determined from formulas that are weighted in favor of those with low earnings and also vary, to some extent, with length of service, type of work (as to its danger), number of dependents, and place of residence (lower for rural). The pensionable age is 60 for men and 55 for women (lower for dangerous occupations), and there is a retirement test, although it is waived or liberalized for many occupations and geographic areas where labor shortages exist. Survivor pensions are payable to widows at age 55, or if disabled, or with child under age 8 (children are eligible until age 15). Both total and partial disability pensions are payable.

Cash sickness and maternity benefits are directly wage related, but vary by length of continuous service (with any employing organization). The pensions and cash sickness and maternity benefits are financed by employer percentage-of-payroll contributions (varying by industry, generally according to its occupational risk), with the government making up the balance of the cost.

No unemployment benefits are available (it being claimed that there is no unemployment—not even seasonal or frictional). No separate system of employment-injury benefits exists, since this risk is covered by the general medical care, cash sickness, and disability pension systems (with higher cash benefits under such circumstances).

Greece

In Greece, a general system provides for the following benefits: old-age, disability, and survivor pensions; benefits for work-connected injuries; cash sickness and maternity benefits; medical care benefits (on a service basis, with some coinsurance, from facilities of the social security institution); unemployment benefits; and family allowances. This system applies to all employees (and self-employed persons as to pensions, medical care, and cash sickness benefits), except those engaged in agricultural work, for whom there is a separate system of flat-rate benefits. However, there are about 75 contracted-out plans for different occupations in various areas—primarily providing pensions, cash sickness and maternity benefits, and medical care benefits.

The pension benefits are earnings related, with weighting to produce relatively higher amounts for those with lower earnings, and are only indirectly related to length of service. The pensionable age is 62 for men and 57 for women, with reduced benefits available at ages down to 55, and with a retirement test. Widows' pensions are payable regardless of age.

The cash sickness and maternity benefits, the unemployment benefits, and the employment injury benefits are earnings related. On the other hand, the family allowance benefits are paid for each child under age 15, with the benefit being a flat amount plus an additional amount for each day of employment of the worker in the previous year.

The entire package of benefits is financed by earnings-related contributions (with the employer paying about twice what the employee does), with a maximum earnings limit for contributions. Government contributions to meet the balance of the costs for pensions and sickness and maternity benefits are authorized (but nothing in this respect is currently payable). Many of the separate, contracted-out systems are partially financed by third-party taxes (sales taxes on certain commodities, and the like).

Israel

A coordinated compulsory system covers all residents of Israel for old-age, disability, and survivors pensions; all employees and self-employed for cash maternity benefits and employment injury benefits; and all residents for family allowances. Most persons are covered for medical care benefits (and, in some cases, cash sickness benefits) by a few voluntary funds.

The old-age pensions are payable at age 65 for men and age 60 for women, subject to a retirement test for the first five years, with a supplement for a dependent wife regardless of age. Widows' pensions are payable when a child is present or when the widow is disabled or aged 50 or over (reduced pension if aged 40 to 49). The pension amounts are flat, varying to some extent with length of coverage and deferment of retirement. Pensions are automatically adjusted for changes in the cost of living.

The cash maternity and the employment injury benefits are earnings related. The family allowance benefits for all residents are payable for the fourth and higher child present, under age 18 (or under age 25 if disabled), and are flat amounts per child, increasing with the number of eligible children. In addition, such benefits are also available for the first three children of employees.

The benefits are financed by earnings-related contributions (income-related contributions for the self-employed and the nonemployed) subject to a maximum. For pensions, the employer pays about twice what the employee pays (the self-employed and the nonemployed pay the combined employer-employee rate), with the government contributing 10 percent of the contributions of covered persons and employers. For sickness and maternity cash benefits, the employer and employee share the cost equally, with no government contribution. The cost of employment injury benefits is met entirely by the employer, with the rates varying to reflect the differences in risk. The family allowance benefits are financed by the employer (with the self-employed and the nonemployed paying a rate about half as large) and by the government, which pays 20 percent of the direct contributions.

United Arab Republic (Egypt)

Employees in industry and commerce in Egypt have a unified program of old-age, disability, and survivor pensions, cash sickness and maternity benefits, medical care benefits, unemployment benefits, and employment injury benefits. Government employees have a separate system. Earnings-related benefits are payable, with the pension amounts being directly related to length of coverage. The pensionable age is 58 (until recently, 60), with a retirement test (no age requirement for widows' pensions). The system is financed by wage-related employer and employee contributions, with no maximum wage limit and with the employer paying about two thirds of the cost; the government contributes only to the unemployment insurance system (paying one fourth of its cost).

British-Oriented Countries in Africa

Many of the now-independent African nations had previously been colonies or mandates of Great Britain. Their general pattern of social security programs before independence involved only two programs —employment injury benefits and provident funds. The former type of program was similar to those in other countries and was administered through private insurance companies. Since independence, the trend has been toward administration by the government or by autonomous semipublic bodies.

Provident funds are merely compulsory savings programs, usually with the employer and the employee contributing equal percentages of salary. The total account, including accumulated interest, is then payable when a certain contingency occurs, such as attainment of a specified retirement age, permanent and total disability, death, long-term unemployment, or dropping out of the labor market due to such events as a woman marrying or giving birth to a child. As a result, provident funds do not meet very well the lifetime needs for income of retired or disabled workers or survivors of deceased workers.

Before independence, the provident funds were often established on a voluntary basis by employers, rather than through government action. Since independence, in a number of instances the government has required provident-fund coverage, administered through a governmental institution.

Since independence, these countries have generally continued the previous programs, and some have started new programs of other types.

French-Oriented Countries in Africa

Before the independence of many of the French-oriented African nations, there were employment injury and family allowance systems for all employees. The cash benefits under the employment injury programs were earnings related, and these programs were financed entirely by the employers and were administered either by autonomous semipublic bodies or through private insurance companies. The family allowance payments were made to all children, as flat amounts per child (usually under age 14, or a higher age if in school), and were usually financed by wage-related employer contributions (with the government meeting any deficit). Since independence, these programs have been retained, and some of the countries have started programs of other types such as pensions, cash sickness benefits, and medical care benefits.

India

The principal social insurance protection in India covers employees of firms with 20 or more workers. A separate system applies to those in government employment. This general system applies only in certain areas of the country, which are being extended gradually (and now include most of the country). High-paid employees are completely excluded.

Protection against the risks of old age and disability retirement is in the form of a lump-sum return of combined employer-employee contributions plus interest (i.e., a provident-fund type of procedure). The old-age grant is payable upon retirement after age 55. Survivor pensions in an amount dependent upon wage class are available (as are also lump-sum death payments of a uniform amount). The employer and employee contribution rates are equal (although the employer makes an additional contribution to finance the administrative expenses of the system). The government pays an amount equal to somewhat less than 10 percent of the combined employer-employee contributions and also pays the administrative expenses for survivor benefit payments.

A new so-called gratuity-fund system has been established on a nationwide basis covering the same workers as the provident-fund law, except that coverage also applies to firms with 10–19 workers. The benefits are paid by the employer when the employee separates from service (for any reason, including retirement and death) and amount to 15 days of wages for each year of service. Such benefits are in addition to any that might be paid under the program described above and are financed entirely by the employer. This program serves principally as unemployment insurance, but it does not apply to employees with temporary or short service.

Earnings-related cash sickness and maternity benefits and medical care benefits are provided for the same persons who are covered for retirement benefits. The medical care is on a service basis, from public or private doctors and facilities, for workers and dependents, except that the scale of services varies among states. Employment injury protection is included in the foregoing system, with somewhat more liberal provisions for such cases. This program is financed by wage-related contributions from employer and employee (the latter paying about 36 percent of the total rate) and by contributions from state governments, which meet one eighth of the cost of the medical care benefits.

China (Mainland)

In Mainland China, an earnings-related old-age and disability pension system applies to employees in industry with 100 or more employees and to public employees. The retirement age is 60 for men, 55 for salaried female workers, and 50 for other women, with a retirement test. The only survivor benefit is a lump-sum death payment. The system is financed entirely by employer contributions, on a percentage-of-payroll basis.

The employees covered under the pension system are provided earnings-related cash sickness and maternity and medical care benefits for themselves and their dependents (for employees, all services except cost of board in hospitals and cost of ordinary medicine; for dependents, all services except hospitalization and cost of ordinary medicine and only 50 percent of cost of surgery). The employer provides these benefits directly, and at its cost.

Japan

Two separate national systems exist in Japan (in addition to plans for government employees, seamen, teachers, and public utility employees). One system applies to workers in industrial and commercial firms with five or more employees (except for the employment injury benefits, which are applicable irrespective of the size of the firm), and the second applies to all residents who do not otherwise have social security protection.

For the employment-related plan, the benefits are earnings-related pensions (weighted so as to provide amounts not entirely related to length of coverage) for old age, disability, and death; cash sickness and maternity benefits on a wage-related basis; medical care benefits (generally on a service basis with coinsurance, from doctors and facilities of the roughly 1,300 affiliated health insurance societies); employment injury benefits (coordinated with the cash sickness and medical care benefits); and unemployment benefits of a wage-related nature. The pensionable age is 60 for men and 55 for women (for widows—at any age), with a retirement test. These benefits are financed by wage-related employer-employee contributions of equal size (except for employment injury benefits, which are financed entirely by employers through rates that vary by experience) up to a certain maximum earnings limit and by a government contribution related to actual benefit outgo (20 percent for pensions, 25 percent for unemployment benefits, and the administrative expenses of the system of cash sickness and maternity benefits and medical care benefits, plus a further annual subsidy).

The system for other residents provides old-age, disability, and survivor pensions and medical care benefits similar to those under the employment-related plan. The old-age pensions are payable at age 65 after 25 years of contributions (with lower requirements for those initially covered at ages 31 to 50), or at age 70 on a means tests basis (for widows—at age 60 or with children). The pension amounts are based on length of contributions (the means test amounts are uniform —and lower). The pensions are financed by flat contributions from covered adults and by a government contribution equal to half of the contributions of the covered persons. The medical care benefits are financed by contributions levied by the municipal health insurance funds, which also receive a government contribution of 40 percent of the cost of the plan.

Flat-rate children's allowances are available to virtually the entire population, excluding only those with very high incomes. The benefits are payable only to third or higher order children under age 15 (although the first and second children, who do not receive benefits, can be aged 15–17 and qualify younger children). With respect to employees, these payments are financed about 70 percent by the employers and the remainder by the government (two thirds by the national government and one third by local governments); for all other families, the financing is done by the government.

Philippines

A general system in the Republic of the Philippines applies to all employees in industry and commerce and to "permanent" farm workers. (Government employees have a separate system.) The benefits provided are old-age and disability pensions, lump-sum survivor benefits, and cash sickness benefits on a wage-related basis. The pensionable age is 60, with a retirement test until age 65. All benefits are earnings related, with the pension amounts being heavily weighted in favor of those with low wages (no dependents' supplements). The system is financed by wage-related employer-employee contributions (about 40 percent from the employee), with no government contribution, unless the system has a deficit.

Medical care benefits are provided, on an indemnity basis, for workers covered under the general system (and also for government workers) and their dependents. The cost is financed by equal employer, employee, and government contributions.

Cash maternity benefits are paid directly by the employer, under the provisions of the Labor Code.

Employment injury benefits are provided in the same manner as in the United States.

Australia

Family allowances in Australia are provided on a demogrant basis to all permanent residents, with a flat amount per child (with the amount increasing with child order) for all children under age 16 (or under 21 if in school), financed entirely by the government. Old-age, disability, and survivor pensions of a flat amount are also provided on a demogrant basis to all citizens. Initially, these were subject to a means test based on income and assets, but this has been eliminated for persons aged 65 or over (in steps—first for those 75 and over, then for those 70–74, and finally for 65–69). The pensionable age is 65 for men and 60 for women (with a supplement for wives under age 60). A widow's pension is payable while a child under age 16 (or under age 21 if in school) is present, after age 50, or after age 45 if there was an eligible child present when age 45 was attained. The pensions are financed completely by the government.

Unemployment benefits of a flat amount are also payable on an income test basis to all residents capable of work. These are financed entirely by the government. The same is also the case for cash sickness benefits, but lump-sum maternity grants are payable to all residents without a means test.

Medical care benefits are provided on a demogrant basis, entirely paid for by the government, in the form of hospital benefits of a flat daily amount toward such costs and as to medicines (but with a flat amount paid by the individual for each prescription). Most of the population receives other medical care benefits (additional payments toward hospitalization costs and partial—up to 90 percent—reimbursement of doctors' bills) through more than 100 nonprofit voluntary benefit organizations (established by friendly societies, insurance companies, doctors, and so forth). The government subsidizes up to half the benefit costs of these voluntary benefit societies.

Employment injury benefits are provided in the same manner as in the United States, with competitive state funds (except in one state, where the state fund is monopolistic).

New Zealand

Family allowances in New Zealand are provided on a demogrant basis to all permanent residents, with a flat amount per child under age 16 (or under age 18, if in school). Old-age, disability, and survivor pensions of a flat amount are also provided on a demogrant basis, involving certain residence requirements. In general, these pensions are subject to a means test based on income, including imputed income from certain assets, but with a specified, significant amount of income being exempt from consideration. A superannuation pension, payable as a right, is also available at age 65 (whereas the pensionable age for the income test pension is 60, or 55 for unmarried women unable to work). A widow's pension is payable while a child under age 16 is present (or under age 18, if in school), after age 50 (with certain length-of-marriage requirements), or after all children have grown up, and the marriage has lasted 15 years. Also, flat-rate orphans' benefits are available (in addition to the family allowances), with a larger amount for the first child. Supplementary assistance is also available on a needs test basis.

Recently, a money-purchase type of old-age benefits plan has been added on top of the flat-benefit program.

Medical care benefits are available for all permanent residents and are provided by doctors and druggists under contract with the government; most hospitalization is in government hospitals. Full medical care is provided, without any maximum time limits. There is cost sharing, in that doctors may charge whatever they see fit to charge above the amount received from the government, in that only part of the cost is paid for treatment in private hospitals, and in that dental care is available only for children under age 16.

Unemployment benefits of a flat amount, with a supplement for the wife (but with an income test, after exclusion of a certain amount of income) are payable after a one-week waiting period and without any prescribed maximum duration. Cash sickness benefits are available on a similar basis.

All the foregoing benefits are financed on a global basis by a gross income tax, a corporation net income tax, and payments from general governmental funds.

Employment injury benefits are provided in the same general manner as in the United States, except that the medical care benefits are provided through the general system described above. In other words, there are earnings-related benefits, financed entirely by the employer through either private insurance companies or self-insurance.

Appendixes

appendix A

Definition of Social Insurance
Developed by the Committee
on Social Insurance
Terminology of the
Commission on Insurance
Terminology of the American
Risk and Insurance Association*

A device for the pooling of risks by their transfer to an organization, usually governmental, that is required by law to provide pecuniary or service benefits to or on behalf of covered persons upon the occurrence of certain predesignated losses under all of the following conditions:

1. Coverage is compulsory by law in virtually all instances.
2. Except during a transition period following its introduction, eligibility for benefits is derived, in fact or in effect, from contributions having been made to the program by or in respect of the claimant or the person as to whom the claimant is a dependent; there is no requirement that the individual demonstrate inadequate financial resources, although a dependency status may need to be established.
3. The method for determining the benefits is prescribed by law.
4. The benefits for any individual are not usually directly related to contributions made by or in respect of him but instead usually redistribute income so as to favor certain groups such as those with low former wages or a large number of dependents.

---

* As published in Robert W. Osler and John S. Bickley, eds., *Glossary of Insurance Terms* (Santa Monica, Calif.: Insurors Press, Inc., 1972).

5. There is a definite plan for financing the benefits that is designed to be adequate in terms of long-range considerations.
6. The cost is borne primarily by contributions which are usually made by covered persons, their employers, or both.
7. The plan is administered or at least supervised by the government.
8. The plan is not established by the government solely for its present or former employees.

appendix **B**

Views on Individual Equity
and Social Adequacy*

Because of its voluntary nature, then, private insurance must be built on principles which assure the greatest practicable degree of equity between the various classes insured. Not only would the very nature of the case make it basically unfair to have one homogeneous group of insured designedly pay for part of the costs of providing insurance for another group for which the actuarial measure of the risk is quite different, but such a practice would lead to a cessation of insurance soon after the former group came to understand that it could save money by being treated as an independent, financially self-contained unit.

Social insurance, on the other hand, is of vastly different character and is generally assigned a considerably different function. It aims primarily at providing society with some protection against one or more major hazards which are sufficiently widespread throughout the population and far-reaching in effect to become "social" in scope and complexion. Usually these risks are not many in number. Yet, if not guarded against through some organized means, they produce large dependency problems that take their toll in terms not only of financial but of human values as well.

---

* From Reinhard A. Hohaus, "Equity, Adequacy, and Related Factors in Old Age Security," *The Record*, American Institute of Actuaries, vol. 37 (1938).

641

Directed against a dependency problem, social insurance is generally compulsory—not voluntary—giving the individual for whom it is intended no choice as to membership. Nor can he as a rule select the kind and amount of protection or the price to be paid for it. All this is specified in the plan, and little, if any, latitude is left for individual treatment. Indeed, social insurance views society as a whole and deals with the individual only in so far as he constitutes one small element of that whole. Consistent with this philosophy, its first objective in the matter of benefits should, therefore, be that those covered by it will, so far as possible, be assured of that minimum income which in most cases will prevent their becoming a charge of society. Not until this is accomplished should financial resources (whatever, if anything, may remain of them) be considered as available to provide individual differentiation aiming at equity.

Private insurance, then, is adapted to the individual's need for, and his ability to afford, protection against one or more of a large variety of risks. Social insurance, on the other hand, is molded to society's need for a minimum of protection against one or more of a limited number of recognized social hazards. The minimum may be considered as that income which society feels is necessary and economically practicable for the subsistence of individuals comprising it. These payments, it is held, must be met in one form or another anyway, and social insurance endeavors to organize the budgeting therefor and dispensing thereof through systematic governmental processes. Hence, just as considerations of equity of benefits form a natural and vital part of operating private insurance, so should considerations of adequacy of benefits control the pattern of social insurance. Likewise, as private insurance would collapse if it stressed considerations of adequacy more than those of equity, so will social insurance fail to remain undisturbed if considerations of equity are allowed to predominate over those of adequacy. . . .

The foregoing need not necessarily imply that all considerations of equity should be discarded from a social insurance plan; rather the point is that, of the two principles, adequacy is the more essential and less dispensable.

appendix **C**

Summary of Major Provisions of Old-Age, Survivors, and Disability Insurance and Medicare Programs

A. SUMMARY OF OLD-AGE, SURVIVORS, AND DISABILITY INSURANCE SYSTEM

I. **Monthly Benefits Payable to—**

   a. Retired worker aged 62 or over (with a lifetime reduction in benefit of $6\frac{2}{3}\%$ for each year under age 65 at time of retirement).

   b. Disabled worker under age 65, after a five-month waiting period (first benefit after completion of six full calendar months of disability). Individual must have a disability so severe that he is unable to engage in any substantial gainful activity; the impairment must be a medically determinable physical or mental condition that is expected to continue for at least 12 months or to result in death.

   c. Wife or husband (or divorced spouse with at least 20 years of marriage) aged 62 or over of a retired or disabled worker (with a lifetime reduction in benefit of $8\frac{1}{3}\%$ for each year under age 65 at time of initial claim). Spouse, regardless of age, receives monthly benefits if eligible child is present (other than a student beneficiary aged 18 or over) (see I-*f*).

d. Widow or widower (or surviving divorced spouse with at least 20 years of marriage) aged 60 or over, of deceased worker (with a lifetime reduction in benefit of 5.7% for each year under age 65 at time of initial claim), producing a benefit rate of 71½% at age 60 and 82.9% at age 62.

e. Disabled widow or widower (or surviving divorced spouse with at least 20 years of marriage) aged 50–59, of deceased worker (with a lifetime reduction in benefit of the sum of (1) 28.5% and (2) 2.15% for each year under age 60 at time of initial claim), producing a benefit rate of 50% at age 50. The disability must have occurred before 7 years after the death of the spouse (or in the case of a widow or widower, if later, 7 years after last eligible child attains age 18 or ceases to be disabled).

f. Children under age 18 (regardless of age if disabled since before age 22, or attending school at ages 18–21 and through end of school period in which age 22 is attained if an undergraduate) of a retired, disabled, or deceased worker, and the parent (not remarried) of eligible children (other than a student beneficiary aged 18 or over) of deceased worker (i.e., worker's widow, widower, or divorced spouse, regardless of age (but if widow or widower is aged 61 or over, may qualify under I-*d* for a larger benefit). Grandchild of a worker is also eligible if living with and being supported by the worker in the year prior to claim and if the child's parents are dead or disabled.

g. Dependent parents aged 62 or over of deceased worker.

h. Certain persons aged 72 or over who are not insured (designated as being transitionally noninsured) who attained age 72 before 1972 in the case of men and 1970 in the case of women (payable on an individual basis, with no dependents or survivors benefits derived therefrom). Benefit is not payable if receiving public assistance; also it is reduced by amount of any other governmental pension.

No individual can receive, for any month, more than the amount of the largest monthly benefit for which he is eligible.

II. Lump-Sum Death Payment

Lump-sum death payment is payable upon death of an insured worker (including retired and disabled workers). Full amount is paid to surviving spouse if had been living with deceased (otherwise, cannot exceed burial expenses).

III. Insured Status

  a. Insured status is based on quarters of coverage, as follows:
   (1) One quarter of coverage for each calendar quarter in which individual is paid at least $50 of covered non-farm wages, with 4 quarters for maximum creditable wages in a year (see Item X).
   (2) One quarter of coverage for each full $100 of covered farm wages paid in a year, with 4 quarters for $400 or more of such wages.
   (3) Four quarters of coverage for at least $400 of creditable self-employment earnings in a year.
  b. "Fully insured" status gives eligibility for all benefits except disability benefits, which also require disability insured status (see Item III-*d*). A fully insured person is one who at or after attainment of age 62, or at death or disability if earlier, has at least 6 quarters of coverage[1] and who has at least 1 quarter of coverage (acquired at any time) for every year elapsed after 1950 (year of attainment of age 21, if later) and before the year of attainment of age 62, or year of death or disability, if earlier (see Item VI for effect of disability on elapsed period). For men attaining age 62 before 1975, the closing date is later than age 62 (namely, age 63 for those born in 1912, age 64 for 1911, and age 65 for 1910 or before). The maximum number of quarters of coverage which will ever be required is 40.
  c. "Currently insured" status alone (i.e., not fully insured) provides eligibility only for child's, mother's, father's, and lump-sum survivor benefits. Currently insured status requires 6 quarters of coverage within the 13-quarter period ending with the quarter of death or entitlement to old-age benefits (see Item VI for effect of disability on 13-quarter period).

---

[1] Monthly benefits are payable at age 72 or over (but only when such age was attained before 1969 in the case of wives and widows, before 1967 in the case of female workers, and before 1964 in the case of male workers), on the basis of 3 to 5 quarters of coverage, to certain workers (and to their wives and widows) who are designated as being transitionally insured.

d. "Disability insured" status is necessary for disability benefits and for establishment of the "disability freeze" (see Item VI). It requires fully insured status and, in addition, 20 quarters of coverage in the 40-quarter period ending with the quarter in which disability began, with a generally lower requirement, as an alternative, for persons becoming disabled before age 31. For those disabled at ages 24–31, the requirement is twice the number of quarters required for fully insured status (but not twice the minimum requirement of 6 quarters of coverage, which results anyhow for those disabled at age 24);[2] for those disabled before age 24, only 6 quarters of coverage in the last 12 quarters are required. For blind persons, only fully insured status is required.

IV.   Computation of Average Monthly Wage and Primary Amount

a. Average monthly wage is computed for the "n" years after 1950 in which credited earnings were the largest (including years after year of attainment of age 61). "n" equals the number of years after 1955 (or year of attainment of age 26, if later) and before the first year after 1960 in which the individual either died or attained age 62, excluding any years in which the individual was in a period of disability (see Item VI). For men attaining age 62 before 1975, the closing date is later than age 62 (namely, age 63 for those born in 1912, age 64 for 1911, and age 65 for 1910 or before). In no case can "n" be less than 2; for old-age benefits, when there is no "disability freeze" involved, "n" will always be at least 5. In computing the average monthly wage for disability benefits, the individual is considered to have attained age 62 in the year that he was disabled (see Item VI).

b. Primary amount is computed from a benefit table that, for June 1975, is based approximately on the formula: 129.48% of the first $110 of average monthly wage, plus 47.10% of the next $290, plus 44.01% of the next $150, plus 51.73% of the next $100, plus 28.77% of the next $100, plus 23.98% of the next $250, plus 21.60% of the next

---

[2] Such required quarters must be acquired after age 21.

$175, increased slightly for average wages under $94. Minimum primary amount in the benefit table is $101.40. A higher minimum primary amount is payable to those with at least 25 "years of coverage."[3] This term means a year in which the worker had covered earnings equal to at least 25% of the maximum taxable earnings base (see Item X), with a special rule for 1937–50 (years of coverage then equal total covered wages in the period divided by $900, but cannot exceed the 14 years involved). The amount is $9 per year of coverage in excess of 10 years, up to a maximum of 30 years (i.e., $135 for 25 years of coverage, ranging up to $180 for 30 or more years of coverage).

c. Illustrative primary amounts based on the benefit table in effect for June 1975 for various lengths of time in covered employment for a worker who reaches age 62 on January 1, 2010, who does not work thereafter, and who does not have a "disability freeze" are:

Average Wage While Working	Number of Years in Covered Employment		
	35	*20*	*10*
$76 or less	$101.40	$101.40	$101.40
100	130.50	101.40	101.40
200	185.20	145.60	101.40
300	231.60	172.00	111.50
400	279.80	198.60	145.60
500	323.40	224.90	158.90
600	371.50	251.10	172.00
700	410.70	279.80	185.20
800	437.00	304.70	198.60
900	461.00	329.30	211.80
1,000	485.00	356.90	224.90
1,100	506.60	386.00	238.20
1,175	522.80	403.50	249.30

d. Alternatively, the "1939 Law" method (for workers with at least 1 quarter of coverage before 1951, exclusive of those

---

[3] For less than 22 years, the formula for the special minimum produces less than the regular $101.40 minimum. For 22–24 years, for the case with the minimum possible qualifying earnings, the amount computed from the benefit formula will always exceed the amount computed under the formula for the special minimum.

who attained age 22 after 1950 and have at least 6 quarters of coverage after 1950) provides that the average wage be computed in a similar manner, except that 1936 is used as the starting date instead of 1950. The "original" amount is 40% of first $50 of average wage plus 10% of next $200, all increased by 1% for each calendar year before 1951 in which at least $200 of wages was paid. The "original" amount is then increased by a conversion table to give the primary amount, indicated by the following table for certain illustrative cases for June 1975 and after:

Original Amount	Primary Amount	Original Amount	Primary Amount
$10	$101.40	$30	$156.50
15	101.40	35	174.10
20	111.50	40	191.60
25	134.50	45	209.70

e. Beginning with 1975, the benefit table will be automatically adjusted (upward only) as of June of each year for changes in the cost of living, as measured by the Consumer Price Index, if for the first quarter of the preceding year it rises by at least 3% over its level in the second quarter of 1974, or, if later, the first quarter of the year that last triggered such a benefit increase. If Congress enacts a general benefit increase in a year (or effective in a year), this negates the automatic adjustment for the next year; under these circumstances, subsequent measurement of the CPI increase is based on the quarter in which such increase was effective. If the earnings base is also automatically increased (see Item X), the benefit table is extended by applying a 20% factor to the new range of average monthly wages added. The automatic adjustment applies only to the benefit table and not to the special minimum primary amount based on years of coverage (see last three sentences of Item IV-b). In the case of benefits first claimed before age 65 and subject to reduction then, any increases due to the automatic-adjustment provisions are subject to reduction (if any) on the basis of the age attained at the time of such adjustment. The CPI for a quarter is the arithmetic mean of the CPIs for each of the three months in the quarter.

f. "Average current earnings" is largest of (1) $\frac{1}{12}$ of highest annual earnings in covered employment in the last six years, (2) $\frac{1}{12}$ of annual average of earnings in covered work in highest five consecutive years, or (3) the average monthly wage. It is automatically adjusted for changes in the general level of earnings following the worker's disablement.

V. Amount of Benefits

a. Old-age benefit is equal to primary amount, except for retirement before age 65 (see Item I-*a*) and except that an increment at the rate of 1% per year is added for months (after 1970) at ages 65–71 for persons who did not receive benefits before age 65 when benefits are not paid because of earnings test (see Item VII); such increment is not applicable to benefits for dependents or survivors of the insured worker and is not subject to the maximum on family benefits (see Item V-*b*).

b. Disability benefit is equal to primary amount.

c. Benefit for wife, husband, or child of retired or disabled worker is 50% of primary amount, except for spouse without eligible child claiming benefit before age 65 (see Item I-*c*).

d. Benefit for widow or widower is 100% of primary amount, except for widow or widower claiming benefit before age 65 (see Item I-*d*) and except for disabled widow or widower (see Item I-*e*). If the deceased worker was receiving a reduced old-age benefit (because of retirement before age 65), the benefit of the surviving widow or widower cannot exceed the larger of (1) the amount of such reduced old-age benefit or (2) $82\frac{1}{2}\%$ of the primary benefit (the latter alternative being applicable only when the worker had retired between age 62 and $62\frac{1}{3}$).

e. Benefit for child of deceased worker and for child's parent is 75% of primary amount.

f. Benefit for dependent parent is $82\frac{1}{2}\%$ of primary amount, except that two such parents receive 75% each.

g. Lump-sum death payment is three times primary benefit, with $255 maximum; as a result, the amount applicable is $255 in all cases.

h. Maximum family benefit for average wages up to $627 is 126.6% of first $436 of average wage, plus 63.3% of next $191 of average wage (approximately), but not less than 1½ times the primary amount. For average wages above $627, maximum family benefit is 175% of primary amount ($914.80 for $1,175 average wage). Any benefit payable to divorced spouse does not count against the maximum.

i. Minimum amount payable to survivor beneficiary family is $101.40 (except in the case of a widow or widower claiming benefits before age 65).

j. Maximum or combined disability benefits (including dependents benefits) and workmen's compensation benefits is 80% of average current earnings (see Item IV-*f*). If this maximum is exceeded, the OASDI benefits are reduced accordingly (but not so as to reduce the total of workmen's compensation and OASDI benefits below the original OASDI benefits amount).

k. The uniform primary benefit for transitionally insured and transitionally noninsured persons is $69.60 per month ($34.80 for eligible wife and $69.60 for eligible widow of transitionally insured person, and $104.40 when both husband and wife are transitionally noninsured persons). The automatic-adjustment provisions (see Item IV-3) apply to these benefits.

Illustrative monthly benefits with respect to insured workers are presented in Tables 1 and 2, applicable for June 1975.

VI. Preservation of Benefit Rights for Disabled ("Disability Freeze")

Periods of disability of at least five months' duration are excluded in determining insured status and average monthly wage, provided the worker is "disability insured" (see Item III-*d*) and so disabled that he is unable to engage in any substantial gainful activity (see Item I-*b* for definition of disability). In addition, blindness is considered to be a qualifying disability for the "disability freeze," although not necessarily for monthly benefits; blind persons become eligible for monthly benefits on an "occupational disability" basis. Determinations of disability are, in general, made by state agencies in charge of vocational rehabilitation.

VII. **Employment Permitted without Suspension of Benefits (Earnings Test)**

a. A beneficiary (other than a disabled beneficiary) can, for 1975, earn up to $2,520 a year in any employment, covered or noncovered, without loss of benefits. For each $2 of covered or noncovered earnings in excess of $2,520, $1

TABLE 1

Illustrative Monthly Benefits for Retired and Disabled Workers

Average Monthly Wage*	Worker Alone	Worker with Spouse Who Claims Benefit at—		Worker, Wife, and One Child†
		Age 62	Age 65	
Disabled Worker or Retired Worker Aged 65 at Time of Retirement‡				
$76 or less	$101.40	$139.50	$152.10	$152.20
100	130.50	179.50	195.80	195.90
200	185.20	254.70	277.80	277.80
300	231.60	318.50	347.40	380.00
400	279.80	384.80	419.70	510.60
500	323.40	444.70	485.10	593.40
600	371.50	510.90	557.30	657.30
700	410.70	564.80	616.10	718.70
800	437.00	600.90	655.50	764.80
900	461.00	633.90	691.50	806.80
1,000	485.00	666.90	727.50	848.80
1,175	522.80	718.90	784.20	914.80
Retired Worker Aged 62 at Time of Retirement				
$76 or less	$ 81.20	$119.30	$131.90	$132.00
100	104.40	153.40	169.70	169.80
200	148.20	217.70	240.80	240.80
300	185.30	272.20	301.10	333.70
400	223.90	328.90	363.80	454.70
500	258.80	380.10	420.50	528.80
600	297.20	436.60	483.00	583.00
700	328.60	482.70	534.00	636.60
800	349.60	513.50	568.10	677.40
900	368.80	541.70	599.30	714.60
1,000	388.00	569.90	630.50	751.80
1,175	418.30	614.40	679.70	810.30

* When the average wage is based on earnings before 1974, it is affected by the lower earnings bases then in effect. Thus, an average wage of $1,175 will be impossible to obtain for many years, except for young disabled workers.

† Also applies where worker, wife, and more than 1 child, where worker and 2 or more children, and where worker, husband aged 65 or over, and 1 or more children.

‡ If worker retires after age 65, his benefit (but not any additional dependents benefit) is increased by 1% for each year of delay, up to a maximum of 7%.

Note 1: In cases when more than two beneficiaries, actual benefit may be slightly higher (10 cents or 20 cents usually) due to rounding.

Note 2: The above figures do not include any possible deferred retirement increment (see Item V-a).

TABLE 2

Illustrative Monthly Benefits for Survivors

*Average Monthly Wage**	*Disabled Widow Aged 50†*	*Widow Aged 60†*	*Widow Aged 62†*	*Widow Aged 65 or Over†*
$76 or less.................	$ 56.80	$ 74.90	$ 84.50	$101.40
100.....................	65.40	93.40	108.20	130.50
200.....................	92.70	132.50	153.60	185.20
300.....................	115.90	165.60	192.00	231.60
400.....................	140.00	200.10	232.00	279.80
500.....................	161.80	231.30	268.10	323.40
600.....................	185.90	265.70	308.00	371.50
700.....................	205.40	293.70	340.50	410.70
800.....................	218.60	312.50	362.30	437.00
900.....................	230.60	329.70	382.20	461.00
1,000.....................	242.60	346.80	402.10	485.00
1,175.....................	261.50	373.90	433.50	522.80

*Average Monthly Wage**	*Dependent Parent*	*One Child*	*Mother and One Child§*	*Maximum Family Benefit‖*
$76 or less.................	$101.40	$101.40	$152.20	$152.10
100.....................	107.70	101.40	195.80	195.80
200.....................	152.80	138.90	277.80	277.80
300.....................	191.10	173.70	347.40	379.90
400.....................	230.90	209.90	419.80	510.50
500.....................	266.90	242.60	485.20	593.30
600.....................	306.50	278.70	557.40	657.30
700.....................	338.90	308.10	616.20	718.70
800.....................	360.60	327.80	655.60	764.80
900.....................	380.40	345.80	691.60	806.80
1,000.....................	400.20	363.80	727.60	848.70
1,175.....................	431.40	392.10	784.20	914.80

* When the average wage is based on earnings before 1974, it is affected by the lower earnings bases then in effect. Thus, an average wage of $1,175 will be impossible to obtain for many years, except for deaths of young workers.

† Also applies to widower. Age shown relates to age at time of a claim. Amounts shown for widows aged 62 or over might be reduced if deceased worker was receiving a reduced old-age benefit (because of retirement before age 65) (see Item V-*d*).

§ Also applies to two children, to father and one child, and to two dependent parents.

‖ Payable to mother or father and two or more children and to three or more children.

Note: In cases when more than two beneficiaries, actual benefit may be slightly higher (10 cents or 20 cents usually) due to rounding.

of benefits is withheld. In no case, however, are benefits withheld for any month in which the beneficiary's remuneration as an employee is $210 or less and in which he rendered no substantial services in self-employment. In the case of a retired worker with dependents who are beneficiaries, the reduction for "excess earnings" is applicable to the total family benefit.

b. For beneficiaries aged 72 or over, there is no limitation on earnings.

c. The annual and monthly exempt amounts are automatically adjusted in the future in the same manner as the earnings base (see Item X) in units of $120 per year and $10 per month, respectively; this is done for the calendar year after an automatic adjustment of the benefit amounts has occurred.

d. For disabled beneficiaries, wages of over $200 per month earned over a period of time will ordinarily prove that the individual is no longer disabled, while wages of $130–200 will result in reconsideration of the case.

VIII. Covered Employment

a. All employment listed in VIII-*b* that takes place in the 50 states, the District of Columbia, American Samoa, Guam, Puerto Rico, or the Virgin Islands, or that is performed outside the United States by American citizens employed by an American employer (or, by election of the employer, by American citizens employed by a foreign subsidiary of an American employer) is covered employment. Also covered, under certain conditions, is employment on American ships and aircraft outside the United States.

b. Individuals engaged in the following types of employment are covered for such employment:

(1) Virtually all employees in industry and commerce, other than long-service railroad workers. Railroad service of those who retire or die with less than 10 years of railroad service is counted as covered wages; for those who have 10 or more years of railroad service, survivor benefits are based on the combination of railroad wages and covered earnings (although generally payable by the railroad retirement system, being based on having a "current connection" with RR), while disability and old-age benefits are payable on a coordinated basis for service after 1974.

(2)   Farm and nonfarm self-employed with $400 or more of net earnings from covered self-employment.

(3)   State and local government employees not covered by a retirement system (excluding policemen, other than in some designated states) can be covered by a referendum in which a majority of the eligibles vote in favor of coverage. In a few designated states, retirement systems can be divided into two groups, those wishing coverage and those not wishing coverage, with all future entrants covered. In any event, the state must elect such coverage.

(4)   American citizens employed in the United States by foreign governments or international organizations (covered as self-employed).

(5)   Federal civilian employees not covered by retirement systems established by law of the United States (other than a few specifically excluded small categories).

(6)   Nonfarm domestic workers (based on having $50 in cash wages from one employer in a quarter).

(7)   Farm workers, including farm domestic workers (based on having $150 or more in cash wages, or 20 or more days of employment remunerated on a time basis, from any one employer in a year).

(8)   Ministers and members of religious orders (other than those who have taken a vow of poverty), either employed by nonprofit institutions (in positions which only a minister can fill) or self-employed (covered as self-employed unless they opt out on grounds of conscience or religious principle). Members of religious orders who have taken a vow of poverty can be covered, on an employee basis, if the order irrevocably elects such coverage for all such members and for its lay employees.

(9)   Employees of nonprofit educational, religious, or scientific institutions (covered on group elective basis; employer must elect coverage, and then all employees concurring in coverage and all new employees are covered).

(10) Members of the uniformed services (on base pay only).

(11)　Groups such as full-time life insurance salesmen, wholesale salesmen, and agent drivers (covered as "employees" under the broadened definition of "employee" from strict common-law rule). Also, industrial homeworkers paid at least $50 in cash during a quarter and working under specifications supplied by the employer are covered.

(12)　Employees receiving tips of $20 or more per month (such tips covered as wages and reported through employer, but only the employee tax is paid).

IX.　Gratuitous Wage Credits for Military Service

World War II veterans and those in service thereafter (including those who died in service) are, with certain restrictions, given wage credits of $160 for each month of active military service in World War II and thereafter through December 1956; for those in service after 1956, credit is given for service after 1950 even if it is used for purposes of other retirement benefits paid by the uniformed services or by the Veterans Administration, but in all other cases credit is not given if service is used for any other federal retirement or survivor system (other than compensation or pension payable by the Veterans Administration). For military service after 1956, an additional $300 of wage credits is given for each quarter of service. Additional cost of benefits arising from such wage credits is met from general funds of the Treasury. (Somewhat similar wage credits are given to U.S. citizens of Japanese ancestry who were interned during World War II.)

X.　Financing

a.　Tax rates are as follows (see HI Item V-*d* for combined OASDI and hospital insurance tax rates):

Calendar Year	Employee	Employer	Employer-Employee	Self-Employed
1974–2010	4.95%	4.95%	9.9%	7.0%
2011 and after	5.95	5.95	11.9	7.0

The self-employed rate is approximately $1\frac{1}{2}$ times the employee rate (result rounded to nearest $\frac{1}{10}\%$), but with a maximum of 7.0%.

b. Maximum taxable earnings base was $3,000 in 1937–50, $3,600 in 1951–54, $4,200 in 1955–58, $4,800 in 1959–65, $6,600 in 1966–67, $7,800 in 1968–71, $9,000 in 1972, $10,800 in 1973, $13,200 in 1974, and $14,100 in 1975. The earnings base will be automatically adjusted (only upwards) for each year following the year in which the benefit table is adjusted (see Item IV-*e*). The adjustment of the base is determined from the changes in average wages in covered employment (in essence, without regard to the dampening effect of the base), measuring from the year before the last year for which the base was increased to the year before the base is to be changed. As in the case of the benefits, current action by Congress will override the automatic-adjustment provisions.

c. Self-employment-income taxes are, in general, based on net income from trade or business. Special optional provisions based on ⅔ds of gross income are available for farmers with gross income of $2,400 or less (for farmers with gross income of over $2,400 and net income of less than $1,600, optional reporting of $1,600 is permitted); a similar reporting procedure can be used for the nonfarm self-employed but on a more limited basis (can be used only five times, only if actual net earnings were at least $400 in at least two of the three preceding years, and only if actual net earnings were less than $1,600 and also less than ⅔ds of gross income).

d. There are two separate trust funds—Disability Insurance Trust Fund (for payment of monthly benefits to disabled workers, including benefits for dependents) and Old-Age and Survivors Insurance Trust Fund (for payment of all other benefits). Total tax rate is subdivided so that the following amount goes to DI Trust Fund (and remainder goes to OASI Trust Fund):

Calendar Year	From Employer-Employee Rate	From Self-Employed Rate
1974–77	1.15%	0.815%
1978–80	1.20	0.850
1981–85	1.30	0.920
1986–2010	1.40	0.990
2011 and after	1.70	1.000

Assets are invested in interest-bearing obligations of the United States, either public issues or special obligations bearing interest at a rate equal to the average market yield (at end of month preceding issue), rounded to nearest ⅛%, on all marketable interest-bearing obligations of the United States not due or callable for four years from end of such month.

e. Payments for vocational rehabilitation of disabled beneficiaries (when such payments will, on the average, be expected to result in a more than offsetting reduction in benefit outgo) can be made from both trust funds. The maximum total such payments is 1½% of benefit outgo for such beneficiaries in the previous year.

f. Board of trustees of the trust funds is composed of the Secretary of the Treasury (as Managing Trustee), the Secretary of Labor, and the Secretary of Health, Education, and Welfare; the Commissioner of Social Security serves as Secretary of the Board.

g. No provision is made for authorizing appropriations from general revenues to assist in financing the program, except that benefits for transitional noninsured persons (other than those with at least 3 quarters of coverage) are reimbursed from this source.

h. Financial interchange with railroad retirement system is provided, so that OASI and DI Trust Funds are placed in same position as if railroad employment had always been covered under OASDI (currently results in sizable annual transfers from OASDI to RR).

B. SUMMARY OF HOSPITAL INSURANCE SYSTEM

I. Coverage Provisions (for payroll tax purposes)

a. All workers who are covered by OASDI.

b. All railroad workers. RR system collects taxes and transfers them to HI Trust Fund through financial interchange provisions; HI Trust Fund pays benefits to suppliers of services.

II. Persons Protected (for benefit purposes):

a. Insured persons. All individuals aged 65 or over who are eligible for any type of OASDI or railroad retirement monthly benefit (i.e., as insured workers, dependents, or survivors), without regard to whether retired (i.e., no earnings test), and all disabled beneficiaries (workers under age 65, widows and widowers aged 50–64, and children aged 18 and over disabled before age 22) who have been on the benefit roll for at least 2 years.

b. Noninsured persons blanketed-in without charge. All other individuals aged 65 or over before 1968 who are citizens or aliens lawfully admitted for permanent residence with at least five consecutive years of residence and who are not subversives or retired federal employees (or dependents of such individuals) covered under the Federal Employees Health Benefits Act of 1959 (including certain individuals who could have been covered if they had so elected). Those in this category attaining age 65 after 1967 must have certain amounts of OASDI or RR coverage to be eligible for HI benefits, namely, 3 quarters of coverage for each year after 1966 and before age 65, so that the provision becomes ineffective after 1974, since then the "regular" OASDI insured status conditions are as easy to meet.

c. Other noninsured persons aged 65 or over. Such persons over age 65 who are enrolled in SMI can elect to enroll in HI under the same conditions applicable to SMI (see Item I under SMI). The entire cost is paid by the enrollees, with the monthly standard premium rate for July 1974 through June 1975 being $36 and that for the next year being $40.

d. Persons with chronic kidney disease, requiring dialysis or renal transplant. Such individuals under age 65 (if fully or currently insured, or if wife or dependent child of such insured person or a monthly beneficiary, or if a monthly beneficiary) are covered under HI, beginning with the 3d month after month in which course of treatment began and ending with the 12th month after month of transplant or after dialysis terminates.

III. Benefits Provided:

a. Hospital benefits. Full cost of all hospital services (i.e., including room and board, operating room, laboratory tests and X rays, drugs, dressings, general nursing services, and services of interns and residents in training) is covered for semiprivate accommodations for up to 90 days in a "spell of illness" (a period beginning with the first day of hospitalization and ending after the person has been out of a hospital and a skilled nursing facility for 60 consecutive days), after a deductible of $92 in 1975 and coinsurance of $23 per day for all days after the 60th one, and also a deductible of the cost of the first 3 pints of blood; lifetime maximum of 190 days for psychiatric hospital care. A lifetime reserve of 60 days with $46 daily coinsurance is available in addition to the 90 days per spell of illness. The deductible and the coinsurance will be automatically adjusted each year to reflect changes in hospital costs.

b. Skilled nursing facility (skilled nursing home or convalescent wing of hospital—formerly called "extended care facility") benefits. Following at least 3 days of hospitalization and beginning within 14 days of leaving hospital, benefits are available for care needed on a daily basis that can only be provided by such a facility on an inpatient basis, for up to 100 days of such care in a spell of illness, with coinsurance of $11.50 per day for all days after the 20th one; the coinsurance will be automatically adjusted each year to reflect changes in hospital costs.

c. Home health services benefits. Following at least 3 days of hospitalization beginning within 14 days of leaving hospital or skilled nursing facility, benefits are available for up to 100 visits in the next 365 days and before the beginning of the next spell of illness. Such services are essentially for homebound persons and include visiting nurse services and various types of therapy treatment, including outpatient hospital services when equipment cannot be brought to the home.

Benefits are not provided for services obtained outside the United States (except for emergency services for an illness occurring in the United States, or in transit in Canada between Alaska and another state, and except for illness of a person treated in a foreign hospital which is nearer his U.S. residence than any U.S. one), elective "luxury" services (such as private room or television), custodial care, hospitalization for services not necessary for the treatment of illness or injury (such as elective cosmetic surgery), services performed in a federal institution (such as a Veterans Administration hospital), and cases eligible under workmen's compensation.

IV. Administration

Administration is by the Department of Health, Education, and Welfare, through fiscal intermediaries (such as Blue Cross, other health insurance organizations, or state agencies) who are able to assist the providers of services in applying safeguards against overutilization of services. Each provider of services can nominate a fiscal intermediary or can deal directly with DHEW.

a. The providers of services are reimbursed on a "reasonable cost" basis, and the fiscal intermediaries are reimbursed for their reasonable costs of administration.

b. The providers of services must meet certain standards, including establishment of utilization review committees for hospitals and skilled nursing facilities and development of transfer agreements between hospitals and skilled nursing facilities.

c. Special reimbursement bases may apply to health maintenance organizations (in essence, group practice prepayment plans) so as to reward them financially for what is believed to be their more favorable operating experience.

V. Financing

a. Insured persons pay taxes which finance the program on a long-range self-supporting basis (just as OASDI) through separate schedule of increasing rates on covered earnings, with same maximum taxable earnings base as scheduled for OASDI (see Item V-*e*); same rate applies to employees, employers, and self-employed (unlike OASDI).

b. HI Trust Fund is a separate trust fund, with separate board of trustees (same membership as for OASI and DI Trust Funds) and with same investment procedures.

c. Noninsured persons have their benefit costs financed from general revenues, through the HI Trust Fund.

d. Tax rates are as follows:

Calendar Year	HI Rate*	Combined OASDI and HI Rate	
		Employer-Employee	Self-Employed
1974–77...................	0.90%	11.70%	7.90%
1978–80...................	1.10	12.10	8.10
1981–85...................	1.35	12.60	8.35
1986–2010................	1.50	12.90	8.50
2011 and after.............	1.50	14.90	8.50

* Rate for employee; same for both employer and self-employed.

e. For taxable earnings bases, see Item X-*b* of OASDI section.

C. SUMMARY OF SUPPLEMENTARY MEDICAL INSURANCE SYSTEM

I. Coverage Provisions (for premium and benefit purposes)

a. Persons aged 65 and over on December 31, 1965, may elect coverage if also eligible for HI benefits, or if a citizen or other alien lawfully admitted for permanent residence with at least five consecutive years of residence (except subversives).[4]

b. Similarly, persons attaining age 65 after 1965 may elect coverage in the seven-month period centering around the month of attainment of age 65 (or first subsequent month when eligibility requirements are met), to be effective for month of attaining age 65 if elected in advance (otherwise, effective for first to third month following election). All persons entitled to HI are automatically enrolled in SMI unless they opt-out.

c. Beginning July 1973, disabled beneficiaries (workers under

---

[4] The constitutionality of this alien residence requirement is now being considered by the courts, with a lower court having declared it unconstitutional.

age 65, widows and widowers aged 50–64, and children aged 18 and over disabled before age 22), including railroad retirement ones, who have been on the benefit roll for at least two years are covered in the same manner as are persons aged 65 or over.

d. Persons with chronic kidney disease, requiring dialysis or renal transplant, who are eligible for HI (see Item II-*d* under HI) are covered in the same manner as are persons aged 65 or over.

e. Persons failing to enroll in initial period can enroll in subsequent general enrollment periods (January–March of each year), to be effective the next July.

f. Termination of enrollment may be either by failure to pay premiums (for premiums not deducted from benefits) or by election to do so. An individual who terminates coverage may reenroll if he does so in a general enrollment period, with reenrollment permitted only once.

II. Benefits Provided

a. Types of benefits provided include physician and surgeon services (including anesthesiologist, pathologist, radiologist, and physical medicine in hospital), home health services (as in HI, but without requirement that they be furnished after hospitalization), outpatient hospital services, and certain other medical services such as diagnostic tests, limited ambulance services, prosthetic devices, physical therapy and speech pathology services, hospital equipment and other durable medical equipment used at home, and supplies used for fractures.

b. The amount of reimbursement is 80% of the reasonable charge (or cost, as case may be) after the participant has paid a calendar-year deductible of $60. There are special limits on out-of-hospital mental care costs (50% coinsurance and $250 maximum annual reimbursement) and home health services (100 visits per calendar year). Inpatient hospital services by pathologists and radiologists are covered without any cost sharing. Home health services are covered without any coinsurance. No more than $100 per year of services of independent physical therapists is covered.

c. Reimbursement is on a "reasonable charge" basis for individual suppliers of services and on a "reasonable cost" basis for institutional suppliers of services. The "reasonable charge" basis for physicians is founded on the customary charge, but is limited by the prevailing charge in the community (which, in turn, is limited by the actual prevailing charge in July 1972 to June 1973 as increased by an economic index reflecting general earnings levels and costs of operation of physicians). When payment is made directly to individual suppliers (by assignment), the bill to the patient may not exceed the reasonable-charge basis; otherwise, payment is made to the participant only upon presentation of an itemized bill.

d. Services not covered include drugs (covered only under HI when receiving covered hospital or skilled nursing facility services), private duty nursing, dental services (except for treatment of conditions resulting from accident), skilled nursing home and custodial care, routine physical and eye examinations, elective cosmetic surgery, services performed by a relative or household member, services performed by a governmental agency, eyeglasses and hearing aids, cases eligible under workmen's compensation, chiropractic services (except under very limited conditions— for treatment of spine, verifiable by X ray showing subluxation), and services outside the United States (except ambulance and physician services in connection with covered HI services—see Item III under HI).

III. Administration

Administration is by the Department of Health, Education, and Welfare through carriers, such as Blue Shield and insurance companies, who are selected by the department, who have had experience in this field, and who will determine the reasonable costs and charges applicable and will assist in controlling utilization. Carriers are paid their reasonable costs of administration. Special reimbursement basis may apply to health maintenance organizations (in essence, group practice prepayment plans) so as to reward them financially for what is believed to be their more favorable operating experience.

IV. Financing

    a. A uniform standard monthly premium rate, determined by the Secretary of Health, Education, and Welfare, is paid by all participants enrolling on a timely basis. The rate is applicable for one-year periods beginning July 1. The rate is the same for all categories (aged and disabled), but any increase is based on the change in the rate determined for enrollees aged 65 or over considered alone, and the increase in the rate over that of the previous year cannot exceed the increase in the cash-benefit level (if any) from the June preceding the promulgation to the next June (based on the law in effect at the time of the promulgation). Because of a technical error in the law, no increase in the premium rate is possible in the future as long as only the automatic-adjustment provisions for the cash benefits apply and no ad hoc increases occur.[5] A rate of $6.70 was promulgated for July 1974 through June 1975, and it remained unchanged for the next year (because of the effect of the provision as to changes in the cash-benefits level). A higher rate is paid by those enrolling late (10% additional for each full year of delay).

    b. Government contribution is, in essence, equal to the sum of:

      (1) The enrollee premiums;

      (2) For those aged 65 or over, twice the excess of what the enrollee premiums would have been, without the restriction based on benefit increases (at a rate determined for this category separately, which was $6.70 for July 1974 through June 1975, and $7.50 for the following year), over what they actually are; and

      (3) For disabled beneficiaries (including those made eligible as a result of chronic kidney disease), twice the excess of what the enrollee premiums (at a rate determined for this category separately, which is $18 for July 1974 through June 1975, and $18.50 for the

---

[5] In March 1975, legislation was actively being considered in Congress that would correct this error. Under this legislation, the standard rate would increase to $7.40 for the year beginning July 1975.

following year) would have been over what they actually are.

c. Payment of premiums is by automatic deduction from OASDI, railroad retirement, or civil service retirement benefits when possible. Otherwise, for persons affected by earnings test and for persons not eligible for such benefits, payment is direct (not necessarily on a monthly basis), with a grace period determined by the Secretary of Health, Education, and Welfare of up to 90 days. Public assistance agencies may enroll, and pay premiums, for public assistance recipients.

d. The SMI Trust Fund is established on same basis as OASI, DI, and HI Trust Funds, with a separate board of trustees (same membership) and with the same investment procedures.

Selected Bibliography*

A. BOOKS

ALTMEYER, ARTHUR J.   *Formative Years of Social Security.* Madison: University of Wisconsin Press, 1966.

AMERICAN ASSEMBLY   *Economic Security for Americans: An Appraisal of the Progress during the Last 50 Years.* New York: Columbia University, Graduate School of Business, 1954.

AMERICAN ENTERPRISE INSTITUTE FOR PUBLIC POLICY RESEARCH   *Private Pensions and the Public Interest.* Washington, D.C.: The Institute, 1970.

—— *Social Security: Universal or Selective?* Rational Debate Seminar, Wilbur J. Cohen and Milton Friedman. Washington, D.C.: The Institute, 1972.

ARMSTRONG, BARBARA N.   *Insuring the Essentials: Minimum Wage, Plus Social Insurance.* New York: Macmillan, Inc., 1932.

BACHMAN, GEORGE W., AND MERIAM, LEWIS   *The Issue of Compulsory Health Insurance.* Washington, D.C.: The Brookings Institution, 1948.

---

* *Key to Abbreviations:* "HEW" denotes U.S. Department of Health, Education, and Welfare; "SSA" denotes Social Security Administration; and "GPO" denotes U.S. Government Printing Office. For more extensive bibliographies, see the pamphlet "Basic Readings in Social Security" listed under HEW and the paper listed under Nancy Davenport.

BECKER, JOSEPH M. *Experience Rating in Unemployment Insurance: An Experiment in Competitive Socialism.* Baltimore: Johns Hopkins University Press, 1972.

────── *Unemployment Insurance: Virtue or Vice.* Kalamazoo: W. E. Upjohn Institute for Employment Research, 1972.

BOWEN, HARBISON, LESTER, AND SOMERS, EDS. *The American System of Social Insurance: Its Philosophy, Impact, and Future Development.* Princeton Symposium. New York: McGraw-Hill Book Co., 1968.

BRITTAIN, JOHN A. *The Payroll Tax for Social Security.* Washington, D.C.: The Brookings Institution, 1972.

BRONSON, D. C. *Concepts of Actuarial Soundness in Pension Plans.* Homewood, Ill.: Richard D. Irwin, Inc. 1957.

BROWN, J. DOUGLAS *An American Philosophy of Social Security.* Princeton, N.J.: Princeton University Press, 1972.

BURNS, EVELINE M. *Toward Social Security.* New York: McGraw-Hill Book Co., 1936.

────── *The American Social Security System.* Boston: Houghton Mifflin Co., 1949.

────── *Social Security and Public Policy.* New York: McGraw-Hill Book Co., 1956.

CARLSON, VALDEMAR *Economic Security in the United States.* New York: McGraw-Hill Book Co., 1962.

CHEIT, EARL F., AND GORDON, MARGARET S., EDS. *Occupational Disability and Public Policy.* New York: John Wiley & Sons, Inc., 1963.

CLARK, ROBERT M. *Economic Security for the Aged in the United States and Canada.* Ottawa: Queen's Printer, 1959.

COHEN, WILBUR J. *Retirement Policies under Social Security.* Berkeley: University of California Press, 1957.

CORSON, JOHN J., AND MCCONNELL, JOHN W. *Economic Needs of Older People.* New York: The Twentieth Century Fund, 1956.

DOUGLAS, PAUL H. *Social Security in the United States: An Analysis and Appraisal of the Federal Social Security Act.* 2d ed. New York: McGraw-Hill Book Co., 1939.

──────, AND DIRECTOR, AARON *The Problem of Unemployment.* New York: Macmillan, Inc., 1931.

DRAKE, JOSEPH T. *The Aged in American Society.* New York: Ronald Press, 1958.

EILERS, ROBERT D., AND MOYERMAN, SUE, EDS. *National Health Insurance.* Homewood, Ill.: Richard D. Irwin, Inc., 1971.

EPSTEIN, ABRAHAM   *Insecurity: A Challenge to America.* New York: Random House, Inc., 1938.

FALK, I. S.   *Security Against Sickness: A Study of Health Insurance.* Garden City, N.Y.: Doubleday, Doran, & Co., 1936.

FOLLMAN, J. F., JR.   *Medical Care and Health Insurance.* Homewood, Ill.: Richard D. Irwin, Inc., 1963.

GAGLIARDO, DOMENICO   *American Social Insurance.* New York: Harper & Bros., 1949.

GORDON, MARGARET S.   *The Economics of Welfare Policies.* New York: Columbia University Press, 1963.

GRANT, MARGARET   *Old-Age Security.* Washington, D.C.: Social Science Research Council, 1939.

HABER, WILLIAM, AND COHEN, WILBUR J.   *Social Security Programs, Problems, and Policies.* Homewood, Ill.: Richard D. Irwin, Inc., 1960.

HARRIS, R.   *A Sacred Trust.* New York: The New American Library, 1966.

HARRIS, S. E.   *Economics of Social Security.* New York: McGraw-Hill Book Co., 1941.

HIRSHFIELD, DANIEL S.   *The Lost Reform: The Campaign for Compulsory Health Insurance in the United States from 1932 to 1943.* Cambridge, Mass.: Harvard University Press, 1970.

HOGAN, JOHN D., AND IANNI, FRANCIS, A.   *American Social Legislation.* New York: Harper & Bros., 1956.

LARSON, ARTHUR   *Know Your Social Security.* Rev. ed. New York: Harper & Bros., 1959.

LESTER, RICHARD A.   *The Economics of Unemployment Compensation.* Princeton: Princeton University, Industrial Relations Section, Department of Economics, 1962.

———, AND KIDD, CHARLES V.   *The Case Against Experience Rating in Unemployment Compensation.* New York: Industrial Relations Counselors, 1939.

MADISON, BERNICE Q.   *Social Welfare in the Soviet Union.* Stanford, Calif.: Stanford University Press, 1968.

MERIAM, LEWIS   *Relief and Social Security.* Washington, D.C.: The Brookings Institution, 1946.

———; MARONEY, MILDRED; AND SCHLOTTERBECK, KARL   *The Cost and Financing of Social Security.* Washington, D.C.: The Brookings Institution, 1950.

MITCHELL, WILLIAM L.   *Social Security in America.* Washington, D.C.: Robert B. Luce, Inc., 1964.

MOYNIHAN, DANIEL P.   *The Politics of a Guaranteed Income; The Nixon Administration and the Family Assistance Plan.* New York: Random House, 1973.

MUNNELL, ALICIA H.   *The Effect of Social Security on Personal Saving.* Cambridge, Mass.: Ballinger Publishing Co., 1974.

MYERS, ROBERT J.   *Medicare.* Homewood, Ill.: Richard D. Irwin, Inc. 1970.

NATIONAL CONFERENCE ON SOCIAL WELFARE   *The Social Welfare Forum.* New York: Columbia University Press, 1972.

NELSON, DANIEL   *Unemployment Insurance: The American Experience, 1915–1935.* Madison: University of Wisconsin Press, 1969.

OSBORN, GRANT M.   *Compulsory Temporary Disability Insurance in the United States.* Homewood, Ill.: Richard D. Irwin, Inc., 1958.

PECHMAN, JOSEPH A.; AARON, HENRY J.; AND TAUSSIG, MICHAEL K.   *Social Security: Perspectives for Reform.* Washington, D.C.: The Brookings Institution, 1968.

PRESIDENT'S COMMITTEE ON ECONOMIC SECURITY   *Social Security in America.* Washington, D.C.: Social Security Board, 1937.

RUBINOW, I. M.   *The Quest for Security.* New York: Henry Holt, Inc., 1934.

SCHOTTLAND, CHARLES I.   *The Social Security Program in the United States.* New York: Appleton-Century-Crofts, 1963.

SOMERS, HERMAN M., AND SOMERS, ANNE R.   *Workmen's Compensation: Prevention, Insurance, and Rehabilitation of Occupational Disability.* New York: John Wiley & Sons, Inc., 1954.

——— *Doctors, Patients and Health Insurance.* Washington, D.C.: The Brookings Institution, 1961.

——— *Medicare and the Hospitals.* Washington, D.C.: The Brookings Institution, 1967.

SPIEGELMAN, MORTIMER   *Ensuring Medical Care for the Aged.* Homewood, Ill.: Richard D. Irwin, Inc., 1960.

STEINER, PETER O., AND DORFMAN, ROBERT   *The Economic Status of the Aged.* Berkeley: University of California Press, 1957.

STEWART, MAXWELL S.   *Social Security.* Rev. ed. New York: W. W. Norton & Co., Inc., 1939.

TURNBULL, JOHN G.; WILLIAMS, C. ARTHUR, JR., AND CHEIT, EARL F.   *Economic and Social Security.* 3d ed. New York: Ronald Press, 1968.

WITTE, EDWIN E.   *The Development of the Social Security Act.* Madison: University of Wisconsin Press, 1962.

WITTE, EDWIN E.   *Social Security Perspectives.* Madison: University of Wisconsin Press, 1962.

WYATT, BIRCHARD E., AND WANDEL, WILLIAM H.   *The Social Security Act in Operation.* Washington, D.C.: Graphic Arts Press, 1937.

B. REPORTS AND PAMPHLETS

ALTMEYER, ARTHUR J., ET AL.   *War and Post-War Social Security.* Washington, D.C.: American Council on Public Affairs, 1942.

BAYO, FRANCISCO AND MCKAY, STEVEN F.   *U.S. Population Projections for OASDHI Cost Estimates.* Actuarial Study No. 72. Washington: HEW-SSA, 1974.

———, AND RITCHIE, WILLIAM D.   *Long-Range Cost Estimates for OASDI System, 1974.* Actuarial Study No. 73. Washington: HEW-SSA, 1974.

BLUE CROSS ASSOCIATION AND AMERICAN HOSPITAL ASSOCIATION   *Financing Health Care of the Aged.* Chicago, 1962.

BOARD OF TRUSTEES OF THE FEDERAL HOSPITAL INSURANCE TRUST FUND   *1974 Annual Report.* House Document No. 93–314. Washington, D.C.: GPO, 1974.

BOARD OF TRUSTEES OF THE FEDERAL OLD-AGE AND SURVIVORS INSURANCE TRUST FUND AND THE FEDERAL DISABILITY INSURANCE TRUST FUND   *1974 Annual Report.* House Document No. 93–313. Washington, D.C.: GPO, 1974.

BOARD OF TRUSTEES OF THE FEDERAL SUPPLEMENTARY MEDICAL INSURANCE TRUST FUND   *1974 Annual Report.* House Document No. 93–315. Washington, D.C.: GPO, 1973.

CALVERT, GEOFFREY N.   *New Realistic Projections of Social Security Benefits and Taxes.* New York: Alexander and Alexander, Inc., 1973.

CANADA, GOVERNMENT OF   *The Canada Pension Plan.* Ottawa: Information Canada, 1970.

———   *Income Security for Canadians.* Ottawa: Department of National Health and Welfare, 1970.

———   *Working Paper on Social Security in Canada.* Ottawa: Ministry of National Health and Welfare, April 1973.

CARROLL, JOHN J.   *Alternative Methods of Financing Old-Age, Survivors, and Disability Insurance.* Ann Arbor: University of Michigan, Institute of Public Administration, 1960.

CHAMBER OF COMMERCE OF THE UNITED STATES   *Improving Social Security.* Washington, D.C., 1953.

CHEN, YUNG-PING   *Reforming Social Security: Certain Approaches and Issues.* Los Angeles: Institute of Industrial Relations, University of California (Reprint No. 194), 1969.

—— *General Revenue Financing for Social Security: A Negative View.* Los Angeles: Institute of Industrial Relations, University of California (Reprint No. 213), 1971.

CONSULTANTS ON SOCIAL SECURITY *A Report to the Secretary of HEW on Extension of OASI to Additional Groups of Current Workers.* Washington, D.C.: GPO, 1953.

GORDON, MARGARET S., AND AMERSON, RALPH W. *Unemployment Insurance.* Berkeley: University of California, Institute of Industrial Relations, 1957.

INTERNATIONAL LABOUR OFFICE *Unemployment Insurance Schemes.* Geneva, 1955.

—— *Social Security, a Worker's Education Manual.* Geneva, 1958.

—— *The Cost of Medical Care.* Studies and Reports, New Series, No. 51. Geneva, 1959.

—— *The Cost of Social Security 1949–1957.* Geneva, 1961.

KRISLOV, JOSEPH *A Survey of State and Local Government Retirement Systems Covering Workers Also Covered under the Federal OASDI Program, 1961.* Washington, D.C.: HEW-SSA, 1962.

MALISOFF, HARRY *Cost Estimation Methods in Unemployment Insurance, 1909–1957.* New York: New York State Department of Labor, 1958.

—— *The Insurance Character of Unemployment Insurance.* Kalamazoo: W. E. Upjohn Institute for Employment Research, 1961.

MERRIAM, IDA C. *Social Security Financing.* Bureau Report No. 17. Washington, D.C.: Federal Security Agency, SSA, 1952.

MYERS, ROBERT J. *The Financial Principle of Self-Support in the OASI System.* Actuarial Study No. 40. Washington, D.C.: HEW-SSA, 1955.

—— *Methodology Involved in Developing Long-Range Cost Estimates for the OASDI System.* Actuarial Study No. 49. Washington, D.C.: HEW-SSA, 1959.

—— *Medium-Range Cost Estimates for OASDI under Increasing-Earnings Assumption.* Actuarial Study No. 53. Washington, D.C.: HEW-SSA, 1961.

—— *The Role of Social Security in Developing Countries.* Washington, D.C.: U.S. Department of State, Agency for International Development, 1963.

—— *Actuarial Cost Estimates for Hospital Insurance Bill.* Actuarial Study No. 57. Washington, D.C.: HEW-SSA, 1963.

—— *Estimated Amount of Life Insurance in Force as Survivor Benefits under the Social Security Program.* Actuarial Note No. 71. Washington, D.C.: HEW-SSA, 1970.

—— *Coverage of Out-of-Hospital Prescription Drugs under Medicare.*

Washington, D.C.: American Enterprise Institute for Public Policy Research, 1972.

——, AND BAYO, FRANCISCO   *Long-Range Cost Estimates for OASDI System, 1966.* Actuarial Study No. 63. Washington, D.C.: HEW-SSA 1967.

——, AND HSIAO, WILLIAM C.   *Actuarial Cost Estimates for Hospital Insurance Program.* Actuarial Study No. 70. Washington, D.C.: HEW-SSA, 1970.

NATIONAL COMMISSION ON STATE WORKMEN'S COMPENSATION LAWS   *Report of Commission.* Washington, D.C.: GPO, July, 1972.

NATIONAL COMMITTEE ON HEALTH CARE OF THE AGED   *A National Program for Financing Health Care of the Aged.* New York, 1963.

NIESSEN, A. M.   *Twelfth Actuarial Valuation of the Assets and Liabilities under the Railroad Retirement Acts as of December 31, 1971.* Chicago: Railroad Retirement Board, 1973.

PRESIDENT'S COMMISSION ON VETERAN'S PENSIONS   *Veteran's Benefits in the United States.* Washington, D.C.: 1956.

SAXER, ARNOLD, AND MYERS, ROBERT J.   *Old-Age Insurance.* Geneva: International Social Security Association, 1959.

U.S. ADVISORY COUNCIL ON HEALTH INSURANCE FOR THE DISABLED   *Health Insurance for the Disabled under Social Security.* Washington, D.C.: GPO, 1969.

U.S. ADVISORY COUNCIL ON SOCIAL SECURITY   *Final Report.* Senate Document No. 4, 76th Congress. Washington, D.C. GPO, 1939.

——   *Recommendations for Social Security Legislation.* Senate Document No. 208, 80th Congress. Washington, D.C.: GPO, 1949.

——   *The Status of the Social Security Program and Recommendations for Its Improvement.* Washington, D.C.: GPO, 1964.

——   *Reports of the 1971 Advisory Council.* House Document No. 92–80. Washington, D.C.: GPO, 1971.

——   *Reports of the Advisory Council on Social Security.* Washington, D.C.: GPO, 1975.

U.S. ADVISORY COUNCIL ON SOCIAL SECURITY FINANCING   *Financing OASDI.* Washington, D.C.: GPO, 1959.

U.S. COMMISSION ON RAILROAD RETIREMENT   *The Railroad Retirement System: Its Coming Crisis—Report to the President and the Congress.* House Document No. 92–350. Washington, D.C.: GPO, June 30, 1972.

U.S. CONGRESS, HOUSE OF REPRESENTATIVES, COMMITTEE ON WAYS AND MEANS   *Issues in Social Security.* Washington, D.C.: GPO, 1946.

—— SUBCOMMITTEE ON SOCIAL SECURITY   *Social Security after 18 Years: A Staff Report.* Washington, D.C.: GPO, 1954.

—— *Analysis of Health Insurance Proposals Introduced in the 92nd Congress.* Washington, D.C.: GPO, 1971.

—— *Actuarial Cost Estimates for OASDI, HI, and SMI Systems as Modified by Public Law 92–603.* Washington, D.C.: GPO, March 2, 1973.

U.S. CONGRESS, SENATE, COMMITTEE ON FINANCE   *Report of the Panel on Social Security Financing.* Washington, D.C.: GPO, 1975.

U.S. DEPARTMENT OF HEW   *Hospitalization Insurance for OASDI Beneficiaries; Report Submitted to the Committee on Ways and Means.* Washington, D.C.: GPO, 1959.

—— *A Report on Social Security Programs in the Soviet Union.* Washington, D.C.: HEW-SSA, 1960.

—— *Basic Readings in Social Security.* Publication No. 28. Washington, D.C.: HEW-SSA, 1960.

—— *Annual Statistical Supplement, 1971, Social Security Bulletin.* Washington, D.C.: HEW-SSA, 1973.

—— *Social Security Programs Throughout the World, 1971.* Washington, D.C.: HEW-SSA, 1972.

—— *State and Local Government Retirement Systems, 1965 (covered by OASDHI).* Research Report No. 15. Washington, D.C.: HEW-SSA, 1966.

—— *State and Local Government Retirement Systems, 1966 (not covered by OASDHI).* Research Report No. 23. Washington, D.C.: HEW-SSA, 1967.

—— *Report of the State-Federal Task Force on Costs of Medical Assistance and Public Assistance.* Washington, D.C.: HEW, October 14, 1968.

—— *Relating Social Security Protection to the Federal Civil Service.* Washington, D.C.: HEW, January, 1969.

—— *Finding of the Department of HEW Respecting Drugs.* House Document No. 91–43. Washington, D.C.: GPO, January 14, 1969.

—— *Final Report—Task Force on Prescription Drugs.* Washington, D.C.: HEW, February 7, 1969.

—— *Report of the Secretary's Review Committee of the Task Force on Prescription Drugs.* Washington, D.C.: HEW, July 23, 1969.

—— *Basic Readings in Social Security.* Washington, D.C.: HEW-SSA, 1970.

—— *Report of the Task Force on Medicaid and Related Programs.* Washington, D.C.: GPO, 1970.

U.S. Department of HEW   *Actuarial Cost Estimates for OASDI and HI System As Modified by the Social Security Provisions of Public Law 92–336.* Washington, D.C.: HEW-SSA, September 1972.

——— *Social Security in the United States.* Washington, D.C.: HEW-SSA, 1973.

——— *Railroad Retirement Legislation in 1973.* Research and Statistics Note No. 15–1973. Washington, D.C.: HEW-SSA (Office of Research and Statistics), 1973.

——— *History of the Provisions of OASDHI, 1935–1972.* Washington, D.C.: HEW-SSA (Office of the Actuary), 1973.

——— *Social Security Programs in the United States.* Washington, D.C.: HEW-SSA, 1973.

——— *Social Security Handbook on OASDI, July 1973.* Washington, D.C.: HEW-SSA, 1974.

U.S. Department of Labor   *State Workmen's Compensation Laws.* Bulletin 161. Washington, D.C.: The Department, Bureau of Labor Standards, 1969.

——— *Comparison of State Unemployment Insurance Laws.* Washington, D.C.: The Department, Manpower Administration, January 1972 (with periodic subsequent updating inserts).

——— *Comparison of Temporary Disability Insurance Laws.* Washington, D.C.: The Department, Manpower Administration, August 1971.

——— *Unemployment Insurance: State Laws and Experience.* Washington, D.C.: The Department, Manpower Administration, 1973.

——— *Handbook of Unemployment Insurance Financial Data, 1938–1970.* Washington, D.C.: The Department, Manpower Administration, 1971 (with periodic updating inserts).

——— *Unemployment Insurance Tax Rates by Industry, 1969.* Washington, D.C.: The Department, Manpower Administration, 1972.

U.S. Executive Office of the President, Committee on Retirement Policy for Federal Personnel   *Retirement Policy for Federal Personnel.* Senate Document No. 89, 83rd Congress. Washington, D.C.: GPO, 1954.

U.S. House of Representatives, Committee on Ways and Means   *Committee Staff Report on the Disability Insurance Program.* Washington, D.C.: GPO, July 1974.

U.S. National Resources Planning Board   *Security, Work, and Relief Policies.* Washington: GPO, 1942.

U.S. Railroad Retirement Board   *The Railroad Retirement and Unemployment Insurance Systems.* Chicago, 1959.

——— *Legislative History of the Provisions of the RRA, 1935–1970.* Actuarial Notes, No. 2–71, February 1971.

—— *Provisions of RUIA.* Research and Statistics Notes, No. 7–71, June 1971.

—— *Railroad Unemployment Insurance Program Compared with State Unemployment Programs, January 1973.* Research and Statistics Notes, No. 4–73, February 1973.

WILLIAMS, WALTER *The Supplemental Security Income Program: Potentially the Next Crucial Step toward Social Security and Welfare Reform.* Seattle, Wash.: Institute of Governmental Research, University of Washington, 1973.

C. PAPERS AND ARTICLES

BALL, ROBERT M. "Social Security Amendments of 1972: Summary and Legislative History." *Social Security Bulletin,* vol. 36, no. 3 (March 1973).

—— "Social Security Perspectives." *Social Security Bulletin,* vol. 31, no. 8 (August 1968).

BROWN, J. DOUGLAS "The Role of Social Insurance in the United States." *Industrial and Labor Relations Review,* vol. 13 (October 1960).

CLARE, JAMES L. "What's Still Wrong with the Canada Pension Plan." *Canadian Business,* April 1973.

COHEN, WILBUR J. "Social Security Act Amendments of 1952." *Social Security Bulletin,* vol. 25, no. 9 (September 1952).

—— "Some Issues and Goals in Social Security." *Industrial and Labor Relations Review,* vol. 12, no. 4 (July 1959).

——, AND BALL, ROBERT M. "Public Welfare Amendments of 1962 and Proposals for Health Insurance for the Aged." *Social Security Bulletin,* vol. 25, no. 10 (October 1962).

—— AND —— "Social Security Amendments of 1967: Summary and Legislative History." *Social Security Bulletin,* vol. 31, no. 2 (February 1968).

——, ——, AND MYERS, ROBERT J. "Social Security Act Amendments of 1954: A Summary and Legislative History," *Social Security Bulletin,* vol. 17, no. 9 (September 1954).

——, AND MITCHELL, WILLIAM L. "Social Security Amendments of 1961: Summary and Legislative History." *Social Security Bulletin,* vol. 24, no. 9 (September 1961).

——, AND MYERS, ROBERT J. "Social Security Amendments of 1950: A Summary and Legislative History." *Social Security Bulletin,* vol. 13, no. 10 (October 1950).

CROWLEY, FRANCIS J. "Financing the Social Security Program—Then and Now." *Studies in Public Welfare No. 18,* Joint Economic Committee, U.S. Congress, December 1974.

DAVENPORT, NANCY   "Origin and Development of Social Security Financing in the United States, 1932–73: Selected References." *Studies in Public Welfare No. 18,* Joint Economic Committee, U.S. Congress, 1974.

FAULKNER, EDWIN J.   "Social Security and Insurance—Some Relationships in Perspective." *The Journal of Insurance,* vol. 30, no. 2 (June 1963).

GEORGE, DENIS R. J.   "Experience Rating Unemployment Insurance." *Proceedings,* Canadian Institute of Actuaries, vol. 4, 1974.

HART, MARICE C.   "OASDI: Early Retirement Provisions." *Social Security Bulletin,* vol. 24, no. 10 (October 1961).

HOHAUS, R. A.   "Observations on Financing Old Age Security." *Transactions, Actuarial Society of America,* vol. 38 (1937).

————   "Equity, Adequacy and Related Factors in Old Age Security." *Record, American Institute of Actuaries,* vol. 27 (1938).

INTERNATIONAL LABOUR OFFICE   "Gradual Extension of Social Insurance Schemes in Latin American Countries." *International Labour Review,* vol. 78, no. 3 (September 1958).

————   "Social Security in Asia." *International Labour Review,* vol. 82, no. 1 and no. 2 (July and August 1960).

————   "Social Security in Africa South of the Sahara." *International Labour Review,* vol. 84, no. 3 (September 1961).

LINTON, M.A.   "Reserve Provisions of the Federal Old Age Security Program." *Transactions, Actuarial Society of America,* vol. 36 (1935).

MURRAY, ANGELA J.   "Social Security Act Amendments of 1946." *Social Security Bulletin,* vol. 9, no. 9 (September 1946).

MYERS, ROBERT J.   "Cost Estimates for the Old-Age Insurance System." *Record, American Institute of Actuaries,* vol. 28 (1939).

————   "Railroad Retirement Act Amendments of 1951: Financial and Actuarial Aspects." *Social Security Bulletin,* vol. 15, no. 3 (March 1952).

————   "OASDI Cost Estimates and Valuations." *Proceedings, Casualty Actuarial Society,* vol. 46 (1959).

————   "Preparation and Presentation of Actuarial Cost Estimates for Long-Range Social Insurance Benefits." *Proceedings, Conference of Actuaries in Public Practice,* vol. 9 (1959–60).

————   "OASDI: Financing Basis and Policy under the 1961 Amendments." *Social Security Bulletin,* vol. 24, no. 9 (September 1961).

————   "Social Security Taxes and Total Payrolls." *Social Security Bulletin,* vol. 26, no. 8 (August 1963).

————   "Age and Sex of Persons Receiving Both OASI Benefits and OAA Payments." *Social Security Bulletin,* vol. 26, no. 10 (October 1963).

———— "Earnings Test under OASDI: Basis, Background and Experience." *Social Security Bulletin,* vol. 27, no. 5 (May 1964).

———— "Employee Social Insurance Contributions and Regressive Taxation." *Journal of Risk and Insurance,* December 1967.

———— "Government and Pensions." *Symposium on Private Pensions and the Public Interest.* Washington, D.C.: American Enterprise Institute for Public Policy Research, May 1969.

———— "Administrative Expenses of the Social Security Program." *Social Security Bulletin,* vol. 32, no. 9 (September 1969).

———— "Social Security at the Crossroads." *Reader's Digest,* April 1970.

———— "The Role of Government in Providing Economic Security." *1970 CLU Forum Report.* Bryn Mawr, Pa.: American Society of Chartered Life Underwriters, September 1970.

———— "Does the Young Worker Get His Money's Worth under Social Security?" *Pension and Welfare News,* April 1970.

———— "New Insight as to the True Basis of Social Security Benefits." *Pension and Welfare News,* August 1971.

———— "Where Will the Pending Social Security Amendments Take the Program?" *CLU Journal,* October 1971.

———— "Fallacies Expounded by Advocates of National Health Insurance." *New York Medicine,* November 1971.

———— "Coverage of Out-of-Hospital Drugs." Washington, D.C.: American Enterprise Institute for Public Policy Research, April 1972.

———— "Social Security's Hidden Hazards." *Wall Street Journal,* July 28, 1972.

———— "How They've Perverted the Medicare Payment System." *Medical Economics,* February 19, 1973.

————, AND COHEN, WILBUR J. "Railroad Retirement Act Amendments of 1951: Benefit Provisions and Legislative History." *Social Security Bulletin,* vol. 15, no. 2 (February 1952).

————, AND ———— "Social Security Payments to Noninsured Persons." *Social Security Bulletin,* vol. 29, no. 9 (September 1966).

————, AND HART, MARICE C. "Automatic Cost-of-Living Increases in Federal Benefit Plans." *Pension and Welfare News,* March 1970.

NIESSEN, A. M. "Measure of Actuarial Soundness in a Pension Plan of the Railroad Retirement Type." *Transactions, Society of Actuaries,* vol. 6 (1954).

PETERSON, RAY M. "Misconceptions and Missing Perceptions of Our Social Security System." *Transactions, Society of Actuaries,* vol. 11 (1959).

RAILROAD RETIREMENT BOARD   "The Railroad Retirement Act of 1974." *The RRB Quarterly Review*, July–September 1974.

RATCLIFF, A. R. N.   "State and Private Pension Schemes in the European Economic Community and the United Kingdom." *Journal of the Institute of Actuaries*, vol. 89, no. 383 (1963).

RETTIG, A., AND NICHOLS, O. R.   "Changes in Social Security Benefits under Public Law 93–233." *Actuarial Note No. 85*, SSA, April 1974.

——   "Some Aspects of the Dynamic Projection of Benefits under the 1973 Social Security Amendments." *Actuarial Note No. 87*, SSA, April 1974.

RICHTER, O. C., AND WILLIAMSON, W. R.   "The Social Security Act of 1935 and the Work of the Committee on Economic Security." *Transactions, Actuarial Society of America*, vol. 36 (1935).

ROBBINS, R. B.   "Railroad Retirement Act." *Record, American Institute of Actuaries*, vol. 23 (1934).

——   "Retirement Plans Created by Federal Legislation." *Record, American Institute of Actuaries*, vol. 28 (1939).

ROBINSON, G. B.   "Accounting Error in Social Security." *Journal of Accounting* (November 1944).

SCHOTTLAND, CHARLES I.   "Social Security Amendments of 1956: A Summary and Legislative History." *Social Security Bulletin*, vol. 19, no. 9 (September 1956).

——   "Social Security Amendments of 1958: A Summary and Legislative History." *Social Security Bulletin*, vol. 21, no. 10 (October 1958).

SEIDMAN, BERT   "Welfare Reform and the Work Ethic." *AFL-CIO American Federationist*, February 1973.

SMEDLEY, LAWRENCE T.   "Changing Patterns in Social Security." *AFL-CIO American Federationist*, January 1973.

U.S. DEPARTMENT OF HEW, SSA   "International Issue." *Social Security Bulletin*, vol. 27, no. 9 (September 1964).

——   "Social Security Protection After Thirty Years." *Social Security Bulletin*, vol. 28, no. 8 (August 1965).

——   "Three Decades of Social Security Research Publishing." *Social Security Bulletin*, vol. 31, no. 3 (March 1968).

WATSON, A. D.   "Current Cost and the Contributory Old Age Annuity Scheme in the Social Security Act." *Transactions, Actuarial Society of America*, vol. 38 (1937).

WEST, HOWARD   "Five Years of Medicare—A Statistical Review." *Social Security Bulletin*, vol. 34, no. 12 (December 1971).

Willcox, Alanson W.   "The Contributory Principle and the Integrity of OASI: A Functional Evaluation." *Industrial and Labor Relations Review*, vol. 8 (April 1955).

Wollenberg, Elmer F.   "Vested Rights in Social Security Benefits." *Oregon Law Review*, vol. 37 (June 1958).

Zelenka, A.   "Some Remarks on Special Social Security Schemes for Agriculture." *International Labour Review*, vol. 88 (October 1963).

INDEXES

Index of Persons and Organizations

683

Index of Subjects

A

Actuarial cost estimates; *see also specific program*
long-range programs, 157–65, 305–11
Medicare, 335–48
methodology, 157
OASDI, 335–48
short-range programs, 311–14, 428–29, 523–26
statistics, Medicare, 357–68
statistics, OASDI, 351–57, 364–70
Actuarial soundness, 139–43
Actuarial valuations, 136–43
"balance-sheet" method, 158–61
earnings assumptions, 167
intermediate estimates, 161
level-costs, 159–61, 177
Medicare, 335–51
OASDI, 335–51
projection method, 158–61
RR, 484–89
variability, 161
Administration
Medicare, 253–56
OASDI, 81–82
Administration Account, UI, 503

Administrative costs
general, 11
Medicare, 254, 366
OASDI, 76, 365
public assistance, 421
UI, 493, 502, 504, 533
Africa
British-oriented countries, 629
French-oriented countries, 630
Aid
to the blind, 402–6
to families with dependent children, 402–6
to permanently and totally disabled, 402–6
Armed forces; *see* Military
Assignment, Medicare, 247
Australia, 633
Automatic-adjustment
benefits
CSR, 577
federal employees compensation, 586
military, 593
earnings base, OASDI and HI, 79
earnings test, OASDI, 75

685

This book has been set in 10 and 9 point Janson, leaded 2 points. Part numbers and chapter titles are 18 point Bulmer. Part titles are 18 point Bulmer italic. Chapter numbers are 16 and 24 point Bulmer. The size of the type page is 26 × 41½ picas.